W9-CNN-383

Unemployment Insurance in the American Economy

The Irwin Series in Risk and Insurance

EDITORS

EDISON L. BOWERS   DAVIS W. GREGG
The Ohio State University   The American College of Life Underwriters

ATHEARN   *General Insurance Agency Management*

BLACK, KEIR, & SURREY   *Cases in Life Insurance*

BRAINARD   *Automobile Insurance*

DICKERSON   *Health Insurance*   Revised Edition

DONALDSON   *Casualty Claim Practice*

EILERS & CROWE   *Group Insurance Handbook*

FOLLMANN   *Medical Care and Health Insurance: A Study in Social Progress*

FRAINE   *Valuation of Securities Holdings of Life Insurance Companies*

GOSHAY   *Information Technology in the Insurance Industry*

GREGG   *Life and Health Insurance Handbook*   Second Edition

GREIDER & BEADLES   *Law and the Life Insurance Contract*

HABER & COHEN   *Social Security: Programs, Problems, and Policies*

HABER & MURRAY   *Unemployment Insurance in the American Economy*

LONG & GREGG   *Property and Liability Insurance Handbook*

MAGEE   *Life Insurance*   Third Edition

MAGEE   *Property Insurance*   Third Edition

MAGEE & BICKELHAUPT   *General Insurance*   Seventh Edition

McGILL   *Legal Aspects of Life Insurance*

McGILL   *Life Insurance*

MEHR & CAMMACK   *Principles of Insurance*   Third Edition

MEHR & HEDGES   *Risk Management in the Business Enterprise*

MYERS   *Social Insurance and Allied Government Programs*

REDEKER & REID   *Life Insurance Settlement Options*   Revised Edition

SNIDER   *Readings in Property and Casualty Insurance*

STALNAKER   *Life Insurance Agency Financial Management*   Revised Edition

Unemployment Insurance

in the

American Economy

AN HISTORICAL REVIEW AND ANALYSIS

William Haber
The University of Michigan

and

Merrill G. Murray
The W. E. Upjohn Institute for Employment Research

1966

RICHARD D. IRWIN, INC.

HOMEWOOD, ILLINOIS

80399

© 1966 BY RICHARD D. IRWIN, INC.

ALL RIGHTS RESERVED. THIS BOOK OR ANY PART
THEREOF MAY NOT BE REPRODUCED WITHOUT
THE WRITTEN PERMISSION OF THE PUBLISHER

First Printing, June, 1966

PRINTED IN THE UNITED STATES OF AMERICA

To
Arthur J. Altmeyer
who provided intelligent and inspiring leadership
in the formative years of
unemployment insurance in the United States

Foreword

This book on unemployment insurance is the result of a generation of observation and reflection by the authors. It also represents over two years of laborious work. It has had the benefit of advice and criticism from many competent sources. It is an important contribution to the understanding of the problem of job security. The Upjohn Institute is pleased to have supported its preparation and hopes it will serve to provide better general understanding concerning this highly complex and significant subject.

HAROLD C. TAYLOR,
Director,
The W. E. Upjohn Institute
for Employment Research

Preface

Much has been written about unemployment insurance in the United States. Its contribution to the wage earners, its costs to the employer, its role in contributing to economic stability, its shortcomings and the abuses alleged to be occurring in our jobless insurance program—all these have been reviewed in monographs and technical papers. Congressional committees and state legislators have taken thousands of pages of testimony. However, despite this wealth of material, there have been few attempts at a comprehensive review of the history and problems of unemployment insurance in this country.

The reasons are not difficult to find. Our economy has been undergoing rapid changes in employment and unemployment. The unemployment insurance program itself is complex in its provisions and in its administration. Its substantive features have been changed almost annually in the 50 state legislatures. The very volume of the provisions and their complexity discourage any attempt at an overall appraisal of its provisions and historical development.

There appeared, therefore, to be a need for a comprehensive study of unemployment insurance in the American economy, including the nature of the unemployment which it is designed to alleviate, the principles on which it is based, its historical development, and the issues that have developed with respect to virtually every phase of the program. This book is an attempt to make such a study. Since the authors are primarily interested in the policies that govern the program, only incidental attention has been given to the administration of the program and it is hoped that someone with special administrative interests will fill that gap. It has, of course, also been necessary to deal with many aspects of the program rather briefly, and the reader interested in delving more deeply into these aspects is referred to the writings cited in the footnotes and bibliography.

In the course of writing this book, we have been faced with the problem of keeping abreast of a program in the process of change. Many amendments are made in the state laws each year, so that we have had to describe the laws as of a specified date, with the realization that the facts given might be changed before this book is printed. We are also faced, as this book goes to press, with the fact that the Congress is actively considering the federal administration's bill, which if enacted will make a number of rather significant changes in the program. With the possible exception of extensions of coverage, however, the issues and problems with which these proposed federal amendments deal will not be permanently or conclusively settled. The discussion of these issues and problems in this volume will therefore still be pertinent, even if most of the proposals in the administration's bill are enacted.

This book was made possible through financial grants from the W. E. Upjohn Institute for Employment Research. The authors are deeply indebted to Dr. Harold C. Taylor, Director of the Institute, for his understanding of the nature and significance of this problem and for recognizing the need for the historical study and appraisal that this book provides. We also appreciate the encouragement of Dr. Herbert E. Striner, Director for Program Development for the Institute in Washington, whose cooperation has eased the problem of preparing this volume.

We are in debt to many people who have written on this subject. We relied upon many persons who offered to review our analysis of the controversial issues which are found in this area. We are especially indebted to a group of men who read portions of the manuscript and who assisted us with critical comments. These include Norman C. Barcus, Director of the Research and Statistical Division, Michigan Employment Security Commission; Dr. Sar A. Levitan of the Washington staff of the Upjohn Institute; and Raymond Munts, Assistant Director, Department of Social Security, AFL-CIO, who read the entire manuscript. In addition, Marion B. Folsom, former Secretary of the Department of Health, Education, and Welfare and Director of the Eastman Kodak Company, who served on the Advisory Council to the Committee on Economic Security in 1935 and on other state and federal advisory groups, managed to squeeze some time into a crowded schedule and to send us valuable comments on several of the chapters. S. W. Wirpel, Assistant Director, Employee Benefits Department, Inland Steel Company, gave helpful suggestions on a number of chapters. We are indebted to Robert C. Goodwin, Administrator of the Bureau of Employment Security, whose interest in this volume made it easier for us to exploit the knowledge of the Bureau staff, especially William R. Curtis, Deputy Administrator; Louis Levine, Director of the United States Employment Service; Margaret M. Dahm, Special Assistant to the Administrator; and Ralph Altman, Ely M. Artenberg, Saul J. Blaustein, and Leo M. Orwicz of the Unemployment Insurance Service.

We expecially wish to thank Mrs. Joyce L. Kornbluh of Ann Arbor, Michigan, who substantially improved the style and readability of this book by careful and imaginative editing of the entire manuscript.

Needless to say, the responsibility for errors of fact and in judgments on policy matters clearly belong only to the authors.

April, 1966   WILLIAM HABER
                                          MERRILL G. MURRAY

Table of Contents

80399

Introduction

Unemployment insurance is the keystone in the growing number of programs to aid the unemployed. Each year it helps millions of workers to bridge the gap between jobs. Available without proof of need, it aids workers to maintain self-respect at a time when their morale is low. By providing a regular though reduced income, it saves the unemployed worker from the gnawing fear of destitution.

The program has been in continuous operation for over a quarter of a century. Following the enactment of the first state law in Wisconsin in 1932, unemployment insurance laws were enacted in all other states during 1935-37 under the stimulus of the 1935 federal Social Security Act. Since that time, federal programs have been provided for railroad workers, federal civilian workers, and those in military service.

Uemployment insurance has won general acceptance and is taken for granted as one of our American institutions. Labor considers it to be one of our most valuable social programs. And although most employers originally opposed the enactment of unemployment insurance laws, today, for the most part, management accepts the program and recognizes its value.

Yet the program is subject to continual criticism from every side. Labor criticizes the program as inadequate. Management is also critical, observing that many laws are too loose in their eligibility and disqualification provisions. Almost every "man on the street" has some example of a person who, he believes, drew benefits without justification. Periodically, the program is criticized in magazine articles or the press, usually by calling attention to alleged abuses in the system. Most critics would agree, however, that the assistance provided by unemployment insurance to millions of unemployed workers and the increased stability it gives the economy far outweigh such criticisms.

After more than a quarter of a century, there is still much controversy and disagreement about many provisions of unemployment insurance even among those who have been closely involved with the program for many years. Although today nearly everyone agrees there should be a program, the particulars of the program arouse considerable disagreement.

Why is there so much controversy about unemployment insurance? First, disagreements spring from differences in social philosophy or points of view. Workers, who receive the benefits of the program, put more emphasis on the adequacy of such benefits. Employers, who pay the cost of the program, are more concerned with restrictions on those eligible for benefits and on the prevention of what they consider to be unwarranted benefit payments. In addition, there are differences in political points of view as to whether the program should include greater state autonomy or more federal participation.

Unemployment insurance is a dynamic program which needs to keep adapting to the changing character of a tremendously complex economy. It reflects the problems presented by a changing and growing labor force and by new and different types of unemployment growing out of advancing technology. These problems must usually be solved on the basis of incomplete information and in the midst of conflicting interests.

Much has been written over the years on specific controversial issues. But few comprehensive studies have been made of the unemployment insurance program in the United States. After more than a quarter century of experience, such a study of the unemployment insurance system seems desirable. Great changes are taking place in the labor force to which unemployment insurance should be adjusted. Recent years have seen a large influx of married women and youth into the job market. The growing number of workers who are subject to persistent and long-term unemployment challenges a program designed particularly for short-term unemployment. The continuing relatively high level of unemployment, although on the decline as this is written, is straining the financial structure of the unemployment insurance system in some states and raising basic questions as to how it can be more adequately financed.

It is the authors' belief that a contribution can be made through a comprehensive review of *all* the issues of the unemployment insurance program. Hopefully, such a review will bring out the interrelationships of many problems. Valuable new data, especially the study of the characteristics of the claimants under the Temporary Extended Unemployment Compensation Act of 1961, have recently become available and should throw new light on many old issues in the present context of a changed and changing labor market.

The authors have lived more or less closely with this program from its inception. They have had an extraordinary opportunity to help preside at its birth, watch its growth into maturity, and participate in the solution of some of its problems. They hope that this work will contribute toward a better understanding of the problems that are constantly emerging in this dynamic program and will result in improvements in its character and operation.

Part I

Unemployment and Its Insurability

Chapter 1

The Changing Unemployment
Problem and Its Implications
for Unemployment Insurance

Some unemployment is inevitable in a free, dynamic society. Even if "full employment" were attained, there would still be some unemployment due to changing demands for products, seasonal variations in business activity, movement of workers into the labor force, and a multitude of other causes. To paraphrase the late Lord William H. Beveridge, "full employment" does not mean "no unemployment." And it appears to be unlikely that we will or want to have full employment in the sense that everyone is working all the time. Enormous changes are occurring in our economy and are likely to continue, perhaps at an accelerating pace. The appearance of new products, changes in materials, geographical shifts in the location of industries, and changes in technology—of which automation is the most spectacular—all result in dislocations of labor. Unemployment results for some wage earners from increased productivity; other unemployment is due to the inability of displaced workers to fit into new types of jobs. Even if the workers who are dislocated by industrial change are re-employed in some new process or industry, most suffer a period of unemployment. Many must be retrained before they can be re-employed.

We are faced with the compound problem of increasing the demand for products and services fast enough to absorb those displaced by increased productivity at the same time that we must provide jobs for a labor force which is rapidly expanding and changing its makeup. The result has been a relatively high rate of unemployment and large numbers who are unemployed for long periods of time. Although we seem to be making inroads on this problem, even the most optimistic foresee a long road ahead before we can bring unemployment levels down to what would be the irreducible minimum of "frictional" unemployment under a "full employment" economy.

3

Unemployment insurance is the "first line of defense" against unemployment, whether it be large-scale unemployment or only frictional unemployment. As unemployment has increased in numbers, duration, and complexity, new problems have been created and old problems have grown more difficult to solve. An understanding of trends in the extent, duration, and nature of unemployment is therefore of primary importance to those interested in an effective unemployment insurance program.

INCREASES AND CHANGES IN THE LABOR FORCE

By 1947, the postwar readjustment was about over and the period was one of prosperity and comparatively full employment. The year 1947, therefore, is a good starting point for the purposes of considering those changes in the labor force that affect the operation of the unemployment insurance program.

Between 1947 and 1965, the civilian labor force grew from 60,168,000 to 75,635,000,[1] by 15.5 million or 25.6 percent.[2] This growth was not steady and reflected changing economic conditions. The average annual growth was about 800,000, but it was only 100,000 in 1961 and 1.8 million in 1965.

Of special significance was the number of women who entered the labor market during this period. From 1947 to 1965, there was an increase of 9.7 million women in the labor force (from 16.9 million to 26.6 million) as compared to an increase of 5.7 million men. During these years the proportion of women in the civilian labor force rose from 28 to 35.2 percent. From 1947 to 1962, the number of married women, living with their husbands, in the labor force increased from 7.5 to 14.8 million.[3]

Because of their pattern of moving in and out of the job market, the increase in married women workers presents special problems to the unemployment insurance program. For example, 8.5 million women who had worked at some time during 1962 were out of the labor force during part of the year because they were taking care of their homes.[4] Presumably, most of these were married women.

It is expected that the total labor force will grow to about 86 million by 1970 and to 101 million by 1980.[5] The increase in the number of women in the labor force will continue through the 1960's, reaching a projected total

[1] Alaska and Hawaii are included in the 1962 data and thereafter but were not available in previous years.

[2] *Manpower Report of the President and a Report on Manpower Requirements, Resources, Utilization and Training by the United States Department of Labor, March, 1966* (Washington, D.C.: U.S. Government Printing Office), p. 153, table A–1.

[3] *Manpower Report of the President and a Report on Manpower Requirements, Resources, Utilization and Training by the United States Department of Labor, March, 1963* (Washington, D.C.: U.S. Government Printing Office), p. 12.

[4] Samuel Sabin, "Work Experience of the Population in 1962," *Monthly Labor Review*, Vol. LXXXIV, No. 1 (January, 1964), p. 23, table 7.

[5] Sophia Cooper and Denis F. Johnston, "Labor Force Projections for 1970–80," *Monthly Labor Review*, Vol. LXXXVIII, No. 2, p. 130, table 1.

of over 30 million in 1970. The most rapid growth will be among females 14 to 24 years of age—2.7 million as compared with 0.3 million in the 1950's —reflecting the greater numbers of maturing youth in the population. Projections for 1970 to 1980 show almost as large an increase in the number of women entering the labor force as in the 1960's—an increase of over 6 million. In the 1970's, there will be a smaller increase among young women under 24—1.5 million—and an increase in those 25 to 34 years of age—2.5 million—reflecting the older ages of young girls who entered the labor force in the 1960's. The number of women aged 45 and over in the labor force will increase by 3 million in the 1960's and by 3.5 million in the 1970's.[6]

The greatest change in the composition of the labor force during this period will be in the number of youth entering the job market. In the 1950's, the increase in the number of youth 14–24 years of age in the total labor force was minor, netting only 366,000, reflecting the low birth rate during the depression of the 1930's and the World War II years. During the 1960's, however, the youth who were born during the "baby boom" following World War II are old enough to be available for jobs. In the decade from 1960 to 1970 the *net* number of youth in the labor force will grow from 13.7 million to 20.3 million, an increase of 48 percent.[7] But in 1970– 1980 the increase in youth in the labor force (18.3 percent), will be only slightly larger than the increase in the total labor force (17.9 percent).

Male workers aged 25 to 34 years will increase in numbers as the young men entering the labor force in the 1960's mature. This age group, which actually dropped by 100,000 in the 1950's, will be added to by over a million in the 1960's and by 5.5 million in the 1970's—a total rise of 45.8 percent. In fact, despite the large numbers of women continuing to enter the labor force, there will be a greater rise among males of all ages in the labor force than among females. Between 1964 and 1970, males of all ages will account for slightly over half of the additional workers in the labor force; between 1970 and 1975, about 58 percent; and between 1975 and 1980, 60 percent.[8] This shift will also reflect the slowing down in the number of married women entering the labor force and the withdrawal of a larger proportion of young women from the job market by their late teens or mid-twenties when they have children.

These changes will have broad effects on unemployment insurance. Primarily, the numbers of workers who will be covered by unemployment

[6] Sophia Cooper and Denis F. Johnston, "Labor Force Projections for 1970–80," *Monthly Labor Review,* Vol. LXXXV, No. 2 (February, 1965), pp. 129–40.

[7] Since a large number of those entering the labor force in the 1960's will be young students and older women who are seeking part-time employment or have low skills, the numbers given above may not materialize unless part-time employment and jobs requiring lower skills expand correspondingly.

[8] United States Department of Labor, *Manpower Report of the President and a Report on Manpower Requirements, Resources, Utilization and Training, March, 1965* (Washington, D.C.: U.S. Government Printing Office), p. 49. See also pp. 46–50 on labor force growth.

insurance will rise. However, large numbers of youth who will be covered by the program in the 1960's will be out of work before they can become sufficiently established job-wise to qualify for unemployment benefits. As for the additional number of working women, their tendency to move in and out of the job market will increase the problem for the unemployment insurance program of guarding against unwarranted drawing of benefits after withdrawal from the labor force. The increased numbers of working men will be an offsetting factor because of their greater job stability.

EMPLOYMENT TRENDS

From 1947 through 1963, the growth in employment of 11 million fell short by 1.8 million of the labor force growth of 1.8 million. This was reversed in 1964 and 1965, during which employment grew by 3.4 million, while the labor force grew by 2.6 million, narrowing the discrepancy to only one million. As this is written, it is too early to tell whether this is a permanent reversal in trends.

Actually, the increase in non-agricultural employment from 1947 to 1965 was 18 million, since agricultural employment declined by 3.7 million. These over-all employment figures also hide dramatic changes in some manufacturing industries. As a result of increased productivity, some manufacturing industries have actually reduced their work force. In most industries, the total number of workers has not decreased as much as would have been the case had not total output increased during the period. But even with additional output, the total number employed has declined in most producing industries in the last decade and a half. In addition, the number of white-collared workers in sales and clerical work has gone up, and, therefore, the relative decline in production workers is even sharper than the net reduction in the number of employees in these industries would indicate. While total manufacturing employment increased from 15,545,000 in 1947 to 17,984,000 in 1965, employment of production and related workers grew only slightly from 12,990,000 in 1947 to 13,376,000 in 1965. These totals, moreover, hide considerable decreases in the employment of production workers in specific industries. The number of production workers in petroleum and related products, for example, decreased from 170,000 in 1947 to 110,000 in 1965, and in textile mills from 1,220,000 to 821,000 during the same period.[9]

In contrast to the shrinking job opportunities for production workers, job openings have increased in the service-producing industries, employing predominantly white-collar workers. In fact, of the 14.4 million net increase in employment from 1947 to 1965, 8.7 million occurred in trade, finance, insurance, real estate, and service industries. The increase in these industries was 50 percent.

Government is another sector of the economy that has experienced a

[9] *Manpower Report, 1965, op. cit.,* pp. 233–34, tables C–1 and C–2.

large expansion in employment. Government employment increased from 5.5 million in 1947 to 9.2 million in 1962, a growth of more than 65 percent. Nine tenths of this growth was at state and local levels, reflecting the increased need for teachers as school registrations have mounted, and the increased need for additional urban services as cities have expanded following World War II.

If present trends continue, a further contraction in blue-collar jobs can be anticipated. With increased mechanization and the introduction of automation into clerical activities, a slowing down or even a reduction in clerical employment may also eventually occur. In fact, the development of phonetic automatic typewriters may soon affect one of the shortage occupations, that of stenographers. Mechanization of retail operations through vending machines and further automation of supermarket and department store operations can be expected. The only sector of the economy that may show marked increases in employment is government, and even there mechanization is making inroads on employment.

Part-Time Employment

The increase in part-time employment,[10] deserves special discussion. Between 1950 and 1960, the number of part-time workers in nonagricultural industries went up from 7.1 to 10.8 million or by 52 percent, while full-time employment increased from 43.0 to 48.6 million or by only 13 percent. The number employed part time continued to grow in the 1960's.

In order to analyze part-time employment meaningfully for unemployment insurance, it is necessary to distinguish three groups of part-time workers: those who normally work full time but are temporarily working part time for "noneconomic reasons," those on part time for "economic reasons," and a third group who usually work part time out of choice.

The first group, which has only minor significance for the unemployment insurance program, includes those working short time because of bad weather, labor disputes, vacation, illness, holidays or other temporary events—about 2 million persons. Workers who are employed part time for economic reasons represent underemployment. Their number, which ranges from 2 to 2.5 million, fluctuates with economic conditions. This group includes those who usually work full time and those who usually work part time.[11] Those normally working full time are of most significance for unemployment insurance since some may be working short enough hours to qualify or be able to qualify for partial unemployment insurance benefits. Some persons who usually work part time may also qualify for

---

[10] Part-time work is defined in the *Monthly Report of the Labor Force* of the United States Department of Labor as work on a schedule of less than 35 hours.

[11] The latter group in turn are composed of those who work part time by choice but do not have as much part-time work as they would like and those who once worked full time but have been on short time for so long they can no longer be regarded as full-time workers. These two subgroups are about equally divided in size.

unemployment insurance, either on the basis of former full-time employment or by reason of liberal qualifying requirements for unemployment benefits.

The third, and largest group of part-time workers are those working part time out of choice. The group has grown significantly in recent years. An average of 4.7 million were voluntarily working part time in 1955. The number, 8.5 million, had almost doubled by 1964.

Those working part time by choice are largely women, students, partially retired persons, and those unable to work full time because of partial disability. They are mainly concentrated in sales work (24.1 percent), private household work (46.5 percent), and other service work (21.0 percent). In a detailed analysis of part-time employment in May, 1960,[12] it was found that over 80 percent or 1.6 million of employed boys and girls aged 14 to 17 were working part time. Only 1.5 percent of the men 25 to 64 years of age, or less than half a million, were working part time voluntarily, but 17.7 percent, or 1.3 million working women within this age group were employed part time. Of those aged 65 and over who were working, 26.4 percent, or about 425,000 of the men, and 42.5 percent, or about 340,000 of the women were voluntarily engaged in part-time jobs.

The implications of these changes for unemployment insurance are difficult to predict. With increases in employment in the service industries and in the white-collar occupations, it may be expected that a larger proportion of claimants will be women whose attachment to the labor market is generally more difficult to determine than that of the men. Secondly, there will be a growing problem of dealing with claimants who have been employed only on a part-time basis—a growing phenomenon, especially in retail trade. A third problem area may develop from the growing numbers of state and local government workers, only a fraction of whom are now protected by the unemployment insurance program.

TRENDS IN UNEMPLOYMENT

Unemployment was at fairly low levels in the first decade following World War II, except for temprorary increases in unemployment during the recessions of 1949–50 and 1953–54. This trend shifted, however, following the recessions of 1954 and 1958, and high levels of unemployment continued to be a problem even during prosperous years. Following 1958, unemployment did not drop below 5 percent until 1964 (see Table 1–1), and although it fell below 4 percent early in 1966, it promises to remain a stubborn problem for large numbers in view of the prospective increases in the labor force and the trends in employment already discussed.

The higher levels of unemployment that occurred after 1953 were accompanied by an increase in the number of persons experiencing long

[12] Robert L. Stein and Jane L. Meredith, "Growth and Characteristics of the Part time Work Force," Special Labor Force Report No. 10, *Monthly Labor Review*, November, 1960, pp. 1166–75.

periods without work. The average number unemployed 15 to 26 weeks increased from 132,000 in 1953 to a peak of 785,000 in 1958 and was still 491,000 in 1964. The number unemployed 27 weeks or more was particularly pronounced, increasing from an average of 79,000 in 1953 to a peak of 804,000 in 1961. By 1964, it had dropped to 482,000 (see Table 1–2).

Table 1–1

Unemployed Persons and Unemployment Rates
1947–64

Year	Number Unemployed (in thousands)	Unemployment Rate
1947	2,142	3.6
1948	2,064	3.4
1949	3,395	5.5
1950	3,142	5.0
1951	1,879	3.0
1952	1,673	2.7
1953	1,602	2.5
1954	3,240	5.0
1955	2,654	4.0
1956	2,551	3.8
1957	2,936	4.3
1958	4,681	6.8
1959	3,813	5.5
1960	3,931	5.6
1961	4,806	6.7
1962	4,007	5.6
1963	4,166	5.7
1964	3,876	5.2

Source: *Manpower Report of the President*, March, 1965, p. 264, table A–11.

Data on unemployment tend to be understated, since they are based on monthly counts of the unemployed through the sample surveys conducted by the Bureau of the Census. During the course of a year, several times as many persons experience unemployment as are unemployed at any one time. In 1962, for example, an average number of 4 million were unemployed at any one time, but a total of 15.3 million experienced some unemployment during the year.[13] Similarly, the number of long-term unemployed is much higher over a year's period than the monthly average. Turnover among the unemployed and the large numbers of persons who experience two or more spells of unemployment, which together amount to 15 or more weeks of unemployment, swell the rate of long-term unemployment during any one year. Thus, in 1962, a total of 2,768,000 experienced from 15 to 26 weeks of unemployment and 2,020,000 experienced 27 weeks or more.[14]

[13] Sabin, *op. cit.*, p. 18.
[14] *Ibid.*, p. 19, table 2.

Table 1–2

Unemployed Persons and Percent Distribution of the Unemployed, by Duration of Unemployment: Annual Averages, 1947–64

| | | Duration of Unemployment | | | | | | |
| | | Number (in thousands) | | | | Percentage Distribution | | |
Year	Total	Less than 15 Weeks	15 to 26 Weeks	27 Weeks and Over	Total	Less than 15 Weeks	15 to 26 Weeks	27 Weeks and Over
1947	2,356	1,959	234	164	100.0	83.1	9.9	7.0
1948	2,325	2,018	193	116	100,0	86.7	8.3	5.0
1949	3,682	2,999	427	256	100.0	81.5	11.6	7.0
1950	3,351	2,570	425	357	100.0	76.7	12.7	10.7
1951	2,099	1,799	166	137	100.0	85.6	7.9	6.5
1952	1,932	1,700	148	84	100.0	88.0	7.7	4.4
1953	1,870	1,660	132	79	100.0	88.7	7.1	4.2
1954	3,578	2,766	495	317	100.0	77.3	13.8	8.9
1955	2,904	2,202	367	336	100.0	75.8	12.6	11.6
1956	2,822	2,210	301	232	100.0	81.0	10.7	8.2
1957	2,936	2,375	321	239	100.0	80.9	10.9	8.1
1958	4,681	3,230	785	667	100.0	69.0	16.8	14.2
1959	3,813	2,771	469	571	100.0	72.7	12.3	15.0
1960	3,931	2,974	502	454	100.0	75.7	12.8	11.5
1961	4,806	3,272	728	804	100.0	70.1	15.1	16.7
1962	4,007	2,868	534	585	100.0	72.1	13.3	14.6
1963	4,166	3,078	535	553	100.0	73.9	12.8	13.3
1964	3,876	2,903	491	482	100.0	74.9	12.6	12.4

Source: *Manpower Report of the President*, March, 1965, p. 209, table A–17.

TYPES OF UNEMPLOYMENT

Any classification of unemployment into types of unemployment is necessarily arbitrary. For convenience, however, unemployment will be discussed under the headings of short-term or "frictional" unemployment, cyclical unemployment, and unemployment due to structural and technological developments.

Short-Term Unemployment

Although the problem of long-term unemployment is serious, most unemployment is still of short duration. The proportion varies with business conditions, but about three fourths of the unemployed at any time have been out of work less than 15 weeks, and from 40 to 50 percent have been unemployed less than 5 weeks. Over a 12-month period, the proportion with short-duration unemployment is lower, since many have two or three spells of short-duration unemployment which may add up to a yearly total of 15 or more weeks. Thus, of the 15.3 million unemployed during 1962, 8.5 million, or 56 percent, had less than 15 weeks of unemployment: 4 million had from 1 to 4 weeks of unemployment, 2.8 million from 5 to 10 weeks, and 1.7 million had from 11 to 14 weeks.[15]

[15] *Ibid.*, p. 19, table 2.

A large part of this short-duration unemployment is what is ordinarily referred to as "frictional unemployment." A minimum amount of frictional unemployment is a necessary ingredient of a dynamic economy. If it does not rise above 2 or 3 percent of the labor force, it need not be a source of worry. A fairly large part of frictional unemployment consists of people entering and leaving the labor market, or being idle while changing from one job to another. Such mobility of labor characterizes a healthy economy. Some of this unemployment can be reduced or shortened through improved organization of the labor market; it cannot be eliminated.

The bulk of "frictional" or short-term unemployment, however, is caused by constant changes in the demand for workers during the year due to temporary changes in consumer demand, model changeovers, and a host of other reasons. This usually takes the form of short layoffs after which the workers return to their former jobs.

Seasonal Unemployment

One of the major types of short-term unemployment is due to seasonal changes in employment because of weather or seasonal changes in consumer demand. The seasonal adjustment factors used by the United States Bureau of Labor Statistics for unemployment rates during 1958–60 in the *Monthly Report on the Labor Force* ranged from 118.6 in February to 78.2 in October.[16] This means that unemployment resulting from seasonal influences alone may cause total unemployment to fluctuate by about 40 percent during a calendar year—from almost 20 percent above the average in February to more than 20 percent below the average in October.

Seasonal unemployment has always been a problem for unemployment insurance. Attempts have been made in some states to identify seasonal industries and pay benefits only during the normal season, but without significant results. Although the bulk of seasonal employment is covered by unemployment insurance, some industries that operate for only a short season are not included under those state laws that cover only employers who operate for 20 or more weeks in the year. The bulk of seasonal employment, however, is covered by unemployment insurance. There is some evidence that the availability of unemployment compensation has actually increased worker attachment to seasonal employers and some type of seasonal unemployment.[17]

In the future, some lessening in seasonal unemployment may be anticipated. Modern technological improvements, such as in the making of

[16] Morton S. Ruff and Robert L. Stein, "New Seasonal Adjustment Factors for Labor Force Components," *Monthly Labor Review,* August, 1960, p. 823, table 1.

[17] Richard A. Lester, *Economics of Unemployment Compensation* (Princeton: Industrial Relations Section, Princeton University, 1962), pp. 49–50. This observation is made in an informative and thoughtful chapter on "Implications of Labor Force Developments for Unemployment Benefits" (also appearing in the *Quarterly Review of Economics and Business,* May, 1961, pp. 47–56).

concrete, have made it possible to continue many types of construction throughout the year, even in cold weather. No doubt, other seasonal industries, particularly manufacturing, will provide more stability of employment by diversification of products and other devices, or through better management. On the other hand, the trade and service industries, which are heavily seasonal, are expanding and may result in an increase in total seasonal unemployment. Such expansion will be counteracted to some extent by a movement to iron out seasonality in the service industries. For example, seasonal hotels in the South have been kept open during summer by a movement to reduce rates, and Northern hotels have attracted winter guests by increasing their skiing facilities. But although there can be some reduction in it, seasonal unemployment will continue to be an important problem for unemployment insurance.

Unemployment among Part-Time Workers

The household data on unemployment published in the *Monthly Report on the Labor Force* include those looking for part-time as well as full-time work.[18] Those looking for part-time work (an average of 676,000) included about one sixth of the totally unemployed in 1964. This reduces significantly the number of the totally unemployed who would be of primary concern to unemployment insurance—those normally looking for full-time work. The latter, for instance, averaged 3,201,000 out of the gross average figure of 3,876,000 unemployed during 1964.

Between 1957 and 1964 the rate of unemployment of those looking for part-time work increased more than the rate of those looking for full-time work. In May, 1957, the unemployment rate was 3.7 percent for part-time workers and 4.0 percent for full-time workers; in May, 1964, the rate was 5.7 percent for part-time workers and 4.7 percent for full-time workers. The number of part-time women workers aged 20 and over who were unemployed had doubled to 160,000 from May, 1957, to May, 1964, but in the latter month, the rate of unemployment for women part-time workers aged 20 and over was only 3.3 percent[19] and for men aged 20 and over it was 4.2 percent.[20]

Since unemployment insurance was originally designed for full-time workers, the implication of the growing volume of part-time unemployment needs to be faced. Only a few states have any positive policy regarding the payment of benefits to part-time workers, but in all states some unemployed workers no doubt earn enough to qualify for benefits on the basis of part-

[18] A breakdown of those totally unemployed by those looking for full-time work and those looking for part-time work became available in the *Monthly Report on the Labor Force* beginning in January, 1963.

[19] The rate of unemployment of part-time women workers is low because many apparently can afford to remain out of the labor market when not employed.

[20] Robert L. Stein and June L. Meredith, "Unemployment among Full-Time and Part-Time Workers," *Monthly Labor Review*, September, 1964, p. 1011.

time employment. It is important that vigilance is exercised so that part-time workers who do meet the qualifying requirements and file claims for benefits are available for work.

Cyclical Unemployment

When it occurs, cyclical unemployment causes national concern. Unemployment caused by business recessions receives the most attention because it is usually nation-wide in scope and more in the public view. Business recessions since World War II have been relatively mild and of short duration. Unemployment during these recent recessions has been concentrated largely in manufacturing, particularly in the durable-goods manufacturing industries. Declining employment in manufacturing, construction, and trade, however, has been partially offset by employment gains in government and in finance and service industries. Thus, in February, 1961, at the trough of the recession, an employment drop of 1.5 million in the first three industry groups was partially offset by a gain of 400,000 in the last three.

The average number of unemployed increased by 1.7 million in 1954; 1.7 million in 1918; and 0.9 million in 1961.[21] Percentagewise, unemployment rose from 2.9 percent in 1953 to 5.6 percent in 1954; from 4.3 percent in 1957 to 6.8 percent in 1958; and from 5.6 percent in 1960 to 6.7 percent to 1961.

During recessions, unemployment increases not only in number but also in duration. Between 1960 and 1961, the average number of unemployed 27 weeks or more rose from 454,000 to 805,000, although this was a relatively mild recession. During 1961, the total number unemployed 27 weeks or more was 2,209,000.

This rise in long-duration unemployment is reflected in the claimants for unemployment insurance. Between 1960 and 1961, the number of claimants exhausting their benefits increased from 1.6 million to 2.4 million. In a more severe recession, such as that of 1957-58, the number of claimants exhausting their benefits rose from 1.1 million in 1957 to 2.5 million in 1958.

It is to be hoped that recessions will continue to be moderate, of short duration, and followed by longer periods of prosperity as they have been in the postwar years. However, recessions will continue to be a major source of unemployment, particularly unemployment of long duration. Permanent unemployment insurance policies and measures are required to deal adequately with the longer duration of unemployment that is characteristic of recessions.

[21] *Economic Report of the President, January, 1963*, table C–19. (The differences between the decrease in employment at the trough of the recession in 1958 and 1961 and the increase in unemployment in those years is because the unemployment figures are averages for the year.)

UNEMPLOYMENT FROM TECHNOLOGICAL AND STRUCTURAL CHANGES

Serious unemployment problems are being created by the tremendous transformations taking place in employment due to changes in materials, consumer demand, new and improved products, shifts in defense policy, and many other aspects of the economy. Technological innovations, however, are having the greatest impact on employment, leading to the most severe unemployment problems.

Structural Changes in Industry

Changes have occurred in materials used, such as the shift from coal to oil, steel to aluminum, wood to glass, and the substitution of plastics for other materials. Depletion of natural resourses has left whole areas depressed. For instance, depletion of iron ore has caused a large drop in employment in the Mesabi range of Minnesota. On the other hand, the development of new materials, such as plastics, has made possible the development of new products that have expanded employment.

Major shifts in defense policies, such as the shift from aircraft to missiles and radical changes in consumer demand are creating obsolete industries, products, and processes at an unprecedented rate, leaving displaced workers in their wake. Although new industries have rapidly developed, they are usually located in different geographic areas and demand different skill requirements. Thus, the last few decades have witnessed mass shutdowns in some sections of the country and the creation of entirely new industries in other areas.

Large-scale geographical movements of industries are continuing—the generation-long exodus of textile plants from the North to the South; the shift of furniture production from Michigan to Georgia; and the diffusion of Chicago-centered meat packing and meat processing operations to Iowa, Nebraska, and other Western states. All of these have resulted in a great reduction in the number of workers in the affected areas. Mergers of corporations also cause consolidation of plans and displacement of workers in abandoned, less efficient plants.[22]

Technological Changes

Increasing attention has focused on those changes in employment and the displacement of workers caused by technological advances, especially automation. However, there are many advances being made in technology besides automation per se. Extension of mechanization to operations still largely done by hand has contributed to increased productivity. New models of automatic machinery, such as for bottling or packaging, require less labor through simpler controls, variable motor speeds, and larger

---

[22] For an elaboration of these changes, see William Haber, Louis A. Ferman, and James R. Hudson, *The Impact of Technological Change*, (Kalamazoo, Mich.: W. E. Upjohn Institute for Employment Research, September, 1963), pp. 2–8.

machines. In many cases, a number of operations are integrated into a single machine. Materials handling has been increasingly mechanized. New metal processes are being developed; the basic oxygen process in steel-making, for example, is producing steel at least six times faster than the open hearth process. Technological advances in transportation including diesel-electric locomotives, large jet airplanes, and mechanization of traffic control are reducing manpower needs. Technological advances in power production, including nuclear power, are in various stages of development. Spectacular developments in communication, including the communications satellites, have improved the scope, efficiency, and speed of the transmission of votes, sight, and documents. The development of new synthetic materials, especially the plastics, and improved uses of older materials are resulting in the creation of new products and the displacement of others.[23] Many of these technological developments are akin to automation or have been automatized, but automation in the stricter sense is adding a new dimension to technological development.

Automation

What is automation? In the words of a recent Congressional report on the subject:

Automation is the third phase in the development of technology that began with the industrial revolution of the 18th century. First came mechanization, which created the factory system and separated labor and management in production. In the early 20th century, mass production brought the assembly line and other machinery so expensive that the ownership of industry had to be divorced from management and atomized into millions of separate shareholdings. Finally, since World War II, automation has added the elements of automatic control and decision making, turning the factory from a haphazard collection of machines into a single, integrated unit and requiring production on an enormous scale. Mechanization was a technology based on forms and applications of power. Mass production was a technology based on principles of production organization. Automation is a technology based on communication and control.[24]

The basic component of automation is the electronic computer. First introduced commercially in 1951, the number of computers has increased phenomenally since then. In addition, automation may include other components, including instrumentation, automatic controls, and numerical controls. Systems of recording and control instruments in plants where gases, fluids, and other chemicals are processed measure and record such factors as pressure, temperature, humidity, and flow and activate the opening and closing of valves and the operation of pumps. Computers are being increasingly applied to process control in industry. Numerical control in metal-

[23] For a fuller description of these technological developments, as well as automation, see *Manpower Report, 1964, op. cit.*, pp. 52–61.

[24] *Impact of Automation on Employment,* Report of the Subcommittee on Unemployment and the Impact of Automation of the Committee on Education and Labor, 87th Cong., 1st sess., Washington, D.C., June, 1961, p. 3.

working industries is achieved by the operation of machine tools and other types of equipment through numerically coded information recorded in advance on punched cards, magnetic tape, or punched paper tapes. This recorded information is often prepared with the help of a computer.[25]

The foregoing technological developments are interrelated. For example, the integration of long-distance transmission of data, electronic computers, and materials-handling equipment makes possible the automatic handling of customer orders, inventory control, and warehouse shipping.[26]

Dire predictions have been made of wholesale wiping out of jobs by automation. No doubt, large numbers of clerical jobs are being eliminated in business and government data processing, as well as numerous semiskilled and unskilled jobs and some supervisory positions in manufacturing. On the other hand, the manufacture, operation, and maintenance of computers is creating thousands of new jobs. Expanding reporting and control systems made possible by computers create additional employment openings. The facilitation of research and development through computers is contributing to the creation of new products and even of new industries.

No one knows as yet what the net effect of automation on employment will be, but it is certain that it will result in major changes in occupational and industrial employment. It is also certain that large numbers of workers will experience either temporary or long-duration unemployment in the process. As President Johnson said in his 1964 *Manpower Report* to the Congress: "Automation offers the possibility of rapid economic progress— even greater freedom from want and freedom from toil. But it brings with it problems of dislocation and readjustment for large numbers of individuals."[27]

Technological Changes Increase Productivity

The effect of technological changes can be measured by increases in productivity or output per man-hour. Our history has been marked by a continual increase in productivity. From 1909 to 1963 productivity per man-hour increased at a rate of 2.4 percent a year in the private economy. In the postwar years 1947 to 1963, the average annual increase per man hour was 3 percent. The 1965 *Manpower Report* had this to say about the effects of this rise in productivity, combined with the expected expansion of the labor force:

If we assume no more than a continuation of the long-term productivity trend, and no significant changes in the work week or work year, the combined requirements for additional real gross national product to compensate for just these two factors imply the need for an average annual increase well above 4 percent between now and 1970 . . . at no time in our recent peacetime history

[25] *Manpower Report*, 1964, *op. cit.*, pp. 55–56.
[26] *Ibid.*, p. 53.
[27] *Manpower Report*, 1964, *op. cit.*, p. 1.

have we been able to sustain a rate of increase in gross national product of over 4 percent for more than a brief period.

Altogether, taking into consideration the need to create jobs to reduce the unemployment rate from the current level of 5 percent to a more acceptable level, it will be necessary to sustain an annual average rate of increase in real gross national product about equal to this year's high rate of growth (4¾ percent) for the next half dozen years.[28]

Inadequate Economic Growth or Structural Unemployment?

There are two schools of thought as to the reasons for the relatively high levels of unemployment in recent years. These were set forth in the statements of William McChesney Martin of the Federal Reserve Board and Walter W. Heller of the Council of Economic Advisors who testified before the Joint Economic Committee of Congress on March 6 and 7, 1961. Mr. Martin maintained that the continued high rate of unemployment was due to structural changes, which resulted in persistent unemployment of large numbers of those affected. Mr. Heller held that the high level of unemployment was due to inadequate economic growth.[29]

The arguments over these two points of view have continued. It has been argued that too much stimulation of economic growth will result in inflation and adversely affect our international balance of payments. It has also been argued that economic growth can be stimulated without these adverse effects through tax cuts or appropriate incentives for capital investments, liberal depreciation allowances, and similar measures primarily designed to create favorable situations for profits. The stimulating effect of a federal tax cut on economic growth was demonstrated in 1964.

Others believe that structural factors represent the principal reason for continued high levels of unemployment. There is much truth to this. The ranks of the long-term unemployed are heavily weighted with semiskilled and unskilled workers, workers with low education, and workers under the handicaps of age or color. Large numbers of inexperienced and poorly educated youth swell the ranks of the unemployed. Most of the jobs that are disappearing as a result of automation and other types of advanced technology are jobs that have been held by the unskilled and poorly educated.

Large numbers of the structurally unemployed, through additional education and training or retraining, can be re-employed, especially in the growing service trades. But without an expanding economy, those displaced through technological changes and the larger numbers entering the labor market in the 1960's and 1970's cannot all be absorbed into jobs. It is therefore necessary both to keep expanding the economy and to educate and retrain workers for the kinds of jobs that are created in a dynamic and

[28] *Manpower Report, 1965, op. cit.,* p. 47.
[29] Hearings before the Joint Economic Committee, 87th Cong., 1st sess., February–April, 1961, pp. 321–41, 470–71.

changing industrial society. In our opinion, economic growth is the more important of these.[30]

There are reasons to believe that, in the long run, technological changes combined with economic growth will create the new jobs that are needed to absorb the growing labor force and to reduce the number of unemployed. Gloomy forecasts of the effects of technological change have been made ever since the invention of the steam engine. Similarly, despite the permanent decreases in the size of manufacturing employment which were forecast in the 1920's, manufacturing employment grew to twice the size it was then. There are a number of reasons for present-day optimism.

First, growth in the labor force is largely a reflection of population growth. An ever-growing population requires a continuing expansion in the production of goods and services. With projections of the population of from 180 million in 1960 to 214 million in 1970, there will be a great growth in employment to provide goods and services for this increased population.

Second, continued improvement in living standards is indicated for most Americans. This will create more employment through a greater demand for material goods, higher education, improved health services, better housing, more social services, and more convenient transportation. Americans have been conditioned not only to expect that their basic needs will be satisfied, but also to have insatiable wants.

Perhaps the most promising activity is the increased investment in research and development. Expenditures for research and development have totaled about $15 billion annually in recent years. In addition to the increased employment of those engaged in research and development, this activity should lead to the creation of new jobs in large numbers.[31]

There is hope, then, that, in the long run, the forces mentioned above, combined with sound government policies to promote economic growth, will result in sufficient expansion in employment to keep unemployment down to manageable levels.

However, even if economic growth is sufficient to keep unemployment at more tolerable levels—3 or 4 percent—automation and other technological developments will continue to result in the displacement each year of large numbers of workers. Also, the new opportunities for employment will require skills that many of these workers do not possess. While many workers displaced through technology find new jobs, there is usually an interval of unemployment. For large numbers of workers there is a long and difficult period of readjustment before another job is found, if ever one is found.

For those workers who find re-employment before too long a period of

---

[30] See the discussion by one of the authors, William Haber, "Unemployment: Inadequate Demand or Structural Imbalances," *Michigan Business Review* (Ann Arbor: University of Michigan, November, 1964), pp. 10–15.

[31] *The Impact of Technological Change, op. cit.*, pp. 9–10.

unemployment transpires, unemployment insurance fills an important role of providing partial income maintenance. One of the most important questions facing the unemployment insurance program is how long that period of protection should be. It is evident that the increased numbers who are unemployed for six months or longer include many technologically displaced workers.

While it is recognized that retraining is necessary for many if they are to find re-employment, this may not be available for some unemployed workers. Some will lack the basic education needed for retraining. Many will be unwilling to leave their homes and relocate where new jobs have opened. How long should unemployment insurance carry such workers on its rolls? Certainly, the great increase in technological unemployment in recent years has important implications for unemployment insurance. And, if adequate economic growth is not maintained, the long-range financing of unemployment insurance will have to be adjusted to the higher costs of long-term high levels of unemployment.

THE INSURED UNEMPLOYED

Thus far we have discussed the problem of unemployment in terms of total unemployment as revealed by the monthly household data given in the *Monthly Survey of the Labor Force,* issued by the United States Department of Labor.[32] Before leaving the discussion of unemployment, it is important to know something about the number and characteristics of unemployed claimants for unemployment insurance. Weekly reports are secured on "insured unemployment," that is, the number of persons filing claims for unemployment benefits certifying to a week of total or partial unemployment.[33] The number of insured unemployed under the state unemployment insurance laws is usually used for comparison with the Census household sample data on the unemployed. Weekly data on the number of insured unemployed under the federal programs for federal civilian workers, ex-servicemen, and railroad workers are also secured and published.

The figures on state insured unemployment are much lower than the figures for total unemployment.[34] State insured unemployment amounts to a higher proportion of total unemployment in periods of recession than in periods of prosperity. In recessions, it reaches 60 percent or more in some months. In prosperous years, the proportion ranges between 40 and 50

[32] This data is collected through a monthly sample survey of households, collected and tabulated by the Bureau of the Census, United States Department of Commerce for the Bureau of Labor Statistics of the United States Department of Labor.

[33] Weekly reports are also secured on the number filing "initial claims," that is, persons filing notices that they are starting periods of unemployment. Part of these are re-employed before they have completed a week of unemployment.

[34] The data on total unemployment are subject to a sampling error, whereas insured unemployment is an actual, complete count. This may result in a smaller or larger difference between Census and insured unemployment data, depending on whether there is a plus or minus error in the Census data.

percent. Insured unemployment also fluctuates more seasonally than total unemployment and reaches a peak in the winter months. Total unemployment reaches a peak in June, due to the influx of students into the labor market at that time (see Table 1–3).

Table 1–3

State Insured Unemployment, Total Unemployment, and Insured Unemployment as a Percent of Total Unemployment

Year	Insured Unemployment	Total Unemployment	Insured Unemployment* as Percent of Total Unemployment
1956	1,212	2,551	43
1957	1,450	2,936	49
1958	2,509	4,681	54
1959	1,683	3,813	44
1960	1,906	3,931	44
1961	2,290	4,807	48
1962	1,783	4,008	44
1963	1,806	4,166	43
1964	1,605	3,876	41

* For Census week.

Source: United States Department of Labor, Bureau of Employment Security.

There are a number of reasons for the large difference between the number of total and insured unemployed. First, the difference would be somewhat smaller if insured unemployment under the regular federal programs were included. These programs, however, would add less than 10 percent to the state insured unemployment totals. A second difference is that total unemployment figures include new entrants and re-entrants into the labor force who have not yet found jobs. For example, in 1963, unemployed entrants with no work experience were 17.5 percent of the total number unemployed. The number of re-entrants who have not yet found jobs is not known.

In the third group who are not in the insured unemployment figures are, of course, those who have been in self-employment, unpaid family employment, or in employment not covered by unemployment insurance. While employment that is not covered by unemployment insurance is almost a fourth of all wage and salaried employment, unemployment in the noncovered groups would add only about 15 percent to the insured unemployment figures. The rate of unemployment among those who have been in noncovered employment is somewhat lower than the rate of insured unemployment because a large proportion of the noncovered workers are employed by state and local governments and nonprofit organizations which have a low rate of unemployment.

A fourth group includes those who have worked in covered employment but not enough to qualify for benefits, who have been disqualified from benefits for various reasons, or, although qualified, have not yet filed or may never file for benefits. This, again, represents a small proportion of the total and would add not more than 5 or 6 percent to insured unemployment if they were counted. Sometimes, particularly when layoffs are expected to be short, the number qualified for benefits who do not file claims may be significant.

An important fraction of the total number unemployed are those who have exhausted their unemployment benefits. This proportion varies with the total amount of unemployment, being larger in recessions. During recent years, between recessions, the proportion who have exhausted their benefits has been higher than before 1958.

Finally, the total number of unemployed in 1964 incuded about two thirds of a million workers who normally worked only part time. Since most states require a claimant for benefits to be available for full-time employment, most of these persons would not qualify for unemployment benefits.[35] On the other hand, insured unemployment includes those who are normally employed full time but are partially unemployed and therefore file for partial benefits. They represent 8 or 9 percent of the insured unemployed. These are not counted as unemployed by the Census totals.

The Geographical Location of Insured Unemployment

Another aspect of insured unemployment data needs to be noted. Since unemployment insurance is mostly a federal-state system, it is important to know something about the geographical distribution of unemployment. Insured unemployment data are superior to monthly data on total unemployment in that the insured data are available on a state basis.

The *range* of insured unemployment is quite wide among the states. With a national rate of 5.7 in the recession year 1961, insured unemployment ranged from 2.8 percent in Nebraska and South Dakota to 8.1 percent in Pennsylvania and 8.8 percent in West Virginia (leaving Alaska aside, which is not typical because of its high unemployment in the winter season, and Puerto Rico which has a serious problem of underdevelopment). In the recovery year of 1963, insured unemployment had dropped to a national rate of 4.3, but ranged from 1.5 percent in Nebraska and Virginia to 5.9 percent in California (see Table 1–4).

[35] Estimates were made in 1962 by the Bureau of Employment Security, adjusting insured unemployment upward for all the factors listed above except the Census figures on unemployed part-time workers. The difference between the adjusted estimates of insured unemployment and the Census figures on total unemployment, using two methods of adjustment, still left differences ranging from one half to three fourths of a million. (See President's Committee to Appraise Employment and Unemployment Statistics, *Measuring Employment and Unemployment* [Washington, D.C., 1962], pp. 104–112 and Appendix H.) Apparently if these figures had been available on the part-time workers who were unemployed, they would have accounted for practically all of the difference.

Table 1–4

Annual Rate of Insured Unemployment by State
1961 and 1964

	1961	*1964*
United States	5.7	4.3
Alabama	6.2	4.2
Alaska	12.6	10.2
Arizona	4.5	3.7
Arkansas	7.4	4.9
California	6.3	5.4
Colorado	2.9	2.9
Connecticut	5.1	3.6
Delaware	4.3	2.7
District of Columbia	2.5	2.3
Florida	4.7	3.1
Georgia	5.1	2.8
Hawaii	4.0	4.6
Idaho	6.1	4.9
Illinois	4.3	3.1
Indiana	4.9	2.7
Iowa	3.4	2.0
Kansas	3.7	2.9
Kentucky	8.0	4.5
Louisiana	6.3	4.1
Maine	8.3	5.8
Maryland	5.4	3.5
Massachusetts	5.7	5.5
Michigan	7.9	3.5
Minnesota	5.2	4.2
Mississippi	7.0	4.5
Missouri	5.1	3.6
Montana	7.8	4.3
Nebraska	2.8	2.5
Nevada	5.4	3.6
New Hampshire	5.1	4.5
New Jersey	6.0	5.3
New Mexico	5.3	3.8
New York	5.9	5.3
North Carolina	5.2	3.7
North Dakota	6.2	4.6
Ohio	6.0	3.6
Oklahoma	5.7	4.5
Oregon	6.9	4.6
Pennsylvania	8.1	5.8
Rhode Island	6.4	5.6
South Carolina	4.3	3.1
South Dakota	2.8	3.2
Tennessee	6.9	4.6
Texas	3.4	2.8
Utah	3.7	3.5
Vermont	6.3	5.8
Virginia	3.0	1.8
Washington	7.5	6.5
West Virginia	8.8	5.8
Wisconsin	4.7	3.1
Wyoming	4.7	4.5
Puerto Rico	6.4	6.6

Source: *Handbook of Unemployment Insurance Financial Data*, United States Department of Labor, Bureau of Employment Security.

In short, insured unemployment is three or four times as much in some states as in others. This is partly due to differences in the state laws, particularly with respect to their provisions which affect the duration of benefits. It is mainly due, however, to differences in economic conditions in different states. This has important implications for the financing of unemployment insurance benefits.

SUMMARY AND CONCLUSIONS

Beginning in 1958, high unemployment has been one of our most important economic problems. There have been important changes in the volume and character of the labor force and of employment in the postwar period. More changes are in prospect. All this has important implications for unemployment insurance.

The major part of the growth in the labor force from 1947 to 1964 was among women. Married women accounted for most of the increased number of women workers. While the number of youth rose only slightly during the 1950's, there will be a large growth in the proportion of youth entering the labor market in the 1960's. In the 1970's, the number of women entering the labor market will slow down, and most of the labor force growth will be among men in the 25 to 34 age group.

Manufacturing has been marked by reductions in the number of production workers, partially offset by increases in clerical and sales forces. Employment has expanded in the service industries and particularly in employment for state and local governments. Part-time employment, especially among those who work part time by choice, has increased more proportionately than full-time employment. The growth in employment in the service industries, and in part-time employment—in both of which women predominate—will accentuate the problem of abuse in unemployment insurance because of the greater difficulty of verifying women's attachment to the labor force.

From 1958 to 1964 unemployment was at high levels. Long-term unemployment increased. Most unemployment, however, continued to be short term—the kind of unemployment for which unemployment insurance functions best. Unemployment among part-time workers has also increased. Seasonal unemployment which is still prevalent continues to be largely an unsolved problem for unemployment insurance.

Recessions since World War II have been relatively mild. Unemployment has increased during recessions, but the chief problem has been the increased number experiencing long-duration unemployment during recessions. This has created a need for permanent measures for longer duration of unemployment benefits during such business slumps.

Much unemployment is caused by the displacement of workers due to the structural and technological changes in the economy. Technological changes, especially automation, are generating intense apprehension that large numbers of jobs will be destroyed. The great technological advances are accelerating increases in productivity. The GNP has been increasing, but some believe that economic growth is not fast enough to offset increased productivity and the growth in the labor force. Others believe that persistent unemployment is largely structural in nature—that it is due to the inability of poorly educated and low-skilled workers to perform the new jobs created by the new technology, and to the difficulty of older workers and Negroes in finding employment because of discrimination. There is some truth on both sides, but while retraining and the breakdown of prejudices will help in the re-employment of the structurally unemployed, the greater need is for increased economic growth. Fortunately, there are factors favoring economic growth, such as increases in population, improved standards of living, and the creation of new products through research and development. There is also increased understanding of the ability of government to stimulate economic growth, as through the tax cut of 1964. Even with adequate economic growth, however, there will be continued need for the provision of a longer duration of unemployment benefits for those displaced by technological changes, to enable most of those who are displaced to find re-employment.

Because of a variety of reasons, insured unemployment is much lower than total unemployment. Two of these reasons do give concern. Part of the difference between insured and total unemployment reflects the large number of workers who are not covered by unemployment insurance. Another important part stems from the exhaustion of benefits by large numbers of insured workers. These two facts raise questions as to the need for extending unemployment insurance coverage to more workers and providing more adequate duration of benefits. Insured unemployment data also reveal large differences in the rate of insured unemployment in different states. Differences in state laws account for part of this difference. Most of it is due to differences in the economies of different states and underlines the importance of federal financial measures to protect the solvency of the funds of those states which have heavy insured unemployment.

While some of the implications for unemployment insurance of the past and prospective trends in unemployment have been indicated, other implications can only become evident as the various issues and problems in unemployment insurance are discussed in detail. The program must be enlarged in coverage and must provide adequate duration of benefits if unemployment insurance is to play its role more effectively in meeting the problems of unemployment.

Developments in the labor market will make it more difficult for unemployment insurance to function without criticism. One problem is the increased number of women, especially married women, in the labor market who are not too firmly attached to the labor force. Others, such as pensioners, present similar problems. Measures will have to be taken to tighten eligibility conditions so that those who attempt to draw benefits improperly will not bring the program into disrepute. At the same time, this should not be done at the expense of providing an adequate program for the great bulk of the unemployed who are honest and genuinely attached to the labor market, and for whom unemployment insurance fulfills a real need in providing them with a measure of security when they become unemployed.

Chapter 2

The Objectives
of Unemployment Insurance

The primary objective of unemployment insurance is to alleviate the hardships that result from the loss of wage income during unemployment. Other objectives are secondary.

The objectives of unemployment insurance were succinctly set forth in a statement issued by the United States Department of Labor in 1955:

Unemployment insurance is a program—established under Federal and State law—for income maintenance during period of involuntary unemployment due to lack of work, which provides partial compensation for wage loss as a matter of right, with dignity and dispatch, to eligible individuals. It helps to maintain purchasing power and to stabilize the economy. It helps to prevent the dispersal of the employers' trained work force, the sacrifice of skills, and the breakdown of labor standards during temporary unemployment.[1]

There are three types of programs for dealing with unemployment: preventive, alleviative, and curative. Preventive programs include private efforts by employers to stabilize their employment, and public efforts such as sound credit policies, regulation of the stock market, and other measures that have been developed for stabilizing the economy. Curative programs include such broad government measures as tax reductions, acceleration of public works, and programs of retraining and relocation of unemployed workers.

Unemployment insurance has preventive aspects, including the provision of incentives for employers to stabilize their employment, and the partial maintenance of purchasing power to help stabilize the economy by putting a brake on the downward spiral of business and employment during a recession. It has curative aspects, such as the use of the public employment office to assist the claimant in finding a job. Unemployment insurance is primarily alleviative in that it assists the unemployed worker,

[1] United States Department of Labor, Bureau of Employment Security, *Major Objectives of Federal Policy with Respect to the Federal-State Employment Security Program*, General Administration Letter No. 305, April 25, 1955.

26

when preventive and curative measures fail, to meet his nondeferable expenses. It is an insurance program that provides partial replacement of a worker's wage loss during unemployment in a manner that will maintain his self-respect. It is designed to enable the worker to bridge the gap between jobs without becoming destitute and without having to experience the mental and social degradation of seeking public relief.

In this chapter, we will (1) briefly describe how unemployment insurance came to be recognized during the depression of the 1930's as superior to relief for unemployed workers; (2) look at why the unemployed need unemployment insurance, and at the difference it makes in helping them meet expenses; (3) review the extent to which unemployment insurance has encouraged the stabilization of employment and has assisted in maintaining purchasing power; and (4) discuss some other objectives of unemployment insurance, such as helping the worker to preserve his status and the employer to maintain his trained work force.

UNEMPLOYMENT INSURANCE AS A PROGRAM FOR ALLEVIATING UNEMPLOYMENT

Problems of Providing Relief during the Depression of the 1930's

Unemployment insurance was enacted in the 1930's after five years of bitter experience with the difficulties and inadequacies of relief as a means of alleviating unemployment. It is difficult for anyone who did not live through the depression of the 1930's to appreciate how unprepared the nation was for the large-scale unemployment growing out of the drop in business activity and how much the unemployed suffered as a result.

There was little or no public provision for the unemployed at the beginning of the depression. Unemployment was left largely to public charity and efforts were made to raise additional private funds through the Community Chest and other organizations. In most places, the public relief that was provided was poorly organized and pitifully inadequate. Relief was often offered in the form of soup kitchens or, at best, in the form of food parcels which the relief client had to seek and carry home in the full view of his neighbors. The following description of one type of relief administration is taken from the report of an investigation published in 1931 in Wisconsin:

One of the most deplorable situations was found in one of our medium-sized cities where each applicant for relief was compelled to appear before the monthly meeting of the poor committee composed of the mayor and aldermen and be cross-examined by these 8 or 9 city officials. This winter when so many were needing help, the meetings sometimes lasted until 2 or 3 o'clock in the morning. One can imagine how much sympathetic consideration an applicant, after waiting for 8 hours to be heard, would get at 2:30 A.M.[2]

[2] Don D. Lescohier and Florence Peterson, *The Alleviation of Unemployment in Wisconsin* (Madison: Industrial Commission of Wisconsin, July, 1931), p. 35.

As unemployment increased, the traditional methods of providing unemployment relief through private charities and local public poor relief became inadequate. The exhaustion of resources for providing relief by cities that faced bankruptcy because of tax delinquencies gradually led the state governments to take over the responsibility of relief, often through the appointment of state emergency relief commissions. In turn, state resources became overstrained or exhausted and the federal government had to take over the burden, first through loans from the Reconstruction Finance Corporation, and then through the direct financing of relief by the Federal Emergency Relief Administration.

As the states and the federal government assumed the major responsibility for financing unemployment relief, the methods of administration and the kind of relief provided improved. Staffs were trained and relief was granted under less humiliating circumstances. Relief was provided in cash, and work programs were developed, such as the emergency Civil Works Administration of 1933–34, the Civilian Conservation Corps, the Works Progress Administration, and the National Youth Administration.

Superiority of Unemployment Insurance over Relief

Although it had been proposed for a generation and tried out on a limited scale by some unions and employers, unemployment insurance was not seriously considered in this country until the inadequacies. of relief as a means of providing for the unemployed became widely appreciated in the 1930's. The superiority of unemployment insurance over relief was eloquently stated by Leo Wolman in 1931:

The alternatives before us, then, are reliance on the hastily devised machinery for the distribution of doles during the time of crisis, or systematic provision for unemployment compensation out of reserves set aside for this purpose in advance. . . . Our present method reduces a multitude of our fellow-citizens to a state of poverty, forces them into breadlines and soup kitchens, and reduces to starvation those self-respecting and timid workingmen who prefer hunger and cold to the ministrations of eleemosynary agencies. The second alternative, wisely conceived and expertly managed, represents . . . a decent and far-sighted approach to the problem of protecting the standards of living of American employees which are our proud boast.[3]

The methods of determining the need for relief and of providing relief, and the adequacy of relief payments have no doubt been greatly improved since the early 1930's. Employable persons are still not eligible for public relief, however, in a large number of states and cities (see Chapter 23). And where relief is provided, under the best of circumstances, it is inferior to unemployment insurance as a means of providing for the unemployed. The basic differences between the two methods is that relief is provided only on the basis of proven need, whereas unemployment insurance bene-

[3] Leo Wolman, "Unemployment Insurance for the United States," *American Labor Legislation Review*, March, 1931.

fits are provided without regard to need, provided that the worker has worked for a substantial period in employment covered by unemployment insurance, and is able and available to work. It is not necessary for the unemployed worker to become destitute when his savings and resources are exhausted in order to be eligible for unemployment insurance. Instead, unemployment insurance is designed to prevent destitution by immediately providing a cash payment to meet the worker's nondeferable expenses.

After graphically relating his experience as Mayor of Youngstown in struggling with the problem of providing relief for the unemployed in 1930–31, Joseph L. Heffernan gave this description of what happens to the unemployed who must go on relief:

> With quiet desperation they will bear hunger and mental anguish until every resourse is exhausted. Then comes the ultimate struggle when, with heartache and an overwhelming sense of disgrace, they have to make the shame-faced journey to the door of public charity. This is the last straw. Their self-respect is destroyed; they undergo an insidious metamorphosis, and sink down to spiritless despondency.
>
> This descent from respectability, frequent enough in the best of times, has been hastened immeasurably by 2 years of business paralysis, and the people who have been affected in this manner must be numbered in millions. This is what we have accomplished with our breadlines and soup kitchens. I know, because I have seen thousands of these defeated, discouraged, hopeless men and women, cringing and fawning as they come to ask for public aid.[4]

One of the values of unemployment insurance as compared with public relief is that it not only prevents destitution but enables those drawing unemployment compensation to maintain their self-respect.

Although unemployment insurance in this country has many shortcomings, nevertheless, the program is accepted as the best method of alleviating the strains and stresses of unemployment. There may be a widespread feeling that many persons are receiving unemployment insurance who are not genuinely unemployed, but few would advocate abolition of the system. It is generally recognized that unemployment is unavoidable in a dynamic and free society and that most workers do not have adequate resources to tide them over spells of unemployment.

THE UNEMPLOYED NEED UNEMPLOYMENT COMPENSATION

During the depression of the 1930's, when millions were unemployed for long periods of time and eventually had to seek public relief, there was no question that most of the unemployed could not live on their own resources. Today, however, with our high-wage economy, some people may believe that workers should be able to accumulate sufficient savings to tide them over periods of unemployment. Others may hold that large numbers of the unemployed do not need unemployment compensation because

[4] Joseph L. Heffernan, "The Hungry City, A Mayor's Experience with Unemployment," *Atlantic Monthly*, May, 1932.

80399

someone else in the family is working. This question is more frequently raised when both husband and wife have been employed.

The Unemployed Cannot Get along on Savings

The pressure on the worker today is to spend, not to save. With high pressure advertising and the encouragement of installment buying, it is surprising how many workers do accumulate liquid savings.

Some data are available on the savings of unemployment insurance beneficiaries. Sample studies of beneficiaries, made in six states during 1954–58, showed that (depending on the state) from 14 to 42 percent of the beneficiaries who were heads of households used some savings while drawing benefits. One of the studies showed that three fourths of the household heads used whatever savings they had. If this proportion held for the other studies, it meant that from about 20 to 55 percent of the household heads had some savings. Or stating it the other way around, from 45 to 80 percent of the household heads had no savings.[5]

Unemployment Beneficiaries Have Little Other Income

It is also true that most unemployed workers do not have much income, aside from what unemployment compensation they may qualify for. In five of the six studies of unemployment beneficiaries referred to above, heads of households with no other earner in the household had other income ranging from $25 to $75 a month in the different states. Single claimants averaged from $12 to $43 a month in other income.[6] Other income obviously is inadequate to provide support for unemployed wage earners when there is no other wage earner in the household.

The Working Wife's Benefits Are Needed

Questions are most frequently raised as to whether working wives or other workers in the family need benefits when they become unemployed if the husband is working. In the beneficiary studies previously referred to, when a nonhead of the family was unemployed, total cash outlay exceeded total cash income (including the unemployment compensation received by the nonhead) by an average of $75 a month in Florida, $51 a month in South Carolina, $86 a month in Oregon, and $56 a month in Missouri.[7]

These averages do not mean, of course, that every unemployment claim-

[5] United States Department of Labor, Bureau of Employment Security, *Unemployment Insurance and the Finances of the Unemployed, Analysis of Six Benefit Adequacy Studies, 1954–1958,* BES No. U–203 (July, 1961, p. 81, table E1. Other information from these studies is given in Chapter 11.

[6] Includes income from self-employment, pension and welfare payments, unemployment benefits of family members other than the sample claimant, cash gifts or contributions, net proceeds from sale of real estate or other property, income tax refunds, and any other income of family members. *Ibid.,* pp. 72–76, table D–4.

[7] *Ibid.* p. 71, table D–3. This data was not available from the Pittsburgh, Pennsylvania study and in the New York study the data were distorted by the purchase of an automobile by one claimant in the sample.

ant "needs" his or her benefit. But one of the purposes of unemployment insurance is to get away from a determination of individual need in determining eligibility for unemployment compensation, and to substitute a system in which the benefit is an indemnity for wage loss.

INCENTIVE FOR EMPLOYERS TO STABILIZE EMPLOYMENT

A second objective of unemployment insurance, urged quite frequently at the beginning of the program but not mentioned much today, is to stimulate the stabilization of employment by individual employers. It was expected that stabilization would be encouraged by providing lower tax rates through "experience rating" for employers who regularized their employment.

Considerable effort was put into promoting the idea of stabilization of employment, particularly in Wisconsin, during the early days of the program. Evidently, at the beginning of the program, many employers did make efforts to stabilize their employment. However, after the initial impact of unemployment insurance taxes wore off, experience rating seems to have provided little incentive for employment stabilization.[8]

STABILIZATION OF THE ECONOMY

A third objective of unemployment insurance is a broader version of the idea of stabilization of employment—namely, to assist in minimizing recessions through the maintenance of purchasing power. This objective has been emphasized in more recent years, but was also included in early statements of the purposes of unemployment insurance. Thus, in the draft bill that the Social Security Board issued in 1936, a suggested "Declaration of State Public Policy" contained this clause: "...thus maintaining purchasing power." As elaborated by the Bureau of Employment Security in 1950: "By maintaining essential consumer purchasing power, on which production plans are based, the program provides a brake on down-turns in business activity, helps to stabilize employment, and lessens the momentum of deflation during periods of recession."[9]

This objective of unemployment insurance was stated in both the majority and minority reports of the Senate Special Committee on Unemployment Problems in 1960. The majority report stated: "the payment of unemployment benefits has the secondary effect of maintaining purchasing power and cushioning the shock of unemployment to the community and to the national economy."[10]

The minority report of the Committee made an even stronger statement: "In regard to cyclical unemployment, unemployment compensation payments have constituted an important antirecessionary measure available

[8] This will be discussed at length in Chapter 17.

[9] United States Department of Labor, Bureau of Employment Security, *Unemployment Insurance: Purposes and Principles* (Washington, D.C., December, 1950), p. 1.

[10] *Report of the Special Committee on Unemployment Problems,* 86th Cong., 2d sess., Senate Report No. 1206, 1960, p. 87.

to the Federal government . . . of all the counter-measures—the so-called built-in stabilizers—which have served to sustain buying power and cushion recessions, this is the most important single measure."[11]

An analysis of the validity of the stabilization objectives has been made by Richard A. Lester which demonstrates that the contribution of unemployment insurance to the stability of the economy is limited but important.[12]

In his study, Lester found that total unemployment benefit payments were less than 1 percent of labor income, of consumer expenditures, and of disposable personal income in the years 1950–60, except in 1954, 1958, and 1960 when the payments rose above 1 percent of labor income, and in 1958 when they rose above 1 percent of consumption expenditures and disposable income. Unemployment compensation, as a percentage of labor income, rose from 0.77 to 1.56 percent from 1957 to 1958, which Lester considered "a significant increment."[13]

Dr. Lester also measured the countercyclical effect of unemployment compensation. This countercyclical effect, which occurs without legislation, has classed unemployment insurance as an "automatic stabilizer." During the upswing of the cycle, tax intake increases and benefit outflow decreases, while in the trough of the cycle, benefit outflow increases and tax intake decreases. To get the net countercyclical effect, Lester subtracted the payment of state taxes from the payment of state benefits. At the time of his writing, the maximum effect had occurred in 1958, when benefits exceeded taxes by over $2 billion ($3.5 billion in benefits minus $1.4 billion in taxes.)[14] During 1961, when a milder recession occurred, $3.4 billion was paid out in benefits. However, $2.4 billion was paid in unemployment taxes, so that the net effect was only $1 billion.[15]

Dr. Lester does go on to say, however, that when the incidence of the unemployment tax and the spending patterns of beneficiaries are considered, unemployment insurance has a greater countercyclical effect than is indicated by the foregoing. In his words, "part of the tax does, under experience rating, rest on profits and the benefits are in large part spent for current goods and services. Thus, even if taxes and contributions exactly balanced, quarter by quarter, the system would probably cause (by itself) some shift from investment to consumption."[16]

The Council of Economic Advisors described the effects of unemployment insurance on the economy in more concrete terms in its 1965 report:

[11] Ibid., pp. 165–66.

[12] Richard A. Lester, The Economics of Unemployment Compensation (Princeton: Industrial Relations Section, Princeton University, 1962), chap. 2.

[13] Ibid., p. 10.

[14] Ibid., p. 20 and table 2.

[15] These figures do not include the $600 million in extended benefits paid from June, 1958, to July, 1959, under the Temporary Unemployment Compensation Act of 1958 or the $770 million paid from April, 1961, through June, 1962, under the Temporary Extended Unemployment Compensation Act of 1962.

[16] Lester, op. cit., p. 24.

In postwar recessions, built-in stabilizers have worked primarily through changes in corporate profits, the corporate tax yield, and transfer payments.

The 1960–61 recession can serve as an illustration. During that recession, national income fell by $4.5 billion (annual rate), but personal income actually rose by $5.2 billion. Corporate profits bore the brunt of the decline, but reductions in corporate tax liabilities helped to maintain dividends. Increased transfer payments, including a $1.4 billion (annual rate) rise in unemployment benefits, offset some losses in earnings.

Strengthening the unemployment compensation system deserves high priority among possible steps to increase the automatic resistance of the economy to recessions. The most important reasons for improving the system are to increase individual security and reduce the unnecessary human costs of unemployment. But a strengthened system would also sustain consumer purchasing power more effectively, thereby reducing the amount of unemployment as well.[17]

The value of the program as a stabilizer of the economy can also be augmented if coverage is made more universal and benefits are made more adequate.

Professor Arthur F. Burns of Columbia University, when Chairman of the Council of Economic Advisors, stressed the importance of increasing coverage and benefits. In the 1954 *Annual Report* of the Council, recommendations were made for increasing coverage and increasing the maximum weekly benefit amount (a recommendation discussed at length in Chapter 11), and providing at least 26 weeks' duration of benefits. In support of these recommendations, the Report stated: "Unemployment insurance is a valuable first line of defense against economic recession. . . . When set at appropriate levels, they can sustain to some degree the earner's way of life, as well as his demand for commodities. Thus, its payments can help to curb economic decline during an interval of time that allows other stabilizing measures to become effective."[18]

The extent to which unemployment insurance can help stabilize the economy by maintaining purchasing power during recessions is limited. Nevertheless, it is substantial and the stabilization of the economy can legitimately be considered as one of the objectives of unemployment insurance.

Other Objectives

Several other objectives or values of unemployment insurance should be listed. One is to provide an orderly method of meeting the cost of unemployment since financing public unemployment relief has always been difficult and unsatisfactory. Not only is there a reluctance to appro-

---

[17] *Economic Report of the President together with the Annual Report of the Council of Economic Advisers, January, 1965* (Washington, D.C.: U.S. Government Printing Office), pp. 101–2.

[18] *Economic Report of the President together with the Annual Report of the Council of Economic Advisers, January, 1954* (Washington, D.C.: U.S. Government Printing Office), p. 96.

priate adequate funds, but the costs of unemployment relief fall most heavily on the community during periods of low business activity at a time when tax revenues have fallen. Unemployment insurance, on the other hand, is a device for building up reserves in good times which are automatically available for the increased payment of benefits in bad times.

Unemployment insurance is of value to the worker, not only as a partial replacement of his lost earnings, but as an aid in preserving his skills for a reasonable period until he can find suitable work. The unemployment insurance claimant can refuse unsuitable work and still receive his benefits. He thus can avoid having to take jobs far below his skill and abilities which may downgrade his status and make it more difficult for him to "land" a suitable job when it becomes available.

Through the requirement that he register with the public employment service, the unemployment insurance claimant can be reabsorbed more speedily into employment—or at least this has been the objective of such a requirement. In actuality, only a small percentage of unemployment insurance claimants are placed by the employment service, but this does not negate the soundness of the objective. What is needed to make this objective more effective is an improved employment service and greater utilization of it by employers—but that is another story which will be discussed in Chapter 21.

Finally, the payment of unemployment compensation to his former employees is of advantage to an employer during short layoffs, since it tends to preserve his labor force intact until he can re-employ it. Workers are not forced to scatter in search of jobs, at least during short layoffs. While this restricts the mobility of labor, it is of value to the employer, as well as to the worker and the community.

This does not exhaust the list of objectives or values of unemployment insurance. Others have been set forth from time to time, but the objectives we have discussed are those which have most influenced the character of the program.

SUMMARY

In summary, the main objective of unemployment insurance is to provide an orderly way of partially replacing the loss of income by the unemployed without damage to their self-respect. Unemployment insurance is far superior to relief as a method for alleviating the problems of unemployment. It is needed by most beneficiaries because of their limited savings or resources, as indicated in studies of beneficiaries of unemployment insurance.

Apparently, variations in unemployment insurance taxes through experience rating have not stimulated much stabilization of employment by individual employers, although this was urged as an important objective in the early years of the program.

A third objective of unemployment insurance is to operate as a "built-in" stabilizer of the economy. Its value in this respect has perhaps been somewhat exaggerated, but it is nevertheless significant.

These objectives of the program are only being partially fulfilled, and the authors will have much to say later as to how this situation can be improved. Nevertheless, notwithstanding its shortcomings, unemployment compensation makes a significant contribution in bringing a measure of security and income to millions of unemployed workers.

Chapter 3

The Insurance Character
of Unemployment Insurance

When proposals for unemployment insurance legislation were being debated in the early 1930's, many critics claimed that unemployment was too unpredictable to be insurable. In the midst of the worst depression in history, unemployment had reached heights never before experienced. Critics pointed to the heavy debt incurred by the British unemployment system to show that unemployment insurance could not be kept on a solvent basis. These fears, however, proved to be unfounded. In the United States, only three state funds have ever borrowed money and only one of these states needed to use the money it borrowed. During World War II large unemployment insurance reserves were built up, and although a number of state funds dropped to dangerous levels in recent years, this developed after those states excessively reduced their tax rates. Moderate increases in taxes would rebuild these state funds to safe levels.

The risk of unemployment meets the tests of insurability. Unemployment insurance no longer needs to be justified, but it is desirable to understand the insurance principles that apply to both private and social insurance.

Another matter that needs discussion at the outset is whether unemployment insurance can meet its social objectives and yet maintain its insurance character. Unemployment insurance is *social* insurance and so has some features that could not be written into a private insurance policy. Why such social features do not destroy the "insurance character" of the system needs to be understood.

Pressures are being continually brought to bear to introduce features or administrative practices to safeguard the system from abuse. Some of these proposals would place the system in jeopardy of becoming a welfare system, rather than an insurance system. Such features tend to destroy one of the chief values of unemployment insurance—that unemployment compensation can be claimed as a matter of right without any loss of self-respect by the claimant.

This chapter, then, is designed to do three things: (1) show that unemployment is an insurable risk; (2) discuss some of the features that make the program "social insurance"; and (3) indicate the danger of adopting certain features or practices that would tend to make unemployment insurance a relief rather than an insurance system.

DOES UNEMPLOYMENT MEET THE TESTS OF INSURABILITY?

Most insurance textbooks define insurance as a mechanism, rather than in terms of its function.

A useful textbook definition for our purposes is that given by Riegel and Miller: "From the functional standpoint, insurance is a social device whereby the uncertain risks of individuals may be combined in a group and thus made more certain, small periodic contributions by the individuals providing the fund out of which those suffering losses may be reimbursed."[1]

There are three types of risk against which insurance is issued: those involving (1) personal loss, (2) property loss, and (3) liability for damage to a third person. Unemployment insurance is insurance against the risk of personal loss (wage loss) due to unemployment.

Much confused thinking has resulted from the mixture of liability and personal loss concepts in the state unemployment insurance laws. In framing an unemployment insurance program, one school of thought put the emphasis on the third type of risk, i.e., the liability of the employer for the damage he did to his workers by laying them off, and sought to confine the risk only to unemployment for which the employer is directly responsible. Those who are concerned with the wage loss of the worker focus on compensating involuntary unemployment, whatever its economic cause, while those concerned with the employer's liability seek to restrict compensation to unemployment which the employer has directly caused.

Tests of Insurability

In order for the insurance scheme to be successful, it must meet a number of tests.

Involuntary Risk. First, there must be a pure, not a speculative risk. In other words, insurance should assume only a risk that already exists, and not a risk that may be created, as, for example, a gambling bet, which involves the creation of a speculative risk. In order to be sure that the unemployment insured against is a pure risk and not a risk that is created by the insured, the laws in general provide that benefits be paid only when the unemployment is involuntary. No question is raised when the worker is laid off for lack of work—the risk of so being laid off always exists.

Questions, however, arise in cases where the worker may have caused, or contributed to, his unemployment by his own actions. Unemployment insurance generally restricts benefits in such cases, or denies them entirely.

[1] Robert Riegel and Jerome B. Miller, *Insurance Principles and Practices* (4th ed.; Englewood Cliffs, N.J.: Prentice-Hall, Inc., 1959), p. 26.

Unemployment insurance departs somewhat, however, from this principle in paying benefits when certain types of voluntary action result in unemployment, for example, when a worker voluntarily quits a job for "good" cause. As will be discussed later, this can be justified in a social insurance program.

Economic Loss Involved. A second test of insurability of a risk is whether an economic loss is involved. Unemployment involves wage loss. Therefore, at first glance, there would appear to be no problem in unemployment meeting this test. However, questions do arise in some cases. For example, if a student is laid off at the end of his summer vacation and returns to school, has he incurred a wage loss? The answer in this case is not difficult—obviously he hasn't. Or suppose a housewife has worked at a cannery only during the canning season for some years. When she is laid off has she suffered a wage loss? Such cases, however, are in the minority; the majority of workers who are laid off would have kept on working if possible and thus do suffer an economic loss. Their unemployment, therefore, meets the second test of insurability.

Risk Is Verifiable. Still another test is whether the occurrence of the risk—in this case unemployment—is verifiable. In other types of insurance, a greater degree of objectivity is possible in verifying the occurrence of the hazard insured against. There is no difficulty in verifying that a person is dead, although even life insurance companies at times have problems in verifying whether an insured person has actually died, as, for example, in drownings when a body may not be recovered. In unemployment insurance, the reason given by a worker for his unemployment can be verified through a report from the employer. But there still may be difficulty in determining whether the worker was separated from his job for a reason that makes his unemployment compensable. If he quit, why did he? Was it because his working conditions were unbearable?

Even more difficult is the problem of verifying whether a claimant is still unemployed. Various techniques have been developed to determine whether a claimant is working on another job. But difficulties arise in determining whether a person who is not working is really available for work. Is the claimant genuinely looking for work or is he in effect taking a vacation?

It is true that a "moral hazard" may exist that a claimant will misrepresent his situation, but extended experience has shown that the hazard materializes only in a small minority of cases. A "moral hazard" exists in all insurance; fires may be started in order to collect fire insurance, and even life insurance is sometimes taken out with the intent of killing the insured. More akin to moral hazards in unemployment insurance, however, is the moral hazard in workmen's compensation that a person drawing compensation may malinger. Doctors will admit that it is often very difficult to determine whether an injured man is able to return to work. It may be more difficult to verify unemployment in borderline cases than to verify

the occurrence of other hazards. In the great majority of situations, however, the genuineness of the claimant's unemployment can be easily
verified.

Meets Law of Large Numbers.   A fourth test is that the risk of unemployment must be subject to the Law of Large Numbers,[2] which states
that if the number of cases is large enough, there is a tendency for mass
phenomena to operate in accordance with the theory of probability. This
theory is popularly illustrated by the random tossing of a coin 1,000 times.
The probability is that "heads" will come up 500 times and "tails" 500
times. There is no certainty that this will occur. But the larger the number
of times the coin is tossed, the greater is the probability that the Law of
Large Numbers will apply. This law can be applied to human risks if
enough cases are involved. Mortality tables have been constructed on the
basis of a large number of deaths so that it can be predicted with considerable accuracy what proportion of 100,000 can be expected to die at each
year of age.

Unemployment insurance can easily meet the Law of Large Numbers
since a sufficiently large number are insured under every state law to make
the laws of probability operative. Even Alaska, the state with the smallest
coverage, had 38,274 workers in covered employment in June, 1962, a much
larger number than is necessary to meet the Law of Large Numbers. This
law is also met in that there is also a random selection of the workers covered, at least to the extent that all of certain classes of workers are insured.
Contrary to present practices in most states which exclude certain classes
from the program, the random nature of the insured group would improve
if all workers in every state were covered, although some who are poorer
risks than most now covered might be included. If all workers in the United
States were covered under one system, the random nature of the coverage
would improve still further since the industries covered would be more
highly diversified than they presently are in most states.

Only Part Unemployed at One Time.   Another test of insurability is
that the contingency happens to only a portion of the insured, at any one
time. A large proportion of the labor force never experiences any unemployment, and although a sizable proportion may have some unemployment during a recession, only a small proportion are unemployed at any
one time. Although in the 12-year period 1950 through 1962 average
weekly insured unemployment reached a peak of 6.4 percent in 1958, and
monthly unemployment in figures peaked at 8.4 percent in February,
1961, such peak figures are not significant. Focus should be placed on
unemployment over a period of time. Average insured unemployment over
recent business cycles has been several points lower than in the peak

---

[2] See Harry Malisoff, *The Insurance Character of Unemployment Insurance* (Kalamazoo, Mich.: W. E. Upjohn Institute for Employment Research, 1961), chap. ii. Dr.
Malisoff also discusses other aspects of the insurability of unemployment in a somewhat
different manner than is done in this chapter.

months or years and although the proportion in some states is higher than others, unemployment still affects only a small proportion of workers. For example, Michigan had average insured unemployment of 6.8 percent in the years 1957 through 1961 with a rate of 12.1 percent in the peak year of 1958. However, from July, 1963, through June, 1964, insured unemployment averaged only 3.1 percent in Michigan. It is true that over a period of a year several times as many have some unemployment as are unemployed on the average. But even in states with the worst experience, unemployment insurance meets the test that the risk happens to only a fairly small portion of the insured at any one time.

Unemployment Predictable.   The final and most important test of insurability is whether the occurrence of the contingency (in this case unemployment) can be predicted within reasonable limits. As has already been indicated, there were fears in the 1930's that unemployment was not insurable because of the unexpected and unprecedented numbers of unemployed workers at that time. But since then, unemployment figures have been only a fraction of those in the great depression. Unemployment was very low during World War II and since that time, despite several mild recessions, it is believed that enough safeguards have been built into the economy to prevent a depression such as that of the 1930's. The pattern of unemployment during the postwar years has also been sufficiently regular to permit predictions of its incidence within a reasonable margin of error.

A vast amount of information on the characteristics and behavior of unemployment has been accumulated as a byproduct of the operation of unemployment insurance. Detailed studies of the individual state economies enable projections of employment and unemployment trends. Actuarial techniques for estimating the cost of unemployment insurance have been developed and constantly improved. The costs of unemployment insurance over a period of time can therefore be predicted with sufficient accuracy so that the unemployment insurance funds can be kept solvent— provided that the actuarial predictions are translated into adequate tax income.

Predictions, however, must be made over a period of years in unemployment insurance systems. Unemployment fluctuates with the business cycle. This does not invalidate its insurability. Business cycles have become shorter and milder in recent years so that the margin of error is reduced and can be discovered more quickly. But allowances must be made for recessions, and actuarial estimates must be made over a long enough period of time to include at least one business cycle.

Before leaving the discussion of the insurance aspects of the program, one additional characteristic of unemployment insurance should be pointed out. In social insurance, as contrasted with private insurance, the contract can be changed without the individual consent of the insured or of those who finance the program. If unemployment changes so that the actuarial estimates do not work out, contributions or taxes can be increased to take care of the changed situation. About two thirds of the states have two or more tax schedules, so that tax rates increase automatically when reserves fall below a state level. In other states, experience rating is suspended automatically when the unemployment fund drops to a dangerously low level. If these automatic measures prove inadequate, the state legislatures can increase the unemployment taxes. In this respect, unemployment insurance has an advantage over private insurance which risks the loss of business if it raises rates. Unemployment insurance has a "captive" group of contributors, whose only way of avoiding a necessary tax rate increase is by pressure on the legislature not to take action. The real test, in the last analysis, of the insurability of unemployment is whether the state legislatures will make changes in the unemployment taxes when increased costs necessitate such changes.

DO THE SOCIAL OBJECTIVES OF UNEMPLOYMENT INSURANCE ALTER ITS INSURANCE CHARACTER?

There are many features in the unemployment insurance program that could not be written into a private insurance contract. In private insurance, the emphasis must be on individual equity, and benefit protection must be directly related to the amount of contributions. In a social insurance program, the emphasis is on "social adequacy," that is, on providing the insured with benefits related to their presumed needs.[3] For example, minimum benefits are set in some unemployment insurance state laws at a level that gives many unemployed workers a much higher proportion of their former weekly wages than higher-paid workers receive. Also, some state formulas "weight" benefits at the lower end of the scale, i.e., pay as a benefit a higher percentage of low wages than of high wages. Such variations from private insurance practice are justified on the basis of the relative needs of lower and higher paid workers. When dependents' allowances are added to benefits, with no differentiation in premiums, there is a further departure from private insurance principles. But dependents' allowances serve a social purpose in providing more adequate benefits where there are more mouths to feed. As Reinhard Hohaus, Actuary for the Metropolitan Life Insurance Company, has written: "Just as considerations of equity of benefits form a natural and vital part of operating private insurance, so should considerations of adequacy of benefits control the pattern of social insurance."[4] Another departure from private insurance principles is the payment of benefits under certain circumstances for unemployment that is created by the claimants' own actions. For example, benefits are paid for unemployment which may follow the voluntary quitting of a job, providing the claimant can establish that he had "good cause" for leaving.[5]

[3] See Robert J. Myers, *Social Insurance and Allied Government Programs* (Homewood, Ill.: Richard D. Irwin, Inc., 1965), p. 6.

[4] Reinhard Hohaus, "Equity, Adequacy and Related Factors in Old Age Security," in William Haber and Wilbur J. Cohen, *Readings in Social Security* (Englewood Cliffs, N.J.: Prentice-Hall, Inc., 1948), p. 77.

[5] "Good cause" in many states is restricted to causes attributable to the employer or connected with the work.

A further departure from private insurance principles occurs when a worker who quit *without* good cause or was discharged is allowed to draw benefits after a period of disqualification. The justification given for such benefit payments is that after a certain period following separation from a job, unemployment becomes involuntary if the claimant has been unsuccessful in his genuine attempts to find a job.

These departures from private insurance are on the lenient side. On the other hand, there are certain departures from private insurance principles that are more restrictive. For example, most state laws vary the duration of benefits in proportion to previous employment or earnings on which contributions have been paid. This makes unemployment insurance more of a savings plan than an insurance plan. In other types of insurance, the amount of indemnity is not limited by the length of time the contributor has been paying premiums. In practically all insurance, the full amount of insurance becomes effective from the moment the insured signs the insurance contract.

Another restriction is that benefits are paid only to workers who have had a minimum period of qualifying employment or earnings. This is no doubt necessary in order to establish evidence that the claimant has been genuinely and substantially attached to the labor market. Such a test is more necessary than in other types of insurance because the fact of unemployment cannot be established as objectively as the fact of an accident or a death. Nevertheless, it must be recognized that a qualifying requirement is unique to social insurance.

DOES UNEMPLOYMENT INSURANCE DIFFER ENOUGH FROM RELIEF?

In order to preserve the insurance character of unemployment insurance, some curbs must be put on the social features of the program. On the other hand, the legislative and administrative restrictions placed on the payment of unemployment compensation should not be so restrictive as to make the unemployed think of it as relief or welfare, rather than an insurance program.

The concern of the claimants may be whether there is much difference between unemployment insurance and welfare programs, not whether unemployment insurance departs from private insurance principles. One of the principal advantages of unemployment insurance is that the unemployed worker is not subjected to a needs test such as is applied to a relief applicant. The application of a needs test, as one writer has put it, is the "watershed" dividing social insurance from public assistance.[6]

A related advantage put forward for unemployment insurance over welfare payments was that unemployed workers felt that their benefits would be paid "as a matter of right." But even this "right" may be undermined, as Harry Malisoff pointed out, if the questions asked of an unem-

[6] Valdemar Carlson, *Economic Security in the United States* (New York: McGraw-Hill Book Co., Inc., 1962), p. 7.

ployment insurance claimant are so detailed or personal that he feels his private life is invaded.[7] The personal questioning about the economic needs of applicants for public welfare is one of the reasons that people avoid applying for relief if possible. In the same way, many unemployed workers do not file for unemployment compensation in a few states where the practice of extensive personal questioning makes them feel that unemployment insurance is no better or no different from relief.

SUMMARY

Although at the beginning of the program many persons feared that unemployment was not insurable, experience has proved their fears unfounded.

Unemployment insurance insures against the risk of personal loss of income due to unemployment, although much controversy has arisen over the concept that only unemployment for which the employer is liable or responsible should be insured.

Unemployment insurance meets the accepted tests as to whether a risk is insurable. It insures unemployment that is involuntary, and does not compensate for unemployment created by the insured himself, except under certain restricted conditions, such as voluntary leaving for "good" cause. It meets the test that the occurrence of the risk must be verifiable. It is subject to the Law of Large Numbers, which makes it possible to apply statistical techniques of probability. The contingency insured against, unemployment, happens to only a portion of the insured at any one time. The risk of unemployment is predictable within reasonable limits, and techniques for estimating costs are being constantly improved. Several tax schedules are written into the laws of most states so that tax rates will be increased automatically if the condition of the unemployment fund requires it, or experience rating will be suspended. Since unemployment insurance is a public program, the state legislature can change tax rates if necessitated by increased costs.

Unemployment insurance is a social insurance program, and, thus can contain features that could not be written into private insurance policies. It can compensate for a higher percentage of the wage loss of low wage earners and pay additional benefits for dependents. Even some types of voluntary unemployment can be compensated. On the other hand, it can impose requirements for the receipt of benefits that are not found in private insurance, such as a qualifying period of earnings before benefits can be received.

The unemployment insurance system is kept distinct from relief by basing eligibility for benefits as much as possible on objective "rights," rather than on the determination of personal need. The introduction of a test of personal need would destroy the insurance character of the program.

[7] Malisoff, *op. cit.*, pp. 25–27.

Part II

How
Unemployment Insurance
Developed

Chapter 4

European Experience
with Unemployment Insurance

There was considerable foreign experience to draw upon when unemployment insurance began to be seriously considered in the United States. Altogether, 19 European nations, Australia, Canada, and Queensland had initiated nation-wide unemployment insurance programs, either of a compulsory or voluntary nature. The voluntary programs were of interest to American planners mainly in the degree of national control and the methods of national assistance to local plans. The experience under the compulsory systems of Great Britain and Germany was of most value in planning both federal and state legislation.

FOREIGN VOLUNTARY PLANS

Lawmakers in Basle Town, Switzerland, were the recipients of the first unemployment insurance plan in 1789, but this plan lasted only a few years. Apparently there were no further attempts to create an unemployment insurance plan during the next century. About the middle of the 19th century, trade-unions began to pay benefits to their unemployed members and some plans were also operated by mutual benefit or fraternal societies. Starting with Dijon, France, in 1896, municipalities began to subsidize voluntary plans. The Belgian cities of Liege (1897) and Ghent (1901) subsidized trade-union funds, for the purpose of increasing their benefits. Subsidies were granted annually on the basis of benefits paid the preceding year. This system of municipal subsidies spread widely.[1] In the early part of the twentieth century, many provinces and cantons began to add their subsidies to those of the cities, and some national governments added grants. In only three countries having solely voluntary plans did employers make any contributions. In two of these, Switzerland and Spain, employers contributed to joint employer-employee plans, and in Denmark in 1921,

---

[1] With some modifications it was emulated in other municipalities in Belgium, France, Germany, Switzerland, Italy, the Netherlands, Norway, Denmark, Finland, and Great Britain.

47

employers were required to contribute to a central fund to provide emergency benefits to those who had exhausted trade-union benefits. Some communal voluntary plans were also established, notably in Switzerland, where they were subsidized first by the cantons and eventually by the federal government. Where government subsidies were provided, government control varied from practically none in Belgium and the other countries which used the "Ghent" system, to very detailed requirements and controls in Switzerland. In Belgium, during the depression of the 1930's, administration became so loose that in 1933 the federal government introduced rigid controls, defining membership, contributions, and benefit requirements on a uniform basis.[2] By the time the Social Security Act was under consideration in the United States, 11 countries had laws providing for subsidies to voluntary unemployment insurance plans. By 1961, seven of these had changed to compulsory laws.[3] Only Denmark, Finland, Sweden, and two cantons of Switzerland had voluntary systems (Table 4–1). Czechoslovakia had repealed its legislation.

FOREIGN COMPULSORY PROGRAMS

The first attempt at a compulsory unemployment insurance system was made in the Swiss commune of St. Gall in 1894, but it ceased to function in 1897 after workers with stable employment began moving to other towns to avoid paying contributions. The first national compulsory system was enacted in Great Britain in 1911. The second was established eight years later in Italy and was followed by compulsory legislation in seven other countries during the 1920's.[4] The German law of 1927 was the most recent before the Social Security Act was passed. By 1964, 32 countries had compulsory laws. Four other countries (Australia, New Zealand, France, and Luxembourg) had unemployment assistance schemes (see Table 4–1). Since the British and German systems were both the largest and most intensively studied[5] and publicized, their experience will be described in some detail.

[2] The Belgian experience was studied in detail by Constance A. Kiehl, *Unemployment Insurance in Belgium* (New York: Industrial Relations Counselors, Inc., 1932) and the Swiss experience by T. C. Spates and G. S. Rabinovitch, *Unemployment Insurance in Switzerland* (New York: Industrial Relations Counselors, Inc., 1931).

[3] Belgium, Czechoslovakia, Denmark, Finland, France, Greece, the Netherlands, Norway, Spain, Sweden, and Switzerland (12 cantons).

[4] Australia (Queensland), Austria, Bulgaria, Germany, Irish Free State, Poland, Switzerland (13 cantons).

[5] For a description of foreign systems prior to the Social Security Act, see Industrial Relations Counselors, Inc., *An Historical Basis for Unemployment Insurance* (Minneapolis: University of Minnesota Press, 1934) and *Unemployment-Benefit Plans in the United States and Unemployment Insurance in Foreign Countries,* Bulletin No. 544 (Washington, D.C.: U.S. Department of Labor, Bureau of Labor Statistics, 1931). For more up-to-date information, see International Labour Office, *Unemployment Insurance Schemes* (Geneva, Switzerland, 1955); and U.S. Department of Health, Education and Welfare, Social Security Administration, *Social Security Programs Throughout the World, 1964* (Washington, D.C.: U.S. Government Printing Office, 1964).

Table 4-1

Unemployment Insurance Systems (1961) with the Year of Enactment of the Legislation in Force

Compulsory Insurance Systems		Voluntary Insurance Systems		Noninsurance Systems	
Austria	1949	Denmark	1933	Australia	1947
Belgium	1945	Finland	1934	France	1951‖
Canada	1955	Sweden	1934	Luxembourg	1945
Chile	1937*	Switzerland	1924‡	New Zealand	1938
Cyprus	1954				
Ecuador	1954				
East Germany	1947				
Federal Republic of Germany	1927				
Greece	1954				
Iceland	1956†				
Italy	1935				
Japan	1947				
Netherlands	1949				
Norway	1938				
Spain	1961				
Switzerland	1951‡				
Union of South America	1946				
United Kingdom	1946				
United States	1935§				
Yugoslavia	1952				

* Salaried employees only.
† Trade-union employees only.
‡ Date of latest federal law. Seventeen cantons have compulsory insurance covering their whole territory, ten have compulsory insurance covering only their communes, and two (Appenzell Innen-Rhoden and Aargau) have only voluntary insurance, established under 1924 federal law.
§ Date of federal law.
‖ Also large collectively bargained insurance scheme, for commerce and industry.

The British Experience[6]

The original British unemployment insurance act was passed in 1911. As has usually been the case with countries adopting unemployment insurance, there had already been a considerable development of trade-union plans. In Great Britain the payment of unemployment benefits by unions to their unemployed members reached back at least 70 years. About one hundred of the principal unions paid unemployment benefits in 1892. The number had grown to about 680 unions with a membership of 1,839,000 in 1908. On the other hand, about 380 unions, with a membership of about 525,000, paid no benefits. Two fifths of the latter were in mining, quarrying, and the transport trades. Trade-union members, in turn, represented only about an estimated 14 percent of all wage earners in Great Britain.

The British unemployment insurance act was passed after the Royal Commission on the Poor Laws and Relief of Distress reported in February, 1909, following an exhaustive four-year study. The majority report recommended the establishment of some form of unemployment insurance, especially among unskilled and unorganized labor. However, it recommended that this be accomplished through encouragement of voluntary schemes by government subsidy. The minority report, while recommending government subsidies to trade-union plans, argued strongly against a national system as impractical and probably harmful. Nevertheless, a national scheme of unemployment insurance was enacted in 1911.

The 1911 Act covered only about 2½ million workers in half a dozen industries that had a high incidence of unemployment. These industries were building and construction, shipbuilding, foundries and machine shops, construction of vehicles, and sawmilling. Seasonal industries, such as cotton manufacturing and coal mining, were excluded. The program was limited in coverage because it was considered to be experimental in nature.

The original program was also quite limited as to benefits. A modest weekly benefit was payable. The duration of benefits was limited to a maximum of 15 weeks in a 12-month period and was further limited to one week of benefits for each five weeks of contributions. Employers and workers contributed equal amounts, with a government contribution equal to one fourth of the total. Refunds of the surplus of contributions over benefits were to be made to workers at age 60 who had made 500 contributions, and rebates to employers with good employment records.

The program was extended in 1916 to munitions workers (for whom unemployment was expected after the war) and to certain other industries, including the chemical, leather, metal, and rubber industries. This enlarged the coverage to above 3,700,000 workers.

[6] For detailed information on the British experience prior to 1935, see Eveline M. Burns, *British Unemployment Programs, 1920–1938* (Washington, D.C.: Social Science Research Council, 1941) and Mary B. Gilson, *Unemployment Insurance in Great Britain* (New York: Industrial Relations Counselors, Inc., 1931).

Up to 1920, when the Act was extended to most wage earners, the program was on a solvent basis. In fact, with the low unemployment during World War I, a substantial surplus accumulated in the unemployment insurance fund. In the middle of 1919, this surplus amounted to about £18,000,000.

The 1920 Amendments. In 1920, the coverage of the Act was extended to all workers between age 16 and 65 except those in agriculture (covered by a separate scheme in 1936), domestic service, civil servants, railway and public utility employees, and white-collar workers earning over £250 a year. Benefits were increased to 15s. for men and a lower benefit of 12s. for women was introduced.

Although the 1920 Act was enacted in a favorable economic climate, unemployment began to rise almost immediately after it took effect on November 8, 1920. In the next month, the unemployment rate was 7.8 percent and the following year rose to an average of 16.6 percent. During the next 10 years, unemployment averaged 12.7 percent and fell below 10 percent only in 1927. In 1931 it had risen to 21.1 percent.

Early Relaxations in Eligibility Requirements. The British were faced during the 1920's with a continuing large volume of unemployment and only local relief as an alternative program to unemployment insurance to provide income for the unemployed. The conditions for receipt of local relief were onerous and the local governments were unable to finance it for the large numbers who were unemployed. With the constant hope that employment conditions would improve, the British therefore used the unemployment insurance system to provide for the unemployed. This was done through a bewildering succession of relaxations in conditions for benefits and extensions of the duration of "covenanted" and "uncovenanted" benefits. Such actions began to be taken almost immediately after the expansion of the unemployment insurance system under the 1920 Act. Even that Act provided that, for a temporary period, a worker could draw eight weeks of benefits if he paid contributions for only four weeks. Because increasing unemployment was preventing many from meeting even this mild qualification during the month following enactment, the law was changed. A worker could now qualify for eight weeks of benefits if he had had 10 weeks since December 31, 1919, during which he worked in what would have been "insurable employment" if the 1920 Act had been in force, or four such weeks since July 4, 1920.

Standard Benefits. The eligibility requirements for standard or "covenanted" benefits were tightened on July 3, 1921, to 20 weeks of contributions since the beginning of the last preceding insurance year. Again, this was waived if the claimant could show that he was normally in insured employment and genuinely seeking fulltime employment. By the Unemployment Insurance Act (No. 2) of 1924, the qualifying requirements were further tightened to a requirement of 30 contributions since the beginning of the second benefit year preceding the current one and 20 weeks in the immediately preceding benefit year. However, the Minister of Labor was authorized to waive the new condition of 30 contributions, first until October 1, 1925, and then by two further acts until December 31, 1927. To complicate matters even more, the waiver rules issued by the Minister were progressively relaxed until, beginning in February 1925, a claimant could qualify for covenanted benefits if he had made eight contributions in the last two preceding insurance years or 30 contributions at any time.

The statutory conditions for standard benefits were changed again by the Unemployment Insurance Act of 1927, effective April 19, 1928, by having only one requirement, namely, 30 contributions in the two years preceding application for benefit.

The maximum duration of covenanted or standard benefits varied from 15 to 16 weeks until November 2, 1922, when it was lengthened to 26 weeks. From April 19, 1928, to November 11, 1931, there was no statutory limitation on the number of standard benefits. The rule of one week's benefits for each six contributions was also relaxed in various ways and was abolished by the Act of 1927, effective April, 1928. The unrestricted duration of benefits was recommended by the so-called Blanesburgh Committee (appointed in 1925), which took the position that the unemployed should draw benefits for an unlimited period provided that they were genuinely seeking work. In March, 1930, on the recommendation of the Morris Committee (appointed in 1929), the genuinely seeking work provision was replaced by one disqualifying a worker for failure or refusal to apply for or accept suitable work or failure to carry out the written directions of the public employment office. This latter requirement was very ineffective because of the limited number of job openings due to employment conditions. As a result, the number of persons drawing benefits was considerably increased.

"Uncovenanted Benefits." Even with the temporary relaxing of regulations, large numbers of the unemployed could not meet the contributory rules for regular benefits. Additional benefits, called "uncovenanted" benefits (1921–24), "extended" benefits (1924–28), and "transitional" benefits (1928–31) were therefore paid to persons who could not meet the contribution conditions provided they met certain alternative conditions, which included proof that the claimant would have normally been in insured employment and was genuinely seeking work on a full-time basis. For a time, benefits were paid at the discretion of the Minister of Labor when he deemed it in the public interest. This discretion was used by the Minister to exclude certain classes where the benefit was deemed not to be necessary in view of other resources; that is, by a rough test of need. Even this discretion was abolished by the Act of 1924. The Act of 1927 aimed to abolish "uncovenanted" or "extended" benefits. However, because large numbers of workers could not meet the contributory conditions for unemployment insurance benefits (30 contributions in the two preceding years) and unemployment was still serious, "transitional" payments were pro-

vided. Only eight contributions in the preceding two years were required for such "transitional" payments. Even this contribution requirement was repealed by the Act of 1930.

The maximum duration of uncovenanted benefits was first set at 22 weeks, but this was increased to 44 on November 2, 1922, and then reduced to 41 on October 18, 1923. During this period, no benefits were paid during temporary "gaps" of from one to three weeks after benefits had been paid for specified periods. Beginning on August 1, 1924, when the name of "uncovenanted" benefits was changed to "extended" benefits, there was no statutory limit on their duration. Workers who exhausted their standard or "covenanted" benefits were able to draw uncovenanted benefits for additional weeks to bring their combined benefits up to the statutory limits for uncovenanted benefits. After August 1, 1924, there was no limit to such extension of benefits except that those who had not made 30 contributions at any time needed eight contributions in the two years immediately preceding their claim for benefits.

Retrenchment in 1931. The combination of extensions of benefits and other liberalizations in the program kept the unemployment insurance fund in financial difficulties. The surplus of £22 million which had been built up in the ten years preceding the expansion of the program on November 8, 1920, was exhausted by the following July. During the next ten years, expenditures exceeded receipts in all but two fiscal years. The debt rose especially rapidly beginning with the fiscal year 1930–31. During that year it practically doubled and exceeded £75 million on June 30, 1931. Six months later it reached over £110 million. This occurred despite the payment of the entire cost of transitional payments by the government during fiscal years 1930 and 1931.

The heavy drains that unemployment insurance made on the national treasury led to drastic revision of the unemployment insurance system in 1931. Recommendations of a Committee on National Expenditures resulted in the passage of the National Economy Act of 1931 which authorized Orders in Council[7] to make economies in specified services, including unemployment insurance. Orders in Council increased contributions and decreased the weekly benefit amount, limited the duration of standard benefits to 26 weeks and introduced a requalifying requirement after exhaustion of benefits. "Transitional benefits" were terminated and replaced by "transitional payments" based on need. These payments were restricted to those who had exhausted standard benefits and would have been eligibile for benefits under the 1927 qualifying requirements. Determination of need was to be made by the local assistance authorities.

These changes resulted in drastic reductions in expenditures. Although the deficit in expenditures was not entirely eliminated following June, 1933, the insurance fund began to show an annual surplus and the debt

[7] Orders of the King with the advice of his Privy Council.

began to be reduced. By December 31, 1934, a balance of over £10 million had been built up and the debt reduced to £105,741,000.

The Unemployment Act of 1934. The British provisions for the unemployed were drastically changed by the Unemployment Act of 1934. The transitional payments system was abolished and an Unemployment Assistance Scheme substituted to provide assistance for the unemployed who were not drawing unemployment insurance and were in need. This scheme was to be nationally financed and administered by a National Assistance Board. The unemployment insurance program was liberalized by providing that all insured workers would be eligible for 26 weeks of benefits in a year and additional benefits would be paid to those with a good record of employment in the last five years, up to an additional 26 weeks of benefits. Weekly benefit amounts were increased considerably so that most beneficiaries would not need supplementary relief. The outstanding debt was separated, with provision that it would be repaid out of current income at the rate of £5 million annually. Since then, the unemployment insurance system has been kept on a sound financial basis.

The Present System. Following World War II, the 1946 National Insurance Act unified all types of social insurance in the United Kingdom into a comprehensive scheme. In 1948, unemployment assistance was absorbed into a new national public assistance program by the National Assistance Act. Under this Act, a National Assistance Board was established with regional and area offices, through which national assistance is paid to the unemployed, as well as to other persons whose resources are below needs.

Unemployment insurance now covers all workers, except that coverage is optional for married women. Benefits are financed through an over-all contribution for all types of social insurance, payable in equal amounts by employers and workers, with a government contribution equal to one fourth of these combined contributions. The qualifying requirement is a minimum 26 weeks of employment in the preceding year. Men and women now receive equal amounts of benefits, except that married women and youth receive reduced amounts. Quite substantial dependents' allowances are paid. Benefits are varied up to a maximum of 30 weeks of benefits for those with 50 weeks of employment. Extended benefits are payable up to a maximum of 52 weeks to employees with at least five years of insurance coverage and a good record of employment.

Lessons from the British Experience. The British experience with unemployment insurance was no argument for action in this country in 1935. In fact, the British experience from 1921 to 1931 was fully exploited by those opposed to proposed legislation in the United States. The economies that had been made in 1931, and the revamping of the system in 1934, did not have much counterinfluence in this country before the Social Security Act was passed. So far as the influence of the British plan on American opinion was concerned, the story ended with the heavy debt built up before the National Economy Act of 1931. This was quoted by opponents of unemployment insurance as proof that an unemployment insurance system could not be kept solvent. Coupled with this, the payment of benefits for ten years to large numbers of persons who had never contributed to, or had a very tenuous attachment to the unemployment insurance program, was cited as an example of how an insurance system could deteriorate into a "dole."

Actually, the image of the British system as a dole was created by about one fourth of the beneficiaries in the ten years ending in 1931. About three fourths of the beneficiaries during this period were claimants for regular benefits. It has been estimated that if there had been no changes in the 1920 Act, it would have remained solvent. The estimated cost of uncovenanted, extended, and transitional benefits exceeded £70 million. Estimates of the cost of extension of "regular" duration of benefits beyond 26 weeks, the abolition of the genuinely-seeking-work clause, and increases in benefits and reductions in contributions from 1926 to 1931 totaled £40 million.[8]

As for the continued extensions of benefits to those who had exhausted standard benefits and to those who could not meet the qualifying conditions, the British experience constituted a warning of the political pressures that develop if an alternative method of caring for the unemployed who exhaust their unemployment insurance benefits is not available. The English poor law system was harsh and antiquated and the British government sought to minimize the use of it for the unemployed. Also, if it had been used to care for those unable to qualify for standard unemployment benefits, the local governments that administered poor relief would have been bankrupted.

The planners of unemployment insurance legislation in this country learned a great deal from the British experience. First, they were careful to propose strict qualifying requirements and definite limitations on the duration of benefits in order to avoid any charges that they were proposing a "dole" to all the unemployed. Second, they were extremely prudent and perhaps too conservative in the benefits proposed, in order to assure a solvent system. Finally, the British legislation, being the best known, was most widely copied in drafting the detailed provisions of legislative proposals with respect to qualifying and disqualifying provisions and administrative arrangements.

The German System[9]

The German Unemployment Insurance Act of 1927 differed markedly from the British Act of 1920. The experts who designed the German system

---

[8] Burns, *op. cit.*, p. 70, table 5.

[9] For detailed information on the German experience prior to 1935, see Mollie Ray Carroll, *Unemployment Insurance in Germany* (2d ed., rev.; Washington, D.C.: Brookings Institution, 1930) and National Industrial Conference Board, Inc., *Unemployment Insurance in Germany* (New York, 1932) and briefer and later accounts in the studies of foreign systems listed on page 48.

had studied the British experience and endeavored to profit from its mistakes. Nevertheless, the German system had as hard going from 1929 on as the British system after 1920, and was subject to as frequent changes. The adaptations to heavy unemployment, however, were generally in the opposite direction from those taken by the British. Instead of endeavoring to use the unemployment insurance system to provide for the great bulk of the unemployed, as the British did, the Germans in most respects progressively restricted the unemployment insurance system and changed it more and more into a relief system.

In spite of being the first country to adopt a general social insurance system (in 1889), Germany was late among European countries in adopting an unemployment insurance system. It had had experience, however, with a national unemployment relief system for almost ten years. Immediately after the end of World War I, a national emergency relief system was created. Although it was first enacted as a temporary measure, it was continued up to the time the unemployment insurance law was enacted. In fact, by that time it had taken on some of the characteristics of an insurance system. Beginning October 15, 1923, employers and workers had contributed to its financing. Administrative control had also been gradually shifted from communal relief agencies to the employment exchanges.

This relief system was entirely superseded by the German unemployment insurance law, enacted July 16 and effective October 1, 1927. The new law provided for a three-tier system of assistance to the unemployed. The top tier was an unemployment insurance system financed through employer and employee contributions. The second tier provided emergency benefits, based on a moderate means test and financed four fifths by the federal government and one fifth by the local governments. The bottom tier consisted of local poor relief, which was originally intended to be financed exclusively by local governments, but which was given substantial federal aid during the 1929–33 depression. The plan for emergency benefits was in recognition of the fact that ordinary benefits would not give sufficient protection during depressions. It was to be an intermediate stage between unemployment insurance and poor relief, to be restricted or expanded according to economic conditions, with a needs test less severe than that required for poor relief. It was to be administered by the same organization as that paying regular unemployment insurance benefits.

Instead of flat-rate contributions and benefits, as under the British insurance system, the German unemployment insurance law created eleven wage classes, both for contributions and benefits. The benefits were on a graduated scale that was more generous to the lower-paid workers. Dependents' allowances were provided. Duration was the same as under the British Act of 1927—26 weeks—with a qualifying requirement of 26 weeks of employment. Coverage was almost universal from the start. Manual workers between the school-leaving age and 65 and salaried workers receiving no more than 8400 RM a year were covered. Only agricultural workers and domestic workers were excluded from the system.

The emergency unemployment benefits were payable for a maximum period of 26 weeks during periods of exceptional unemployment, except that nonmanual workers over 40 could receive such benefits for 39 weeks. The benefits were payable to those who had exhausted regular insurance benefits or were unable to qualify for them. At first, the rates of weekly benefits were the same as for regular benefits, but the rates were lowered in November, 1930.

Changes to Meet Heavy Unemployment—1928–1932. The German law of 1927 was enacted in a period of relative prosperity, but severe unemployment set in shortly thereafter, beginning in 1928. Unemployment continued to grow, except for seasonal improvements, until it reached a peak of 6 million workers in 1932. This represented almost half the work force covered by unemployment insurance. Although during its first six months of operation the system built up a surplus of 57 million RM, large federal loans had to be made to the insurance fund in 1928 and 1929. Contributions were increased three times during 1930 from the original combined rate on employers and workers of 3 percent to 6½ percent. Thereafter, the insurance fund had an annual surplus, even though in the fiscal year 1932–33, there was a transfer of 359 million RM to relief funds.[10] Unemployment insurance benefits had been cut so drastically by then, both in amount and the number eligible for them, that the fund still had a surplus.

Despite the drastic increase in contributions, a whole series of laws and Presidential decrees were enacted beginning November 1, 1929, in order to keep the insurance fund solvent. These laws and decrees adjusted coverage, extended the waiting period, tightened the law against abuse, increased the eligibility requirements, and finally cut benefits. In October, 1931, the duration of benefits was reduced to 20 weeks and in June, 1932, a needs test was imposed after the first six weeks of benefits. At the same time, regular weekly benefit amounts were reduced 23 percent.

In contrast to the constant changes in extended benefits made by the British, major changes were made only twice in the German emergency benefit scheme. In November, 1930, insured persons in all occupations other than manual workers in agriculture, domestic servants, and persons under 21 were made eligible for emergency benefits provided they lived in places of 10,000 population or over and provided that they had satisfied the general conditions for standard benefit. On the other hand, the emergency benefit amount was reduced, and the duration shortened from 39 to 32 weeks, with extension in exceptional cases to 45 weeks for persons over 40 years of age. A stricter proof of need was also required.

In October, 1932, supplementary emergency benefits were made pay-

[10] *Unemployment Insurance, A Summary of Some Existing Governmental and Private Plans* (New York: Metropolitan Life Insurance Company, 1935), p. 39.

able to persons with dependents and benefits were continued for those who otherwise would have exhausted their benefits. Intended as a temporary measure, these relaxations were continued indefinitely in March, 1933. Beginning in May, 1933, the cost of emergency benefits was paid out of the contributory unemployment insurance fund. It is interesting that the British took the opposite course the following year, when they separated the financing of regular and extended benefits.

The proportion of the unemployed who drew ordinary benefits was at a peak of 81.1 percent in January, 1929. This had dropped to 31.2 percent in January, 1932. This decrease was probably due in large part to the exhaustion of regular benefits by an increasing number of the unemployed. The peak number drawing ordinary benefits despite this was almost 2.5 million in February, 1932. In June, 1932, when ordinary benefits without a needs test were restricted to six weeks, the number receiving ordinary benefits fell to 950,000, or 17.2 percent of the unemployed. A year later, in June, 1933, only 416,000 drew ordinary benefits, although unemployment still hovered around 5 million.[11] Figures after that date are not comparable.

The number drawing emergency benefits naturally increased as the depression wore on and workers exhausted regular benefits. In January, 1929, a total of 145,000, or only 5.2 percent of the unemployed drew emergency benefits. The number increased steadily except for seasonal fluctuations until it reached a peak of 1.7 million, or 28.9 percent of the unemployed in March, 1932. Thereafter, emergency benefits also declined somewhat in importance with 1,313,000 drawing emergency benefits in June, 1933.

Local relief had to take care of an increasing proportion of the unemployed. Comparable figures are not available before August, 1930, but in that month 450,000, or 15.7 percent of the unemployed received local relief. The number grew to 2.4 million, or 41.7 percent of the unemployed in December, 1932.

The number of unemployed drawing neither benefits or relief was 480,000, or 16.7 percent in August, 1930, and 1.3 million, or 22.4 percent in December, 1932.[12]

Post-War Legislation. No fundamental change was made in the German system during World War II, except that unemployment benefits were paid to workers while cleaning up and putting bombed factories back into production. At the end of the War, and again in 1948, the Allies froze all German government funds, and in connection with currency reform, wiped out accumulated funds so that a fresh start had to be made twice in accumulating a reserve. A new unemployment insurance law was enacted in the

[11] The only change made by the Nazis up to then was to exclude domestic servants in May, 1933. Other restrictions later imposed were to withdraw protection from agricultural workers and all non-Aryans.

[12] Industrial Relations Counselors, Inc., *An Historical Basis for Unemployment Insurance* (Minneapolis, Minn.: University of Minnesota Press, 1934), pp. 278–81, table xiv.

Western zones in October, 1947.[13] The Federal Republic of Germany, on March 10, 1952, set up a new federal placement and unemployment insurance institution to administer unemployment insurance—the pattern of administration used before the War for all of Germany. The 1947 law was amended in 1952, 1953, and 1956. The present law in structure is quite similar to the original law of 1927. Coverage is about the same, except that there are no age limits on workers covered. A separate scheme is provided for dock and construction workers. Contributions are again 1.5 percent each paid by employers and workers. The principal difference is in the duration of benefits. Thirteen weeks of benefits are paid if the worker has had 26 weeks of insurable employment in the preceding year, 20 weeks duration if he has had 39 weeks of insurable employment, and 26 weeks if he has had 52 weeks of insurable employment. Unemployment assistance is provided for those who have had 26 weeks of employment in the preceding two years. Unemployment assistance is payable after exhaustion of regular benefits, subject to an income test.

Lessons from German Experience. While the British badly damaged their unemployment insurance system by using all sorts of devices to keep the unemployed on the benefit rolls and thereby going heavily in debt, the Germans almost destroyed their unemployment insurance system by progressively restricting it in order to keep it solvent. While Germany kept unemployment insurance self-supporting, and also eventually supported emergency benefits out of unemployment insurance income, practically all benefits (all except the first six weeks of benefits) were placed on a needs basis.

The experience of the German system was also used by those opposed to legislation in the United States to demonstrate that an unemployment insurance system could not meet the needs of a depression. There is little evidence that much consideration was given to the German system during the framing of the Social Security Act. The rather favorable experience with emergency benefits might well have been considered, in view of the very modest program of unemployment insurance proposed in this country.

The German system set a precedent for varying contributions and benefits with wages. Doing this by wage classes was considered, but not adopted in this country because no advantage was seen in it. Contributions by both employers and workers, as in Germany, were adopted by ten states, but now employee contributions exist in only three states. This is largely due to the emphasis that has been placed in this country on employer responsibility for unemployment.

[13] An attempt was made in the Allied Control Council to develop a comprehensive social insurance system for all of Germany, but while it was being negotiated, the Russians issued an ordinance of March 28, 1947, providing for a unified social insurance system, including unemployment insurance, for East Germany. The three western Allied powers then decided to let the West Germans develop a revised unemployment insurance law, subject to the approval of the occupying powers.

SUMMARY

The European countries had accumulated considerable experience with unemployment insurance prior to the passage of the Social Security Act. The smaller countries had largely relied on subsidization of trade-union plans, which were much more highly developed than in this country. A few countries had compulsory unemployment insurance systems, of which the British and German are most useful for study.

The British system, started on a limited basis, was at first successful. But the greatly expanded Act of 1920 soon was subjected to continuous changes, in efforts to cope with the heavy and continued unemployment that the British experienced year after year. In the absence of an adequate public assistance program, the unemployed were kept under the unemployment insurance system through progressive relaxation of qualifying conditions. As a result, the system was discredited and ran heavily into debt. Beginning in 1931, however, the system was put on a sound financial basis and from 1934 on, a system of unemployment assistance and later of general public assistance made it possible to restore the British unemployment insurance system to its original purposes. These reforms, however, came too late to be useful in framing the American system.

The German system, although carefully designed to meet the problems of long duration unemployment, was deluged with heavy unemployment soon after its inception. The Germans took opposite measures from the British to keep their program solvent, progressively retrenching the unemployment insurance system and virtually converting it to a relief system.

The unemployment problems that the British and Germans faced and the measures they took to meet them were used by the opponents of unemployment insurance in this country to discredit the insurance method. Because of this, American proponents tended to play down European experience, although they used many technical provisions of foreign laws as models in drafting American legislation. The heavy debt built up by the British system also probably influenced planners to use undue caution, reflected in the limited benefits provided under early American laws. The German experience had less influence on the original American legislation, probably both because of the short German experience and because the Nazi regime had cast a shadow on anything that was German.

The British mistakes of the 1920's and their subsequent successful experience, however, now merit study since they had problems of persistent unemployment now faced in the United States. The early German experience should also be studied in view of the difficulties they experienced, even though they had made advance provision for extended duration of benefits during periods of high unemployment.

Chapter 5

American Forerunners
and Early Attempts
at Legislation

The United States did not entirely lack experience with unemployment insurance before the wave of legislation in the mid-1930's. Some experience had been accumulated through trade-union plans, joint agreement employer-employee plans, and company plans. Attempts at state legislation date back at least to 1916. As the depression of the 1930's deepened, a number of state commissions were created to study unemployment insurance and a large number of bills were introduced in state legislatures. One state, Wisconsin, passed a law in 1932. Some study of the question was also made in Congress and a few bills introduced. The reports of the state commissions, the resulting debates in state legislatures, and these early bills greatly influenced the character of the legislation that was eventually passed.

This chapter will briefly describe the experience with voluntary unemployment insurance schemes in this country and trace the history of attempts to secure legislation prior to the passage of the Social Security Act.

AMERICAN VOLUNTARY PLANS[1]

Trade-Union Plans

In contrast to European countries, very few formal unemployment benefit plans were developed by trade-unions in this country. The earliest known plan was established in 1831. During times of depression in the latter part of the 1800's and the early part of the 1900's, practically all trade-unions gave assistance to their unemployed members and many unemployment benefit or relief plans sprang up, only to be discontinued with improvement in employment conditions. In April, 1931, the Bureau of

[1] For a more detailed description of American voluntary plans up to 1930, see Bryce M. Stewart, *Unemployment Benefits in the United States* (New York: Industrial Relations Counselors, Inc., 1930).

Labor Statistics found only three national unions and 45 local unions that had unemployment benefit plans of a more or less permanent and systematic character.[2] Of the local plans, eight had been established after the depression of the 1930's began.

The three national unions with unemployment benefit plans had a total membership of only about 1,000. The oldest, the Deutsch-Amerikanishe Typographia, started its plan in 1884, and the other two, siderographers and diamond cutters, in 1910 and 1912.

The 45 local unions with plans in 1931 had a total membership of 44,648. They included the following types of local unions: bookbinders; lithographers; electrotypers; photoengravers; pressmen and press assistants; typographical workers; bakery workers; lace operatives; brewery, flour, cereal, and soft drink workers; and wood carvers.

The plans varied widely both as to type and amount of contributions, which were paid entirely by union members. Contributions in some plans equaled a percentage of earnings, in others a flat daily, weekly, or monthly amount was contributed, and in still others, assessments were paid according to need. Contributions in several plans ran as high as $2 a week per member and in one (San Francisco Local No. 8 of the Photoengravers) 10 percent of earnings was contributed.

Benefits also varied widely. The three national union plans, perhaps because they were started in a day of lower wages, paid only $5, $6, and $9 a week, but for durations varying from 16 to 26 weeks. The local union plans paid from $5.50 to $30 a week, the highest benefits being paid by the photoengravers and electrotypers. Duration ranged from eight to 32 weeks, with ten plans having indefinite or unlimited duration.

During 1933, the latest year for which figures are available, a total of $3,700,000 was paid out in benefits, of which $2,150,000 was paid by the electrotypers and photoengravers.[3]

Joint-Agreement Plans

In April, 1961, sixteen unemployment benefit and guaranteed employment plans, worked out by joint agreement between unions and management, covered over 65,000 workers. All were established in the 1920's, except the plan in the wallpaper industry which started in 1894. The 13 benefit plans were all in the needle trades. The most important numerically were the plans of the Amalgamated Clothing Workers in Chicago, New York City, and Rochester, New York, totaling 33,000 workers and the American Federation of Full-Fashioned Hosiery Workers, with 15,000 members. The guaranteed employment plans were in the women's cloth-

---

[2] United States Department of Labor, Bureau of Labor Statistics, *Unemployment-Benefit Plans in the United States and Unemployment Insurance in Foreign Countries*, Bulletin No. 544 (Washington, D.C.: U.S. Government Printing Office, July, 1931).

[3] Metropolitan Life Insurance Company, *Unemployment Insurance, A Summary of Some Existing Governmental and Private Plans* (New York, 1935), p. 67.

ing industry in Cleveland, the wallpaper workers, and the maintenance-of-equipment employees of the Seaboard Airline Railway.[4] By 1933, the hat industry benefit plans, the hosiery industry plan, three of the lace industry plans, and the oldest plan—that of the wallpaper industry—had been suspended or abandoned.[5]

The unemployment benefit plans were supported by employer contributions in five plans and by joint contributions in eight plans. Contributions were usually expressed as a percentage of payroll, the highest being the Amalgamated Clothing Workers plan in Chicago, with a 3 percent employer and 1½ percent employee contribution.

Benefits were more limited than in the plans financed by trade-unions, and were usually aimed at compensating seasonal unemployment. For example, the Chicago plan of the Amalgamated provided for a maximum of 3¾ weeks of benefits in two seasons. Benefits were equal to 30 percent of wages up to a maximum of $15 a week.

The International Ladies' Garment Workers' Union plan in Cleveland guaranteed 38 weeks of employment. The Seaboard plan guaranteed employment for a whole year for a minimum number of workers. The United Wall Paper Crafts plan guaranteed 45 weeks of full pay a year.

Statistics are not available as to amounts paid under these plans, except for the three Amalgamated Clothing Workers plans. From April, 1929, to March, 1934, a total of $883,729 was paid under these three joint-agreement plans.[6]

Company Plans

Beginning with the Dennison Manufacturing Company in 1917, 38 firms had 19 unemployment benefit plans, savings plans, or employment guarantee plans at some time between 1917 and 1933. When the BLS made its survey in April, 1931, 15 plans, including the 14-firm "Rochester Plan," had been adopted or were in operation.[7] About 80,000 workers were covered by these plans. By the end of 1933, four new plans had been adopted, but four others had suspended or ended operations. In addition, seven of the 14 firms had withdrawn from the "Rochester Plan."[8]

The best known of the guaranteed employment plans was Procter and Gamble's. When started in 1923, it guaranteed 48 weeks of employment at full pay for hourly paid employees whose annual earnings were less than

[4] *Unemployment Benefit Plans,* Bulletin No. 544, *op. cit.,* pp. 14–19.

[5] Industrial Relations Counselors, Inc., *An Historical Basis for Unemployment Insurance* (Minneapolis: University of Minnesota Press, 1934), p. 66.

[6] *Unemployment Insurance, A Summary,* etc., *op. cit.,* p. 69.

[7] A dismissal payment plan of the Delaware and Hudson Railroad, which the BLS did not consider as an unemployment-benefit plan, was also reported in *Unemployment Insurance, A Summary,* etc., *op. cit.*

[8] *An Historical Basis for Unemployment Insurance, op. cit.,* pp. 67–70 and appendix v. Also Bulletin No. 544, *op. cit.,* pp. 7–13; *Unemployment Insurance, A Summary,* etc., *op. cit.,* pp. 69–76.

$2,000, who were participants in the company's profit-sharing plan, and who had six months of service. On January 1, 1933, membership in the profit-sharing plan was no longer required, but one year of service was mandatory.

Typical of an individual savings plan was that of the J. I. Case Company of Racine, Wisconsin, which contributed an amount equal to 5 percent of each employee's earnings, matched by a similar employer contribution until one year's earnings accrued in a savings account. During periods of depression, a laid-off employee could (after a 90-day waiting period) withdraw 40 percent of his earnings up to a maximum of $40 for each semimonthly period.

The General Electric Company put two types of plans in effect in 1930 and 1931: a guaranteed employment plan for 8,000 electric light bulb employees in Schenectady, New York, and an employee benefit plan for 40,000 out of 70,000 employees in the balance of the company's plants. Under this plan, employer and employee contributions, each equal to 1 percent of earnings, were to be paid for three years. The original plan provided for benefits equal to 50 percent of normal fulltime earnings up to a maximum of $20 a week for ten weeks in any 12 months. The plan was modified several times in the first three years of operation, but not fundamentally changed.

The Rochester Plan also merits a brief description. This plan was uniform for the participating companies, but each company administered its own fund. The companies were to contribute 2 percent of payroll to a company fund until it reached an amount equal to five year's contributions. If the fund proved inadequate after January 1, 1933, all employees of the company would be required to contribute 1 percent of their pay and the company would add an additional amount. Originally, weekly benefits were to be 60 percent of earnings up to a maximum of $22.50 to employees with a year or more of service and earnings not exceeding $50 a week. A two-week waiting period was required, with benefit duration varying from six to 13 weeks for employees with from one to five years of service. In November, 1932, benefits were temporarily reduced to 50 percent of average weekly earnings, up to a maximum of $18.75.

It is interesting that officials of eight of the company plans testified favorably at one or more hearings on state and federal legislation. Their experience had made them believe that unemployment benefits should be generally available, by legislation if necessary. As Marion B. Folsom, Treasurer of the Eastman Kodak Company, a member of the Rochester Plan, testified with respect to the unemployment insurance provisions of the Social Security bill: "The employers who are on this Advisory Council —you will recall they are Mr. Teagle, Mr. Swope, Mr. Lewisohn, Mr. Leeds, besides myself—reached the conclusion that you must have legislation in order to provide security for the workers in general, which many companies are already providing, because voluntary action would be too slow."[9]

ATTEMPTS AT STATE LEGISLATION

Although there was some discussion of unemployment insurance in the United States as early as 1907, there were no attempts at state legislation until 1916.

The earliest known discussion of unemployment insurance was a paper on the "Ghent system" by Professor Henry R. Seager of Columbia University at the first annual meeting of the American Association for Labor Legislation in 1907. At its annual meeting in 1911, Professor Charles R. Henderson discussed the new British unemployment insurance law and a Committee on Unemployment was appointed to consider the problem. In 1913, the Association held the first American Conference on Social Insurance at which Professor Henderson urged unemployment insurance in this country.

There was more widespread interest in unemployment insurance during the depression of 1914–15. In 1914, the American Association for Labor Legislation and its affiliated American Association on Unemployment held two national conferences on unemployment. At a second meeting, a tentative draft was presented, "A Practical Program for the Prevention of Unemployment," principally authored by John B. Andrews, Executive Secretary of the Association. This program, which included unemployment insurance, was endorsed by the conference and supported by several emergency commissions on unemployment appointed during the depression. Thereafter, the American Association for Labor Legislation seems to have lost interest in unemployment insurance for some years.[10]

Two years later, in 1916, the first bill on unemployment insurance was entered in the Massachusetts legislature. In general, it copied the British law. In 1921, a similar bill was introduced in New York by the Socialist Party, and in the same year, a bill of quite a different character was introduced in Wisconsin.

The Huber Bill in Wisconsin

On February 4, 1921, Senator Henry A. Huber of Wisconsin introduced a bill with the unique feature of varying employers' contributions accord-

---

[9] *Economic Security Act,* Hearings before the Committee on Finance, U.S. Senate, 74th Cong., 1st sess., on S. 1130 (Washington, D.C.: U.S. Government Printing Office, 1935), p. 555. (The Advisory Council referred to was that appointed by the President as advisory to the Committee on Economic Security. Mr. Swope was president of General Electric Company and Mr. Leeds of Leeds-Northrup Company, both of which had private plans.)

[10] The above information was supplied by Edwin E. Witte in "Development of Unemployment Compensation," *Yale Law Journal,* Vol. LV, No. 1 (December, 1945), pp. 22–23.

ing to the regularity of their employment. The principal author of this bill was Professor John R. Commons of the University of Wisconsin who had been the first administrator of the Wisconsin workmen's compensation law enacted ten years before. Dr. Commons was impressed with the stimulus that variation in premiums gave to accident prevention, and believed that the stimulus to prevent unemployment would be provided by an unemployment compensation law which based an employer's contributions on his experience with unemployment. Industries covered under the Huber bill were to be classified, and premium rates established according to their regularity of employment. The entire cost of the compensation paid to the unemployed would be borne by employers, who would be required to insure their liability for payments with a mutual insurance company controlled by the State Compensation Insurance Board.

Although the Huber bill had the support of the Wisconsin State Federation of Labor and several employers with unemployment insurance plans of their own, there was a formidable list of employers in opposition to it. The bill was defeated in the Senate by a vote of 19 to 10. However, the Huber measure was reintroduced in each succeeding session of the Wisconsin legislature through 1929, with different sponsors from 1925 on. In 1923, it lost by one vote in the Wisconsin Senate. Although several modifications were made in the bill in succeeding years, its essential features remained intact.[11]

The Huber bill formed the pattern for most bills introduced in other State legislatures during the 1920's: in Connecticut, Minnesota, and Pennsylvania in 1921; Minnesota in 1923 and 1925; and Connecticut in 1927. Altogether, 22 bills in six states were introduced in the 1920's with bills introduced in five states in 1929.[12]

RESURGENCE OF INTEREST IN LEGISLATION IN DEPRESSION OF 1930'S

Interest in unemployment insurance revived with the onset of the great depression of the 1930's.

The Wisconsin Act

In 1931, two bills were introduced in Wisconsin that were quite different from the Huber bill. One was based on a bill called "An American Plan for Unemployment Reserves,"[13] brought out by the American Association for Labor Legislation in 1930. This bill differed from the Huber bill in that it provided for a state fund with flat contributions of 1.5 percent of payroll by employers. Provision was also made for insurance by industry and

[11] For a detailed discussion and history of the Huber bill and its successors, see John B. Ewing, *Job Insurance* (Norman, Okla.: University of Oklahoma Press, 1933).

[12] *An Historical Basis,* etc., *op. cit.,* pp. 72–73, table vii.

[13] For the text, see "Senate Passes Unemployment Bills," *American Labor Legislation Review,* Vol. 20, No. 125 (1930).

industry funds. This bill appealed to J. J. Handley and Henry Ohl, Jr., officers of the Wisconsin Federation of Labor and they urged Robert Nixon, who had introduced the Huber bill in 1929, to use the Association draft. In 1931, Mr. Nixon introduced a bill in the Wisconsin legislature following the Association bill in providing for a state fund, but including the principle of experience rating of contributions.

Professor Harold M. Groves (who had been elected to the state legislature), with the assistance of Professors Paul Raushenbusch and Elizabeth Brandeis and others, drafted a bill with important differences from the Huber bill. The most important change was the provision of a state fund with individual employer accounts to be financed through contributions by the employer. Benefits would be paid to an employee only from his employer's account and benefits were to be reduced or stopped if the employer's reserves was inadequate. This bill was introduced on February 6, 1931.

Hearings were held jointly on the Nixon and Groves bills. No action was taken on the bills but, instead, the legislature authorized an interim committee for the study of unemployment insurance, to report at a special session of the legislature in the fall. At the fall session, the majority of the committee recommended enactment of an unemployment compensation bill with features quite similar to an amended bill that Groves had introduced later in the 1931 regular session. Mr. Handley, Secretary of the Wisconsin Federation of Labor, signed the report.[14]

The American Association for Labor Legislation joined forces with the supporters of the Groves bill. Governor Phil LaFollette in his opening address at the special session which convened on November 24, 1931, disarmed much of the opposition by proposing that the unemployment compensation bill would take effect "conditional upon industry's failure to establish a fair voluntary system in Wisconsin within a reasonable time (i.e., a year and a half)." When the Groves bill was reintroduced, it provided that the Act would not take effect if employers of at least 200,000 workers had adopted systems of unemployment reserves that met stated requirements within the time limit. The bill passed the Legislature by large majorities and was signed by the Governor on January 29, 1932. The main provisions of the Wisconsin Unemployment Compensation Act as passed were as follows:[15]

1. A state fund with individual employer accounts, funds to be invested in government securities by the State Investment Board.
2. Contributions equal to 2 percent of payroll during first two years and thereafter until employer's account averages $55 an employee; thereafter

[14] *Report of the Wisconsin Legislative Interim Committee on Unemployment* (Industrial Commission, State of Wisconsin, 1931).

[15] For an authoritative discussion of the Act, see Paul Raushenbusch, "Wisconsin's Unemployment Compensation Act," *American Labor Legislation Review*, Vol. 22 (1931), p. 11 ff.

1 percent if the account is more than $55 but less than $75; no contributions if more than $75. An additional 0.2 percent from all employers for administrative expenses and employment offices.

3. Coverage of employers with ten or more employees for four months or more in a year. Exemptions of farm workers, railroad employees in interstate commerce, logging workers, government employees and employees receiving more than $1,500 a year.

4. Benefits, after two weeks waiting period, equal to 50 percent of weekly wages with a minimum of $5 and a maximum of $10. Benefits to be reduced $1 a week for each $5 that employer's reserve account is below $50 per employee. Benefits to be paid for a maximum of ten weeks in the proportion of one week of benefits for each four weeks of employment in the last year. Each company's liability limited to the amount in its reserve fund. Benefits of a worker employed by several companies would be charged to last employer first and then in inverse order to other employers.

5. Disqualifications from benefits in cases of discharge for misconduct, voluntary leaving not attributable to the employer, refusal of suitable work, leaving employment because of a labor dispute, unemployment due to an act of God, unemployment by student if he worked only during vacations.

6. Qualifying requirements: two year's residence in the state and 40 weeks of employment during the period.

Legislative Activity in Other States

In the meantime, efforts were stepped up in other states to secure unemployment insurance legislation. A bill authorizing private insurance companies to sell private plans of unemployment insurance was passed by the New York Legislature in 1931, but vetoed by Governor Franklin D. Roosevelt.

In 1931, Governor Roosevelt invited the governors of six other states to explore the possibilities of simultaneous action by the states.[16] As Governor Roosevelt put it in his opening talk to the governors, "All must act, or there will be no action." As a result of the conference, an Interstate Commission on Unemployment Insurance was created, on which each of the attending governors appointed a member.[17] This Commission issued a report on February 15, 1932, unanimously recommending compulsory legislation of the individual employer reserves type, very similar to the Wisconsin law that had just been passed.[18]

---

[16] The conference was attended by the Governors of New Jersey, Connecticut, Ohio, Massachusetts, Pennsylvania, and Rhode Island.

[17] Leo Wolman, Columbia University; A. Lincoln Filene, Boston; William M. Leiserson, Antioch College, Ohio; Charles R. Blunt, Commissioner of Labor, New Jersey; Charles A. Kulp, University of Pennsylvania; and W. J. Couper, Deputy Commissioner of Labor, Connecticut.

[18] Professor Leiserson, although he signed the report, took "exception to any implication in it that an insurance system with pooling of contributions may not be better than a plan of separate plant reserves."

Activity accelerated in individual states. Altogether, 52 bills were introduced in 17 states in 1931.[19] In addition to the interim commission of Wisconsin, study commissions were appointed in California, Connecticut, Massachusetts, New York, and Ohio. Four of them reported favorably.

Ohio's report was the most significant because of the wide attention that it received in proposing a different type of plan than that passed in Wisconsin. The Commission recommended a state pooled fund, although provision was made for variation of employer contribution rates based on experience. Employees were to contribute 1 percent of their earnings, in addition to the 2 percent rate for employers. A "flat" duration of 16 weeks of benefits would be payable to all workers who qualified for any benefits. This bill received wide attention, and became a model for a number of bills introduced in other state legislatures.

Since 1932 was an "off" legislative year, bills were introduced in only five states. High hopes were entertained, however, for state legislation in 1933, with the favorable interstate and state commission reports. Altogether, 68 bills were introduced in 25 states, with several types of bills being introduced in some state legislatures. According to a tabulation of the American Association for Labor Legislation, its "American Plan" (for a state fund but with funds by industry and dividends to employers) was introduced in 16 states and in Congress.[20] Bills for individual employer reserves, such as the Wisconsin Act, were entered in 12 state legislatures and bills for industry pools in six. The Ohio plan for a single state pooled fund was introduced in 16 states.

No state passed a law in 1933, but a bill passed one house in seven states. Of these seven states, four states passed bills for a State pooled fund, one for individual employer reserves, one for industry funds, and one for both establishment funds and industry pooled funds.[21]

According to Edwin E. Witte, 10 out of 11 states study commissions, appointed in 1933 and 1934, made favorable reports.[22] Most of these commissions recommended either the Wisconsin or Ohio type of laws. The Virginia commission recommended individual employer reserves, but with a part of each employer's contribution going to a state guaranteed fund. The Connecticut Commission recommended a dismissal wage. Although

[19] For a state-by-state tabulation of bills from 1916–33, see An Historical Basis, op. cit., pp. 72–73, table viii.

[20] In June, 1933, this Association brought out a new model bill providing for individual employer accounts in state fund, but providing also for pooling by industry when the administrator finds this desirable to safeguard the reserves. Senator Wagner introduced a bill, the same month (S. 1943), for the District of Columbia embodying this new bill with minor modifications.

[21] Memorandum prepared by the American Association for Labor Legislation, Unemployment Insurance, Hearings before a subcommittee of the Committee on Ways and Means, House of Representatives, 73rd Cong., 2d sess., on H.R. 7659 (Washington, D.C.: U.S. Government Printing Office, 1934), pp. 102–6.

[22] Edwin E. Witte, "An Historical Account of Unemployment Insurance in the Social Security Act," Law and Contemporary Problems, Vol. III, No. 1 (January, 1936), p. 158.

no more laws were passed until 1935, these state commissions no doubt influenced the legislation eventually passed in their states.

FEDERAL STUDIES AND PROPOSALS

The federal government gave very little attention to unemployment insurance until shortly before the depression of the 1930's. The earliest known official recommendation was that of the United States Commission on Industrial Relations. In its final report in 1916, the Commission recommended the investigation and preparation of plans for insurance against unemployment "in such trades and industries as may seem desirable."[23]

In February, 1916, Representative Meyer London, New York Socialist, introduced a resolution in the House of Representatives for the "appointment of a national insurance commission and for the mitigation of the evil of unemployment."[24] The Committee on Labor of the House held hearings on April 6 and 11. Although there were several favorable witnesses representing insurance, social legislation, and research organizations, labor opposed action. Samuel Gompers, President of the American Federation of Labor, took a stand against the proposed Commission, but said that if it was established: "I would have them investigate the subject of social insurance of a voluntary character and how far it can be established in the United States with such aid as the Government can give. I am more concerned, as I have tried to indicate, with the fundamental principles of human liberty and refusal to surrender rights to government agencies, than I am with social insurance."[25] This remained his position and the official position of the American Federation of Labor until 1932. The London bill was killed in Committee, but it aroused considerable interest.

In 1921, President Warren Harding called a national conference on unemployment, under the chairmanship of Secretary of Commerce Herbert Hoover. In his opening statement, Mr. Hoover spoke of "direct doles" to individuals as "the most vicious of solutions" and hoped they would find solutions that do not "come within the range of charity." After reviewing private plans in this country, the Economic Advisory Committee on Unemployment and Depression Insurance, appointed at the conference, said that "any form of unemployment insurance which would create an economic motive to regularize unemployment is worthy of consideration." It recommended that reserve funds be created and used in depressions, not to pay part-wages to workers "in idleness" but to keep them employed on making repairs, producing to stock, etc.[26]

[23] United States Commission on Industrial Relations, *Final Report*, 64th Cong., 1st sess., S. Doc. 415 (Washington, D.C.: U.S. Government Printing Office, 1916), Vol. 2, p. 1160.

[24] H.R. 159, 64th Cong., 1st sess.

[25] *Commission to Study Social Insurance and Unemployment*, Hearings on H.R. 159, Committee on Labor, House of Representatives, 64th Cong., 1st sess., p. 172.

[26] Report of the President's Committee on Unemployment, *Business Cycles and Unemployment* (New York: McGraw-Hill Co., 1923).

In 1928, the first federal unemployment insurance bill (H.R. 12205) was introduced in Congress by Representative Victor Berger. This received no attention, but the Senate on May 3, 1928 adopted S. Res. 219, introduced by Senator James Couzens of Michigan, "providing for an analysis and appraisal of reports on unemployment and systems for prevention and relief thereof." The Committee on Education and Labor held hearings in December, 1928 and January and February, 1929. Dr. John R. Commons of the University of Wisconsin was one of the principal witnesses, and testified at length on how unemployment compensation could serve to stabilize employment. In its report the Committee thought that government should encourage private industry in its responsibility to stabilize employment. Its second recommendation was that: "Insurance plans against unemployment should be confined to the industry itself as much as possible. There is no necessity and no place for Federal interference in such efforts at this time. If any public insurance scheme is considered, it should be left to the State legislatures to study the problem."[27]

As the depression of the 1930's deepened, Senator Robert F. Wagner secured the adoption of Senate Resolution 483 on February 28, 1931, providing for the appointment of a Select Committee on Unemployment Insurance. Senator Felix Hebert of Rhode Island was appointed chairman, and Senator Otis F. Glenn and Senator Wagner members of the Committee. Hearings were held in April and the last three months of 1931. The Committee secured the services of Hugh S. Hanna of the Bureau of Labor Statistics who supplied members with extensive information on foreign systems and American plans. In a rather comprehensive report, Senators Hebert and Glenn took the position that a federal system of unemployment insurance would be unconstitutional and undesirable. Although they favored voluntary plans, they recognized that these were being established so slowly that state compulsory legislation might be necessary. They suggested (as was done in the Wisconsin law) that state legislation fix a period during which employers could formulate their own plans. Their only recommendation for federal action was that "the Federal Government contribute to such systems of private unemployment reserves to the extent of permitting employers who maintain them to deduct some portion, if not all, of the contributions thereto out of their income for tax purposes."[28]

In a minority report, Senator Wagner concluded that "unemployment insurance or wage reserves, to be successful, should be inaugurated under compulsory State legislation and be supervised by State authority"; that "each system should be organized to provide incentives to the stabilization of employment"; and that the federal government should allow employers

[27] *Causes of Unemployment,* Report No. 2072, United States Senate, 70th Cong., 2d sess. (February 25, 1929), p. xv.
[28] *Unemployment Insurance,* Report No. 964, United States Senate, 72d Cong., 1st sess. (June 20, 1932), pp. 51–52.

to deduct from income tax their payments into unemployment reserves or insurance plans.[29] He differed from the majority in recommending that 30 percent of such payments be deductible from the tax itself, rather than from gross income. Senator Wagner also introduced his income tax proposal in the same session of Congress (S.J. Res. 26, 72d Cong.).[30]

Besides these bills, Senator Wagner also introduced a bill in January, 1931 (S. 5634), to apportion $100 million among the states in proportion to each state's contributions to unemployment reserves. In 1933, two bills on unemployment insurance were introduced in Congress and four bills were introduced the following year.[31] Of these, the identical bills introduced by Senator Wagner and Congressman David J. Lewis of Maryland are discussed below in detail because of their influence on the unemployment insurance features of the Social Security Act.

The Wagner-Lewis Bill

The failure of any state to enact an unemployment insurance or reserves law in 1933, despite the widespread and intensive effort in the states, pointed to the necessity of federal action.[32] The strongest obstacle to state action was the argument that legislation by individual states would place industry in such states at a competitive disadvantage with industry in states without legislation.

A type of federal legislation that would secure state action was reportedly suggested by Supreme Court Justice Brandeis while his daughter, Elizabeth Brandeis and her husband, Paul Raushenbusch, of Wisconsin were visiting him at Christmastime, 1933. This was the method used in the Federal Estate Tax Act of 1926. The State of Florida had been inducing wealthy persons to move to Florida by publicizing that they had no inheritance tax law. The Federal Estate Tax Act imposed a federal inheritance tax, but with a provision that 80 percent credit would be given for taxes paid under a state inheritance tax law. Although the federal estate tax was passed in order to induce Florida to pass a similar law and thus remove her competitive advantage with other states, the Supreme Court of the United States unanimously declared the federal law to be constitutional.[33] Justice Brandeis' suggestion was implemented by Secretary

[29] *Unemployment Insurance,* Report No. 629, United States Senate, 72d Cong., 1st sess. (April 29, 1932), p. 26.

[30] In December, 1930, Senator Wagner had introduced a bill (S. 5350), 71st Cong., which was similar to the recommendations of the majority of the Select Committee.

[31] H.R. 4887 by Dunn, April 11, 1933; H.R. 5271 by Lewis, April 26, 1933; H.R. 6467 by Cannon, January 5, 1934; H.R. 7598 by Lundeen, February 2, 1934; S. 5480 by Tydings, 1933; H.R. 7659 by Lewis, February 5, 1934; S. 2616 by Wagner, February 5, 1934.

[32] In fact, during 1933, resolutions were introduced in the Maine, Minnesota, Montana, and Wisconsin legislatures memorializing Congress to enact unemployment insurance legislation.

[33] *Florida* v. *Mellon,* 273 U.S. 12.

Francis Perkins assigning Thomas H. Eliot, Associate Solicitor of the Department of Labor, to work with Paul Raushenbusch in drafting a bill along the lines of the Federal Estate Tax Act. The bill was introduced early in 1934 by Senator Wagner and Congressman Lewis.

The Wagner-Lewis bill, as it came to be called, imposed an excise tax of 5 percent of payrolls on about the same types of employers and employment as were covered by the Wisconsin act. An employer covered by the federal act, if the state law met prescribed conditions, could receive 100 percent credit against the federal tax, even if his contributions under the state law were lower than the federal tax because of favorable unemployment experience. It is significant to note that the bill had minimum benefit standards. In order for their employers to get federal tax credit, the state laws would have to provide minimum compensation of not less than $7 a week or not less than average earnings for 20 hours of work. Partial benefits would have to be paid to supplement actual earnings up to the benefit amount for total unemployment. Benefits would have to be provided for a duration of at least ten weeks in a year, or if paid in proportion to previous weeks worked for a maximum of at least 15 weeks. The state law would have to provide that workers could not be denied benefits for refusing to accept new work in case of (1) a labor dispute; (2) an offer of substandard wages, hours, or working conditions; or (3) if acceptance of the employment would require joining a company union or interfere with joining or retaining membership in a bona fide labor organization. This last provision was the only real standard that was contained in the Social Security Act when it was passed the following year. Other requirements in the Social Security Act related to investment of funds, provision for proper administration, etc.

From March 21 to March 30, 1934, hearings were held on the Lewis bill (H.R. 7659) by a subcommittee of the House Committee on Ways and Means. An impressive array of witnesses, including several employers, testified in favor of the bill. Opposition was mainly by employer organizations. The bill also had the blessing of the administration, with the President writing a letter of endorsement and Department of Labor Secretary Perkins serving as the leading witness. Nevertheless, no action was taken on the bill. According to Edwin E. Witte, the opposition, which came mainly from employers, was stronger than had appeared at the hearings on the Wagner-Lewis bill. In addition, various people seem to have gone to the President and pointed out weaknesses in the bill and urged that it be given further study. The President was particularly impressed by the argument that the large unemployment reserves that would be built up might increase the severity of the depression unless the reserves were under federal control. He was also not completely satisfied with the Dill-Connery bill, providing for the subsidies of state old-age pensions, which had passed the House. Accordingly, during May, 1934, the President informed a number of supporters of these two bills that he thought the best thing was to delay action and prepare a comprehensive program for presentation at the beginning of the first session of the next Congress.[34]

SUMMARY

Unlike the wide development of trade-union plans for unemployment benefits in Europe, only a few formally organized union plans ever existed in the United States, and most of these were local union plans. In addition to plans financed solely by trade-unions, 16 unemployment benefit and guaranteed employment plans had been formed by 1931 under joint union-management agreements, mostly in the needle trades. Between 1917 and 1933, 19 unemployment benefit or guaranteed employment plans were developed by individual companies. The best-known guaranteed-employment plan was that of Proctor and Gamble, and the largest unemployment benefit plan that of the General Electric Company. In Rochester, 14 firms developed and adopted an identical plan in 1930.

As early as 1907, the American Association for Labor Legislation held discussions on unemployment insurance. The earliest bill was introduced in Massachusetts in 1916. During the depression of 1920–21, bills were introduced in New York, Wisconsin, and several other states. The Wisconsin bill, introduced by Senator Huber and developed by John R. Commons, would have varied employer contributions in accordance with the regularity of their employment. The Huber bill was reintroduced in successive legislative sessions during the 1920's and bills were introduced in several other states during this period, but without action.

There was a resurgence of interest in state unemployment insurance legislation with the onset of the depression of the 1930's. In Wisconsin, the Huber bill, now sponsored by Senator Harold M. Groves, was revised to provide for individual employer reserve accounts in a state fund; this bill passed in 1932.

In 1931, New York's Governor Franklin D. Roosevelt called a conference of governors of six neighboring states, resulting in an Interstate Commission on Unemployment Insurance which issued a unanimous report recommending legislation of the Wisconsin type. Despite the appointment of study commissions in other states and introduction of a large number of bills in a number of states between 1931 and 1934, no legislation was passed in any state other than Wisconsin until 1935. Most bills were of the Wisconsin type, but the Ohio Commission recommended a bill providing for a state pooled fund, with variation of employer contributions. The measure also differed from the Wisconsin bill in providing for employee contributions. It provided for uniform duration of benefits for all workers, as contrasted with the Wisconsin provision of variation in duration of benefits

[34] Edwin E. Witte, *The Development of the Social Security Act* (Madison: University of Wisconsin Press, 1962), pp. 4–5.

with length of previous employment. This bill received wide attention and became a rival to the Wisconsin act in state legislative proposals.

The earliest federal attention given to unemployment insurance was a recommendation by the U.S. Commission on Industrial Relations in 1916 for the development of unemployment insurance plans. A bill for a national plan of unemployment insurance was introduced in Congress the same year by Representative Meyer London. At the national conference on unemployment, called by President Warren Harding in 1921, Herbert Hoover spoke against the provision of "direct doles," but a committee appointed by the conference was favorable to any form of unemployment insurance that would encourage regularization of employment.

In 1928, hearings were held by the Senate Committee on Education and Labor, pursuant to a resolution by Senator James Couzens of Michigan, and the Committee recommended that private unemployment insurance plans be developed, free from federal interference. Pursuant to a resolution by Senator Robert F. Wagner, a Select Committee on Unemployment Insurance was appointed in 1931, which recommended that income tax credit be given for contributions to private unemployment reserve plans. In a minority report, Senator Wagner took the position that state legislation was necessary and should be encouraged by deductions of the cost of contribution from the income tax itself.

In 1934, Senator Wagner and Congressman David J. Lewis introduced a bill providing for a federal unemployment tax, against which 100 percent credit could be secured by employers for contributions to a state law that met prescribed minimum benefit standards. The bill was supported by President Roosevelt, but no action was taken on it after he announced that he proposed a comprehensive study of social insurance.

Chapter 6

The Social Security Act
Breaks the Stalemate

By 1934, it became evident that there would be little or no progress in unemployment insurance legislation unless there was federal action. High hopes had been entertained for the 1934 Wagner-Lewis bill, which, if passed, would have stimulated the enactment of state legislation. While disappointed that the Wagner-Lewis bill did not pass, the friends of unemployment insurance had their hopes revived when the President appointed the Committee on Economic Security on June 29, 1934.

Soon after the Committee began its deliberations, it became clear that there were strong differences among the friends of legislation as to what form the legislation should take. There was disagreement as to whether there should be a federal or a federal-state system. If it were to be the latter, there was controversy as to the type of federal legislation. These disagreements grew out of contrasting views as to the extent of federal control that should be provided. The alternatives presented to the Committee on Economic Security by its Technical Board, Advisory Council, and staff, and the process by which decisions were reached will therefore be described in some detail in this chapter which will also highlight the Congressional considerations of the unemployment insurance proposals and changes in the legislation.

DELIBERATIONS OF THE COMMITTEE ON ECONOMIC SECURITY

Formation of the Committee

On June 8, 1934, in a special message to the Congress, President Roosevelt listed what he considered to be the unfinished legislative goals of his administration. Among these were the "furthering of the security of the citizen and his family through social insurance." He held that the various types of social insurance were interrelated and difficult to solve piecemeal. "Hence, I am looking for a sound means to provide at once security against

76

several of the great disturbing factors in life—especially those which relate to unemployment and old age."[1]

The President followed up this message with an Executive Order on June 29, 1934, creating the Committee on Economic Security.[2] The only directive given the Committee was that it "shall study problems relating to the economic security of individuals"; it was generally understood that this would include consideration of unemployment insurance.

The Committee on Economic Security consisted of the Secretary of Labor (Chairman), the Secretary of the Treasury, the Attorney General, the Secretary of Agriculture, and the Federal Emergency Relief Administrator. The Executive Order also provided for an Advisory Council of citizens, a Technical Board of "qualified representatives" from federal agencies, and an Executive Director.

A 23-man Advisory Council was appointed, chaired by Frank P. Graham, President of the University of North Carolina. High-ranking representatives of labor and management were appointed to the Council, as well as other national figures from interested groups. Dr. Arthur J. Altmeyer, then Second Assistant Secretary of Labor, was made Chairman of the Technical Board which consisted of 25 members. Dr. Edwin E. Witte, Professor of Economics at the University of Wisconsin, was appointed Executive Director of the Committee on July 24. During the next month, a staff of experts in many fields was assembled, including Dr. Bryce M. Stewart, Research Director of Industrial Relations Counsellors as director of the unemployment insurance staff.[3]

Disagreements on Unemployment Insurance

Soon after the Technical Board and Committee staff began their work, it became evident that there was disagreement as to what type of unemployment insurance program should be recommended. The President had stated his views in his Congressional message of June 8, but they were rather ambiguous:

I believe there should be a maximum of cooperation between States and the Federal Government. I believe that the funds necessary to provide this insurance should be raised by contribution rather than by an increase in general taxation. Above all, I am convinced that social insurance should be national in scope, although the several States should meet at least a large portion of the cost of management, leaving to the Federal Government the responsibility of investing, maintaining and safeguarding the funds constituting the necessary insurance reserves.

This would indicate that the President was thinking in terms of a federal-state system.

[1] H. Doc. No. 397, 73d Cong., 2d sess. (1934).

[2] Executive Order No. 6757.

[3] One of the authors, Dr. Murray, was appointed associative director of the unemployment compensation staff.

Late in August, President Roosevelt had his first conference with the Secretary of Labor, Dr. Witte, and several others. Dr. Witte reported that the President "expressed decided preferences for state administration of unemployment insurance, but stressed again that the reserve funds must be handled by the federal government; also, that unemployment insurance should be set up to give encouragement to the regularization of employment."[4] However, Dr. Witte said that the President did not insist that the Committee should necessarily recommend his ideas.

Proposal for Federal System

Despite the President's views, Dr. Bryce M. Stewart, director of the unemployment insurance staff, in a preliminary report in September, recommended a national system because of his belief that most unemployment was due to national rather than local causes. The plan he recommended, however, would have permitted entire industries and, perhaps, large nation-wide employers to have their own funds. This report was presented to the Technical Board late in September, together with recommendations by Dr. Witte for a federal-state plan along the lines suggested by the President.

The arguments for a national system that were put forward in Dr. Stewart's report and subsequent discussions included the following: (1) it would provide uniformity of protection to all employees in the United States exposed to the same risk of unemployment; (2) it would provide an easy and uniform method of handling the problem of employees who worked in several states; (3) it would also be preferable for employers who operated across state lines, who would not have to pay taxes and make reports under a multiplicity of state laws and regulations, as would occur under a federal-state system; (4) it would permit the pooling of reserves on a national basis; and (5) it would provide a superior basis for actuarial estimates, since state statistics on unemployment were practically nonexistent.

On the other hand, the arguments of those who favored a federal-state system included the following: (1) a national system would be cumbersome to operate, and centralization of administration might paralyze action; (2) a national system would require immediate decisions on such controversial issues as employee contributions, methods of experience rating, and variable versus uniform duration of benefits, whereas under a federal-state system these could be left for discussion and decision by individual states; (3) a federal-state system would permit wide latitude for experimentation by the states which would be desirable in the absence of experience with unemployment insurance in the United States; and (4) if mistakes were made in individual states in their legislation, they would not have as

---

[4] Edwin E. Witte, *The Development of the Social Security Act* (Madison: University of Wisconsin Press, 1962), p. 18.

serious repercussion in a federal-state system as mistakes made in legislation for a federal system.

The Technical Board set up an unemployment insurance committee,[5] to which it referred the question as to whether a federal or federal-state system should be recommended. This committee reported to the executive committee of the Technical Board a few days later in favor of a federal system, differing in some details from Dr. Stewart's plan. In October, the executive committee, in turn, presented a statement of principles regarding unemployment insurance to the Committee on Economic Security. One of these principles read: "If constitutional, a nationally administered system of unemployment insurance is to be preferred to a State system, but the Committee should be satisfied that a nationally administered system is constitutional before commitments in favor of such a system are made to the public."[6]

Federal-State System Decided on

Eventually, the unemployment insurance committee of the Technical Board reversed its position and voted unanimously for a plan similar to the Wagner-Lewis bill of 1934; i.e., provision for a federal unemployment tax against which tax credits could be secured for taxes paid under a state unemployment insurance law. The executive committee of the Technical Board, however, was still divided on what plan to recommend. A report was therefore made to the Committee on Economic Security on November 9 setting forth the pros and cons for the three alternatives of a federal system, a tax-credit plan of the Wagner-Lewis type, or a federal-state subsidy plan (which had been injected into the discussions). The Committee voted unanimously to give up any further consideration of a federal plan, but reached no conclusions on the relative merits of a tax-credit or subsidy plan for a federal-state system.

The Committee's decision for a federal-state system was conveyed to the President. A few days later, on November 14, a National Conference on Economic Security was held, attended by about 150 experts and representatives of various interests. In his address to this conference, President Roosevelt said that in the program recommended to Congress, unemployment insurance would be proposed as "a cooperative federal-state undertaking," but he was no more specific than this. The alternatives of a tax-credit plan such as the Wagner-Lewis bill or a subsidy plan continued to be discussed.

---

[5] Alvin H. Hansen, Chief Economic Advisor, Department of State, Chairman; William M. Leiserson, Chairman, National Mediation Board; Jacob Viner, Assistant to the Secretary, Treasury Department; Thomas Eliot, Associate Solicitor, Department of Labor; and E. Willard Jensen, Executive Secretary, Business Advisory Council, Department of Commerce.

[6] Quoted in Witte, op. cit., p. 114.

Subsidy Plan

During the discussions by the Technical Board in October, a "subsidy plan" had been suggested, under which a federal tax would be collected from employers, with the proceeds from each state to be returned to the state if it met standards for unemployment compensation prescribed by the federal government.[7]

This subsidy plan would have met the conditions laid down by the President and was favored as a second choice by those who were for a federal system. The subsidy plan was seen as having the advantages of a federal plan in that it would permit the writing of definite standards on benefits into the federal law without endangering its constitutionality. The lawyers thought that if standards were put in a tax-credit type of law, its constitutionality would be endangered. The subsidy plan was opposed, however, by some members of the staff and Technical Board who did not think it would be possible, without practical experience, to prescribe standards for the state laws.

Advisory Council Views

The Advisory Council held its first meeting on November 15 and 16, immediately following the National Conference on Economic Security. The Council's discussion was devoted to unemployment insurance. In view of the President's announcement that unemployment insurance would be on a federal-state basis, discussion of the type of system was confined to the Wagner-Lewis (tax-credit) and subsidy plans. The Advisory Council appointed a committee to consider this issue and other questions discussed at its meeting.[8] During the next month, this committee held several meetings. Although the next Advisory Council meeting was delayed until December 7, the committee made no formal report to the Council. Instead, it presented individual views and a mass of other material. The Council voted nine to six in favor of the subsidy plan. Since five members of the Council were absent, the Council qualified its vote the next day to the effect that the vote represented individual views, that the tax-credit and subsidy plans each had their good features, and the issue should be decided by the Committee on Economic Security. The Advisory Council completed its report on December 15.

The Committee Adopts Tax-Credit Plan

The Committee on Economic Security, in the meantime, had become worried about the delays in reaching decisions on unemployment insur-

[7] According to Dr. Witte's recollection, this was suggested by Mr. Emerson Ross of the Federal Emergency Relief Administration. *Ibid.*, p. 115.

[8] The members of the Committee were Frank P. Graham, President of the University of North Carolina; Miss Grace Abbott of the University of Chicago; Marion B. Folsom, Assistant Treasurer of Eastman Kodak Company; Morris E. Leeds, President of Leeds

ance. The President had asked for a report by December 1 so that he could include the Committee's proposals in his legislative program for the coming session of Congress. The Committee, therefore, had gone ahead with final consideration of its recommendations. When it made its final decisions during December it had the report of the Advisory Council, but had not yet received the report of Bryce Stewart and his unemployment insurance staff. The Committee, however, knew his views favoring a federal system as a first choice and the subsidy plan as a second choice. The Committee once more thoroughly reviewed the alternatives of a subsidy or tax-credit plan and voted for the latter.

The history of the discussions regarding the three alternative types of federal legislation has been given in some detail to show that there was considerable division of opinion as to the degree of participation by the federal government in the unemployment insurance system. The decision to have a federal-state system was in accord with the President's own predelictions, and so was decided more readily than what type of federal plan should be recommended. What tipped the scales in favor of the Wagner-Lewis tax-credit plan was the belief that it had a better chance of being approved by the Supreme Court as constitutional. It was recognized that a subsidy plan with federal benefit standards would have a better chance with the Supreme Court than a tax-credit plan with standards. But since the Committee had decided to have as few standards as possible, the Wagner-Lewis plan had the advantage in the arguments over constitutionality of the two plans. Moreover, under the tax-credit plan, the states would have their own self-sustaining laws, should the federal legislation be declared unconstitutional.

Secondary Issues

Other issues that arose included whether to have employee or government contributions, whether to permit the Wisconsin system of individual employer accounts, and what should be the rate of and timing of employer contributions.

Employee Contributions. After extended discussion, a majority of the Advisory Council voted against employee contributions. However, four of the employer members of the Council along with Raymond Moley felt so strongly about employee contributions that they wrote a separate statement advocating them. They believed that employee contributions would make it possible to have more adequate benefits, as well as a more effective administration, since the workers would have a clearer conception of their responsibilities.[9] The consensus of the Council was that there should not be

---

and Northrop Company; William Green, President of the American Federation of Labor; Paul Scharrenberg, Secretary-Treasurer of the Calfiornia State Federation of Labor.

[9] *Economic Security Act,* Hearings before the Committee on Ways and Means, House of Representatives, 74th Cong., 1st sess., on H.R. 4120, pp. 873–74.

government contributions, especially in view of the large outlays being made by the government for general relief at the time.[10]

Experience Rating. The President's desire to encourage stabilization of employment through the experience rating of unemployment insurance contributions was generally accepted. The difficulty was in deciding how to do it. Bryce Stewart, who supported the subsidy plan after a federal system was rejected, argued that "merit rating," as it was called then, could be accomplished under a subsidy plan through federal tax refunds to "any insurance unit" that had built up a sufficient reserve. (As "insurance units," he proposed individual employers, groups of employers, or industries.) Dr. Witte reported that the issue of pooled funds versus individual employer accounts was not settled until the final meeting of the Committee on Economic Security.[11] Several members of the Committee were opposed to individual employer accounts, such as were provided for in the Wisconsin law, but it was finally agreed to permit state laws to have employer accounts provided the state required employers to contribute at least 1 percent of their payrolls to a central pooled fund—a recommendation of Dr. Altmeyer.

Rate and Timing of Employer Tax. Although there was general agreement that there should be employer contributions, it was felt that the imposition of an employer tax should be so timed as not to impede industrial recovery. The Advisory Council also felt that the tax rate of 5 percent of payrolls proposed in the Wagner-Lewis bill of 1934 was too high, and reached agreement on a 3 percent rate. The unemployment insurance committee of the Technical Board proposed that the rate of contributions be increased over a three-year period by steps geared to the level of the Federal Reserve Board index of industrial production. This would assure that increases in the tax would take effect only as business recovered. This idea was adopted by the Committee.

REPORT OF THE COMMITTEE ON ECONOMIC SECURITY

In its report to the President, the Committee stressed the need of federal legislation on unemployment insurance in order to remove the chief obstacle to state action; namely, the fear of each state that if it imposed a tax on its employers, it would place them at a competitive disadvantage with other states. The Committee recommended that this fear be removed through a uniform federal excise tax on employment, with a tax credit to employers for their contributions under a compulsory state unemployment insurance law. This tax credit would not only remove the chief obstacle to state legislation, but would encourage state action in order for their employers to secure the tax credit. The second major recommendation of

[10] Paul Kellogg, editor of *The Survey*, a member of the Advisory Council, felt so strongly that there should be government contributions that he urged them at every opportunity.

[11] *Development of the Economic Security Act, op. cit.,* p. 127.

the Committee was that the federal government grant the states sufficient funds for proper administration of their unemployment insurance laws. The specific legislative recommendations of the Committee were directed to these two major proposals.

Unemployment Tax

The Committee recommended a federal excise tax on employers who employ four or more workers for 13 or more weeks in a year. It recommended that this tax be equal to 1 percent of total payrolls in 1936 and 3 percent by 1938, with increases in the interim geared to increases in the index of industrial production of the Federal Reserve Board. The Committee recommended that no industries be exempted. It stated, however, that it favored a separate federal system for railroad employees and maritime workers.

A credit up to 90 percent of the federal tax would be allowed employers for contributions under a state unemployment compensation law, provided the state is cooperating with the federal government in the administration of unemployment compensation, is depositing contributions collected in an unemployment trust fund in the federal Treasury, and is using such contributions solely for benefits. These were the only conditions mentioned in the Committee report that a state would have to meet.

Not mentioned in the Committee report, but included in the bill presented to Congress was the so-called "labor standards" provision that had to be included in the state laws, in order for them to be approved for tax-credit purposes.[12] This standard was designed to protect claimants from having to accept offers of work that entailed certain employment conditions disadvantageous to themselves or to their labor union. This was the only real standard relating to benefit rights included in the bill. Although it was recognized that any standard as specific as this might give the tax a regulatory nature and thus might endanger the constitutionality of the Act, it probably was included to allay labor's fear that unemployment insurance might be used to break unions or weaken labor standards. This was the principal fear that had caused the American Federation of Labor to oppose compulsory unemployment insurance until its Convention of 1932.

"Additional Credit" toward Federal Unemployment Tax

The Committee further recommended that, if a state allowed lower contribution rates to employers with stable employment, additional credit toward the federal tax be allowed for the taxes that otherwise would be paid under the state law. The Committee recommended stiff requirements for such additional credit: a reserve equal to at least 15 percent of annual payrolls in individual reserve accounts and a reserve of at least 7½ percent

---

[12] See condition (5) for approval of state laws under "Title IX" given in the Appendix to this chapter.

in guaranteed employment accounts. In addition, employers contributing to such accounts would have to contribute 1 percent of payroll to a state pooled fund. Employers contributing solely to state pooled funds could not be allowed lower rates until the state law had been in operation for five years.

Unemployment Trust Fund

The Committee recommended that all money collected by the states for unemployment compensation be deposited with the federal Treasury and placed in a trust fund with an account to the credit of each state. The Secretary of the Treasury would invest the money in the trust fund as a whole. Interest on the average amount in each state account should be allowed at the average rate of interest on primary obligations of the United States.

It was recommended that the collection of the federal tax and the investment of reserves be under the control of the Secretary of the Treasury and that other federal aspects of the legislation be administered by a social insurance board of three members, housed in the Department of Labor.

Grants for Administration

The other major recommendation of the Committee was for the federal government to grant the states money for administration of their laws "under conditions designed to insure competence and probity." Among these conditions, the Committee considered it vital that the selection of personnel be on a merit basis, which at that time was a practice in very few states. Another condition should be that the states accept the provisions of the Wagner-Peyser Act for a federal-state employment service system and pay unemployment compensation through employment offices. It was assumed that the funds for administrative grants would be financed from the 10 percent of the federal unemployment tax that would be collected by the federal government. For constitutional reasons, however, it was not recommended that the taxes be earmarked for this purpose.

Although, in his Congressional message of June 8, 1934, the President had suggested that "the several states should meet at least a large portion of the cost of management," the Committee recommended that the federal government pay the entire cost of administration. The Committee recommended this, evidently, because of a fear that state legislatures would not provide adequate funds for administration and that standards of administration would not be high enough to insure successful operation of the program. Yet they trusted the state legislatures fully with respect to providing proper benefits and benefit conditions.

In its report, the Committee justified the proposed federal-state system on the grounds that, since considerable controversy had grown up over such questions as pooled funds versus individual employer reserves, a federal-state system would permit variations in state laws "so that we can learn through variation what is best." The Committee recognized that a federal system would be superior in some respects, particularly in relation to workers who move from state to state. It also recognized that in other respects "State administration may develop marked inadequacies." If experience showed that a federal system was desirable, the Committee rather blithely stated: "It is always possible by subsequent legislation to establish such a system." In order that this be possible, the Committee recommended, that the states be required to include in their laws a reservation of power to modify or repeal the law and that the federal law contain a similar reservation.

With respect to the choice of the tax-credit type of federal-state legislation in preference to the subsidy type, the Committee said:

We prefer a tax credit device to one in which the tax would be wholly collected and then remitted, as grants-in-aid, to the States, because under the latter system the States would not have self-supporting laws of their own, and as with all compensation having its source in Federal grants there would be great and constant pressure for larger grants exceeding the money raised by the tax, with a consequent confusion of compensation and relief.[13]

CONSIDERATION OF UNEMPLOYMENT INSURANCE BY CONGRESS

The Committee on Economic Security's report to the President was not ready until January 15, 1939. The report was promptly submitted to the Congress on January 17, with a special message in which the President urged that legislation "should be brought forward with a minimum of delay."

A bill had been drafted by Mr. Eliot (Associate Solicitor of Labor) which was immediately introduced by Senator Wagner, and by Congressman Lewis and Congressman Robert L. Doughton, who vied for the honor of its introduction in the House. Since the latter was chairman of the Committee on Ways and Means, the hearings were conducted on his Economic Security bill (H.R. 4120). The bill was referred to his Committee and the Senate Finance Committee because of its tax features.[14]

It had been hoped that Congress would pass the legislation in time for the states to act in their 1935 legislative sessions, since only a few states would hold legislative sessions in 1936. Congress proceeded, however, with what might be termed deliberate speed. Hearings by the Committee on Ways and Means on the Doughton bill began promptly, starting January

---

[13] *Report to the President of the Committee on Economic Security* (Washington, D.C.: U.S. Government Printing Office, 1935), p. 17.

[14] The Chairman of the House Labor Committee, Congressman William P. Connery, Jr., tried to get the bill referred to his Committee. When this was not done, he held hearings on the "Lundeen bill" (H.R. 2827) which provided for unemployment compensation equal to the difference between earnings, if any, and average local wages for as long as a person able and willing to work was unemployed or underemployed. Such benefits were to be paid out of federal general funds, to be increased if necessary through increases in inheritance and income taxes. Hearings were held on this bill and it was reported favorably by the Labor Committee but was never acted upon by the House.

21, but were not concluded until February 12, although the Committee met almost daily. The Committee thereafter held 20 executive sessions and did not report the bill until April 5. Part of this slow progress was due to the meticulous work of the legislative counsel to the Committee, Mr. Middleton Beaman, who spent hours in conference with his staff and Thomas Eliot,[15] discussing single phrases of the bill.

Only after Mr. Beaman had completely redrafted several titles of the bill was it taken up in executive session by the Committee. The bill contained titles on a number of other measures, including old-age insurance, public assistance for the aged, dependent children and the blind, other child care services, and public health measures. As a result, only a fraction of the time was devoted to unemployment insurance. In fact, during the entire Congressional consideration of the bill, major attention was given to the old-age insurance and old-age assistance titles of the bill.

Debate in the House commenced on April 11 and lasted until April 19, when the bill was passed by a vote of 371 to 33.

The Senate Committee on Finance had already held hearings from January 22 to February 20 on the bill introduced in the Senate (S. 1130) but at the time the social security bill passed the House, the Senate Finance Committee was busy with bonus and tax bills. The Finance Committee reviewed the House bill thoroughly and made a number of changes. As a result, the Committee did not report the bill back to the Senate until May 20. Another three weeks' delay ensued before the Senate commenced consideration of the bill due to the precedence of other bills on the calendar. The Senate debated the bill from June 14 to June 19, passing it by a vote of 77 to 6.

The biggest controversy in the Senate had developed over the so-called "Clark amendment," which would have exempted employer pension plans meeting certain standards from coverage under the old-age insurance provisions of the Act. The Conference Committee of the House and Senate was deadlocked over this amendment for weeks, so that its report was not filed until early in August. The Conference report was adopted by the House on August 8 and by the Senate on August 9. The bill was signed by the President on August 14, 1935.

Practically all the state legislatures had long since gone home, so the hope that the bill would result in widespread action by the states in 1935 was frustrated.

The principal change made by the House in the federal unemployment tax part of the bill was to strike out the provisions for "additional credit" for lower tax rates under experience rating. During the hearings of the Committee on Ways and Means, Congressman Jere Cooper had perceived the inconsistency between the proposal for a uniform federal tax in order

---

[15] An amusing but informative account of his participation in the drafting of the bill was given by Mr. Eliot, now Chancellor of Washington University, in "The Social Security Act—25 Years After," *Atlantic Monthly*, August, 1960.

to meet the problem of unequal costs in interstate competition and the proposal to permit variation of contributions in the states, which would eliminate such uniformity. He was therefore able to persuade the Committee to report the bill without the "additional credit" provisions.

At the hearings on the bill by the Senate Committee on Finance, employer witnesses had strongly advocated the "additional credit" provisions in the bill because of the desirability of permitting experience rating in state laws.[16] These provisions were subsequently restored by the Senate Committee on Finance through an amendment proposed by Senator Robert LaFollette, Jr., of Wisconsin.

The amendment was unanimously adopted by the Committee and accepted by the Senate without much debate. Subsequently it was agreed to in conference. In the process, the requirement in the bill as introduced in the House, of a minimum contribution of 1 percent of payroll to a state pooled fund was eliminated. The requirements were eased for experience rating under individual reserve accounts and state pooled funds. The proposal that increases in the tax from 1 to 3 percent of payroll be tied to increases in the index of industrial production was eliminated and an increase to 2 percent for 1937 and to 3 percent beginning in 1938 was substituted.

The bill emerged from Congress with a much more restricted coverage than that proposed by the administration. The Committee on Ways and Means changed the coverage to employers with ten or more employees in 20 weeks. The Senate changed it back to the original bill's coverage of employers with four or more employees in 13 weeks. The conference committee agreed to a compromise coverage of eight or more in 20 weeks.

The Committee on Ways and Means also restricted the unemployment insurance coverage by excluding agricultural workers, domestic servants, and employees of nonprofit organizations, members of the immediate family of the employer, and government workers. The Committee on Economic Security's recommendation that railroad workers in interstate commerce and maritime workers be covered by a separate system was not followed. Maritime workers employed on the navigable waters of the United States were exempted, but railroad workers were covered by the tax.

Finally, although one of the principal objectives of the Committee on Economic Security in providing for federal administrative grants was to be able to require the employment of personnel on a merit basis, Congress specifically excepted the "selection, tenure of office, and compensation of personnel" from the methods of administration that the Social Security Board could require of the states.[17]

[16] See testimony of Marion B. Folsom, representing the employer members of the Advisory Council to the Committee on Economic Security, in *Economic Security Act,* Hearings before the Committee on Finance, United States Senate, 74th Cong., 1st sess., pp. 557 ff.

[17] This was amended in 1939 to give the Board authority within prescribed limits as will be described in the next chapter.

Although important changes were made by Congress in the unemployment insurance features of the Social Security Act, the basic structure followed the recommendations of the Committee on Economic Security and the administration. While there were many witnesses critical of the proposals, according to Dr. Witte: "The members of Congress throughout took it for granted that if anything was to be done about unemployment insurance, the Administration's proposals would have to be approved."[18]

SUMMARY

The appointment of the Committee on Economic Security in June, 1934, raised the hopes of the supporters of unemployment insurance that legislation would be forthcoming.

As soon as the Committee and its Technical Board and staff commenced deliberations, it became evident that there was serious disagreement over the form that the federal legislation on unemployment insurance should take. The President had expressed his preference for a federal-state program, but had indicated he would not insist on this. The preliminary report of Dr. Bryce M. Stewart, chief of the unemployment insurance staff, advocated a federal system. This proposal was at first supported by a subcommittee of the Technical Board and presented to the executive committee of the Board. After weeks of deliberation, including extensive study and debate by the staff and Technical Board, the Committee rejected the idea of a federal system and definitely decided on a federal-state system. The Committee conveyed its decision to the President, who announced it at a National Conference on Employment Security held early in November.

An alternative to the tax-credit plan of the Wagner-Lewis bill, was suggested in the course of the deliberations which was referred to as the "subsidy plan." Under this plan, the full federal unemployment tax would be collected by the federal government and distributed to the states in the amount of taxes collected with respect to employment in each state. This subsidy plan was supported by those who had favored a federal system, since it was thought that the states could be required to meet more standards under such a plan without endangering its constitutionality. A majority of the Advisory Council to the Committee voted for the subsidy plan. Nevertheless, the Committee on Economic Security decided on the tax-credit plan such as had been in the Wagner-Lewis bill. The Committee made this decision after agreement that there should be a minimum of federal standards and maximum freedom for the states to experiment. Without federal benefit standards, the tax-offset plan was thought to have a better chance of being upheld as constitutional by the Supreme Court.

In its report, the Committee in addition to advocating the tax-credit plan, recommended a subsidy plan for financing the total cost of state administration. It was expected that the latter would be financed out of the

[18] Edwin E. Witte, "Development of Unemployment Compensation," *Yale Law Journal*, Vol. XXXV, No. 1 (December, 1945), pp. 31–32.

10 percent of the federal unemployment tax that would be collected by the federal government.

In a special message to Congress on January 17, 1935, President Roosevelt urged enactment of the Committee's recommendations. The President asked for speedy action, as it was hoped legislation would be enacted in time for state legislatures to pass unemployment insurance laws in 1935. However, Congress did not complete action on the legislation until August, 1935, after most state legislatures had adjourned.

The unemployment insurance provisions in the Social Security Act were not basically different from the recommendations of the Committee on Economic Security. The requirements for experience rating were changed somewhat. The federal unemployment tax was made applicable only to employers with at least eight employees in at least 20 weeks in a year. Large groups of workers, including agricultural and household workers, employees of nonprofit institutions, and government workers were exempted. In the provisions for administrative grants to the states, the Social Security Board was prohibited from requiring methods of administration with respect to the selection, tenure, or compensation of personnel, although one of the principal objectives of the provisions for grants for administration was to secure personnel merit systems in the states.

Although many were disappointed with the limitations of the federal legislation, it provided an effective means for securing state unemployment insurance legislation.

APPENDIX

Unemployment Insurance Provisions of Social Security Act of 1935

The Social Security Act as passed contained two titles regarding unemployment compensation: Title IX providing for the federal unemployment tax and its related provisions; and Title III providing for federal administrative grants. A summary of these titles follows:

TITLE IX

Title IX provided for an excise tax on employment by employers of eight or more persons in 20 or more weeks in a year. The tax would be equal to 1 percent of total payroll in 1936; 2 percent in 1937; and 3 percent in 1938.

Employment excluded from the tax were:

(1) agricultural labor;

(2) domestic service in a private home;

(3) services by the crews of vessels on navigable waters of the United States;

(4) service by specified immediate members of the family of the employer;

(5) service for the federal government or federal instrumentalities;

(6) service for state and local governments and instrumentalities;

(7) service for nonprofit organizations of a religious, charitable, scientific, literary, or educational nature or for the prevention of cruelty to children or animals.

Employers making contributions to approved state unemployment compensation laws could receive credit for such contributions up to 90 percent of the federal tax, if the state law met the following conditions:

(1) All compensation is to be paid through public employment offices or such other agencies as the Social Security Board (established by the Act) might approve.

(2) No compensation is to be paid for two years after contributions commence.

(3) All money received in the state unemployment fund is to be immediately deposited in the Federal Unemployment Trust Fund created by the Act, (to be credited to the state's account in the fund).

(4) All money withdrawn from the Trust Fund is to be used solely in the payment of unemployment compensation.

(5) Compensation will not be denied to any otherwise eligible unemployed worker for refusing to accept new work under any of the following conditions:

(A) if the position offered is vacant due directly to a strike, lockout, or other labor dispute;

(B) if the wages, hours, or other conditions of the work offered are substantially less favorable to the individual than those prevailing for similar work in the locality;

(C) if as a condition of being employed the individual would be required to join a company union or to resign from or refrain from joining any bona fide labor organization.

(6) All the rights, privileges and immunities created by the state law are subject to the power of the legislature to amend or repeal the law at any time.

"Additional credit" would be given against the federal tax for state contributions not made because of a lower experience rate under the following conditions:

(1) If the employer was contributing to a state pooled fund, he has had three full years of "compensation experience";

(2) if he is contributing to a guaranteed employment account, he has fulfilled the guarantee (at least 30 hours of wages for at least 40 weeks in the preceding year) and his account equals at least 7½ percent of his total payroll in the preceding year; or

(3) if he is contributing to a separate reserve account in the state fund for one or more employers,

(A) compensation was payable from the account throughout the preceding year;

(B) the account is not less than five times the largest amount of compensation paid out of the account in any of the last three preceding years;

(C) the account is equal to 7½ percent of total wages payable in the preceding year.

The Unemployment Trust Fund was created in the Treasury of the United States. The act provided that deposits in the fund must be invested in federal securities that would yield the average rate of interest being paid on all federal securities. It also provided that funds could be invested in special obligations issued to the Trust Fund that yielded such average rate of interest.

Title IX would be administered by the Treasury Department, except that the Social Security Board would determine whether the state unemployment compensation laws met and continued to meet the prescribed conditions. The Board was required to give reasonable notice and a fair hearing to the state before it refused to certify a state that did not meet the conditions.

TITLE III

Grants were authorized to be made to each state in such amounts as the Social Security Board determined to be necessary for the proper administration of its unemployment compensation law. The Board's determination was to be based on (1) the population of the state; (2) an estimate of the number of persons covered by the state law and of the cost of proper administration of such law; and (3) such other factors as the Board found relevant. Dollar limitations were placed on the amounts that could be granted—not more than $4 million for the fiscal year ending June 30, 1936, and not more than $49 million in any fiscal year thereafter.

In order for a state to receive administrative grants, its law had to be approved under Title IX, and also had to include provisions for:

(1) Such methods of administration (other than those relating to selection, tenure of office, and compensation of personnel) as were found by the Board to be reasonably calculated to pay benefits when due;

(2) an opportunity for a fair hearing, before an impartial tribunal, for unemployed workers whose claims for benefits were denied;

(3) the making of such reports as the Social Security Board might require; and

(4) making available upon the request of any federal agency charged with public works or assistance through public employment information under the state law.

In addition to these conditions, the first three conditions listed above for approval under Title IX were also included in Title III.

The state law not only had to meet these conditions but a state could also be denied administrative grants if the Board after reasonable notice and opportunity for hearing found that the state had failed to comply substantially with the specified conditions or had denied compensation in a substantial number of cases to persons entitled to it.

Chapter 7

Federal
Legislative Developments[1]

Considerable federal legislation on unemployment insurance has been enacted over the years. Most of the legislation has expanded the federal role; some has restricted it. Coverage of the federal unemployment tax has been expanded in some respects, restricted in others. Federal programs have been established for railroad employees, federal civilian employees, ex-servicemen, and temporarily for seamen. Temporary programs for extended benefits to those exhausting regular benefits were enacted during the recessions of 1958 and 1961. A federal loan fund has been established to strengthen the financial structure of the program. Changes both of a positive and of a restrictive nature have been made in the financing of administration. But while there have been numerous legislative enactments, none of them has changed the basic federal-state character of the system.

Rather than give a chronological history, it will be more useful to review various categories of federal legislation. Only changes of some importance will be mentioned.

COVERAGE: EBB AND FLOW

The coverage of the federal taxes for unemployment and for old-age insurance were largely the same in the original Social Security Act. The unemployment tax, however, did not cover small employers but did cover railroad workers.

The 1939 amendments to the Social Security Act made some important as well as detailed exclusions from the taxes for both old-age insurance and unemployment insurance.[2] Several hundred thousand workers were excluded by broadening the definition of agricultural labor (which was al-

---

[1] Some of the federal legislation will be discussed more fully in later chapters, but is outlined in this chapter so as to bring all federal legislation together in one place.

[2] On February 10, 1939, these taxes, originally in Titles VIII and IX of the Social Security Act were made part of the Internal Revenue Code.

ready excluded) to encompass the packing and processing of fruits and vegetables if done in connection with their preparation for market. Employment in the production of maple sugar, turpentine or gum spirits, mushrooms, the hatching of poultry, and the ginning of cotton was specifically excluded. Nonprofit organizations such as fraternal organizations, horticultural and agricultural organizations, and voluntary beneficiary associations were added to the list of nonprofit organizations already excluded.[3] Also excluded were students, including student nurses, and part-time workers for nonprofit organizations not otherwise exempted, and employees of foreign governments and instrumentalities of foreign governments. In addition to those exclusions made for both old-age and unemployment insurance, insurance agents and solicitors on a commission basis and newsboys under 18 were excluded from coverage under the federal unemployment tax. The only major gain under the 1939 amendments was the extension of coverage to certain government instrumentalities, including national banks and state bank members of the federal reserve system. Instrumentalities wholly owned by the federal government were covered by the unemployment compensation program for federal employees enacted in 1954 and the states were authorized to cover the others. The Bonneville Dam Authority was similarly covered in 1945. All remaining federal government instrumentalities were brought under coverage in 1961.

After the Supreme Court ruled in 1947 that the language of the 1935 act permitted a broader interpretation of "employee" than would have been possible under the common-law "master-servant" relationship,[4] Congress passed a "status quo" amendment in 1948 to confine the definition of employee to the common-law rules. Fortunately, many of the states had broader definitions of employee spelled out in their laws, the so-called "ABC" tests,[5] but several hundred thousand workers were still excluded by the federal amendment, and, consequently, by those states whose laws followed the federal definition.

The only real advance in coverage through federal legislation was not made until 1954, when Congress extended the coverage of the Federal Unemployment Tax from employers with eight employees to employers of four employees in 20 weeks in a year, effective January 1, 1956.[6] Many of the states had already gone this far or further in covering small employers, but still about 1.4 million workers were given coverage under state laws as a result of the amendment.[7]

Puerto Rico was not included in the original federal legislation. The

---

[3] Most of these except employees earning less than $50 a quarter, were again covered in 1961.

[4] *United States* v. *Silk*, 331 U.S. 704, 712–14 (1947).

[5] See Chapter 10.

[6] Public Law 83–767, approved September 1, 1954.

[7] The states have almost universally gone as far as the federal act in coverage because of the tax-credit provisions for state coverage.

inclusion of Puerto Rico as a "state" should be noted here, although this was more than an extension of coverage. Puerto Rico enacted an unemployment insurance law in June, 1956. The Puerto Rican government was anxious to come under the federal-state system, but Congress did not act to give it this status until 1960.[8]

Extension of the coverage of the program will be discussed in greater detail in Chapter 10.

PROGRAMS FOR SPECIAL GROUPS

Railroad Workers

Although the Committee on Economic Security recommended that railroad workers be covered by a federal system, they were originally covered under the federal-state system. In 1938, however, a federal railroad unemployment insurance system was created[9] effective January 1, 1939, under a bill worked out jointly between the railroads and the railroad unions, with the assistance of Murray W. Latimer, Chairman of the Railroad Retirement Board. Since all the states had covered railroad workers, the act provided for the transfer to an unemployment insurance account in the Unemployment Trust Fund of the excess of contributions by the railroads over benefits paid to railroad workers from the state funds. All the states passed the necessary legislation to implement the act.

The original Railroad Unemployment Insurance Act was less liberal than most state laws, but by subsequent amendments over the years, has become a much more liberal law than most of the states provide. The basic principles of the 1938 Act, however, have been retained.

Because railroad employment operates on a seven-day-a-week basis, the benefit provisions of the Railroad Unemployment Insurance Act are considerably different from state benefit provisions. Benefits are on a daily basis, and are paid biweekly. Since 1959, all days of unemployment in excess of four in a two-week period are compensable. Daily benefits range from $4.50 to $10.20 a day. The daily benefit rate is based on annual creditable earnings in the base year. The minimum of $4.50 a day is paid to claimants with earnings of $750–$999 in the base year. The daily benefit is increased by 50 cents for each additional $300 in earnings, with the maximum of $10.20 being paid to those earning $4,000 or more a year. Alternatively, if it would result in a higher benefit, the claimant may receive 60 percent of his daily rate or pay for his last railroad job in the base year. Since most claimants earn more than $4,000 a year, over 90 percent have been eligible for the maximum in recent years. In 1963–64, the average daily benefit was $10.09.

Benefits are payable on a uniform basis for a maximum of 130 days (26 weeks) in a year. To qualify for normal benefits, the claimant must have

---

[8] Public Law 86–778, approved September 13, 1960.
[9] 52 Stat. 1094 (1938).

earned $750 in railroad employment in the preceding (base) year and if he has not worked in the railroad industry previously, must have worked in at least seven months of the base year in railroad employment. If a claimant has had 10–14 years of railroad service and has exhausted normal benefits, he can receive an additional 65 days of benefits; if he has had 15 or more years of service, he can receive 130 additional days. These additional benefits were enacted in 1959.[10]

With the continuing shrinkage of employment in the railroad industry since World War II, the number of workers drawing benefits has been high, reaching a peak of 470,000 in 1949–50. The number of beneficiaries has fluctuated widely, however, ranging from as few as eight beneficiaries per 100 eligible covered workers in prosperous years to as high as 28 per 100 in recession years. Since the 1961 recession, the number of beneficiaries has been decreasing. This reflects both the continuing decline in the number of workers attached to the railroad industry as well as more favorable re-employment opportunities. During fiscal year 1963–64, there were 152,-000 beneficiaries, or 15 per 100 qualified employees. Of these, 23,000 were drawing extended benefits for which they were eligible because of ten years or more of railroad service.

The railroad unemployment insurance system is financed through employer contributions. Unlike the state systems, there is no experience rating. The rate of contributions was originally 3 percent of the first $300 of monthly earnings, which paid for both benefits and administration. During World War II, like the state systems, the railroad unemployment insurance system built up large reserves because of the very small amount of unemployment. The reserves reached a peak of $950 million in 1948. Under amendments passed that year, the rate of contributions was geared to the size of the fund, and the lowest rate provided, ½ percent, took effect. Beginning in 1956, since the fund had fallen because of the large number of claims due to decreasing railroad employment, the tax rate was increased to 1½ percent. The rate was increased annually thereafter until, in 1959, it reached the maximum of 3¾ percent. In that year, the fund was virtually exhausted and, thereafter, loans were made from the Railroad Retirement Fund. By December, 1963, the unemployment insurance fund owed the Retirement Fund $136 million and the United States Treasury $2 million. Under amendments passed in 1963,[11] the contribution rate was raised to 4 percent. As a result of this increased contribution rate and a reduction of claims during 1964, the indebtedness of the unemployment insurance fund was reduced to $301 million.

Sickness and maternity benefits, as well as normal and extended unem-

---

[10] Public Law 86–28, approved May 19, 1959. In the same law, temporary extended benefits were provided for 65 days for those with less than ten years of service. These benefits were provided retroactively to June 19, 1958, for persons who had exhausted benefits and were unemployed during this 11 months. Temporary extended benefits were also paid to those exhausting normal benefits in the 1960–61 recession.

[11] Public Law 88–133, approved October 5, 1963.

ployment benefits, are financed out of the 4 percent employer contribution and paid out of the same account. In 1963–64, out of each $1 of benefits paid out, 55 cents was paid in normal unemployment benefits, 9 cents in extended unemployment benefits, 34 cents in sickness benefits, and 2 cents in maternity benefits.

Seamen

The story of the coverage of seamen is rather complex. The Committee on Economic Security originally recommended exemption of seamen from the federal-state system in the expectation that a federal system would be provided for them and railroad workers. Instead, however, they were exempted from the federal unemployment tax.

After a federal system was established for railroad workers, a Seamen's Unemployment Insurance bill was introduced in 1941 and hearings were held before the Senate Maritime Committee. Nothing came of the effort. In the meantime, several states had covered crews on the navigable waters of the United States. Such coverage was contested by maritime employers, but was ruled to be constitutional by a decision of the United States Supreme Court in 1943.

By an act in 1946,[12] Congress formally gave the states permission to cover maritime workers employed on American vessels operating on navigable waters within or without the United States with the proviso that they would receive equal treatment with other workers covered by state laws.[13] Maritime workers were covered by the federal unemployment tax, but Congress exempted fishing vessels, except those fishing for salmon and halibut, and vessels of more than ten net tons. It also exempted service by crews of foreign vessels while in ports of the United States.

The 1946 act also provided for a temporary program for readjustment benefits for seamen (RUBS) on ships controlled by the War Shipping Administration. After the war, unemployment was heavy among seamen formerly employed on such vessels. The legislation provided that seamen on such ships could draw benefits under the terms of the state law where the seamen filed a claim but the federal government would pay the cost. This special program expired on June 30, 1950.

During the Korean War, the problem again arose through the reactivation of some Maritime Administration ships. These were operated under general agency agreements with private operators. This time, the seamen's service was covered by the federal unemployment tax and the states were authorized to cover the seamen on such ships, beginning July 1, 1953.[14]

[12] *Social Security Amendments of 1946*, Title III, approved August 10, 1946. (See Sec. 3305 [f] of Internal Revenue Code of 1954.)

[13] This proviso has been ignored, however, by Ohio which enacted a special seasonal provision for Great Lakes seamen. The federal government has been helpless to enforce the nondiscrimination provision because of the lack of any sanction in the federal legislation.

[14] Public Law 82–196, approved August 5, 1953.

FEDERAL CIVILIAN EMPLOYEES

The largest expansion of unemployment insurance coverage occurred in 1954, when federal civilian employees obtained coverage.[15] Beginning January 1, 1955, a separate federal program was provided for them in a new Title XV of the Social Security Act. Although it was to be financed entirely by the federal government, the benefits provided were in accordance with the law of the state in which the federal employee last worked. There was considerable objection to this feature by the federal unions, because it meant different protection in different states for federal employees with identical salaries and employment records. The unions, however, agreed to and supported the legislation when it became clear that they could get nothing better. The legislation provided for payment of the benefits under agreements between the Secretary of Labor and the states. The law covers service in the employ of the United States or its wholly owned instrumentalities, with certain specified exceptions, the principal ones now being elected officials and aliens working for the government outside the United States. Only a small percentage of the workers covered have drawn benefits. Most of these have been "blue-collar" workers and temporary employees. In the fiscal year ending June 30, 1964, when an estimated 2,530,000 employees were covered, a weekly average of about 32,000 unemployed government workers drew a total of $60.7 million in benefits.

EX-SERVICEMEN

Workers who have been withdrawn from the civilian labor market for a period of military service often upon return have a difficult time finding civilian work. This is particularly true of the young person who has never had a civilian job. Temporary unemployment compensation programs following World War II and the Korean War and then a permanent program was provided to meet this problem.

Servicemen's Readjustment Allowances—1944

Title V of the Servicemen's Readjustment Act of 1944 provided benefits for those who were unemployed after discharge, up to a maximum of 52 weeks. In addition, if "self-employed" veterans had a net profit of less than $100 in any month, they were entitled to receive a readjustment allowance equal to the different between earnings and $100. The program lasted from 1944 to 1950.

Although the SRA program was administered on the national level by the Veterans Administration, the state employment security agencies paid the benefits as the agents of the federal government.

[15] Public Law 83–767, approved September 1, 1954.

Unemployment Compensation for Veterans—1952

Following the Korean conflict, a program of Unemployment Compensation for Veterans (UCV) was again enacted in 1952.[16] This program was more closely coordinated with unemployment compensation than SRA. Benefit payments of $26 a week were provided up to a total of $676. However, if a veteran qualified for unemployment compensation under either federal or state law, this was subtracted from the UCV payment. Also, while the 1944 law had its own eligibility and disqualification provisions, the 1952 act provided that such provisions in the law of the state in which the veteran was drawing benefits would apply. The only exception was that, if the state law cancelled all benefit rights under a disqualification provision, this did not apply to UCV payments. The program was ended by Presidential proclamation on January 31, 1960.

Unemployment Compensation for Ex-Servicemen—1958

While the UCV program was still in existence, the Bureau of Employment Security of the Department of Labor proposed a permanent program of unemployment benefits for men discharged from the armed services. This seemed particularly appropriate because of compulsory military service under the Selective Service Act. But it also seemed appropriate for those who enlisted voluntarily, since a large percentage of these had enlisted to avoid the draft. Most importantly, it was evident that for the indefinite future large numbers would serve a period of military service and face unemployment on discharge. Accordingly, the Ex-servicemen's Unemployment Act was passed in 1958. This amended Title XV of the Social Security Act, which provides unemployment compensation for federal civilian employees, to provide the same benefits for ex-servicemen.

In order to avoid duplicating payments on discharge, it is provided that any accrued leave or mustering-out pay[17] shall be used before drawing ex-servicemen's unemployment compensation, and also that an ex-serviceman shall be ineligible for benefits while receiving an education or training allowance under the Veterans Readjustment Assistance Act of 1952.

Finally, the benefit is paid according to the law of the state in which the ex-serviceman files a claim. The benefit amount is determined on the basis of a schedule of remuneration for each pay grade, periodically revised by the Secretary of Labor after consultation with the Secretary of Defense. This differs from benefits paid to ex-civilian federal employees in recognition that an ex-serviceman may be discharged far from his home or place of last employment.

---

16 Title IV, Veterans' Readjustment Assistance Act of 1952, Public Law 82–550, approved July 16, 1952.

17 Mustering-out pay for peacetime forces expired and was repealed by Public Law 87–675, approved September 19, 1962. Korean veterans, however, are still eligible for such pay.

The unemployment compensation program for ex-servicemen has filled a real need. During the fiscal year ending June 30, 1964, an average of 53,500 ex-servicemen drew benefits each week, with total payments for the year amounting to almost $89 million.

TEMPORARY EXTENDED BENEFIT PROGRAMS

Temporary Unemployment Compensation Act of 1958

The recession of 1958 resulted in an unprecedented number of the unemployed exhausting their unemployment insurance benefits. To meet this problem, Congress enacted a temporary program of extended benefits for persons exhausting benefits under federal or state laws.[18] The legislation provided that funds would be advanced to states entering into agreements with the Secretary of Labor to pay extended benefits to unemployed workers who had exhausted their regular benefits. Extended benefits would be payable up to a maximum duration equal to one-half the duration of the regular benefits paid each claimant. The extended benefits would be reduced by the amount of any temporary extended benefits payable to an individual under a state law. The weekly benefit amount would be the same as that received in regular benefits. The program retroactively made any unemployed person who had exhausted his regular benefits after June 30, 1957, eligibile for extended benefits for unemployment occurring after the Act was passed.

The benefits were to be financed out of federal general revenues, but in a state agreeing to pay such benefits, the amounts paid in extended benefits to workers who had exhausted benefits under the state's law would have to be restored to the United States Treasury either by a transfer from its unemployment fund or out of other funds. In case such restoration was not made by November 10, 1963, the credits against the federal tax paid by employers in the state would be reduced progressively by 5 percent in 1963, by 10 percent in 1964, by 15 percent in 1965, and so on until the full amount paid out by the state in extended benefits was restored.[19] Payments of extended benefits could be made for weeks of unemployment beginning 15 or more days after enactment of the legislation and up to April 1, 1959.[20]

Temporary Extended Unemployment Compensation Act of 1961

When President Kennedy took office in January, 1961, a recession had been under way for some months. Within three weeks after taking office,

[18] Public Law 85–441, approved June 4, 1958.
[19] Public Law 88–173, approved November 7, 1963, provides that reduction in tax credit shall continue to be 10 percent each year after 1964 until the advance is repaid.
[20] The legislation was extended in 1959 so that persons who had filed claims before April 1, 1959, but had not used up all the extended benefits to which they were entitled, would have up to July 1, 1959 to draw them. (Public Law 86–7, approved March 31, 1959.)

he transmitted a bill to Congress (on February 6), which was passed and signed by him on March 24, 1961, only seven weeks later.[21]

In many respects the new act was similar to the 1958 act. Persons who had exhausted state or Title XV benefits after June 30, 1960 were eligible for extended benefits. The extended weekly benefit amount would be the same as for regular benefits. Extended benefits were payable equal to one-half the duration of regular benefits, except this time the duration was limited to a maximum of 13 weeks, and the over-all maximum duration of regular and extended benefits was limited to 39 weeks. These limitations were made because nine states were now paying regular benefits in excess of 26 weeks—in fact, one state had a maximum of 39 weeks—and without the limitation it was thought regular plus extended benefits might be unnecessarily long. The new act provided for termination of the program on April 1 of the following year, except for a phasing out by July 1 of those that commenced extended benefits before April 1, 1962. The benefits would again be administered by the states under agreements with the Secretary of Labor.

The big change in the new act was in the method of financing. Instead of the federal government merely making repayable advances of money to states that signed agreements to pay the benefits as in the 1958 act, the new act provided for payment of the entire cost by the federal government. This was to be financed by a temporary increase in the federal tax, which would be pooled to finance benefits in any state. Thus, there would be a truly federal program of extended benefits although the states would administer the benefit payments.

The pooling of funds was not accepted without a struggle. The bill as it passed the House, provided for an increase of 0.4 percent in the federal unemployment tax for the calendar years 1962 and 1963.[22] The bill passed the House in this form, but was amended by the Senate Finance Committee to provide that the increased taxes would be allocated to the state in which the wages were paid on which the tax was based. At the end of the program, any excess of the increased taxes allocated to a state over extended benefits paid by that state would be transferred to the state's account in the Unemployment Trust Fund. On the other hand, if a state paid out more in extended benefits than its employers paid in increased taxes, that state's employers would have to make up the deficit through future reductions in their federal tax credits. Thus there would be state-by-state financing of the program. When the bill came before the senate, the biggest battle was waged over this amendment, which was narrowly defeated by a vote of 46 to 44.

Since benefits were being financed on a nation-wide basis, another im-

[21] Public Law 87–6.

[22] Since it became evident that the 0.4 percent federal tax increase for 1962 and 1963 would leave a surplus of an estimated $172 million over the costs of the TEUC program, Congress in 1963 reduced the 1963 increase in the tax from 0.4 percent to 0.25 percent. Public Law 88–31, approved May 29, 1963.

portant difference from the 1958 act was to provide that any state paying more than 26 weeks in benefits (whether regular benefits or extended benefits in the six states that provided them) would be reimbursed for benefit payments in excess of 26 weeks. It was thought that this was only fair, in order that states providing more generous duration than 26 weeks of benefits would not be penalized for doing so.

Another change was to reduce weekly benefits by the amount received as a pension which was provided or contributed to by a former "base-period" employer of the claimant. Thus a federal standard of a negative character was added to the bill, although in all other respects benefits were to be paid according to state law.

Finally, because charges were made that a large portion of the benefits would go to secondary workers who did not need them, an amendment was added by the Senate Finance Committee requiring each state to secure, on a sample basis, data on the personal characteristics, family situation, employment background, and benefit experience of those who drew benefits under the new act. Despite the primary purpose of the amendment —to furnish "ammunition" for those who might wish to restrict extended benefits in any future program—this amendment has resulted in the collection of the most comprehensive statistics on long-term unemployment yet available.[23]

In view of the manner of financing the new program, it was a foregone conclusion that all states would enter into agreements to pay the benefits— the principal objective of the financial arrangements.[24]

CHANGES IN FINANCING

Taxable Wage Base

The financial structure of the federal-state unemployment insurance system has never been basically changed.

The most important change in the federal unemployment tax seemed to be a minor change at the time. In the original act, the tax applied to the total payroll of covered employers. On the other hand, only the first $3,000 in annual earnings of workers covered by the federal old-age insurance program was taxed. This limitation was enacted because old-age benefits were based on the first $3,000 of earnings, and with employees also contributing, it was thought that the tax and benefit base should be the same. In the 1939 Social Security Act amendments, the federal unemployment tax base was changed from total payrolls to the first $3,000 in annual earnings. This was done in order to simplify federal tax collections for old-age and unemployment insurance taxes by providing the same taxable wage base

---

[23] For a more detailed history of the passage of this act see Philip Booth, "Temporary Extended Unemployment Compensation Act of 1961—A Legislative History," *Labor Law Journal*, October, 1961, pp. 909–21.

[24] For further discussion of the 1958 and 1961 programs, see Chapter 13.

for them. The change at the time was not considered to be important since it reduced covered wages subject to the unemployment tax by only about 8 percent. The change has grown in significance, however, as wages have increased over the years. The tax base for the employment taxes to finance the federal OASDI program has been changed several times and in 1966 is $6,600. However, corresponding changes have not been made in the federal unemployment tax base. Whether or not the unemployment tax base should be increased has become a major issue in the unemployment insurance program and will be discussed more fully in Chapter 18.

Experience Rating

Only minor changes had been made in the "additional credit" provisions of the federal unemployment tax before 1954. In that year, the most important change was made. Up to then, the federal act required that an employer must have had at least three years of "unemployment experience" before he could receive a lower tax rate. The change in 1954 permitted a state to shorten the period before an experience rating could be given to one year. The change was applicable not only to newly covered employers but also to new employers just starting in business. The change was not mandatory on the state and some states have not taken advantage of it. Experience rating will be discussed in detail in Chapter 17.

Federal Loan Fund

In connection with planning for the reconversion period following World War II, a federal loan fund (the so-called "George Fund") was established.[25] This provided that federal advances would be made to states whose reserves were dangerously low. Such advances were to be financed from the excess of federal unemployment tax collections over and above federal and state administrative expenses. The provision was twice extended, but allowed to expire on March 31, 1952. During its life no appropriation was ever made to the loan fund and no application for a loan had been made.

Agitation continued, however, for some method of assisting states in financial distress. As a result, a new federal loan fund was established on a much firmer basis as a part of the Administrative Financing Act of 1954.[26] Provision was made for automatic appropriation of the receipts of the federal unemployment tax to the Unemployment Trust Fund. The excess of federal unemployment tax receipts over federal and state administrative expenses was to be placed in a Federal Unemployment Account until this account reached $200 million. From this account, a federal advance, interest free, could be made to a state unemployment fund if at the end of any calendar quarter such fund amounted to less than its benefit payments over the preceding four calendar quarters. The amount of the ad-

---

[25] See *War Mobilization and Reconversion Act of 1944*, 58 Stat. 785 (1944).
[26] Public Law 87–567, approved August 5, 1964.

vance might not exceed the highest benefit expenditures in any of the four preceding calendar quarters. Since it was assumed that a state would normally need an advance during an economic recession, it was provided that repayments could be delayed for four years. Such repayment would be through a reduction in the tax credits of the state's employers, equal to 0.15 percent of taxable payrolls in the first year, 0.30 percent in the second year, and so on progressively until the advance was repaid.[27]

The requirements for the receipt and repayment of federal advances were tightened by the Social Security Amendments of 1960.[28] These amendments provided that a state would not be eligible for an advance unless its unemployment fund was so low that it could not meet its estimated benefit payments for the current month or the next month. Moreover, the state would be advanced only sufficient funds (with an allowance for error in the estimated amount needed) to carry it through the month. The advances would be repayable beginning with the second January following the advance, rather than the fourth January, as previously provided. Repayments would also have to be made at double the rate in the 1954 act. In order to assure that the state would increase its taxes so as to get in a sounder financial position, the amendments also provided that while a state has an outstanding advance it must have average contribution rates of 2.7 percent for the third and fourth years after the advance is made, and, thereafter, average contribution rates equal to its average cost rates, or 2.7 percent, whichever is higher, until the advance is repaid.[29]

Paradoxically, at the same time that the requirements for federal loans were so drastically tightened that the likelihood of advances being made was almost eliminated, the maximum size of the loan fund was increased to $550 million or 0.4 percent of taxable wages under all state laws, whichever was a greater amount.[30]

FINANCING OF ADMINISTRATION

Financing of the Employment Service

The Wagner-Peyser Act as passed on June 6, 1933, provided that the federal government would match state appropriations for the employment service. When the states commenced to pay unemployment compensation in 1938, the Social Security Board interpreted the requirement in Title III

[27] Public Law 88–173, approved November 7, 1963, provides that the reduction in tax credit for repayment of advances made before September 13, 1960, shall be at 0.15 percent for five taxable years, 1963–67, after which the tax credit reductions would be increased as prescribed in the permanent legislation. The act also provides that a state can avoid the automatic reductions in tax credit by installment payments made annually before November 10, such annual installment to be equal to the estimated amount of reductions in tax credit that would otherwise apply.

[28] Public Law 86–778.

[29] The repayment provisions of the 1954 act were retained for the advances outstanding at the time these changes were made.

[30] For further discussion, see Chapter 19.

of the Social Security Act that unemployment compensation should be paid through public employment offices to empower it to grant funds under Title III for the operation of the employment offices. It was not long before the entire cost of the state employment services was paid from Title III funds, and the requirement for state matching of funds was waived annually by language in the appropriations for Title III. This was formalized by an act of Congress in 1950, which deleted Sections 6 and 7 of the Wagner-Peyser Act, relating to state matching of federal grants.[31]

Financing Grants for Administration under Title III of Social Security Act

As has been said, the federal unemployment tax was earmarked in 1954, so that it would be used only for employment security purposes.[32] Tax receipts were substantially in excess of the administrative expenses of the employment security program during the next five years. As was provided in the 1954 act, the excess went into the federal loan fund and the loan fund was rapidly built up to its authorized maximum of $200 million. Thereafter $138 million was distributed to the states from the continuing excess federal unemployment taxes. By 1960, however, the federal loan fund was depleted due to advances mainly to Alaska, Michigan, and Pennsylvania. At the same time, administrative costs had risen in the states to where the margin of tax receipts over administrative costs was rapidly narrowing.

Taking both these factors into account, Congress in 1960 increased the federal unemployment tax rate from 3.0 to 3.1 percent, but left the maximum credit against the tax at 2.7 percent, thus increasing the federal "share" from 0.3 to 0.4 percent of taxable wages.

To prevent the increase in the federal tax "take" from being exhausted in administrative costs, Congress also placed a ceiling of $350 million on the annual amount that could be granted to states for administration. While the bill was under consideration, Department of Labor officials remonstrated, since administrative grants were rapidly approaching this ceiling. In fact, each following year, it became necessary to lift or waive the ceiling. An amendment was enacted in 1963[33] which provided for a "flexible" ceiling equal to 95 percent of estimated receipts from the federal unemployment tax (exclusive of the temporary increases in the tax for 1962 and 1963 for the TEUC program). The flexible ceiling should permanently avoid any necessity of further change in the basic legislation if tax income is adequate. However, it was evident by 1965 that the tax yield would not be adequate to finance unemployment insurance administration and the Employment Service if state administrative costs continued the upward trend that had persisted since the program commenced. This will be further discussed in Chapter 20.

[31] Public Law 81–775.
[32] Public Law 83–567.
[33] Public Law 88–31, approved May 29, 1963.

SUMMARY

While there has been considerable federal legislation over the years, much of it has been of a minor nature and the basic character of the federal-state program has not been changed. The coverage of the federal unemployment tax has been extended in some respects and contracted in others. The federal unemployment tax has been extended from employers of eight or more in 20 weeks in a year to employers of four or more in 20 weeks. Other extensions of coverage have not been large and have been more than counterbalanced by restrictions in coverage, notably of quasi-agricultural employment and of workers whose relation to their employer is of a border-line character. Railroad workers have been transferred to a separate federal system. A program of unemployment compensation for federal civilian employees and ex-servicemen has been added.

As to the financing, the taxable wage base of the federal unemployment tax was limited in 1939 to the first $3,000 of each worker's annual earnings. This limitation has not been raised, despite steady and substantial increases in wages since 1939. Protection against insolvency of state benefit funds has been provided through a federal loan fund, although recent amendments have made the conditions for loans so stringent that they can be secured only under extreme circumstances and on a month-to-month basis.

Administrative financing has been placed on a firmer basis by automatic appropriation of all federal unemployment tax receipts to the Unemployment Trust Fund and provision that use of the taxes for meeting administrative costs of the program shall have first priority. However, the need for an increase in the federal unemployment tax receipts was becoming evident by 1965 to meet increasing administrative costs.

The most far-reaching federal legislation has been of a temporary character: the programs for extended benefits to those who exhausted regular benefits during the recessions of 1958 and 1961.

Much more extensive changes in the federal legislation have been proposed, including extensions in coverage, minimum federal benefit standards, and plans for reinsurance and equalization grants to high cost states. Proposals for permanent legislation for extended benefits are at the top of the list of proposed changes under current discussion as this book is written. We will consider these proposals in detail in subsequent chapters.

Chapter 8

State Legislation:
Beginnings and Developments[1]

The expectations were fulfilled that the Social Security Act of 1935 would result in universal state action. By July, 1935, all the states, as well as the District of Columbia and the Territories of Hawaii and Alaska, had enacted unemployment compensation legislation. This was not accomplished, however, without some heel-dragging. While five state laws were passed in 1935 during the consideration of the Social Security Act, only a few more were enacted during the balance of the year and during the early months of 1936. There was a rush in the closing months of 1936 by many states to pass legislation in order to "get under the wire" so that employers could receive credit for state taxes against the federal unemployment tax payable that year. A few states still held out, in the hope that the federal legislation would be ruled to be unconstitutional. After the Supreme Court, on May 24, 1937, handed down its decision upholding the federal legislation,[2] and on the same day declared the Alabama unemployment insurance law constitutional,[3] the remaining states passed laws. Illinois was the last state, its law being signed on June 30, 1937.

Although considerable thought and study had gone into the legislation of some of the states, particularly of those that had had study commissions, most states were ill prepared for legislation. The Committee on Economic Security had recognized this and in its report had suggested some considerations that should be taken into account by the states. It presented actuarial estimates as to what duration could be provided under different assumptions. It also emphasized the importance of requiring adequate reserves in the accounts of individual employers when experience rating was permitted, to assure that benefit liabilities could be met. The Com-

---

[1] Much of the information in this chapter is discussed in detail in later chapters dealing with specific subjects. It is presented here in order to give a panoramic view of state legislative developments in one place.

[2] *Steward Machine Co. v. Davis*, 301 U.S. 548 (1937).

[3] *Carmichael v. Southern Coal & Coke Co.*, 301 U.S. 495 (1937).

mittee also had draft bills prepared setting forth alternative provisions under pooled fund and individual employer reserve account laws.[4]

These draft bills and later revisions prepared by the staff of the Social Security Board were used extensively by the states. As a result, most of the early laws were very similar in language, although there was still considerable variation in content. Since then, through a multitude of amendments, the state laws present a variety of provisions on almost every feature of the laws.

In the following pages, we will describe the original provisions in the state laws and the changes that have been made over the years, without dwelling excessively on detail. It is desirable to review the original legislation, because it set patterns that persist to the present time. There has, however, been a vast amount of change in the laws over the years. It would not be possible to trace these changes in detail. The original provisions will, therefore, in general, be compared with the laws as of a recent date. So as to give concreteness to the various provisions, statistics on the number of states with particular provisions will be given as of January 1, 1966, even though later amendments to the state laws may soon make these statistics obsolete.[5]

COVERAGE

Size of Firm Covered

A bare majority of the state laws originally covered the same size of firms as was covered by the federal unemployment tax—employers who had eight or more employees at some time of each of 20 or more weeks in a year. The District of Columbia law went the whole way in covering employers with one or more employees at any time, while nine other states covered employers of one or more in 20 weeks. Coverage in the other states scattered between these extremes, with a small concentration of nine states covering employers of four or more. As experience was gained in collecting contributions, additional states covered smaller employers, many covering employers of one or more workers. After 1946, however, there was no state action until 1954 when the federal coverage was changed to employers of four or more in 20 or more weeks. Following the 1954 federal extension, all states followed the federal act, while several that had not previously done so went a little further. As of January 1, 1966, 20 states cover employers of one or more, four cover employers of three or more, and 28 cover employers of four or more.[6]

---

[4] These were prepared by Assistant Secretary of Labor, Arthur J. Altmeyer, Paul Raushenbush of Wisconsin, and Merrill G. Murray.

[5] For later amendments, see the latest edition of the following publication: United States Department of Labor, Bureau of Employment Security, *Comparison of State Unemployment Insurance Laws*, BES No. U–141 (Washington, D.C.: U.S. Government Printing Office). This publication is revised annually.

[6] Of those covering employers of one or more, 13 cover only employers with a minimum specified payroll or a minimum amount of time that workers are employed.

Agricultural Labor

As to types of employment excluded from coverage, the state laws have followed the federal unemployment tax with few exceptions. The states generally follow the federal definition of agricultural labor, either by statutory definition or regulation. Only the District of Columbia (which has no agriculture), Puerto Rico, and Hawaii cover agricultural workers, the latter exempting employing units with less than 20 agricultural workers in 20 weeks.[7]

Domestic Service

Only New York and Hawaii cover domestic service in private homes. In New York the employer must have a payroll of at least $500 in a quarter to be covered and in Hawaii, a payroll of at least $225 in a quarter. Domestic service in college clubs and fraternity and sorority chapters is excluded in 40 states.

Nonprofit Organizations

Alaska, Colorado, the District of Columbia, and Hawaii cover nonprofit organizations, but with some important exceptions such as religious workers. The rest of the states follow the original exemptions of nonprofit organizations, but vary considerably in the extent to which they have followed the detailed exemptions made by the 1939 federal amendments, or the restorations in coverage made in 1960.

Definition of Employee

The principal deviation from federal coverage results from differences in the definition of "employee." In 1946, Congress countered a broad interpretation by the Supreme Court of the meaning of "employee" by specifically limiting the definition to those in the common-law master-servant relationship. Most of the states had followed the board definition of "employee" spelled out in the Social Security Board's draft bills (the so-called "ABC" test).[8] Despite the restriction of the federal definition to the common-law rules in 1948, 26 of the states still have the ABC test, and 15 others apply one or two of the tests. Under the broader tests, commission salesmen, milk-drivers, filling station lessors, and the like are covered.

[7] Agricultural employers may elect coverage under a separate agricultural unemployment compensation law in Hawaii. In Puerto Rico sugar workers, who were formerly under a separate law, receive a flat weekly benefit of $5.50.

[8] This test is that a worker is considered an employee unless his employment meets all three of the following: (A) the worker is free from control or direction in the performance of his work under his contract of service and in fact; (B) the service is performed either outside the usual course of the business for which it is performed or is performed outside of all places of business of the enterprise for which it is performed; and (C) the individual is customarily engaged in an independent trade, occupation, profession, or business.

State and Local Government Employment

An area in which coverage is growing in the states is employment in state and local governments. (For constitutional reasons, such employment is not covered by the federal act.) Thirty-four states have some coverage of their state or local government employees. Ten states have mandatory coverage of state employees and two of them have mandatory coverage of local government employees; the rest provide for coverage if the local government elects it. In some cases, coverage is limited to certain types of governmental units or occupations. Despite the growing amount of legislation, however, only about one tenth of state and local government service was covered in 1964, since there had not been much elective coverage.

WEEKLY BENEFIT AMOUNT

Benefits Based on Quarterly Earnings

The original state laws provided that the weekly benefit amount would be 50 percent of full-time weekly earnings. As the states began to collect and post the weekly wages of covered workers, the bookkeeping work soon bogged down. Wisconsin's solution to this problem was to secure "separation reports" from employers which gave the necessary information on wages and weeks of employment at the time employees were separated from the firm. However, the Social Security Board decided to advise the states to collect quarterly wage reports, which could be identical with the quarterly wage reports being collected for the old-age insurance program and to determine the weekly benefit amount for unemployment compensation as a fraction of quarterly earnings. In order to get an approximation to full-time earnings, the Board advised use of the quarter of highest earnings in the period used for determining total benefits.[9] As to the fraction to be used, 1/26th of quarterly earnings would be the same as 50 percent of full-time weekly earnings. But since there might be some unemployment or short working weeks even in that quarter, the Board advised using a larger fraction than $\frac{1}{26}$th, such as $\frac{1}{24}$th or $\frac{1}{20}$th. During the next few years, most of the states adopted quarterly wage formulas. Most used larger fractions than $\frac{1}{26}$th. Now only 16 have a larger fraction than $\frac{1}{26}$th and 12 of these use $\frac{1}{25}$th. Some states use a weighted schedule, providing a larger fraction of wages for low paid wage earners than for high paid.

Annual Earnings Formulas

As of July, 1966, six states have a plan which uses a percentage of annual earnings to determine weekly benefits. The number of states using this plan has fluctuated somewhat. Oregon adopted this plan in 1963;

---

[9] Preferably the first four of the last five completed calendar quarters. A "lag" of a quarter was advised so that the quarterly wages reports needed would have been received and processed.

but Minnesota and Maine abandoned it in 1966. Oregon pays weekly benefits equal to 1.25 percent of annual earnings, up to a maximum of $44 a week. The other five states have a range of fractions, with larger fractions for lower earnings. For example, in North Carolina the fraction ranges from 2.0 percent for the lowest paid workers to 1.0 percent for the highest paid workers up to a maximum of $42 a week.

Weekly Earnings Formulas

As has been said, Wisconsin never changed from using average weekly earnings as a basis for determining weekly benefit amounts. Eight other states have shifted in the last few years from either the quarterly or annual basis to an average weekly basis. In order to get an approximation to average full-time weekly earnings, these states ignore weeks with earnings below a stated amount. For example, Ohio, which shifted to a weekly basis in 1963, uses only weeks with $20 or more of wages. Four of these states also pay a larger fraction of weekly earnings to low-paid workers. The most liberal fraction is New York's—from 67 percent for those drawing minimum benefits down to 50 percent for those at the maximum.

Dependents' Benefits

Originally, only the District of Columbia paid benefits for dependents—$1 each for a maximum of three dependents. A maximum of 12 states eventually paid dependents' benefits, but this number had been reduced to 10 by January 1, 1966. All 10 pay benefits for dependent children under 16 or 18, and all but one pay benefits for older children or other dependent relatives, but in most states only if they are not able to work. Weekly dependents' benefits vary from $1 to $6. Maximum dependents' benefits payable to one worker range from $3 to $25, except in Massachusetts where the augmented benefit can equal the average weekly wage. In Illinois and Michigan benefits are increased for claimants with dependents, depending on the height of former earnings of the claimant.

Maximum and Minimum Benefits

The state laws also provide for both a maximum and a minimum weekly benefit amount. Originally, all but three states adopted the maximum recommended in the draft bills, namely, $15 a week, which approximated about 60 percent of average covered wages in the United States at that time. Michigan provided a maximum of $17 and Wyoming of $18. Wisconsin moved its original maximum of $10 up to $15 in 1938.

As earnings rapidly increased following the beginning of World War II, there was a distinct lag by the states in adjusting the maximum benefit amounts to increasing wages. As a result, more and more of the claimants drew maximum benefits. The ratio of average wages to the average weekly benefit amount also kept dropping. In December, 1939, the maximum weekly benefit in 49 states had been 50 percent or more of average weekly wages of all covered workers; in all but three states in 1952, the maximum was below 50 percent. Since then, maximums have been increased in all the states. As of the beginning of 1966, all states have maximums of $30 or more, except Puerto Rico whose maximum is $16. Maximum benefits range up to $65 in California. Nevertheless, 32 states, as of January 1, 1966, still have maximums equal to less than 50 percent of average covered wages in their states. If dependents' allowances are taken into account, the distribution of maximums provided in the laws was of course higher, up to $75 in Connecticut. As wages have kept rising, the states, time after time, had to face the issue of moving up the maximum benefit amount. In order to avoid this perennial adjustment, an increasing number of states have geared the maximum to the average weekly wage in covered employment. Sixteen states have such flexible provisions; 11 of them have a maximum equal to 50 percent.[10] The maximum is adjusted annually in 10 states and semiannually in two states.

Practically all the states wrote minimum benefits of $5 a week into their original laws. The most common minimum now is $10 (29 states). Nine states pay less than $10, and the balance pay higher minimums up to $25 in California.

Benefits for Partial Unemployment

In order to provide an incentive for a beneficiary to accept even minor or temporary jobs, all the states disregard some earnings in computing weekly benefits. At the beginning, all but six states had such provisions. Originally, the most common provision (28 states) was to reduce the weekly benefit amount by the amount of earnings to the point where benefits plus earnings would be equal to 120 percent of the weekly benefit amount. The second most common provision (13 states) was to disregard $2 of earnings in reducing benefits by the amount of earnings. All but one of the states now use the latter method. The amount of benefits for a week of partial unemployment is the weekly benefit amount less wages earned, but from $2 to $36 of weekly earnings is disregarded.

DURATION OF BENEFITS

In its report to the President, the Committee on Economic Security stressed the importance of not providing longer duration of benefits than could be financed out of contributions. The Committee was heavily influenced by what proved to be overconservative estimates by its actuaries of what duration could be provided. Two sets of estimates were prepared: one based on 1922–30 employment and unemployment estimates and the other on 1922–33 estimates. On the basis of 1922–33 statistics, which included the first four years of the depression, it was estimated that a 3 per-

---

[10] In one of the latter, Mississippi, a dollar maximum of $30 held the maximum to 42 percent of average wages in 1963. Hawaii's maximum of $55 (not a flexible maximum) was equal to 62 percent of wages in 1963.

cent contribution rate would finance only eight weeks of benefits with a two-week waiting period, and only 10 weeks with a four-week waiting period. On the basis of 1922–30 statistics, it was estimated that 12 weeks of benefits could be paid with a two-week waiting period and 15 weeks with a four-week waiting period.[11] The estimates also allowed for an additional week of benefits for each six months of employment in the last five years during which no benefits were drawn. The Committee's draft bills used the more optimistic estimates based on 1922–30 statistics. In revisions of the draft bills issued in January, 1936, the Social Security Board recommended 12 weeks of benefits after a two-week waiting period.[12] The Board suggested a somewhat more liberal ratio for additional benefits; namely, one additional week of benefit for each 20 uncharged weeks of employment in the preceding 260 weeks.

The states were more optimistic than the actuaries of the Committee on Economic Security as to the benefits that could be financed. Four states provided for a 20-week maximum duration; one for 18 weeks; 28 for 16 weeks; and the balance for a shorter duration. Only three states had a maximum as low as 12 weeks. Five states originally provided additional weeks of benefits for long-term employment, but these provisions have all been repealed.

There has been more improvement in the duration of benefits than in any other aspect of unemployment insurance. As it became evident that a longer duration of benefits could be financed within the framework of the tax structure, and as labor pressed for the need for longer duration, a duration of 26 weeks became something of a standard. Even that has been exceeded in some states as the recurrent recessions have demonstrated the need for an even longer duration than 26 weeks. All but three states, as of January 1, 1966, have a maximum duration of at least 26 weeks, and nine states have durations ranging from 28 to 39 weeks. In addition, seven states provided for extended duration of benefits up to 13 more weeks if insured unemployment reaches stated percentages.

Uniform versus Variable Duration

One of the disagreements over duration has been whether to provide uniform duration, that is, the same maximum duration for all claimants who qualify for any benefits, or to vary duration in proportion to former earnings or employment. Originally, only one state (Ohio) had uniform duration of benefits. By 1941, 15 additional states had shifted to uniform duration. Since then, there has been a gradual reduction in the number of states with

[11] These estimates assumed among other specifications that benefits would be paid at 50 percent of average weekly wages up to a weekly maximum of $15, and that the duration of benefits would be limited to one week of benefits for each four weeks of contributions.

[12] In a footnote, however, it stated that the 12-week duration was merely illustrative and that the duration that could be financed in any state depended on the contribution rate, length of waiting period, and many other factors.

uniform duration. Counting the shift of Maine in April, 1966, to variable duration, only eight states still provide uniform duration of benefits. Originally, there were a great variety of provisions for varying the duration of benefits. Now the duration is usually varied by limiting the total amount (weekly amount $\times$ duration) to a fraction or percentage of the claimant's wage credits or weeks of employment in his "base year" used for calculating benefits. The most common provision is one third of base year earnings.

Waiting Period

A waiting period of two weeks of total unemployment accumulated over a period of 13 weeks, was recommended in the draft bills of the Social Security Board. In a footnote, an alternative of a four-week waiting period in 52 weeks was suggested; it was pointed out that the savings that would result would make a longer duration of benefits possible. Thirty states initially provided for a two-week waiting period; 19 for a three-week waiting period and only two for a four-week waiting period. It was originally thought that a minimum waiting period of two weeks would be necessary, to provide time for processing a claim. These long waiting periods did not last. By 1941, all four-week waiting periods had been abandoned and only three states still had a three-week waiting period. Twenty-two states had already shortened their waiting periods to one week. By 1951, only two states required a waiting period of two weeks. Three states had abolished the waiting period altogether. By 1966, three states had no waiting period, and the balance had a one-week waiting period for a benefit year.

QUALIFYING REQUIREMENTS

All the states require a certain amount of employment or earnings in a "base period"[13] prior to filing a claim. The aim is to assure that the claimant has had substantial attachment to the labor market, and to eliminate workers who work only casually or intermittently. It would not be worthwhile to go into the original qualifying requirements, since they were changed as the states shifted to determining wages on the basis of quarterly or annual wages. Such a shift made it impossible to use weeks of employment as a qualifying test. Most states that adopted a quarterly wage basis for determining benefits chose an amount equal to a multiple of the weekly benefit amount as a qualifying requirement, ranging from 13 to 40 times the benefit amount. Some required a minimum amount of earnings in the base year, ranging from $100 to $300. All the states adopting an annual wage formula used a minimum amount of earnings as a qualifying requirement.

In general, the states now follow the same types of qualifying require-

---

[13] The base period is usually the equivalent of four calendar quarters, and in many laws is the first four out of the last five completed calendar quarters preceding the first claim for benefits.

ments for benefits; more, however, are shifting to a week-of-employment test. Eighteen states require a multiple of the weekly benefit amount. The most common multiple is 30, which (assuming that the benefit is one-half weekly wages) is the rough equivalent of 15 weeks of employment. Seven of these states also require earnings in at least two quarters in the base period. Ten states as of January 1, 1966, use a multiple of high-quarter earnings, most commonly 1½ times. Such a requirement assures substantial earnings in more than one calendar quarter. Thirteen states require flat amounts of earnings. The minimum wages required range from $300 to $800, with higher amounts required for benefits above the minimum. The eight states that determine benefits on a weekly wage basis use weeks of employment as a qualifying test, as do five other states. These states require from 14 to 26 weeks of employment in which a minimum amount of wages has been earned, ranging from $15 to $20. Three of these still retain a quarterly benefit formula.

ELIGIBILITY REQUIREMENTS

After having qualified for benefits, the claimant must be able to work and be available for work in order to keep eligible for benefits. This has been required in all states from the beginning. In addition to proving availability by registration at the local employment office, 30 states, as of January 1, 1966, require that the claimant must be actively seeking work or making a reasonable effort to obtain work. On the other hand, in nine states, the availability for work requirement is not applied if there is temporary illness or disability during an uninterrupted period of unemployment, so long as no suitable work is available. Twenty-two states hold a claimant available for work during the time he is attending a training or retraining course approved or recommended by the employment security agency. The number of states permitting this has rapidly increased in the last few years.

DISQUALIFICATIONS

There is strong and widespread disagreement both as to what acts should result in a disqualification and as to what the disqualification should be. The most universal causes for disqualification are (1) voluntarily leaving work without good cause, (2) discharge for misconduct connected with the work, (3) refusal of suitable work, (4) involvement in a labor dispute, and (5) fraudulent misrepresentation to obtain benefits. Other reasons for disqualification, fall into the two general classifications: disqualification of special groups and disqualifying income.

Voluntarily Leaving Work

If a worker leaves work voluntarily in any state, he must have good cause for leaving or he will not be eligible for benefits. "Good cause" originally appeared in the laws as a general term and was interpreted to include good personal causes for leaving. Almost half the states (24 as of

January 1, 1966) restrict "good cause" to a cause attributable to the employer or connected with the work. A few states provide for specific exceptions to such a restriction, such as voluntary leaving to accept other work.

Period of Disqualification. From the beginning, the states had a great variety of provisions as to the period of disqualification for voluntarily quitting without good cause. Twenty-nine states followed the Social Security Board's draft bills in disqualifying claimants from receiving benefits for the week during which they left their jobs and for from one to five weeks (plus the waiting period) thereafter. Seventeen states disqualified such a worker for a fixed number of weeks. New York originally provided for no disqualification. Wisconsin cancelled the benefit rights based on employment which the worker quit, and, in addition, made the worker ineligible for benefits from the previous employer's account for the week of leaving and the next four weeks.

The trend, however, has been to lengthen the disqualification. Thirty-one states still postpone benefits for a specific period. Of these, 14 do so for a fixed period ranging from three to 12 weeks. Of the 17 states that postpone benefits for a variable number of weeks, all but three have a maximum disqualification in excess of six weeks, running up to 26 weeks in one state. Twenty-three states disqualify for the duration of unemployment, almost all of them requiring a claimant to have a period of earnings in a subsequent job before he can again be eligible for benefits. In addition, benefit rights are reduced by the number of weeks of disqualification or cancelled entirely in 16 states.

Discharge for Misconduct

Although the original draft bills merely used the words "discharge for misconduct" this has been generally interpreted as meaning misconduct "connected with the work." This additional wording has been recommended by the Bureau of Employment Security for some years. Some of the states define misconduct more explicitly, such as "willful misconduct" or "deliberate misconduct" in willful disregard of the employing unit's interest. Some states disqualify during a disciplinary suspension as well as for discharge of misconduct.

Period of Disqualification. A somewhat longer maximum disqualification in the Social Security Board draft bills was recommended for discharge for misconduct connected with the work than was recommended for voluntary quits—nine weeks. Most states, however, considered nine weeks too severe, and only 17 states followed the draft bill recommendation. Eleven states provided the same penalty as for voluntary quitting without good cause, from one to five weeks, and all but three of the others provided for some variation between five and nine weeks as a maximum. New York imposed a flat disqualification of ten weeks, Washington disqualified for the duration of unemployment, and Wisconsin cancelled all benefit rights with the discharging employer and disqualified for three weeks based on employment with previous employers. Pennsylvania originally had no disqualification.

More of the states (24) now provide for a variable number of weeks of disqualification for discharge than provide variable duration for voluntary quits. This is to enable the agency to vary the length of the disqualification with the "seriousness of the misconduct" that caused the discharge. Eighteen states have a fixed period of disqualification of from three to 12 weeks, depending on the state. Twenty-three disqualify for the duration of unemployment, and almost all of these require a stated amount of earnings or work in a new job before the claimant is again eligible for benefits. Almost a third of the states (24) cancel some or all of the claimant's benefit rights.

In line with the idea of varying the disqualification with the seriousness of the offense, 22 states, as of January 1, 1966, have more stringent provisions for gross misconduct, which includes, but is not limited to, unlawful actions. The states vary a good deal in their definitions of gross misconduct. The most usual penalty is cancellation of all wage rights.

Refusal of Suitable Work

A worker is disqualified in all states for failure, without good cause, to apply for or accept suitable work when the worker is referred to it by the public employment office. Some states disqualify for refusal "to return to customary self-employment."

It will be recalled that the Federal Unemployment Tax Act specifies certain conditions (the so-called "labor standards") under which a state, in order for its law to be approved, cannot disqualify a claimant for refusal of new work.[14] These conditions are designed to enable a worker to refuse a job where a labor dispute exists, where wages, hours, or working conditions are substandard, or where his right to join a bona fide labor union would be restricted. All states contain these conditions. In addition, most of the state laws list certain criteria for testing the suitability of the work. The usual criteria include the degree of risk to the claimant's health, safety, or morals; his physical fitness and prior training, experience, and earnings. Some states take into consideration the length of the claimant's unemployment and, after a certain period, require him to take less suitable employment than he previously had. The claimant's prospects of securing local work in his customary occupation and the distance of available work from his residence must be taken into consideration in some states.

Period of Disqualification. The same period of disqualification for refusal of suitable work as for voluntary quitting without good cause—from one to five weeks plus the waiting period—was proposed in the draft bills. Thirty-one states followed this recommendation, while most of the other

---

[14] Section 3304 (a) (5) of The Internal Revenue Code of 1954. See Appendix to Chapter 6, Condition (5) for the wording of this provision.

states disqualify for lesser periods. Four states disqualified for the duration of unemployment, and Missouri and Wisconsin cancelled all benefit rights. There is a tendency toward shorter disqualifications for refusal of suitable work. Fifteen states cancel or reduce benefit rights for refusal of suitable work, as compared to 16 states for voluntary quits and 24 states for discharges. Most of these states reduce benefit rights by the number of weeks of disqualification, and such reduction in benefit rights is optional in three states.

Labor Disputes

There is general agreement that a worker should not receive benefits during a labor dispute. Forty-eight of the states originally disqualified a worker for any week of unemployment due to a labor dispute. Three states disqualified for a stated period: New York for ten weeks, Rhode Island for eight weeks, and Pennsylvania for three weeks. New York has since shortened the period to seven weeks and the waiting period, and Rhode Island to six weeks; Pennsylvania no longer pays benefits during a strike. Thirty-one states apply the disqualification during the plant's stoppage of work due to the dispute and 12 while the dispute is in active progress. The balance of the states use other definitions of the duration of a dispute. The most important change in the labor dispute qualifications is that 12 states[15] exclude lockouts from labor disputes. A few do not disqualify if the dispute is due to the employer's failure to conform to the labor contract or labor law.

Individuals are not disqualified in a plant involved in a labor dispute if they or others of the same grade or class are not participating in the dispute (42 states), financing it (30 states) or directly interested in it (42 states). Other circumstances under which an individual is not disqualified are spelled out in a few state laws; for example, if the dispute did not cause the worker to lose or leave his employment.

Fraudulent Misrepresentation

Originally, all but four of the states relied upon court prosecution in cases of fraudulent misrepresentation to obtain benefits. The range of fines and maximum periods of imprisonment was specified in the laws. Convictions were so difficult to obtain or so long in being obtained that almost all the states now have statutory disqualifications. These disqualifications do not free the claimant from repayment of the benefits unlawfully obtained or absolve him from possible fine and imprisonment. Disqualification from benefits is usually up to a year although a few states vary the penalty with the number of weeks of fraudulent claims. Benefits are reduced by the number of weeks of the disqualification or are cancelled entirely. If the fraud is discovered after the benefits have been paid, recovery of the fraudulent payments is secured if possible.

[15] Three by judicial construction of statutory language.

Disqualifying Income

Forty-five of the states originally followed the draft bill with minor variations in reducing benefits by the amount of income received in the form of wages in lieu of notice, workmen's compensation for temporary partial disability, and old-age insurance benefits received under the Social Security Act.

This is an area in which many of the states are less restrictive than originally. Only 19 states reduce unemployment benefits by the amount of federal old-age insurance benefits received. This presumably reflects amendments to the Social Security Act which have permitted more and more earnings from employment without suspension of such benefits. Almost two thirds of the states take into account the receipt of pensions under private plans. Sixteen of these reduce unemployment benefits by the amount of a pension received from any employer and 17 states reduce benefits only if the pension is received from a base-period employer. Some of these states reduce the benefit by only one-half the pension if the claimant contributed to it.

Twenty-four states reduce benefits or disqualify a worker if he is receiving workmen's compensation, although about one half of these apply the disqualification only in cases of partial temporary disability.

Thirty-three of the states disqualify a worker or reduce the benefits of a worker by the amount of wages received in lieu of notice. Twenty states have the same disqualification for dismissal payments. In many states dismissal wages are treated as wages for contribution purposes, as they have been treated under the Federal Unemployment Tax Act since 1951.

By 1964, all but six states had taken action to disregard supplementary unemployment benefits paid under private agreements. Two states specifically prohibit supplementation: Virginia by statutory amendment, Maine by a ruling of the Attorney General.

All the state laws disqualify a worker from receiving benefits during a week in which he is receiving or seeking unemployment benefits under another state or federal law. This is to avoid duplication of benefits. No such disqualification is imposed if benefits are denied under the other law.

Disqualification of Special Groups

Disqualification for Pregnancy. All the states, of course, disqualify a woman because of pregnancy or childbirth if she cannot meet the general requirements of ability to work or availability for work. Thirty-seven of the states now disqualify a woman for specific periods before and after childbirth. Originally, there were no such specific disqualifications, but the number of states with such provisions has gradually increased over the years. Apparently the principal reason these provisions have been enacted is because it may be administratively difficult to determine ability to work in such cases. No two states agree as to the period of disqualification. The length of disqualification varies from four weeks to four months before and from two weeks to three months after childbirth. In some states, re-employment after childbirth is necessary before a woman who has had a pregnancy can become eligible for benefits.

Unemployment Due to Marital Obligations. Instead of applying the availability-for-work test, 23 of the states disqualify a person who has quit work to fulfill marital obligations, until he or she has been re-employed for a specified period. One state also cancels all wage credits. No state had such a provision originally.

Students. Some states exclude from coverage students doing part-time work or working for the institution they are attending. In addition, about a third of the states have provisions limiting the benefit rights of students who have had covered employment. Several disqualify an individual for leaving work to attend school and others, for the period the student is attending school.

The above recital of disqualification provisions, while complicated enough, is an oversimplification, as the states in their detailed provisions vary much more than has been indicated.

FINANCING

Contributions

All states naturally provide that employers covered by the law shall contribute to the state fund, since such employers would otherwise pay the full Federal Unemployment Tax. Whereas, on principle, it generally has been agreed that employers should contribute, there has been much less agreement that employees should contribute. Ten states originally provided for employee contributions varying from one-half percent to 1.5 percent of wages, with most providing for 1 percent. Three states provided for experience rating of employee contributions. All but two of the ten states have since repealed their provisions. Alabama has an employee contribution rate of 0.25, which is raised to 0.5 percent if the employer's contribution is at the maximum under specified fund conditions. In California, New Jersey, and Rhode Island, the employee contribution has been diverted to a temporary disability program, but New Jersey has retained part of the employee contribution (0.25 percent of taxable pay) for unemployment insurance. Alaska introduced an employee contribution in 1955 along with other actions needed to put its fund on a sound actuarial basis. The rate varies from 0.3 to 0.9 percent of the first $7,200 of the worker's pay, depending on the employer's experience rating.

The original District of Columbia law was the only law that ever provided for a government contribution. Appropriations of $100,000 were made in 1936 and of $125,000 in 1937, but the provision has since been repealed.

Types of Funds

The most hotly contested issue in the formation of the original state laws was whether to have the Wisconsin type of individual employer reserves or a completely pooled fund. It was argued that individual employer reserves gave maximum incentive to stabilization of employment. The pooled-fund advocates, on the other hand, maintained that individual accounts could easily be exhausted and that there should be pooling of funds to give maximum protection to the worker. Many of the pooled-fund advocates also contended that there should be no experience rating. The draft bills of the Social Security Board offered compromises between the two extremes. One bill provided for individual employer reserve accounts within the state unemployment insurance fund, but with a partial pooling of contributions; the other bill provided for a pooled fund, but with experience rating of contributions of individual employers. Both bills proposed a reduction of the contributions rate for 2.7 percent to 1.8 percent if the excess of contributions by an employer over benefits paid to his former employees exceeded 7.5 percent of payroll, and a reduction to 0.9 percent if the excess was 10 percent or more of payroll.

Despite the early example of the Wisconsin law, only seven states provided for individual employer reserves, of which two provided for partial pooling of contributions. The rest provided for pooled funds, all but 11 of them with experience rating of employer contributions. Of the 11 without experience rating, provision for study of experience rating was made in nine states. Four states provided for guaranteed employment plans and three for "contracting out" of employers who provided benefits equal to or larger than those provided by the state law. There is no record of these latter provisions ever having been used, and they were subsequently repealed.

All states now provide for completely pooled funds and all state laws also provide for experience rating of employers' contributions to such funds. The provisions vary widely, but all have certain common characteristics. The objective, of course, is to measure the amount of unemployment or cost of benefits resulting from layoffs by employers, and to compare the experience with a measure of the exposure of the firm's employees to unemployment—usually payrolls—in order to determine the relative experience of various-sized firms. The methods of measurement vary widely, but can be classified into five types. These are called reserve-ratio, benefit-ratio, benefit-wage-ratio, compensable-separations, and payroll-variation plans.[16] Reserve-ratio formulas are by far the most popular, and are used in 32 states.

[16] These plans are described in Chapter 18.

Experience Rating

Maximum Rates. In the 40 states originally providing for experience rating, 27 provided for maximum rates above the "standard" rate of 2.7 percent. Eight states had a maximum rate of 4 percent. In 1951, the number of states with maximum rates above 2.7 percent was reduced to nine. In recent years, as reserves have been depleted, an increasing number of states have provided for maximums above 2.7 percent. There are now 35 states with maximum rates above 2.7 percent and 27 with maximum rates of 4.0 percent or more.

Minimum Rates. Whereas the minimum rate recommended in the Social Security Board draft bills was 0.9 percent, nine states provided that the rate could be reduced to zero and two states to 0.5 percent. Twenty-five states provided for minimum rates of 0.9 or 1.0 percent. Fifteen states, as of January 1, 1966, provide for zero rates, 13 for minimums of 0.1 percent, and 16 for minimums of from 0.15 to 0.8 percent. Oregon has a minimum of 1.2 percent, Alaska of 1.5 percent, and Rhode Island of 1.6 percent.

Taxable Wage Base

Originally, total wages were taxed. In 1939, the annual wages of employees subject to taxation was limited to the first $3,000. The states followed suit in changing their laws but in recent years, as wages have increased, a growing number of states have raised their taxable wage base. As of January 1, 1966, 18 states have higher wage bases, of which six were enacted during that year. In 13 of these states, the wage base is $3,600. The highest base is that of Alaska, $7,200, which can be explained both by the high wage rates in Alaska and by the necessity of taking all possible measures to become solvent.

SUMMARY

The Social Security Act was very effective in stimulating the passage of state unemployment insurance laws. By July, 1937, all the states had passed laws that met the federal requirements. Because of the use in most states of draft bills issued by the Social Security Board, the original laws had many similarities in content and language. Still, there were important differences.

From the beginning some states went further than the federal act in covering small employers. With the extension of the federal coverage to four or more in 1954, all states have at least that coverage and 21 states cover employers of one or more persons as of January 1, 1966.

Very few states have varied from the federal exemptions of agricultural labor, domestic service, and most nonprofit organizations. Most states have a broader definition of "employee" than the common-law definition in the federal act. An increasing number of state laws are covering some or all state and local government employees, but mostly on an optional basis.

Thus, the state laws have gone somewhat further than the federal tax in covering workers, but in recent years they have generally waited for the federal government to take the lead.

After experience indicated that it was impractical to base weekly benefit amounts on full-time weekly wages, all states except Wisconsin shifted to formulas that based benefits on quarterly or annual wages. In recent years, a few states have turned to the use of average weekly wages as a basis for benefits. Increases in maximum weekly benefits have lagged behind increases in wages, although since 1953, all states have increased their maximums. An increasing number of states are adopting provisions making the maximum a percentage of average covered wages in the state so as to automatically increase the maximum as average wages rise.

Because of overconservative cost estimates of duration of benefits that were made for the Committee on Economic Security, the durations originally ranged from only 12 to 20 weeks. Today, almost all states have a duration of 26 weeks or more, and a few states extend the duration during periods of high unemployment. Most states vary duration with the amount of previous wages or employment, but some provide uniform maximum duration for all.

Most of the states orignally had a two-week waiting period and some a three-week or four-week waiting period before benefits could start; today all have only one week except for a few states that have eliminated the waiting period entirely.

While the states originally required a stated number of weeks of employment to qualify for benefits, most now have requirements based on a stated amount of former quarterly or annual earnings. But an increasing number of states are shifting back to a weeks-of-employment test.

In order to remain eligible for benefits, all states require a claimant to be able to work and available for work. Availability is now tested in a majority of the states by whether the claimant is actively seeking work. A few states continue benefits if a claimant becomes ill after starting to draw benefits, and an increasing number permit the claimant to take training while drawing benefits.

The states have been increasingly stringent in their provisions for disqualification from benefits, both in the reasons for disqualification and the length of disqualifications. For the most common reasons for disqualification—voluntarily leaving work without good cause, discharge for misconduct, and refusal of suitable work—the states are fairly equally divided between disqualifying for a variable number of weeks, for a fixed temporary period, or for the duration of unemployment. Many states cancel benefit rights or reduce benefits by the number of weeks of disqualification. Causes for voluntary leaving which are not disqualifying are now limited in many states to good cause attributable to the employer or connected with the work. More severe penalties are imposed in some states for gross misconduct.

In all but two states, workers are not eligible for benefits during labor disputes in which they are involved. A few states pay benefits during lockouts. There are variations among the states in the degree of involvement in the dispute that results in disqualification.

In cases of fraudulent misrepresentation to obtain benefits, the states mainly rely on disqualification from benefits, because of unsatisfactory experience with getting court convictions. Disqualifications range up to a year.

Fewer states than originally did so reduce benefits if a worker is drawing federal old-age insurance benefits. In about one half of the states benefits are reduced if a private pension is received. Many states also reduce benefits by the amount received in workmen's compensation, especially in partial temporary disability cases. Wages in lieu of notice, or dismissal payments, are deducted from benefits in a number of states.

Specific disqualifications have been added in many states in cases of pregnancy, unemployment due to marital obligations, or periods when a student leaves work to attend school.

Practically all states rely entirely on employer contributions. While some states originally had employee contributions, only three do so today. Only the District of Columbia ever required government contributions and this lasted only a few years.

While a few states originally followed Wisconsin in providing for individual employer reserve accounts, most states provided for pooled funds. Most of the latter provided for experience rating. Today, all states have pooled funds with variation in contributions in accordance with the employer's experience with unemployment. Almost every state has a different formula for varying contribution rates. As benefit costs have increased and reserves have been depleted, more and more states are providing for contribution rates above the "standard" rate of 2.7 percent, as was originally done in most of the states. Minimum rates have been reduced to zero or 0.1 percent in most states.

The taxable wage base originally covered the entire payroll of the employer. In 1939, it was limited to the first $3,000 of each worker's earnings. Until recently, this base had not been changed as wages have risen; now over a third of the states have raised the base somewhat, usually to $3,600.

The state laws are so complex and vary so greatly that it is hard to summarize them. It is therefore difficult to make any over-all evaluation as to the extent the laws have been improved over the years. In some respects, they have been improved; in other respects, in our opinion, they have retrograded. The evaluation must be made in detail and, even then, there will be disagreements as to what is to be considered improvement and what changes represent a retreat. There are also disagreements as to the alternative courses of action that can be taken where changes are needed in the program. The balance of this book will be devoted to a detailed consideration of the different features of unemployment insurance and the issues that surround almost every one of these features.

Part III

Issues
in Unemployment Insurance—
Coverage and Benefits

Chapter 9

Why So Many Issues
in Unemployment Insurance?

Today, unemployment insurance is well established in the American economic structure, aiding millions of people during difficult and often critical periods of their working lives. The program is looked upon as one of the important "built-in" stabilizers that helps maintain purchasing power during periods of business decline. Wage earners consider it one of the great bulwarks of their economic security. Employers, who as a group were strongly opposed to unemployment insurance before it was enacted, and now are critical of one or another aspect of the program, generally accept it as desirable and necessary.

Most of the disagreements that arise in unemployment insurance are about specific provisions in the program—how much should be provided in weekly benefits, what the qualifying requirements should be, under what conditions a worker should be disqualified from the receipt of benefits and for how long, what the tax base should be. But underlying these specific questions are more general disagreements, such as the extent of federal participation in the program or whether changes in the program should be made through federal legislation or throught state action. Disagreements arise between management and labor as well as between federal and state officials administering the program. Even the nongovernment experts who have no vested interest in the program often disagree about these issues.

On most topics many specific arguments are marshalled for and against the provision at issue. But often, if not always, these specific arguments are used because they support general attitudes. Some of these attitudes are deep-seated and show that ideas and viewpoints that have long existed in a society die slowly.

This is true of attitudes toward unemployment. When compulsory unemployment insurance was proposed during the depression of the 1930's, it was a relatively new idea that unemployment was anything more than a temporary problem occurring periodically during depressions. But after

127

business recovered, the problem of unemployment was thought to be of no importance, or was entirely forgotten.

The many millions who were unemployed during the depression of the 1930's brought home the realization that unemployment was due to other than personal reasons. When unemployment reached into the homes of executives, white-collar workers, skilled mechanics who had been efficient and reliable and who had heretofore not been touched by unemployment, it was realized that unemployment strikes the efficient as well as the inefficient, the industrious as well as the lazy worker.

Moreover, government intervention in the form of a compulsory system of insurance to protect the unemployed was a new idea for almost everyone in this country, although bills had been introduced in a few legislatures as early as 1916. Before the depression of the 1930's, there was little provision even for public relief for the unemployed. For many decades, private welfare agencies had contended that relief of the unemployed was within their province, and such public provision as existed for unemployment relief was provided by local government.[1] Most employers did not consider provision for the unemployed as a responsibility of business, and those who did, with few exceptions, thought that unemployment benefit plans should be provided by employers on a private, voluntary basis.

These ideas—that unemployment is a problem only during business depressions (or recessions as we call them now); that unemployment is due to the personal deficiencies of the individual; and that government intervention to provide for the unemployed is not justified or needed—die hard. While unemployment insurance is accepted as a permanent public program and is never likely to be repealed, there are millions of Americans who still find it difficult to accommodate themselves philosophically to the idea that unemployment insurance benefits should be claimed as a matter of right by unemployed workers who do not appear to need them.

These attitudes toward unemployment and unemployment insurance have undergone considerable modification over the years. Unemployment is recognized as a continuing problem, though more acute during business declines than at other times. Most unemployment is recognized as due to impersonal, economic causes, but during periods of prosperity, the belief that much unemployment is the fault of the worker comes to the fore again. Unemployment insurance as a government program is accepted, but there is resistance to specific proposals to increase the protection it provides.

It is difficult to sort out in logical sequence the reasons why so many features of unemployment insurance are controversial, since many of them overlap or are intertwined. The detailed discussion of them will, therefore, not follow precisely the order in which they have been discussed so far.

[1] See Frank R. Breul, "Early History of Aid to the Unemployed in the United States," In *Aid of the Unemployed*, Father Joseph Becker (ed.) (Baltimore: Johns Hopkins Press, 1964), pp. 6–21.

First, we think it is desirable to point out that the resistance to government intervention in the form of unemployment insurance is part of the resistance to the transition of the American economy into welfare capitalism, a transition that is by no means complete. Second, we will discuss the attitudes toward unemployment and unemployment insurance in more detail, including some employer attitudes, some labor attitudes and some commonly held attitudes such as that unemployment is the personal fault of the worker. Then we will discuss more intangible sources of disagreement, including the question of the effect of unemployment benefits on the incentive to work, the problem of proving or disproving whether a person is genuinely unemployed in many situations, and the problem of disagreements over the extent of abuse of unemployment insurance. The difficulty in reaching agreement on issues because of the chronic lack of adequate information and the necessity of exercising personal judgment also needs discussion. Finally, we will discuss the issues that arise because unemployment insurance in this country is mostly a federal-state system.

There is considerable overlapping in the various reasons behind these controversial issues in unemployment insurance. Also, as we have sought to present them, the issues do not fall into a neat pattern. But that is one of the difficulties about unemployment insurance problems: none of them can be solved in a neat and logical manner. This is, of course, true of all human and social problems, but we believe it is particularly true of unemployment insurance.

THE LARGER ISSUE OF WELFARE CAPITALISM

Unemployment insurance is not unique in being controversial. Many of the issues in unemployment insurance are common to other social insurance or labor legislation. Less is heard about it publicly, but many features of workmen's compensation are still controversial. Its coverage is still limited. Controversy is rife particularly over whether industrial illnesses, as well as industrial accidents, should be covered by the program. Minimum wage legislation also has aroused controversy. It is even more difficult to secure increases in the level of the minimum wage than in the level of unemployment insurance benefits. There is similar opposition to the extension of coverage under both programs. Disagreement is as strong over whether extension of the minimum wage, for example, should be through federal or state action as over whether extensions or improvements in unemployment insurance should be through one level of government or another.

The disagreements over unemployment insurance can be put in a larger setting. Resistance to the enlargement and improvement of unemployment insurance is a part of the resistance that has been going on for over half a century to the transition of America from *laissez faire* capitalism to welfare capitalism. Max Lerner in his study of *America as a Civilization* wrote:

Since the area of security necessarily involved the emergence of a welfare state to carry part of the burden and responsibility, storms and turbulences have raged around it ever since the turn of the twentieth century. It has been the arena of the great reform movements of America and administrative efforts of Democratic and liberal Republican administrations alike have had to meet resistance of interest groups.[2]

As unemployment insurance has come to be accepted as a program, it has also been subject, along with other types of social insurance and other measures for social reform, to typical American approaches to such programs. Quoting Max Lerner again, Americans

have responded piecemeal and in irregular fashion to the need for workmen's compensation, unemployment benefits, old-age insurance, subsidized low-cost housing (etc.) . . . what has emerged in each area of welfare is the acceptance of the principle of responsibility but with the least challenge to private enterprise, the least burden on the tax structure, and the greatest reliance on the voluntary principle. The broad formula has been for the government to set a floor below which security and welfare cannot fall, to use government funds for the more clamant forms of social insurance but to let the others go, to give the states the widest possible discretion, to steer away from centralized authority and administration . . . to put the burden of expanding the programs upon continued popular pressures.[3]

In that paragraph, Lerner captured the quintessence of the reasons there have been controversies in unemployment insurance. Its progress has been piecemeal, irregular, and inadequate. Employers have sought to keep their responsibility for financing the compensation of unemployment as narrow and limited as possible. The program has been geared to the private enterprise system by giving incentives to stabilize employment and by seeking to allocate the costs of unemployment insurance as much as possible on the basis of unemployment caused by the individual employer. There are constant pressures to keep unemployment taxes to a minimum, and a general attitude that benefits should be kept down to a minimum floor of protection and limited to short-term unemployment between jobs. From the beginning, the states have been given the widest possible discretion as to the provisions in their laws and there has been resistance to any attempts at federal legislation to set minimum standards or to any strengthening of federal authority in the program. Expansions and improvements in the program have occurred only when organized labor has been strong enough, or when unemployment has been widespread enough, to bring sufficient pressure on the state legislatures to act.

These reasons for the controversial nature of the unemployment insurance program could equally apply to other social insurance and labor legislation. In addition, there are certain reasons unique to unemployment

[2] Max Lerner, *America as a Civilization* (New York: Simon & Schuster, 1957), p. 130.
[3] *Ibid.*, p. 131.

insurance, largely growing out of the attitudes toward, and the unique characteristics of, unemployment.

THE ATTITUDE THAT UNEMPLOYMENT IS THE FAULT OF THE WORKER

There is always a cultural lag between a change in social or economic conditions and public recognition of the change. Such a lag exists in the recognition that unemployment is due, in large measure, to economic causes. Until the depression of the 1930's brought home to almost every family in America that unemployment could stem from impersonal economic conditions, unemployment was considered by most to be due to the deficiencies of the individual.

Clinch Calkins, in a book written in 1930 analyzing case studies of unemployed persons, said, "There are several widely held ideas about unemployment which this book should dispel. One of them is that unemployment comes only in hard times. . . . A second presumption is that under unemployment only those suffer who have been too thriftless to save. And still a third, the most pervasive of all, is that if a man really wants to find work, he can find it."[4]

Over thirty years later, a large proportion of Americans still hold the last idea Miss Calkins listed. During a recession, there may be a general recognition that a large amount of the unemployment results from economic causes, but as soon as prosperity returns, many believe that if people are unemployed it is their own fault. This is true even among employees.

An indication of present-day thinking on this point is given by the results of a 1962 sample household survey made in six Ohio cities by the Research Foundation of Ohio State University. In answer to the question, "Whose fault is it when people become unemployed?" 58.1 percent of the employers and 38.2 percent of the self-employed in the survey replied that it was the fault of the unemployed. This reply might be expected from these groups but the surprising thing is that 36.8 percent of the employees interviewed gave the same answer![5] The highest proportion of persons who thought unemployment was an individual's own fault was in employee groups that tend to have the least difficulty with unemployment. Thus, 47.8 percent of those in professional occupations believed unemployment was the worker's own fault. About half as many—23.2 percent—of the unskilled, who experience the most unemployment, believed this (but even that many is surprising). The same relationship existed between levels of income and attitudes toward the unemployed. Of those in the sample with incomes of $10,000 or over, 50.4 percent thought unemployment was

---

[4] Clinch Calkins, *Some Folks Won't Work* (New York: Harcourt, Brace & Co., 1930), pp. 20–21.

[5] Research Foundation, The Ohio State University, *Use of and Attitude toward the Ohio Bureau of Unemployment Compensation: A Research Report*, Project 1472 (Columbus, 1963), p. 32.

the fault of the unemployed, as compared with 28.4 percent of those with incomes of $2,500 or less.

The proportion thinking that unemployment was the fault of the unemployed rose with the educational level of those interviewed. Thus, while about 30 percent of those with less than eight years of education thought this, 44.0 percent of those with three or four years of college education, and 46.9 of those who had had postgraduate college educations held this view. The writers of the report had this to say about this latter finding:

The people with the greater amounts of formal education, presumably the most informed people, are those who most likely have been exposed to the ideas of economics, including the widely-held notion of involuntary unemployment. Yet this seems to make little difference regarding their beliefs about the reasons for unemployment. It must be, therefore, that this attitude is the manifestation of a more-or-less deeply held belief that is not susceptible to alteration or modification merely through exposure to the thinking and opinions of those generally regarded as "experts."[6]

If this is the general situation, it is not surprising that the management group, who have little fear of unemployment, who are well paid, and who are usually well educated, tend to favor any unemployment insurance restriction that is based on the assumption that the kind of unemployment in question is the fault of the worker.

EMPLOYER ATTITUDES AS A CAUSE OF DISAGREEMENTS

At the time the Social Security Act and the original state unemployment insurance laws were passed, employers, with few exceptions, strongly opposed the enactment of the laws. Part of their opposition stemmed from their viewpoint that unemployment insurance was a further step toward welfare capitalism. Many went further and considered it socialistic. They were opposed to government action and to what they considered to be government interference with the free enterprise system.

Part of their opposition was due to the taxes levied on them to pay the costs of the system, or, at least, most of the costs in those states that enacted employee contributions. They opposed these taxes, not only as an increased cost at a time when they were struggling to keep their businesses from going bankrupt, but because they felt that such taxes meant that they were being held responsible for unemployment and for the welfare of employees they had "let go." This was a radical reversal of a trend that had been going on for several centuries, during which employers had been progressively relieved of any feeling of responsibility for their employees. The breakup of the feudal system first relieved the employer of any legal responsibility for the welfare of his employees. The rise of the factory system as a substitute for the small craftsman's shop, and particularly the

[6] *Ibid.*, p. 33.

rise of the modern corporation, had completed the process of depersonalizing the relationship between the employer and the worker.

Classical economics had also given the employer a theoretical basis for feeling little responsibility for the unemployed. Classical economics explained unemployment as being due to imperfect functioning of a free market. Under perfect functioning, the economy would automatically reach an equilibrium through the adjustment of wages to a level where all would be employed. The employer might be personally sympathetic to the plight of the unemployed worker, but the alleviation of that plight was none of his economic responsibility. Nor was the elimination of unemployment his affair; it would be eliminated if the market were permitted to function freely. Lord William Beveridge's ringing challenge that "unemployment remains . . . a problem of industry, not an Act of God," originally made in 1909 and repeated in 1930, had not reached all employers' ears.[7] There were outstanding exceptions. Employers like Henry Dennison of the Dennison Manufacturing Company, Marion B. Folsom of the Eastman Kodak Company, and Gerard Swope of the General Electric Company had developed unemployment benefit plans for their companies, such as were described in Chapter 5. When the prospects of unemployment insurance were being debated in the early 1930's, the attitude of most employers toward paying the costs of the program was expressed by Noel Sargent of the National Association of Manufacturers in 1931: "Penalization of employers because of unemployment resulting from conditions over which the employer has little control is both ethically and economically unjustified."[8]

The injection of experience rating into the unemployment insurance system, which varies the employer's tax rate with his "experience with unemployment," was probably the major factor in bringing employers to accept unemployment insurance. It led, however, to no more than a limited acceptance of the program by most employers. While experience rating was designed to be an incentive for employers to regularize their employment, experience rating for most employers has merely meant that they should be charged only for layoffs brought about by the vicissitudes of their own business. The original objective of encouraging the stabilization of employment has largely dropped out of sight.

The concept that employers should pay the cost only of benefits to workers whose unemployment is due to layoffs is one of the principal reasons that employers generally have advocated a whole series of restrictions on the payment of unemployment insurance. These include the payment of bene-

[7] William Beveridge, *Unemployment a Problem of Industry (1909 and 1930)* (London: Longmans, Green & Co., 1930), p. 419.

[8] *Unemployment Insurance,* Hearings before a Select Committee on Unemployment Insurance, United States Senate, 72nd Cong., 1st sess., pursuant to S. Res. 483, 71st Cong., (Washington, D.C.: U.S. Government Printing Office, 1931), p. 441.

fits to a worker who voluntarily quits only if his reason for quitting was attributable to the employer; the disqualification for the duration of his unemployment of a worker who quits without such good cause or is discharged for misconduct; the automatic disqualification of a pregnant woman as she approaches childbirth even though she may be able to work and available for work. The attitude that employers should pay only for unemployment for which they are responsible is also one of the reasons that, in most states, an employer is charged for benefits only in proportion to the length of time the worker was in his employ.

Many employers also support these restrictions on benefits from a sincere conviction that a worker should not draw benefits when the unemployment is due to the worker's own actions. Also, in recent years, employers have sought legislation to curb alleged abuses by the growing number of temporary seasonal workers, married women, and pensioners who are drawing benefits. (See discussion on the problem of abuse in a later section of this chapter.)

The Effect of Costs on Employer Attitudes

Employers naturally look at proposals for changes in unemployment insurance from the standpoint of whether the change will cost or save them money. Experience rating gives them more motivation to do this, but employers would look at changes from a cost standpoint in any case. Often millions of dollars are involved. Although it is argued that employers can pass the cost of unemployment insurance on to the consumer in increased prices, or back to labor through lower wages (or at least smaller wage increases), employers usually do not act as if they believed this, except when employers with stable employment are arguing for higher taxes for those with high rates of unemployment.

Certainly in the short run, business must bear the cost of increases in benefits or other increased costs of the program. And, as will be brought out more fully in the chapter on experience rating, it can be argued that experience rating has made it more difficult to pass on the costs of unemployment insurance. In any case, to the average employer, any change in unemployment insurance that will result in an increase in costs and, therefore, an increase in taxes is to be resisted like an increase in any other kind of tax. To him, it will represent an increase in the cost of doing business and, to the extent that the increase is made in his state alone, the average employer believes that it will put him at a competititve disadvantage with employers in other states. Changes in the program that will increase costs are almost automatically opposed by employers.

Employers and their representatives are sensitive to many elements of their costs, but especially those costs that result from legislation. Since they pay the costs of unemployment insurance, the detailed provisions of the state law are of prime importance to employers, individually and collectively. Few sophisticated employers feel they can candidly discuss these concerns, and others are not (or will not permit themselves to be) aware of this concern over costs. For this reason, most discussion focuses upon, and much heated debate can be generated over, "principles of insurance," "equities," "abuses," "preserving incentive to work," etc. Such intangibles are useful arguments in legislative maneuverings.

There are exceptions to such attitudes. The Committee on Economic Development, with a membership of outstanding employers, has taken positive positions for improvements in the unemployment insurance program. Individual employers have also taken a constructive attitude.[9]

ATTITUDES OF LABOR A CAUSE OF DISAGREEMENT

Labor naturally wants to get as much protection as possible out of unemployment insurance, and unions are constantly advocating increases in the amount and duration of benefits. Since labor naturally wants as few restrictions on the payment of benefits as possible, the unions take a stand against restrictions that they consider to be inequitable or unnecessary. They oppose the narrowing of "good cause" for voluntarily leaving to causes attributable to the employer; they oppose disqualifications for the duration of unemployment; they oppose varying the duration of benefits with the duration of previous employment. Organized labor also has been opposed to experience rating because unions look on it as the motivating force behind most of the resistance of employers to increases in benefits and behind the advocacy of provisions restricting benefits. Labor also puts more emphasis on the *social* insurance aspects of unemployment insurance, while employers tend to put more emphasis on the *insurance* aspects.

Thus, labor and management are lined up against each other on practically every substantive change proposed in unemployment insurance laws. It is true that, at times, the two groups come before the state legislature with an agreed bill—in a few states this is the usual practice—but such agreed bills are often the result of bargaining in which both sides have made concessions and compromises. Too frequently these have been agreements by employers to an increase in benefits in return for labor refraining from opposing tax cuts, with the solvency of the state fund weakened in the process.

THE QUESTION OF THE EFFECT OF BENEFITS ON THE INCENTIVE TO WORK

Disagreement as to the extent to which a claimant's incentive to work will be affected plays an important part in controversies over particular

[9] Marion B. Folsom, Director of the Eastman Kodak Company, in an address to the Annual Meeting of the Interstate Conference Employment Security Agencies in Miami, Florida, on October 7, 1964, advocated a number of improvements in the program. He told the authors that he did not receive a single criticism of his address from other employers.

provisions of unemployment insurance. For example, disagreements arise over how high weekly benefit amounts can go without affecting the incentive to work, or for how long a period they can be paid before the incentive to seek work decreases. There are also disagreements over the extent to which certain classes of workers, such as married women, would rather draw benefits than seek work. Employers tend to emphasize the effect of benefits on work incentives; labor to minimize the effect. Those who are prone to stress that workers will malinger if benefits are too high tend to hold the view that people are inherently lazy and will work only if there is a substantial differential between benefits and wages. Those who minimize the effect of benefits on incentives stress that there is psychological demoralization and a loss in social prestige in this work-oriented civilization if one is unemployed, and, thus, that people will work if it is at all possible. One of the reasons these differences persist is that the motivation to work is a subjective matter that can never be measured, and disagreements will continue over the effect of different features of unemployment insurance on the incentive to get and hold a job.

THE PROBLEM OF THE SUBJECTIVE ELEMENT IN UNEMPLOYMENT

When a worker is laid off by an employer for lack of work, there is no question that he is unemployed. At least, there is no question on the day he is laid off. Whether the worker is still unemployed from then on is, to a lesser or greater degree, a matter of his state of mind as to whether he wants to work. Perhaps this point would become clearer if we said, "her state of mind." Unemployed women workers, especially if they are wives or daughters living at home, are immediately suspect as not genuinely wanting to work or, at least, as not wanting very much to work. But women are not alone in being suspect. The pensioner, the student, the worker laid off a seasonal job are also open to question because of the subjective element in unemployment, the state of mind of the jobless person toward work. Unemployment is not as concrete and easy to prove as an industrial accident or the fact that one is aged 65. Week after week, a worker comes into the employment security office and files a claim for benefits; how can one know whether he is earnestly desirous of getting a job rather than merely going through the motions of seeking work?

Because unemployment is difficult to prove in so many situations, one school of thought holds that the provisions of the unemployment insurance law should be tight enough to give benefits only to those who unquestionably and demonstrably are involuntarily unemployed. Another school of thought holds that the unemployed worker should be given the benefit of the doubt and the law should be liberal in testing the readiness of the worker to find employment. As a result, there are a whole series of provisions in the state laws that differ from state to state because of these differences in point of view. The first school of thought under certain conditions favors disqualifications for the duration of unemployment; the other school of thought favors temporary disqualifications. Those adhering to the first school of thought would disqualify all pregnant women, all persons who quit to fulfill marital obligations, all pensioners. Those holding to the second school of thought would permit the payment of benefits if such workers demonstrate that they are available for and able to work.

The subjective character of unemployment is an important contributing factor that causes these differences in the treatment of claimants.

ABUSE OF THE PROGRAM AS A SOURCE OF CONTROVERSY

The question of the extent to which beneficiaries abuse unemployment insurance affects attitudes toward many unemployment insurance provisions. Periodically, the program is subject to attack in articles which attempt to prove that benefits are being paid to large numbers of "loafers, quitters, schemers and cheaters."[10] The examples of abuse given in these attacks run the gamut of situations that involve specific provisions found in many, and sometimes in a majority, of the state laws. Thus, there are examples of students, pregnant women, women who have quit their jobs to fulfill marital obligations, seasonal workers, and/or vacationers who, in the opinion of the critic, have abused the system. Disqualification provision for voluntary quitting or discharge for misconduct, are attacked as being too lenient and leading to abuse of the system. The kind of cases cited are not situations in which outright fraud is perpetrated but ones in which the worker is alleged to have taken advantage of some provision or interpretation of the law in a manner that constitutes an abuse of the system.

It is sometimes darkly hinted that there is a great deal of outright fraud in the program which is being hidden from the public. Actually, the amount of fraud in the sense of willful misrepresentation is small. Although some fraud no doubt escapes detection, its volume can not be large. As part of their vigorous programs for uncovering fraud, the states spend millions of dollars each year in investigating suspected claims. In fiscal year 1964, only 12 out of every 1,000 beneficiaries were found to have made fraudulent claims that resulted in "overpayment" of benefits. Of every $100 paid out in benefits during the year, only 31 cents was an overpayment resulting from fraud and 64 percent of these overpayments due to fraud were recovered from the claimants by the state agencies.

The kinds of cases that are generally cited in these articles attacking the program are not cases of fraud. They are cases in which individuals have legally drawn benefits under the law. What are attacked are legislative provisions. The cases usually cited are not run-of-the mill examples, but unusual cases that have been the subject of review by appeals tribunals, even by the courts, and in which benefits have been awarded. Such cases

[10] See, for example, Kenneth O. Gilmore, "The Scandal of Unemployment Compensation," *Reader's Digest*, April, 1960, pp. 37–43; "The Scandal in Unemployment Insurance," (Anonymous) *Atlantic Monthly*, February, 1964, pp. 84–86.

are usually on the borderline; otherwise, they would not have reached the appeal stage. The Bureau of Employment Security has often found that the facts cited in the articles are taken out of context and fail to include the extenuating circumstances that led to the final award of benefits.[11] The cases are often selected because they support an attack on the provisions of law, the public policy, that permits the payment of benefits in such cases.

One example in differences in public policy is the variation of treatment of a wife who quits her job to move with her husband when he gets a job in a distant location. If the woman promptly registers for work at the public employment office when she arrives in the new location and is genuinely ready to work and able to work, she is awarded benefits under some state laws. The public policy in such states is that a woman should not be penalized by the loss of benefits if she fulfills her legal and social obligation to live with her husband. In a number of states, however, the wife must first find another job in the new location and work for a minimum period of time before she is again eligible for benefits if laid off. The public policy in states with such provisions is that the wife must demonstrate by actually finding a job that she is available for work in the new location. Those who charge the system is being abused in states which follow the other policy are merely disagreeing with the policy.

There is no doubt that, in many cases, claimants take advantage of provisions in the state laws that permit some latitude in interpretation. It is easier to abuse the program in those states that pay benefits after a disqualification for a temporary period. Under such a provision, a woman may quit her job without good cause and following the disqualification period of, for example, six weeks, apply for benefits although she has no intention of working. If she is clever enough, she can find ways of avoiding work, even when she is referred to a job for which she is qualified by the employment office. For example, she may dress or conduct herself in such a manner that the prospective employer does not hire her. In the states that have temporary disqualifications for voluntary quitting for good cause or for discharge for misconduct, the public policy is based on a judgment that, if the disqualified claimant is unemployed and genuinely seeking work after a certain number of weeks, his unemployment is no longer due to the reason that he left his former job. These states place importance on the ability of such persons to draw benefits after the disqualification period, even though it may permit a few dishonest persons to abuse the system by drawing benefits while not genuinely seeking work. In other states, it is believed that disqualifications for a temporary period are too subject to abuse. It is also believed that the reason for the disqualification continues to be the reason for the unemployment until another job is found. These differences represent another area of controversy.

[11] For example, see *Analysis of Reader's Digest Article "The Scandal of Unemployment Insurance"* in William Haber and Wilbur J. Cohen, *Social Security; Programs, Problems, and Policies* (Homewood, Ill.: Richard D. Irwin, Inc., 1960), pp. 309–22.

There is no doubt that proposed liberalizations in the program, particularly in the amount of benefits, are hindered because of the widespread opinion that there is much abuse in the unemployment insurance program. As long as this opinion prevails, the program will remain controversial.

THE ELEMENT OF JUDGMENT AS A SOURCE OF DISAGREEMENT

Even if there were no conflicts of interest in unemployment insurance, it would be difficult to settle many issues on a basis satisfactory to everyone.

First, there is practically no issue in unemployment insurance on which there are data that give satisfactory and adequate answers to all the questions involved. Much information has been assembled over the years, but it is often in a form that does not give the precise information needed. For example, the most comprehensive information that has ever been assembled on the characteristics of unemployment insurance beneficiaries was collected, under mandate of Congress, with respect to the beneficiaries of the Temporary Unemployment Compensation Act of 1961. Voluminous reports have been issued by the Bureau of Employment Security and the states on the mass of data secured through this study. But when one looks for the answer to some concrete problem, such as the issue of pensioners who drew benefits under the program, one does not find sufficient information to form an unqualified position on the question. Intensive surveys of the personal circumstances of the pensioners and their efforts to secure work would be necessary before adequate information would be available.

But even if more complete information were available, judgments have to be made as to its meaning and policy implications. In making such judgments, people will differ because no one is free from predilections or prejudices; or stating it more positively, people differ in the values they hold.

Take, for example, the issue as to what is an adequate weekly benefit amount. What do we mean by "adequate?" One's answer will depend on what criteria he uses as a measure of adequacy. As Father Joseph M. Becker, who has put a great deal of study and thought into the question of the adequacy of unemployment benefits, states: "Adequacy is a normative concept rooted in a value system, and in any large society there will be many different value systems. Reflecting these values, the concept will vary from user to user, often in unstated ways. Many a disagreement about the 'adequacy' of a given benefit provision is really a disagreement about the definition of adequacy and stems fundamentally from different value systems."[12] In applying a "norm" that benefits are adequate if they meet "nondeferable expenses," Father Becker has used items that had been selected by the Bureau of Employment Security: food, shelter, clothing, and medical expenses. The selection of these particular items was a matter of

[12] Joseph M. Becker, "The Adequacy of Benefits in Unemployment Insurance" in *In Aid of the Unemployed*, Joseph M. Becker (ed.) (Baltimore: Johns Hopkins Press, 1965), p. 79.

judgment, since the beneficiaries on the average had continued expenditures in all the twelve categories in which expenditures were classified, and had not reduced expenditures drastically in any category. What were classified as deferable expenses were those that the classifiers, in their judgment, thought beneficiaries could have deferred. Thus, judgment had to be exercised as to what is a good norm of adequacy, and, then, for each norm of adequacy selected, judgment had to be exercised as to what went into the norm. Finally, it was a matter of judgment as to whether the norm was being met. Was it being met if 50 or 67 or 90 percent were getting "adequate" benefits?

In short, personal judgment has to be used in deciding on almost every provision in unemployment insurance. In nearly every feature of the program, there are multiple choices as to what the provision should be. What provision has been passed by the legislature represented a choice among alternatives based on a judgment, the judgment of the majority of the legislators.

FEDERAL–STATE CONTROVERSIES

When the unemployment insurance features of the Social Security Act were worked out, one of the most vigorous controversies developed over whether unemployment insurance should be a federal or a federal-state program.[13] Although the Social Security Act settled the issue by the creation of a federal–state system, many—including the authors—continued to hold the conviction that it should have been a federal system. In fact, the CIO throughout its history advocated the federalization of the system, and the Social Security Board, at one time during the 1940's, advocated federalization in its annual report. Although those who believed, or still believe, that a federal system would be superior have long since given up any hope of or effort to federalize the system, the ghost of federalization hovers over any proposal by the federal administration to improve the program. Proposals by federal authorities for any nation-wide change in the system are rarely considered purely on their merits. Any proposal that contains any measure of additional federal responsibility or control is charged as being an attack on states' rights and a "camel's nose under the tent" to federalize the system. In fact, almost every proposal for federal legislation, if proposed by federal authorities, is muddied by such suspicions.

Since national organizations of labor usually initiate or support proposals for federal legislation, employers generally oppose these proposals, falling back on the argument that they are a matter for state action. Also, the almost automatic opposition by employers to federal legislation for unemployment insurance is due partly to the traditional attitude of the business community that any federal program or legislation for improve-

13 See Chapter 6.

ment of a program is another move toward centralization of government, considered an evil in itself.

Unfortunately, some issues over federal legislation for unemployment insurance are also complicated by a fear on the part of state administrators that the national officials are seeking to increase their power and authority or to decrease that of the state administrators. Some, if not most, state administrators, therefore, align themselves with employers in opposition to measures for federal action to improve the program, not so much on the merits of the proposal from a program standpoint as on the question of whether it will increase federal authority. Labor, often frustrated in its effort to improve state laws because of the make-up of the state legislatures (a situation that will undoubtedly be improved by reapportionment in the state legislatures), in turn, aligns itself with the federal administration. Within these alignments such issues are seldom decided entirely on their merits.

SUMMARY

Unemployment insurance has demonstrated its worth and is accepted as an American institution. Such disagreements as now exist focus on specific provisions of the unemployment insurance program. General attitudes lie behind and influence the specific reasons for disagreements about particular provisions, and even the ideas that originally caused opposition to the program are still latent: that unemployment is a problem only during recessions; that much, if not most, unemployment in prosperous times is the fault of the worker; and that government intervention should be resisted.

Many of the issues in unemployment insurance are common to other social insurance and labor legislation. The resistance to enlargement or improvement of unemployment insurance is also a part of the resistance to the transition of the American economy from laissez faire capitalism to welfare capitalism.

The attitude that unemployment is the fault of the unemployed worker is still held by a surprisingly high proportion of American employers and employees. This frequently held assumption has led to the passage of provisions which deny benefits when there is any possibility that the worker may be responsible for his or her unemployment. This attitude is particularly strong among employers.

Employers were especially opposed to unemployment insurance before it was enacted because, for centuries, business had been progressively released from any feeling of responsibility for its employees. The imposition of a tax on employers to pay the cost of unemployment insurance was, therefore, strongly resisted because of the inference that employers were responsible for the unemployment of their workers. While employers now accept unemployment insurance, as far as possible most continue to seek to restrict their responsibility to paying the cost of benefits only to employees whom they have laid off. This has caused them to advocate many restrictions on the payment of unemployment benefits. Employers also resist increases in benefits which, they claim, will increase the cost of doing business, just as they resist any other increases in cost. The positive purpose of experience rating, to encourage the stabilization of employment, has been subordinated to employer policing of the system to prevent unwarranted payment of benefits.

Labor, on the other hand, naturally wants to get as much protection as possible from unemployment insurance and resists any efforts to restrict benefits. Unions have opposed experience rating of employer taxes largely because they feel that the desire to get lower tax rates influences employers to resist liberalizations in the program.

There are certain intangibles that increase the difficulty of management and labor agreeing on certain provisions. One of these is the effect of an increase in benefits on the incentive to work. Another is the subjective element in unemployment, the fact that one cannot see inside the mind of the unemployed worker and know whether he really wants to get back to work. Thus, disagreements continue as to whether or not unemployment insurance provisions should be designed to give the unemployed worker the benefit of the doubt. Periodic attacks on the program encourage the widespread feeling that there is much abuse in unemployment insurance, which has an effect on progress in legislation and reinforces the position of those who would further restrict the system.

Even if there were no conflicts of interest between management and labor with respect to unemployment insurance, it would be difficult to reach agreement on many specific provisions. This is partly due to the lack of adequate information on many questions. But even if information were complete, in the last analysis, personal judgment has to be used to determine many of the unemployment insurance provisions. For example, in determining what is an adequate benefit, it is necessary to first select a norm or criterion of adequacy. Judgment must then be exercised as to what goes into the norm. Finally, judgment must be used in determining whether enough persons are meeting the norm for the benefits to be adequate.

The fact that unemployment insurance in this country is mostly under a federal-state system aggravates certain controversies, particularly when increased federal authority or federal action to change standards in the state programs is involved. One or more of these many sources of disagreement enter, to a greater or lesser degree, into almost every unemployment insurance issue. While in the following chapters the issues in unemployment insurance will be examined on their merits, it will have to be realized that some of the factors just discussed may be more influential than the specific reasons given for or against particular issues in unemployment insurance.

Chapter 10

Issues in Coverage Extension

When the federal-state unemployment insurance system was started, it was assumed that all work subject to the risk of unemployment would eventually be covered by the system. The original social security bill submitted to Congress covered all wage and salaried workers except the employees of firms with a small number of employees. Even this exception was expected to be temporary. On principle, the Committee on Economic Security believed that all employees should be covered, regardless of the size of firm by which they were employed. The limitation was recommended because it was believed that initially it would be difficult to administer a program covering employers with very few workers.

In the original Social Security Act, Congress exempted from the federal unemployment tax employers who did not have at least eight employees in each of 20 weeks during a year. It also excluded large groups of workers: agricultural workers, domestic workers in private homes, employees of nonprofit organizations, and government employees. By and large, the states followed the federal coverage, except that almost half of them covered smaller firms.

In the ensuing years, Congress, on the one hand, narrowed the coverage of the tax in certain respects, and, on the other, removed the exclusion of some groups of workers. The principal restriction, made in 1948, limited the definition of employees covered. The principal enlargement in coverage, made in 1954, changed the exemption of small employers from those with eight or more to those with four or more employees in each of 20 or more weeks. It also provided unemployment compensation for federal civilian workers in 1954 and for ex-servicemen in 1958.

The states have largely followed the lead of the federal government in further restricting or extending coverage. Notable exceptions include the 20 states which now cover employers of one or more, and about half the states which have covered more-or-less limited numbers of state and local government employees. After 30 years of experience, however, only three fourths of those who work for others are covered by unemployment insurance.

Why has the extension of unemployment insurance coverage been so limited? The coverage of the Federal Old-Age, Survivors and Disability Insurance program has been progressively extended until practically the only workers who are not covered are government employees protected by more liberal civil service retirement systems. Why the difference? Is it because unemployment insurance is more difficult to administer for the uncovered groups? Is it because some of them do not incur much risk of unemployment, while everyone faces the risk of old age, disability, or death? Is it because OASDI is a federal program and the responsibility of one level of government while the federal-state unemployment insurance program has divided responsibility for action, which leads to "buck-passing" from one level of government to the other? As we discuss the problems of covering particular groups of workers, we shall see that the reasons for noncoverage vary from group to group.

EXTENT OF THE COVERAGE PROBLEM

Some perspective can be gained by looking at the number who are now protected and the number now excluded by the unemployment insurance program. The number of workers covered by unemployment insurance has grown from slightly less than 20 million in 1938 to 48.4 million in 1963 (see Table 10–1). Most of this increase results from growth in the labor

Table 10–1

Employment Covered by Unemployment Insurance
1938–63

Year	Total All Programs	State UI	Federal Civilian Government	Railroad
		(in 000's)		
1938	21,022	19,929		1,093
1940	24,291	23,096		1,195
1945	30,087	28,407		1,680
1950	34,308	32,887		1,421
1955	40,018	36,591	2,188	1,239
1960	46,334*	40,523	2,388	909
1963	48,434*	42,371†	2,536	790

* Includes Puerto Rico.
† Includes Unemployment Compensation for Ex-Servicemen Program, not shown separately.
Source: U.S. Department of Labor, Bureau of Employment Security, *Employ-ment and Wages of Workers Covered by State Unemployment Insurance Laws and Unemployment Compensation for Federal Employees, First Quarter 1964*, p. C–2.

force. Extensions of coverage to smaller firms, federal civilian employees, ex-servicemen, and other groups account for from 7 to 8 million of the increase.

The portion of employees covered by unemployment insurance varies from state to state. In 1962 it was estimated that the proportion of nonagricultural wage and salaried workers covered by state laws ranged from 61 percent in North and South Dakota to 100 percent in Hawaii. Thirty states covered less than 80 percent of nonagricultural workers. If agricultural workers had been included in the estimate, the percentages would, of course, have been lower and the range of the proportion covered would have been wider.

In 1963, about 15 million were not covered by unemployment insurance. These were in six major groups: firms with only a few employees (in most states); employees of nonprofit organizations; farm workers and agricultural processing workers; domestic or household workers in private homes; state and local government employees; those in borderline employment who are working on a commission or similar basis; and a few minor groups (Chart I).

Chart I

Unemployment Insurance Coverage of Wage and Salary Employment Calendar Year 1963

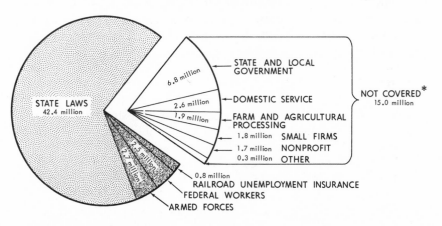

* Excludes clergymen and members of religious orders, student nurses, interns, and students employed in schools where enrolled.
Source: United States Department of Labor, Manpower Administration, Bureau of Employment Security, Unemployment Insurance Service.

PAST EXTENSIONS OF COVERAGE

Although some states have extended coverage over the years, this has been mainly coverage of smaller firms and coverage of state and local government employees. The major extensions of coverage have come from federal action in three areas: extension of coverage to smaller firms, federal civilian workers, and members of the Armed Forces. In 1954, Congress broadened the coverage of the federal unemployment tax from employers of eight or more in 20 weeks to employers of four or more in 20 weeks.[1]

[1] Public Law 83–767, approved September 1, 1954.

About half the states already had covered or had extended coverage to firms of this size or smaller firms. The remaining states changed their coverage to the larger coverage of the federal act or went further. The practical effect was to extend coverage to 1.4 million workers in 26 states.

In the same 1954 amendments, Congress added Title XV to the Social Security Act, providing for a program of unemployment compensation for federal civilian workers. In 1958, Congress extended this program to ex-servicemen who experience unemployment after separation from the Armed Forces.[2]

Since then, there have been only minor extensions of coverage. In 1960, Congress completed the coverage of "federal instrumentalities," effective in 1961, and gave coverage to employment on aircraft outside the United States, employment for commercial enterprises owned by nonprofit organizations (the so-called "feeder" organizations), and most employment for fraternal, agricultural, horticultural, and employee benefit organizations.

The states also made some minor extensions of coverage, and several states covered nonprofit organizations and agricultural workers. An increasing number of states either covered the employees of state and local governments on a compulsory basis or permitted election of coverage; however, less than a tenth of all such workers are covered. In 1963, only five states made any extensions of coverage and these were minor in character.

It appears, therefore, that, with the possible exception of state and local government employees, there will be no major extension in coverage unless some new approaches are taken to the problems involved.[3] Apparently, a fresh look at all noncovered groups needs to be taken. Have labor market or other changes affected the need for coverage of certain groups so that there is a stronger or weaker case for covering them? With electronic data processing, is it becoming administratively more feasible to cover the groups that heretofore have presented administrative difficulties for coverage? Are there alternative ways to cover them? Each of the major noncovered groups will be taken up in turn to see what the answers are to these and other questions.

WHO SHOULD BE COVERED?

As a matter of principle, everyone who seeks gainful employment should be protected against the risk of loss of income due to unemployment. If anyone is unemployed and seeking work, it is presumed that he needs the income from a job. If he cannot find work, it is presumed that he needs some substitute type of income.

[2] Public Law 85–848, approved August 28, 1958.
[3] Both the Republican and Democratic Administrations have been trying to secure federal extension of coverage to employers of one or more and to nonprofit organizations since 1954, but without success up to the time of writing.

This principle could be applied even to the self-employed. The Monthly Survey of the Labor Force of the United States Department of Labor shows a small number of self-employed among the unemployed.[4] But, again, as in other areas of unemployment insurance, it is necessary to qualify statements of principle when considering the self-employed. Even though some self-employed persons become unemployed, they would present problems of coverage because of the difficulty of determining what earned income they have lost and whether they are genuinely unemployed.[5] For example, if a self-employed storekeeper operates at a loss until he "eats up" his assets and finally closes his store, he is then unemployed. But how could one measure his income loss and provide partial compensation for it? Or suppose a self-employed person operates a real estate business and fails to make a sale for three months? He has suffered a complete loss of income during these three months. Should he be considered as unemployed? Or, if he is defined as unemployed only when he quits trying to sell real estate, again, how can his income loss be determined? What about farmers with one crop sold at the end of the growing season, who are idle most of the time in the winter? It is obvious that, for practical reasons, the self-employed cannot be brought under unemployment insurance.[6]

Another category of workers must also be dropped from consideration—unpaid family workers. When the head of the family no longer has work for them, how can they be compensated for income loss when previously they received no salary?

No attempt has ever been made to provide unemployment insurance coverage for still another class of employees: workers, and particularly youths, who are entering the labor market for the first time and have not yet found employment. They are unemployed in the sense that they cannot find work. In fact, unemployed youth who have never had a job represent one of the most serious social problems. Yet, it would do serious violence to the insurance principle to consider protecting them through unemployment insurance until they have had a job in covered employment and have suffered an income loss through the loss of a job.

The statement that there should be universal coverage must accordingly be qualified: unemployment insurance should cover all persons who are working for others and so presumably face the risk of unemployment. In addition, there are large numbers who work on a commission or similar basis who should also be covered.

[4] About 2.5 percent of the unemployed each month are self-employed or unpaid family workers.

[5] In California, an employer subject to coverage of his employees under the law may apply for coverage of his own services. If his election is approved, his wages for purposes of contributions and benefits are deemed to be $1,410 per quarter and his contribution rate is fixed at 1.25 percent of such wages.

[6] The Servicemen's Readjustment Allowance program of 1944 paid self-employed veterans of World War II $100 a month less earnings for the month with unfortunate results. A number of self-employed, especially farmers, drew benefits under conditions that brought criticism of the program.

COVERAGE OF SMALL EMPLOYERS

Eliminating the exemptions of employers with a small number of employees from the federal unemployment tax and from the unemployment insurance laws of all states is the most obvious and feasible step in the extension of unemployment insurance coverage. Many states do not have such exemptions and have demonstrated the feasibility of covering employers with one, two, or three workers. As of January 1, 1966, 21 states covered employers of one or more, seven without any limitation and 14 with other conditions imposed such as a minimum payroll in a calendar quarter. Four states covered employers with three or more under varying conditions.[7] The balance followed the federal act in covering employers of four or more in 20 or more weeks.[8] Puerto Rico covered employers of four or more at any time.

If the exemption of small employers were completely removed, as was proposed in the 1965 Administration bill (H. R. 8282), it would add about 1.8 million workers to the unemployment insurance system.[9]

In the initial stages of the program, the principal reason for limiting coverage was administrative. It was believed that initially it would be too difficult and too expensive to collect taxes from the large number of very small employers and to receive accurate reports from them as to employment and wages. The states that have successfully covered employers of one or more at any time have demonstrated that these reasons for excluding small employers are no longer valid. Large states and small states, states with dense population and states with sparse population cover employers of one or more.

Actually, if employers with one or more employees *at any time* are covered, the procedure is simplified. The need is eliminated for employer audits or investigations to determine whether specific employers are covered. In borderline cases, it is no longer necessary for the state to wait until the end of the year to determine whether the employer is covered. Determination of benefits is speeded up in many cases where previously it was necessary to determine whether the employer of the claimant was covered by the law. Following the initial step of covering numbers of employers who were not previously covered, the only problem is the larger volume of employers from whom taxes must be collected.[10]

---

[7] Arizona and Vermont covered employers of three or more in each of 20 weeks; Connecticut, three in each of 13 weeks; Ohio, three at any one time.

[8] Eight of these also had alternative measures of coverage, usually in terms of payroll, designed to cover larger employers who employed workers for a shorter part of the year. For example, Nebraska covered employers with a payroll of $10,000 in a quarter.

[9] If the federal unemployment tax act were amended to cover employers of one or more at any time, it would cover an additional million workers who are now covered in the states with broader coverage of small employers.

[10] See Vernon G. Graham, "California's Experience in Changing to Coverage of One or More," *Employment Security Review*, Vol. XXI, No. 8 (August, 1954), pp. 15–17, 25; William I. Walsh, "Maryland's Experience in Changing Coverage of Employers," *Employment Security Review*, Vol. XXI, No. 8 (August, 1954), pp. 12–15.

The administrative problem of covering small employers should not be minimized. The Bureau of Employment Security estimated that 1,041,500 employers were exempted by the statutory employer coverage provisions in effect in 1961. Coverage of employers of one or more at any time would increase the number of covered employers by one third for the country as a whole, and by an average of 54.2 percent in the 33 states with more restricted coverage.

However, with modern electronic data processing equipment, it becomes less of a problem and less costly to secure and process taxes and wage reports from small employers. Employers of one or more at any time have been covered from the start by the federal OASDI program with much less advanced data processing equipment than is available today.[11] Administrative feasibility, the original reason for excluding small employers, is, therefore, no longer valid.

A second argument is also pressed by the opponents of extension of coverage; namely, that employment with small employers is too much of a risk to be insurable. They point to the high number of business failures as evidence that small employers would be a liability to the system. In rebuttal, it can be said that, although there may be a higher turnover rate of small employers while they are getting started, once they are established, a higher percentage provide stable employment than do large employers. In an analysis of employer accounts distributed by size of payroll in 1953, 23.4 percent of the firms with less than $5,000 of taxable payroll were paying the "standard" rate of 2.7 percent because they had been covered for less than three years, while only 13.5 percent of firms with taxable payrolls of $50,000 or over were paying the standard rate. This reflects the high initial turnover of small employers. Of those in business long enough to have experience rates, 23.6 percent of the smaller firms had rates of 2.7 percent or higher, while only 13.5 percent of the large firms had experience rates of 2.7 percent or higher. At the other end of the rating scale, however, a larger percentage of the small than the large firms had rates of less than 1 percent (57.4 and 48.5 percent respectively).[12]

Fairly comparable results were obtained from a study by 14 states covering employers with one or more in 1958 and 1959.[13]

Seven of the 14 states also tabulated data on the beneficiary experience of workers by size of firm (see Table 10–2). In five of the seven states, a larger proportion of the workers in small firms than in large firms drew some benefits. However, this did not materially affect the total proportion of

[11] The employer coverage under OASDI helps ease the problem of covering employers under unemployment insurance. Many states accept carbon copies or duplicate punch cards of employer reports for OASDI. In fact, the Federal Internal Revenue Service receives many federal unemployment tax returns from small employers not covered by the federal unemployment tax and has the added administrative burden of making refunds to them.

[12] *Unemployment Compensation*, Hearings *op. cit.*, p. 65, table 6.

[13] United States Department of Labor, Bureau of Employment Security, *Selected Charts and Tables Relating to Unemployment Insurance Legislative Planning*, September, 1961, p. 25, table C–5.

Table 10–2

Beneficiary Experience of Workers, by Size of Firm,[a]
Seven States Covering Employers of One or More Workers

State	Total	Proportion of Workers Drawing Benefits[b]		Benefits Drawn Average Weekly Benefit		Average Duration (Weeks)	
		Small Firms	Large Firms	Small Firms	Large Firms	Small Firms	Large Firms
Arkansas[c]	15.6	12.5	16.0	$ 21.25	$ 21.96	11.2	11.7
Delaware[d]	4.8	9.1	4.5	....	....	8.6	8.5
District of Columbia[e] ..	6.0	7.2	5.9[f]	236.02[f]	265.10	...	...
Idaho[g]	19.5	33.1	17.8	31.45	35.76	12.3	12.0
Montana[e]	26.5	55.8	21.7	24.48	28.15	16.1	14.0
Utah[c]	13.9	20.2	13.3	29.46	32.68	11.1	10.7
Washington[e]	24.1	17.7	24.7	29.18	30.73	12.5	12.1

[a] For Idaho, small firms are those with fiscal 1958 taxable payrolls under $10,000; for other states, firms with fewer than four workers. Size of firm and total covered employment by size of firm based on employment in the following periods: Arkansas, March, 1959; Delaware, February, 1959; District of Columbia and Utah, March, 1958; Idaho, average month, fiscal 1958; Montana, first quarter 1959; and Washington, September, 1958.
[b] Relationship, by size of firm, between total covered workers in a month and total beneficiaries in a one-year period.
[c] Calendar 1958 experience.
[d] February 1959 experience.
[e] Fiscal year 1959 experience.
[f] Average benefits paid per beneficiary during fiscal year 1959.
[g] Fiscal year 1958 experience.
Source: U.S. Department of Labor, Bureau of Employment Security, *Selected Charts and Tables relating to Unemployment Insurance Planning*, September, 1961 (mimeo), p. 24, table C–4.

workers in the states drawing benefits. With the exception of one state, Montana, the higher unemployment in small firms did not raise the proportion of all workers drawing benefits as much as 2 percent above the proportion of workers in large firms who drew benefits. In all of the seven states, the average benefit amount was smaller for former employees of small firms, but not significantly so. The average duration was slightly longer in six of the seven states. The results of this study must be accepted with some caution, since they represent experience during an economic recession, which may have affected small employers more than large. The higher costs may also be due to the large number of small firms that are in the construction industry. If, however, the results of this study are representative, the somewhat more serious unemployment that was indicated in most states was not enough to significantly affect total costs in the state. In addition, this information underlines the need of workers in small firms for unemployment insurance protection.

An additional argument raised *against* federal extension of coverage is that the states should be left free to experiment and fit their legislation to the needs of the state. A counterargument holds that small firms are very much alike in every state so that one state has no more justification for excluding small employers than any other. All types and sizes of states cover employers of one or more workers.

It is true that federal action in advance of state action is not essential. Interstate competition is certainly not a factor in determining whether small employers should be covered, since practically all small firms are local in character. According to testimony by James T. O'Connell,[14] 45 percent in 1959 were in retail trade, 9 percent in finance, real estate, and insurance, and 26 percent in service activities. The other 20 percent was broadly distributed, with a large proportion serving as secretaries or receptionists in the offices of doctors, dentists, and lawyers.

Dr. Richard A. Lester has suggested: "Experience in many states indicates that expansion of coverage to employers of two or one is strongly resisted in the State legislatures, partly, it appears, because lawyer legislators do not wish to cover their secretaries or clerical assistants."[15] If this is true, it would argue for consideration of coverage of small firms through federal action, since Congressmen would not be personally affected as much as state legislators, and, it is hoped, would take a broader view of the question.

The self-interest of the federal government should also lead it to cover employers of one or more workers. The administrative cost of the coverage of employers not covered by the federal unemployment tax is nevertheless paid out of the proceeds of that tax. If the federal tax covered employers of one or more, taxes received from the small employers in the states with broader coverage than the federal tax could be used for the state's administrative costs of covering them.

Another aspect, not often recognized, pertains to the exemption of employers who do not have four or more employees *in each of at least 20 weeks in the year*. The latter part of the exclusion may exempt very large firms indeed. In states that have this exemption, an employer can employ hundreds if he does not employ them in more than 19 weeks in the year. In fact, many large seasonal hotels are open for less than 20 weeks just to avoid coverage.[16] And such a provision does not operate solely as a means of exempting seasonal employers. As an extreme example, a construction employer can start a project 19 weeks before the end of one calendar year and complete it in the nineteenth week of the next and not be covered. It is therefore important to look at the total provision under which employers are covered or excluded. This is the reason that eight states that have the standard coverage of employers of four or more in 20 weeks stipulate alternative provisions designed to cover larger employers who operate for shorter periods. It is also the reason that many of the states that

[14] *Unemployment Compensation*, Hearings, *op. cit.*, p. 22.

[15] Richard A. Lester, *The Economics of Unemployment Compensation* (Princeton: Industrial Relations Section, Princeton University, 1962), p. 126.

[16] On the other hand, some seasonal hotels plan to keep their employees on the payroll long enough to qualify for benefits. For a discussion of the problems of seasonal unemployment, see Chapter 12.

cover smaller employers cover them if they employ the specified number for shorter periods—many if the employer has an employee at any time—or use the amount of payroll as a measure of coverage.

There is some justification for providing that small employers will be exempted unless they have had a minimum amount of employment or payrolls. As has already been stated, 13 of the states that covered employers of one or more in 1964 specified added conditions, the most usual being a minimum payroll of several hundred dollars during a calendar quarter. Such limitations eliminate casual or incidental employment, most of which probably is never reported. A payroll requirement rather than a time requirement also makes it easier both for the employer and the state agency to determine whether an unemployed worker is covered.

The foregoing adds up to a conclusion that there is no sound reason for excluding all small employers. There may be some merit in excluding employers who on a very casual or intermittent basis hire a person for a day or two, by having some minimum payroll or employment requirement. Aside from this, the employees of very small firms should be covered in all the states, as they are now in two fifths of the states.

NONPROFIT ORGANIZATIONS

Employees of nonprofit organizations are the second largest group for which the federal executive branch has been urging coverage in recent years.

The recommendations of the Committee on Economic Security did not specify the exemption of nonprofit organizations. This exemption was added to the bill by the House Committee on Ways and Means without any explanation in the report. The president of the American Hospital Association was the only witness in the Committee's hearings asking exemption from any taxes imposed under the bill, but evidently his request prevailed.

Originally, the exemption was limited to service in the employ of nonprofit religious, charitable, scientific, literary, or educational institutions subject to income tax exemption. In 1939, a number of other types of nonprofit organizations were exempted, including fraternal, agricultural, horticultural, and employee mutual benefit organizations. The 1960 amendments restored the latter organizations to coverage, except that individuals who earned less than $50 a quarter from such organizations were still exempted.[17] The original exemption was also narrowed by covering "feeder" organizations; that is, organizations operated for profit whose income is used by the parent nonprofit organization.

Only four states cover service in nonprofit organizations that are exempted under the federal act: Colorado, the District of Columbia, Alaska,

---

[17] The exemption now is in terms of service for nonprofit organizations described in Section 501 (e) (3) of the Internal Revenue Code which are exempt from federal income tax under Section 501 (a) of that Code.

and Hawaii. All four exempt the clergy and members of religious orders; the District of Columbia goes further and exempts all employees of religious organizations. Colorado exempts all professional employees of nonprofit hospitals and members of the faculty of a nonprofit college or university. Those earning less than a specified amount ($45 or $50 in a quarter) are exempted in Alaska, the District of Columbia, and Hawaii. Colorado exempts certain part-time workers and those employed less than 12 weeks in seasonal camps. The four laws differ in other minor respects.

Seven states in 1961 made their exemption contingent on exemption from the federal income tax and two on exemption from the federal unemployment tax. Most of the other states include any service covered by the federal unemployment tax and so, automatically, included nonprofit organizations covered by the 1960 federal amendments.

In bills sponsored by the executive branch since 1958, the federal government has proposed coverage of employees of nonprofit organizations except members of the clergy and religious orders and handicapped workers in sheltered workshops. The present exemptions of certain students and interns, and employees who earn less than $50 a quarter would be continued. After hearings in 1959, the House Ways and Means Committee voted against such extension of coverage, but the proposal has been included in the Administration bills introduced since the mid-1950's.

Nonprofit organizations were originally exempted on the basis of their traditional freedom from taxation, and because of the financial difficulties they would experience in paying the required taxes. In the 1959 hearings before the House Committee on Ways and Means the testimony for continued exemption stressed the lack of unemployment risk for employees of nonprofit organizations which, accordingly, would be subjected to unnecessary taxation, at least until their taxes would be reduced through experience rating.

The nub of the question of covering nonprofit organizations is whether there is an unemployment risk for nonprofit employees. Unfortunately, information on this is inadequate and much that exists consists of statistics from which only inferences can be drawn. No information is available on the experience with coverage in Colorado and the District of Columbia and only limited data on the experience with coverage in Alaska and Hawaii. In addition, the experience in Alaska and Hawaii may not be typical. The following available information, however, throws some light on the question of coverage.

Employment rates in different kinds of nonprofit institutions were secured from OASDI data by the Bureau of Employment Security. In the first quarter of 1956, nonprofit organizations that had voluntarily elected coverage under OASDI reported total employment of 1,361,158 employees. Of these, the largest group was in hospitals—646,463, and the next largest group was in colleges and universities—201,685. Religious organizations reported 122,112 and charities 99,315. By size of employing units, 36,000 with less than 100 employees employed 325,000 workers. The 325 units with 500 or more employees employed a total of 307,000.

The OASDI data has limitations. Not all nonprofit organizations have elected coverage under OASDI, and there has been some growth in employment, especially in hospitals, since the above tabulation. As Chart I illustrates, an estimated 1.7 million employed in 1963 by nonprofit organizations were exempt from coverage under unemployment insurance.[18]

In a sample tabulation of workers covered by OASDI in 1952, nonprofit workers showed less year-round employment than all workers covered by OASDI. The proportion of the nonprofit workers with four quarters of coverage was 43.5 percent as compared with 66.4 percent of all workers in 1952. On the other hand, 25.9 percent of the nonprofit workers had only one quarter of coverage as compared with 10.8 percent of all covered workers. The percentage of those with two quarters of coverage was 18.8 in 1952; those with three quarters of coverage was 11.8. The high proportion with less than year-round employment with nonprofit organizations probably indicates both high turnover and a large amount of temporary and seasonal employment, such as employment in financial campaigns and in summer camps. No figures are available to indicate whether the large number with less than four quarters worked in other types of employment in the balance of the year, nor the number who were available for work only a part of the year; thus, this information as indicative of the extent of unemployment should be discounted considerably.

In order to find out how much of an unemployment problem nonprofit organizations have in 1961, a special committee of the National Social Welfare Assembly made a survey of national organizations with state and local units in California, Illinois, and Pennsylvania. The Committee reported: "The central finding is that employees of non-profit organizations do experience significant unemployment, although less than the labor force as a whole."[19]

The National Social Welfare Assembly study did not include hospitals. Turnover in nonprofit hospitals was 60 percent in 1955.[20] Turnover data are of limited value, especially in the case of hospitals which seldom reduce their personnel. Such data would include, however, some quitting for good cause, which, if it resulted in unemployment, might be compensable under unemployment insurance. Turnover data may also include some layoffs of temporary personnel hired during peak loads of patients.

One final piece of inferential information: covered proprietary hospitals had a significantly lower tax rate than the average tax rate of all covered

[18] This estimate did not include members of religious orders, student nurses, interns, and students employed in schools where enrolled.
[19] National Social Welfare Assembly, *Report, Special Committee on Unemployment Insurance Coverage of the Committee on Social Issues and Policies, January, 1964* (New York, 1964), p. 7.
[20] E. Levine, and Stuart Wright, "Analyzing Turnover among Hospital Personnel," Part Two, *Hospitals*, September, 1957.

employers in a 14-state study in 1961.[21] It can be inferred that nonprofit hospitals, if covered by unemployment insurance, would also have low tax rates as a result of low unemployment.

The experience of Alaska and Hawaii would certainly indicate that the unemployment risk is low in nonprofit organizations. Benefit payments in Alaska in 1955 represented only 0.3 percent of taxable wages in nonprofit organizations. Hawaii had an even lower cost rate in 1958, with total benefits representing only 0.17 percent of taxable wages. The cost rate by types of nonprofit organizations was 0.27 percent for religious, 0.07 for charitable, 0.09 for hospital, 0.25 for elementary school, and 0.70 for college organizations.

All the data given above indicate that there is *some* unemployment arising out of nonprofit employment. Other industries, such as insurance and public utilities, that have a very low rate of unemployment are covered by unemployment insurance.

The most serious objection to coverage of nonprofit organizations is that they would be required, in view of their low unemployment, to build up unnecessary reserves before they could get experience rating. This problem has been diminished in those states that took advantage of the 1954 amendment to the Federal Unemployment Tax permitting a lower rating after one year of coverage. Not all the states, however, have shortened the period from the former requirement of three years of coverage, and most of those that have amended their laws still require something more than a year of coverage. Even with a lower tax rate after a year, all nonprofit organizations would accumulate a reserve of 2.7 percent of taxable payrolls during the first year. If the state does not provide "zero" tax rates, additional reserves would be accumulated by some institutions in subsequent years.[22]

In order to get around the problem of excess financing, New York and California have proposed that nonprofit organizations be covered on a reimbursement basis, that is, pay for unemployment benefits that have actually been disbursed. The United States Department of Labor's opinion was that this would not meet the experience rating requirements of the federal act. Senator Jacob Javits of New York accordingly introduced a bill in 1962 to amend the act to permit reimbursement. The Department of Labor also objected on policy grounds to financing by reimbursement, pointing out that there would be no spreading of the risk. It contended that most unemployment would occur when the nonprofit organization was least able to pay, since most layoffs occur because of failure of nonprofit organizations to raise their budgets or because of the closing of the organization. The New York agency countered by proposing that the general

[21] United States Department of Labor, Bureau of Employment Security, *Financial Experience of Covered Hospitals as Compared with Total State Financial Experience in Selected States*, 1961.

[22] The portion of the federal unemployment tax not creditable (0.4 percent of taxable payrolls in 1964) would still have to be paid.

unemployment fund of the state pay the cost if the nonprofit organization failed to reimburse the state. They argued that this should not be unacceptable to other employers contributing to the fund, most of whom are already contributing to one or more of the nonprofit organizations that would be covered.

In 1965 the federal administration evidently agreed that alternative methods of financing for nonprofit organizations was desirable or, at least, should be permitted. The 1965 Administration bill (H.R. 8282) provided that a state may use special methods for determining the contributions payable by nonprofit organizations; this would permit a state to provide that nonprofit organizations would reimburse the state after benefits are paid. It further provided that the state could reduce contribution rates for nonprofit organizations on any basis it chose without regard to federal requirements for other employers. This proposal, if it becomes law, would leave little reason for a state not covering nonprofit organizations and thus protecting their workers against such unemployment as may occur.

If nonprofit organizations are covered by unemployment insurance, it would still be necessary to exempt members of the clergy and members of religious orders. Certainly those religious workers who have taken the vow of poverty should be exempted. There is also some justification for exempting interns, student nurses, and students employed by the schools that they are attending, although for many students loss of such employment would spell the loss of ability to continue in school and the need for finding another job.

The National Social Welfare Assembly study would indicate that some seasonal workers, such as students acting as camp counsellors, should be exempted from coverage. On the other hand, large numbers of these temporary and seasonal workers who are hired and separated each year, no doubt are in the labor market the year around. There should be no blanket exemption for such workers; reliance should be placed on qualifying requirements for benefits toward those not regularly in the labor force.

The United States Department of Labor's proposal to exempt clients in sheltered workshops recognizes that these are handicapped workers not generally considered to be "able to work" and, thus, are ineligible for benefits. Exemption of part-time workers earning less than $50 a quarter should also be continued. These, however, are details. The coverage of nonprofit organizations, many of which have been in the forefront in advocating unemployment insurance, is long overdue, and will become increasingly important as employment in nonprofit organizations further expands.

AGRICULTURAL WORKERS

The coverage of agricultural workers involves diverse problems with respect to regular, seasonal, and borderline occupations. The original exclusion in the Social Security Act consisted of two words: "agricultural labor." In 1939, the Social Security Board recommended that large agricultural employers be covered by unemployment insurance and that the exception of agricultural labor "apply only to the services of a farmhand employed by a small farmer to do the ordinary work connected with a farm."[23] Instead, Congress enacted an elaborate definition of agricultural labor that: (1) included the handling, processing, storage, and transportation of agricultural commodities to market if incidental to ordinary farming operations, or in the case of fruits and vegetables, incidental to the preparation for market; (2) expanded the concept of a farm to include greenhouses and fur-bearing animal farms; and (3) defined as agricultural a miscellaneous group of activities, including the harvesting of maple sugar, turpentine and other gum naval stores, mushroom growing, poultry hatching, cotton ginning, and certain irrigation operations.

In 1950, Congress removed from the definition of agricultural labor and covered under the OASDI program, services performed off the farm, particularly with respect to drying, packing, and processing plants. The definition under the federal unemployment tax, however, was left unchanged, so that about a quarter of a million workers in "factories" off the farm are still excluded from coverage. An attempt to extend coverage of unemployment insurance to such workers was made by the federal Administration in 1954, but without success. Representatives of several fruit growers' associations objected to the extension of coverage on the grounds that the change would discriminate against small farmers whose grading and packing of fruit was done by cooperative or commercial packing firms, in contrast to the large grower who packed his own produce and would continue to be exempt. Another objection was that most of the packing was seasonal employment. The small added cost of unemployment insurance coverage of the packing houses, however, should not have materially affected the cost to small growers of having their products packed off the farm. States could handle the seasonality of the packing work, by following procedures similar to those set for other food packing and processing plants that operate on a seasonal basis.

Both California and Florida, which have large numbers of workers in processing operations, have a narrower definition than the federal act. The District of Columbia act has never excluded agricultural labor, but this has had little meaning in the virtual absence of agricultural operations. Under its regular law, Hawaii covers employers of 20 or more agricultural workers in each of 20 or more weeks, but permits them to elect coverage under its separate agricultural labor unemployment insurance law. Puerto Rico, which had an unemployment insurance law for sugar workers, brought them under the new more comprehensive law passed in 1962. The other states, however, have generally followed the federal definition of agricultural labor, either by statutory definition or by regulation.

[23] Social Security, Hearings before the Committee on Ways and Means, House of Representatives, 76th Cong., 1st sess. (Washington, D.C.: U.S. Government Printing Office, 1939), Vol. 1, p. 11.

Agricultural labor was originally excluded mainly on the grounds that coverage was not administratively feasible. The broadening of the definition in 1939 was largely the result of pressures by agricultural interests. Although most agricultural labor was covered by the OASDI program in 1950, which should considerably diminish the administrative problem of collecting unemployment insurance taxes for agricultural workers, administrative problems would still remain, especially with respect to the coverage of migrant seasonal labor. Economic considerations, however, loom larger.

It is claimed that there is a shortage of year-round farm labor so that no unemployment problem exists in their case; on the other hand, it is claimed that seasonal labor is composed of either (1) local labor that temporarily comes into the labor market or (2) migrant interstate labor that works for so short a time in each state that a worker could not acquire enough covered employment to qualify under individual state laws. For them, it would be necessary either to be covered under an interstate agreement or a national system.

It is often assumed that, with the great shrinkage in the number of people working on farms, the number of hired agricultural laborers has also greatly diminished. The number of self-employed farmers dropped from 4,973,000 in 1947 to 2,366,000 in 1964 and the number of unpaid family workers dropped from about 1,677,000 to 813,000 in the same period. But the number of hired farm workers has not significantly declined. While there have been fluctuations from year to year, the number of wage and salary workers in agriculture, averaging 1,582,000 in 1964,[24] was only 75,000 less in that year than in 1947.

Nevertheless, there have been great changes in the employment of agricultural workers. Increased mechanization, especially of harvesting operations, has reduced the need for harvest labor. Importation of Mexican laborers, particularly in the states bordering Mexico,[25] the importation of some British West Indians, and the migration of Puerto Ricans to the mainland has created additional employment problems. Today, agricultural workers are still employed seasonally for the cultivation and harvest periods. The great majority work on a relatively few farms, since the number of small farms has sharply declined, and small units have consolidated into large farms that can afford expensive machinery and modern scientific techniques. The need for year-round farm workers has decreased, except in dairying, greenhouses, and other continuous operations. Because of the decline of year-round workers and the increase in the seasonal farm labor,

[24] *Manpower Report of the President and A Report on Manpower Requirements, Resources, Utilization, and Training by the United States Department of Labor,* Transmitted to the Congress, March, 1965 (Washington, D.C.: U.S. Government Printing Office), p. 200, table 8.

[25] This source of labor has been drastically reduced, except for specialized workers, since the expiration at the end of 1964 of the importation program under "Public Law 78."

total man-hours of farm labor declined by one third in the 1950's. During the same period, the use of mechanical power and agricultural machinery increased by one fifth.

State Studies of Agricultural Employment

In order to get a factual basis for determining the need for and feasibility of covering agricultural labor under present-day conditions, the Bureau of Employment Security obtained the cooperation of several states in making detailed studies of agricultural labor. The results of the surveys in Arizona, Connecticut, and New York, were available at the time of writing.[26]

Since New York is a good example of a state with diversified farming and Arizona an example of a state with large numbers of migrant seasonal farm workers, the results of the surveys in these two states are summarized below, and are useful for some insights into the administrative feasibility of coverage.

From their experience, it would appear that securing adequate reports on employed workers would not pose much of a problem. Both New York and Arizona reported that employers kept better records than had been expected. New York thought that this was mainly due to the prevailing method of paying wages by check. New York farm employers paid 81 percent of their regular workers and 74 percent of seasonal workers by check.[27] In Arizona, when farmers directly employed workers, they paid 99 percent of the regular workers and 91 percent of the seasonal workers by check. Arizona reported, however, that crew leaders, who employed most of the workers used, paid mostly in cash, which would present more problems if the farm workers were covered. Crew leaders could not or would not give as much information on earnings of the members of their crew as the farmers could. New York gave a similar report on crew leaders.

The fact that crew leaders ordinarily have a sizable number of workers should make it more possible to identify them and secure their reports.[28] Crew leaders are responsible for keeping records and making reports for

[26] Research and Information, Employment Security Division, Connecticut Labor Department, *A Study of the Feasibility of Covering Farm Workers under Unemployment Compensation* (Hartford, Conn., July, 1961), 239 pp.

Research and Reports Section, Unemployment Compensation Division, Employment Security Commission of Arizona, *Study of Employment and Unemployment of Agricultural Workers* (Phoenix, Ariz., December, 1960), 3 vols.

Institute of Labor Relations and Social Security, New York University, in cooperation with the Division of Employment, New York State Department of Labor, and the Bureau of Employment Security, United States Department of Labor, *The Pattern of Farm Employment in New York State: Implications for Unemployment Insurance Coverage* (New York: New York University, 1962), 75 pp.

[27] Regular workers were defined as those who worked or expected to work 150 days or more in a year; seasonal workers were those who worked or expected to work less than 150 days.

[28] In New York, 168 crew leaders employed 7,954 workers. In Arizona, 630 crew leaders employed over 40,000 workers, with few employing less than ten workers and 10 percent employing 100 or more.

OASDI for all workers whom they pay more than $150 a year, and this should facilitate getting their reports for unemployment insurance.[29] The studies concluded that crew leaders would be able to provide adequate reports, but enforcement of unemployment insurance regulations, and education as to the crew leaders' responsibilities would be at least an initial problem for the program's administrators.

One such problem would arise over the reporting of perquisites. The most common perquisite for regular farm workers is the provision of housing or room and board. Arizona employers provided this perquisite for 70 percent of regular workers and New York for over one half. In both states, fewer than half of the seasonal workers were provided with perquisites which were largely in the form of transportation and produce. The New York report recommends that only board and housing be defined as perquisites and other perquisites be considered as fringe benefits that need not be reported. The housing and food items were the only ones that would substantially add to the wages that the workers could have counted toward benefits.

One of the discoveries favorable to coverage was that there was less mobility of farm workers than had been expected. About seven out of ten regular workers in New York, and one out of five seasonal workers were employed by only one farmer. It was rare for either a regular or seasonal worker to work for more than two employers. In Arizona, also, about two thirds of the regular workers had only one farm employer. More than half of the seasonal workers, however, worked for three or more employers.

The proportions of regular workers (those with over 150 days of employment with one employer) was over 70 percent for farm operators in New York, but only slightly over a third in Arizona. On the average, regular workers held jobs for a high proportion of the weeks in the year: 49 in Arizona and 47.2 in New York. About 12 percent of the regular workers in New York combined other jobs with farm work, working a shorter period in agriculture and averaging 21.3 weeks in other employment.

Seasonal workers in Arizona averaged 37 weeks of some kind of employment, of which 21 weeks was agricultural work within the state. In New York, seasonal workers held their in-state farm jobs an average of only 13.8 weeks and spent 22.8 weeks in other in-state employment. Female seasonal workers averaged 10.4 weeks of farm work, and only a small number held other jobs in the state, which lasted an average of 37 weeks for those who were so employed.

In New York, almost 80 percent of the seasonal workers reported some unemployment. However, during 70 percent of the weeks they did not work, they were not seeking other employment. New York estimates that unemployed seasonal workers looked for work an average of only 5.5 weeks during the year.

[29] Public Law 88–582, requiring interstate crew leaders to register with the United States Department of Labor, should also help overcome this problem.

In Arizona, no breakdown is given between regular and seasonal workers as to the average number of weeks unemployed. It was found that those unemployed who sought work averaged 15 weeks of unemployment; those who withdrew from the labor force were out of work an average of 18 weeks.

Each state estimated the cost of covering agricultural workers on the basis of their own law. In Arizona, it was estimated that benefits for regular workers would have cost 1.4 percent of taxable payroll in the year of the survey; benefits to seasonal workers would have cost 7.91 percent of payroll. The average cost for all agricultural workers in Arizona would have been 3.77 percent. However, after making allowance for the benefits their workers would have received on the basis of other than agricultural work, the average cost would have been 2.78 percent of payroll. In New York, the estimated costs were: for regular workers, 2.73 percent of taxable payrolls, for seasonal workers, 4.55 percent. The combined average cost for both types of workers was 3.27 percent.

It would appear from the data given above that the cost of covering agricultural workers would not be prohibitive, at least for regular workers. The costs for seasonal workers could be lower if they were covered by some kind of interstate scheme under which all their employment could be combined. This, of course, leads to other problems.

On the basis of these studies, the authors would conclude that regular agricultural workers could be and should be covered immediately by unemployment insurance. The surveys show that regular workers still experience a considerable amount of unemployment, although they average a considerable number of weeks on their jobs. The amount is not excessive, however, and unemployment benefits should not be unduly costly. It might be well, then, to begin by covering only regular agricultural workers, even though many seasonal workers are more in need of coverage.[30]

A large part of seasonal work is performed by students and housewives who enter the labor market only temporarily and do not need coverage. Qualifying requirements for benefits should be high enough to exclude such workers. Those who most need unemployment insurance are the migrant workers who rely solely on agricultural labor for a livelihood. Before they are covered, however, many problems will have to be met: securing data to test the common assumption that they only want to work during the farm season; arranging to combine records of their earnings in different states; and providing more continuity of employment through scheduling their movements from place to place as crops ripen. Most difficult of all, would be to work out some interstate or national plan for covering migrant labor.

[30] It may be necessary for administrative reasons to collect taxes on all the employment of farm employers who are covered and restrict benefits for seasonal workers by qualifying employment requirements or special seasonal provisions, as is done to restrict benefits for seasonal workers in other industries.

A "wage combining plan" for combining the wages earned in presently covered employment in several states has been worked out. Agreed to by almost all the states, this interstate "wage combining plan" probably offers the most promising way of making coverage of migrant workers practicable, although a national plan would be less cumbersome. However, the special problems of dealing with seasonal workers discussed in Chapter 12, would probably continue.

In addition to starting by insuring only regular farm workers, it might be desirable also to start by covering only larger farm employers. With the increasing concentration of farming in large units, a large proportion of farm labor could be insured if only farm units were covered that had, say, four or more regular employees.

In addition, the definition of agriculture should be amended in the federal unemployment tax act to correspond with the definition in OASDI so as to cover nonfarm activities, such as poultry hatching, and the packing, processing, or other handling of agricultural products performed off the farm, now defined as agricultural, but essentially industrial in character.[31]

DOMESTIC SERVICE WORKERS

Probably the most difficult group to cover will be household workers. The original Social Security Act excluded "domestic service in a private home" from the coverage of the Federal Unemployment Tax Act. The 1939 amendments added the exclusion of domestic service in a "local college club or local chapter of a college fraternity or sorority." Originally only New York included household workers, covering employers of four or more during at least 15 days in a year; this was revised in 1936 to four or more within 13 weeks in a year. New York now covers employers who employ a payroll of $500 or more a quarter and Hawaii any employer who has a payroll of $225 or more a quarter.

Household workers in private homes are probably being given less thought than any other group not covered by unemployment insurance. Perhaps one reason for lack of attention to the problem of covering household workers is a general impression that there has been a decline in the use of household help. However, in the 15 years 1947–62, there was a steady growth in the number of household workers in private homes from average employment of 1,730,000 in 1947 to 2,322,000 in 1963.[32]

[31] The Administration bill of 1965 (H.R. 8282) proposed coverage of farm employers using 300 or more man-days of hired farm labor in any calendar quarter in a year. This might be a simpler criterion of coverage and would approximate the wages of four regular workers. H.R. 8282 also provides for the substitution of the OASDI definition of agriculture.

[32] *Manpower Report of the President and A Report on Manpower Requirements, Resources, Utilization, and Training by the United States Department of Labor,* Transmitted to the Congress, March, 1965 (Washington, D.C.: U.S. Government Printing Office, 1965), p. 202, table A–10.

The explanation for this situation evidently lies in a decrease in full-time workers and an increase in the number of part-time household workers. Data are available only from 1957 to 1960, but the trend toward part-time employment was clearly marked during this period. The number of household workers who were seeking only part-time work increased from 968,000 in April, 1957, to 1,030,000 in May, 1960. There was also an increase in those who were working part time because they could not find full-time work—from 240,000 in 1957 to 290,000 in 1960. The proportion working full time has also decreased about 100,000 during this period—from 962,000 to 858,000.

The employment situation of household workers added up in May, 1960, to 38.7 percent working full time, 1.1 percent of those usually work-full time who were partially unemployed, 11.9 percent usually working part time because they could not find full-time work, and 46.5 percent working part time out of personal choice.[33]

The years 1957–60, admittedly, are a short span of time and if data were available for a longer period, more of a change might be observed. Also, if the 1957 to 1960 trends have continued, there would be a still greater shift from full time to part time in household work.

These household data, as well as some nonstatistical considerations, add up to some difficult problems that would be encountered in covering domestic workers.

The first problem would be the securing of contribution and wage reports on the large number of household workers who either work part time for one or several employers. Housewives, the typical employers of household workers, have been educated in reporting wages and paying social security taxes under the OASDI program. Those administering that program, however, recognize that there is a great deal of underreporting of domestic labor. This continues despite the fact that the most casual and intermittent employment need not be reported because of the exemption of workers earning less than $50 a quarter from one employer. During 1960, only 1.3 million household workers had their wages reported by 1.1 million employers.[34] The situation is further complicated for OASDI by the need for paying an employee tax as well as an employer tax. It has been difficult to educate domestic workers on the value of paying social security taxes. In fact, there is little advantage for the three quarters of a million married women employed in household work, since most of their husbands are covered by OASDI and few can get more in benefits by working than they can get in wife's benefits under the present law.

It is possible that a better record of reporting could be secured under unemployment insurance coverage, where no employee contribution is

[33] Robert L. Stein and Jane L. Meredith, "Growth and Characteristics of the Part-Time Work Force." Special Labor Force Report No. 10, *Monthly Labor Review*, Vol. LXXXIII (November, 1960), table A–7.

[34] An unknown number may have been reported by husbands on their wage reports for industrial employees.

involved. New York, one of the two states that cover household workers, has been successful in collecting unemployment insurance taxes, but this is probably because only households employing four or more workers are covered.[35]

The large amount of part-time employment would also make it difficult to determine whether household workers were working only part time out of choice or because of inability to find full-time work. While all states pay benefits for partial unemployment, this is a difficult area of administration in any case and would be even more difficult in the area of household employment. The problem would probably not be too great, however, since large numbers of part-time workers do not have enough employment or earnings to qualify, particularly if qualifying requirements are high enough to exclude those not regularly attached to the labor force. The qualifying requirements would need to help weed out intermittent workers, but cover persons who are fully employed by working for several employers during a week. In view of the lack of standards as to wages, hours, and conditions of work for household employees, another problem would be to determine whether a claimant for benefits had justifiably turned down an offer of work as unsuitable or whether a voluntary quit was for "good cause."

Household workers often have serious unemployment problems, and despite the issues indicated above, should be covered by unemployment insurance if possible. Their unemployment rate for total unemployment has been at least 4.8 percent since 1957, while part-time work for economic reasons, which really is partial unemployment, has ranged between 12 and 15 percent in recent years. Other countries have successfully covered household workers in private homes and it should be possible to successfully cover them here.

STATE AND LOCAL GOVERNMENT EMPLOYEES—THE GROWING GROUP

State and local government workers represent the most promising area for extension of coverage. Employment by state and local governments and their instrumentalities was not covered by the federal unemployment tax because of the constitutional proscription against taxing states and their subdivisions. Any coverage of such employees has, therefore, been on the initiative of the states themselves. Wisconsin has long covered employees of the state and its larger cities; other political subdivisions of the state may elect coverage of one or more of their operating units. By 1964, in addition to Wisconsin, Connecticut and New York covered their state employees on a compulsory basis and the District of Columbia had elected coverage of its employees under a permissive provision in its laws. Seven

[35] No information is available as to Hawaii's success in collecting taxes for household workers.

other states permitted election of coverage by state and local governmental units and Massachusetts permitted election by certain instrumentalities.

The provision of unemployment compensation for federal civilian employees by Congressional action in 1954[36] seems to have given an impetus to action by the states. By the end of 1961, 32 states had taken some type of action. The movement, however, seems to have lost its momentum: during the two years 1962 and 1963, only one state took positive action and that was only to permit political subdivisions to elect coverage. Another state that had previously taken action exempted service in certain state parks. By 1964, ten states covered all state employees on a compulsory basis and four covered some employees. Two states on a mandatory basis covered all local government units and six other states some local employing units. Fifteen states permitted election of coverage by both state and local government units and ten more by local government units only.

Employees of state and local government are the largest group not protected by unemployment insurance. In fact, in 1962, they constituted 40 percent of the total noncovered workers. State and local government employment has been constantly growing, and only showed a decrease in one of the 15 years from 1947 to 1962. Government employment during the 15-year period almost doubled from an annual average of 3,582,000 in 1947 to 6,550,000 in 1962, and all signs point to its continued growth.

The U.S. Bureau of Employment Security estimated that, in 1962, only about 400,000 of the total number of state and local government employees were actually covered by unemployment compensation in the 32 states that had some legislation for coverage of these employees. (The actual number covered in 1959 was 296,168 state employees and 60,542 local government employees.)[37] There is apparently a long journey ahead before coverage of government employees is general.

Is there enough risk of unemployment among government employees to justify covering them? Despite the growth of civil service and tenure, the answer is in the affirmative. Some temporary or seasonal governmental activity exists. Personnel must be cut when appropriations are reduced. Work loads, and employment, fluctuate in some operations. Some workers may lose their jobs through changes in operating methods or shifts in government activities, even though total employment grows.

This is borne out by the actual benefit payment experience of the state and local government units which cover employees under unemployment insurance. In 1959, nine states with mandatory coverage of state employees had benefit costs ranging from 0.12 to 0.68 percent of total wages, except Rhode Island, whose costs were 1.37 percent.

Five of these states, however, excluded temporary and seasonal em-

---

[36] Public Law No. 83–767, approved September 1, 1954.

[37] United States Department of Labor, Bureau of Employment Security, "Selected Employment and Cost Data Pertaining to the Unemployment Insurance Coverage of State and Local Government Employees," *Unemployment Insurance Program Letter No. 595* (Washington, D.C., April 1, 1961), attachment (1), table 1.

ployees through a variety of provisions. In the seven states in which coverage had been elected for 500 or more local government employees the average benefit costs ranged from 0.09 percent to 5.35 percent of total wages, with average costs exceeding 1 percent in three of the states. In Wisconsin, the only state with any significant amount of local government coverage (23,697 employees), the cost was 0.44 percent.[38]

The financing of the coverage of state and local government employees, therefore, would not be difficult since the costs involved would be low. The financing of benefits can also be facilitated by reimbursing the unemployment fund for actual benefits paid, rather than by paying contributions in advance. Almost one half of the states with some kind of coverage of state and local employees provide for financing of benefits on a reimbursable basis, several having shifted from advance payment of contributions. While this removes the insurance character of such coverage, it involves no risk that the benefits will not be financed, since there is no risk of a government "going out of business."

With the small costs involved, it would seem that there is no excuse for the states not covering all state and local government employees on a mandatory basis where this is constitutionally possible.

BROADENING THE DEFINITION OF EMPLOYEE

Inclusion of workers in the twilight zone between employment and self-employment is the knottiest coverage problem. Principally, this involves those who are paid on a commission basis, as well as those who work in an endless variety of jobs which have some aspects of an employer-employee relationship and some aspects of self-employment. In 1948, it was estimated by the Federal Security Administrator that this twilight zone included about a million and a quarter individuals.[39] About half of these were "outside" salesmen; the balance included taxi-drivers, owner-operators of trucks, filling station operators, private-duty nurses, industrial homeworkers, entertainers, and agent drivers. Undoubtedly, the number of "twilight zone" workers has increased substantially since then.

The original Social Security Act did not define "employee," it merely stated that the term "includes an officer of a corporation." In the absence of any definition in the law, the Treasury Department and Social Security Board issued regulations defining "employee." Emphasis was placed on the legal right to control, but other significant factors were also taken into account. The most difficulty was encountered in applying these regulations to outside salesmen. In considering the 1939 amendments to the Social Security Act, the House included a definition of "employee" that would have covered more salesmen than the regulations did. The Senate, however, would not agree to this definition for the old-age insurance program.

[38] *Ibid.*, attachment (3), table 2.
[39] *H. J. Res. 296*, Hearings before the Senate Finance Committee, 80th Cong., 2d sess. (Washington, D.C.: U.S. Government Printing Office, 1948), pp. 152–53.

As for the federal unemployment tax, the 1939 amendments specifically excluded insurance salesmen operating on a commission basis.

In 1941, the Supreme Court narrowed the definition of the employer-employee relationship in the case of *Texas Co.* v. *Higgins* (188 F. (2d) 636), largely guided by the formal language of the contracts between employers and their agents. The Treasury Department, accordingly, adopted a narrower interpretation of "employee," but still did not confine coverage to the narrow common-law test of a "master-servant" relationship. During the following years, about 250 cases were litigated in which courts applied standards which varied widely from narrow to liberal interpretations of what constituted an employer-employee relationship.

Finally, the Supreme Court took jurisdiction in several cases. In its opinion on one of the cases, the Court stated that the interpretation of individual arrangements must be in the light of the purpose of the legislation. It summarized its interpretation as follows: "We concluded that . . . 'employees' included workers who were such as a matter of economic reality. . . . We rejected the test of the 'technical concepts pertinent to the employer's legal responsibility to third persons for acts of his servants. . . .' "[40] It was estimated that between one half and three quarters of a million workers would be covered under the Court's new interpretation. Its ruling, however, was not sweeping in character. In another case, it held that the majority of two groups of owner-operators of motor trucks were "small businessmen," and placed reliance on the terms of written contracts without investigating whether the "economic reality" meant that workers under such contracts still had an employee relationship.[41]

After the Court decision, the Treasury Department once more drafted a proposed revision in its regulation which incorporated the "economic reality" test. When the proposed regulation was published in the Federal Register on November 27, 1947, it aroused a storm of protest. The chairmen of the House Ways and Means and Senate Finance Committees accordingly asked the Treasury Department to refrain from releasing the regulation until Congress could study the question. On January 15, 1948, Representative Gearhart of California introduced House Joint Resolution 296 to "maintain the status quo . . . pending action by Congress on extended social security coverage" and, in the meantime, to exclude from coverage under both the OASDI and unemployment tax provisions, "(1) any individual who, under the usual common-law rules applicable in determining the employer-employee relationship, has the status of an independent contractor, or (2) any individual (except an officer of a corporation) who is not an employee under such common-law rules."[42] The resolution was passed over a veto by President Harry S Truman, and became Public Law 642 (80th Congress).

[40] *United States* v. *Silk*, 331 U.S. 704, 712–14 (1947).
[41] *Bartels* v. *Birmingham*, 332 U.S. 126 (1947).
[42] The wording now included in Sec. 3306 (i) of the Federal Unemployment Tax Act.

It was understood that this was a temporary amendment pending thorough Congressional consideration of the question. Action on the OASDI program was taken in the 1950 amendments which reaffirmed the common-law rules, but listed a number of borderline occupations that were covered. No similar action has been taken with respect to the Federal Unemployment Tax Act.[43]

Fortunately, when the "Status Quo Amendment" was passed by Congress, most of the states had written into their laws definitions of employment that included what is generally known as the "ABC" test. The original Wisconsin law included such a definition, which was also incorporated into revised draft bills issued in January, 1937 by the Social Security Board. The provision in the draft bill read as follows:

(1) Employment . . . means service . . . performed for wages or under any contract of hire, written or oral, express or implied. . . .
(2) Services performed by an individual for wages shall be deemed to be employment subject to this act unless and until it is shown to the satisfaction of the commissioner that—
   (a) such individual has been and will continue to be free from control or direction over the performance of such service, both under his contract of service and in fact; and
   (b) such service is either outside the usual course of the business for which such service is performed or that such service is performed outside of all the places of business of the enterprise for which such service is performed; and
   (c) such individual is customarily engaged in an independently established trade, occupation, profession or business.

Following the adoption of the "Status Quo Amendment," three states repealed their "ABC" clauses.[44] As of January 1, 1962, 29 state laws still contained the "ABC" tests, and 12 more contained one or two of the tests.

In a few states having the "ABC" tests, the courts have interpreted the provisions so narrowly that they actually do not go beyond the common-law rules. Other states have been restrictive in their application of the tests. The majority of the state courts, however, have taken the tests at their face value. Even with the tests, the states are often presented with difficult cases of interpretation. As Alanson W. Willcox, formerly General Counsel of the Federal Security Agency, has written: "The 'ABC' test has not solved the insoluble. In the hands of some courts it has accomplished little or nothing. Applied by other courts with an understanding of legislative purpose and economic realities, it has accomplished more than any other test yet de-

[43] For a full discussion of this history and the issues involved, the authors have drawn on the article by Alanson W. Willcox, "The Coverage of Unemployment Compensation Laws," *Vanderbilt Law Review*, Vol. VIII, No. 2 (February, 1955), pp. 245–55; and Wilbur J. Cohen, *The Social Security Act Amendments of 1950: Legislative History of the Coverage Provisions of the Federal Old Age and Survivors Insurance Program* (Washington, D.C.: Federal Security Agency, Social Security Administration, June, 1961), pp. 59–67 (mimeographed).
[44] Arizona (1947), Florida (1947), and North Carolina (1949). Two states had previously repealed their provisions: Colorado (1941) and Michigan (1943).

vised toward bringing the law into harmony with the actualities of our economic life."[45]

It is our view that the "ABC" tests should be included in the federal unemployment tax law, and applied in those states whose laws do not contain the tests or contain only one or two of them. This should eventually result in a broader interpretation of the tests in the state courts that now interpret them narrowly. Such a federal amendment would bring under coverage probably an additional quarter of a million workers now not covered by state law or interpretation. This appears to be an area in which the state employment security agencies could join hands with the federal agency so as to bring uniformity of coverage. Without such action, a large number of workers do not have the protection of unemployment insurance although in "economic reality" they are employees.[46]

VOLUNTARY ELECTION OF COVERAGE

One possible avenue for extending the coverage of unemployment insurance is through voluntary election of coverage. Under all state laws except Alabama, Massachusetts, and New York, employers may elect coverage, with the approval of the state agency, of services excluded from the definition of employment. There have been reports of a limited amount of elective coverage of highly mechanized wheat farms in South Dakota and of some religious publishing houses at the insistence of their printing unions.

All the states that limit the size of firms covered permit the election of coverage by the excluded firms. Most states also permit election of coverage by an interstate employer who has enough employees to be covered by the federal tax, but not enough in-state employees to be covered. For example, there has been some election of coverage by small firms in Michigan. About one half of the elections in Michigan have been by construction firms which have difficulty in getting workers unless they are covered. In 1962, the total number of employees in elective coverage in Michigan was 3,050 or only 0.18 percent of the total coverage in the state.[47]

SUMMARY AND CONCLUSIONS

In principle, everyone working for a living and having a risk of unemployment should be covered by unemployment insurance. However, it would be extremely difficult, if not impractical, to consider covering the self-employed, unpaid family workers, and those without a job who are seeking employment for the first time. About 15 million workers whom it would be feasible to cover, are still excluded from unemployment insur-

[45] Willcox, op. cit., pp. 266–67. See his full discussion of these problems, pp. 255–67.
[46] The Administration bill of 1965 (H.R. 8282) proposed that the OASDI definition of employee be substituted for the present definition in the Federal Unemployment Tax Act. This definition is more specific, but somewhat more restricted than the ABC test.
[47] Michigan Employment Security Commission, Elective Coverage, A Study prepared for Governor George Romney (Detroit, November 1, 1963), p. 21.

ance protection. The largest groups include employees of small firms in most of the states, farm and agricultural processing workers, household workers, employees of nonprofit institutions, employees of state and local governments, and large numbers of workers who, in economic reality, are employees but who do not meet the common-law rules as to what constitutes an employee.

The most progress has been made in covering employees of small firms. The federal unemployment tax, which originally covered only employers who employed eight or more workers in each of at least 20 weeks in a year, now covers employers of four or more workers in each of at least 20 weeks. About two fifths of the states go further, four covering employers of three or more and 20 covering employers of one or more. Originally small employers were exempted because of fear of the administrative problem of covering them. Today, the administrative feasibility of covering employers regardless of how few workers they employ has been amply demonstrated.

Exemption of employers who cover less than four or more workers (or a lesser number) for a minimum of 20 weeks (or some other number of weeks) can exempt very large employers who operate for only a limited period in the year. As their recognition of this grows, states are amending their laws to cover employers whose payrolls exceed a stated amount during a calendar quarter or year.

Employment in nonprofit organizations has been exempted from coverage because of the traditional exemption of such organizations from taxation, because of the contention that they have little or no unemployment, and because of the argument that they will have to pay taxes they can ill afford. The benefit experience of Alaska and Hawaii in covering nonprofit organizations, shows that, although there is some unemployment, benefit payments are a very small fraction of payroll. It has therefore been proposed that nonprofit organizations be covered and that they reimburse the state unemployment fund for benefits actually paid to their former employees, instead of paying contributions in advance.

Agricultural workers have been exempted from coverage principally because administrative complexities and higher benefit costs were predicted as a result of their inclusion in the program. Studies of agricultural workers in New York and Arizona revealed, however, that agricultural employers keep much better employee wage records than was anticipated; it was also found in those states that the costs of coverage would not be excessive. With the increasing consolidation of farms into larger units, regular workers on large farms might be covered first. Coverage of seasonal and migrant workers will no doubt present the principal problems in extending coverage to agricultural labor. Some method of combining the wages earned by migrants in different states would need to be worked out before their coverage would be feasible. Qualifying requirements would need to be high enough to weed out workers not regularly in the labor force. Agricultural labor has been so broadly defined that hundreds of thousands of workers in packing and processing plants are excluded, even though they are actually factory workers. Such exemptions should be eliminated.

Of all the excluded groups, domestic workers in private households are probably most in need of unemployment insurance protection. The large increase in part-time workers, however, has aggravated the problems of securing tax payments and wage records from the employer (usually the housewife) and of determining when part-time workers are genuinely unemployed. Intermittently employed household workers would also be a problem. Much more study needs to be carried out to determine whether these problems can be solved.

The most promising area for extension of coverage lies with state and local government employees, the largest and fastest growing group of exempted workers. Some states cover all or some of their own employees and a number of states permit local governments to elect coverage. The number actually covered, however, is still small. Coverage for government employees would be no problem, both because of the low cost and because it would not be necessary to contribute and build up advance reserves.

Workers whose arrangements with the employer do not meet the common-law rules as to what constitutes an employer-employee relationship present the knottiest coverage problem. Most of these employers are paid on a commission basis. Most of the states apply three "ABC" tests, to cover workers who are "in economic reality" employees, although they do not meet the common-law "master-servant" tests. The federal definition restricts coverage to those who meet the common-law tests and some state courts have tended to apply such tests even though the state unemployment compensation law includes "ABC" tests. The solution apparently lies in amending the Federal Unemployment Tax Act to include the "ABC" tests now in most state laws, after which, it would be hoped, that all states would adopt such tests, and the courts would interpret them more liberally.

Practically all of the states permit workers excluded from coverage to elect coverage and all states that limit the size of covered firms permit election of coverage by the excluded small firms. Only limited use has been made of voluntary election of coverage.

The road to universal employee coverage is long and filled with many obstructions. It is our hope, however, that the analyses presented in this chapter will be helpful in advancing some way along that road. Extensions in the coverage of small firms, nonprofit organizations, and state and local government employees seem most possible, but the more difficult stretches of the road, especially those that encompass agricultural and household workers and borderline employments, should not be neglected because of the large obstructions to coverage that must be cleared away.

The most hopeful place to look for leadership in the extension of coverage is the federal government. The states have made very minor progress in the extension of coverage in recent years, except with respect to state and local government workers. The states have largely taken their cue from the federal legislation in the coverage of their acts, mainly to cover employment newly included under the Federal Unemployment Tax Act to prevent the entire employer's tax from going to the federal government. In order to facilitate adaptation to federal coverage, all but four states that do not cover employers of one or more workers have provisions to automatically cover any employing unit to which federal coverage is extended. Similarly, over three fifths of the states have provisions for including any service to which the federal unemployment tax is extended.

Chapter 11

Benefit Amount—
The Problems of
Wage Increases and Adequacy

The weekly benefit amount and the duration of benefits are the two most important elements in unemployment insurance. One of the most controversial issues in the program has been the adequacy of the benefit amount. This is because there is no general agreement as to the principles that should govern its size.

There has never been any controversy over the basic concept of varying the benefit amount in accordance with previous earnings. This may be surprising since flat benefit amounts are paid in the United Kingdom, and many other features of the British unemployment insurance law were used as models in this country. The primary argument for relating benefits to earnings rather than providing flat amounts of benefits, as in the United Kingdom, was the wide variation in wages in different areas of this country as well as greater wage differentials between different skill groups in the same area. Probably, the precedent of relating workmen's compensation payments to wages also had a major influence.

A second generally accepted concept was that the weekly benefit amount should be 50 percent of former wages. There is no record as to why this percentage was originally chosen, particularly as workmen's compensation benefits were generally set at 66⅔ percent of former earnings. A few states have weighted the benefit amount in inverse proportion to earnings, in a few cases paying up to two thirds of wages at the lowest end of the benefit scale. Nevertheless, 50 percent of wages has become so firmly established as a concept that it is often referred to as the *"principle"* of 50 percent of wages.

It has also been taken for granted that there should be a maximum limit on weekly benefits. A maximum limit was accepted as necessary both in order to conserve funds and to avoid paying more than was "needed." There is also agreement that the maximum should be high enough so it

173

would not adversely affect the great majority of claimants. But there is little agreement as to what the maximum benefit amount should be in concrete figures.

Although, curiously, the Committee on Economic Security recommended no minimum, it was also agreed that a minimum benefit amount was necessary. The minimum amount has never received much attention in discussions of what benefits should be.[1]

The concept has generally prevailed that weekly benefits should be based as nearly as possible on full-time weekly earnings. Technically, this has been very difficult to accomplish, and has at best been no more than approximated. An alternative idea that was vigorously pushed for a while and written into some laws, was that weekly benefits should be a fraction of annual earnings. This idea was based on the argument that annual earnings rather than weekly earnings determine a worker's standard of living.

Finally, a few states provide additional allowances for dependents. There is disagreement over whether such allowances introduce an element of need into the program.

Actually, there was no widespread controversy about the weekly benefit amount until weekly earnings rose rapidly after World War II, making the original benefit maximums rather obsolete. At that time, the effort of those interested in the adequacy of the weekly benefit amount was confined to restoring the original relationship between the maximum and the general average of weekly wages. But this effort stirred up discussion of what principles should govern the adequacy of the benefit amount, principles that were not defined at the beginning of the program. It became evident that people held a variety and often a mixture of concepts, and agreement has still to be reached on which of these concepts should govern.

To recapitulate, the weekly benefit amount in state laws has these elements: (1) it varies with the former earnings of the claimant; (2) it is designed to approximate one half of weekly earnings; (3) it is based in most states on full-time weekly earnings; (4) it is limited by a maximum benefit amount; (5) it is based on an established minimum below which benefits will not fall; and (6) it is supplemented in some states with allowances for dependents.

This chapter will discuss how the original structure of the benefit formula has been changed, the controversies that have developed, particularly over the benefit maximum, and the difficulties involved in determining what is an adequate benefit amount.

THE ORIGINAL STRUCTURE OF THE WEEKLY BENEFIT AMOUNT

The weekly benefit amount did not receive much attention at the beginning of the program. Since millions of unemployed had been out of

---

[1] More attention has been given to minimum qualifying requirements, with which minimum benefit amounts are closely associated.

work for a long time, concern focused on the duration for which benefits could be provided, and an attempt was made to provide benefits for as long a period as possible.

The weekly benefit amount recommended by the Committee on Economic Security and included in the draft bills of the Social Security Board was 50 percent of the average full-time weekly wages received by the claimant immediately preceding his unemployment. Most of the states accepted this without question, along with a recommended weekly maximum of $15, which was adopted by all but three of the states. Michigan provided a maximum of $16; Wyoming of $18; and Wisconsin increased its original maximum of $10 to $15 in 1938.

WEEKLY, QUARTERLY, AND ANNUAL FORMULAS

The attempt to base the benefit amount on former full-time weekly wages was soon abandoned, as has been described in Chapter 8, because of difficulties in accumulating weekly earnings data on every covered worker. With the exception of Wisconsin, the states therefore shifted to either a quarterly or annual wage formula. In recent years, however, states have gradually shifted back to a weekly wage formula. Let us look at the relative merits of these three approaches.

Quarterly Benefit Formulas. On the advice of the Social Security Board, most states shifted to benefit formulas based on quarterly earnings. Earnings for each calendar quarter were easy for the states to secure because quarterly earnings were reported for the federal old-age insurance program. Weekly benefits were provided that were equal to a fraction of earnings in the calendar quarter in the "base period" in which earnings were highest. In turn, the base period was usually made the first four out of the last five completed calendar quarters before the first claim for benefits was filed.[2] This "lag" between the base period of earnings and the beginning of the benefit period was necessary in order to give the state time to collect and post the quarterly wage information.

The quarterly wage formula has the advantage of simplicity in securing and recording quarterly wages. It also is likely to result in a benefit based on full-time weekly wages through use of the quarter during the "base year" in which earnings are highest.

The quarterly wage formula has several disadvantages, however. First, the "lag period" results in a substantial gap between the time when benefits are claimed and the time used for determining benefits. If the "high quarter" occurs earlier than the last quarter in the base period, the gap will be quite substantial, as long as a year or more. At the time of layoff, the worker's weekly wage may have been substantially different from the wage used for determining benefits, so that the benefit does not reflect his wage loss. On the other hand, if a worker's hours have been reduced and his

---

[2] Four states in 1964 used the last four completed calendar quarters; on the other hand, four states used earnings in the preceding calendar year.

earnings consequently lowered prior to layoff, the "lag period" and use of high-quarter earnings would be more likely to result in the use of earnings that more nearly reflected his normal earnings.

Another objection to using quarterly earnings is that some unemployment may have occurred even in the quarter of highest earnings, so that the benefit will reflect less than 50 percent of full-time weekly earnings. If one works full time, $\frac{1}{26}$th of quarterly earnings will give a benefit equal to 50 percent of weekly earnings. Some states use a larger fraction of quarterly earnings, such as $\frac{1}{20}$th, to allow for some underemployment. This results, however, in workers who have had full-time employment getting a larger fraction than 50 percent of full-time weekly earnings.

Still another objection to using high-quarter wages is that they may represent more than full-time earnings because of overtime earnings or year-end bonuses. In such cases, the claimant's benefit may be more than 50 percent of his full-time earnings.

Annual Wage Formulas. When the states were considering shifting from a weekly wage formula to one that was more feasible to administer, an annual wage formula for determining the weekly benefit amount was aggressively pushed by Mr. Frank B. Cliffe, of the General Electric Company. He argued that an annual formula would not only be simpler to administer, but would base benefits on what really determined a worker's standard of living, his annual earnings. This was a highly questionable assumption since most workers live on a week-to-week basis. Nevertheless, a few states accepted his plan.

While these states presumably adopted Mr. Cliffe's theory in principle, their present formulas do not apply it in practice. A worker full employed during a year would need a weekly benefit equal to approximately 1 percent of his annual earnings in order to receive 50 percent of his weekly earnings. But as is shown in the following table, all but two states with annual wage formulas provide higher fractions than 1 percent at the highest earnings brackets, and all but Oregon have weighted benefit formulas so that the lower the annual earnings, the larger the fraction that is paid in benefits.

The higher fractions serve a dual purpose of allowing for some unemployment or underemployment and of providing a higher proportion of

Annual Wage Formulas for Weekly Benefits in April, 1966

State	Weekly Benefit as Percentage of Annual Earnings
Alaska	1.8–1.1*
New Hampshire	1.7–1.1
North Carolina	2.0–1.0
Oregon	1.25
Washington	2.0–1.1
West Virginia	1.8–1.0

* Plus dependents' allowances.

earnings as a benefit for lower-paid workers. Under these formulas, it is possible for a worker who is employed full time during the year to get more than 50 percent of his full-time weekly wages.[3]

In fact, a worker in the lowest earning bracket who was employed full time in the base year can get up to 100 percent or more of his former earnings in four of the annual wage states. These seemingly generous formulas, however, have worked out in practice to produce lower-than-average benefits, indicating that most claimants had unemployment in their base years. In 1963 the ratio of average weekly benefits to average weekly wages was lower than the national average in all the states with an annual wage formula. The smallest ratio was 23.2 percent and the highest was 30.1 percent, compared with a national ratio of 34.6 percent.[4] The annual wage formulas evidently are resulting in a very large proportion of beneficiaries receiving benefits equal to less than 50 percent of the weekly wages they earned when working.

Weekly Wage Formulas. In 1938, when the Social Security Board recommended that the states abandon their full-time weekly wage formulas, the states were attempting to secure and post wage reports from all employers on a weekly basis. Wisconsin, instead, was receiving "separation reports"; i.e., reports of employment and earnings on workers only at the time they left their jobs. Because the Social Security Board was skeptical that accurate and full reports could be secured, it was critical of separation reports, especially for workers who had had more than one employer. The Board, therefore, recommended that the states shift to a quarterly wage formula.

But Wisconsin persevered, demonstrating that it was practical to secure wage and employment reports after the worker became unemployed.[5]

In the early 1950's, employer groups began to push for a return to the use of average weekly earnings. By 1965, nine states had an average-weekly-wage formula. In the calculation of the benefit these states disregard weeks with no earnings and most disregard weeks with earnings of less than $15 to $20, depending on the state. In order to get an approximation of full-time weekly earnings, the formulas eliminated weeks in which earnings were below a stated amount. Most of them either provided for a

---

[3] Except for workers in the highest earning brackets in North Carolina and West Virginia who get 1 percent of annual earnings, and except for those with higher earnings than are necessary to get maximum benefits in all states.

[4] United States Department of Labor, Bureau of Employment Security, *Handbook of Unemployment Insurance Financial Data, 1946–1963*, BES No. U–73. Revised May, 1964 (Washington, D.C.: U.S. Government Printing Office).

[5] Wisconsin's success was facilitated by a unique provision in its law; namely, that the weekly benefit amount is calculated separately for employment with each of the worker's former employers, beginning with the latest employer. Many multijob workers return to work before the wage and employment information from employers other than the last is needed. All such workers need to report is the name and address of the last employers. This minimized the Social Security Board's chief objection to separation reporting—that the worker might be unable to recall all employers for whom he had worked during the preceding year.

weighted benefit formula that would give a higher fraction of average weekly wages to low-paid workers, provided for dependents' allowances, or provided for both.

The weekly benefit formulas have the advantage of using only earnings during actual weeks of employment in determining the weekly benefit amount. Since weeks of low earnings are eliminated, these formulas are much more likely to provide benefits based on full-time weekly earnings. They have the second advantage of making it possible to use a base period immediately prior to the beginning of unemployment, since the weekly wage information needed can be secured within a few days after the claim is filed. While the inclusion of some weeks of underemployment may result, this is partially avoided by the elimination of weeks of low earnings.

On the other hand, unless a worker has had full-time employment in all the weeks used for computing benefits, his benefit will be less than 50 per-cent of full-time weekly earnings. Even though weeks with very low earn-ings are eliminated in most of the states with average weekly wage formulas, weeks in which the claimant worked less than full time can be included in the computation of the average weekly wage. Also, since only weeks with less than $15–$20 are eliminated, the higher the wage rate of the worker, the greater will be the amount of underemployment in the computation. For example, a worker earning $1.25 an hour will have only weeks with less than 12–16 hours of work eliminated from the computation; a worker earning $2.50 an hour will have weeks with less than 6–8 hours eliminated.

The administrative problem of obtaining separation reports, so that weekly wages can be secured and used to calculate weekly benefits, seems to have been pretty well solved. States have stiff penalties for employers who do not promptly send in separation reports, and use the further "in-ducement" that benefits will otherwise be based on the wages the worker claims to have earned. Although for some years, the Bureau of Employment Security opposed the principle of weekly formulas because of the fear that many workers would lose benefits through unreported earnings, Bureau experts have become convinced that separation reporting gives satisfac-tory results.[6]

It appears to the authors that, despite their weaknesses, weekly benefit amount formulas based on average weekly wages are superior to quarterly and annual wage formulas; the fears regarding such formulas do not have a firm foundation.

THE MAXIMUM WEEKLY BENEFIT AMOUNT CONTROVERSY

Wages have steadily increased since the beginning of the unemployment insurance program. In 1939, the first year in which all the states paid bene-

[6] Use of separation reporting may complicate the problems of extending coverage to agricultural and household workers, whose employers may not keep weekly records, especially of temporary workers whom they employed months before a separation report would be requested.

fits, average weekly wages were $26.15 in employment covered by the program. By 1964, average weekly wages increased to $106.48, an increase of 307 percent. Between 1939 and 1965,[7] average weekly benefits went from $10.66 to $37.19, an increase of 249 percent. Since average benefits increased less than average wages, the ratio of average weekly benefits to average weekly wages dropped from 41 percent in 1939 to 35 percent in 1965. Leaving aside for the moment whether weekly benefits were ever adequate, it is clear that they were relatively less adequate in 1963 than at the beginning of the program.

The decrease in average benefits in relation to wages has not been steady. The ratio of benefits to wages dropped from 41 percent in 1939 to 34 percent in 1943, increased to 42 percent in 1945, and then declined again to a ratio of 32 in 1953. The ratio seesawed in the following ten years, but gradually increased to 35 percent in 1965 as indicated above. This does not mean that every claimant's benefit has fallen in relation to his earnings. Between the minimum and maximum benefit levels, all the states aim to provide benefits equal to at least 50 percent of wages.[8] In fact, in some states, the formulas are designed to provide a higher percentage than 50 percent for lower-paid workers.

The principal factor that reduced the relative effectiveness of the weekly benefit amount was the failure to increase the maximum weekly benefit amount as much as wages increased. As an increasing number of workers earned more than twice the maximum, the average benefit as a percentage of average wages dropped. This is shown by the following table, which gives the distribution of the maximum benefit amounts provided by the states at the close of 1939, 1953, and the beginning of 1966, expressed as a percentage of average weekly covered wages.

Maximum Benefits as a Percentage of Average Weekly Wages

Percent of Average Weekly Wages*	December 1939	December 1953	January 1966
20–29	—	2	1
30–39	—	17	16
40–49	2	29	18
50–59	15	2	16
60–69	17	1	1
70–79	7	—	—
80–89	7	—	—
90–99	3	—	—

* Excludes dependents' allowances, since such allowances in most states are added to a basic benefit of 50 percent of wages in recognition that a worker with dependents needs more than 50 percent of wages in benefits.

In 1939, the maximum was 50 percent or more of average weekly wages in all but two states, and above 70 percent in about a third of the states. In

[7] 1964 is used for average weekly wages because the wages for (roughly) the preceding year are used in calculating benefits.

[8] A few states add dependents' benefits, as will be discussed later.

1953, only three states had maximums of 50 percent or more of average weekly wages and over a third had maximums of less than 40 percent. Although the maximums expressed as dollars had been increased in every state, by January, 1966, wages had also increased so that the relationship of the maximum to average weekly wages in covered employment had not greatly improved. In that year 17 states had maximums of 50 percent or more of average weekly wages as compared with three in 1953, but 19 states still had maximums equal to less than 40 percent of average wages.

In 1939, only 25.8 percent of benefit payments had been at the maximum; in 1953, the proportion had increased to 58.8 percent. In 1963, 45 percent of the claimants were receiving maximum benefits as a result of increased maximums.

Recommended Maximum Benefit Amount in Economic Report of the President

The need for increasing maximum weekly benefit amounts was recognized in President Eisenhower's Economic Report to Congress in January, 1954. In a discussion of needed improvements in unemployment insurance, it was suggested "that the States raise these dollar maximums so that the payments to the great majority of the beneficiaries may equal at least half their regular earnings."

Arguments immediately arose over the interpretation of this recommendation. What was meant by the "great majority"? No official answer was ever forthcoming. What was meant by "regular earnings"? Did it mean "gross earnings" or "net earnings after taxes"? In an off-the-cuff answer to a question by a reporter, Secretary of Labor James P. Mitchell said that "regular earnings" meant "net earnings." However, in a letter to the state governors on November 27, 1954, discussing the President's recommendation, Secretary Mitchell used the words "average gross earnings." He also wrote: "In order to achieve this goal, it is our belief that the maximum benefit level, which is the principal limiting factor on weekly benefits, should be geared to the average gross earnings of *all workers covered by the program*, not just of those who are drawing benefits at any particular time." (Italics supplied.) In the Economic Report for 1955, the wording of the recommendation was changed to read: "the great majority of *covered workers*" should be eligible for payments equal to at least half their regular earnings. (Italics supplied.) Arguments continued, however, as to whether the wages of beneficiaries or covered workers should be used.

To continue the argument over what was meant in the recommendation would be useless. The questions, however, did raise important issues which need discussion, since the issues are still alive today.

The recommendation has been repeated annually for some years in the Economic Report of the President. This recommendation—that the maximum be high enough to cover the great majority of eligible workers with benefits equal to half their regular earnings—cannot be translated into a precise percentage. But, certainly, "great majority" means at least 75 percent, or it could be even argued, at least 90 percent. Conversely, not more than from 10 to 25 percent will have their benefits reduced below 50 percent of their former weekly wages by the operation of the maximum if the "great majority" are eligible for 50 percent of their wages in benefits.

Yet in 1963, after ten years of prodding by the federal government and labor for higher maximums, only three states had a maximum high enough to provide the recommended maximum benefits for 25 percent or less of the claimants. From 26 to 50 percent of the claimants were at the maximum in 28 states and 51 percent or more were at the maximum in 21 states. In one state, Iowa, 80 percent were at the maximum. It would be difficult to defend such a situation and argue that there was no room for improvement unless one believed in the British system of flat-rate benefits.

Gross Earnings versus Net Earnings. What should be used as a measure in determining benefits: gross earnings or net earnings after income and social security taxes are deducted? The states have always used gross earnings, but the laws were enacted at a time when both federal income and social security taxes were low. Today because of these taxes, net earnings are significantly less than gross earnings, particularly for single persons.

Those who have advocated paying benefits as a proportion of net earnings (principally representatives of employers) point to the fact that benefits are nontaxable. As a result, workers getting less than maximum benefits may be getting more than 50 percent of take-home pay. It is also pointed out that a single person with the same gross wage as the head of a family gets a benefit that is a higher percentage of take-home pay than the family man. If benefits were based on net instead of gross pay, the difference can appear exaggerated unless the difference is actually computed. For example, in February, 1965, gross average weekly earnings of factory workers were $106.19. Net spendable earnings after deduction of federal income and social security taxes were $88.00 for single persons, and $95.65 for persons with three dependents. A benefit of 50 percent of gross earnings would have been $53.00. This would have been 60 percent of net earnings for a single person and 55 percent for a person with three dependents.

Those who believe that gross wages should continue to be the basis of benefits, and especially representatives of labor, argue that a worker loses more than cash wages when he is laid off; he also loses many of the fringe benefits connected with his job. They argue that if net wages are going to be used as a basis for determining benefits, the cost of fringe benefits the claimant is losing should be added to his take-home pay before applying the benefit formula. This, however, does not completely meet the argument of those advocating take-home pay as a basis for benefits since the differential between the man without dependents and the man with dependents would still remain unless dependents' benefits are provided. It is also urged that a worker who is only temporarily laid off would not lose many of his fringe benefits.

Benefits based on take-home pay would have to be higher than 50 percent of such pay in order to be adequate. As will be brought out later in this chapter, sample studies of beneficiaries in 1954–58 disclosed that single persons without dependents spent about 50 percent of gross pay on non-deferrable expenses and heads of families spent much more.

The administrative problems in determining take-home pay, moreover, would be so great that they would outweigh any possible advantages that the take-home pay formula might have. States that use quarterly or annual earnings would have no way of applying the take-home pay concept. Only states that secure and use weekly wage data as a basis for determining the weekly benefit amount could use take-home pay as a basis for determining benefits. Even for these states, there would be many problems. The actual income taxes withheld each week may be more or less than the final tax on the employee. For example, the final tax may be reduced because of excessive medical expenses, etc. As a result, a large number of employees get refunds at the end of the year. It would be administratively impossible to adjust net wages for the income tax finally paid. But it would be inequitable to calculate the weekly wage on the basis of "take-home pay" unless such adjustments are made.

The *concept* of "take-home pay," nevertheless, can be useful in measuring the adequacy of benefits, as will be discussed in the next section.

The next question is whether the great majority of *covered workers* or of *beneficiaries* should be able to receive at least half their regular earnings in benefits. In 1955, as has been said, the recommendation in the Economic Report of the President was changed to make it clear that the measure of adequacy was to be the potential benefits of all *covered* workers. In an insurance system, it was argued, one measures what *potential* protection is provided. Part of the security provided by unemployment insurance is the knowledge of the employed worker that his unemployment compensation will be an adequate proportion of his former earnings.

Although few statistics are available to test it, there is some evidence that average wages of beneficiaries are lower in prosperous times than the average wages of all covered workers. But during a recession, the average wages of covered workers more closely approximate the wages of beneficiaries, even though workers with least seniority are laid off first. This is indicated by the increase in average weekly benefits during recessions and by the higher proportion of claimants receiving maximum benefits.

The argument for using net wages, however, never got beyond the theoretical stage. As a practical matter, the proportion of claimants receiving maximum benefits has been used as a measure of the adequacy of the maximum, since data on this are readily available.

Federal Advisory Council Recommendation

As phrased in the President's 1955 Economic Report the recommendation, although sound in principle, used terms that were subject to different interpretations, and terms that were difficult to measure in practice. It was only possible to determine whether a state met the recommendation after the fact, when statistics became available on the proportion receiving maximum benefits.

The recommendation had the additional weakness of being stated in terms that could not be written into law. Shortly before the recommendation was made in the 1954 President's Economic Report, a majority of the Federal Advisory Council on Employment Security made an independent recommendation which Secretary of Labor Mitchell interpreted as being equivalent to the President's recommendation. The Advisory Council recommended that the maximum should be equal to from three fifths to two thirds of the state-wide average weekly wage. The Council arrived at these fractions on the basis of a statistical analysis made by one of its members, Dr. Richard B. Lester, who estimated that the maximums in the original state laws would have been the equivalent of from three fifths to two thirds of average weekly wages in manufacturing in 1939.

The Secretary of Labor was criticized, especially by the employer members of the Federal Advisory Council, for saying that this recommendation "supported" the President's recommendation. Mitchell had based his statement on the data from 1939, the reference point for the Council's recommendation, which showed that only 25.8 percent of claimants received maximum benefits for the country as a whole, so that the great majority of claimants were presumably getting half their weekly wages in benefits. The Council's recommendation, the goal of the Department of Labor and both Republican and Democratic Administrations, is still far from achievement although the position of the federal government has no doubt had some influence in developing pressures for increasing the state maximums.

Flexible Maximums

One of the reasons it has been difficult for states to keep their maximums in pace with increasing wages is that they must continually take legislative action to raise their maximums if expressed in dollar terms. To avoid this, an increasing number of states, totaling 16 in 1966, have adopted "flexible maximums" which are adjusted anually or semiannually according to fluctuations in average weekly covered wages. Most states set the maximum at 50 percent of average weekly wages. Idaho and Wisconsin set it at 52.5 percent. Wyoming first set its maximum at 55 percent, but in 1964 reduced it to 50 percent. This type of provision introduces a stabilizing factor into the state laws that prevents the benefits from falling behind wage increases.

How high does the maximum weekly benefit amount need to be in order for the great majority of workers to receive at least one half their weekly wages? The following table gives the proportion of beneficiaries at the maximum in 1963 in those states with an automatic adjustment of the maximum to a percentage of the state-wide average weekly wage:

State	Maximum as Percent of Average Weekly Wages 1963	Percent Beneficiaries Receiving Maximum 1963
Arkansas	50	32
Colorado	50	62
District of Columbia	52½	38
Idaho	50	48
Kansas	50	50
North Dakota	50	65
South Carolina	50	25
Utah	50	52
Vermont	50	34
Wisconsin	52½	36
Wyoming	55	54

In six of the 11 states, 50 percent or more of the beneficiaries were at the maximum. It should be the other way around—in these states the great majority should *not* have been at the maximum in order to get 50 percent of *their* average wages in benefits. This table shows that in many states a higher percentage than 50 or even 55 percent of average wages would be needed as a maximum if the great majority of beneficiaries are to get half their wages.

Effect of Different Maximums

Thirteen states made a sample study which showed what proportion of claimants in 1961 had wages higher than twice the maximum if the maximum had been 50 percent of the average weekly wage or if the maximum had been 66⅔. If the weekly benefit amount formula provided for a benefit equal to one half the weekly wage, these claimants would have received less than half their wages.[9] As will be seen from Table 11–1, the proportion whose benefits would have been reduced by a maximum of 50 percent of average wages would have been high in most of these States (as was the actual experience of the states having an automatic 50 percent maximum). A maximum equal to two thirds of average weekly wage would appear to be a little higher than necessary for the "great majority" of the claimant group as a whole to get 50 percent of their weekly wages, if the "great majority" is considered to be 25 percent of all claimants.

[9] The proportion receiving the maximum would have been 1 or 2 percent more, since some claimants would get exactly half their wages in benefits.

Table 11-1

Effects of Different Maximum Basic[a] Weekly Benefit Amounts on Unemployment Insurance Claimants, by Family Status, 1961[b]

State and Basis of Maximum Weekly Benefit Amount (AWW = Average Weekly Wage)	Maximum Weekly Benefit Amount	Percent of Claimants with Weekly Wage Higher than Twice the Maximum Weekly Benefit Amount				
		All Claimants	Primary Earners	Married Secondary Earners	Claimants in Families Living Alone	
					Men	Women
Arizona						
Current—1961 ....$35		62%	77%	28%	74%	34%
½ state AWW—1961 ... 49		42	57	4	52	11
⅔ state AWW—1961 ... 65		19	27	1	27	3
California						
Current—1961 55		34	48	7	43	7
½ state AWW—1961 ... 55		34	48	7	43	7
⅔ state AWW—1961[c] .. 73		14	23	1	14	2
Georgia						
Current—1961 35		29	45	11	18	12
½ state AWW—1961 ... 38		28	41	10	16	7
⅔ state AWW—1961 ... 50		16	26	4	5	0
Illinois						
Current—1961 38		60	76	26	67	27
½ state AWW—1961 ... 53		37	53	8	37	4
⅔ state AWW—1961[c] .. 71		13	20	1	14	0
Indiana						
Current—1961 36		66	80	32	70	13
½ state AWW—1961 ... 50		35	49	4	42	3
⅔ state AWW—1961 ... 66		12	17	1	17	0
Louisiana						
Current—1961 35		45	55	15	40	11
½ state AWW—1961 ... 43		29	37	6	21	0
⅔ state AWW—1961 ... 57		17	20	3	10	0
Maryland[d]						
Current—1961 35		48	67	19	49	22
½ state AWW—1961 ... 44		32	48	8	29	10
⅔ state AWW—1961 ... 59		10	17	0	11	4
Michigan						
Current—1961 30		90	97	67	91	59
½ state AWW—1961 ... 55		31	40	1	23	0
⅔ state AWW—1961 ... 74		12	16	0	8	0
New York						
Current—1961 50		26	45	5	28	9
½ state AWW—1961 ... 53		23	40	4	25	8
⅔ state AWW—1961[c] .. 71		10	19	1	10	3
Ohio[d]						
Current—1961 42		67	74	23	59	18
½ state AWW—1961 ... 52		35	50	6	33	3
⅔ state AWW—1961 ... 69		14	20	2	12	0
Oregon						
Current—1961 40		62	80	14	75	11
½ state AWW—1961 ... 47		46	63	6	50	5
⅔ state AWW—1961 ... 63		18	26	1	15	3

Table 11-1 (Continued)

State and Basis of Maximum Weekly Benefit Amount (AWW = Average Weekly Wage)	Maximum Weekly Benefit Amount	Percent of Claimants with Weekly Wage Higher than Twice the Maximum Weekly Benefit Amount				
		All Claimants	Primary Earners	Married Secondary Earners	Claimants in Families Living Alone	
					Men	Women
Pennsylvania						
Current—1961 40	40	49	67	8	61	8
½ state AWW—1961 ... 46	46	35	50	4	44	5
⅔ state AWW—1961 ... 61	61	12	16	1	15	1
Vermont						
Current—1961 40	40	25	38	7	33	3
½ state AWW—1961 ... 40	40	25	38	7	33	3
⅔ state AWW—1961 ... 54	54	9	14	1	12	0

a Excludes dependents' allowances.
b May and September, 1961, and January, 1962, surveys combined.
c Percentages shown on these lines include all claimants with weekly wages of $140 or more, somewhat less than twice the maximum set at ⅔ the state average weekly wage.
d Higher benefits payable to those with dependents in these states not taken into account.
Source: United States Department of Labor, Bureau of Employment Security.

Since emphasis has been increasingly placed on the importance of pro-viding an adequate benefit for the primary wage earner in families, let us look at Table 11-1 which gives the proportions by family status. It shows that 25 percent of primary wage earners with families would have received benefits of less than half their wages in three states, even at a maximum of two thirds of average weekly wages. It will also be seen that men living alone require a maximum higher than one half of average weekly wages. While a maximum of two thirds of average weekly wages may appear to be higher than necessary for all claimants, it is certainly necessary for pri-mary wage earners and men living alone.

On the other hand, it may be argued that a maximum equal to two thirds of average wages would result in too small a proportion of married sec-ondary workers and women living alone receiving maximum benefits. But this small percentage would do no harm. It must be kept in mind that none at the maximum would get more than 50 percent of *their* wages. A very small proportion of women would be at the maximum because of their low earnings. The study samples of claimants revealed that the median earnings of women were about two thirds of the median earnings of men. It can be presumed that a higher proportion of these lower paid women need to get full benefits (50 percent of their earnings) than do claimants as a whole.

WHAT IS AN ADEQUATE BENEFIT AMOUNT?

Thus far, the discussion has proceeded on the assumption that a benefit equal to 50 percent of average weekly wages is adequate. But, as has been said earlier, this percentage was generally accepted and written into the state laws without determining whether it would be adequate to meet unemployed workers' needs. In order to get a factual basis for determining whether benefits were adequate, six sample studies of beneficiaries were conducted between 1954 and 1958. The samples were drawn from the following cities: Pittsburgh, Pennsylvania (August, 1954); Tampa and St. Petersburg, Florida (October, 1956); Anderson, Greenville, and Spartanburg, South Carolina (March, 1957); Albany-Schenectady-Troy, New York (Spring, 1957); Portland, Oregon (March, 1958); and St. Louis, Missouri (April, 1958.)[10]

The study samples contained four categories of beneficiaries: unemployed single persons, and four-person families with (1) the unemployed head of household the sole wage earner, (2) the head of household unemployed and the spouse working, and (3) the head of household working and the spouse unemployed.

Criteria of Adequacy. In an analyisis of these beneficiary studies[11] Father Joseph M. Becker applied four criteria of adequacy; benefits are adequate if they (1) equal half or more of wages; (2) keep the beneficiaries from experiencing "too much" hardship; (3) keep beneficiaries off the relief rolls; and (4) meet "nondeferrable" expenditures.[12] He thought these would be the most useful, although other criteria could also be applied.[13]

Criterion of Fifty Percent of Wages. In applying the first criterion of whether the claimants received 50 percent of their former wages, Father Becker computed the following table giving the proportions, by family status of the beneficiary, on the basis of gross and net wages:

[10] For a summarization and analysis of these studies, see United States Department of Labor, Bureau of Employment Security, *Unemployment Insurance and the Family Finances of the Unemployed, An Analysis of Six Benefit Adequacy Studies, 1954–58,* BES No. U–203 (Washington, D.C., July, 1961). Information from these studies on the savings of these beneficiaries is given in Chapter 2.

[11] Joseph M. Becker, S.J., *The Adequacy of the Benefit Amount in Unemployment Insurance* (W. E. Upjohn Institute for Employment Research, Kalamazoo, Michigan, May, 1961), 64 pp. Father Becker has given a further analysis in somewhat different form in chapter 5 of the book of which he was the editor, *In Aid of the Unemployed* (Baltimore: Johns Hopkins Press, 1965).

[12] In his analysis, Father Becker used the four studies whose format was sufficiently similar to facilitate summarization: the studies in Florida, New York, Missouri, and Oregon.

[13] Richard A. Lester has suggested other tests, namely, whether the benefit amount provides the beneficiary with the necessary sense of security from the risk of unemployment (a psychological test); whether the benefits are sufficient to maintain an essential flow of consumer payments in the locality to merchants and others (a community purchasing-power test); or whether the benefits provide a cushion to brake economic downturns by helping to maintain purchasing power throughout the country (a national purchasing power test). The latter two tests, however, cannot be used as tests of the adequacy of individual benefits, but rather of the program as a whole. The first test could be gauged only by an opinion poll. See his discussion in *The Economics of Unemployment Compensation* (Princeton: Industrial Relations Section, Princeton University, 1962), chap. 3.

Family Status (Beneficiary Type)	Percent of Claimants with Weekly Benefit Amount Equal to 50 Percent or More of Weekly Earnings							
	Florida		New York		Oregon		Missouri	
	Gross	Net*	Gross	Net*	Gross	Net*	Gross	Net*
Single	28	65	51	70	52	79	34	57
Head of household ...			26	39	25	40	15	27
	27†	52†						
Nonhead			64	90	42	79	40	68

* Earnings are less federal income and social security taxes withheld, as of the time of the studies (1955–59).
† Includes head and nonhead of household claimants.
Source: Becker, *op. cit.*, 1961, p. 34, table 2.

It will be seen that on the basis of *gross* wages, the basis on which benefits are determined, a bare majority of single claimants in two states, and only about a third of them in the other two states, received 50 percent or more of their weekly earnings. About two thirds of the nonheads of families, the unemployed wives, received 50 percent or more of their gross weekly earnings in New York, but only 40 percent in Oregon and Missouri. However, a high proportion (although not a great majority in all states) of both single persons and nonheads of households received half or more of their *net* earnings. On the other hand, fewer than a majority of the heads of households, except in Florida, received half of *either* their gross or net earnings.

Regardless of their family status, the proportion of beneficiaries who received benefits of 50 percent of former wages on the basis of gross wages was far short of being a "great majority." On the basis of *net* wages, far less than a majority of family heads received half their former wages, although the benefits of single persons and nonheads of families came nearer to meeting this goal.[14]

A benefit equal to 50 percent of earnings, however, is no real criterion of adequacy. One must know what 50 percent of earnings means to a worker in meeting his needs. Let us see if the other criteria used by Father Becker are more meaningful.

Criterion of "Too Much Hardship." In applying criterion (2), Father Becker defined a measure of hardship as the extent to which expenditures exceeded income of all types, including unemployment insurance, and the expedients used to make up the discrepancy. He found that no class of beneficiaries decreased their expenditures substantially. He also found that there was no significant correlation between the reduction of expenditures during unemployment and the factors of income, age, or even duration of unemployment. Both Father Becker and Richard A. Lester observed that

[14] Net wages would have shown a smaller difference after the income tax cuts of 1964–65, although this would have been slightly offset by increases in social security taxes.

the unemployed made greater financial adjustments during recession years than during prosperous periods.[15]

Most commonly, the unemployed met the discrepancies between expenditures and income by using their savings and other assets, and going in debt by running up bills at stores, borrowing money, or both. A considerable proportion received help from friends and relatives. According to Lester, about two fifths of all expenditures were financed by these expedients, "which in some instances involved considerable strain." He cites the Oregon survey which showed for the survey year a total of net decreases in savings and other assets and net increases in debt averaging $291 for single beneficiaries and $507 for family units with one wage earner.[16] Father Becker's conclusion was similar to Lester's: "the general picture is not one of catastrophe but is definitely one of considerable strain."[17]

Whether Beneficiaries Kept off Relief. Father Becker quickly disposed of the criterion of whether unemployment compensation kept beneficiaries off relief. Except in a small percentage of cases, this criterion was met. The proportion going on relief was less than 10 percent; it averaged less than 5 percent in all cities and categories of beneficiaries, except in the case of single beneficiaries in Florida, 18 percent of whom received relief in kind. It is significant, however, that a substantial proportion of the claimants in the sample studies received help from friends or relatives, which is a form of relief. About a third of the heads of households received such help in South Carolina, Oregon, and St. Louis.[18] The amount of such help is not given, but the very fact that such help was received indicates that benefits plus resources and credit were inadequate for some beneficiaries. In the absence of such help, in many cases, the claimant might have had to apply for public relief. No doubt the reluctance of people to seek public relief except as a last resort, and the need to exhaust all assets in order to be eligible for public welfare, also minimized the number applying for relief.

Criterion of Nondeferrable Expenses. Whether or not the beneficiary was able to meet his nondeferrable expenses proved to be the most useful criterion. Father Becker selected the same expenses used by the Bureau of Employment Security in its analysis of the studies: food, housing (including utilities), clothing, and medical care. Using these nondeferrable expenditures as a criterion, Father Becker found that the benefits were adequate for most single persons, since they averaged somewhat more than

---

[15] Becker, *op. cit.*, 1961, pp. 40–41; Lester, *op. cit.*, pp. 34–35.

[16] Lester, *op. cit.*, p. 34. See Carl M. Stevens, *The Adequacy of Unemployment Benefits, Experience of Unemployment Compensation Beneficiaries in the Portland Metropolitan Area* (Salem: Oregon Unemployment Compensation Commission, March, 1959), pp. 27–29.

[17] Becker, *op. cit.*, 1961, p. 40.

[18] *Unemployment Insurance and the Family Finances of the Unemployed*, *op. cit.*, p. 81, table E–1.

such expenditures in all states except in Florida, where benefits were 95 percent of such expenditures. The benefits of the unemployed wives of working household heads were 40 percent or less of the family's nondeferrable expenditures. Since family expenditures were highest in this category because the husband was employed, Father Becker adjusted these figures so that the adjusted amount of nondeferrable expenditures would bear the same ratio to the unadjusted amount as the beneficiary's wage had borne to the total family income. On this basis, the wife's benefit was equal to, or more than, the adjusted nondeferrable expenditures in all states but Florida where wives' benefits still averaged only 52 percent of expenditures. In most of the studies, the primary beneficiary's benefit was only about two thirds of family nondeferrable expenditures, except when the benefit could be adjusted for the earnings of another worker in the family. In the latter case, it met from 80–90 percent of expenditures in all the studies, except in that of Florida.[19]

The choice of nondeferrable expenses used for the analysis were, as Father Becker said, "necessarily somewhat arbitrary." The Bureau Report had also stated: "Just what constitutes 'basic living costs' or 'nondeferrable expenses' is debatable." The items selected for comparison are intended to be illustrative, not definitive, of nondeferrable expenses.[20] When one looks at the other eight types of expenditures of the claimants in the samples,[21] a good argument could be made for including other types of expenditures. For example, if a claimant is going to seek work, he needs money for transportation. Most of the claimants, especially family heads, indicated that they continued to use their automobiles. Expenditures for transportation were reduced, but such reduced expenditures were evidently nondeferrable. Personal care, which averaged $1 or $2 a week, is also a nondeferrable expense since a claimant needs to keep himself presentable as a job applicant. Life insurance premiums cannot be deferred, particularly on "industrial insurance" or term insurance. Evidently some beneficiaries had to give up their life insurance.[22]

If expenditures for transportation, personal care, and life insurance are added to the list of nondeferrable expenses, the benefits were inadequate even for single persons and secondary workers in families. Thus, for single workers, the benefit rate expressed as a percent of nondeferrable expenses shows the following differences when the items used by Father Becker and the Bureau of Employment Security are compared with the expanded list just suggested:

[19] *Ibid.*, p. 44, table 5.
[20] *Ibid.*, p. 45.
[21] *Ibid.*, pp. 77–79, table D–5.
[22] A similar survey to those being discussed was made in Utica, New York, in the fall of 1958. In that survey, a criterion of "recurrent" expenditures was used, which included food, housing, medical care, installment payments, and other regularly required payments.

Average Monthly Benefits as a Percent of Nondeferrable Expenses for Single Persons

State Sample	Average Monthly Benefit	Ratio of Monthly Benefits to:	
		BES/Becker List of Expenses*	Expanded List of Expenses
Florida ....$ 85		91%	75%
New York 130		103	83
Oregon 130		107	88
Missouri 113		100	75

* Percentages are from Father Becker's earlier study. Percentages were somewhat higher in his analysis in *In Aid of the Unemployed*, p. 86, table 5–2.

If the adjustment Father Becker made for other family income is made for the expanded list of nondeferrable expenditures, in the case of unemployed wives who were the secondary earners in their families, the ratio of the adjusted amount to benefits fell substantially below 100 percent, shown as follows:

Average Monthly Benefits as a Percent of Adjusted Nondeferrable Expenses for Unemployed Wives

State Sample	Average Monthly Benefit	Ratio of Monthly Benefits to:	
		BES/Becker List of Expenses	Expanded List of Expenses
New York $120		100%	77%
Oregon 116		112	80
Missouri 110		105	72

It could be argued that *all* the expenditures that the beneficiaries generally considered to be nondeferrable should be used as the criterion of adequacy. The beneficiary studies showed that moderate reductions were made in all categories of expenditures, except that a small proportion of the beneficiaries dropped life insurance and a considerable proportion postponed medical or dental care. This should not be passed over lightly. The fact that the beneficiaries were willing or compelled to use up their savings or go into debt rather than to reduce expenditures further might be interpreted as meaning that to them, at least, what they spent was nondeferrable.

In discussing the fact that more was spent during unemployment than was received in benefits and other cash income, the Bureau observed: "This result is not surprising. People are likely to resist lowering their standard of living even if, at times, they cannot meet their costs out of current income. Such behavior is likely if income loss is considered temporary, a tendency noted in other research."[23]

An appropriate list of nondeferrable expenses would probably be somewhat different from a relief budget, which is based on the assumption that the period of relief will be indefinite. Relief budgets, however, would be a good starting point. Probably the answer would lie somewhat above a relief budget and somewhat below the City Worker's Family Budget of the Bureau of Labor Statistics.

The City Worker's Family Budget (CWFB) is composed of goods and services necessary for a four-person family to maintain ". . . a level of adequate living according to prevailing standards of what is needed for health, efficiency, the nurture of children, and for participation in social and community activities. . . ."[24] The Bureau of Employment Security compared the CWFB with the expenditures of the claimants *before* unemployment in Portland, Oregon, and St. Louis Missouri, and found the amounts and spending patterns were roughly comparable. The reduced expenditures of the beneficiary households *during* unemployment were, therefore, definitely below the CWFB standard.[25] Relief budgets for these cities were not given.

Need for More Research

The beneficiary studies were useful in supplying valuable information on the adequacy, or rather inadequacy, of unemployment compensation. They did not provide precise answers, however, as to how much would have been required in benefits in order for the average beneficiary to meet the test of nondeferrable expenditures. Much more research needs to be done on the subject of benefit adequacy. More current and more extensive surveys are needed. It seems almost incredible that, in a program expending billions of dollars in benefits, so little has been spent on studies of the adequacy of the benefits being paid.

No matter how much additional study is done, however, decisions will still have to be made on the basis of "value" judgments as to what benefits should be paid. This is illustrated by the preceding discussion of what constitutes "nondeferrable expenses."

DEPENDENTS' BENEFITS

Supplementary benefits for the dependents of a beneficiary (or dependents' allowances as they are frequently called) are provided in a few states. They are paid in recognition that a person with dependents needs a larger replacement of his lost wages than a person without dependents.

---

[23] *Ibid.*, p. 34.
[24] Helen H. Lamale and Margaret S. Stotz, "The Interim City Worker's Family Budget," *Monthly Labor Review*, Vol. LXXXIII (August, 1960), p. 785.
[25] *Unemployment Insurance and the Family Finances of the Unemployed, op. cit.*, pp. 46–49.

There is much disagreement, however, as to whether such benefits are appropriate in an unemployment *insurance* program.

Originally, only the District of Columbia law provided for dependents' benefits. By 1955, eleven states had added dependents' benefits, but in the next ten years only three additional states had enacted provisions for dependents' benefits and three states had repealed their provisions.

The laws have a variety of provisions for dependents' benefits. All include allowances for dependent children under either 16 or 18 years of age; most provide for older children not able to work. About one half provide for nonworking wives or disabled nonworking husbands, and a few for a dependent parent, brother, or sister.

In 1966, the weekly dependent's benefit varied from a minimum of $1 to a maximum of $9 per dependent, with the limitation on total allowances to a beneficiary ranging from $3 to $29. Massachusetts may pay even more in some cases, since the amount of dependents' benefits is only limited by a provision that the combined basic and dependents' benefits cannot exceed the average weekly wage of the beneficiary. Most state laws provide for a flat weekly benefit per dependent. Two states (Illinois and Michigan) vary the amount of the additional benefits with the amount of earnings of the worker; the higher the earnings, the higher the additional benefits.[25a] The provisions of these two states will be described later in more detail.

Do Dependents' Benefits Introduce a Principle of Need?

Dependents' benefits have been opposed principally on the argument that they introduce an element of need into the program, since it is assumed that the claimant with dependents needs larger weekly payments than does the claimant without dependents. The counter argument is that dependents' benefits only introduce the concept of *presumptive* need; that is, a presumption that an unemployed worker with dependents needs more in benefits than a worker without dependents. The vital difference that still exists between unemployment insurance and relief is that no individual inquiry and determination is made as to whether the claimant actually needs the dependent's benefit in order to house, feed, and clothe the dependent. The claimant merely has to establish that he has legal dependents; his personal affairs are not investigated.

This principle of presumptive need is contained in many other provisions of unemployment insurance. For example, it is inherent in benefit formulas that provide a benefit equal to a higher percentage of earnings for lower paid workers than for higher paid workers. In fact, the imposition of a maximum benefit is partly based on the presumption that no worker needs more than the maximum amount. When a state provides dependents' benefits, it is merely placing a higher value on social adequacy than on individual equity. As has been discussed in Chapter 3, this is perfectly

---

[25a] Iowa for a time also provided such "variable maximums," but changed its law in 1965.

legitimate in a social insurance system, as distinguished from a private insurance system.

Dependents' benefits have been paid under several workmen's compensation laws and are paid under the OASDI program without any criticism that the benefits have turned either workmen's compensation or OASDI into programs based on need. Both are considered social insurance programs. An unemployment insurance program that provides dependents' benefits is also a social insurance program.

Dependents' benefits are objected to on the ground that they are inappropriate to a wage-related program. Additional benefits for dependents result in paying different total benefits to workers with the same wage. This objection is countered with the contention that, since the basic benefit is related to the claimants' former wages, the program is still wage-related.[26]

Are Dependents' Benefits Desirable?

There should not, then, be any objection to dependents' benefits on the basis of principle. What about their desirability? Dependents' benefits are desirable simply because persons with dependents need a higher proportion of their lost wages than single persons or secondary workers in families. It is true that heads of households average higher wages than either married or single secondary workers. But family heads need a higher percentage of their higher earnings to meet nondeferrable expenses, as indicated by the beneficiary studies.

Dependents' benefits can also be a means of providing total benefits for the family head without raising the basic benefit to a level that would weaken the incentive of workers without dependents to find jobs. For example, if basic benefits were increased to 80 percent of gross weekly wages in order to provide adequate benefits for heads of families, a working wife who is laid off while her husband is working might be strongly tempted to "take it easy" in looking for work. Also, a single man who averages almost as much as male heads of families might lack incentive to work, particularly since a benefit of 80 percent of gross wages would provide an income more closely approximating his former net wages.

The principal argument for dependents' benefits is that an unemployed worker with dependents needs more in benefits than a person without dependents. This need for higher benefits by workers with dependents was the main conclusion that Father Becker drew from his analysis of the beneficiary studies. In his words: ". . . the clearest lesson taught by the sample studies, namely, that the needs of the two groups—those with dependents and those without dependents—differ significantly. Any benefit that is proportioned to the needs of one group will not be proportioned to the needs of the other. Since the beneficiary universe is about equally divided

---

[26] In Illinois and Michigan, the additional benefits are also related to the claimants' former wages. The provisions in these states, however, are objectionable in the authors' opinion for reasons to be discussed on page 196.

between these two groups, any benefit structure that does not distinguish between them will be inappropriate for half the beneficiaries."[27]

Dependents' benefits are also an economical way of providing an adequate benefit for persons with dependents. For example, Nevada provides an allowance of $5 a week up to four dependents,[28] and defined dependents to include not only dependent children and dependent wives, but dependent husbands, parents, brothers, or sisters if disabled. In the last quarter of 1963, 36 percent of the beneficiaries in Nevada had compensable dependents, and the dependents' allowances increased the average augmented benefit by 31.8 percent over the basic weekly benefit for claimants with dependents. Yet the average benefit payment for *all* claimants, those with and without dependents, was increased by only 12.9 percent.

In other states paying dependents' benefits, the increase in the average payment for all claimants was less than half the increase in the payments to claimants receiving dependents' benefits. Such additional benefits appear to be an economical way to increase the effectiveness of the benefits paid.

How Best Provide Dependents' Benefits?

If a state chooses to pay dependents' benefits, the question remains as to what is the best way to do so. Most of the states have chosen to set dependents' benefits at specific dollar amounts. However, the benefits have to be periodically raised to take account of increases in the cost of living. It would be more convenient, and also more in accord with the philosophy of a wage-loss system, to set the amount of the dependent's benefit as a percentage of the former wages of the claimant. Benefits as a percentage of wage loss are based on the concept that a worker's standard of living varies with his wage income and that his adjustment during unemployment should be in proportion to his standard of living. If dependents' benefits are geared to former earnings, the same proportionate adjustment can be made across the board for all expenses of the family.

The larger benefits paid to claimants with dependents under the Michigan and Illinois laws result from their adoption of the concept of gear-

---

[27] Becker, *op. cit.*, 1961, p. 53. Father Becker suggested in his later analysis (*op. cit.*, 1965, p. 96) that a state with an inadequate maximum might both increase the maximum and provide dependents' benefits through a system of "variable maximums." In an expanded version of the last chapter of this book this is elaborated in the recommendation of "the wider adoption of the system of variable maximums—always with the understanding that the *basic benefit be set sufficiently high to assure that the majority beneficiaries without dependents receive at least 50 percent of their wage.* (Italics supplied.) (Joseph M. Becker, William Haber, Sar A. Levitan, *Programs to Aid the Unemployed in the 1960s,* [Kalamazoo: W. E. Upjohn Institute for Employment Research, January, 1965] p. 15.) William Haber agreed to this recommendation only with the addition of the qualification in italics in the quotation.

[28] The augmented benefit, however, could not exceed 6 percent of high-quarter wages.

ing allowances to former earnings. However, their methods of paying additional benefits were so different from other states that they require a detailed description.

In Michigan, under its 1963 amendments, benefits were paid to claimants according to six family classes. Class A was for claimants with no dependents. Class B was for claimants with one adult dependent; Classes C through F were for claimants with one to four dependent children, or from two to five dependents. Allowances varied from $1 to $6 per dependent, depending on the wages of the claimant. The maximum benefits payable is based on the number of dependents, as well as on average weekly wages. A maximum benefit of $33 was payable to a claimant with no dependents and average weekly wages of $81 or more; for claimants with the maximum number of four or five dependents, that is, a claimant who was in Class F, the maximum benefit of $60 was payable only if the claimant's average weekly wage was $120 or more. The basic criticism of the Michigan benefit structure is that no worker could receive more than 50 percent of average weekly benefits when such benefits were above $43, no matter how many dependents he had. Such a scale of benefits is inadequate if the beneficiary studies previously discussed are any guide.

The Illinois law pays larger benefits only to those claimants with dependents whose high-quarter wages are above the amount required for a single person to receive maximum benefits. According to the Illinois law as of January 1, 1964, the highest benefit a claimant without dependents could receive was $38, based on high-quarter earnings of $911.25. The weekly dependent's benefit varied from $1 to $9 per dependent according to the high-quarter wages of the claimant. The maximum amount that could be received for all dependents varied from $1 to $21, also according to the amount of high-quarter earnings. The highest amount payable in basic benefits plus dependents' benefits was $59. This was payable to a claimant with four dependents and high-quarter wages of $1,508.26 or more.

The benefit structure under the Illinois provisions is open to the criticism that no dependents' benefits are paid to lower-paid workers, only to those with earnings higher than the earnings required of a single person to secure maximum benefits. These laws provide a facade for what appear to be very generous laws with high maximums. Benefits in Illinois and in Michigan were increased substantially, effective January 1, 1966. The range in maximum benefits is now $42–$70 in Illinois and $43–$72 in Michigan. The maximum benefit for a person without dependents is still so low in these two states, however, that it was only 36 percent of average 1964 weekly wages in Illinois and 34 percent in Michigan.

If properly structured, benefit schedules with additional benefits for dependents can provide adequate but not overgenerous benefits for persons without dependents and higher benefits for persons with dependents to allow for the higher living costs of workers with families. This can be done without violence to social insurance policies by providing a basic benefit of at least 50 percent of average weekly wages and adding dependents' benefits above that.

SUMMARY AND CONCLUSIONS

A weekly benefit equal to 50 percent of average weekly wages was accepted as the norm at the beginning of the unemployment insurance program in this country. Because of the difficulty of keeping weekly wage records, the formulas for determining the weekly benefit amount were soon changed in most states to formulas based on calendar quarter or annual earnings. The quarterly earnings formulas are unsatisfactory because of the time lag between the quarter used and the date of the claim, and because the weekly benefit can be based on only an approximation to weekly earnings. These faults are even greater when annual earnings are used. Successful techniques have been developed for securing information on earnings from employers at the time of layoff so that an increasing number of states are again using weekly wage information in determining the weekly benefit amount. While these states still do not use full-time weekly wages as a basis for benefits, most use the most recent weekly wages of the worker, a system superior to the quarterly and annual wage formulas for benefits.

As wages increased, particularly after World War II, the states failed to increase the maximum benefit amount proportionately. As a result, the general level of benefits deteriorated in relation to earnings. To correct this, President Eisenhower in 1954 recommended that the states increase maximums so that the great majority, when unemployed, would get at least half their weekly earnings. Controversy raged over the interpretation of his recommendation, particularly over what percentage was meant by the "great majority."

Since that time, arguments have also arisen over the specific formula recommended by the federal Administrations to achieve this objective: that the maximum be equal to two thirds of average weekly wages of covered workers in the states.

Discussion of these goals has stimulated pressures for action so that the level of maximum benefits was somewhat increased in relation to wages for a few years. From 1958 to 1965, increases in benefits just about kept pace with increases in weekly wages, the ratio remaining at 35 or 36 percent, as compared with 41 percent in 1939.

An increasing number of states are setting the maximum as a percentage of state-wide average wages, usually 50 percent. These "flexible maximums" avoid the need of constant legislative action to keep the maximum abreast of increasing wages. The percentages used, however, are too low to permit the "great majority" to get half their weekly earnings in benefits.

Sample studies of beneficiaries were made in six states in the 1950's in order to get a factual basis for determining what is an adequate benefit amount. The average benefit was found to be far below 50 percent of wages for heads of four-person families, and approximately 50 percent for secondary family workers (usually wives) and single workers. Benefits for secondary and single workers averaged more than 50 percent of net earnings, after federal income and social security tax deductions.

Total expenditures, although reduced during unemployment, far exceeded benefits especially of the family heads. The principal expedients to meet the difference between benefits and expenditures were to draw on savings and other assets, run into debt, or get help from friends and relatives. Although not a catastrophe, the picture was one of considerable strain, but only a small percentage needed public relief.

The proportion that benefits bear to nondeferrable expenses is the best measure of adequacy. Food, housing, utilities, clothing, and medical care were selected as nondeferrable expenses in analyzing the beneficiary studies. On this basis, benefits were adequate for single persons and secondary workers, but inadequate for family heads. It is questionable whether these items are the only ones that are nondeferrable expenses. If transportation, personal care, and insurance expenses are added, benefits were inadequate for all categories of beneficiaries. More research is needed as to what expenses are not deferrable during unemployment.

The principal finding of the beneficiary studies was that different rates of benefits are needed for persons with and without dependents. Some states take account of this by paying additional benefits for dependents. This does not introduce an element of need into the program since dependents' benefits are based on *presumptive* need, not demonstration of actual need.

Eleven states provide additional benefits for dependents. Most states pay flat amounts as dependents' benefits. Two states, Illinois and Michigan, in effect vary the amount of dependents' benefits according to the former earnings of the claimant. One of these states paid dependents' benefits only to claimants whose wages were above what is required for single workers to draw maximum benefits. This disregarded the dependents of low-wage earners who needed the extra benefits most. In the other state, benefits were so structured that a claimant with dependents who received more than $43 in benefits got only 50 percent or less of his former wages in total benefits. For persons with dependents, the basic benefit should be at least 50 percent, in addition to dependents' benefits.

The adequacy of the weekly benefit amount is crucial to the effectiveness of the unemployment insurance program. Benefits are generally inadequate, particularly for heads of families. Increased maximum weekly benefits and the provision of meaningful dependents' benefits need special consideration.

Chapter 12

The Duration
of "Regular Benefits"

The amount of weekly benefits is one dimension of the protection that unemployment insurance provides; the other dimension is the duration of benefits.

Unemployment insurance was originally designed to provide income protection for short-term rather than long-term unemployment. How to find the proper demarcation between short-term and long-term unemployment is one of the major problems of the program.

The length of the waiting period after unemployment commences and before benefits begin was once an important factor in determining the duration of benefits. Any discussion of the duration of benefits would therefore be incomplete without a discussion of the waiting period.

In this country, a major duration issue is whether there should be "variable duration" (whether the duration should be varied with the amount of recent previous employment of the beneficiary) or whether there should be "uniform duration" (whether all beneficiaries who qualify for any benefits should be eligible for the same duration provided in the law).

A special problem is presented by seasonal workers. Some believe that seasonal workers should not qualify for any benefits, others that the duration of benefits should be different for seasonal than for other workers. Still others believe that there should be no distinction between seasonal and other workers in the duration of benefits for which they should be able to qualify.

The questions that will be discussed in this chapter will therefore be: What function should be played by the waiting period before benefits commence? How long should the duration of "regular benefits" be? Should duration of benefits be uniform for all claimants or vary with previous employment or earnings? What, if any, special limitations should be placed on the duration of benefits of seasonal workers?

WAITING PERIOD

At the beginning of the unemployment insurance program, a long waiting period was advocated as a device to conserve funds for the payment of a longer duration of benefits. Since a large amount of unemployment is of very short duration, however, large numbers of workers would draw no benefits if the waiting period was two or three weeks long.

The Committee on Economic Security made no specific recommendation on the length of the waiting period, but presented estimates based on waiting periods of two, three, and four weeks. Thirty-one of the original state laws required a waiting period of two weeks; 17 required three weeks; and three required four weeks. All the states with a minimum waiting period of two weeks, and some with a minimum of three weeks, required additional waiting periods during the year under specified conditions such as the beginning of another spell of unemployment.

Experience showed, however, that a much longer duration of benefits could be financed with lower contribution rates than 3 percent, and that it was not necessary to conserve funds through a long waiting period. Since any waiting period results in lack of income between the time of layoff and the time when benefits commence, the states shortened or even eliminated their waiting periods to reduce further hardship for the unemployed.

In 1966, no state required a waiting period of more than one week for total unemployment and three states had eliminated the waiting period altogether. Four states require a longer waiting period for partial unemployment. In a few states, a benefit is retroactively paid for the waiting week if unemployment lasts for a specified period. All states now require only one waiting period during a benefit year; about half the states do not require an additional waiting period if a second benefit year immediately follows the first.

From the beginning of the program, the need for time to process the initial claim for benefits was one of the reasons for a waiting period; today, it is the principal reason. The length of the waiting period is no longer an issue in the program.

HOW LONG SHOULD DURATION BE?

There have been no clear-cut guiding principles for determining the duration of unemployment insurance benefits. Should any limitation be set on the duration of unemployment insurance as long as the worker is still unemployed? Some other types of income insurance have no duration limitation as long as the risk insured against continues. Under the social security program, old-age insurance benefits are paid until death. Permanent disability insurance benefits are paid for the duration of disability, and the same is done for permanent disabilities under some state workmen's compensation programs. One consideration in limiting the duration of unemployment insurance is that, as unemployment lengthens, many workers become less and less employable, both psychologically and physically. Whether and when a worker becomes unemployable, however, varies with the individual and is difficult to determine. The duration of benefits, therefore, cannot be based on this consideration.

Perhaps the closest we can come to giving a guiding principle is to say that the duration of benefits should be long enough that the great majority of claimants can find employment before exhausting their benefits.

DURATION OF UNEMPLOYMENT

Some light can be thrown on the problem of the duration of unemployment compensation benefits by looking at the duration of unemployment in recent years. It is better for this purpose to use the statistics issued by the Bureau of Labor Statistics on total unemployment, since the statistics on insured unemployment are limited to those filing claims for the payment of unemployment compensation. Since 1957, statistics have been secured on total yearly unemployment, whether incurred in one or more periods. This is the most useful information for our purpose, since unemployment compensation is paid over a "benefit year" and the maximum duration for which a worker is eligible can be used during several spells of unemployment.

Table 12–1 shows that during the years 1957 to 1963, about 85 percent

Table 12–1

Number and Percent Distribution of Unemployed Persons with Work Experience during the Year, 1957–63

Extent of Unemployment	1963	1962	1961	1960	1959	1958	1957
Total number (in millions)..	12.4	13.4	13.4	12.6	10.9	12.4	10.6
Total (percent distribution)	100.0%	100.0%	100.0%	100.0%	100.0%	100.0%	100.0%
1 to 4 weeks	31.8	30.8	30.8	31.1	31.3	28.7	33.4
5 to 10 weeks	19.4	20.6	19.1	21.5	21.6	19.0	22.0
11 to 14 weeks	12.9	12.7	12.4	12.1	12.9	11.9	13.1
15 to 26 weeks	21.1	20.7	21.2	19.6	19.1	20.5	17.8
27 weeks or more	14.8	15.1	16.5	15.8	15.0	19.9	13.7

Source: United States Department of Labor, *Manpower Report of the President and a Report on Manpower Requirements, Resources, Utilization and Training*, March, 1965, table B–19.

of the unemployed with work experience had an accumulated total of less than 27 weeks of unemployment in a year and about 20 percent were unemployed from 15 to 26 weeks during the year.[1]

[1] The data also show a remarkable regularity in the distribution of the unemployed by duration of unemployment, variations in recession years being largely in the *numbers* unemployed. We can assume that these distributions would be similar to those for unemployed covered by unemployment insurance, although the numbers covered by unemployment insurance would be smaller.

DEVELOPMENTS IN DURATION OF BENEFITS

Maximum Duration

Unemployment insurance in this country was originally designed to provide benefits for only a short length of time. In the words of the Committee on Economic Security, it was "a first line of defense" against unemployment. The Committee thought that a cash benefit should be provided "for a limited period during which there is an expectation that the claimant will soon be re-employed." If the unemployed person does not find work before exhaustion of his benefits, the Committee recommended that his further unemployment should be met by a "work benefit." The Committee report states: "in periods of depression public employment should be regarded as a principal line of defense. Even in prosperous times it may be necessary, on a smaller scale, when 'pockets' develop in which there is much unemployment."[2]

The actuary of the Committee on Economic Security advised that only from 12 to 15 weeks of benefits (depending on whether a waiting period of two, three, or four weeks was used) could be financed with a contribution rate of 3 percent of payrolls. Therefore the Committee thought it had no choice but to recommend a program of short-term benefits. The Committee suggested that the states provide for an additional ten weeks of benefits for workers with long records of steady employment and that these could be financed from the savings realized by shortening the maximum regular duration by one week.

The actuarial estimates given the Committee were based, however, on rates of unemployment that were much higher than the actual rates that have occurred since the program has been in operation. Experience proved that benefits could be financed for a longer duration than was originally thought possible. The duration of "regular" unemployment insurance benefits has gradually been increased beyond the 15 or 16 weeks originally provided. A maximum of at least 26 weeks of benefits in a year—the objective that the United States Department of Labor set during the 1950's—was provided as of January, 1966, in all but two states (South Carolina and South Dakota) and Puerto Rico.

A few states have gone beyond this in recent years. As of January 1, 1966, nine states had maximums of from 28 to 39 weeks. The enactment of the federal law providing for "extended benefits" during the recession of 1958, no doubt stimulated the enactment of provisions for durations beyond 26 weeks in some of these states.

Does the fact that an increased proportion of the unemployed have more than 26 weeks of unemployment in a year mean that the objective for the maximum duration of *regular* unemployment compensation should

[2] *Report to the President of the Committee on Economic Security* (Washington, D.C.: U.S. Government Printing Office, 1935), p. 8.

be reset at, say, 39 weeks? We will leave this question for consideration in the next chapter, when extended unemployment benefit programs are considered.

Minimum Duration

In discussions of the adequacy of the duration of benefits, little attention has been given to the minimum duration of benefits provided by the state laws. Attention has focused on increases in the maximum duration, but minimum durations have also been significantly increased as will be seen from the following table:

Minimum Potential Duration of Benefits	Number of States with Specific Durations	
	1951	1965*
4–5 weeks	2	
6–7 weeks	12	1
8–9 weeks	5	3
10–11 weeks	11	17
12–13 weeks	3	11
14–15 weeks	4	3
16–17 weeks		2
18–19 weeks		5
20 weeks		2

* In five states, longer minimum durations are provided for those with minimum weekly benefit amounts, the minimum duration varying with the distribution of wages within the base period.

UNIFORM VERSUS VARIABLE DURATION OF BENEFITS

The duration provisions of the state laws can be divided into two main groups: those that provide uniform potential duration for all eligible claimants, and those that limit the duration by the amount of wage credits or weeks of employment the claimant has had during the base period. The latter group of states provide what is called "variable" duration of benefits. Whether to provide uniform or variable duration of benefits has been one of the chief bones of contention since the beginning of the program. Originally, 16 states provided uniform maximum duration of benefits. Although there has been some switching from variable to uniform duration, more states have switched from uniform to variable duration. As of April, 1966, only eight states still provided for uniform duration of benefits.

Arguments for Variable Duration

Those favoring variable duration of benefits argue that this method is inherent in the insurance "principle." In reality, uniform duration of benefits is more in accord with most other types of insurance and variable duration is incompatible with the insurance "principle." In most types of insurance one is insured for the full amount from the first payment of premiums; the amount of insurance does not vary with the length of time that contributions are paid. Under workmen's compensation, a worker is entitled to full benefits if injured at any time after the moment of hiring. In the case of retirement benefits, length of service determines the weekly or monthly *amount* of benefits, but not the duration of benefits.

On the other hand, private benefit plans more closely related to unemployment compensation—supplementary unemployment benefits and dismissal wages—increase duration with length of service. But these plans operate more like savings than insurance.

A second argument for variable duration is that it provides greater equity for those with long periods of previous employment. There would be some substance to this argument if employees contributed to the system. But in the absence of employee contributions, there is no logical reason why workers who have had longer previous employment should get a longer duration of benefits. From the standpoint of presumptive need, those who have had the shortest periods of employment probably need the longest periods of benefits since they have had less time to accumulate savings and have had longer periods without work. And unemployment insurance is more concerned with meeting needs and with providing social adequacy than with individual equity.

Another argument for variable duration is that an employer should be "liable" for benefits only in proportion to the employment has has provided the unemployed worker; therefore, the duration of benefits should be proportioned to previous employment. This "employer liability" argument probably has had the greatest influence in causing states to provide for variable duration of benefits. The "liability" of the employer, as reflected in his experience rating, will be directly affected in most states by the length of benefits paid to his former employees. Therefore, employers have sought to limit the duration of benefits by the amount of employment the worker has had. However, it could also be argued that the more regular employment the employer has provided the worker, the less he should be "liable" for benefits.

Another consideration, as some states recognize, is that the employer has little control over the *duration* of the worker's unemployment, once he has been laid off—unless, of course, the employer rehires the worker. Such states charge all benefits to the last employer, except benefits to employees who have been given only casual or short-time employment.

Perhaps the strongest argument for variable duration is the uncertainty as to whether the qualifying (wages or employment) requirement in any state law effectively tests adequate attachment to the labor market for all claimants. Even though the claimant has enough weeks of employment to qualify for benefits, it is still uncertain whether he is attached to the labor market on a year-round basis. The uncertainty is greater if former wages instead of weeks of employment are used as a qualifying requirement since the amount of wages earned is only a rough indication of the length of post-labor-market attachment. Proportioning the duration of benefits to the length of employment or amount of earnings, permits greater assurance that those who draw benefits for longer periods have been more firmly attached to the labor market. Conversely, those who have had limited employment are more likely to have been less firmly attached to the labor market. Under variable duration there is less danger of paying these workers benefits during the period when they would normally withdraw from the labor force. On the other hand, the qualifying requirement supposedly determines whether the claimant is firmly attached to the labor force. If there is a question as to whether it is performing this function, the qualifying requirement should be strengthened.

In addition, there are continuing tests of the claimant's availability for work once he has qualified for and is receiving benefits. Chapter 14 will discuss the effectiveness of these tests.

Arguments for Uniform Duration

Several of the arguments for uniform duration have just been discussed indirectly. The leading argument for uniform duration of benefits is that it provides greater security for the worker. The ability to draw the maximum duration of benefits provides as much security for the unemployed worker who has not been able to secure regular employment as for the worker who has had a steady job. Uniform duration also gives the employed worker a greater sense of security, since he knows how long he can receive benefits if he loses his job.

Uniform duration of benefits is also simpler to explain and justify to the claimant. Under variable duration it is difficult for worker A to understand why fellow worker B who has been more fortunate in getting work is also more fortunate in getting longer benefits. It would seem more equitable to A if he was entitled to as long duration as B.

Uniform duration is also easier to administer, since it requires less information from the employer, less record keeping, and fewer computations. But in this computerized age, this is no longer a significant argument.

It can be seen from this brief review of the arguments pro and con that there are good reasons for both variable and uniform duration. Choice of either alternative depends on the value one attaches to the various considerations that have been outlined.

Experience with Uniform and Variable Duration

How have the provisions for variable and uniform duration of benefits worked out in actual practice?

First, it is necessary to know something about the methods of computing the potential[3] duration of benefits for each claimant in the variable duration states. The method used in each state is given in Table 12–2. Those states that use former earnings as a basis determine the potential duration

---

[3] By potential duration is meant the maximum number of weeks of benefits that a claimant can receive if he remains unemployed that long.

Table 12-2

Method of Computing Potential Duration and Maximum Weeks Payable, December, 1963

State	Method of Computing: Proportion of Base-Period Earnings or of Weeks of Employment	Maximum Weeks Payable
Alabama	⅓	26
Alaska	30–29%†	26
Arizona	⅓	26
Arkansas	⅓	26
California	½	26*
Colorado	⅓	26
Connecticut	⅓	26*
Delaware	37%	26
District of Columbia	½	34
Florida	½ weeks of employment	26
Georgia	¼	26
Hawaii	Uniform	26*
Idaho	30–29%†	26*
Illinois	35–34%†	26*
Indiana	¼	26
Iowa	⅓	26
Kansas	⅓	26
Kentucky	⅓	26
Louisiana	⅖	28
Maine	Uniform	26
Maryland	Uniform	26
Massachusetts	36%	30
Michigan	⅔ weeks of employment	26
Minnesota	42–33%†	26
Mississippi	⅓	26
Missouri	⅓	26
Montana	†	26
Nebraska	⅓	26
Nevada	⅓	26
New Hampshire	Uniform	26
New Jersey	¾ weeks of employment	26
New Mexico	⅗	30
New York	Uniform	26
North Carolina	Uniform	26*
North Dakota	†	26
Ohio	20 weeks for first 20 credit weeks of employment plus 1 week for each 2 additional credit weeks	26
Oklahoma	⅓	39
Oregon	⅓	26
Pennsylvania	Uniform	30*
Puerto Rico	Uniform	12
Rhode Island	⅗ weeks of employment	26
South Carolina	⅓	22
South Dakota	32–26%†	24
Tennessee	⅓†	26
Texas	27%†	26

Table 12–2 (Continued)

State	Method of Computing: Proportion of Base-Period Earnings or of Weeks of Employment	Maximum Weeks Payable
Utah	Weighted schedule of base-period wages in relation to high-quarter wages	36
Vermont	Uniform	26*
Virginia	¼	24
Washington	⅓	30
West Virginia	Uniform	26
Wisconsin	⁷⁄₁₀ weeks of first 20 weeks of employment and ⁸⁄₁₀ of additional weeks up to 45	34
Wyoming	³⁄₁₀	26

* Benefits are extended under certain conditions.

† For states with weighted schedules, percent of benefits based on bottom of lowest and highest wage brackets. In states noted, percentages vary for other brackets. In Montana 13, 20, and 26 weeks depending on quarters of employment. In North Dakota 18, 22, and 26 weeks depending on amount of base-period earnings.

Source: United States Department of Labor, Bureau of Employment Security, *Summary Tables for Evaluation of Coverage and Benefit Provisions of State Unemployment Insurance Laws as of December 31, 1963* (BES No. U–235, September, 1964).

of benefits for a claimant by taking a fraction (such as one third) or a percentage (such as 37 percent) of the claimant's total annual earnings. For example, if the worker's base period earnings are $1,800, and if the fraction used is a third, the total benefits payable are one third of $1,800 or $600. If the weekly benefit amount is $30, the duration of benefits would be 20 weeks. If former employment is used as a basis for determining potential duration for a claimant, a fraction such as three fifths of the weeks of employment in the base period is used. For example, if a worker had 30 weeks of employment and a fraction of three fifths is used, the claimant's potential duration would be 18 weeks.

Exhaustion Rates

The most frequently used measure of the adequacy of duration—the only universally available one in the states—has been the "exhaustion ratio," that is, the proportion of claimants who exhaust their benefits.[4] This is not a perfect measure since it is influenced by employment conditions. The proportion who exhaust benefits is higher in periods of high unemployment than in periods of low unemployment. Even in a prosperous year, the rate of unemployment is higher in some states than others and the exhaustion rate may therefore be higher. Statutory differences also play an important part in producing different exhaustion ratios. However, in the opinion of the International Labour Office, the percentage of claimants exhausting benefits should not be more than 10 percent in normal

---

[4] Technically, the exhaustion ratio is determined by expressing total exhaustions during a 12-month period as a percent of first payments of unemployment benefits during a corresponding 12-month period.

times.[5] A more conservative norm might be no more than 20 percent who exhaust benefits in any year in which insured unemployment is below 5 percent.

Chart II gives the percentage of workers in each state who exhausted their benefit rights during the 12-month period July, 1963–June, 1964, when insured unemployment averaged 4 percent. Eight of the nine states that provided uniform duration of 26 weeks or more of benefits during this period had exhaustion ratios of less than 20 percent. Vermont was the only exception with an exhaustion ratio of 24 percent.[6] On the other hand, only three of the 43 states with variable duration of benefits—Michigan, Missouri, and Wyoming—had exhaustion ratios of less than 20 percent. Seven of the states with variable duration had exhaustion ratios in excess of 30 percent.

If the proportion who exhaust their benefits is a good criterion, Chart II shows that uniform duration more effectively meets the needs of the unemployed.

The effect of variable duration is even more striking if the exhaustees are distributed by the duration of benefits they received. Such a distribution is given in Table 12–3 which shows the percentage distribution of claimants who exhausted benefits in 1963, grouped by those receiving less than 15 weeks of benefits, 15 to 25 weeks, and 26 weeks or more.[7]

In 15 states with variable duration, more than 25 percent of the exhaustees qualified for less than 15 weeks of benefits. In three of these states, more than half of the exhaustees qualified for less than 15 weeks. Unfortunately, too much importance cannot be placed on the last column in Table 12–3, which gives the proportion receiving 26 weeks or more in benefits, because the spread of 15 to 25 weeks' duration in the next to last column is too broad. It is possible that a considerable proportion drew from 20 to 25 weeks. This is indicated by the fact that the average duration for all exhaustees was 20 weeks or more in 18 of the variable duration states. Nevertheless, Table 12–3 shows that it is important to look at more than the maximum duration of benefits provided in the law in determining its effectiveness. It makes a big difference whether there is uniform or variable duration.

In variable duration states, the adequacy of the law also depends on how the maximum duration is determined for each individual. Of the three states with over 25 percent receiving less than 14 weeks' benefits (see Table 12–2), Georgia and Indiana limited total benefits to one fourth and Idaho to 29–30 percent of base period earnings; these were among the smallest proportions in any state law. Therefore, the fraction used to determine the

[5] International Labour Office, *Unemployment Insurance Schemes* (Geneva, Switzerland, 1955), p. 178.

[6] Puerto Rico, the other state with uniform duration, provided a maximum of 12 weeks of benefits.

[7] In order to give greater comparability, the table does not include those states that provided less than 26 weeks' maximum duration of benefits in all or part of 1963.

Percent of Beneficiaries Who Exhausted Their Benefit Rights, July, 1963–June, 1964

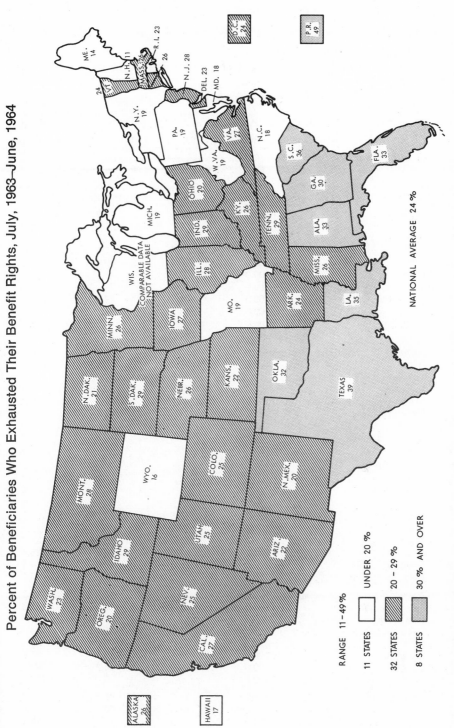

NATIONAL AVERAGE 24 %

RANGE 11–49%

11 STATES	☐	UNDER 20 %
32 STATES	▨	20 – 29 %
8 STATES	▤	30 % AND OVER

Source: United States Department of Labor, Manpower Administration, Bureau of Employment Security, Unemployment Insurance Service.

potential duration of benefits of claimants is quite important in variable duration formulas. In California, which limits total benefits to one half of base-year earnings, only 10.2 percent drew less than 15 weeks of benefits.

Table 12–3

Distribution of Exhaustees by Duration of Benefits Received, in States Providing Uniform or Variable Duration of 26 Weeks or More, 1963

State	Total	Percent Receiving Benefits for		
		Less than 15 Weeks	15–25 Weeks	26 or More Weeks
Alabama	100.0	14.0	41.6	44.4
Alaska	100.0	0	26.5	73.5
Arizona	100.0	27.5	41.6	30.9
Arkansas	100.0	27.6	47.8	24.6
California	100.0	10.2	49.6	50.2
Colorado	100.0	15.9	45.7	39.4
Connecticut	100.0	22.9	37.1	40.0
Delaware	100.0	13.5	49.4	37.1
District of Columbia	100.0	4.3	38.9	56.8
Florida	100.0	42.7	44.3	13.0
Georgia	100.0	51.3	44.1	4.6
Hawaii*	100.0	0	0	100.0
Idaho	100.0	57.5	36.3	6.2
Illinois	100.0	32.5	39.4	28.1
Indiana	100.0	58.4	34.3	7.3
Iowa	100.0	43.7	42.7	13.6
Kansas	100.0	24.1	41.7	34.2
Kentucky	100.0	0	65.6	34.4
Louisiana	100.0	24.4	46.8	28.8
Maine*	100.0	0	0	100.0
Maryland*	100.0	0	0	100.0
Massachusetts	100.0	17.5	40.0	42.5
Michigan	100.0	36.7	36.0	27.3
Minnesota	100.0	0	66.7	33.3
Mississippi	100.0	15.3	53.6	31.1
Missouri	100.0	23.2	43.4	33.4
Montana	100.0	45.0	29.3	25.7
Nebraska	100.0	33.9	37.7	28.4
Nevada*	100.0	26.3	39.3	34.4
New Hampshire*	100.0	0	2.6	97.4
New Jersey	100.0	16.5	47.2	36.3
New Mexico	100.0	5.7	40.5	53.8
New York*	100.0	0	0	100.0
North Carolina	100.0	1.0	25.3	73.7
Ohio	100.0	‡	0.2	99.8
Oklahoma	100.0	10.7	51.7	37.6
Oregon	100.0	6.6	54.2	39.2
Pennsylvania*	100.0	0	0	100.0
Rhode Island	100.0	18.9	45.2	35.9
Texas	100.0	41.0	50.9	8.1
Utah	100.0	39.5	42.4	18.1
Vermont*	100.0	0	0	100.0
Washington	100.0	0	47.4	52.6

Table 12–3 (Continued)

| | | Percent Receiving Benefits for | | |
| | | Less than 15 | 15–25 | 26 or More |
State	Total	Weeks	Weeks	Weeks
West Virginia*	100.0	‡	11.7	88.3
Wisconsin†	100.0	NA	NA	NA
Wyoming	100.0	27.8	48.1	24.1

* Uniform duration.
† Excluded; comparable data not available.
‡ Less than 0.05 percent.
NA—Not available.
Source: United States Department of Labor, Bureau of Employment Security, *Summary Tables for Evaluation of Coverage and Benefit Provisions of State Unemployment Insurance Laws as of December 31, 1963* (BES No. U–235, September, 1964).

Post-Exhaustion Studies

Exhaustion ratios, however, are an inadequate test of whether or not there should be variable or uniform duration of benefits. Another test is whether the exhaustees would have left the labor force if they had been unable to draw unemployment benefits. Sample studies in a number of states provide a clue to the post exhaustion experience of claimants. Summaries of 17 state studies made at various times between 1954 and 1956 and summaries of 15 state studies made between 1956 and 1959 were compiled by the Bureau of Employment Security in 1958 and 1961.[8]

Table 12–4 gives data from the second group of studies on the proportions who were employed, were still unemployed, or had withdrawn from the labor force two months after exhaustion of benefits. The usefulness of the information is limited because all exhaustees in each variable duration state are lumped together without regard to the duration of their benefits. There is still no consistent difference between uniform and variable duration states in the percentage who withdrew from the labor market during the two months after exhaustion of benefits. This would indicate that there is not much danger that claimants in uniform duration states will be more prone to draw all benefits for which they are eligible before withdrawing from the labor market than claimants in states that vary duration with the amount of previous employment.

Although some claimants who had withdrawn from the labor market might still report that they were unemployed, as Father Joseph M. Becker suggests,[9] the number of such statements would be no more in uniform duration states than in variable duration states.

More intensive surveys in depth are needed before any conclusions can be drawn as to the labor force attachment of benefit exhaustees. The in-

[8] United States Department of Labor, Bureau of Employment Security, *Experience of Claimants Exhausting Benefit Rights under Unemployment Insurance, 17 Selected States*, BES No. U–178, December, 1958; *Major Findings of 16 State Studies of Claimants Exhausting Unemployment Benefit Rights, 1956–1959*, April, 1961.
[9] Joseph M. Becker, S.J., *In Aid of the Unemployed* (Baltimore: Johns Hopkins Press, 1965), p. 106.

212   UNEMPLOYMENT INSURANCE IN THE AMERICAN ECONOMY

Table 12–4

Labor Market Status of Exhaustees Two Months after Exhaustion, 13 States

State Study	Statutory Maximum Duration (Weeks)*	Total	Employed	Unemployed	Withdrawn from Labor Market
Arizona—1958–59 26		100%	27%	64%	9%
Arkansas—1957 18		100	41	51	8
Indiana—1957 20		100	34	54	12
Maine—1956–57 ....23U		100	20	62	18
Mississippi—1956–57 .:..20U		100	34	57	9
Missouri—1957 24		100	41	50	9
Missouri—1958 26		100	34	61	5
New Jersey—1957 26		100	31	53	16
North Carolina—1957 ....26U		100	20	69	11
North Dakota—1957 .....20U		100	37	58	5
Oregon—1958 26		100	34	62	4
Pennsylvania—1957–58 ..30U		100	13	71	16
South Dakota—1957–58 ..20		100†	38	55	7
Vermont—1958 ....26U		100	23	64	13

* Maximum duration of benefits applicable at the beginning of the period surveyed in the study.
† Data shown reflect labor market status six weeks after exhaustion.
U—Uniform duration.
Source: United States Department of Labor, Bureau of Employment Security, *Major Findings of 16 State Studies of Claimants Exhausting Unemployment Benefit Rights 1956–1959*, table 1.

tensive studies by Professor Ronald S. Johnson of the University of Michigan and by Professor William S. Devino of Michigan State University were both made in a state with variable duration of benefits and are thus not useful for our present purpose.[10] Comparable studies in depth of the experience in uniform duration states and variable duration states are needed to determine whether variable duration more effectively screens out those who are not regularly attached to the labor market.

More information is necessary on the labor force attachment of beneficiaries during the base period as well as after exhaustion of benefits before a clear case can be made for either uniform or variable duration of benefits. The large numbers of unemployed persons who are affected by the variable duration provisions and the large proportion of women who do not work on a year-round basis add to the importance of such research. Pending such research, the data available on exhaustion rates must be our principal guide. They indicate that states with variable duration of benefits generally fail to provide adequate duration of benefits for too high a proportion of the jobless, and that uniform duration more effectively meets the needs of the unemployed.

[10] Ronald S. Johnson, *A Study of People Who Have Exhausted Unemployment Benefits in an Active Labor Market* (Ann Arbor, Mich.: Bureau of Business Research, University of Michigan, January, 1951); William S. Devino, *Exhaustion of Unemployment Benefits during a Recession* (East Lansing, Mich.: Labor and Industrial Relations Center, Michigan State University, 1960).

DURATION OF BENEFITS FOR SEASONAL UNEMPLOYMENT

Since unemployment insurance is primarily designed for temporary unemployment, one could assume that it should compensate seasonal unemployment. But there is wide disagreement as to whether seasonal unemployment should be compensated or not, and if so, for what duration.

Some would deny benefits to all seasonal workers who became unemployed, on the grounds that a seasonal worker has suffered no wage loss when he is not working. Others would deny benefits during the "off-season," but would pay benefits to workers attached to a seasonal industry if they are unemployed part of their normal working season. They reason that there is a wage loss in the latter case but no wage loss for unemployment occurring outside the normal season of operation.[11]

Those favoring a denial of benefits, at least during the off-season, frequently argue that higher wages are customarily paid in seasonal occupations to enable the worker to save money to carry him over slack periods. They point to the construction industry as the classic example. Even if seasonality rather than superior bargaining power is the reason for higher wages in construction work, the differential between average weekly earnings of construction and other workers is not enough to offset much loss of earnings during seasonal unemployment. May is usually a month when contract construction is in full swing from a seasonal standpoint. Yet in May, 1963, average weekly earnings of production workers in contract construction were only about a fourth higher than weekly earnings of production workers in manufacturing—$127.25 as compared with $99.47. Even if construction workers received unemployment benefits for the full "off-season," the higher pay they receive plus unemployment benefits would probably be less for many of them than the year-round pay of a skilled factory worker in a nonseasonal industry.

Construction and mining are about the only seasonal industries that have higher-than-average wages. In fact, weekly wages in some seasonal industries are less than in year-round industries. Low wage scales are more prevalent in short season industries such as canning and other food processing, summer and winter hotels, and summer camps.

Workers in construction, mining, and other seasonal industries are also subject to the hazards of cyclical and technological unemployment. If all workers in a seasonal industry are denied benefits in the off-season, those who lose their jobs for cyclical and technological reasons would be discriminated against as compared to workers in other industries.

Restriction of benefits in the off-season would also lead to inequities for workers in the same industry since unemployment in these industries is not evenly distributed: some workers have slack time during the busy

[11] This is the position of the International Labour Office. See *Unemployment Insurance Schemes, op. cit.*, pp. 88–90.

season, others lose work outside the busy season, and still others work the year round.

It has also been argued that seasonal workers should not receive benefits in the off-season because of the drains it would make on the fund at the expense of other workers. To the extent that an industry cannot regularize because of weather conditions or fluctuations in consumer demand, it should theoretically meet the cost of benefits to seasonal workers through higher tax rates. Presumably, such higher tax rates would then be passed on to the consumer in higher prices.

According to Richard A. Lester, however, employers can shift taxes under experience rating only to a limited extent.[12] States have also hesitated to set rates as high as would be necessary for some seasonal industries to carry the whole load of benefits to their workers; it is feared that this would place such industries at a disadvantage in interstate competition.

Popular opinion sides with those who would restrict or deny benefits to seasonal workers. The average citizen is critical of the program when he sees a seasonal worker regularly draw unemployment compensation every year in the off-season without making any evident effort to secure alternative employment. It can be argued that this is the fault of the administrative agency in not applying the "work test" more effectively. But if a seasonal worker is in a one-industry town or in an occupation that cannot be carried on in the winter months, it is not possible to apply a "work test." Public policy must them determine whether such a seasonal worker should be supported by public funds on a "presumptive need" basis.

Stories also circulate that some employers in, for example, the canning industry openly advertise or point out to prospective employees that they will be able to draw unemployment benefits when the plant closes down in addition to the wages they earn during the season. When housewives work only for such employers, it should be possible for the administrative agency to disqualify them in the off-season as unavailable for work, but there are many cases that are not as clear-cut.

Methods of Restricting Benefits to Seasonal Workers

Several courses of action are open to states that wish to deny or restrict benefits to seasonal workers. First, industries such as seasonal hotels or canneries that shut down in the off-season, can be excluded from coverage. This is accomplished today in many states which exclude employers who do not employ a minimum number of workers for 20 or more weeks in the year. However, exclusion of seasonal industries by this method may result in inequities. A waiter or cook who works in Northern hotels in the summer and Southern hotels in the winter, for example, would be unfairly treated as compared with a worker employed for the same length of time in a year-round hotel. A more equitable device could be a qualifying requirement

---

[12] Richard A. Lester, *The Economics of Unemployment Compensation* (Princeton: Industrial Relations Section, Princeton University, 1962) pp. 60 ff.

that excludes workers who are in the labor market only during a short seasonal operation. It can operate effectively, however, only if the qualifying requirement is in terms of weeks of employment.

While methods described above would deny benefits to seasonal workers, the following devices would restrict their duration of benefits. A device used in several European countries[13] and suggested in an early treatise in the United States by Paul H. Douglas [14] is a longer waiting period for seasonal workers. Douglas pointed out that those seasonally unemployed for more than the average time and those thrown out of work from cyclical and technological causes would still be protected under this device.

Another method, used by the United Kingdom and Canada, imposes additional conditions on seasonal workers. Canada also pays special seasonal benefits to certain classes of workers from January 1 to April 15, because of the severe weather conditions during this period.

A method enacted in 1964 by the state legislature of South Dakota, was to relate the amount of benefits paid to a worker during a calendar quarter to his earnings in the corresponding calendar quarter in the preceding year. This enactment, however, was defeated in a 1964 election referendum. A somewhat similar proposal was made in 1962 by the Canadian Committee of Inquiry into the Unemployment Insurance Act[15] which recommended identification of seasonal workers rather than designation of seasonal industries.

The most common method used in the United States is to designate seasonal industries, determine their normal busy season, pay benefits for unemployment occurring during the busy season, and deny benefits during the off-season. Seventeen state laws provide for this method and authorize the administrative agency to make such determinations. In practice, such provisions have not been utilized to any great degree, and when utilized, the number affected has not been large. The provisions usually apply or are applied only to industries that shut down completely in the off-season.

Any provision restricting seasonal benefits is bound to be arbitrary and create anomalies and inequities. Qualifying requirements should exclude workers who enter the labor market for only a short period of seasonal employment. The seasonal workers who have substantial attachment to the labor force and therefore qualify for benefits should receive the special

---

[13] *Unemployment Insurance Schemes, op. cit.*, p. 118.

[14] Paul H. Douglas, *Standard of Unemployment Insurance* (Chicago: University of Chicago Press, 1933), p. 56. An excellent discussion of the problem of compensating seasonal employment is found on pp. 52–56.

[15] The Committee of Inquiry recommended that any gap of five weeks or more in a worker's contribution during the first of the two years preceding his claim that is matched by a corresponding gap at the same time during the preceding year would establish an off-season for him. He would be ineligible for benefits during this period. However, seasonal benefits would be paid, under special conditions and limitations, through an extended benefit plan to be financed by the National Government. See *Report of the Committee of Inquiry into the Unemployment Insurance Act* (Ottawa, Canada: Queens Printer, November, 1962), p. 132.

attention of the administrative agency as to their continuing availability for work during the off-season.

SUMMARY AND CONCLUSIONS

The duration of unemployment benefits is one of the most important aspects of the unemployment insurance program. Unemployment insurance was originally designed in this country to provide short-term benefits. While it might be argued that there should be no limit to the duration of benefits, financial and other considerations make some limitation necessary. Experience has shown, however, that a longer duration can be provided than was originally estimated. Twenty-six weeks has become the generally accepted standard, although some states provide even longer duration. Alternative programs of "extended benefits" have been developed to supplement "regular benefits" during recessions or at all times for workers with long attachment to the labor force. These programs will be considered in the next chapter.

Originally, a long waiting period was advocated to conserve funds with which to finance a longer duration of benefits. Today, no state has a longer waiting period than one week in a year and several states have eliminated the waiting period altogether. The waiting period has ceased to be an issue.

A major duration issue is whether to provide a uniform maximum duration for all claimants who qualify for benefits, or to vary the maximum for each individual in proportion to his previous earnings or employment. It has been argued that "variable" duration is more in accord with insurance principles but in many types of insurance, the full amount of insurance is payable without regard to the length of time the person has been insured. It has also been argued that to vary duration with former employment is consonant with charging benefits to employers' experience rating in proportion to employment formerly given the claimant. Uniform duration is justified on the ground that workers who have had less than full employment need as long a period of protection as regularly employed workers. Uniform duration gives all workers a greater sense of security, is simpler to explain and easier to administer.

Comparison of states with uniform and with variable maximums of 26 weeks of benefits shows that the states with uniform duration do not have excessive numbers exhausting benefits in contrast to the high proportion of exhaustees in some states with variable duration. In states with variable duration, there are wide differences in the number who exhaust their benefits depending on their states' duration formulas. Some states have a high proportion of exhaustees who were eligible for less than 15 weeks of benefits. These are mainly states that limit duration to too small a proportion of previous employment or earnings. Before a final judgment can be made, more information is needed on the labor market attachment of workers who qualify for only a short duration of benefits in variable states, but the weight of available evidence, especially the high rates of exhaustion of benefits in most states with variable duration of benefits, points toward the desirability of providing uniform maximum duration of benefits for all workers who qualify for benefits. If uniform duration is provided, however, it is important that enough previous employment or wages be required to assure that the claimant is firmly attached to the labor force.

Opinions differ over the problem of restricting the duration of benefits to seasonal workers or denying them benefits altogether. The case is stronger for restricting unemployment benefits during the "off-season" rather than during the busy season. There are a number of ways of restricting benefits to seasonal workers. About a third of the states make an administrative determination of the normal season of an industry and deny benefits outside that season. This device has not been extensively used by the administrative agencies, however, and has not resulted in much saving in benefits. It would appear that the seasonal problem can be controlled if sufficient employment is required for a worker to qualify for benefits so that workers who temporarily enter the labor market only to work in short-season industries are not eligible. The administrative agency must effectively test the continuing availability for work of seasonal workers during the slow or off-season of the industry. Variable duration of benefits will also provide some safeguard against excessive payments to workers who are not in the labor force throughout the year.

The duration of "regular" unemployment benefits has been liberalized more than any other feature of unemployment insurance, but there is still much room for improvement. The state formulas for limiting duration should also be liberalized. Too many workers are getting too few benefits in too many states.

Chapter 13

Extended Duration
of Unemployment Benefits

The postwar economy has been characterized by relatively mild and short recessions rather than deep depressions. Nevertheless, these recessions have been marked by sharp increases in the number of insured wage earners suffering long periods of unemployment. Consequently, "exhaustion ratios" phenomenally increased. The number of long unemployed claimants who exhausted benefits almost doubled between 1948 and 1949, and more than doubled between 1953 and 1954. In 1958, the number not only increased by 120 percent over 1957, but was also three quarters of a million more than in 1954, totaling 2.5 million under the state programs. In 1961, exhaustions numbered 2,370,000.

In addition, the number of long-duration unemployed increased between recessions, particularly after the 1958 recession. Over 1.6 million jobless workers had exhausted their benefits in 1959 and 1960. Again, in the years after the 1961 recession, exhaustions remained at much higher levels than in the years between the recessions of 1950 and 1954 (see Table 13–1). The increases in exhaustions partly reflected the increase in the number of covered workers, but primarily resulted from levels of unemployment. The increased volume of workers exhausting their unemployment insurance created a strong interest in longer duration of unemployment compensation in order to provide protection for the very long-term unemployment.

In 1958, Congress and the state legislatures could not ignore the numbers of claimants who still remained unemployed after the receipt of their last benefit check. Only three fourths of the unemployed had their needs met by the duration provisions under the state programs. State action to extend benefits was slow in coming, however. Individual states felt that they could not take the risk of the added cost to the employers which would place them at a competitive disadvantage with employers of other states. Therefore, federal action appeared imperative. In 1958, Congress passed the Temporary Unemployment Compensation Act; in

218

Table 13-1

Claimants Exhausting Benefits under
State Unemployment Insurance Programs

Year	Number of Exhaustions	Percent of First Payments*
1948	1,027,520	27.5
1949	1,934,759	29.1
1950	1,853,336	30.1
1951	810,580	20.4
1952	931,362	20.3
1953	764,420	19.2
1954	1,768,927	28.8
1955	1,272,232	23.9
1956	979,684	22.9
1957	1,138,389	23.8
1958	2,504,469	33.3
1959	1,674,902	28.2
1960	1,603,372	26.1
1961	2,370,833	30.4
1962	1,628,359†	27.4†
1963	1,653,862†	25.4†
1964	1,370,796†	23.8†

* First payments means claimants paid at least one week of benefits. For years prior to 1953, first payments of benefits for 12 months ending September 30; for 1953-64, first payments for fiscal year ending June 30.

† Includes Puerto Rico which became subject to the Federal Unemployment Tax Act beginning January 1, 1961.

1961, Congress followed the recommendation of President Kennedy and passed the Temporary Extended Unemployment Compensation Act. Both of these federal laws extended the duration of benefits by roughly 50 percent, for those who had exhausted their regular benefits or whose benefit years had expired. A few states passed extended benefit programs of their own to be operative during periods of high unemployment; other states lengthened the duration of their regular benefits beyond 26 weeks. The pressures for improvisation and speedy action that accompanied the temporary federal acts resulted in a consensus among state employment security administrators that there should be a permanent program of extended benefits that would become automatically available during high unemployment periods accompanying recessions. This view was shared by Congressional leaders who handled the temporary acts of 1958 and 1961.

The continuing high volume of long-term unemployed during the recovery period following the 1961 recession led the federal Administration to propose also a program of extended benefits that would be available at all times, not just in recessions. The extent to which unemployment insurance should provide protection for long-term unemployment was one of the principal preoccupations of employment security administrators and others concerned with unemployment insurance during the early 1960's. This interest will no doubt continue throughout the 1960's.

There appears to be general agreement that unemployment benefits should be temporarily extended during recessions. As this book is written, it is not known how far agreement can be reached on providing extended benefits in recovery or boom years as well as in recession years. However, sentiment for extended benefits even in recessions is not unanimous. A few voices have been raised questioning whether unemployment insurance should attempt to deal at all with very long-duration unemployment, and maintaining that such unemployment calls for other types of programs such as retraining or relocation. If income maintenance is necessary, such persons recommend an unemployment assistance program midway between insurance and relief.

This chapter will first review the experience of foreign countries with extended benefits, the early proposals in this country for dealing with long-duration unemployment, the attempt to provide "reconversion benefits" following World War II, and the experience with the temporary programs in 1958 and 1961. It will then consider whether extension of unemployment insurance benefits is the proper method of providing income protection for the long-term unemployed, and, if so, whether extended benefits should be provided at all times or only during recessions. A discussion of the issues that must be dealt with in framing a program effective only in recessions or a continuous program will then be discussed in detail.

FOREIGN EXPERIENCE WITH EXTENDED BENEFITS

Much can be learned from the British experience in dealing with persistent and prolonged unemployment between 1920 and 1930 (see Chapter 4). As heavy unemployment continued, qualification requirements were progressively loosened and benefits were extended for longer and longer periods. By 1927, 96 weeks of "transitional benefits" were available to those who had paid eight contributions in the preceding two years; those who had paid 30 contributions at any time were eligible for an unlimited number of weeks of "transitional benefits," provided they met other conditions, including a genuinely-seeking-work requirement. This trend was reversed in 1931, when these benefits were replaced by "transitional payments" based on need. A Royal Commission on Unemployment Insurance was appointed to review the complicated history of the attempts during the 1920's to cope with the problem of long-duration unemployment. The Majority's Final Report, issued in 1932, pointed out that, although the purpose of unemployment insurance is to pay benefits as a right for a limited period, subject to specified conditions, experience has shown that a depression creates irresistible pressures to ignore the limits of unemployment insurance unless a satisfactory alternative is established. As such an alternative, the majority of the Royal Commission recommended a national system of unemployment allowances based on a needs test. This recommendation was followed by the enactment of the National Unemployment Act of 1934 which provided assistance to insurable persons between the ages of 16 and 65 who were in need and who satisfied certain other conditions, such as being capable of and available for work.[1] The same Act thoroughly reorganized the unemployment insurance system, and provided 26 weeks of benefits in a benefit year to all insured workers. However, not all unemployed workers with more than 26 weeks of benefits were transferred to the unemployment assistance scheme. Additional days of benefits were provided for workers with a good record of past employment. This 1934 Act allowed three additional days of benefit for every five contributions paid in the five insurance years immediately preceding the current benefit year, minus one day for every five days of benefit drawn during the same period. Thus, an additional 156 days or 26 weeks of benefits was possible. This provision has been liberalized several times; since 1953, benefits are extended by three days for each five weeks of contributions in the last ten years, minus one day for each ten days of benefit received in the last four years, for employees with at least five years of insurance coverage. Thus, 312 additional days or 52 weeks of extended benefits are possible, or a maximum duration with regular benefits of 492 days or 78 weeks.[2] With the careful surveillance of a committee whose principal responsibility is to keep the system solvent, these additional benefits have been adequately financed and the system has avoided criticism.

Other countries vary widely in their provision for long-duration unemployment. In 1931, the International Labour Office listed eight countries with "emergency" provisions.[3] By 1955, only Switzerland provided for extension of unemployment insurance during periods of severe unemployment. The extension, however, was only for 30–60 days after 90 days of regular benefits. Italy provided "extraordinary allowances" to workers who had exhausted their 180 days of insurance benefits. Several countries allowed additional weeks of benefits for workers with long periods of contributions, similar to the system in the United Kingdom. Others provided unemployment assistance on a needs basis. Five countries set no limitation on duration of benefits, but of these, three (France, Australia, and New Zealand) applied a needs test to claimants for any benefits, and one (Belgium) placed restrictions on the duration of benefits for married women, and administrative termination of benefits in certain circumstances. The fifth (Yugoslavia), had no limitations on the duration of its benefits.[4]

AMERICAN APPROACHES TO LONG-TERM UNEMPLOYMENT BENEFITS

Many years ago, several students of unemployment insurance in the United States anticipated the need for some program to provide for the un-

[1] The National Assistance Act of 1948 brought the unemployed under a liberalized assistance act applicable to all needy persons.

[2] Employees contribute equally with employers to the British system, which makes it easier to justify paying additional benefits to those who have not made heavy drains on the fund.

[3] "Unemployment Insurance: Tabular Analysis of the Legislation in Force," *International Labour Review*, Vol. XXIII (January, 1931), pp. 48–66.

[4] *Unemployment Insurance Schemes*, International Labour Office (Geneva, Switzerland: 1955), pp. 180–84.

employed who exhausted regular unemployment insurance benefits. One of them, Senator Paul H. Douglas, prophetically stated: "Unless an adequate supplementary system of relief is built up which is not humiliating in character, there will be a strong movement for a further extension of benefits under the insurance system to those who have exhausted their standard claims."[5] Douglas advocated a supplementary program that blended aspects of insurance and relief, providing benefits only for those who could meet a means test, but paying the benefits and applying a work test through the public employment offices.

A similar plan for those exhausting unemployment insurance benefits was recommended during the early 1930's by Hansen, Murray, Stevenson, and Stewart. This plan provided for a limited means test under which the worker would not have to exhaust his savings, but any income would be deducted from benefits.[6]

The Committee on Economic Security, however, ignored such recommendations and suggested instead that a work program be provided for the unemployed after exhaustion of unemployment benefits.

Proposal for Postwar Reconversion Benefits

The first attempt to extend unemployment insurance benefits was made at the close of World War II. In order to provide more adequate benefits during the unemployment that was expected to accompany the reconversion from war to peacetime production, Senator Kilgore tried abortively in 1955 to secure very liberal unemployment benefits for a duration maximum of two years. The following year on May 28, 1945, President Truman sent a special message to Congress recommending that the federal government supplement state unemployment compensation in order to bring the total duration of benefits up to 26 weeks and the maximum weekly benefits up to $25. The Senate passed a bill (S. 1274)[7] providing for supplementation only of benefit duration, but the House Committee on Ways and Means did not even report a bill. President Truman's proposal for supplementation of state benefits during the postwar reconversion period was essentially an attempt to bring regular unemployment benefit duration up to an adequate level. Except for the 1944 Kilgore bill, no proposal to extend benefits for long-duration unemployment was made until 1958.

Temporary Unemployment Compensation Act of 1958

On March 25, 1958, President Eisenhower sent a message to Congress requesting enactment of a program to extend the duration of benefits for all workers who exhausted their unemployment benefits during the follow-

---

[5] Paul H. Douglas, *Standards of Unemployment Insurance* (Chicago: University of Chicago Press, 1932), p. 90.

[6] Alvin H. Hansen, Merrill G. Murray, Russell A. Stevenson, and Bryce M. Stewart, *A Program of Unemployment Insurance and Relief in the United States* (Minneapolis: University of Minnesota Press, 1934), Part III.

[7] Committee on Finance, Senate Report 565, September 17, 1945, 79th Cong., 1st sess. (Washington, D.C.: U.S. Government Printing Office, 1945).

ing 12 months. The message was motivated by the rapid increase in the number of workers who were exhausting their regular benefits and the estimate that a total of 2.3 million workers would exhaust their benefits during 1958. The Administration bill presented to Congress provided for the temporary extension by 50 percent of the duration benefits a worker had received prior to his exhaustion of benefits. The benefits were to be federal, and were to be financed by reductions in employers' federal unemployment tax credits, beginning in 1963, until enough additional federal taxes had been collected to finance the benefits paid. The benefits were to be disbursed by the state employment security agencies under agreements with the Secretary of Labor, but with the proviso that if a state would not enter into an agreement, the Secretary of Labor was authorized to use a federal agency to pay the benefits.[8]

The Administration plan was drastically revised by Congress. The Temporary Unemployment Compensation Act of 1958, as finally enacted,[9] provided that federal loans would be made to states wishing to pay extended benefits. The loans (or "advances," as they were called) would cover the cost of extending by 50 percent the duration of "regular" benefits that workers had exhausted. For example, if a worker had exhausted 26 weeks of benefits and was still unemployed, the loans would finance 13 more weeks of benefits. Nothing would happen in a state that did not wish such loans. The Act, therefore, advanced interest-free money to the states to pay extended benefits. Such advances were to be repaid through reduction in the tax credits of the employers of the state, or in any other manner decided upon by the state. Together with the political pressure that had been built up, the availability of these loans proved to be sufficient inducement for 17 states to join the program. In addition, five states independently enacted extended benefit programs of their own. These 22 states contained 70 percent of the workers covered by regular state programs. Twelve additional states agreed to act as agents of the federal government to pay extended benefits to unemployed federal civilian workers and ex-servicemen. From June, 1958, when the program took effect, to July 1, 1959, slightly over two million workers drew just over $600 million in extended benefits.

Temporary Extended Unemployment Compensation Act of 1961

Faster action to provide extended benefits was taken in the next session of 1961. On February 6, 1961, President Kennedy sent a special message

---

[8] Many alternative bills were introduced into Congress. The most far-reaching (H.R. 11634) was introduced by Senator Winston L. Prouty, then in the House, which would have both increased the benefit amount and provided for unlimited duration of benefits during the recession then being experienced. John K. Galbraith developed the same idea in his book, *The Affluent Society*. He recommended that during periods of high unemployment, the weekly benefit amount be progressively increased to a top of four fifths of the worker's last weekly wage, perhaps when unemployment reached 4 million, and be decreased again when unemployment fell. The higher benefits would be paid for the duration of the unemployment of the individual. See John K. Galbraith, *The Affluent Society* (Boston: Houghton Mifflin Company, 1958), chap. 21.

[9] Public Law 85–441, approved June 4, 1958.

to Congress requesting enactment of a temporary program of extended benefits. A bill, speedily enacted by Congress, was signed by the President on March 24, 1961.[10] This Temporary Extended Unemployment Compensation Act of 1961 differed from its predecessor in that it was truly a federal program. The benefits were financed by an increase in the Federal Unemployment Tax for all employers for the calendar years 1962 and 1963, the resulting taxes to be pooled for the payment of benefits in the country as a whole. This feature of the bill was enacted only after a substitute amendment, which would have allocated the taxes collected in each state for payment of benefits only in that state, was defeated by a small margin. The Acts differed from the 1958 Act in only one other important respect—extended benefits were payable for a maximum of 13 weeks and the combined state and federal benefits were limited to an over-all maximum of 39 weeks. Since nine states had laws providing for maximum durations in excess of 26 weeks and six states had their own laws for paying extended benefits, the bill also provided for reimbursement to a state for any benefits it paid in excess of 26 weeks during the life of the program, April, 1961, through June, 1962. The number of claimants who received benefits under the TEUC program totaled 2,782,000. Claimants received an average of nine weeks of benefits. A total of $817 million was paid out in benefits under the program, including $46 million in reimbursement to states for benefits paid out in excess of 26 weeks.

IS IT SOUND TO PROVIDE EXTENDED UNEMPLOYMENT INSURANCE BENEFITS?

Some persons thing it is neither sound nor advisable to extend unemployment insurance benefits beyond the duration considered to be adequate for regular benefits. This point of view has been forcefully and brilliantly expressed in a 1962 article by Dr. Eveline M. Burns,[11] one of the leading authorities on unemployment insurance. In her article, she argued that unemployment insurance is "peculiarly well suited to meet needs for income during periods of short-run unemployment." However, there are types of long-duration unemployment for which other kinds of programs are better suited. These types include (1) long-duration unemployment due to a permanent decline in the demand for the skill or occupation of the worker, such as unemployment in depressed areas or in jobs that have become extinct due to technological change; (2) long-duration unemployment in a prolonged recession; and (3) long-period unemployment resulting from the characteristics of certain workers which make it difficult to secure employment except in periods of high demand. The latter type of unemployment is prevalent among young workers, older workers, those not possessing the education or skill required by modern

[10] Public Law 87–6.
[11] Eveline M. Burns, "New Guidelines for Unemployment Insurance," *Employment Security Review*, Vol. XX, No. 2 (August, 1962), pp. 5–9.

industry, or those under the handicap of discrimination because of race. Mrs. Burns also points out that there are employed workers who do not seek employment on a full-time or year-round basis who present a problem, especially in any extended duration program.

A short-term program is one with a duration that is now generally accepted in the regular state programs, namely, a maximum duration somewhere between 26 and 39 weeks. For unemployment of longer duration, Mrs. Burns writes:

considerations of the long-run interests of society and of the individuals concerned suggest that other policies must now be applied. Benefits higher than the typical unemployment insurance benefit may be necessary. Also society may demand more rigorous testing of the genuineness of the desire for work than is possible under the formal, objective tests of unemployment insurance. If there is a long continued recession, the community may even decide to ration the help it provides by requiring some form of needs test (one form of which would be a decision to limit payments to 'primary' workers). . . . For some long-period unemployed, especially among the older groups or workers in depressed areas, a program of public works may be indicated.[12]

The case that Mrs. Burns has made against extended benefits is formidable if we repeat the errors of the British. Basically, she poses the problem of setting the outer limits of the duration of unemployment so that unemployment insurance will not become a catch-all program. To her, that outer limit is somewhere between 26 and 39 weeks. The test of whether that outer limit is being reached is whether too many unemployed workers are being continued on benefits who have little prospect of re-employment (1) because of a permanent decline in the demand for their skill or occupation; or (2) because of handicaps of youth, old age, lack of education or skill, or race. Mrs. Burns lists a third group—the increasing number who work part time or only part of the year—which constitutes a problem of unemployment insurance protection, no matter how short the duration of benefits. Therefore, this group shall not be taken into account in determining the outer limits of unemployment insurance protection. From the data available, we shall look at the sex, age, color, occupational, and industrial characteristics of the long-term unemployed, and when available, any other characteristic that will give some indication of their employability. We can, however, only do this in broad strokes of the brush. A much more thorough and detailed examination is needed of the questions Mrs. Burns raises.

Characteristics of the Long-Duration Unemployed

What are the characteristics of those who drew extended benefits under the Temporary Extended Unemployment Compensation program of 1961 and is there any indication that this program exceeded the bounds of the protection that unemployment insurance should provide?

[12] *Ibid.*, pp. 8–9.

A superficial analysis of the results of the surveys of the characteristics of claimants under the Temporary Extended Unemployment Compensation program of 1961–62 indicates that the characteristics of these claimants did not greatly differ from regular claimants for unemployment insurance.[13] Table 13–2 compares the characteristics of claimants for regular State benefits and extended benefits under the TEUC program for September, 1961. Table 13–2 indicates that the sex, age, industrial, and occupational characteristics of the regular and TEUC claimants were quite alike. Both programs included similar proportions of men and women. The age distribution was about the same in both programs except that there was a larger proportion of both male and female workers age 65 and over receiving TEUC benefits. The occupational distribution was similar, except that there was a smaller proportion of skilled and a larger proportion of unskilled workers among the TEUC claimants. The handicaps of advanced age and lack of skill were already becoming more significant among those drawing extended benefits, but not enough so to be decisive.[14]

By and large, characteristics of the claimants for TEUC indicate that a program of extended benefits in a short recession, such as that of 1961, will provide additional protection for the same types of workers as draw benefits for shorter periods, those whose chances of re-employment are good.

Can it be expected that those who are unemployed more than 26 weeks during nonrecession years will have characteristics making them less employable than workers similarly unemployed in recession years? Let us compare those unemployed 26 weeks or more in 1964, and in the recession period of 1961.

Since separate data are not available on the characteristics of the insured unemployed who were out of work for 27 weeks or longer in 1964, the household sample data on total unemployment published in the *Monthly Report on the Labor Force* will be analyzed.

Table 13–3 gives the composition of experienced wage and salary workers in nonagricultural industries and in selected occupations comparable to those covered by unemployment insurance. Those unemployed 27 weeks or more are compared with all the unemployed in 1964. A higher proportion were unemployed for 27 weeks or more in mining and manufacturing, the industries most affected by technological changes. The proportion of long-duration unemployment that exists in manufacturing, however, is not much higher than the proportion that workers in manufacturing represent

[13] For a fuller analysis of the characteristic of TEUC claimants, as well as a discussion of the issues considered in this chapter, see Paul J. Mackin, *Extended Unemployment Benefits* (Kalamazoo: W. E. Upjohn Institute for Employment Research, 1965). See also *The Long-Term Unemployed; Comparison with Regular Unemployment Insurance Claimants*, BES No. U–225–3 (U.S. Department of Labor, Bureau of Employment Security, in cooperation with Georgia Department of Labor, Employment Security Agency, November, 1965).

[14] The large proportion of those 65 and over who were drawing pensions under the Social Security Act or other programs constituted a special problem that will be dealt with in Chapter 15.

Table 13–2

Selected Characteristics of Claimants of Regular and TEUC Benefits, United States, September, 1961

Characteristic	Regular Claimants	TEUC Claimants
Age in Years by Sex:		
Men	60.2	60.6
Under 25	13.5	12.0
25–44	42.0	41.0
45–64	34.5	34.0
65 and over	10.0	12.0
Women	39.8	39.4
Under 25	15.2	14.0
25–44	44.7	46.0
45–64	35.3	33.0
65 and over	4.7	7.0
Industry:		
Total	100.0	100.0
Mining	2.2	2.0
Contract construction	11.2	11.0
Manufacturing	51.3	49.0
Public utilities	4.0	4.0
Wholesale and retail trade	17.0	21.0
Finance, insurance, and real estate	2.5	3.0
Services	9.6	9.0
All other and information not available	2.2	1.0
Occupation:		
Total	100.0	100.0
Professional and managerial	4.4	4.0
Clerical and sales	16.9	19.0
Service	8.6	10.0
Skilled	16.0	14.0
Semiskilled	27.2	27.0
Unskilled	26.2	28.0
Information not available	0.7	—

Sources: United States Department of Labor, Bureau of Employment Security, *The Insured Unemployed*, October, 1962, pp. 7–8, table 2; *Family Characteristics of the Long-Term Unemployed*, TEUC Report Series No. 4, January, 1963 (BES No. U–207–4), tables C, 1, 4a, and 11c.

in the labor force, as will be seen from the last column in Table 13–3. The two occupational groups that are reputed to be most affected by technological changes, operatives and nonfarm laborers, actually constituted a smaller proportion of those unemployed 27 weeks or more than of all the unemployed. This may be explained for operatives by the large increase in their employment since 1961.

Table 13–3 also gives distributions by occupation and industry for 1961, so that a prosperous year like 1964 can be compared with a recession year. Unemployment was less represented in manufacturing in 1964 than in 1961, both among all the unemployed and among those unemployed 27 weeks or more. This is to be expected, since unemployment is heavier in manufac-

Table 13–3

Selected Industrial and Occupational Distribution of All Unemployed and Unemployed 27 Weeks or More, 1961 and 1964

Characteristics	Total Unemployed		Unemployed 27 Weeks or More		Civilian Labor Force
	1961	*1964*	*1961*	*1964*	*1964*
Industry					
Experienced wage and salary workers—nonagricultural	81.2%	77.2%	86.8%	81.3%	83.2%
Mining, forestry, fisheries	1.6	1.3	2.4	2.5	0.9
Construction	11.7	10.5	7.7	9.5	5.5
Manufacturing	28.8	24.4	37.1	29.5	25.7
Transportation and public utilities	4.9	3.9	6.6	5.0	6.2
Wholesale and retail trade	16.4	16.2	15.2	15.6	15.5
real estate	1.9	2.0	13.2	17.3	24.3
Service industries	13.9	16.0			
Finance, insurance and Public administration	1.9	2.2	3.3	2.7	5.1
Occupation					
Total, selected occupations	85.7	83.2	86.4	84.2	89.6
White-collar workers	20.6	23.8	19.1	22.7	43.0
Professional and technical	3.3	3.0	2.5	3.3	11.7
Managers, officials, and proprietors	2.8	4.4	2.9	4.0	10.2
Clerical	9.9	10.2	10.0	11.2	14.9
Sales	4.6	6.2	3.7	4.2	6.2
Blue-collar workers	51.4	48.3	56.2	46.6	36.7
Craftsmen and foremen	12.1	9.2	12.6	10.0	12.6
Operatives	26.0	26.5	27.8	25.4	18.6
Nonfarm laborers	12.3	12.6	15.8	11.2	5.5
Service workers, other than household	10.1	13.4	11.1	12.9	9.9

turing than in other industries during recessions. Outside of manufacturing, construction was the only industry more heavily represented among the long-term unemployed in 1964 than in 1961.

Another significant fact that stands out in Table 13–3 is that the unemployed are as broadly distributed both by industry and occupation in 1964 as in 1961. There is also less difference in 1964 than in 1961 in this distributions between those unemployed 27 weeks or more and the total group of unemployed.

Table 13–4 reveals a concentration of older male workers among those unemployed 27 weeks or over, almost twice as many as among the unemployed as a whole in 1964. But, surprisingly, males aged 45 and over represented the same proportion of the long-duration unemployed in 1964 as in 1961. In other words, the problem of the unemployed older male worker is no more serious in prosperous times than in recessions. Referring back to Table 13–2, it might also be noted that older workers were as heavily represented among regular unemployment insurance beneficiaries as among those drawing extended benefits in 1961. In other words, older workers would not constitute a special problem if extended benefits were provided in a nonrecession period.

Table 13–4

Selected Characteristics of All Unemployed and Unemployed 27 Weeks or More, 1961 and 1964

	Total Unemployed		Unemployed 27 Weeks or More		Civilian Labor Force
	1961	1964	1961	1964	1964
Age in years by sex	100.0%	100.0%	100.0%	100.0%	100.0%
Male	63.7	58.6	70.7	64.8	65.2
14–19	11.3	14.5	6.5	8.8	5.1
20–24	15.2	8.1	8.1	6.4	6.4
25–44	9.5	17.2	24.8	16.0	28.3
45 and over	22.7	17.2	33.0	33.5	25.4
Female	36.3	41.4	29.3	35.2	34.8
14–19	7.9	10.6	3.1	4.9	3.7
20–24	5.5	7.1	3.6	5.6	4.3
25–44	13.5	14.0	12.0	12.1	13.2
45 and over	9.4	9.8	10.7	12.6	13.6
Color	100.0%	100.0%	100.0%	100.0%	100.0%
White	79.5	79.1	76.4	74.7	88.8
Nonwhite	20.5	20.9	23.6	25.3	11.2

Table 13–4 also shows that the unemployment problem of the Negro is the same at any stage of the business cycle. The Negro has twice as high a rate of unemployment as the white worker and a greater problem of long-duration unemployment both in recessions and in boom years.

If extended benefits are justified in recessions, they are also justified in prosperous years, at least as long as unemployment is 5 percent or more. Extended benefits might also be justified when unemployment is 4 percent, as the characteristics of the long-duration unemployment would probably not be much different than they were in 1964.

From a practical standpoint, a program of extended benefits should be thoroughly tested before substitutes such as Mrs. Burns has set forth are proposed.

While extended benefits seem justified, other measures should also be initiated for the long-term unemployed. Long-duration claimants should be given special counseling and assistance in finding jobs. Where retraining or relocation appears necessary, the jobless worker should be guided into this long before he exhausts his benefits. These measures, however, are no substitute for an extended benefit program. Retraining and relocation will not be available for all claimants with a long duration of unemployment, and many will need to draw the full duration of extended benefits. Extended benefits will at least give them a few more months of financial security before they face the possibility of becoming indigent.

ISSUES IN EXTENDED BENEFITS

Experience with the enactment and administration of the temporary extended benefit programs of 1958 and 1961 leads to the conclusion that stopgap approaches should cease and that a permanent program should be enacted. The hurried decisions that determined the nature of the temporary 1958 and 1961 measures, and the inevitable delays in getting them enacted and into operation, are potent arguments for a permanent program. In addition, once a permanent program is initiated, proper methods of financing can be provided through regular contributions made in advance over the business cycle.[15]

It is conceivable that the duration of unemployment insurance payments should not involve a separate program of extended benefits at all. Like the British plan, regular benefits might be extended for 26 or perhaps 39 weeks and longer for those whose attachment to the labor force has been continuous and substantial. Some other method of meeting the income loss might be provided for those who "fall out" of the system—who "exhaust." This would be an ideal situation. However, the enactment of a 39-week period of "normal," universally applicable duration by the states or even by the federal government is not likely to take place immediately. Consequently, we are compelled to explore the practicability of a program which combines both "regular" and "extended" benefits.

To be sure, any permanent program of extended benefits raises a number of important questions. Should the extended benefits be available only during recessions or at all times? What should be the duration of extended benefits? Should all claimants who exhaust regular state benefits be eligible for extended benefits, or only those who have been unemployed for a minimum period of time? Should a test of firmer attachment to the labor market be required as a qualifying condition for extended benefits than for regular benefits? Should extended benefits be paid under a federal program, a federal-state program, or exclusively state programs? Should benefits be financed solely through employer contributions, or should there be employee contributions? Should benefits be financed out of general revenues of the government? If the program is in effect only during recessions, should it be "triggered in" on a national or state-by-state basis?

---

[15] In the case of the advances under the 1958 program, their repayment through reductions in the federal unemployment tax commenced in 1963 while the temporary increase in the federal tax was in effect to finance the 1961 program retroactively.

The Proposals of Interstate Conference and Administration Bills

Before discussing these questions, it will be desirable to review the main features of two bills for extended benefits which are being proposed at the time of writing. The differences in these two bills point up many of the questions just listed. One of these bills (H.R. 12771) was prepared by and sponsored by the Interstate Conference of Employment Security Agencies and introduced by Congressman Wilbur D. Mills (Dem.) near the end of the 88th Congress "for discussion purposes." An identical bill (H. R. 12772) was introduced by Congressman John W. Byrnes (Rep.) of Wisconsin.

This bill would provide for the payment of extended benefits during recessions on an automatically "triggered" basis. During a recession period, the federal government would finance 50 percent of the cost of the extended benefits. The benefits would be payable only in accordance with state legislation but the federal sharing would be limited to additional benefits not to exceed one half of the beneficiary's regular benefits or 13 weeks, whichever is less, the combined total of regular plus extended benefits not to exceed 39 weeks of benefits for total unemployment. If a state pays regular benefits in excess of 26 times the weekly benefit amount during the "federal sharing period," the federal government would reimburse the state for half of such excess. The period during which the federal government shared in the financing of benefits would be determined on an individual state basis, and would be "triggered in" after the rate of insured unemployment for a 13-week period had risen to 115 percent of average insured unemployment for the same period in the two preceding years, and triggered out after insured unemployment fell below this percentage. The federal government's share of the benefits would be financed by an increase of 0.1 percent in the federal unemployment tax. The state could finance its share in any way it chose.

This bill is different from the extended benefit acts of 1958 and 1961 in significant respects. It resembles both acts in restricting extended benefits to recession periods, but defines such periods in terms of the rate of unemployment in individual states. It is like the 1961 act in restricting extended benefits to a maximum duration of 13 weeks and regular and extended benefits to 39 weeks.

The Administration bill (H.R. 8282, 89th Congress) takes a much broader approach. It would provide a maximum of 26 weeks of benefits and an over-all maximum of 52 weeks of regular and extended benefits at all times and in all states. The federal government would entirely finance the extended benefits which would be payable under the terms and conditions of the state laws. The proposed federal unemployment adjustment benefits (FUAB) would be restricted to workers who have had at least 78 weeks of employment in the preceding three years and at least 26 weeks in their state "base periods." The benefits would be payable over a three-year period which started with the worker's state benefit year. The benefits would be financed both by a government contribution and by employer contributions through an increase in the federal unemployment tax and an increase in the wage base of the federal unemployment tax to $5,600.[16]

When Should Extended Benefits Be Provided?

It is not difficult to justify the extension of unemployment benefits during periods of recession, since a larger proportion are unemployed for longer periods than in prosperous times.

If unemployment should continue to drop as it did in 1965, would long-duration unemployment also drop? The Bureau of Labor Statistics has determined that there is an extremely close relationship between total and long-term unemployment (defined as unemployment of 15 or more weeks) over a period of time. The correlation coefficient between the two series in the 1948–64 period was .94 on an annual average basis. The Bureau of Labor Statistics concluded: "assuming the same relationship, if the total unemployment rate could be reduced to the 4.0 percent level that prevailed in the first half of 1957, the long-term jobless rate could be expected to drop to less than 1 percent of the civilian labor force (about 600,000 persons)."[17] Actually, in December, 1965, when unemployment dropped to 4.1 percent, the long-term unemployed (those out of work 15 weeks or more) were 600,000, and those unemployed 27 weeks or more were 266,000.

If experience in recent years is a guide, an average of 300,000 would mean that several times that number would accumulate 27 or more weeks of unemployment in the course of a year, as is seen in the following table:

Table 13–5

Average and Total Number Unemployed 27 Weeks or More
1957–63

Year	Unemployment Rate	Average Number (000)	Total Number (000)	Number Exhausting UI Benefits (000)
1957 .... 4.3%		239	1,454	1,450
1958 .... 6.8		667	2,482	2,505
1959 .... 5.5		571	1,633	1,674
1960 .... 5.6		454	1,982	1,603
1961 .... 6.7		585	2,209	2,370
1962 .... 5.6		553	2,020	1,638
1963 .... 5.7		482	1,840	1,568

Sources: Sophia Cooper, "Work Experience of the Population in 1959," *Monthly Labor Review*, Vol. LXXXVIII (December, 1960), table 2. Samuel Saben, "Work Experience of the Population in 1963," *Monthly Labor Review*, Vol. LXXXVII (January, 1965), table 2.

[16] The exact increase in the federal unemployment tax to finance the extended benefit program is not specified in the bill, since a proposed increase of 0.3 percent would also finance "matching grants for high-cost states" provided in the bill.

[17] United States Department of Labor, *Monthly Report on the Labor Force*, September, 1964, p. 13.

Of course, not all these long-duration unemployed qualified for unemployment insurance, and a much smaller proportion qualified for 26 weeks of benefits because of the variable duration of benefits. It is interesting, however, that the number of workers exhausting unemployment benefits has closely paralleled the total number unemployed 27 weeks or more each year, as will be seen in the last column of the preceding table.

The 1,568,558 who exhausted benefits in 1963, drew an average of 21.6 weeks of benefits. If those who qualified for only a short duration of benefits are subtracted, assuming this reflects limited past employment, at least a million were workers with at least 27 weeks of unemployment and a previous record of substantial and regular employment.

Even with unemployment at 4 percent, the number of long-term unemployed is still high enough to justify a program of extended benefits at all times, not just during recessions.

In drawing this conclusion, it must be underlined that extended benefits between recessions are justified, provided that the qualifiying requirements weed out those who are not regularly and substantially attached to the labor market. It must also be underlined that such a program would pay benefits only to those who could not benefit from or were not available for retraining and relocation. In fact, extended benefits should be denied to a claimant who refuses suitable training to which he is referred by the employment security agency. Special attention should also be given to long-term beneficiaries, including testing and counseling, to improve their chances of re-employment.

What Should Be the Duration of Extended Benefits?

How long should the combined duration of regular and extended benefits be to adequately protect the long-term unemployed?

As a general principle or goal, the combined duration of regular and extended benefits should be long enough to cover the period during which the great majority of the long-term unemployed can reasonably be expected to find re-employment. This goal was far from attainment during the TEUC program, even in those states which uniformly paid regular benefits for 26 weeks and TEUC benefits for 13 weeks; i.e., for a total of 39 weeks. Fifty-eight percent of the long-term unemployed exhausted even this duration of benefits.

Thirteen states made a sample survey of the labor force status of those exhausting benefits under the TEUC program, three months after exhaustion. The number who were employed ranged from 24 to 37 percent, except in one state, Maryland, in which only 16 percent had found work again (see Chart III).[18]

What was the experience in New York State where all TEUC exhaustees had drawn 39 weeks of benefits?

[18] United States Department of Labor, Bureau of Employment Security, *The Long-Term Unemployed; Labor Force Status after Exhaustion of Benefits*, BES No. U–225–2.

Chart III

Percentage Distributions of TEUC Exhaustees in 13 States by Sex and Labor Force Status Three Months after Exhaustion

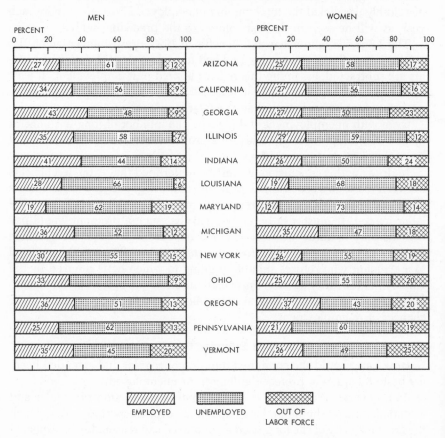

	MEN			WOMEN		
	EMPLOYED	UNEMPLOYED	OUT OF LABOR FORCE	EMPLOYED	UNEMPLOYED	OUT OF LABOR FORCE
ARIZONA	27	61	12	25	58	17
CALIFORNIA	34	56	9	27	56	16
GEORGIA	43	48	9	27	50	23
ILLINOIS	35	58	7	29	59	12
INDIANA	41	44	14	26	50	24
LOUISIANA	28	66	6	19	68	18
MARYLAND	19	62	19	12	73	14
MICHIGAN	36	52	12	35	47	18
NEW YORK	30	55	15	26	55	19
OHIO	33		9	25	55	20
OREGON	36	51	13	37	43	20
PENNSYLVANIA	25	62	13	21	60	19
VERMONT	35	45	20	26	49	25

Source: U.S. Department of Labor, Bureau of Employment Security, *The Long-Term Unemployed: Labor Force Status after Exhaustion of Benefits*, BES No. U-225-2, chart 3.

In New York State, 28 percent (30 percent men and 26 percent women) were working three months after exhaustion of TEUC, or 52 weeks after becoming unemployed.[19] Fifty-five percent were still looking for work and 17 percent had withdrawn from the labor market.

Fifty-five percent seems a large proportion to be still unemployed after 52 weeks of unemployment. But these represented only about 6 percent of those who drew any benefits in 1961. This 6 percent figure is arrived at as follows: In 1961, 22 percent of the New York claimants exhausted their regular benefits. Of these, about one half exhausted TEUC benefits, bring-

[19] Backlog claimants, i.e., claimants who had exhausted benefits between July, 1960, and April, 1961, when the TEUC program began, were unemployed up to 90 weeks.

ing the proportion of the original exhaustees who were still unemployed down to about 11 percent of all New York beneficiaries in 1961. Of these, somewhat over one half were still unemployed three months after exhaustion of TEUC benefits. Thus, about 6 percent of those who drew some regular benefits in 1961 were still unemployed after 52 weeks. This would indicate that if regular benefits were provided for 26 weeks and extended benefits were provided for another 26 weeks, 90 percent of unemployment insurance claimants would be provided with benefits for the duration of their unemployment during a recession.

Extended Duration in Nonrecession Periods

In the absence of any general program of extended benefits in nonrecession periods, the state studies of the post-exhaustion experience of exhaustees of regular benefits[20] are the best available indicators of what the duration of extended benefits should be in such periods. The studies made between 1954 and 1956 are more suitable for this purpose, since all but one were made in the prosperous years 1955–56 (about half the studies made in the 1956–59 period included the recession of 1958).

In using the 1955–56 studies, the states with variable duration should be excluded, since claimants drawing less than the maximum were included in their data. Practically all the exhaustees in five of the states which had uniform duration of benefits therefore drew the same maximum duration of benefits in each of these states.[21] The results for these five states are given in the following table:

Percentage of Exhaustees by Labor Force Status

State	Maximum Duration (Weeks)	Two Months after Exhaustion			Four Months after Exhaustion		
		Em-ployed	Unem-ployed	With-drawn	Em-ployed	Unem-ployed	With-drawn
Maine (1955–56) 23		N.A.	N.A.	N.A.	31.2*	51.4*	17.4*
New York (1954–55) ... 26		40.3	35.2	24.5	46.1	28.6	25.3
North Carolina (1955–56) 26		26.0	67.0	7.0	34.8	56.8	8.4
Tennessee (1956) 22		30.2	56.8	13.0	38.2	47.6	14.2
West Virginia (1956) ... 24		33.7	57.2	9.1	43.1	45.3	11.6

* Three months after exhaustion.
Source: United States Department of Labor, Bureau of Employment Security, *Experience of Claimants Exhausting Benefit Rights under Unemployment Insurance, 17 Selected States*, BES No. U–178, December, 1958.

A substantial proportion were employed two months after exhaustion of benefits, but only a small additional proportion were employed after four months. Although it is not shown in the table, from 20 to 30 percent of those still unemployed after four months had some interim employment. One might conclude from this data that an extension of duration of not

[20] See Chapter 12.
[21] The proportion was less than 100 percent because of loss of benefits through disqualifications, etc.

much more than three or four months would have been justified (at the time these studies were made). The data are too old and too limited in scope, however, to be the basis for final conclusions.

The foregoing does not give much guidance as to what proportion would be re-employed before expiration of the 26 weeks' duration of extended benefits proposed in the 1965 Administration bill. If this bill is enacted, the beneficiaries would be a more select group because of the long qualifying requirements provided for extended benefits, and should be more re-employable than TEUC claimants on the whole. On the other hand, a higher proportion may be displaced by technological changes and may need more time for finding other types of employment.

An extended benefit program of 26 weeks (assuming the first 26 weeks of unemployment is compensated through regular benefits) appears desirable and necessary to adequately meet the need of long-term unemployed persons during nonrecession as well as recession periods. After a study of workers displaced by plant shutdowns, Wilcock and Franke concluded:

Using Beveridge's criterion that unemployment insurance is an appropriate remedy for unemployment only when the unemployed worker has a good prospect of re-employment, our case studies of displaced workers suggest that one year might be an appropriate maximum. Most of the displaced workers who found jobs obtained them within a year of their layoff. Most of those who found no work during this first year were still jobless two and one-half to three years after the shutdowns. At least in nonrecessional periods, a duration period of one year would probably cover most workers who have any reasonable chance of re-employment. This might not be the case, of course, in a recession.[22]

Demarcation between Regular and Extended Benefits

The problem of maximum duration of extended benefits is complicated by what Harry Malisoff has characterized as the "gray area"[23] of maximum regular duration of benefits, which ranged from 28 to 39 weeks in nine states at the time of writing. Should the maximum duration of extended benefits be reduced by the number of weeks in excess of 26 already provided in these states? The answer would be somewhat different if extended benefits are confined to recession periods rather than payable at all times. Those state laws which provide longer duration of benefits (the "gray area") recognize the all-time need for a longer duration than 26 weeks. If extended benefits are provided only for a recession, then it would probably be necessary to have a provision like that in the 1961 act to reimburse states for benefits paid in excess of 26 weeks during the period of the extended

[22] Richard C. Wilcock and Walter H. Franke, *Unwanted Workers* (Institute of Labor and Industrial Relations, University of Illinois) (London: Free Press of Glencoe, Collier-Macmillan, Ltd., 1963), pp. 191–92.

[23] Harry Malisoff, *The Financing of Extended Unemployment Insurance Benefits in the United States* (Kalamazoo, Mich.: W. E. Upjohn Institute for Employment Research, April, 1963), p. 1.

benefit program. This provision was included in the 1961 act in the interest of equity to the "gray area" states and a desire not to discourage them from providing more than 26 weeks at all times. But why should the federal government be responsible for financing or helping to finance benefits in excess of 26 weeks during recessions and not at other times? Putting it another way, why should states be more responsible for a longer duration of benefits in good years than in bad? One reason that could be given is that the states are more able to finance a long duration in prosperous years. But this has been less true in recent years because of the continuing high level of persistent unemployment in good years. The problem can be re-solved only by the states and the federal government agreeing on a line of demarcation between regular and extended benefits so as to eliminate the "gray area," and work out a rational program of extended benefits. It is our belief that 26 weeks is a good dividing line, as we indicated in the preceding chapter.

Should Short-Duration Exhaustees Get Extended Benefits?

States that provide a shorter duration than 26 weeks for many or all claimants create another problem that makes it difficult to set the duration of extended benefits. Two remaining states and Puerto Rico have a shorter maximum duration than 26 weeks, and a much larger group of states have variable duration of benefits. The 1958 and 1961 extended benefit pro-grams made all exhaustees of regular benefits eligible for extended bene-fits, irrespective of how short the duration of their regular benefits had been. Persons barely eligible for the minimum duration of benefits pro-vided in variable duration states received an additional 50 percent dura-tion, even though this meant as few as five or six weeks of extended benefits. In fact, in three states,[24] 30 percent or more of the claimants who exhausted extended benefits under the 1961 program were eligible for less than seven weeks of extended benefits, which meant they had been eligible for less than 13 weeks of regular benefits and less than 20 weeks of total protection.

Although six or seven weeks of extended benefits helped the short-duration claimants for a few weeks, they probably did not help much in bridging the gap before these workers were re-employed.

What should be the cutoff after which extended benefits begin? Any cutoff point will result in anomalies. The 1961 TEUC Act set a precedent by financing all benefits in excess of 26 weeks under the extended benefit program. The Administration bills of 1961–65 took the logical next step in proposing that workers who were eligible for *some* benefits under regular state programs be entitled to commence drawing extended benefits only after their 26th week of unemployment. The bills included the requirement that the claimants continue to be available for work in the interim if they exhausted their regular duration of benefits short of 26 weeks. The bills

[24] South Dakota, Utah, and Virginia.

also were based on the concept that extended benefits should be paid only for long-duration unemployment, and that the states should fill any gap. This would make it possible, however, for persons with low employability to barely qualify for regular benefits, exhaust them, and later draw a few weeks of extended benefits. Therefore, the 1961–65 Administration bills also required that there be a long and substantial period of employment in order to qualify for extended benefits.

It is our belief that this principle of a longer qualifying requirement for extended benefits should be established, even if a "triggered" program such as the Interstate Conference bill prevails. This bill could well be modified to provide that the federal government share in the cost of extended benefits only for claimants who have exhausted 26 weeks of benefits. In states with variable duration, the federal government would share in the cost of extended benefits only for those with a substantial work history. The states could still have variable duration for claimants with lesser qualifying wages or employment. Since the requirements for 26 weeks of benefits differ greatly in the variable duration states, the federal government might provide grants-in-aid only for those claimants who met the qualifying requirements for extended benefits proposed in the Administration bills.

What Should Be the Qualifying Requirement for Extended Benefits?

The 1958 and 1961 temporary extended unemployment compensation acts had no qualifying requirement for extended benefits beyond the fact that the claimant had exhausted his regular benefits or his benefit year had expired. This may have been necessary in a "crash" program. But even in a recession, in the absence of any requirement beyond exhaustion of regular benefits, many persons who are chronically unemployed for long periods would be eligible for extended benefits after a brief period of employment. Other persons who do not look for year-round employment may get a windfall of a few extra weeks of benefits. It is therefore desirable and probably necessary to devise a test that will pay benefits only to those workers who normally are attached year-round to the labor force, but who are suffering an unusually long period of unemployment.

How can a qualifying requirement be devised that will accomplish this objective without going into the personal characteristics of the worker? As in the case of regular benefits, the record of previous employment seems to be the best test.

As has been pointed out earlier in the chapter, the British pay "additional days" of benefits amounting to three days for each five weeks of contribution in the last ten years, minus one day for each ten days of benefits in the last four years, for employees with five years of insurance coverage. Such a provision makes the insurance program something of a savings system for the workers.

Under the Railroad Unemployment Insurance Act, a claimant who exhausts normal benefits can draw an additional 65 days of extended benefits if he has had from 10-15 years of railroad service. He is entitled to a maximum of 130 additional days if he has had 15 or more years of service. Such a program of extended benefits is particularly appropriate for the railroad industry in which great numbers of workers with long service have lost their jobs through technological and other changes.

As a qualifying requirement for extended benefits, the 1965 Administration bill specifies that a worker must have had 78 weeks of employment in the past 156 weeks and 26 weeks in the last 52 weeks preceding his claim for regular benefits. The worker must have a record of substantial recent employment and a sustained period of employment, a much stiffer requirement than the qualifying stipulations under any state law for regular benefits.

Analysis of various available data indicates that the qualifying requirement in the 1965 Administration bill would eliminate about 40 percent of those exhausting regular benefits. Presumably, these would include new entrants, workers with low employability, or those who were not in the labor market on a year-round basis. Only experience can tell whether the qualifying requirement in the Administration bill is a good test. Its effectiveness will be proved if it qualifies only claimants who have a reasonable prospect of finding employment while drawing extended benefits or who will be able to make some readjustment during the extended period, such as starting a retraining course, which will eventually result in their reemployment.

Federal or State Responsibility for Financing Extended Benefits

How should extended benefits be financed—by the federal government, the state governments, or both? Should funds be taken from employer taxes, employee contributions, general government funds, or some combination of these sources?

The jurisdictional responsibility for the raising of funds will have some influence on the source of funds. In the case of the 1958 TUC Act, the federal government had the immediate responsibility for providing funds. Since these were in the nature of advances to the states, however, the ultimate responsibility for financing the extended benefits rested with the states that chose to participate in the program. The situation was more clear-cut with respect to the 1961 TEUC Act, in which the federal government had the sole responsibility for financing the program.

The plan for a permanent program of extended benefits that was proposed by the federal Administration in 1965 provides for exclusive federal financing of the benefits. The bill prepared and sponsored by the Interstate Conference (H.R. 12271, 88th Congress) provided for 50-50 financing by the federal government and those state governments that chose to cooperate in the program.

The official explanation of the 1963 federal Administration bill (H.R.

6339) justified full federal responsibility for extended benefits: "Unemployment of longer duration (than 26 weeks) is made a Federal responsibility because long-term unemployment is a national problem. It results from economic changes and relocation of industry, which transcend State lines. Its impact cannot be confined to the immediate areas of its origin. Its effective treatment is predicated upon both a local and an over-all approach, which utilizes the resources of the entire nation." These statements could also be applied to a considerable amount of short-duration unemployment. Much short-range unemployment stems from national causes, or occurs in connection with products that have a national market. During a recession, the first 26 weeks of unemployment are as much due to national causes as the following 26 weeks, if the drop in business is nationwide. It is true that a large amount of short-duration unemployment is frictional in character and the result of local causes. But much, if not most of it, is due to economic conditions and changes that transcend state lines.

Exclusive or partial federal financing of extended benefits can be justified on another basis; namely, the uneven incidence of unemployment among the states. A recession hits some states much harder than others. In 1961, for example, insured unemployment which averaged 5.7 percent nationally, ranged from a low of 2.5 percent in the District of Columbia to a high of 12.6 percent in Alaska. Heavy unemployment also means longer duration unemployment. While a case can be made for some sharing of the cost of the regular benefits because much unemployment is due to national economic conditions, a much stronger case can be made for national sharing of the cost of the long-duration unemployment, because of the heavier burden it will otherwise place on certain states.

From 1958 on, a few states assumed responsibility for extended benefits by enacting their own programs. Why should not all the states do likewise? The states have assumed responsibility for short-term unemployment, whatever its causes; why should they not assume responsibility for long-term unemployment? Logically, there is little reason. Practically, as has just been argued, the uneven incidence of nationally caused unemployment calls for some sharing, if not total assumption, of the cost of long-duration unemployment by the federal government.

The Interstate Conference plan for federal-state sharing of the cost of extended benefits represented a compromise between the points of view of those who believe that the states should assume full responsibility and those who advocated full federal responsibility for long-duration unemployment. Although this is essentially a political compromise, there is much to be said for joint sharing of the responsibility. While most long-duration unemployment is due to national causes, much of it results from local conditions.

There are also definite advantages in shared financial responsibility when one level of government—the states—has major responsibility for the administration of extended benefits. The state agencies have done an honest and conscientious job in administering many programs that are wholly federally financed, including benefits for federal civilian workers and ex-servicemen, the TEUC program of 1961, training allowances under the ARA, and MDTA programs. Yet state financial participation in a federal-state extended benefits program would no doubt result in more state interest and responsibility in the program's success. Since extended benefits are "triggered" by increases in unemployment in individual states under the Interstate Conference plan, it would also be more logical for a state to pay part of the cost. We therefore believe that a federal-state joint financing of extended benefits makes good sense.

How Should Extended Benefits Be Financed?

Unemployment taxes paid by employers have financed both the 1958 and 1961 temporary extended benefit programs. Federal employer taxes would pay part of the cost in the 1965 federal plan and the federal share of the cost in the Interstate Conference plan. Government funds would partly finance the federal plan. The Interstate Conference plan, however, left it to the states to determine how they would finance their share. If past practice is any precedent, it can be assumed that the states would normally finance their share through past or present employer contributions.

Employer Contributions. Employer financing of extended benefits will require only a modest increase in an existing tax and the same mechanism can be used for its collection at no additional administrative cost. Another argument for employer financing of extended benefits is that much of the unemployment for which the extended benefits is provided is no different in kind from short-duration unemployment, although employers can argue that the longer the duration of unemployment the less they are responsible for it.

If extended benefits are provided for all types of persistent unemployment in good years and bad, other questions arise with respect to exclusive employer financing. Where a plant has automated, it can be argued that the employer is responsible for the unemployment and should pay for the full duration of benefits. If the plant has been relocated in another geographical area, the individual employer is again responsible. But if the unemployment is due to a secular decline in the industry because of changes in consumer tastes, a new invention, or the ascendancy of a competing product, the individual employer cannot be held responsible and the case for employer payment of extended benefits is weakened, even if the costs are spread among all of a state's employers. Individual employers have even less responsibility for unemployment due to a recession.

While employer contributions may be justified for short-term unemployment on the argument that the employer has some control over it, Eveline M. Burns has written: "These justifications for throwing the cost of unemployment benefits solely on employers cannot be urged in the case of long-period unemployment, more especially that which is characteristic of a prolonged recession or of unemployment in depressed areas or in declining industries where an individual employer has almost no control."[25] On the other hand, if employer contributions should not be based on individual employer responsibility but rather on the collective responsibility of the business community, as we have contended later in this book, it is justifiable to finance the cost—or at least part of the cost—of long-duration as well as short-duration unemployment through employer contributions.

Employee Contributions. It is difficult to justify employee contributions for extended benefits when employee contributions are not also required for regular benefits. If employee contributions were imposed to finance extended benefits paid only during periods of high unemployment, this would be, as Harry Malisoff put it, "like paying fire insurance on a house when the policy provided compensation only if a sufficient number of other houses burned down at the same time."[26]

If the plan of extended benefits encompassed all types of unemployment, employee contributions would result in another paradox. The Administration plan provides that a claimant can be disqualified from the extended benefits for six weeks if he refuses to attend or fails to make satisfactory progress in training to which he is referred. If the worker has contributed to the program, he might feel this would be taking away rights he has paid for if he did not want or like the training to which he was referred. The Administration bill provides that the extended benefits can be suspended while training allowances are available. If the training allowances are provided at government expense, the worker would wonder why he had to pay for extended benefits for which he is no longer eligible.

In proportion to the amount of an employee tax it would also be expensive to set up the machinery for the collection and enforcement of an employee contribution if it is limited to financing extended benefits. If employees paid 0.1 percent of taxable wages, their maximum contribution would then amount to only about ten cents a week on a base of $5,600, the base proposed in the Administration bill.

On the other hand, employee contributions can be justified if one uses the analogy of insurance against catastrophic illnesses, rather than Malisoff's analogy. Labor might be more willing to share in paying a premium for protection against catastrophic unemployment of long duration.

Organized labor would also be less opposed to contributing to extended benefits since there would be no experience rating of employer contributions, unlike contributing to the regular state programs in which there is experience rating of employer contributions. The unions believe that since labor cannot aid in the stabilization of employment, one of the purposes of experience rating, it is inconsistent to require employee contributions towards the costs of regular benefits.

[25] Burns, *op. cit.*, p. 8.
[26] Malisoff, *op. cit.*, p. 48.

Government Contributions. A good case can be made for government financing of extended benefits. Although too much emphasis in unemployment insurance has been placed on individual employer responsibility for unemployment, it is legitimate to consider how long industry as a whole should continue to be responsible for unemployment. Workers who suffer prolonged unemployment are usually the victims of general economic changes, as well as the general state of the economy, for which the government is assuming more responsibility.

As Harry Malisoff has written:

General revenue support would reflect our increasing understanding of the nature of the longtime unemployment problem. The longtime unemployed are incidents of changes in the structure of the economy, technological progress, shifting defense contract distribution patterns, occupational obsolescence, and many other factors that are national in scope and origin. The injection of general revenues to whatever extent would constitute an acknowledgement of the national responsibility for persistently extended unemployment.[27]

Malisoff also suggests that a government contribution would facilitate the drawing of distinctions between the conditions for receiving regular and extended benefits, such as requirements of counseling, education, and training as a condition for receiving extended benefits.

As has been pointed out, the 1965 Administration bill provides for a government contribution as well as employer contributions. It includes the provision that a worker will be disqualified from benefits for six weeks if he refuses training, a distinction from the program of regular benefits.

There is a danger, however, that a government contribution would result in the drawing of undesirable distinctions between regular and extended benefits. A case in point is the report of the Canadian government appointed Committee of Inquiry, referred to in the preceding chapter. The Committee recommended a program of extended benefits to be financed entirely out of general revenues of the National Government. The Committee members looked on their plan as intermediate between insurance and assistance. The benefits they recommended would be related to the worker's previous regular benefits. In order to justify government support, it was suggested that the government pay benefits under stricter conditions. The concept of suitable employment would be broadened; the claimant would be required to accept employment for which he is "reasonably capable, whether it is the same as his customary employment or not." Extended benefits would not be available to married women who are not the sole supporters of their households, to persons over 70 who are receiving a pension under the Old-Age Security Act, nor to persons under age 18.

A proposal of government-financed extended benefits in this country may also raise the question whether unemployed workers who have been excluded from unemployment insurance coverage will be eligible for the extended benefit program. As reported to the House in 1958 by the Com-

[27] Malisoff, *op. cit.*, p. 46.

mittee on Ways and Means, the extended benefit bill provided for the financing of the temporary extended benefits out of general revenues. Because of proposed government financing, the Committee felt it necessary to also include, as a separate title in the bill, provision of unemployment benefits for those not covered by the unemployment insurance system. The Committee reasoned that additional benefits should not be provided out of government funds for a privileged group, i.e., workers who have received unemployment benefits, without providing the same benefits for other unemployed persons. Although this bill was defeated and the Administration's proposal was restored, this suggests the possible direction of Congressional thinking on the issue of government financing of extended benefits.

If financing out of general revenues were proposed, it is even possible that the benefits would be subject to a means test. A means test, in fact, could easily be justified if the program is government financed. Even veterans' benefits are payable subject to an income test. If only a moderate income test were provided, such as is in veterans' legislation, it would still result in a very different kind of program than the kind of extended benefits under discussion.

Exclusive government financing may make it difficult to assure that funds for extended benefits are available when there is a sharp increase in claims due to a recession. Congress might balk at appropriating adequate funds except when they were actually needed. Unforeseen increases in long-term unemployment would then require a supplemental appropriation, which might delay benefit payments until such an appropriation was secured.

Despite these objections, financing of extended benefits through government contributions should be seriously considered. Other programs enacted during recent years to deal with the problem of unemployment have been exclusively financed by the government. In the case of the retraining program, this includes the payment of training allowances, which are paid in lieu of unemployment compensation.

A large proportion of those unemployed for prolonged periods are suffering from some handicap that makes it more difficult to find work. Some handicaps are due to discrimination because of age or color. Other handicaps include inadequate education or training, or some physical disability. While it can be argued that employers should bear the cost of unemployment resulting from discriminatory practices, industry cannot be blamed for personal deficiencies and handicaps. Society as a whole should assist such workers. One way society is helping those with personal handicaps, particularly of lack of education or training, is through training programs, including the payment of training allowances. It would therefore be reasonable to expect the government to finance, or at least help finance, the payment of extended benefits, so as to give workers who are handicapped in finding jobs more time to look for work.

This leads to the conclusion that a combination of employer and government contributions should finance extended unemployment compensation, as is proposed in the 1965 Administration bill. Since there is something to be said for both employer and government contributions, and not too strong a case for either party paying the whole cost, we believe the Administration bill of 1965 provides a good compromise.

"Triggering" Extended Benefits during Recessions

If extended benefits are paid only during recessions, it is necessary to have some objective test by which the program can be started and ended, a test which is related to the increase in unemployment incident to the recession. The actual formula by which the extended benefits would be "triggered" is a highly technical matter that must be left to the statisticians. The type of trigger selected for the Interstate Conference bill, however, is open to question by even a nontechnician. As stated earlier, this trigger would be pulled when average insured unemployment for a three-month period was at least 115 percent of the average rate of insured unemployment for the corresponding 13-week periods of the two preceding years. With this trigger, states with a relatively low rate of unemployment which have experienced a 15 percent increase in insured unemployment would be paying extended benefits, while states with persistently high unemployment which have not experienced a 15 percent increase may not be paying such benefits.

A broader question that would have an important bearing on the nature of the program and its effectiveness, is whether the "triggering" should be on a nation-wide or state-by-state basis. If the program is strictly national with funds financed by taxes from all the states, pooled for the nation as a whole, the only logical answer would be a national "trigger" that would put the program in operation simultaneously in all states. But if it is a federal-state program, such as was proposed in the Interstate Conference bill, the issue is pertinent.

It has been reiterated that during a national recession, business decline and unemployment is very uneven among the different states, depending largely upon the extent to which a state contains industries affected by the recession. Some states, especially those without manufacturing, will hardly notice that a recession is in progress; others will be hard hit. Some will suffer a business decline earlier than others, or will recover more slowly. If extended benefits are to be confined to periods of high unemployment, it would appear desirable to develop a test that would be geared to each state's economy. This test would trigger a program on the basis of the rise in unemployment, or whatever the technical measure is, based on the individual state's previous experience.

Such a procedure might still result in inequities. A state may be affected by the recession in only one or a few plants or communities; this may not be sufficient to meet the state-wide test but may result in heavy unemployment in the affected local units of business or government. But if extended benefits are "triggered in" to take care of an individual plant or community, numbers of unemployed elsewhere in the state may receive a windfall if unemployment is no more serious than usual in their particular situation. No statistical device can be used that will not result in anomalies. But the smaller the unit in which extended benefits are "triggered," the less likely that there will be anomalies, or they will be less serious. "Triggering in" of extended benefits for a local community or even an individual plant would carry the triggering concept to its logical limit. But this would result in other problems. For example, with the large numbers of workers commuting from one community to another, some workers with long-duration unemployment in a "triggered in" community would be ineligible for extended benefits because they had worked in a neighboring community. If extended benefits are to be paid on a triggered basis, the state is probably the smallest practical unit.

SUMMARY

The increase in long-duration unemployment both during and between recessions has indicated the need for some provision for income maintenance of the unemployed who have exhausted regular unemployment insurance benefits.

The British experience with emergency provisions for coping with long-duration unemployment indicated the need for permanent legislation, eventually enacted in the United Kingdom. The British extended duration to those with employment against which unemployment insurance benefits had not been charged, and provided an unemployment assistance scheme for those who exhausted unemployment insurance benefits. Some other foreign countries provided emergency extended benefits in the 1930's, but few had such provisions in 1955.

Although the need for income provision for those exhausting unemployment insurance benefits was discussed in this country in the early 1930's, the Committee on Economic Security recommended work programs as a "second line of defense." An unsuccessful attempt was made to provide "Reconversion Benefits" for long-term unemployment following World War II. Extended benefits were provided on an emergency basis in the recessions of 1958 and 1961. Following this, plans were considered for permanent legislation to provide extended benefits during recessions or, alternatively, at all times.

Dr. Eveline M. Burns, an authority on unemployment insurance, has made a strong case against providing a separate program of extended benefits on an insurance basis because of the differing nature of long-duration unemployment at different times and the varying characteristics of many workers suffering long-duration unemployment. She also gives reasons why the unique features of the unemployment insurance program are only suited to short-duration unemployment.

Special studies of the characteristics of those drawing extended benefits under the 1961 TEUC program, however, do not show much difference between them and regular claimants for benefits. If account is taken of the differences in insured unemployed, data on total unemployment in a year of prosperity such as 1964, also indicate that there would not be much difference in the characteristics of regular claimants and those covered by unemployment insurance who experience long-duration unemployment in such a year.

In planning a program of extended benefits, a number of issues arise. Should extended benefits be provided only during recessions or at all times? The increase in long-duration unemployment between recessions indicates that extended benefits should be provided for those who show a firm attachment to the labor force through a long record of substantial employment, but need more time for readjustment before they can find re-employment. A sufficient volume of this type of worker can be anticipated, even when unemployment is 4 percent or less, to justify payment of benefits between recessions.

The temporary programs of 1958 and 1961 demonstrated that 13 weeks of extended benefits is inadequate. The problem of determining what the maximum duration of extended benefits should be is complicated by the different maximum durations in state laws. Agreement is needed between the federal government and the states on a line of demarcation. Twenty-six weeks seems to be the best demarcation, since most states already provide maximum benefits of 26 weeks. In any case, available evidence indicates that the combined duration of regular and extended benefits should be 52 weeks, but no longer.

The 1958 and 1961 programs paid extended benefits to all exhaustees, but analysis shows that the odds were high against those with short duration benefits finding employment before also exhausting their extended benefits. Extended benefits should be paid only to those who have been unemployed for 27 weeks or more, and then, only to unemployed workers whose past records indicate they have some prospect of re-employment.

It is difficult to devise an objective method for determining who should be paid extended benefits which does not go into the personal characteristics of the worker. The qualifying requirements in the 1965 Administration bill, which required 78 weeks of employment in the last 156 and 26 weeks in the last 52 preceding unemployment is a good approach.

The 1958 TUC program was initially financed by the federal government, but with the states responsible for ultimate payment of the cost; the 1961 TEUC program was financed on a national basis through temporary increases in the federal unemployment tax. The strongest argument for federal financing is the unequal incidence of unemployment among the states. Logically, there is no reason why the states should not provide for their own extended benefits, which some have done, since long-term unemployment is an extension of short-term unemployment already compensated by the states. The mixture of local and national causes of long-term unemployment, and the uneven cost among states, argues for federal or federal-state sharing of the cost of funding an extended benefit program.

There are good arguments pro and con for employers continuing to finance the cost of extended benefits. The longer unemployment persists, however, the weaker becomes the argument for employers paying the whole cost.

Workers might question why they should share in the cost of extended benefits if they have not contributed to the regular unemployment insurance system. The administrative cost of collecting employee contributions would also be out of proportion to the small weekly amounts required. On the other hand, extended benefits might be viewed as insurance against a catastrophic risk, and workers might be more willing to pay for this than for regular benefits. Since there would be no experience rating of extended benefits, labor would be less opposed to helping finance costs of an extended benefit program.

A strong case can be made for at least partial financing by the federal government. A government contribution would differentiate extended benefits from regular benefits. Stricter requirements for receiving extended benefits could be imposed with less danger of such requirements "feeding back" to regular benefits. On the other hand, government financing of extended benefits would raise questions as to whether the unemployed not covered by regular benefits should also receive similar benefits. Demands might also arise for a needs test. Finally, it might be difficult to secure Congressional appropriations on a regular basis to finance the benefits.

If extended benefits are confined to recession unemployment, it is necessary to have a "trigger" to automatically set the payment of extended benefits in motion. Whether the "trigger" should start payment of extended benefits on a nation-wide basis or a state-by-state basis, however, is a major policy question. Since the timing and incidence of large-scale unemployment varies geographically, a state-by-state "triggering" and ending of recessional extended benefits would appear to be more realistic than a national "trigger" that simultaneously put the program in operation in all states.

A triggered program for recessional unemployment would result in a discontinuous treatment of long-duration unemployment. There is no sharp break in the volume of long-duration unemployment between one period and another. There does not appear to be much difference in the characteristics of the long-duration unemployed than the unemployed as a whole. A continuing program of extended benefits, carefully circumscribed by qualifying requirements that cull out those without substantial employment and without year-round attachment to the labor market, appears to be necessary and desirable, certainly as long as unemployment continues to be a serious problem.

Chapter 14

The Problem of Testing
Labor Market Attachment

One of the most neglected, yet vital, issues in unemployment insurance is the problem of eligibility requirements for benefits. This includes the requirement of a certain amount of employment or wages before becoming unemployed and the requirement that the worker be available and able to work while drawing benefits. What should be the required attachment to the labor market before unemployment, and what should be the tests of continued attachment to the labor market after the worker becomes unemployed?

The need for a qualifying requirement in terms of former employment or wages is accepted, but few have taken the trouble to think through its objectives. Only recently have there been many studies of the employment history of claimants to determine whether the qualifying requirement was too loose or too tight. The requirements in the state laws have been largely based on guesswork or legislative bargaining. When wages are used as a qualifying requirement, the provisions have become quite technical in order to require enough wages to assure that the claimant has had a substantial amount of employment. Sometimes more attention is given to the technicalities of the requirements than to their substance.

There is general agreement that the qualifying requirements are largely unsatisfactory. This is due to the vagueness of the concepts on which the qualifying requirements are based, the limited knowledge about the employment and wage patterns of covered workers, and the use in most states of quarterly earnings of employees as a basis for qualifying requirements. Nevertheless, only a few states have seriously studied the problem of selecting an effective qualifying requirement.

Qualifying requirements at their best are rough and ready measures for determining the worker's attachment to the labor market. After a worker files a claim, it is necessary to continue to test whether he is still in the labor market and genuinely unemployed. Therefore the laws include requirements that the claimant shall be able to work and available for work. The legislation states these requirements in very general terms and it has been necessary to work out a body of precedents through administrative determination and court decisions to apply these requirements to specific situations. Basic reliance is placed on registration for work at the local public employment office. The legislation or administrative policy of many states also requires an "active" search for work. One of the basic issues of the program is how much effort the claimant should put into an independent search for work in addition to relying on the public employment service to refer him to a job.

The tests of the work record before unemployment and of the availability for work after unemployment commences will be considered in this chapter. The latter test merges into disqualification provisions, particularly with respect to refusal of suitable work, which will be discussed in Chapter 15.

QUALIFYING REQUIREMENT

Objectives of a Qualifying Requirement

The goals and objectives of unemployment insurance should determine the requirements that a claimant must meet to be eligible for benefits. The broad objective of the program is to compensate workers who have been in employment covered by the unemployment insurance program when they are involuntarily without jobs. Those entering the labor market for the first time, re-entering after several years of remaining at home, or seeking to transfer from noncovered employment are not "covered" by the law until they have worked in covered employment. Theoretically, a worker could be protected against unemployment from the day he is hired for a job in covered employment, even if he is laid off the next day. This would follow the rule in accident compensation, under which a worker is protected against accidents on the job from the moment he is employed. If a worker slips on a greasy spot on the floor and suffers an injury an hour after he starts work, he is eligible for workmen's compensation. Suppose, however, that a woman is hired and at the end of the first day is told by her employer that, although her work has been satisfactory, she is no longer needed. The fact that she has been laid off can usually be easily determined, but is she unemployed the following day? Perhaps she had not intended to work more than a few days to earn enough to buy something that could not be bought on her husband's salary. On the other hand, she may have intended to work indefinitely because her husband's wages were inadequate for their growing family. Whether or not she is unemployed depends on her intentions. Unlike an injured worker who can point to his disability, she cannot present objective proof that she is unemployed.

Unemployment insurance planners have therefore had to devise other kinds of tests to determine whether the laid-off worker is suffering a wage loss through his unemployment. One test is to require a substantial amount of covered employment or wages in a recent period, enough to create a presumption that the worker is normally in the labor force and that he would continue to work if he had a job. Substantial and recent employment is normally required in order to eliminate those whose employment has been so casual, brief, or intermittent that it cannot be presumed that they are regularly looking for work.

A qualifying period is also needed for cost reasons. If a substantial amount of previous employment was not required, large numbers of persons with only temporary, casual, or intermittent employment would draw benefits. This would place such large drains on the unemployment funds that much less could be paid in benefits to those who are substantially attached to the labor market and are suffering a real wage loss.

State Qualifying Requirements

Flat Amount of Qualifying Wages. The states that adopted benefit formulas based on quartely or annual wages did so in order to base benefits on the quarterly wage reports required for federal old-age insurance. In addition, this necessitated the development of a qualifying requirement in terms of base period (annual) wages and also, in some states, of "high" quarter wages as well, replacing qualifying requirements based on weeks of employment.

As of January 1, 1966, thirteen states rely entirely upon a minimum amount of annual earnings, ranging from $300 to $800, as a qualifying requirement. This is especially true of states with a benefit formula expressed as a percentage of annual earnings. Eight of these states have additional requirements, such as earnings in more than one calendar quarter.[1]

The principal weakness of such flat dollar requirements is that the amount of time an employee needs to work in order to qualify for benefits depends on his wage level. A $1.00 an hour worker has to work three times longer to qualify than a worker earning $3.00 an hour. Workers with very high earnings can qualify in a few weeks. The required amount also cannot be put high enough to provide an adequate test for a worker with high earnings, since it must be low enough to permit workers with the lowest earnings to qualify for benefits without having to work an unreasonably long period. As a result, for example, many highly paid professional entertainers can earn enough in a few days to qualify for benefits.

Another objection to a flat dollar qualifying requirement is that it can be increased only by legislative action. As a result, increases in the dollar requirement have lagged behind increases in wages and are unrealistically low in some states. In 1966, two states still maintained a requirement of $375 or less. A saving feature of such low requirements is that they qualify workers for only a limited amount of benefits. Those states that require earnings in more than one quarter in addition to a flat dollar amount are

---

[1] Several states have a flat annual earnings requirement above a certain point: California, $750; Oklahoma, $3,000; Rhode Island, $1,200.

setting up some safeguards against admitting temporary workers to benefits.

The importance of requiring earnings in at least two quarters is seen by referring to Table 14–5, presented later in this chapter, which gives the distributions of earnings in West Virginia in 1962. About 16 percent of the workers in the sample worked in only one quarter of the year.

Multiple of Weekly Benefit Amount. In order to have a qualifying requirement that will set approximately the same amount of working time for all workers, some of the states use earnings during the worker's base year equal to a multiple of the weekly benefit amount. Typically, the worker must have earned 30 times the weekly benefit amount to which he would be entitled. Since the benefit amount approximates one half of weekly earnings, a multiple of 30 is assumed to be the equivalent of 15 weeks of full-time employment.[2]

The major weakness of these formulas is that they give only approximations to the amount of employment that is desired as a qualification for benefits. Another weakness is that highly paid workers can earn enough to qualify for the maximum weekly benefit in a shorter period of time than was intended.[3] Some states partially meet this weakness by requiring earnings in at least two calendar quarters during the base year.[4]

Multiple of High-Quarter Wages. An increasing number of states meet the problem of the high wage earner by requiring that a worker earn a multiple of his high-quarter earnings during the "base" year preceding his claim in order to qualify for benefits. The most common multiple is 1½ times high-quarter earnings. Such a multiple will normally require about 20 weeks of earnings to qualify for benefits. This method effectively screens out many workers who are employed for a relatively short time during a year.

Table 14–1 shows that a substantial proportion of covered workers earn less than 1½ times high-quarter earnings, more than a fourth in the three states shown. In fact, Table 14–1 shows that a substantial percentage worked in only one calendar quarter.

When a multiple of high-quarter earnings is used as a qualifying requirement, the minimum annual earnings required is important. If the

---

[2] Some states require a higher multiple than 30 times the benefit amount, especially states with a weighted benefit formula which pays a higher proportion of high-quarter wages to low earnings workers than to high earnings workers. In these cases, a large multiple of the benefit amount is required for the lower benefit amounts. Thus, in 1962, Pennsylvania required 32–45 times the weekly benefit amount.

[3] For example, a state has a maximum weekly benefit amount of $40. The qualifying requirement is 30 times the benefit amount, or $1,200 at the maximum. A worker earning $80 a week must work 15 weeks to qualify for benefits. A worker earning $150 a week could qualify for benefits in eight weeks.

[4] States with a high-quarter formula for determining the weekly benefit amount have also found it necessary to require a minimum amount of earnings in the high quarter. Such provisions eliminate workers whose weekly earnings are less than the minimum weekly benefit amount.

Table 14–1

Proportion of Workers with Annual Covered Earnings Equal to Less than 1.5 Times High-Quarter Earnings, by Selected Industries—Three States

	Percent of Covered Workers with Total Earnings	
	In One Quarter Only	Less Than 1.5 Times High-Quality Earnings
Oregon—1958:		
All industries 18%		27%
Construction 23		36
Manufacturing 15		23
Canning and preserving 33		50
Lumber and wood products ... 13		20
Trade 20		29
Retail trade 22		32
Services 22		33
Oklahoma—1960*:		
All industries 22%		36%
Mining 22		38
Construction 31		49
Manufacturing 15		26
Food processing 22		35
Trade 22		38
Retail trade 25		42
Services 28		40
Pennsylvania—1961:		
All industries 15%		26%
Construction 18		34
Manufacturing 9		23
Durable goods 8		24
Primary metals 11		25
Trade 19		30
Services 21		32

* Based on taxable wages only (up to $3,000).

minimum annual earnings requirement is too low, it will still allow workers who work only on a part-time, casual, or intermittent basis to receive benefits.

For example, if a multiple of 1½ times high-quarter earnings is used, but the minimum annual earnings required is only $300, a worker can qualify by earning only $200 in the high quarter and $100 in another quarter.

Weeks of Employment. Beginning in the 1950's, an increasing number of states (13 states as of January 1, 1966) have been turning from the use of quarterly or annual earnings to the use of weeks of work as a means of determining qualifying requirements. The number of weeks required varies from 14 to 26 weeks, with 20 weeks the most common requirement.[5] Only weeks in which earnings are in excess of a stated amount, varying from $15 to $20, are counted so as to disregard any week of inconsequential employment. This kind of requirement makes it possible to secure a much more accurate measurement of attachment to the labor market. It is more constant than a requirement based on wages in that it requires the same amount of employment from both low-paid and high-paid workers.

The record of weeks of employment is secured in most of these states through "requests" for reports from employers after the worker files a claim for benefits. The principal weakness in the weeks-of-employment requirement is that a worker who has had a number of employers may not be able to recall all of those from whom request of former earnings should be made. The employer may not report, or may report incorrectly. The states, however, impose stiff penalties for nonreporting and use the worker's statement of employment if a report is not received from the employer within a stated period.

The relative effectiveness of the weeks-of-employment test over the multiple-of-high-quarter test was indicated by a study of the 1960 employment patterns of a sample of workers with covered employment in Oregon. A 1½ times high-quarter test is assumed to be the equivalent of a 20 weeks of employment test. But the Oregon study found that 70.1 percent had annual earnings equal to at least 1½ times high-quarter earnings, but only 63.2 percent had at least $20 of earnings in at least 20 weeks. In the canning industry, 49.7 percent met the 1½ times high-quarter earnings test, but only 30.9 percent met the 20 weeks of employment test (see Table 14–2).

The weeks of employment requirement is also somewhat more restrictive than the requirement of a multiple of the weekly benefit amount that would seemingly require the same length of employment. This was shown in a study undertaken by New York State to analyze the effect of changing from a requirement of earnings equal to 30 times the benefit amount to a weeks-of-work test.[6] It was found that a somewhat smaller percentage of workers in 11 of the 18 industries studied could meet a test of 15 weeks of work and $300 in yearly earnings than could meet the old test of 30 times the benefit amount (which required from $300 to $780 in earnings depending on the size of the benefit).[7]

[5] New York and Wisconsin permit use of the two preceding years as a qualifying period if a worker cannot meet the regular requirement. In New York he can qualify with 20 weeks of employment in the 52-week period and a total of 40 weeks in the 104-week period preceding a claim; in Wisconsin with 18 weeks and 55 weeks respectively.

[6] *Employment Patterns of Insured Workers in Selected New York Industries, 1947–51*, Division of Employment, State Department of Labor, New York, October 30, 1953 (Mimeographed). Summarized in *Monthly Labor Review*, September, 1954, pp. 996–97.

[7] At least two states have "pyramided" their qualifying requirements by using two of the methods just described. Thus, Wyoming requires both 1½ times earnings in the high quarter and 26 weeks of employment. This appears to be unnecessarily strict.

Table 14–2

Percentage Comparison of Workers Qualifying for Benefits under Selected Eligibility Requirements, Oregon, 1960

Industry	Percent of Workers Qualifying under	
	$20 in 20 Weeks	Annual Earnings of 1.5 Times High Quarter Earnings
Total, all industries	63.2%	70.1%
Agriculture, forestry, and fishing	30.0	40.0
Mining	55.0	55.0
Contract construction	55.7	62.7
Manufacturing	69.0	74.7
Canning and preserving	30.9	49.7
Other food products	74.7	80.8
Lumber and wood products ...	72.0	79.0
Other manufacturing	79.0	81.7
Transportation, communications, and public utilities	77.8	81.0
Trade	57.8	65.7
Wholesale	67.1	71.2
Retail	54.9	63.9
Finance, insurance, and real estate	73.4	79.5
Service	51.9	63.0

Source: State of Oregon, Department of Employment.

Recency of Employment or Earnings

If an eligibility test of previous employment or earnings is to be effective in weeding out those no longer attached to the labor market, the "base period" must be as near the time of the claim for benefits as possible.

In Chapter 11, we pointed out the disadvantages of having a "lag period" between the base year used to determine benefits and the beginning of a benefit year. The states that use a qualifying requirement in terms of a multiple of the benefit amount or in terms of high-quarter earnings have such a "lag period" in order to give the agency time to post the reports of quarterly wages received from employers. The same is true of those states that stipulate a flat amount of annual earnings as a qualifying requirement, and use records of either quarterly or annual earnings. It was also pointed out in Chapter 11 that when benefits are based on weekly earnings, there need be no lag period since earnings in the 52 weeks immediately preceding the claims can be secured through a report from the employer after the claim is filed. The advantage of avoiding a lag period also applies to using weeks of employment as a qualifying requirement.[8]

[8] It would be possible for a state that has a lag period to secure a "request" report of earnings in the lag period if such earnings were necessary in order for the claimant to qualify for benefits.

Considering the foregoing, it seems to us that the most effective method of determining attachment to the labor force is the use of weeks of employment. In order to be a good test, only weeks of substantial (but not necessarily full-time) employment should be counted. The number of weeks that should be required is discussed later in this chapter.

"Double Dip"

The use of a base period immediately preceding the unemployment avoids what is called the "double dip." This is the ability of a claimant to commence a second benefit year immediately following the end of a benefit year by using as qualifying wages, the "lag period" wages earned in the period between the base period and the beginning of the first benefit year. For example, if a claimant commenced his first benefit year in June, 1964, his base period in some states would be the four quarters of 1963. In June, 1965, his base period would be the four quarters of 1964. If he had earned enough in January through May, 1964, to qualify for benefits, he could establish a new benefit year in June, 1965, in states permitting a "double dip," and draw another year of benefits without any intervening period of employment.

In order to prevent the claimant from qualifying for such a "double dip," about two fifths of the states require additional employment (after he starts a benefit year) before the unemployed worker can qualify for benefits in a second benefit year. These provisions are of two types: one type requires additional earnings at some time during the first benefit year; the other type requires additional earnings after the worker has exhausted his benefits in the first benefit year. The later requirement may work out inequitably. For example, a worker who is eligible for 26 weeks of benefits draws 20 weeks and then gets a job. He is laid off again after 26 weeks and draws his remaining six weeks of benefits. It would be unreasonable to require him to find work again after he has exhausted his benefits, before qualifying for a second benefit year, since he has had enough employment during his benefit year to qualify for a second round of benefits.

On the other hand, to permit a "double dip" on the sole basis of earnings before the first claim is filed would allow the use of earnings more than a year removed from the second benefit year. If the worker has had no earnings during the first benefit year, that is, if he has had no employment for a year or more, unemployment insurance benefits are an inappropriate answer to the unemployed worker's problem.

How Much Wages or Employment Should Be Required?

How much wages or employment represents substantial attachment to the labor force? Again a value judgment must be made on as much knowledge as is available of the employment experience of workers covered by the program.

Work Experience of the Labor Force. Since so few studies have been made of the work experience of covered workers, let us first look at the work experience of the labor force as a whole. Several facts stand out in Table 14–3. One is the enormous number of workers who move in and out of the labor force each year. While the average number in the work force during 1962 was 71,854,000, a total of 82,057,000 were in the work force at some time during the year, a difference of over 10 million. This difference was typical of recent years.

Table 14–3

Work Experience during the Year
by Extent of Employment and by Sex, 1962

Work Experience	Both Sexes	Male	Female
Number (thousands of persons 14 years of age and over):			
Total who worked during the year* . .82,057		50,639	31,418
Full time†			
50 to 52 weeks 44,079		32,513	11,566
27 to 49 weeks 12,102		7,185	4,917
1 to 26 weeks 9,146		4,289	4,857
At part-time jobs			
50 to 52 weeks 5,130		2,114	3,016
27 to 49 weeks 3,368		1,305	2,063
1 to 26 weeks 8,232		3,233	4,999
Percent distribution:			
Total who worked during the year* . . 100.0		100.0	100.0
Full time†			
50 to 52 weeks 53.7		64.2	36.8
27 to 49 weeks 14.7		14.2	15.6
1 to 26 weeks 11.1		8.5	15.5
At part-time jobs			
50 to 52 weeks ⟍ 6.3		4.2	9.6
27 to 49 weeks 4.1		2.6	6.6
1 to 26 weeks 10.0		6.4	15.9

* Time worked includes paid vacation and paid sick leave.
† Usually worked 35 hours or more per week.
Note: Because of rounding, sums of individual items may not equal totals.
Source: See footnote 9.

The second important fact is that only a little more than half (44 million) of those with work experience in 1962 were employed on a full-time basis for 50 weeks or more. Another fourth (over 21 million) worked full time when they were employed, but were either unemployed or out of the labor force for various reasons part of the year. Of these, over 12 million worked from 27 to 49 weeks and the balance, over 9 million, from 1 to 26 weeks.[9]

[9] Samuel Saben, "Work Experience of the Population in 1962," *Monthly Labor Review*, Vol. 87, No. 1 (January, 1964), p. 19, table 1.

The third important fact is that a total of 16,730,000 or 20.4 percent of the work force worked only at part-time jobs in 1962.[10] The number and proportion of part-time workers is also trending upward. The large number of part-time workers raises the question whether, if the part-time work is year-round, the worker should be able to qualify for benefits. Of those working at part-time jobs in 1962, about half worked for 27 or more weeks and almost a third for 50 weeks or more. Part-time work is particularly prevalent among youth under 20 (mostly students), workers 65 and over, and women. In 1962, 39.6 percent of the 2,888,000 working men aged 65 and over were on a part-time schedule. Of the women, 31.8 percent, or almost 10 million of those who worked in 1962, were only on part-time jobs.[11] Should the amount of earnings or employment be set so high that all of these are excluded, or for those who have had substantial employment, should some reliance be placed on testing their availability for work when unemployed?

It is the authors' view that workers who are on a work schedule for a substantial number of hours of the week and who are in the labor market most of the year should be qualified for benefits, *provided that when unemployed they are available for work*. But the large number of part-time workers who have only marginal attachment to the labor market must be kept in mind when setting qualifying requirements.

Finally, it is important to note in the Census data why many millions of workers are employed less than 50 weeks during a year. In 1962, over one fourth (9,643,000) of the 32,848,000 who worked less than 50 weeks on either a full-time or part-time basis gave unemployment as the major reason for not working. Most of the balance worked less than the full year for three reasons: illness or disability (3,261,000); taking care of the home (8,496,000); and going to school part of the year (7,053,000). The remaining 4,395,000 did not work the full year because of retirement, service in the Armed Forces, summer vacations for students, unpaid vacations, strikes, and the like.[12]

Unfortunately, those working full time and those working part time are lumped together in the above figures. It would be desirable to know, for example, what portion of those who were out of the labor market part of the year to take care of their homes were full-time or part-time workers when they were employed.

The Census sample data on the labor force, of course, include workers who are not covered by unemployment insurance. While this limits its usefulness for unemployment insurance purposes, the data presented above can be taken as a general indication that a considerable proportion of covered workers are in the labor force for only a short time, or are unemployed

---

[10] Part-time jobs are defined as those where the worker usually worked less than 35 hours a week.

[11] Saben, *op. cit.* See additional data on part-time employment in chap. 1.

[12] *Ibid.*, p. 23, table 7.

part of the year, or have part-time jobs that are unsubstantial in character. Personal attachment to the labor market, of course, is not the only reason the employment of many workers is limited. As was said in the New York study of insured workers previously mentioned,

There are many reasons why workers are employed intermittently. Some, for their own reasons, drop out of the labor market, quit to look for another job, or are discharged for cause after a brief period of employment. This occurs in all industries. But the very wide variations among industries cannot be satisfactorily explained by these personal factors. The substantial explanation lies in industries' demand for labor, which fluctuates in all industries, within narrow limits in some, and very widely in others.[13]

Therefore, the actual employment experience of workers covered by unemployment insurance must be examined to get the effects of personal attachment or lack of attachment to the labor market, as well as information on the length of time most workers are in covered employment.

State Studies of Employment of Insured Workers. Do the studies that have been made yield information that can help determine what qualifying requirement should be? As of the time of writing, only five states have made a systematic study of their covered workers in order to set or evaluate a qualifying requirement.[14] Unfortunately, these studies are limited to data on the work experience of covered workers and do not include information on what workers are doing when not working. Furthermore, several of the studies are confined to data on quarterly and annual wages and contain no data on weeks of employment.

Let us first look at the data in these studies to see what proportion of workers would be unable to qualify at various levels of annual earnings (Table 14–4). A rule-of-thumb criterion that the qualifying requirement should eliminate about 25 percent of the covered workers, would set this level at somewhere under $800 in Oregon, under $400 in Oklahoma, under $600 in West Virginia, and under $1,000 in Pennsylvania.

Such a flat earnings requirement by itself, however, would be inadequate. In the Pennsylvania study, 15 percent of all the workers studied had only one calendar quarter of coverage and 26 percent had less than 1½ times high-quarter earnings. In Oklahoma, an additional requirement of 1½ times high-quarter earnings was found to be necessary in order to eliminate those who would meet a flat earnings requirement in a short period of time. In its report, the West Virginia agency came to the same conclusion; at least, that some multiple of high-quarter earnings should be considered in addition to its annual earnings requirement of $700.

The West Virginia Department of Employment Security made its study of the earnings of covered workers for the period 1961–63, with special

---

[13] *Employment Patterns of Insured Workers in Selected New York Industries, 1947–51, op. cit.*

[14] New York, Oregon, Oklahoma, Pennsylvania, and West Virginia. Ten more studies were in process in 1965.

Table 14–4

Proportion of Workers with Low Covered Earnings, by Selected Industries—Four States

State and Industry	Percent of Covered Workers with Earnings during Year of Less Than			
	$400	$600	$800	$1,000
Oregon—1958				
All industries	18%	23%	27%	31%
Construction	18	23	28	32
Manufacturing	13	18	22	25
Canning and preserving	39	52	62	68
Lumber and wood products	10	13	16	19
Trade	23	29	34	38
Retail trade	27	34	39	44
Services	28	35	41	45
Oklahoma—1960*				
All industries	25	31	36	40
Mining	16	19	23	25
Construction	32	38	43	47
Manufacturing	15	19	23	26
Food processing	27	33	38	40
Trade	32	39	44	48
Retail trade	36	44	50	54
Services	34	42	49	54
Pennsylvania—1961*				
All industries	13	17	20	24
Construction	13	18	22	27
Manufacturing	7	9	14	14
Durable goods	5	6	8	10
Primary metals	4	5	6	8
Trade	22	28	33	37
Services	26	33	38	43
West Virginia—1962				
All industries	17	21	24	27
Construction	21	27	33	38
Manufacturing	7	9	11	13
Food processing	15	23	26	28
Trade	29	35	40	45
Wholesale trade	16	20	24	28
Transportation, public utilities	10	12	15	17
Service	29	36	43	48

* Based on taxable earnings.

emphasis on earnings in 1962.[15] It was found that in 1962, 16 percent of all covered workers had earnings in only one quarter of the year, 13 percent in two quarters, 13 percent in three quarters, and 58 percent in four quarters.

[15] West Virginia Department of Employment Security, Research and Statistics Division, *Unemployment Benefit Entitlement Security, 1961–1963*, RS–No. 101 (Charleston, February, 1965).

The report tabulated the distribution of workers at different ratios of annual earnings to high-quarter earnings. Table 14–5 shows that at least 150 percent of high-quarter earnings would be necessary as a requirement if one fourth of the covered workers were eliminated by the qualifying requirement. On the other hand, Table 14–5 indicates that an annual

Table 14–5

Ratio of Annual Wages to High-Quarter Wages in Relation to Amount of Annual Wages, West Virginia, 1962

Annual Wages	All Workers No.	%	Percentage Distribution of Workers by the Ratio (Percent) of Annual Wages to High-Quarter Wages								
			100%	101–124	125–149	150–174	175–199	200–249	250–299	300–349	350–400
Total	8,851	100	16	3	5	4	6	8	10	17	31
Less than $200 ..	941	100	78	5	5	5	4	2	1	0	0
$200–399	515	100	49	14	13	8	7	5	2	1	1
$400–599	381	100	32	13	16	12	12	9	3	2	1
$600–799	310	100	25	12	16	12	12	10	4	3	6
$800–999	295	100	19	9	15	15	13	14	6	5	4
$1000–1199	251	100	12	8	9	13	17	16	10	5	10
$1200–1399	239	100	9	5	8	8	17	22	12	7	12
$1400–1599	236	100	10	5	10	5	11	15	17	13	14
$1600–1799	203	100	3	3	6	6	8	26	18	14	16
$1800–1999	197	100	6	2	5	6	13	15	15	16	22
$2000–2499	499	100	3	2	5	7	8	16	16	18	25
$2500–2999	433	100	1	0	1	3	7	13	15	24	36
$3000–3999	930	100	1	1	1	3	5	12	18	22	37
$4000–4999	895	100	0	0	1	1	2	8	16	26	46
$5000–6999 1	1,482	100	0	0	0	0	1	1	8	30	60
$7000 or over ...1	1,044	100	0	0	0	1	1	2	7	27	62

Source: West Virginia Department of Employment Security, Research and Statistics Division, *Unemployment Benefit Entitlement Study*, 1961–63, RS–No. 101 (Charleston, February, 1965) Part A, table 11.

earnings requirement in West Virginia could not be more than somewhere between $600 and $800 without eliminating too many (more than a fourth) who had had three or more quarters of earnings (200 percent or more of high-quarter earnings). In its introduction, the West Virginia report, pointed out that high-quarter wages might include bonuses, overtime, etc., and so distort the quarter. This is an important point, since it was found that 95 percent of the workers had higher earnings in one quarter than in another. The report therefore rather cautiously stated that consideration should be given to using a multiple of high-quarter earnings in addition to a base-period (annual) earnings requirement, but did not recommend what the multiple should be. This illustrates the uncertainties that any state faces when it depends on quarterly and annual earnings, rather than weeks of employment, in devising a qualifying requirement that will not exclude some persons who have had a substantial attachment to covered employment.

The Oregon study (Table 14–2) has indicated that a requirement of $20 in 20 weeks would be superior to a 1½ times high-quarter requirement. The New York study gives a good picture of the weeks of employment that workers have in covered employment and enables us to form a judgment as to how many weeks of employment should be required for a worker to qualify for benefits. Let us look at the distribution of weeks of covered employment as shown in Table 14–6, disregarding the three seasonal industries of canneries, costume jewelry, and seasonal hotels.[16]

Table 14–6

Weeks of Covered Employment of Workers in 1950, New York

Industry	Total	Distribution (in Percent) by Weeks of Covered Employment			
		1–14 Weeks	15–19 Weeks	20–30 Weeks	Over 30 Weeks
Manufacturing					
Canneries	100	34	12	20	34
Costume jewelry	100	27	10	20	43
Women's underwear	100	18	8	19	55
Millinery	100	16	9	25	50
Fur goods	100	15	7	18	60
Women's coats and suits	100	13	8	29	50
Furniture	100	12	5	15	68
Textiles	100	11	5	14	70
Women's dresses	100	11	6	22	61
Men's coats and suits	100	10	4	17	69
Bakeries	100	9	4	11	76
Nonmanufacturing					
Seasonal hotels	100	37	15	27	21
Theaters	100	20	8	19	53
Retail trade	100	20	6	13	61
Laundries	100	18	6	14	62
Cleaning and dyeing	100	17	7	15	61
Restaurants	100	17	9	18	56
Construction	100	11	5	16	68

Source: State Department of Labor, Division of Employment, *Employment Patterns of Insured Workers in Selected New York Industries 1947–51* (Albany, N.Y.: October 30, 1953, Mimeographed).

In the 15 other industries studied, 20 percent or less worked from 1 to 14 weeks. Only an additional 4 to 9 percent had from 15 to 19 weeks of covered employment. Those who worked 20 weeks or more (72 to 87 percent) were a significant percentage of the whole. This raises the question whether workers employed only part of the year in the industry tabulated also worked in some other industry during the year. It was found that from 49 to 90 percent had all or substantially all of their 1950 earnings in one

[16] *Employment Patterns of Insured Workers in Selected New York Industries, op. cit.,* p. 6, table 2.

industry. The lowest percentage was in seasonal hotels; about half worked elsewhere in addition to this seasonal industry.

The New York State study was made to determine whether a new qualifying requirement in the New York law of 20 weeks of employment was more restrictive than the former requirement of 30 times the weekly benefit amount. It was found that a smaller proportion would qualify for benefits under the 20 weeks of employment requirement, or even under a requirement of 15 weeks of employment with earnings of at least $300 a year than qualified under the "30-times" requirement. Nevertheless, if the test is applied that about a fourth should be ruled out by the qualifying requirement, the new 20-week requirement does not appear to have been too high in New York. (That more than 25 percent would be unable to qualify in the three seasonal industries does not bother us. Presumably many of the 25 percent who would be unable to qualify in the three seasonal industries were out of the labor market in the off-season.)

The weeks-of-employment test still has its limitations. Ideally, the test should use weeks of full-time earnings, or at least of substantial employment. Full-time earnings, however, are difficult to determine in many occupations. Most of the states using a weeks-of-employment qualifying requirement count only weeks in which from $15 to $20 are received in earnings. This makes it easier for high-paid workers than for low-paid workers to qualify for benefits.

Conclusions from the Data. Despite these studies, one still has the feeling that much more needs to be known about the work experience of covered workers before any sound judgment can be made as to how much qualifying employment should be required. What prevented the tested workers in the studies from meeting the various qualifications requirements? What proportions were out of the labor market part of the time? What proportions of those with low earnings were part-time workers?

While recognizing these limitations, we believe the data indicate that about 20 weeks of substantial employment in the base year is the best qualifying requirement. It is also clear that if a flat amount of earnings is used as a basis for eligibility, the amount now used in most states is inadequate. If a multiple of the benefit amount is used, the usual requirement of 30 times the benefit amount is inadequate; it probably should be 40 times in order to require the equivalent of 20 weeks of employment. It is also certain that this requirement must include a substantial amount of earnings in other calendar quarters than the quarter in which earnings are the highest, and it appears that "substantial" should be about half again as much; that is, that 1½ times high-quarter earnings should be required.

According to the International Labour Office, experience has shown that not much longer than six months is needed as a qualifying requirement, but if the requirement is much shorter, benefits will be paid to too many workers who are not normally attached to the labor force on a full-time basis. The ILO report further states, however, that the requirement can be somewhat less in "countries with well-developed labour markets where the employment service can function effectively to test regularity of membership in the labour force, the genuineness of unemployment, and the reality of wage loss."[17]

The outstanding fact about the data given on the work experience of the labor force as a whole (Table 14–1), is that only about two thirds had full-time employment for 26 weeks or more in 1962. If this is discounted for the 6.2 million farmers and other self-employed persons who were working on a year-round full-time basis, only about 60 percent of the work force worked full time for 26 weeks or more. Assuming that the work experience of those covered by unemployment insurance is roughly the same as that for the total group of wage and salary workers, this means that only about 60 percent of workers covered by the program could meet a 26-week qualifying requirement. Certainly, some of the 9 million who worked full time 1 to 26 weeks and some of the 8.5 million who worked 26 weeks or more at part-time jobs would have liked to have full-time year-round employment. For example, in 1962 over a million were working part time although they usually worked full time. Should not those who are seeking full-time year-round employment be able to qualify for benefits? If so, a 26-week qualifying requirement is too high.

The New York study indicates that a 26 weeks requirement would be too stringent. Although the New York study did not determine the number with 26 weeks of work, it found that a requirement of over 30 weeks would disqualify from 25 to 50 percent in the nonseasonal industries studied.

On the basis of information that is available, we again conclude that a requirement of 20 weeks of substantial earnings is about right.[18] If a state uses any other measure of earnings or employment as a qualifying requirement, it should still strive to require the equivalent of 20 weeks of substantial earnings. If less is required, there is danger of qualifying too many who are not regularly in the labor market; if much more is required, it will prevent too many who are regularly in the labor force from qualifying for unemployment insurance benefits.

ABLE AND AVAILABLE FOR WORK

The unemployed worker must not only demonstrate his recent and substantial attachment to the labor market, he must demonstrate his continuing attachment. This he does by meeting a requirement (found in all state laws) that he be able to work and available for work. As the Bureau of

[17] International Labour Office, *Unemployment Insurance Schemes* (Geneva, Switzerland, 1955), p. 112.
[18] The Administration bill of 1965 would set a federal standard that any unemployed worker who has had 20 weeks of employment (or its equivalent) shall be entitled to not less than 26 weeks of benefits.

Employment Security has put it, "The qualifying requirement and the requirement that claimants be able and available for work are the two halves of a single requirement that protection be limited to unemployed members of the labor force."[19]

The state employment security agency's application of the test of ability and availability for work has an important bearing on the successful operation of the unemployment insurance program. If the tests are applied loosely or ineffectively so that a substantial number of people draw benefits who are not genuinely in the labor market, it will throw the system into disrepute. On the other hand, if these tests are applied mechanically, inflexibly, and without treating the claimant as a human being, one of the chief values of unemployment insurance, the preservation of the self-respect of the unemployed worker, will be lost. The maintenance of a balance between firm and sympathetic application of the test of availability for work is especially important because unavailability for work is the chief cause of disqualification from benefits. In 1964, there were 920,808 disqualifications because the claimant was unable to work or unavailable for work. This represented only 1 percent of the weekly contacts of the claimants with the employment security offices, but involved about one eighth of the claimants. That this many were disqualified does not mean that they knowingly filed false claims. The weight of the evidence shows that the great majority of claims for unemployment compensation are genuine. For the most part, the administrators of the program are dealing with persons who are anxious to go back to work. Nevertheless, these tests must be continually applied to all claimants.

Factors in Testing Ability and Availability for Work

In determining whether an unemployed worker is able to work and especially is available for work, claims personnel must cope with an infinite variety of situations and with complex human beings. They are dealing with objective situations and with subjective attitudes. At the same time, they have only a minute or two to spend with each person in the line of claimants and must make decisions on the basis of only a few facts.

There is a great variety of factors that affect the claimant's ability to work and availability for work: the existence of a specific disability or illness or general poor health; family or home responsibilities; the promise of a call-back to his former job. The rules of the union to which a claimant belongs may limit his availability to take certain types of jobs. The worker may restrict his availability to a particular type of job and to a particular wage scale because of ignorance of labor market conditions which make his standards unrealistic. Finally, the worker's attitude and efforts to find

[19] United States Department of Labor, Bureau of Employment Security, *Unemployment Insurance Legislative Policy, Recommendations for State Legislation 1962*, BES No. U–212A, October, 1962, p. 44.

work may be affected by ignorance of the consequences if he ignores the requirement that he be available for work.[20]

State Provisions on Ability and Availability for Work

In their requirements that the claimant be able to work and available for work, most states (35 in 1965) do not define "work," but some states (ten in 1965) limit the requirement more specifically to "suitable work" and others (seven in 1965) to work in the claimant's usual occupation or one for which he is reasonably fitted.

Some states have further refinements in their statutory provisions regarding availability for work. For example, Michigan and West Virginia require that a claimant must be available for *full-time* work. Connecticut and New Hampshire specify that women are not required to be available for work between the hours of 1:00 A.M. and 6:00 A.M. Other states have specific provisions with respect to retirees, persons on vacation, persons who have moved to another locality, trainees, students, pregnant women, and persons unavailable due to marital obligations. These provisions are in the form of disqualifications, but involve questions of availability for work. The more important of these special provisions will be discussed later.

Able to Work

In applying the simpler test of ability to work, the claims taker has no problem in the large majority of cases. The normal case is that of a more-or-less healthy person, quite able to work. The claims taker, however, must be constantly on the alert since a claimant may be genuinely ill, yet still able to get down to the local office once a week to file a claim. The claims taker is guided mainly by behavior or appearance and will normally raise a question only in cases of obvious inability to work.

There are disabilities which may or may not restrict a worker's availability to work. An orthopedic impairment such as a stiff joint may be no restriction on certain types of work. Even blindness or poor vision may not be disqualifying if the claimant's employment record has demonstrated his ability to work. Age is usually not taken into account, except that it may raise a question as to whether a worker is receiving a pension, a subject that requires separate treatment.[21]

Should a claimant be disqualified if he has a temporary illness while drawing unemployment benefits, even though no work is available for him? As of January 1, 1965, nine states have provisions that benefits will be continued if the claimant is registered for work and no suitable work is offered during illness. Unless a state has a temporary disability law, the continued

---

[20] Ralph Altman, *Availability for Work: A Study in Unemployment Compensation* (Cambridge: Harvard University Press, 1950), p. 255.

[21] It involves availability to work, but will be treated in the next chapter, in which we will discuss the question of receipt of other income.

payment of unemployment compensation during a temporary illness, particularly when no suitable job is available, is on the side of realism and meets a real need.[22]

Principles in Availability for Work

When we come to the larger question of availability for work, agreement first needs to be reached on the underlying principles that should govern the testing of availability for work before specific methods are considered in the light of those principles.

Ralph Altman, who has made the most comprehensive study of the problem of availability for work, has laid down the following principles:[23] (1) "Claimants should ordinarily be presumed to be available for work." This, unfortunately, is not the attitude of all claims personnel, who frequently are suspicious that claimants tend to avoid work. Such an attitude is unfair to most claimants. On the other hand, if experience has shown certain types of workers to be work-shy, claims personnel are justified in taking a closer look at the claims of such workers. Such a type may be a young woman who has remained in the same locality after recently leaving work to be married. (2) "Claimants must be available for work of which there is a *substantial* amount." The claimant cannot expect to limit his availability to a highly specialized occupation in which few jobs exist. (3) "To demonstrate his availability, the worker must look for work as instructed by the agency." This may or may not mean more than registration for work at the employment office. (This particular point will be discussed at length in the next section.) (4) "If a claimant has unavoidable restrictions on his availability for certain types of work, he should be given the benefit of the doubt that there is a substantial amount of work for which he is available." An example of such unavoidable restrictions is physical inability to do certain kinds of work. (5) "If impersonal causes cut the worker off from suitable work opportunities, he should be considered available for work even though he lacks access to a substantial amount of work." The length of the adjustment period thus granted must be graded to the circumstances. An example is unemployment in a "one-company town" when the company leaves the community where the claimant owns his home.

One overriding principle should apply to all claimants; namely, that the test of availability must be applied individually, taking into account the different circumstances in each case. There should not be any rigid rule enacted into law or developed through regulation that applies sweepingly

[22] A more limited problem is presented by the practice in all states (except New York) of taking claims on a weekly basis. If a claimant is ill for part of the week, the states differ as to whether benefits should be denied. Some deny benefits, others reduce the weekly benefit by a fraction for each work day of disability, and a few allow benefits if the claimant's availability is not materially reduced (see Altman, *op. cit.*, p. 151).

[23] *Ibid.*, pp. 137–38. The discussion of each principle is the authors'.

to all cases. This principle applies particularly to the requirement in many laws that the worker must actively look for work.

Search for Work

When the Social Security Act was passed, it was assumed that if the claimant for unemployment compensation were required to register at a local public employment office, that office could test his availability for work by the offer of suitable jobs. This was the purpose behind the requirement in the original legislation: "Payment of unemployment compensation solely through public employment offices in the State or such other agencies as the (Social Security) Board may approve,"[24] and the Social Security Board's early decision that *only* public employment offices would be approved. Payment of benefits through employment offices did not necessarily mean that the cash or checks would be passed out at the local offices, but it did mean that claims would be filed there and that claimant's would be required to register there for work.

In practice, it has been found that the public employment service cannot adequately apply the "work test." In 1960, it was estimated that only 12 percent of the new hires were made through public employment offices. This "penetration rate" varied from 6 percent for mine workers, 8 percent for skilled workers, 10 percent for professional and managerial, and 21 percent for workers in manufacturing to 30 percent for the unskilled. These are national rates. The percentages are much lower in large cities; in some smaller communities they are higher. Only a portion of these placements are of unemployment insurance claimants.

The many reasons for this will be discussed fully in the chapter on the Public Employment Service. It is sufficient to note at this point that employers place only a small proportion of their job openings with the Employment Service so that the Service is able to offer jobs to only a small fraction of unemployment insurance claimants. Employers fill most of their openings by "hiring at the gate" or from applications filed in their own personnel departments, from persons who are friends or relatives of their employees, from responses to newspaper advertising, or from private employment agencies.

Active Search for Work. A number of the states (30 as of January 1, 1966) have decided that registration at the local public employment office is not enough, and require a claimant to be actively seeking work or making a reasonable effort to obtain work.[25]

The requirement to "actively seek work" has been criticized for several reasons. When required on a blanket basis, it can result in a great deal of

---

[24] *Social Security Act*, Public Law 74–271, Sec. 303 (a) (2).

[25] In Ohio, Oklahoma, Vermont and Wisconsin, the provision is not mandatory; the agency may require the claimant to make efforts to obtain suitable work in addition to registration at the public employment office. In New Jersey, the agency may modify the requirement when warranted by economic conditions. Other states have imposed similar requirements by rules and regulations.

wasted effort that is a nuisance to employers and demoralizing to the worker. When one state administrator required that each claimant apply for work with a stated minimum number of employers each week, there was wide-spread reporting of fictitious visits to employers, probably by many claimants who realized the futility of making actual visits. Large numbers of claimants who have a well-established connection with an employer and a promise that they will be rehired within a few weeks would only be wasting their time and other employers' time looking for work. Such claimants might well be excused from even registering for work with the employment office. In addition, in some trades all hiring is done through the union so that there is no use in the worker independently seeking work.

Just as some of the "actively seeking work" provisions in the state laws have been too rigid and sweeping, the condemnation by some persons of these provisions has also been too rigid and sweeping. Those provisions that are in terms of requiring a reasonable effort to obtain work, if properly administered, can represent a constructive approach to assuring that the claimant is available for work. After a critical analysis of these provisions and their effects, Lee G. Williams quotes the Oklahoma statute as stating the proper rule of construction and the proper role of the employment security agency: "Mere registration and reporting at a local employment office shall not in every case be conclusive evidence of ability to work, availability for work, or willingness to work. In those cases where appropriate, the Commission shall direct and require the claimant to do those things, in addition to registering and reporting to the local employment office, which a reasonably prudent individual could be reasonably expected to do to secure work."[26]

After taking the position that a search for work should not be required if the claimant is on a short layoff, if economic conditions are depressed so that there are no openings for work for which the claimant is suited, or if the employment office has plenty of suitable openings, Ralph Altman recommends that in other cases there be a "guided but active search for work."[27] By "guided" he means that the employment office should give the claimant labor market information that will be helpful to him in looking for work, counseling as to jobs for which he is reasonably fitted, and help in mapping out a plan of job search. Such a "guided but active search for work" is preferable to a wholesale requirement that all claimants actively seek work.

Availability for Work during Training

As late as 1960, a strict interpretation of its law would have required practically every state agency to disqualify a worker as unavailable for

---

[26] Oklahoma Employment Security Act, Oklahoma Stat. tit. 40 #214 (c) Supp. 1953. Quoted by Lee G. Williams, "Eligibility for Benefits," *Vanderbilt Law Review*, Vol. 8, No. II (February, 1955), p. 301.

[27] Altman, *op. cit.*, pp. 115–16.

work if he was taking a course of training. Only North Dakota had a specific provision which considered a student to be available while attending a public vocational training course and Utah considered a student available under certain limited conditions. Two states, Massachusetts and Michigan, had more positive provisions extending the duration of benefits if the claimant was attending an approved vocational training course. The District of Columbia law disqualified an individual under 21 if he failed, without good cause, to accept an agency recommendation that he attend a free vocational or other school.

The discussions of the need of retraining of displaced unemployed workers, which were particularly stimulated by the debates on the Area Redevelopment Act and the Manpower Training and Development Act, resulted in the enactment of provisions in 22 states by January 1, 1966, under which an otherwise eligible claimant was considered to be available for work if he was attending a training or retraining course approved or recommended by the employment security agency.

Some employers have opposed such provisions because they did not want benefits which were paid during training periods to be charged to their experience rating accounts. They justified their opposition on the ground that the employee is, in fact, unavailable for work when taking training. Some have also felt that, although it might be all right for the claimant to take training, he should still be held unavailable for work if he is unwilling to stop his training to accept an offer of suitable employment. Opposition to payment of benefits during training also results from a failure to see unemployment insurance as part of a comprehensive labor market program. It is short-sighted, because in the long run there will be less demand on benefit funds if unemployed workers are retrained for jobs that are in demand.

Under the MDTA program, training allowances are provided while workers are taking training. Nevertheless, all state laws should be amended to permit payment of benefits during training so as to fill the gap if these programs lapse, or to fill present gaps in the provisions for training allowances. There are restrictions on who can qualify for training allowances under the Manpower Development and Training Act. A trainee must have at least two years of worker experience to get a regular training allowance.[28] If a trainee is not the head of the family or household with which he lives, the head must be unemployed. Also, training may be taken that is not under the MDTA program, for which no training allowances are provided. It is probable that this program will not have sufficient funds for a long time to meet all training needs, and the states should encourage claimants to take approved training available through other means.[29]

---

[28] There are special training allowances for inexperienced youth.

[29] The relationship of unemployment compensation and training allowances will be discussed more fully in Chapter 22.

Availability of Students for Work

Closely allied to the question of paying benefits to claimants undergoing training is the question of the treatment of students who work while getting an education. Seven states (as of January 1, 1966) disqualify students who have voluntarily left work to attend school, several for the duration of the unemployment, others during attendance at school. Another nine states disqualify claimants during school attendance, and, in some cases, during vacation periods.[30] With the widely varying conditions under which students attend day and night schools, reliance on a test of the availability of the student for full-time work would seem to be more realistic.

The Availability for Work of Women Claimants

There has been so much attention given to the question of whether women present special problems of availability for work that an extended consideration of this question seems called for. In discussion of abuse of the unemployment insurance system, special emphasis is usually given to cases of women who pretend to be available for work when they are not. Women who are "secondary workers," in the sense that they do not bring the principal income into the home, are especially suspect. It is generally felt that most married women work only to supplement the family income in order to have a higher standard of living. Women move in and out of the labor market more than men, and a high proportion work on part-time jobs. These two facts are pointed to as evidence that women are less firmly attached to the labor market and their "right" to collect is therefore doubtful.

A majority of state laws have special disqualification provisions with respect to voluntary quitting because of marital obligations and pregnancy. Because of these special provisions and because of general suspicions that women are more prone to become unavailable for work, the question of the labor force attachment of working women requires extended treatment.

Some Facts as to the Employment of Women. Any thorough study of women in the labor force and the implications for unemployment insurance would take too much space in this volume.[31] Only a few significant facts can be given.

[30] Although this does not come under the subject of availability for work, as of January 1, 1962, a large amount of work by students was excluded from coverage. Six states excluded part-time work of students and 32 excluded services performed for educational institutions. In five states, benefits were not payable on wages earned while a person was a student, with certain exceptions.

[31] For an excellent study, see Richard C. Wilcock, "Women in the American Labor Force: Employment and Unemployment," *Studies in Unemployment* prepared for the Special Committee on Unemployment Problems, United States Senate, pursuant to S. Res. 196, 86th Cong., pp. 121–72. Also, see Gertrude Bancroft, *The American Labor Force* (New York: Wiley, 1958); National Manpower Council, *Woman Power* (New York: Columbia University Press, 1958); and United States Department of Labor, Women's Bureau, *1964 Handbook on Women Workers* (Washington, D.C., U.S. Government Printing Office.)

First, as has been indicated in Chapter 1, there is the rapidly growing proportion of women in the labor force. The number grew from 16.9 million in 1947 to 25.8 million in 1964. This growth is expected to continue.

Second, the high proportion of married working women should be noted. During the 1947–62 period, the number of married women in the labor force rose from 7.5 to 14.8 million, an even larger growth than the net increase in all women in the labor force.

Third, the large proportion of women who work part time throughout the year should be noted. While 64.2 percent of the men worked 50 or more weeks full time in 1962, only 36.8 percent of the women did so. One half of the women who worked less than 50 weeks gave care of their homes as the reason. Those employed full time from 27 to 49 weeks would normally qualify for unemployment insurance. Of these, 38.2 percent said they had worked less than a full year because of care of the home; only 28 percent of the jobless women said they worked less than a full year because they were unemployed.[32]

Table 14–8 illustrates another striking fact, that over twice as many women as men worked at part-time jobs. This was due to unemployment in 23 percent of the cases for men, but in only 6 percent of the cases for women. "Care of the home" was the reason given for part-time work by 55 percent of the part time women workers.

The following table shows that women have a slightly higher unemployment rate than men. However, when the unemployment rates are determined on the basis of marital status, women (whether with husband present, separated, widowed or divorced, or single) have lower unemployment rates than single men or separate, widowed, or divorced men. Only married men with wives living with them have a lower unemployment rate:

Unemployment Ratio by Sex and Marital Status, December, 1963

Marital Status	Unemployment Rate
Married man, wife present	3.6
Married woman, husband present	4.6
Separated, widowed and divorced: women	6.1
Single women	6.8
Separated, widowed and divorced: men	9.1
Single men	11.7
All men	5.2
All women	5.4

Source: United States Department of Labor, *Monthly Report on the Labor Force*, December, 1963, table 5.

[32] Samuel Saben, "Work Experience of the Population in 1962," *Special Labor Force Report No. 38* (U.S. Department of Labor, Bureau of Labor Statistics, January, 1964), p. A–15, table B–1.

Table 14-8

Major Reason for Part-Year Work in 1962, by Extent of Employment: Part-Year Workers by Sex

Work Experience and Sex	Total Part-Year Workers (in Thousands)	Percentage Distribution of Persons Not Working a Full Year Because of					
		Total	Unemployment	Taking Care of Home	Going to School	Illness or Disability	Other Reasons†
Male							
Total, 14 years and over	16,012	100.0	43.4	( )‡	24.9	12.5	19.9
Worked at full-time jobs	11,474	100.0	51.2	...	15.3	13.7	18.8
27 to 49 weeks	7,185	100.0	60.7	...	2.7	17.0	20.0
1 to 26 weeks	4,289	100.0	35.4	...	36.7	7.3	19.6
Worked at part-time jobs	4,538	100.0	23.4	...	48.8	9.2	18.6
Female							
Total, 14 years and over	16,836	100.0	16.1	50.5	18.2	7.6	7.6
Worked at full-time jobs	9,774	100.0	20.9	47.8	12.1	9.3	9.9
27 to 49 weeks	4,917	100.0	28.2	38.2	3.8	14.3	15.5
1 to 26 weeks	4,857	100.0	13.5	57.2	20.6	4.3	4.3
Worked at part-time jobs	7,062	100.0	9.3	54.2	26.6	5.2	4.7

* Excludes paid sick leave from a job and periods of illness or disability during which the person would not have worked or been in the labor market.
† Includes, among others, retirement, service in the Armed Forces, summer vacations of students, and strikes.
‡ Not available.

Source: Samuel Saben, "Work Experience of the Population in 1962," *Special Labor Force Report No. 38* (U.S. Department of Labor, Bureau of Labor Statistics, January, 1964), p. A–15, table B–1.

A study of married women claimants in Vermont throws some light on the attachment to the labor force of married women claimants for unemployment insurance. This study included a sample of three groups of married women who had drawn (1) temporary extended benefits during the week of May 27, 1961; (2) temporary extended benefits during the week of January 20, 1962; and (3) regular benefits during the latter week. Of the 237 women interviewed during the week of April 14, 1962, 26 percent were currently employed, 55 percent were still unemployed, and 19 percent were currently out of the labor force. The major reasons for being out of the labor force were pregnancy and the necessity of caring for pre-school children. A higher proportion of the May, 1961, groups than the other groups reported that they were out of the labor force. Professor Harris Thurber of Middlebury College, who analyzed the results of the study, suggested that possibly some of these had been unemployed so long they had given up hope of finding jobs. Ninety-four percent of those in the sample felt themselves to have been a part of the labor force for more than 24 out of the 36 preceding months. One half had worked for 24 months or more, and 75 percent had worked more than half the time during the period. Professor Thurber concluded:

the women included in the sample were not 'fly-by-night' members of the labor force . . . the work histories of most respondents proved that they had been fairly steadily employed for considerable periods of time prior to unemployment. More than 90 percent of the respondents unemployed at the time of the survey, for example, indicated a willingness to undergo retraining for other lines of work if retraining programs were available, more than half would be willing to accept jobs which paid less than their normal employment and approximately 85 percent would be willing to accept employment which was different from normal employment. These responses, while again subjective, would seem to indicate a basic desire for employment.[33]

Are Special Eligibility Requirements for Women Needed? Certain general considerations should be kept in mind in considering whether any special measures should be taken to prevent women, especially those with home care responsibilities, from establishing eligibility for benefits when they are not genuinely attached to the labor market. First, the unemployment insurance system should continue to be an insurance program against wage loss, free from any test of need, and free from inquiries into the individual's reasons for working. This means that women should continue to have equal rights with men to benefits.

Second, no distinction in qualifications for benefits should be based on the assumption that just because men are usually the principal wage earners in families, married women are loosely attached to the labor market and work only to supply the household with extras. Studies show that

---

[33] Harris Thurber, in cooperation with Research and Statistics Division, *Special Study of the Long-Term Unemployed Married Secondary Wage Earners* (Montpelier: State of Vermont, Department of Employment, December, 1962), p. 11.

most women work out of economic necessity or to improve the family's standard of living.[34] A recent analysis based on the BLS 1950 Survey of Consumer Expenditures indicated that employed married women who worked the entire year raised their family's total income by 61 percent.[35]

Third, the value of women's work should be recognized, not only for the contribution that it makes to their own support or that of their families, but the contribution it makes to the economy. The country cannot do without the skills that women bring to the labor market, and unemployment compensation should do its part in helping them to remain in the labor market so that their skills will not be lost to society.

Suggestions for safeguarding against abuse of unemployment insurance by women have included the enactment of tighter qualifying requirements for all workers and tighter tests of the availability for work of women who are drawing benefits. With respect to tighter qualifying requirements, Professor Richard A. Lester suggests that higher qualifying requirements be imposed so as to eliminate part-time and part-year workers. Here he agrees with the authors that the qualifying requirement should be increased from the prevalent requirement of 15 weeks or less to 20 weeks.[36]

This would render ineligible the great bulk of women who are out of the labor market part of the time. Let us look back at the statistics in Table 14–8 of women working from 1 to 26 weeks at full-time jobs. Of these, six gave home care as the reason for not working year-round for every one who gave unemployment as the reason. On the other hand, those who worked 27 to 49 weeks, the ratio was three to two. Ten of the women who worked part time gave home responsibilities as the reason for each part-time woman worker who gave inability to find a full-time job as the cause of working part time.

Another suggestion, which Richard C. Wilcock believed as deserving of serious consideration[37] is to have stiffer qualifying requirements for persons without dependents. This has been suggested because of the difficulty of distinguishing whether many secondary family workers are unemployed or have withdrawn from the labor force to take care of the home. Lester notes, however, that different qualifying requirements for those with dependents and those without dependents would be a step away from a program of compensation for wage loss.

The recommendation of the Committee on Social Insurance and Taxes of the President's Commission on the Status of Women is worth quoting at this point: "No distinction in qualifications for unemployment compen-

---

[34] Vernon T. Clover, *Net Income of Employed Wives with Husband Present*, Studies in Economics and Business (Texas Technological College, School of Business Administration, 1962), p. 23.

[35] Margaret S. Carroll, "The Working Wife and Her Family's Economic Position," *Monthly Labor Review*, Vol. LXXXV (April, 1962), pp. 366–74.

[36] Richard A. Lester, *The Economics of Unemployment Compensation* (Princeton: Industrial Relations Section, Princeton University, 1962), p. 126.

[37] Wilcock, *op. cit.*, p. 126.

sation should be made between men and women workers on the ill-
founded assumption that men are the primary workers in households and
that women, particularly married women, are secondary workers. The
problem of payment of benefits to persons with a loose attachment to the
labor market should be met by the adoption of more realistic measures
of labor market attachment applicable to men and women alike."[38]

Testing Availability for Work of Women. Chief reliance must be placed
on the tests of ability to work and availability for work in determining when
women claimants are unavailable for work because of home duties.

At the same time, this should be done on an individual basis, rather than
through statutory disqualifications of women in certain categories. Those
whose availability is in doubt, particularly if their job separations or restrictions as to work for which they are available are due to domestic
responsibilities, should be required to give affirmative evidence of their
availability. In their case, the presumption on availability should not apply.
They should give positive proof of their availability through an active
search for work, re-employment after a voluntary leaving of a job or the
work force, or rearrangement of their marital or domestic duties so as to
be more able to accept suitable employment.[39]

Women whose employment is prolonged should receive special attention. There is a tendency to prolong attachment to the labor force if unemployment benefits are available. This is indicated by the fact that in all
studies of claimants who have exhausted their benefits, a larger proportion
of women than men have withdrawn from the labor market two months
after exhaustion of benefits. In the analysis of 17 state studies of exhaustees
(previously referred to in the chapter on benefit duration), the withdrawal
rate was from half again as much up to four times as much for women as
for men. The proportion of women withdrawing from the labor market
range from a low of 6.9 percent in one state to 27.4 percent in another.[40]

Disqualifications for Unemployment Due to Marital Obligations

As of January 1, 1966, 23 states have special provisions that disqualify
those persons from benefits who quit their jobs because of marital obligations, such as attending to a sick child or moving with a husband who had
been transferred to another state. Such causes, of course, usually involve

[38] *Report of the Committee on Social Insurance and Taxes* (Washington, D.C.: The
President's Commission on the Status of Women, October, 1963) (Processed), p. 42.
[39] Altman, *op. cit.,* p. 237.
[40] United States Department of Labor, Bureau of Employment Security, *Experience
of Claimants Exhausting Benefit Rights under Unemployment Insurance,* BES No.
U–178, table 15. Since the information was secured for these studies from replies to
mail questionnaires rather than through personal interviews, the statistics are open to
question. Father Joseph M. Becker believes they understate the extent that women
withdraw from the labor force, basing his belief on the much higher percentages of
women who withdraw from the labor force as revealed by the monthly sample survey
of the labor force made by the Bureau of the Census (see Joseph M. Becker (ed.), *In
Aid of the Unemployed* [Baltimore: Johns Hopkins Press, 1965], p. 106).

women, but not always. The availability for work requirements in all states disqualify persons from benefits during periods when they are unavailable for work because their time is taken up with home duties. A few of the 22 states disqualify for a certain period of time after which the worker can draw benefits if again available for work. Most of the states, however, require re-employment, usually for a specified amount, before the person can again qualify for benefits. One state law has gone so far as to cancel all existing wage credits when the person left his work to fulfill marital obligations.

No doubt these statutory provisions are easier to administer than general availability-for-work provisions. There can, however, be cases in which a person can give a clear demonstration that, after taking care of the family problem, he or she is back in the labor market and would be working, if work was available. A rigid statutory provision cannot take account of such cases. Several states have, in fact, modified their provisions to take care of cases such as that of a wife who follows her husband to a new residence and immediately makes a reasonable effort to secure work (Arkansas); or that of the claimant who is the sole or major support of his or her family. If a state feels it must have a statutory provision, it would be more advisable to have one such as that of Idaho which requires the claimant to demonstrate a desire for and availability for work or show that he or she is the main support of self or family. Taking note of these provisions, the President's Commission on the Status of Women recommended that "unemployment compensation should be available to persons seeking work who are temporarily jobless because of a family move, but we recommend that such compensation be drawn from the general unemployment fund of the state rather than charged against the account of the former employer."[41] The later part of the recommendation should make the first part more palatable, particularly to those who are concerned that employers be charged only with benefits for unemployment for which they are directly responsible.

Disqualification for Pregnancy

Thirty-seven states have special provisions disqualifying women for stated periods before and after childbirth. These disqualifications range from four weeks to four months before childbirth and up to three months following delivery. Several states disqualify pregnant women for the duration of their unemployment, and others require a specified period of re-employment after childbirth before subsequent unemployment is compensable.

Obviously such provisions are easier to administer than the general provisions on ability to work and availability to work. On the other hand, they can result in gross injustices. For example, employers may have an inflexible policy as to periods beyond which pregnant women must quit or take

[41] *American Women,* Report of the President's Commission on the Status of Women (Washington, D.C.: U.S. Government Printing Office, 1963), p. 43.

maternity leave, although women vary greatly in the time they can safely work prior to childbirth. Anomalies can also occur under these provisions, for example, when there is a general layoff because of lack of work and those laid off include pregnant women who are within the disqualification period. Also, the time that women are able to continue working while pregnant will vary according to the job. The unscientific character of the periods for which women are disqualified is indicated by the fact that almost every state law has a different period of disqualification.

A New York State survey of women claimants who were pregnant when they filed their initial claim for benefits or who became pregnant while drawing benefits revealed that about 1 percent of all new claimants in New York State are pregnant. Eight out of every ten claimants in the survey were laid off. Most of them had been laid off for lack of work, but about one fourth had been laid off because of company restrictions on the employment of pregnant women. About 30 percent of the pregnant women claimants were ruled invalid at the start. This was true of 67 percent of those who had quit their jobs and 22 percent of those who were laid off. Three fifths of the survey claimants were disqualified at some stage of their pregnancy, 90 percent because they were found to be unavailable for or incapable of work. Of those who received benefits, 37 percent received their last benefit payment before the eighth month of pregnancy, 40 percent during the eighth month, and 23 percent during the ninth month.

Within three months after the end of pregnancy, 14 percent were back at work, 20 percent had refiled for benefits, 43 percent expected to return to work, and 23 percent had withdrawn from the labor market.[42]

Admittedly, it is difficult to make an individual determination of the continued ability of a woman to work before childbirth or when she can resume work following delivery. Administrative devices such as the requirement of a physician's certificate in questionable cases, however, are to be preferred to wholesale disqualification of pregnant women for arbitrary periods. Again, in the words of the President's Commission on the Status of Women, "Wide variations among types of jobs and physical capacities of individuals suggest the desirability of flexible means of determining the period which a woman is in fact unable to work."[43]

The President's Commission also called attention to the need for another type of insurance program which would generally take care of the problem of the pregnant women—maternity benefit insurance. It pointed out that 70 countries provide maternity benefits for a period before and after childbirth, usually as a part of programs of insurance against income

---

[42] Ruth Estes, *A Study of Pregnant Women as Unemployment Insurance Claimants* (Albany, N.Y.: Research and Statistics Office, Division of Employment, New York State Department of Labor, November, 1963); summarized in: Ruth Estes and Albert Ross, "Pregnant Women as UI Claimants in New York State," *Unemployment Insurance Review*, April, 1964, pp. 1–5.

[43] *Ibid.*, p. 43.

loss due to illness or temporary disability. It further pointed out that working women are provided in this country with such insurance only through the temporary disability insurance laws of four states, and only to a limited extent through two of them, and through private sources. Maternity benefits would be a desirable addition to our social insurance system for wider reasons than any disqualification provisions in unemployment insurance laws.[44]

SUMMARY AND CONCLUSIONS

Eligibility for unemployment insurance benefits is primarily based on a record of recent and substantial covered employment and a continuing attachment to the labor force during unemployment as shown by ability to work and availability for work.

Most of the states have qualifying requirements in terms of previous earnings in a recent "base year." These are of three types: flat amounts of qualifying wages, wages equal to multiples of the weekly benefit amount, and wages equal to a multiple of high-quarter wages. An increasing number of states are adopting a qualifying requirement in terms of weeks of employment in the 52 weeks immediately preceding unemployment. Such a requirement has the advantages of more precise measurement of previous employment, the ability to use more recent employment, and the avoidance of a "double dip" of two consecutive years of benefits through use of wages earned in the "lag period" between the base year and the beginning of the benefit year.

It is difficult, if not impossible, to fix a wage or employment qualifying requirement on any scientific basis. The compilation of statistics on the annual work experience of the entire labor force gives broad information indicating the large movement in and out of the labor force, the great amount of part-time employment, and the large proportion of part-time employment. Few state studies of the work experience of covered workers have been made. Those that do exist indicate that qualifying requirements have been too low in most states, yet they cannot be set very high without disqualifying too large a proportion of covered workers. The requirement evidently should be as much as, but not more than, about 20 weeks of substantial employment.

The large proportion of part-time workers raises the question of whether they should be able to qualify for benefits. Those who work a substantial number of hours a week for most of the year should qualify, provided they remain available for work when unemployed.

It is necessary to effectively test continuing ability to work and availability for work to prevent abuse of the system. Tests should be on an individual basis rather than by statutory classifications. Establishment of

[44] Maternity benefits are provided under the railroad employment and sickness insurance system.

ability to work has not created serious problems except when a worker becomes ill while drawing benefits. Temporary disability insurance is the best solution for this problem.

In most instances, registration for work at the public employment offices is not an adequate test of availability for work. Many states require an active search for work, but this can be a wasteful and unreasonable requirement. When necessary, an active search for work, guided by the employment office through labor market information and counseling, appears to be a good compromise.

In recent years, states are increasingly providing that a worker is considered available for work during training. Despite the MDTA training allowances, such provisions are necessary in order to fill the gaps in such allowances. The states have generally excluded student work from coverage, and some states deny benefits to students attending school, in some cases during vacation periods. The availability or unavailability of a student for full-time work should be the determining factor.

The increasing number of married women in the labor market and the large number working part time, has aroused suspicion that many may not be available for work when unemployed, although such studies as have been made do not confirm this as a fact. More stringent qualifying requirements for women than for men would be inequitable, but special attention should be given to testing the availability of certain types of women workers. Statutory disqualifications for stated periods before and after childbirth, or disqualification of those quitting work to meet marital obligations until after re-employment can create inequities. Instead of blanket disqualifications, each case should be treated on an individual basis.

Maternity benefits such as are provided under most social insurance programs would remove the problem of income for unemployed pregnant women in most instances, as well as meeting a broader social need.

Chapter 15

Trends in Disqualifications

Disqualifications are a necessary part of any unemployment insurance system. Hundreds of thousands of wage earners eligible for benefit payments who worked in covered employment and earned "qualifying wages" may nevertheless be disqualified for a variety of reasons. At least six classes of disqualifying actions are common to the state unemployment insurance acts. These provide for denial of benefits in cases of voluntary leaving without good cause, discharge for misconduct connected with the work, refusal of suitable work, participation in labor disputes, the receipt of disqualifying income, and making fraudulent claims.

In a system involving cash payments for wage loss due to unemployment, it is not illogical for the legislation to deny such payments to workers whose unemployment is voluntary. Unemployment insurance is not designed to make up the wage loss of workers whose behavior leads to unemployment for which neither the community nor the employer has a responsibility. Payments of unemployment compensation are neither a dole, nor a handout. Entitlement to benefits may be lost by actions which convert unemployment into idleness, for example, the refusal to accept the offer of a suitable job.

In spite of the logic which underlies the disqualification provisions in our unemployment insurance laws, controversy has developed over what acts should be disqualifying and what should be the length of the disqualification. The disqualification features of the laws of many states have become unduly harsh. It has been claimed that the existence of experience rating has led many employers to urge legislatures to pass provisions designed to exclude from benefits persons otherwise eligible but whose employment is not attributable to the employer. Since early in the program there has been a clear trend to exclude jobless persons from benefits for causes which previously had not been considered to be disqualifying.

The magnitude of the problem can be appreciated when we realize that every year there are over two million disqualifications from benefits.[1]

[1] These are not counts of individuals, but of disqualifying actions. The ratios are in terms of number of "claimant contracts" (i.e., claimant visits to the office to file claims) or of new spells of unemployment, of which an individual may have several during a year.

(Almost one half of these are determinations of inability to work or unavailability for work, discussed in the last chapter.) This is not a full measure of the number of disqualifying acts committed under the laws. Many who commit such acts do not apply for benefits; some secure other work. Nevertheless, the statistical evidence of formal disqualifications is enough to suggest that the increasing harshness of the state disqualification provisions and their administration has led to the denial of benefits to many whose unemployment is involuntary.

Although this has fluctuated with economic conditions, there has been a trend toward an ever-increasing number of disqualifications, as will be seen from Table 15–1. This results partly from the growth in the number of unemployed over the years. However, the *proportions* of disqualifications have also grown for two of the principal types of disqualifications. The proportions of inability to work or unavailability for work have tended to increase in recent years. The proportions denied benefits for refusal of suitable work have actually fallen. But there has been a pronounced growth in both the numbers and the proportions of disqualifications under the voluntary quit and discharge for misconduct provisions of the state laws.

The growing proportion of disqualifications for voluntary quitting without good cause is particularly marked. The ratio to spells of unemployment grew rapidly from 1945 to 1953, then leveled off. Following 1960, it shot upward again and in 1964 was almost double the 1945 ratio. The ratio of disqualifications was generally higher in states that restricted "good cause" for quitting to causes connected with the work or attributable to the employer. In 1964, when there were 48.5 disqualifications for voluntary quit for every 1,000 new spells of "insured unemployment," 20 of the 25 states with "restricted" provisions had ratios above 50 per thousand, the highest ratio being 184.3 per thousand. On the other hand, only 10 out of 27 states that recognize good *personal* cause for leaving had ratios above 50 per thousand spells of unemployment. In addition, the proportion of the total weeks of unemployment that are not compensated (not shown in Table 15–1) has no doubt increased because of the increased length of disqualifying periods.

The increasing severity of disqualifications is the major area in which there is conflict of opinion. Another area of conflict, the scope of the reasons for disqualification, is mainly centered on the limitations placed on "good cause" for voluntary quitting.

THE RATIONALE OF DISQUALIFICATIONS

In any insurance policy, the risks insured against and the conditions under which compensation is paid are spelled out in detail. The policy will also list the exceptions or conditions under which compensation will not be paid. These include actions taken by the insured which bring about the insured event (such as deliberately setting fire to an insured barn). The insurer here seeks to protect itself against the moral hazard of the insured

Table 15–1

Total Number of Disqualifications and Ratio to Claimant Contacts and New Spells of Insured Unemployment by Issue—1945–64
(absolute figures in thousands)

Item	1945	1947	1949	1951	1953	1955	1957	1959	1960	1961	1962	1963	1964
New spells of insured unemployment	5,608	8,860	16,352	10,046	10,543	11,079	13,276	13,532	16,061	16,865	14,513	14,958	12,910
Number of claimant contacts	36,241	60,599	109,408	54,835	57,229	72,312	84,534	95,586	109,350	128,899	102,070	103,174	90,971
Total disqualifications*	574	1,063	1,313	1,097	1,207	1,460	1,562	1,721	2,024	2,261	2,151	2,346	2,139
Per 1,000 claimant contacts	15.9	17.5	12.0	19.3	21.1	20.2	18.5	18.0	18.5	17.5	21.1	22.7	23.5
Not able or not available for work	300	564	593	488	493	636	674	765	893	970	932	1,058	921
Per 1,000 claimant contacts	8.3	9.3	5.4	8.6	8.6	8.8	8.0	8.0	8.2	9.5	9.1	10.3	10.1
Refusal of suitable work	88	113	88	91	88	86	68	77	79	90	90	86	78
Per 1,000 claimant contacts	2.4	1.9	0.8	1.6	1.5	1.2	0.8	0.8	0.7	0.7	0.9	0.8	0.9
Voluntary quits	134	263	422	313	393	394	464	480	567	649	624	662	625
Per 1,000 spells of insured unemployment	23.8	29.7	25.8	31.1	37.2	35.6	35.0	35.5	35.3	38.5	43.0	44.3	48.5
Discharge for misconduct	30	83	143	91	122	150	164	176	205	235	213	225	214
Per 1,000 spells of insured unemployment	5.3	9.4	8.8	9.0	11.6	13.5	12.3	13.0	12.8	13.9	15.7	15.1	16.5

* In addition to the four issues shown, also includes miscellaneous disqualifications which do not apply in all states. Excludes labor dispute disqualifications.
Source: United States Department of Labor, Bureau of Employment Security, Washington, D.C.; *Employment Security Review*, August, 1960; *Labor Market and Employment Security* and supplements, 1961–63; Unemployment Insurance Statistics, 1964.

deliberately creating the risk in order to collect the insurance. In line with this in unemployment insurance laws (the laws in effect being insurance policies), the three main disqualifications—voluntary quitting without good cause, discharge for misconduct connected with the work, and refusal of suitable work—are designed to limit the extent to which an individual can collect compensation when he has caused the unemployment or its continuance by his own actions. Thus, while these disqualifications are partly designed to discourage a person from causing his unemployment in the hope of drawing benefits, the main purpose is to limit the payment of compensation to unemployment that is involuntary. At the same time, it is not the purpose to disqualify workers for all voluntary actions that cause unemployment. A worker is disqualified from benefits only when the voluntary leaving is *without good cause*,[2] or when discharge with misconduct is *connected with the work*, or if he refuses *suitable* work. Thus, the laws allow for cases in which quitting, discharge, or refusal of work is justified and so is not disqualifying.

There are situations in which most people would consider the worker's action to be reasonable, the sort of action any reasonable person would take under the circumstances. For example, most people would consider it reasonable for a person to quit if he finds a better job, or if his health no longer permits him to continue heavy work, or if a death in the family makes it necessary for him to temporarily withdraw from the labor market. If he continues to show a genuine desire to work, or if he seeks work as soon as circumstances permit, and is not attempting to get benefits to take a "vacation" from work, the disqualification provisions—at least as originally designed—would not apply. As Professor Paul H. Sanders of Vanderbilt University states: ". . . in the normal statement of the voluntary quit, misconduct discharge, and work refusal trio of disqualifications a balance has been struck between these legitimate controls of the risk and the values that inhere in mobility of labor and freedom of choice."[3]

Some states have also injected an element of penalty into the three main causes of disqualification, especially in the reduction or cancellation of benefit rights in connection with these disqualifications. Penalties have no place in an unemployment insurance program. Quoting Professor Sanders again: "The principles applicable to control of the risk do not, normally, permit the operation of anything that can be classified as a penalty or forfeiture as such. Insurance company practices which tended in this direction have properly been condemned and brought under control by legislation and court decision."[4]

The purpose of disqualifications in connection with labor disputes is essentially the same as disqualification for voluntary quits, except that, in

---

[2] In some states good cause attributable to the employer or connected with the work.
[3] Paul H. Sanders, "Disqualification for Unemployment Insurance," *Vanderbilt Law Review*, Vol. VIII, No. 2 (1955), p. 312.
[4] *Ibid.*, p. 313.

most states, the question of whether the workers were justified for their actions does not arise. Disqualifications because of fraudulent misrepresentation are of still another character: they are in the nature of a forfeiture or penalty, justified in this instance because of the slowness or difficulty in getting punishment through fine or imprisonment. Disqualification from or reduction of benefits because of the receipt of pensions, dismissal pay, or certain other types of income is designed to prevent the duplication of the payment of benefits for the same event.

THE QUESTION OF EMPLOYER FAULT

The disqualification of workers from receiving benefits for any unemployment for which the employer is not responsible has been one of the increasing trends in the program. Because of the influence of the concept of "employer fault" on both the nature and the extent of disqualifications and their interpretation, we will discuss the concept at length before considering the specific disqualifications.[5]

Workmen's compensation was designed to break with the judicial practice of deciding accident cases on the basis of whether the employer was negligent or "at fault" in causing the accident. The concept of workmen's compensation has been stated by Herman and Anne Somers as follows:

Workmen's compensation, the new body of law designed to supplant the common law and employers' liability statutes, involved an entirely new economic and legal principle—*liability without fault*. It abandoned the moral and legal concept of individual fault as a basis for public policy.The cost of industrial accidents was to be socially allocated to the employer, not because of any presumption that he, or the corporation, was responsible for every accident which affected the employees, but because industrial accidents were recognized as one of the inevitable hazards of modern industry. The costs were, therefore, a legitimate cost of production.[6]

Unemployment insurance or compensation was based on the same principle: unemployment is a hazard of industry that should be compensated as a cost of production. Nevertheless, the question of "employer fault," which workmen's compensation was designed to get away from, was raised from the very beginning with respect to unemployment compensation.

The constitutionality of the original state unemployment compensation laws was challenged because they did not relate the burden of employer contributions in every instance to the responsibility for causing unemployment. In passing on the validity of the Alabama act, however, the United States Supreme Court held that it was no valid objection that "those who pay the tax may not have contributed to the unemployment. . . ." The

---

[5] For a brilliant discussion of the implications of the concept of employer fault for the program, see Earle V. Simrell, "Employer Fault vs. General Welfare as the Basis of Unemployment Compensation," *Yale Law Journal*, December, 1945, pp. 181–204.

[6] Herman M. Somers and Anne R. Somers, *Workmen's Compensation* (New York: John Wiley & Sons, Inc., 1954), pp. 26–27.

majority opinion pointed out that "nothing is more familiar in taxation than the imposition of a tax upon a class or upon individuals who enjoy no direct benefit from its expenditure, and who are not responsible for the condition to be remedied."[7]

Despite the Supreme Court decision, the idea that employers should be taxed only for unemployment for which they are responsible pervades the disqualification provisions. It is the principal motivation for restricting the payment of benefits after a voluntary quit to cases where the good cause for quitting is attributable to the employer or connected with the work. It undoubtedly has influenced the increased length of disqualifications, and particularly disqualifications for the duration of unemployment. It is most directly reflected in provisions for reduction or cancellation of benefit rights, so that the employer will not be charged with any benefits that the worker might otherwise draw after he has served his disqualification period.

There has never been any attempt to carry through the idea that an employer should only be charged with unemployment for which he is directly responsible. Even in the original Wisconsin law where the concept has been carried the farthest, the employer was charged with benefits paid to laid-off workers, whether or not the lack of work was within the control of the employer. The original law also provided that, after the unemployed worker had used up his benefit rights with his last employer, his rights based on employment with previous employers could be drawn upon in inverse chronological order. Later, Wisconsin had to recognize the impracticality of limiting a worker's benefits to the money that had been accumulated in his former employer's account. For purposes of paying benefits it pooled the entire state unemployment fund.

IS EXPERIENCE RATING TO BLAME?

The "experience rating" provisions in the state laws, which vary an employer's contributions with his "experience with unemployment," have commonly been blamed for the increasing stringency of disqualification provisions. It is charged that experience rating has provided the incentive for employers to secure the passage of stringent provisions in order to keep their taxes down.

However, Wisconsin, which led the vanguard in advocating experience rating as an incentive to stabilization of employment, took the position at an early date that the purpose of experience rating was not to narrow the payment of benefits to instances where the employer was at fault. In a case involving the discharge of a taxicab driver who had had three accidents in eight weeks, two of which he had not reported, the Industrial Commission of Wisconsin awarded benefits. It resolved that the actions which caused the discharge could not be considered to be misconduct connected with the work. The employer appealed because he did not feel

[7] *Carmichael* v. *Southern Coal & Coke Co.*, 301 U.S. 495 (1937), pp. 521–22.

he should be charged with any benefits paid to the employee since he was justified in discharging him. In its brief to the Supreme Court, the Commission stated that it interpreted the disqualification as having "nothing to do with the question of rightness or wrongness of the employer's act in discharging." Representing employers and employees, the State Advisory Committee on Unemployment Compensation and the Wisconsin Association of Manufacturers supported the Commission's position in briefs filed as *amici curiae.* According to Earle V. Simrell, "all three briefs were clear and emphatic in arguing, not only the consistency of their construction with experience rating, but its downright necessity to the purposes of experience rating." The purpose of experience rating, the Advisory Committee brief said, was to encourage the stabilization of employment, and not to avoid the payment of benefits. In its brief the Commission stated, " 'Experience rating' was certainly not designed for the purpose of allowing employers to restrict and sabotage the efficient operation of the primary purpose of any unemployment compensation law, namely, the payment of benefits to out-of-work employees. Nothing could strike the cause of experience rating a more grievous blow than to have it prostituted to this purpose."[8] In a strong opinion, the Wisconsin Supreme Court affirmed the Commission's award of benefits, holding their interpretation of "discharge for misconduct" as essential to the "principal purpose and object under the act of alleviating the evils of unemployment."[9]

In early cases involving disqualifications from benefits, the Supreme Courts of Michigan and Minnesota also made it clear that their unemployment insurance laws were not framed to exclude the payment of benefits for unemployment which was not the employer's fault. In a case involving a voluntary quit which will be discussed later, the Minnesota Supreme Court looked to the legislative declaration of policy in its law and concluded: "There is nothing in this language to justify the conclusion that benefits under the act accrue only when unemployment is the result of some *wrongful* act or fault of an employer."[10]

Unfortunately, it is evident that the position of the Wisconsin Industrial Commission and Wisconsin Supreme Court has faded away along with the fading of the emphasis on stabilization of employment as the purpose of experience rating. With the current emphasis on the value of experience rating in encouraging employers to "police the system," it would appear that too many employers view experience rating in the way the Commission was seeking to combat. In Simrell's words, "the ghost of employer fault as a test of compensability has haunted the unemployment compensation program as it previously haunted workmen's compensation."[11]

[8] For a more detailed discussion of this case, see Simrell, *op. cit.,* pp. 185–88.
[9] *Boynton Cab Co.* v. *Neubeck,* 237 Wis. 249, 258–59, 296 N.X. 636, 640 (1941).
[10] *Fannon* v. *Federal Cartridge Corporation,* 18 N.W. (2d) 252 (Minn. 1945). (Emphasis the Court's.) See Simrell, *op. cit.,* pp. 188–98 for a discussion of this and other cases cited below.
[11] Simrell, *op. cit.,* p. 196.

The argument of "employer fault" is that an employer is unfairly "penalized" if his experience rating account is charged with benefits for which he is not responsible. Yet unemployment following an ordinary layoff due to lack of work is compensated and the benefits are charged to the employer without regard to whether or not he was at fault in causing the unemployment. Therefore, to seek to disqualify a worker unless the voluntary quit, discharge for misconduct, or refusal of suitable work is the fault of the employer, is no more logical than to refuse to compensate a worker when he is laid off for lack of work unless the lack of work is the fault of the employer.

REFUSAL OF SUITABLE WORK

The overwhelming majority of disqualifications are cases of individual actions rather than cases of group action such as labor disputes. These include refusal of suitable work, voluntary quitting without good cause, and discharge for misconduct. It goes without saying that earning wages in suitable employment is preferable to drawing unemployment compensation because of lack of work. The Employment Security system has therefore always provided for the claimant to register for work at the local public employment office in order to maximize the extent to which he can be offered a suitable job when one becomes available. Reinforcing this aim to get the claimant re-employed, the laws all provide for the disqualification of the claimant from benefits if he refuses an offer of suitable work.

State laws differ only minutely as to the criteria for determining whether work that is offered is suitable. They all include almost identical statements as to the conditions under which "new work" may be refused without disqualification.[12] The major differences in the laws are with respect to the extent of the disqualification that is imposed if "suitable" work is refused. Since the issues regarding the extent of disqualification are similar for all three of the disqualifications for personal actions, these will be discussed together in later sections of this chapter.

While there is little significant difference in the provisions of the state laws governing disqualification for refusal of suitable work, interpretation of the provisions in specific situations has often been difficult and in some cases has led to diametrically opposite decisions.

Interpretations fall into three groups: (1) was the work suitable; (2) was there an offer of work; (3) was the offer refused?

What Is Suitable Work?

When the Social Security Act was passed in 1935, it contained provisions designed to protect labor standards. It was feared that unemployment insurance could be "exploited" by denying benefits to eligible claimants who reject job offers at substandard wages or disadvantageous working

12 See p. 289.

conditions, who refuse to act as strike breakers, or refuse to join a company-dominated union or sign a "yellow-dog" contract as a condition of being employed. The federal law, therefore, required that state laws, as a condition of federal approval, provide the following so-called "labor standards":

compensation shall not be denied in such State to any otherwise eligible individual for refusing to accept new work under any of the following conditions:

(A) If the position offered is vacant due directly to a strike, lockout, or other labor dispute;
(B) if the wages, hours, or other conditions of the work offered are substantially less favorable to the individual than those prevailing for similar work in the locality;
(C) if as a condition of being employed the individual would be required to join a company union or to resign from or refrain from joining any bona fide labor organization.[13]

All the state laws contain such provisions.

For the most part, these provisions have been rather uniformly interpreted, since the Secretary of Labor has taken the position that to make these federal provisions meaningful, the state laws must be given the same meaning in actual construction and application as the federal law. This position, however, has not gone unchallenged. The first conformity issue that resulted in formal hearing and ruling by the Secretary of Labor involved California's interpretation of the meaning of "new work" in the federal labor standard.[14] In this case, the principal issue was whether the state's or the federal government's interpretation of the words of the standard, which were identical in the federal and state statutes, should govern.

In addition to these labor standards, the state laws contain specific lists of criteria which the administrative agency should take into account in determining whether work is suitable. The typical state law follows the Social Security Board's original draft bills, and reads: "In determining whether or not any work is suitable for an individual, the commission shall consider the degree of risk involved in his health, safety, and morals, his physical fitness and prior training and experience, his length of unemployment and prospects for securing local work in his customary occupation, and the distance of the available work from his residence."

There are, however, a few variations from these criteria. Two states make no reference to the suitability of work offered and, instead, provide for disqualifications for refusal of work for which a claimant is reasonably fitted (Delaware and New York). There are also several deviations from the criteria of suitability listed in the state laws. Alabama and West Virginia provide that distance shall not be a factor if the work is in substantially the same locality as the claimant's last regular employment, and he

13 Section 3304 (a) (5) of the Internal Revenue Code of 1954.
14 See discussion of this issue in Chapter 23.

left his last employment without good cause connected with his work. These provisions tend to tie claimants to the locality where they last worked and limit their mobility.

When it comes to the interpretation of such criteria of suitability as the degree of risk to the worker's health, safety, or morals, or physical fitness, there seems to be less divergence of interpretation than over questions of what constitutes a valid offer of work or a refusal of work.[15] With respect to physical fitness, as indeed with respect to the other criteria, the test of suitability is not the suitability of the *job* but the suitability of the work for the individual in the light of his circumstances. For example, an office worker accustomed to inside sedentary work cannot be expected to take an outside job involving heavy work.

The most difficult question is how long the claimant must be unemployed before considerations of prior training or prior earnings shall be given less weight. There are also differences as to how great an adjustment the worker shall be required to make. A worker is usually given a temporary period in which he can seek work that is commensurate with his prior training, experience, and prior earnings. But as his unemployment lengthens, he is ordinarily expected to be willing to take a job involving lower skills or lower earnings. When is a reasonable period of time before he should be disqualified for refusal to accept lower wages? Courts have ruled that three days, five days, or nineteen days are insufficient in specific cases, and that a month or a ten-week period is sufficient in other cases.[16] Some state agencies have set up definite periods of time after which the standards for a suitable job are to be lowered for the claimants. Arthur W. Menard argues that, while a specific period may be convenient as a rule of thumb, there are too many factors to be taken into account to use inflexible rules as a guide.[17]

Questions also arise as to how large an adjustment a worker can be expected to make after the passage of time. Sanders quotes a case of a carpenter previously earning the union scale of $1.58 an hour who was disqualified for refusing without good cause an "open shop" job paying only $1.02 to $1.20 an hour.[18]

Similarly, there are wide differences of opinion as to how far away a new job must be for a worker to regard it as unsuitable.[19]

It is evident that during a slack labor market, the criteria for suitable work are applied more flexibly. In other words, the phrase "suitable work" means something different under different economic conditions. Annual data show that the relative number of disqualifications for refusal of suit-

[15] See Arthur W. Menard, "Refusal of Suitable Work," *Vanderbilt Law Review*, Vol. VIII, No. 2 (December, 1945), pp. 138–47.
[16] Sanders, *op. cit.*, p. 329.
[17] Menard, *op. cit.*, p. 142.
[18] Sanders, *op. cit.*, p. 330.
[19] "Suitable Work—How Far Away?" in United States Department of Labor, Bureau of Employment Security, *Issues Reflected in Appeals Decisions on Unemployment Benefits*, First Series, BES No. 7–180 (July, 1959), pp. 55–59.

able work definitely dropped in the recession years 1949, 1954, 1958, and 1961.[20] This may also be due to fewer jobs being available, so there is less opportunity to apply the "work test" of the offer of a suitable job.

The Offer of Work

Before it can be considered that a worker has refused suitable work, there must be a definite offer of work. The laws do not specify what shall constitute an offer. It is generally agreed that it must be clear to the claimant that he is being asked to take a job, that the conditions of the job are specified, and that definite acceptance or rejection of the offer is required. Problems arise, however, when the employment service does not complete a referral to a job because the claimant indicates that he is not interested in the type of work offered. The decision often turns on the conclusion reached by the employment office interviewer as to whether the worker would have refused the job if he had definitely been referred to it. In some cases, it is ruled that there was a "constructive referral"; in other cases, the decision has been that there was no definite offer of work.[21]

The employment office may initiate the referral to the job or the offer may come directly from the employer. The offer can be by mail. Problems arise, however, if the worker does not receive the offer because he has not notified his former employer of a change of address. This arises most frequently when there is a union agreement that the employer will notify workers by mail in order of seniority and the worker loses his seniority if he does not respond to the recall notice. Different state courts have reached opposite conclusions in such cases.[22]

It is generally agreed that an offer of work must be a bona fide attempt to secure a claimant's service and not merely an offer given in an attempt to secure the disqualification of a worker. Cases are particularly suspect when the employer makes an offer after an appealed ruling has been made against him.[23]

What Is a Work Refusal?

Refusal of suitable work can include failure to apply for such work. The usual state provision reads that the worker is disqualified "if the commissioner finds that he has failed, without good cause, either to apply for available, suitable work when so directed by the employment office or the commissioner or to accept suitable work when offered him. . . ."

When referred to a job, the claimant must make a genuine effort to secure the employment if it is suitable for him. If he deliberately seeks to avoid being hired by acting in a way which causes the employer to withdraw the offer, he will be disqualified in most cases. Delicate questions

[20] This is not brought out clearly in Table 15–1 which uses only semiannual date.

[21] See "Avoiding Referrals or Offers of Work," *Issues*, etc., First Series, *op. cit.*, pp. 71–74.

[22] "Recall Notice Not Received—Refusal of Work," *Issues*, etc., *op. cit.*, pp. 71–74.

[23] Menard, *op. cit.*, p. 136.

arise, however. For example, if a claimant tells the prospective employer that he expects a recall to his former job in a few weeks and will only work until he is recalled, should he be disqualified if the prospective employer does not hire him under such conditions? The decision may turn on whether the claimant made the statement in order to avoid being hired or because he felt he should be honest in advising the prospective employer of his intentions.[24]

VOLUNTARY LEAVING WITHOUT GOOD CAUSE

The second major reason for disqualification from benefits is for voluntarily quitting a job *without good cause*. One unfamiliar with unemployment insurance may be surprised that anyone who voluntarily quits his job under any circumstances can draw benefits, since unemployment insurance is designed to compensate a worker for *involuntary* unemployment. It is a cardinal rule that insurance does not cover losses willfully caused by the insured. There are circumstances, however, under which it has been considered to be reasonable and justifiable for the worker to have quit his job, and unemployment benefits are payable if he cannot find other work. There has never been any disagreement that the laws should permit payment of benefits in some cases of voluntary leaving. The disagreements have arisen over what constitutes good enough cause for leaving.

Good Personal Cause

Originally, almost all states permitted the payment of benefits if unemployment followed good *personal* cause for quitting. Two approaches are taken in determining what constituted good personal cause. The more liberal approach is to ask, "Did the claimant act as a 'reasonable person would have acted in the circumstances?" The more conservative approach is to ask, "Was the cause of a necessitous or compelling nature?" Pennsylvania has incorporated the latter into its statute. The appeals tribunals or courts of other states have used this concept in their interpretation of the meaning of "good cause." In fact, the North Dakota Appeal Tribunal has made the "reasonable person" and "compelling reason" concepts virtually synonymous. It reasoned as follows: "Good cause, in our opinion, is a compelling reason, such a reason as would impel the same or a similar action by an ordinary reasonable individual under the same or similar reason." This case concerned a woman whose earnings, except in the summer months, were so reduced that she could not support herself. She therefore quit and moved to another area to live and share expenses with a sister. The Appeal Tribunal denied benefits, saying "She may have good reasons for leaving the job but not a compelling personal reason" (AT-1-6563, dated 1-10-62).[25]

24 "Claimants Awaiting Recall by Former Employers," *Issues*, etc., *op. cit.*, pp. 63–64.
25 "Compelling Personal Reasons—Good Cause?" *Issues Involved in Appeals Decisions on Unemployment Benefits*, Third Series, BES No. U–213 (January, 1963), pp. 87–88.

Good Cause Attributable to the Employer

More and more states (24 as of January 1, 1966) have restricted good cause for voluntary leaving to good cause connected with the work or attributable to the employer.[26] Whether to limit good cause for quitting to work-connected or employer-connected reasons, or to allow benefits when there is good personal cause for quitting is the big issue in voluntary quit disqualifications.

Only West Virginia has explicitly limited good cause for leaving to situations where the employer is *at fault*. Nevertheless, the other states which allow benefits only if the cause of leaving is attributable to the employer implicitly are seeking to achieve the same end, to pay benefits only when the employer is at fault.

"Attributable to the employer," however, does not necessarily mean that the employer is at fault. In a case where a woman had to quit her job at an ordnance plant because she became severely ill as a result of her work, the Minnesota Supreme Court ruled that she had quit with good cause attributable to the employer. Whether the claimant had "good cause attributable to the employer" was held to be independent of the test of whether there was "any wrongful act, negligence, or failure on the part of the employer." It is a question of relations, said the court, rather than responsibility for sins of either omission or commission. "Factors or circumstances directly connected with employment" are attributable to the employer.[27] In effect, the Court's interpretation made the phrases "attributable to the employer" and "connected with the work" synonymous.

Nevertheless, employers continue to contest claims that a voluntary leaving was "attributable to the employer" on the basis that the employer was not at fault. This has harmful effects on the program as a whole in narrowing compensable unemployment to that for which the employer is directly responsible. Whether or not the question of employer fault is injected, states in which good cause for leaving is restricted to causes attributable to the employer or connected with the work take markedly different positions than states in which good cause is "unrestricted." This is illustrated by different interpretations of what is "good cause" in such common causes for leaving as quitting to take another job.

Voluntariness of the Quit

All but six of the state laws[28] include the word "voluntary" in their quitting without good cause provisions. In laws that do not disqualify for quitting for good personal cause, the question of whether the leaving was voluntary or not usually does not enter into the decision. But when the cause must be attributable to the employer or connected with the work, the interpretation of "voluntary" may be critical when the quit is for

[26] About half of these states make one or more exceptions to this restriction such as if the worker had to quit because of illness or disability.

[27] *Fannon* v. *Federal Cartridge Corporation*, 18 N.W. (2d) 252 (Minn. 1945).

[28] Colorado, Connecticut, Louisiana, Montana, Ohio, and Wisconsin.

personal reasons. At one extreme in court interpretations, "voluntary" means no more than an indication of who initiated the work separation. At the other extreme, it has been held that any quitting of a job, unless it is for good cause attributable to the employer, is voluntary and therefore subject to disqualification.[29]

Quitting to Take Another Job

When a worker voluntarily quits one job to take another job, the question of disqualification from benefits usually arises if the new job fails to materialize or lasts only a short time. In states that recognize good personal causes for leaving, benefits are awarded in such cases. Thus, in Rhode Island, a worker who quit a part-time job to take a full-time job was informed when he reported for work that he would not be hired because his physical examination had disclosed diabetes and high blood pressure. The Board of Review awarded him benefits (No. 3602 UC, dated February 7, 1964).

Some states that restrict good cause to that attributable to the employer have recognized the harshness of disqualifying a worker for quitting to take a better job, and provide exceptions in certain circumstances. Such exceptions, however, do not always give relief in particular situations. For example, the Michigan law restores wage credits lost if a worker quits to take another job but is laid off the new job for lack of work. In one case, a worker was released from his new job because, on the testimony of his employer, he was not catching on fast enough and did not do the necessary work. The Michigan Circuit Court disallowed benefits because the separation was not a layoff due to lack of work, the condition specified in the Michigan statute under which wage credits would be restored (*Patrick Alexander* v. *Detroit Divco Truck Sales, Inc. et. al.*, No. 32633, Wayne County, March 19, 1963).[30] State provisions which disqualify a worker for quitting a job to take another discourage the mobility of labor, one of the treasured advantages of a free-enterprise economy.

Unsuitability of the Work

If a claimant can *refuse* work that is unsuitable without being disqualified, it would seem to follow that if a worker *quits* unsuitable work, he should not be disqualified. Twelve states specifically provide (with some variations) that the unsuitability of the work may be good cause for leaving it. In other states, however, it has been ruled that the unsuitability of the work is not a good cause for leaving. Frequently, such cases involve low wages. And these divide into cases where the worker has quit because his wages have proved to be too low to meet expenses, and cases where there has been a wage cut. The decision in such cases sometimes turns on how

[29] See "The Problems of Voluntariness in Quit Cases," *Issues*, etc., Third Series, *op. cit.*, p. 81.
[30] "Quit to Go to Another Job—Good Cause?" *Unemployment Insurance Review*, April, 1964, pp. 34–37.

long the worker has continued to work at the wage that was the cause of his leaving the job, or on what prospects there are of his wage situation improving. The states have differed in their rulings in such cases, some awarding benefits and other denying them in situations that involve the same basic questions.[31]

Observance of Union Rules

Troublesome questions arise when union rules are involved. Mere compliance with a union order or rule has generally not been considered to be a good cause for leaving. In his study of disqualifications, Paul H. Sanders found that "employees who refuse to cross the picket line of another union on the basis of union orders have been found disqualified by voluntary leaving. But refusal to cross a belligerent picket line from fear of bodily harm was found to be a leaving with good cause 'attributable to the employer.' "[32]

Some states have also taken the position that unions, as the bargaining agents of their members, bind the members in all matters affecting employment. Within a period of four weeks, in 1958, court decisions in three states took the position that a worker has voluntarily quit if he is mandatorily retired on reaching a specified age under a union pension agreement.[33] There were prompt reactions in other states. After the California Superior Court of San Francisco made a similar decision (*Regal Pal Brewing Co. v. Appeals Board and Wenzelburger*, No. 474,268), the California legislature in 1959 amended their law to specifically provide that a worker compulsorily retired under a collective bargaining agreement shall not be deemed to have left his work without good cause. The Pennsylvania Supreme Court in a decision on July 24, 1959 (*Warner Co. v. Board of Review and Gianfelice*, 153 A. [2d] 906) made a sweeping ruling that a retired worker should not be disqualified because of a union agreement.[34] By no means, however, has this issue ended and it will become more important as the number of retirements under collective bargaining agreements continues to increase. (This has important implications for policy making with respect to the broader question of whether or not benefits should be denied to pensioners.)

Marital Obligations

States that do not restrict good cause for voluntary quitting to causes attributable to the employer or work are not free from a "hard-boiled"

---

[31] See "Quitting Work Because of Earnings Reduction," *Issues*, etc., First Series, *op. cit.*, pp. 91–94; "Voluntary Quit—Low Wages," *Issues*, etc., Second Series, BES No. U–201 (July, 1961), pp. 93–97; "Quitting an Unsuitable Job," *Unemployment Insurance Review*, June, 1964, pp. 18–21.

[32] Sanders, *op. cit.*, p. 322.

[33] "Compulsory Retirements under Union Agreements—Voluntary Quits?" *Issues*, etc., First Series, *op. cit.*, pp. 87–90.

[34] "Compulsory Retirements under Union Agreements—Second Round," *Issues*, etc., Second Series, *op. cit.*, pp. 77–80.

attitude toward certain kinds of quits. For example, a common cause for quitting a job is to fulfill marital obligations. This may involve the necessity of quitting to care for a sick husband or child, or to follow a spouse to another locality. Most frequently these cases involve women workers. Many states by statute disqualify workers in such cases. Most of these (15 states as of January 1, 1966) recognize good personal cause for leaving. In the other eight states, except Maine, the reason for a special disqualification for unemployment due to marital obligations is to impose a more severe disqualification than is imposed for other causes for voluntary leaving. Since these special disqualifications also involve the question of availability for work, they have already been discussed in the preceding chapter.

Space does not permit a discussion of all the kinds of questions that arise in connection with voluntary quits, or even all the important questions.[35] Before leaving the subject of voluntary leaving, however, let us return to the major issue of whether personal reasons should be recognized as good cause for leaving, or whether the reason for leaving must be attributable to the employer or connected with the work in order to constitute good cause for leaving. That the latter type of provision is resulting in large numbers of disqualifications in cases that would be considered good cause for leaving in other states is shown by the following table:

Ratio of Disqualifications for Voluntary Quits to 1,000 New Spells of Unemployment in Seven States with Highest Ratios, 1962–64

State	1962	State	1963	State	1964
U.S. Average	43.0		44.3		48.5
So. Carolina*	168.1	So. Carolina*	181.8	Nebraska	217.7
Colorado	147.7	Georgia*	146.5	So. Carolina*	184.3
Georgia*	144.5	Texas*	138.6	Georgia*	176.5
Texas*	129.7	Colorado*	133.7	Oklahoma*	142.3
Oklahoma*	124.6	Oklahoma*	133.1	Texas*	140.8
Montana*	88.9	Montana*	91.9	Colorado*	115.9
Arizona*	80.0	Arizona*	86.8	Iowa*	110.4

* Good cause for leaving restricted to causes attributable to the employer or connected with the work.

With the exception of Colorado in 1962 and Nebraska in 1964, all these states restricted good cause for leaving to cause attributable to the employer or connected with the work (South Carolina by following a court ruling).

While ratios are not the sole criteria for judging a provision good or bad, these ratios were so much higher than the national average that they indi-

35 This is indicated by a mere listing of articles that have been written on other voluntary quit issues in the Bureau of Employment Security's series of studies, *Issues Reflected in Appeals Decision on Unemployment Benefits*: "Leaving Work Before End of Trial Period," "Quitting to Avoid Layoff or Discharge," "Trouble with the Boss— Good Cause for Leaving Work?" and "Leave of Absence—Voluntary Quits and Discharges."

cate that these states were overly restrictive. No doubt some states have higher ratios of disqualifications because of conservative administrative or court rulings, but it is evident that the restrictions on good cause for leaving are the principle reason for higher disqualification rates.

DISCHARGE FOR MISCONDUCT

Discharge from the job is the third major reason for disqualification from unemployment benefits. The initial reaction of an employer unfamiliar with unemployment insurance would probably be that no worker whom he has discharged should be entitled to benefits. It must be recognized, however, that discharges are frequently because of inefficiency or inability of the worker to do the work properly. Sometimes, however, a worker is released for rather capricious reasons. In many, if not most, of these cases, the worker is in fact involuntarily unemployed. Disqualification in case of discharge, therefore, has been circumscribed so as to be consistent with the purpose of unemployment insurance, to compensate for involuntary unemployment. To be disqualifying, the discharge must be for misconduct. Some laws say, "for just cause," but this is usually interpreted to mean the same as misconduct.

Meaning of Misconduct

To be disqualifying, misconduct must be willful or deliberate. Several state laws are explicit in this respect. The Connecticut and Pennsylvania laws use the words "willful misconduct" and the Massachusetts law specifies "deliberate misconduct in willful disregard of the employing unit's interest." The other states have generally interpreted their laws to have this meaning.

The leading court opinion that is most quoted in this respect is the Wisconsin Supreme Court decision in *Boynton Cab Co.* v. *Neubeck*, previously discussed in connection with the question of employer fault. In its opinion, the Court said:

The application of the term "misconduct" . . . is limited to conduct evincing such wilful or wanton disregard of an employer's interest as is found in deliberate violations or disregard of standards of behavior which the employer has the right to expect of his employee, or in carelessness or negligence of such degree or recurrence as to manifest equal culpability, wrongful intent or evil design, or to show an intentional and substantial disregard of the employer's interests or of the employee's duties and obligations to his employer. On the other hand mere inefficiency, unsatisfactory conduct, failure in good performance as the result of inability or incapacity, inadvertencies or ordinary negligence in isolated instances, or good faith errors of judgment or discretion are not to be deemed "misconduct" within the meaning of the statute.[36]

In quoting the above, Professor Paul H. Sanders has written:

[36] 237 Wis. 249, 296 N.W. 636, 640 (1941).

It seems clear that we are not looking simply for substandard conduct under this disqualification but for a wilful or wanton state of mind accompanying the engaging in substandard conduct. It may be pointed out that an employee could scarcely have the state of mind requisite for "misconduct" under the *Boynton* language and not foresee the termination or suspension of his employment as a reasonable and probable consequence of engaging in the conduct.[37]

While there has been rather wide acceptance of the position that simple negligence with no harmful intent is not misconduct connected with the work, the seriousness of the result of negligence may be taken into consideration. Thus, the Michigan Supreme Court (*Ora H. Bell v. ESC and McInerney Spring & Wire Co.*, 103 N.W. 2d) held that a boiler room attendant who was discharged for sleeping on the job was discharged for misconduct connected with the work. The court rejected the claimant's argument that his sleeping was unintentional, because the claimant was taking medicine for a heart condition that made him sleepy so that his sleeping was foreseeable. It also took into consideration the seriousness of the results that would have followed if the boiler had exploded while the claimant slept.

Repetition of the negligence that eventually leads to discharge may or may not result in disqualification. In a Colorado referee's decision (RD–13477–59, August 31, 1959, MC–255.1–17 BSSUI), it was ruled that a bank teller should be disqualified for misconduct connected with his work after he had repeatedly failed to follow the bank's printed rules to verify checks before payment. On the other hand, a glass-products selector and packer who was fired on the employer's charge that she had willfully persisted in packing imperfect bottles was awarded benefits under a California court decision on the basis that the claimant said she had not packed defective bottles intentionally. On the night when she was discharged, she was working the "graveyard shift," had a headache, and there was a high percentage of defective glassware coming down the assembly line. (*Maywood Glass Co. v. Director*, California District Court of Appeals, Second District, Division Two, May, 1959.)[38]

It is often difficult to determine when poor work ceases to be the result of lack of skill or ability and becomes intentional and, therefore, a proper reason for disqualification from benefits. When an employee has been discharged for poor or damaged work because of failure to follow instructions, especially after warning, it has been ruled to be misconduct, but when damaged work or loss to the employer is due to an honest error of judgment, it has been ruled not to be misconduct. The general trend of decisions has held the employer responsible for proper selection, training, instruction, and supervision, and if there is a failure by the employer to

---

[37] Sanders, *op. cit.*, pp. 334–35.
[38] "Employee Negligence—Misconduct?" *Issues*, etc., Second Series, *op. cit.*, pp. 61–64.

provide any of these, the worker should not be disqualified from benefits if discharged for unintentional poor or damaged work.[39] A bank clerk discharged for making mistakes due to poor eyesight was not disqualified when it was found that the employer had never investigated her ability to do the job (Ohio Board of Review, Appeals Docket No. 215580, April 23, 1958). Neither did the Virginia Commission disqualify a truck driver who was discharged when he made the mistake of taking the wrong route in delivering a load of steel, since the driver was a man of extremely limited education (Decision No. 3187-C, January 31, 1958).

"Since we can have no general guide in the laws of the land," wrote Professor Sanders, "the 'wrongness' of the conduct must be judged in the particular employment context." Identical conduct might be treated as an "intentional and substantial disregard of the employer's interest in one environment and not in another."[40]

Violation of Company Rules

When an employee is discharged for violating a company rule, some states consider this as almost conclusive evidence that there has been misconduct connected with the work. Thus, in a New Mexico case, a truck driver was discharged for breaking the employer's rule that all accidents, no matter how minor, must be immediately reported. The discharged truck driver admitted having backed into another company truck, but considered the accident so insignificant that he did not report it. Nevertheless, the Appeals Referee upheld the denial of benefits, saying that "Failure to follow known company policy is considered misconduct connected with the work." In other states, the employer's right to discharge a worker for violation of a company rule is recognized, but the nature of the violation is examined to decide whether it is misconduct connected with the work. In one case, the Michigan Supreme Court stated that whether violation of a company rule is misconduct depends upon whether both the rule and its violation have a reasonable relationship to the "task" or work performance.[41]

In this connection, Professor Sanders wrote that "those (the employer's) interests and obligations can be made concrete, however, only in terms of the 'industrial law,' the 'going' standard of conduct, established and maintained, in fact, for the particular plant, warehouse, store, or office. This industrial law may largely result from the unilateral determination of the employer. If there is a collective bargaining agency present, this 'industrial law' will be conditioned, impliedly, and perhaps expressedly, by that fact."[42]

[39] "Poor or Improper Work," *Issues*, etc., Second Series, *op. cit.*, pp. 51–54.
[40] Sanders, *op. cit.*, p. 335.
[41] "Discharge for Violation of Company Rule—Reasonableness of the Worker's Action." *Issues*, etc., Third Series, *op. cit.*, pp. 43–48.
[42] Sanders, *op. cit.*, p. 336.

Other Types of Misconduct

Other common types of conduct that result in disqualification include insubordination, refusal to perform assigned work, and absence from work. The first two do not raise any particular difficulties in determining whether a disqualification should be imposed. Decisions on whether absence from work is misconduct often turn on such considerations as the amount of inconvenience it has created for the employer, the necessity or justification for the absence, whether a company rule requires notice, or whether consideration for the employer's interests has been demonstrated by securing prior permission for or by giving immediate notice of the absence.[43]

"Connected with the Work"

Although it is usually recognized that disqualifying misconduct must have been performed on the job, cases arise in which conduct off duty is considered to be connected with the work. Such cases are usually associated with drinking. When there is drinking on the job, or the employee arrives on the job unable to physically perform his duties as a result of drinking, discharge is normally ruled to be for misconduct connected with the work. The tendency has been not to disqualify a worker if the drinking is off the premises of the employer. For example, a salesman, who had told his employer that he considered drinking with a customer a part of the job, was discharged by the employer after repeated warnings that the claimant was drinking too much. The referee awarded benefits on the basis that "Nowhere in the evidence do we find that the employer was injured in any way by the employee's conduct." In another case, an employer who maintained vending machines in taverns, restaurants, and other establishments, could get liability insurance only on the basis specified by one insurance company that he hire only teetotalers. An employee was discharged after he had become intoxicated several times while off duty although he had agreed in writing that he would not drink on or off the job. While the Wisconsin Appeal Tribunal and Commission awarded benefits on the basis that there was no evidence that the employer's insurance coverage was jeopardized by such private drinking, the court reversed the ruling and denied benefits on the basis that the employer had every right to exact cooperation from his employees in fulfilling the teetotaler condition in the liability insurance contract.

Other types of misconduct besides drinking, of course, occur off the job. Usually benefits are awarded in such cases even though the employee may be discharged. For the conduct to be disqualifying, there must be a strong connection between such conduct and the employer's business.

Discharge for stealing from the employer usually results in disqualification. The only exceptions are for such minor cases as one in which an employee put a can of apple juice in his pocket. The court ruled that the

---

[43] "Absence from Work," *Issues,* etc., Third Series, *op. cit.,* pp. 49–52.

"de minimis" doctrine applied. (*Parke, Davis and Co.* v. *Michigan Employment Security Appeal Board*, Circuit Court, Wayne County. No. 289,321, December 31, 1957, MC 140.3–11). Discharge for suspected stealing on the basis of a lie detector test has, in more than once case, been ruled to be too uncertain evidence of misconduct to justify disqualification from benefits.[44]

PERIOD OF DISQUALIFICATION

The paramount issue in connection with disqualifications for refusal of suitable work, voluntary leaving without good cause, and discharge for misconduct is the severity of the disqualification imposed. Originally, most of the states provided for temporary periods of disqualification after which the worker, if still unemployed, could draw benefits. This was for a fixed period in some states and for varying periods, within prescribed limits, in other states. For instance, 29 states originally disqualified a worker in case of voluntary leaving without good cause for the week in which the leaving occurred and the next one to five weeks (plus the waiting period). This was also the most common period of disqualification for refusal of suitable work. The period was usually longer in cases of discharge for misconduct, up to nine weeks plus the week of discharge and the waiting period. The length of the period in these states was discretionary with the administrative agency. Some states provided for a flat period of disqualification. From the beginning, a few states have gone further. Six states disqualified a claimant for the entire duration of his unemployment for refusing suitable work, two for discharge for misconduct, and one for voluntary quitting.

Several definite trends are observable with respect to the period of disqualification. One is a change in a number of state laws from a variable number of weeks of disqualification to a fixed number of weeks. Such changes were partly made to simplify administration. The agency, and particularly the individual claims adjudicators, are in no position to fix the length of the disqualification in proportion to the seriousness of the disqualifying action. A fixed disqualification period does take away some flexibility, such as the ability to impose the minimum disqualification in cases where there is a narrow balance between those factors in a situation that justified the claimant's actions and those that did not. But it also removes the undesirable connotation that the disqualification is a penalty or punishment.

A second observable trend is towards longer periods of disqualification. This is particularly true of states that still have variable periods of disqualification. Fourteen of the 17 states with variable duration of disqualification for voluntary quits, disqualify for more than six weeks, the maximum period being 26 weeks in Texas.

The most significant trend in the duration of disqualifications, however,

[44] "Acts of Dishonesty Toward Employer," *Issues*, etc., Second Series, *op. cit.*, pp. 65–68.

has been in the number of states disqualifying for the duration of unemployment. In 1937, only one state disqualified for the duration of unemployment in voluntary quit cases, two in discharge cases, and six in refusal of suitable work cases; in 1966; 26 did so for voluntary quits, 24 for discharges, and 23 for refusal of suitable employment. More than that, most of these states also continued the disqualification until the claimant again earned an amount varying from four times the weekly benefit to qualifying wages. This requirement of some re-employment is evidently aimed at assuring that the worker has actually terminated his unemployment by finding work. However, the amount of work required by some states seems unnecessarily long to accomplish this purpose.

The Administration bill of 1965 (H.R. 8282) would establish a federal standard (as a condition for approval of the state law for federal tax credit) that disqualifications shall not be for more than six weeks, except for fraud, labor disputes, and conviction of a crime arising in connection with a claimant's work.

Arguments for Limited Disqualification. Disqualification for the duration of unemployment and disqualification for a temporary period, whether fixed or variable, represent sharp differences in points of view. Those favoring a disqualification for a temporary period, in effect a postponement of benefits, believe that after a time the reason for a worker's continued unemployment is no longer the disqualifying action but lack of available work. In the case of disqualification for a voluntary quit without good cause, for instance, the voluntary nature of the unemployment undergoes a metamorphosis into involuntary unemployment, as has been stated by the International Labour Office.[45]

Those holding this point of view argue that the disqualification should be no longer than the average period that it takes for a worker to secure employment, about six weeks. This position certainly is more humane. It also takes into account the many disqualifications that are based on a set of facts which, if slightly different, might have resulted in an award of benefits. The preceding discussion of the many issues involved in disqualifications showed that appealed decisions are often decided on fine differences in circumstances. Also, courts in different states often make diametrically opposite decisions on cases that are almost identical as to the facts.

Limitations on the duration of disqualification can also be justified from a social standpoint. If unemployment insurance is designed to alleviate hardship due to unemployment, it can be argued that it is in line with that purpose to pay benefits if unemployment continues beyond a certain point, despite the originating cause of the unemployment. Other countries have universally taken this point of view and commonly do not disqualify claimants for more than two months, or for even shorter periods.

Arguments for Unlimited Disqualification. On the other hand, disquali-

---

[45] International Labour Office, *Unemployment Insurance Systems* (Geneva Switzerland, 1955), p. 123.

fication for the duration of unemployment is consistent with the purpose of unemployment insurance—to compensate involuntary unemployment. If a worker has voluntarily brought about his unemployment through his own actions, it can well be argued that his continued unemployment is due to his original act, and benefits should be denied for its duration. In our opinion, this argument is on more solid ground than the argument that after, for example, six weeks, unemployment due to the voluntary and unjustified action of the worker somehow becomes involuntary unemployment.

It is no doubt true that some persons "work" the system when disqualifications are temporary. A bride, for example, can voluntarily quit her job when she marries and, after a temporary disqualification, draw benefits if she files a claim, registers for work at the employment office, and is clever enough to appear to be genuinely seeking work. Studies on abuses in unemployment insurance all contain such examples. While many of the cases that are used in these studies had extenuating circumstances that justified the payment of benefits, other cases could be found in which this is not so. With the great number of women who are in and out of the labor market and the limited ability of the public employment service to offer them suitable jobs, it is possible that some may abuse the system. Nor is this possibility confined to women. The numbers who take advantage of the system are probably greatly exaggerated, but evidently many state legislatures have become convinced there is enough abuse to justfy lengthening disqualification periods. From 1962 to 1964, the number of states disqualifying claimants for the duration of their unemployment increased by about one third; there was a slight decrease in 1966.

The motivation behind disqualifications for the duration of unemployment and after often does not have the interests of the worker or the program at heart. Too frequently the motivation is to save the employer from being charged with any benefits paid to workers whose unemployment was at least originally due to a disqualifying action. Nevertheless, those who wish to preserve a good reputation for the program need to reexamine the position that disqualifications should merely postpone benefits for a few weeks, after which, if the worker is still unemployed, he can qualify for benefits. From the standpoint of protecting the system against abuse, disqualification for the duration of unemployment has some justification.

The arguments are particularly cogent for disqualifying for the duration of unemployment in cases of voluntary quitting without good cause and in cases of discharge for misconduct. In such cases, the employment relationship has been severed through the worker's own actions and he has caused his own unemployment. While the worker may genuinely seek work after quitting or being fired, he still has himself to blame if he remains unemployed.

At the same time, we would advocate paying benefits in cases where the voluntary quit is due to good personal cause as well as in cases where it is attributable to the employer.

We would recommend against disqualification for the duration of unemployment in cases of refusal of suitable work. In some cases it is true there may be a deliberate avoidance of work. But too often it is debatable whether or not the refusal was justified. When it is debatable, disqualification for the duration of unemployment is too severe a penalty, even though the weight of the evidence is against the claimant. At least the administrative agency should be able, at its discretion, to impose only a temporary disqualification in debatable cases.

Reduction or Cancellation of Benefit Rights

When a claimant is disqualified from benefits, he is still eligible in most states for the number of weeks of benefits for which he was eligible before the disqualification, if he is still unemployed or becomes unemployed again after serving the disqualification period. On the other hand, about a dozen states reduce the number of weeks of benefits for which the worker was eligible. A few states go further and cancel all benefits for which the worker was eligible. As of January 1, 1966, 16 states reduce or cancel benefit rights when disqualifications are for voluntary quits, 24 for discharge for misconduct, and 15 states take such action for refusal of suitable work. In 1963, three states abandoned their reduction in benefits provisions, while two states added such provisions. In most instances of cancellation of benefit rights, the disqualification is for the duration of unemployment. The Administration bill of 1965 would prohibit reduction or cancellation of benefit rights.

The reduction and especially the cancellation of benefit rights in connection with disqualification from benefits, represent the culmination of efforts to save the employer from being charged with any unemployment for which he is not responsible. The injustice rendered to the worker by these penalties may be illustrated by two simple examples. A worker who has enough wage credits to qualify for 26 weeks of benefits, quits to look for a better job. He cannot find one immediately; applies for benefits; is disqualified for six weeks, and his rights to benefits reduced by six weeks. Later he finds a job, but is subsequently laid off for lack of work. He is now eligible for only 20 weeks of benefits instead of 26 because of the reduction of his benefit rights by the prior disqualification of six weeks. Or suppose the worker voluntarily quits without good cause in a state that disqualifies for the duration of unemployment and cancels all rights accumulated with his former employer. Since he had worked for his previous employer during the entire "base year," his benefit rights have been wiped out. If he is laid off his new job before he can accumulate enough new rights to qualify for benefits, he can draw no benefits, even though his unemployment is clearly involuntary. The harshness of such a provision is obvious. Reduction or cancellation of benefit rights is punitive in character and has no proper place in an insurance program. If a worker is disqualified from benefits but goes out and finds another job, he should have the full protection of unemployment compensation to which he was entitled before the disqualification if he is later laid off for lack of work.

Longer Disqualification for Gross Misconduct

As of January 1, 1966, 22 states impose heavier disqualifications for dishonest or criminal acts, or for "gross, flagrant, willful, and unlawful misconduct," or for "forgery, larceny, or embezzlement," or for "arson, intoxication, sabotage, or dishonesty."

Longer periods of disqualification are imposed in some states; in 12 states benefit rights or wage credits are canceled.

Varying the length of the disqualification with the seriousness of the misconduct and especially canceling benefit rights for gross or aggravated misconduct introduces the concept of a penalty into the disqualification. Punishment of the worker for the offense that caused the discharge lies outside the unemployment insurance program. If the offense is serious enough, it can be punished through the courts. But the worker should not be punished by a longer period of disqualification, or cancellation of benefit rights. Why this should not be done has been well stated by Professor Paul H. Sanders: "The sliding-scale disqualification, determined by the circumstances of employee conduct, is apt to center on regulating the conduct rather than its relationship to the risk of unemployment. The complete cancellation of benefit rights, such as in the Tennessee gross-misconduct disqualification affords an excellent illustration of the back-handed attempt to regulate something outside of the principal business of unemployment insurance."[46]

LABOR DISPUTES

From time to time, questions have been raised as to whether there should be any disqualification in labor disputes, but this never became a serious issue.[47] All the states have provisions disqualifying workers involved in labor disputes. Two states limit the disqualification to a specific number of weeks: New York for seven weeks and the waiting period; and Rhode Island for six weeks plus the waiting period. Pennsylvania originally had such a provision but has abandoned it.

There has been some unfavorable publicity regarding the payment of benefits to strikers by these two states and the impression has been created by critical articles that payment of unemployment compensation to strikers is general. Actually, in the years 1959–62, only 1.1 percent of all benefits

[46] Sanders, *op. cit.*, p. 314.
[47] See Fierst and Spector, "Unemployment Compensation in Labor Disputes," *Yale Law Journal*, Vol. 49 (1940), pp. 167 ff; Leonard Lesser, "Labor Disputes and Unemployment Compensation," *Yale Law Journal*, Vol. 55 (1945), pp. 167–81; Shadur, "Unemployment Benefits and the 'Labor Dispute' Disqualification," *University of Chicago Law Review*, Vol. 8 (February, 1955), pp. 338 ff.

paid in New York were paid to those who had been involved in a labor dispute, and from 1938 to 1962, only about one half of one percent of all benefits in Rhode Island were paid to strikers after the initial disqualification period. Such small amounts were paid in benefits because few labor disputes last as long as the disqualification periods in these two states.

·As in other parts of their legislation, most of the states originally followed the wording in the Social Security Board's draft bills with respect to the labor dispute disqualification; many of the original provisions are still intact. In addition, as has happened with other provisions of the state laws, there has been increasing divergence and diversity.

There are differences in the state laws as to (1) what constitutes a labor dispute, (2) the length of the disqualification (usually involving the test as to whether the dispute has ended), (3) the types of individuals or classes of workers who are not subject to disqualifications, and (4) the location of the dispute, particularly in the definition of what constitutes an establishment of the employer.

In considering what should be the proper provisions in a labor dispute disqualification, it must be remembered that this is a situation in which a group of workers rather than an individual is involved and in which there is not a severance of the employer relationship.

Definition of "Labor Dispute"

What should be considered a labor dispute? Most states have no statutory definition or limitation on the nature of the dispute. In most states, a labor dispute is considered to include both strikes and lockouts, and the merits of the dispute have no bearing on the disqualification from benefits. As of January 1, 1966, 12 states exclude lockouts. While presumably the purpose in excluding lockouts is to protect the worker against actions by the employer for which the workers are not responsible, at times a lockout is justified. This can be true in a "whipsaw" strike, in which a union which is bargaining with several employers, strikes only one of them. The employers may counter by locking out the workers in other plants. The National Labor Relations Board has legalized employer lockouts in such situations.[48]

It is frequently difficult to determine whether the dispute is a strike or lockout, and thus, whether the workers are subject to disqualification. The principal method of resolving this question has been through determining which side is attempting to change the status quo; if the workers are trying to get a raise in wages or improving working conditions, it is a strike; if the employer is attempting to cut wages or otherwise worsen the situation of the workers, it is a lockout. But this does not resolve all the difficulties.[49]

[48] *Buffalo Linen Supply Co.*, 109 N.L.R.B. No. 69 (July, 1954).
[49] See Jerre S. Williams, "The Labor Dispute Disqualification—A Primer and Some Problems," *Vanderbilt Law Review*, Vol. VIII, No. 2 (February, 1955), pp. 338–75.

A few states have excluded disputes when the workers strike because the employer has violated the provisions of a labor contract or when the employer has failed to conform with any federal or state law relating to wages, hours, working conditions, or collective bargaining. An argument against such provisions is that unemployment insurance should not be used to enforce a contract or the law. A more valid objection is that the National Labor Relations Board or a court may find after payment of benefits that there has been no violation by the employer. It has been suggested that this problem can be obviated by not charging the employer's experience rating account with the benefits paid.[50]

Duration of Disqualification

Another problem is to determine how long the disqualification because of the dispute should be in effect. Most states (30 in 1966) provide that the disqualification shall continue during the stoppage of work due to the dispute; another 12 provide that the disqualification shall be effective while the dispute is in active progress. Eight states have variants of these two concepts, and New York and Rhode Island, as related above, disqualify for a specific number of weeks and thus avoid the necessity of determining when the dispute is terminated. The "stoppage of work" provision is much to be preferred, not only because it is frequently difficult to determine when a dispute has terminated, but also because workers can be disqualified under the "active progress" provision, if the striking workers still try to continue to negotiate with their employers, long after the employer has replaced the striking workers and resumed normal production.

Exclusions of Individual Workers from Disqualification

Most of the states do not disqualify individuals who are unemployed because of a labor dispute if neither they nor any of the same grade or class are (a) participating in the dispute (42 states as of January 1, 1966); (b) financing the dispute (30 states); or (c) directly interested in the dispute (41 states).[51]

The principal issue in the "participating in the dispute" clause has been the crossing of a picket line. Refusal to cross is generally ruled to mean participation unless the reason is fear of physical violence. It has generally been held that mere payment of union dues is not financing a dispute. As to the "directly interested" clause, it has been interpreted to prevent payments of benefits to workers who are thrown out of work in a plant when only a few key men who are essential to the plant's operation go on strike. In the absence of the "directly interested" clause, others thrown out of work by such a strike can draw benefits even though they would benefit from a successful strike. Interpretations of the clause have also held that

[50] *Ibid.*, p. 373.
[51] New York is among the 10 states that put none of these restrictions on the individuals involved in this dispute.

anyone benefiting from the strike is "directly interested," even if he may be opposed to the strike.

Location of the Dispute

Under the usual wording, the labor dispute, the work stoppage, and the employee involved in the dispute must all be at the same "factory, establishment, or other premises." Disputes have arisen over the meaning of "establishment" when an employer operates plants that are geographically separated, sometimes in different states, but are so integrated that a stoppage of work in one plant halts work in others. In a 1950 case, for example, three Ford Motor Company plants in Detroit had to shut down because of a strike at the company's forge plant at Canton, Ohio.[52] Seven states have amended their laws in the direction of including in a dispute all plants of an employer whose operation is affected by a strike in any one of his plants. The problem has by no means been settled and continues to be the subject of cases carried to court.[53]

Space does not permit a discussion of all the problems that have arisen in connection with the labor dispute disqualification provisions. After a review of the provisions and court interpretations, Professor Jerre S. Williams of the University of Texas concluded in 1955 that "the provision has been interpreted in surprisingly broad strokes."[54]

DISQUALIFYING INCOME

Another group of disqualifications aims primarily to avoid duplicate benefits. This includes disqualification from benefits or reduction of benefits if compensation is received under some other social insurance legislation or as a fringe benefit under a collectively bargained or employer-sponsored plan. The latter include private pension plans, wages in lieu of notice or dismissal payments, supplementary unemployment benefits, and vacation pay. Disqualifications because of the receipt of other social insurance benefits and of supplementary unemployment benefits will be considered in Chapter 23, which discusses coordination with other programs.

Wages in Lieu of Notice and Dismissal Wages

More states disqualify for weeks in which wages in lieu of notice are received than for any other type of income (33 states as of January 1, 1966,

[52] See Willard A. Lewis, *Unemployment Compensation Law in Labor Disputes; Michigan Compared with Seven Selected States, 1936–1964* (Kalamazoo: W. E. Upjohn Institute for Employment Research, November, 1964), pp. 24–31.

[53] See "Functional Integration and the Labor Dispute Disqualification," *Unemployment Insurance Review*, January–February, 1964, pp. 27–30. Also see "Location of Labor Dispute and Its Effect on Claimant's 'Establishment,'" *Issues*, etc., First Series, *op. cit.*, pp. 23–27.

[54] Williams, *op. cit.*, p. 375. In addition to Professor Williams' article, the reader is referred to Lewis, *op. cit.*, to other articles listed in footnote 47, and to articles in the series on *Issues Reflected in Appeals Decisions on Unemployment Benefits*. See also other articles listed in footnote 1 to Professor Williams' article.

of which 10 totally disqualify and the balance reduce the unemployment benefit). The argument for such a disqualification is that a worker should not receive benefits for a period for which he is receiving wages. However, it can be argued that benefits should be payable in full for such a period since the worker could receive full-time wages from another employer if he immediately found a full-time job with another employer.

Dismissal wages are closely related to wages in lieu of notice. The former are usually paid according to a formal plan, frequently relating the amount of the dismissal payment to the length of service, and are usually for longer periods than wages in lieu of notice. Dismissal wages are usually in recognition of past services, whereas wages in lieu of notice are often paid so that the employer will not have the unpleasant situation of a work force, probably with low morale, staying on after they have been given formal notice of separation.

The 1950 Social Security Act amendments changed the definition of wages in the federal unemployment tax act so that all dismissal wages were defined as wages and became subject to the act, effective after 1951. Prior to this, dismissal wages, not legally required from the employer, were not counted as wages. Many states changed their laws to conform to the change in the federal act, but others did not. In those states that made the change, dismissal wages are subject to contribution; in effect, the worker is treated as still employed, or partially employed if the dismissal payment is less than former wages. As of January 1, 1966, 20 states specially provided for disqualification from or reduction of unemployment benefits. The treatment of dismissal payments as disqualifying income is illogical since they are payments, in addition to wages due, usually made in connection with permanent separation of the employee by the employer.[55] Dismissal payments are often made in the form of lump-sum payments, so that the computation to weeks for purposes of denying or reducing unemployment benefits may be artificial. In view of the increasing number of workers covered by dismissal wage plans, estimated at five million in 1960,[56] the question of whether dismissal wages should be taken into account in the payment of unemployment compensation requires more thoughtful consideration than it has thus far received.

Retirement Payments

The payment of unemployment compensation to workers who are receiving retirement benefits under the Social Security Act has become increasingly important. An increasing number of older workers who have retired continue to work to supplement their pensions. Many states treat the receipt of pensions under private employer plans differently than the

[55] See E. D. Hawkins, *Dismissal Compensation* (Princeton: Princeton University Press), 1940.

[56] Turnbull, Williams, and Cheit, *Economic and Social Security* (2d ed; New York: Ronald Press Co., 1962), p. 225.

receipt of federal old-age insurance benefits. Thus, the problem of private pensions has relevance to the issue of disqualifications; the problems of federal old-age insurance benefits and public retirement plans will be discussed in Chapter 23.

A growing number of states (33 as of January 1, 1966) reduced unemployment compensation when the claimant is receiving a private pension. In 17 states the reduction is made only if the unemployment benefits are based on service with a base-period employer or if a base-period employer contributed to the financing of the retirement plan. In the other 16 states, unemployment compensation is reduced if any employer contributed to the plan.

The issue of simultaneous receipt of unemployment compensation and retirement benefits was injected into Congressional consideration of the Temporary Extended Unemployment Compensation Act of 1961. Senator John J. Williams of Delaware secured the passage of a Senate amendment which provided for the reduction of extended benefits payments by the amount received as a retirement benefit under the Social Security Act, any federal or state retirement system, or any private retirement plan contributed to by the employer. A compromise was agreed to in conference. This limited the reduction by the amount received from any public or private pension plan to which any base-period employer had contributed, except disability pensions, veterans' pensions, or pensions received under Title II of the Social Security Act.[57]

This amendment reduced the extended benefits payable under the TEUC Act of 1961 for 4 percent of the claimants who were receiving pensions. The percentages varied from less than 1 percent in some states up to 12 percent in one state. The proportions whose extended benefits were reduced because of the receipt of pensions were not substantially different in those states that had already reduced *regular* unemployment benefits than in those states that had not.[58] This indicates that the receipt of private pensions is as yet not a very large problem in most states. The proportion drawing federal old-age insurance benefits was much larger, as will be shown in Chapter 23.

One point of view holds that all pensioners should receive unemployment compensation if they can demonstrate that they are able to work and available for work. It is argued that pensions are payments for past services and to reduce unemployment benefits by the amount received as a pension is to inject an income test into the unemployment insurance program. Those holding this view believe that there is an especially strong argument for paying unemployment compensation to those who have been

---

[57] *Conference Report* (to accompany H.R. 4806), Temporary Extended Unemployment Compensation Act of 1961, Report No. 183, House of Representatives, 87th Cong., 1st sess. (March 21, 1961).

[58] *Family Characteristics of the Long-Term Unemployed*, TEUC Report No. 4, BES No. U–207–4 (Washington, D.C.: United States Department of Labor, March, 1963), table 15–A.

compulsorily retired but are still available for work as well as anxious to work. It is also argued that there is a presumptive need for unemployment compensation on the part of pensioners who claim benefits because their continuance in the labor market is prima facie evidence that their pensions are inadequate.

On the other hand, it is argued that many pensioners take advantage of the fact that it is difficult to prove unavailability for work. Thus, it is claimed, they draw unemployment compensation based on employment before retirement in the initial period of their retirement, and then withdraw from the labor market.[59]

Disqualifications of all retirees from unemployment compensation would be harsh for those whose pensions are so inadequate that they cannot make ends meet. The compromise worked out by Congress in connection with the TEUC Act of 1961 seems reasonable with respect to private pensions. This aims to deduct the amount of any pension to which a base-period employer has contributed from any unemployment compensation received by a retiree. Otherwise, such employer would be simultaneously financing two benefits for the worker. Perhaps an even more equitable provision would be to reduce the unemployment benefit by one-half the pension if the employee had contributed to the latter.[60]

FRAUDULENT MISREPRESENTATION

Any insurance program must protect itself against fraudulent claims. All state unemployment insurance laws have provisions for fines or imprisonment for fraudulent misrepresentation in order to obtain or increase benefits (in the case of workers) or to prevent or reduce benefits (in the case of employers). In most states, the limits of the fine are specified (from $50 to $1,000) and usually specify minimum and maximum amounts. Both fines and imprisonment are usually higher for employers. The most frequent fines on workers are $20 to $50, and $20 and $200 on employers. Maximum imprisonment varies from 30 days to a year for workers, and from 60 days to a year for employers.

Because of the difficulty or slowness in obtaining court convictions, all the states have added special disqualifications from benefits for fraudulent misrepresentation to obtain benefits. In most states, the disqualification can be applied as an alternative to court action or both courses of action can be taken. In a few states, the disqualification is contingent on court conviction or is increased in case of conviction. If a claimant is fined by a court and is also disqualified from benefits, this results in a double penalty for the same act and seems hardly justified.

Most states provide for a fixed disqualification for fraud. In 11 states the

---

[59] For a study of pensioners drawing unemployment compensation in one state, see: New York Department of Labor, Division of Employment, *Pensioners and Unemployment Insurance*, February, 1960.

[60] For further discussion of the pension problem, see Chapter 23.

disqualification is for 52 weeks; in others it may last longer.[61] In those states in which the duration of the disqualification is varied with the gravity of the offense, the maximum disqualification is usually 52 weeks. Some states, however, have much milder penalties. In some states the worker is disqualified for one or two weeks of benefits for each week of fraud.

Disqualification from benefits for fraudulent misrepresentation is punitive in character. Although we have taken a position against disqualifications being punitive, an exception is justified in the case of willful misrepresentation which aims to defraud the program. A variable duration for the disqualification is also justified and desirable, so that the penalty can be fitted to the gravity of the offense.

Thirty-two states (as of January 1, 1966) cancel or reduce benefit rights when a worker is disqualified for fraud.[62] A few states cancel all wage credits earned prior to the fraudulent act. Some states cancel rights retroactively, a procedure which works out unequally, depending on when the fraudulent act was committed during the benefit year. The Federal Bureau of Employment Security suggests that a more equitable provision would be to cancel the amount of benefits that would otherwise have been paid to the worker during the period of disqualification.

In addition to disqualification from benefits, all states provide for recovery of benefits fraudulently received. A few states also disqualify the worker from any future benefits until the benefits obtained fraudulently are repaid. In about half the states, provision is made for recovery of overpayments whether or not the overpayment is due to misrepresentation by the worker. This seems rather harsh if the overpayment is due to an error of the administrative agency since the unemployed worker may have spent the overpayment and may find it hard to repay. Almost all states provide that fraudulently received overpayments be recovered by cash repayment or offset against future benefits.

SUMMARY AND CONCLUSIONS

There is much controversy over the increased severity of disqualification provisions in many laws, which has given organized labor, as well as many students of the program, much concern. The question as to whether compensation should be paid only when the employer is responsible runs through much of the disagreement over disqualification provisions.

Employer opinion has not been greatly influenced by court rulings that compensation should not be confined to cases where the employer is responsible. The ghost of employer fault still haunts the program.

A claimant can be disqualified for three principal reasons: refusal of suitable work; voluntary quitting without good cause; and discharge for

---

[61] The Administration bill (H.R. 8282) prohibits a disqualification of more than 36 months, beginning with the discovery of the fraud.

[62] In 13 other states benefits in effect are reduced if, before the disqualification period ends, the benefit credits have expired in whole or in part.

misconduct. Disagreement centers on the disqualification for voluntary quitting without good cause. Should this include good personal cause, or be limited to cases attributable to the employer or connected with the work?

Most disagreement arises over the period of disqualification. At the beginning of the program, most states imposed a disqualification for a limited number of weeks and disqualified for a varying number of weeks according to the seriousness of the disqualifying act. One to five weeks, plus the waiting period, was the most common duration. Currently, however, a flat period, such as six weeks, is gaining favor in the case of temporary disqualifications, since a flexible period has a punitive connotation and is more complex to administer. More and more states are disqualifying for the duration of unemployment and some disqualify until there has been a minimum period of re-employment.

The main argument for a limited disqualification is that, after a few weeks, unemployment originally caused by the individual becomes involuntary. In addition, disqualification for the duration of unemployment is harsh in borderline cases and may lead to hardship.

On the other hand, disqualification for the duration of unemployment is more logical in a program that is designed to compensate for involuntary unemployment. It is also a protection against abuse because of the ease with which availability for work can be established after a temporary disqualification has run its course. It is our view that disqualification for the duration of unemployment is justified for voluntary quits without good cause and discharges for miscondct, but not for refusal of suitable work. On the other hand, we believe that reduction or cancellation of benefit rights is unjustified. Since reduction or cancellation of rights can affect a worker who is laid off from a subsequent job, it runs contrary to the program's purpose of protecting the worker against unemployment. Many injustices can result from such provisions. More stringent disqualifications for "gross misconduct" are also out of place in the program because they introduce a punitive concept.

Disqualification provisions for loss of work in connection with labor disputes are justified, at least with respect to strikes, on the ground that the worker has taken voluntary action. Some states define a labor dispute to exclude lockouts on the ground that the resulting unemployment is involuntary. A few states also do not disqualify workers if the strike is due to the employer's violation of the labor contract or any federal or state law relating to wages, hours, or working conditions.

The majority of states disqualify workers during a stoppage of work due to a labor dispute. This is preferable to the provision used in a dozen states which disqualifies while the dispute is in active progress. New York and Rhode Island disqualify workers for only a few weeks. This has been criticized as putting the program in an un-neutral position in favor of the workers in a long, drawn-out dispute.

The state laws differ in the extent to which they reduce or deny unemployment compensation in order to avoid duplication with payments received under other types of income maintenance programs. The most common provision with respect to "fringe benefits" received from the employer is the disqualification from benefits if the worker is receiving wages in lieu of notice. Less common is disqualification if the worker is receiving dismissal wages. About half the states have followed a 1950 amendment to the Federal Unemployment Tax Act under which dismissal wages are counted as wages. The situation with respect to dismissal wages is confused and needs study.

The dual receipt of unemployment compensation and pensions is receiving most critciism. With respect to private pension plans, a good solution is the provision in the 1961 TEUC Act which reduced unemployment compensation only when the pension was based on earnings from the same base-period employer with whom the worker earned qualifying wages for unemployment compensation.

Because of the difficulty of getting court convictions for fraud, all states have provisions disqualifying workers from benefits obtained as a result of fraudulent misrepresentation. These provisions can be used as an alternative to court prosecution. Most states disqualify workers up to 52 weeks and about two thirds of the states also cancel or reduce wage credits in such cases. Disqualification for fraudulent misrepresentation is the only kind of disqualification that should be punitive, although punitive concepts have crept into other disqualification provisions.

Part IV

Financing
Issues and Problems

Chapter 16

The Changing
Financial Picture

Although the financing of unemployment insurance has been one of the principal areas of controversy, the source of financing unemployment insurance has never been a major issue. Since the beginnings of the program, employer contributions (taxes) have been regarded as the major source of revenue. While many have advocated employee contributions, only 10 states have required them at any time and only three states now have them. When employee contributions have been stipulated, they have always been only a small fraction of the rate set for employers. Only the District of Columbia law once provided for government contributions and this provision was soon repealed.[1]

The principal controversy originally focused on the method of employer financing, whether it should be through flat rate contributions or variable rates based on experience with unemployment. Eventually, experience rating won the day and is now incorporated into every state unemployment insurance law. However, experience rating continued to be criticized, first as an impediment to adequate benefits and in recent years as an obstacle to sound and adequate financing. Issues about experience rating will be discussed in the next chapter.

The limitation on the amount of wages that are subject to employee taxes (the wage base), has also become a subject of controversy. Although wages have tripled since 1939, the wage base for the federal unemployment tax has remained the same as the one enacted in that year, the first $3,000 of each worker's earnings. It has been particularly difficult, however, to reach an agreement on whether the base should or should not be raised. A growing number of states have made modest increases and one state raised its wage base by a substantial amount. But the issue of the wage base is bogged down in a morass of arguments on the relative merits of increasing the wage base or the tax rates when additional funds are needed.

[1] Government contributions are proposed as one source of revenue for extended benefits in the Administration bill of 1965.

There has always been some apprehension to whether the unemployment insurance system could be kept financially solvent. Originally, this resulted in overconservative actuarial estimates and the enactment of meager benefits. As it became evident that most states could easily finance much more adequate benefits, concern over solvency receded.

However, the possibility of individual states getting into financial difficulty was not overlooked. Proposals for national reinsurance of state funds were considered by the Committee on Economic Security and studied by the Social Security Board. Nothing was done about this risk, however, until a plan for federal loans to states was enacted in 1944 and re-enacted in modified form in the 1950's. The recent indication of weaknesses in many state funds has given new importance to the consideration of measures to protect the adequacy of state unemployment insurance funds. This has principally taken the form of plans for reinsurance or the equalization of costs through federal grants to states with high benefit costs.

In order to understand the background and scope of these issues, it is necessary to review the financial history of the unemployment insurance program. At the end of World War II, the unemployment insurance system was in a very strong financial position. The amounts paid out in benefits had been very low during the war since there had been almost no unemployment. Although they were decreasing, unemployment tax rates were still relatively high at the end of the war. As a result, reserves had been built up to levels that in some states were higher than foreseeable needs.

During the first dozen years following the war, the financial situation of the system appeared to be good. Although average tax rates were steadily decreased, tax income was larger than total benefit payments, except in the recession years of 1949–50 and 1953–54. Reserves continued to increase in dollar terms through 1957, although the ratio of reserve to total payrolls fell steadily after 1945.

The financial tide began to turn during the 1953–54 recession. Total benefit payments remained at higher levels following that period and rose to an unprecedented level in the recession of 1958. As a result, reserves fell drastically. Since then, because of high rates of unemployment, benefits have continued at high levels and, despite increased unemployment taxes, reserves continued to fall until after the recession of 1961. The total reserves of all the states grew somewhat in the next three years, but in spite of this growth, at the end of 1964 the reserves in no less than 20 states were below what the Bureau of Employment Security suggested as a minimum adequate reserve.[2]

As of 1965, therefore, the unemployment insurance system is faced with some important financial questions unless unemployment is drastically reduced. Can states whose reserves have dropped to dangerous levels regain a sound financial position without putting too heavy a tax burden on

[2] United States Department of Labor, Bureau of Employment Security, *Unemployment Insurance Program Letter No. 800*, March 5, 1965.

their employers? What is the best way to raise more unemployment taxes, through higher tax rates, a higher tax base, or both? In what ways could experience rating systems be improved or modified so as to contribute toward sounder financing? Should a state be permitted to try out some alternative to experience rating? Can the states with high rates of unemployment and high benefit costs finance their systems without cutting benefits or without some federal financial assistance? What is the best method of providing help to states in financial difficulty? These questions will be explored at length in later chapters. As a basis for discussing these questions, the financial history of the program will be traced in some detail in this chapter. In addition, the current costs of unemployment benefits will be compared with other costs of employers in order to put unemployment benefit costs in proper perspective.

FINANCIAL HISTORY OF THE STATE UNEMPLOYMENT INSURANCE PROGRAM

The Prewar Years (1936–41)

After the federal unemployment tax became effective on January 1, 1936, all the states imposed unemployment taxes for 1936.[3] Some states that had delayed passage of unemployment insurance laws in the hope that the federal tax would be held to be unconstitutional, collected their initial taxes retroactively.

The states generally set their contribution or tax rates at 90 percent of the federal tax, the maximum for which employers could get credit against the federal unemployment tax. Since the federal tax was 1 percent of covered wages in 1936, 2 percent in 1937, and 3 percent in 1938 and thereafter, the corresponding state tax rates were 0.9 percent in 1936, 1.8 percent in 1937, and 2.7 percent in 1938 and thereafter (until experience rating resulted in different rates).

Only 23 states started paying benefits on January 1, 1938, the earliest date possible under the federal requirement that state unemployment taxes be collected for two years before benefits could commence. The balance of the states had to start benefits later because of delays in passing their laws. Illinois and Montana, the last two states to pass laws, did not commence benefit payments until July 1, 1939.

The 23 states commencing benefits at the beginning of 1938 had accumulated the equivalent of 2.7 percent of a year's payroll during 1936 and 1937. The other states had more reserves when they commenced paying benefits in 1939, because the full tax rate of 2.7 percent came into effect in 1938. In addition, nine states had collected some employee contributions during one or more years prior to the payment of benefits, at contribution rates ranging from 0.5 percent to 1.5 percent of taxable wages.

[3] Wisconsin commenced collecting employer taxes in 1934.

The first 23 states[4] commenced benefit payments during a sharp recession. Benefit payments ranged from 0.83 percent of payrolls in the District of Columbia to 4.52 percent in Rhode Island. Nevertheless, the $394 million the 23 states disbursed in benefits in 1938 was less than the $570 million collected by them that year. The states not paying benefits collected another $250 million. As a result, reserves rose during the year to $1.1 billion or 4.24 percent of total covered wages on December 31 (see Table 16–1).

Table 16–1

Employer Contributions Collected, Benefit Disbursements and Year-End Reserves, 1938–64
(dollars in millions; ratios to total wages in covered employment)

Year	Contributions Employer		Benefit Disbursements		Year-End Reserves	
1938 ....$	819	2.69%	$ 394	2.11%	$1,111	4.24%
1939	825	2.66	429	1.55	1,538	5.29
1940	854	2.50	519	1.60	1,817	5.60
1941	1,006	2.37	344	.82	2,525	5.99
1942	1,139	1.98	344	.63	3,388	6.18
1943	1,325	1.86	80	.12	4,716	7.13
1944	1,317	1.67	62	.09	6,072	8.78
1945	1,162	1.50	446	.67	6,914	10.37
1946	912	1.24	1,095	1.49	6,860	9.35
1947	1,096	1.19	775	.90	7,303	8.43
1948	1,000	1.01	790	.82	7,603	7.91
1949	987	1.07	1,736	1.85	7,010	7.47
1950	1,191	1.18	1,373	1.33	6,972	6.76
1951	1,493	1.20	840	.71	7,782	6.56
1952	1,368	1.08	998	.78	8,328	6.52
1953	1,348	.93	962	.69	8,913	6.41
1954	1,136	.79	2,027	1.48	8,219	6.00
1955	1,209	.81	1,350	.91	8,264	5.56
1956	1,463	.88	1,381	.84	8,574	5.21
1957	1,544	.85	1,734	1.00	8,662	4.99
1958	1,471	.86	3,513	2.05	6,953	4.05
1959	1,956	1.05	2,279	1.22	6,892	3.69
1960	2,289	1.17	2,727	1.40	6,643	3.41
1961	2,449	1.23	3,423	1.72	5,802	2.91
1962	2,959	1.39	2,675	1.23	6,272	2.95
1963	3,019	1.35	2,775	1.24	6,648	2.98
1964	3,047	1.3 *	2,522	1.10	7,296	3.17

* Estimated.
Source: U.S. Department of Labor, Bureau of Employment Security.

Benefit disbursements were relatively lower in 1939 and 1940, although the total amounts paid out were higher because all the states paid benefits in these years. With rearmament in full sway in 1941, benefit disbursements dropped even more to only 0.82 percent of payrolls. In that year, tax col-

[4] Including Wisconsin, which commenced benefit payments July 1, 1936.

lections totaled almost three times as much as benefit disbursements. The resulting surplus raised the states' reserves to over $2.5 billion or 5.99 percent of total wages at the end of 1941.[5]

The War Years (1942–45)

During World War II, unemployment was so low that unemployment benefit disbursements dropped to fantastically low levels, amounting to only 0.1 percent of wages in 1944. By 1945, many states had initiated experience rating and, therefore, collections were down to 1.74 percent of total wages. These collections included special "war risk contributions" for which 12 states had adopted provisions in anticipation of high unemployment that was expected to result from large scale postwar layoffs. The number of benefit claims moderately increased after hostilities ceased in 1945, but total benefit disbursements were equal to only 0.67 percent of total wages in 1945. During 1942–45, tax collections were almost $5 billion compared to benefit payments of less than $1 billion, so that at the end of 1945 unemployment reserves, including accumulated interest on reserves, stood at over $6.9 billion. This was equivalent to 10.77 percent of total covered payrolls for the country as a whole, the all-time high reached in reserves when measured as a ratio of total wages. In the individual states, reserves varied from 6.54 percent of total wages in Michigan to 16.14 percent in Alaska. All states, therefore, entered the postwar period with large, or excessive reserves.

The Early Postwar Years (1946–53)

The heavy unemployment that was expected to follow the cessation of war production did not materialize. Industries reconverted to peacetime production more rapidly than was expected, and with the pent-up demands for consumer goods, peacetime business was soon booming. Unemployment increased for only a few months and the number of unemployment insurance beneficiaries totaled 1.6 million during January, February, and

[5] It is preferable to express benefits, taxes, and reserves as ratios of *total* wages rather than *taxable* wages to get any realistic comparisons. In most states, taxable wages have remained at the first $3,000 of each worker's earnings since Congress placed this limit on taxable wages by the Social Security Amendments of 1939. As wages have increased, the taxable portion has steadily declined from 97.7 percent of total wages to about 58 percent in 1963.

Since unemployment benefits are not related to taxable wages, it is not possible to realistically compare the relationship of benefits to income or reserves in terms of taxable wages. Since by 1963, 14 states had increased their taxable wage bases in varying degrees, it is impossible to get any comparability between states or any national comparisons over time except by using total wages. This was recognized by the Interstate Conference of Employment Security Agencies in 1962, when it passed a resolution at its annual meeting urging "all States, whether or not they enact a change in their wage base, to study and utilize unemployment insurance financing ratios based on total wages." (Resolution X, Unemployment Insurance Financing Ratios, *Proceedings* of 26th Annual Meeting of Interstate Conference Employment Security Agencies, Portland, Oregon, October 1–3, 1962, p. 78.)

March, 1946, but dropped following that date. As a result, benefit payments during 1946 were only 1.49 percent of total wages. In the years that followed, benefit disbursements were even lower. Except for the recession years of 1949–50, benefit payments were less than 1 percent of total wages in every year from 1947 through 1953 and dropped to 0.69 percent of total wages in 1953 (see Table 16–1).

Pressures for tax reductions built up during these years, not only in states with excessive reserves, but in other states as well. The six states that had held out against experience rating adopted rating systems during this period and lowered their average tax rates. Tax schedules in other states were revised downward. Employee contributions were dropped in all but two states. Except for 1951, collections were below 1.3 percent of total wages in every year, and dropped to 0.97 percent of total wages by 1953.

Since tax collections still exceeded benefits except during the 1949–50 recession, the taxes collected plus interest on reserves built up the total reserve to a dollar peak of more than $8.9 billion by the end of 1953. But this increase in dollar reserves was misleading. Reserves as a proportion of total covered wages had dropped to 6.41 percent, as will be seen by referring to Table 16–1. This, however, aroused little concern since reserves in all states except Rhode Island appeared to be adequate.[6]

Years of Increasing Financial Stress (1954–64)

The recession of 1953–54 turned the financial tide in the unemployment insurance system. Since then, there has been an upward trend in benefit expenditures, reflecting higher levels of unemployment between as well as during recessions. This can best be seen if benefit costs are averaged by business cycles rather than annually.

Average Annual Benefit Costs by Business Cycles as Percent of Total Wages, 1947–61

Years	Benefits to Total Wages
1947–50	1.22
1951–54	0.91
1955–58	1.20
1959–61	1.46

As unemployment increased from 1954 on, total benefit payments rose in each succeeding business cycle. Benefit expenditures continued to be high after the recession of 1961 and equaled about 1.1 percent of total payrolls in 1964, even though unemployment by the end of 1964 had fallen to the lowest level since 1957.

Increases in average tax rates lagged behind increases in benefit costs after the recession of 1953–54. Annual average tax rates (as will be seen in Table 16–1) did not reach annual average cost rates until 1962, except for

---

[6] In Rhode Island, benefit payments in 1949 were equal to 5.25 percent of total wages, leaving a reserve at the end of the year of only 4.18 percent of total wages.

a slightly higher tax rate than benefit cost rate in 1956. By 1964, the average tax rate was 1.3 percent of total wages.

As a result of this lag in tax increases, unemployment reserves declined continuously from 1953 to the end of 1961. The drop during these years was from 6.41 percent to 2.9 percent of total payrolls. While reserves were rebuilt by $1.5 billion during 1962–64 to $7.3 billion at the end of 1964, this was only 3.17 percent of total payrolls.

THE FINANCIAL SITUATION IN INDIVIDUAL STATES

Reserves for the country as a whole, however, are not a good indication of the system's financial situation, since each state must rely on its own unemployment reserve fund to meet its own benefit liabilities. The reserve situation in the individual states must therefore be examined.

According to the criterion applied by the Bureau of Employment Security, the reserve funds of 20 states were low at the end of 1964. The BES criterion judges that a state's reserve is in jeopardy of being exhausted during an ensuing recession if its reserve is less than 1½ times the highest 12-month benefit cost rate during the preceding ten years.[7]

Chart IV gives the state reserve ratio as of the end of 1964 as a multiple of the highest 12-month benefit cost rate in the 10-year period 1954–63. The 20 states whose reserves were below the "warning point" of less than 1.5 were usually states with much heavier benefit expenditures than states with reserves above the warning point. For instance, Pennsylvania which had next to the lowest reserves in proportion to benefit costs, had average costs in the ten years ending December 31, 1963, equal to about 3½ times those of the District of Columbia which had the highest relative reserves. On the other hand, some of the states, even though their benefit costs were moderate, had low reserves because of extremely low average tax rates. For example, Minnesota's average benefit costs of 1.09 percent of total wages were less than the national average of 1.27 percent. Yet Minnesota was at the bottom of the list from the standpoint of adequacy of reserves because its average tax rates had been reduced during the 10-year period to only 0.8 percent of total wages.

The states with inadequate reserves are faced with the need to increase unemployment taxes, not only to meet the higher benefit expenditures of recent years, but also to rebuild their reserves to levels that will be adequate to tide them over future recession periods. In addition, three of these states face the necessity of repaying loans advanced from the federal unemployment (loan) account, as provided under Title XII of the Social Security Act.[8]

[7] Footnote omitted in proof.
[8] Alaska had secured several loans, repayment of which will take until 1975 and will build up to a maximum repayment rate of 1.35 percent of taxable payrolls. Michigan and Pennsylvania had received federal loans during the 1958–59 recession, which would not be paid off until 1970 at a maximum rate of 0.6 percent in Michigan and until 1969 in Pennsylvania at a maximum rate of 0.45 percent, if taxable payrolls under the federal unemployment tax remain at $3,000.

Chart IV

State Reserve Ratio* as a Multiple of Highest 12-Month Benefit Cost Rate† as of December 31, 1964

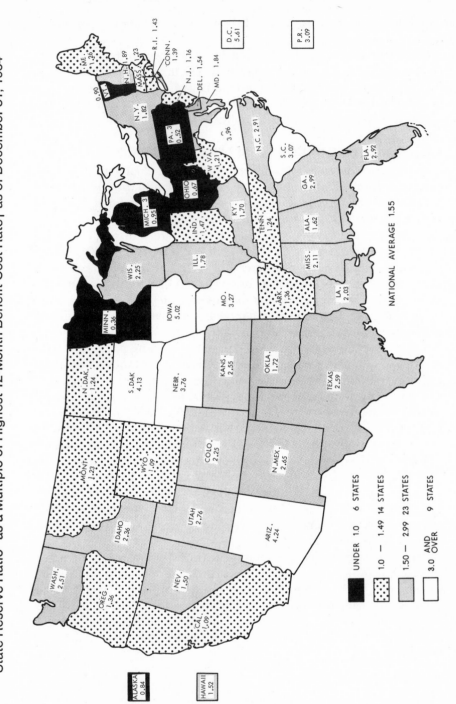

NATIONAL AVERAGE 1.55

■	UNDER 1.0 6 STATES
▨	1.0 — 1.49 14 STATES
▨	1.50 — 2.99 23 STATES
▢	3.0 AND OVER 9 STATES

ME. 1.26
N.H. 1.89
MASS. 1.23
R.I. 1.43
CONN. 1.39
VT. 0.90
N.J. 1.16
DEL. 1.54
MD. 1.84
D.C. 5.61
P.R. 3.09
N.Y. 1.82
PA. 3.0.52
W.VA. 1.21
VA. 3.96
N.C. 2.91
S.C. 3.07
FLA. 2.92
MICH. 3.0.95
OHIO 0.67
IND. 1.47
KY. 1.70
TENN. 1.24
GA. 2.99
ALA. 1.62
WIS. 2.25
ILL. 1.78
MO. 3.27
ARK. 1.36
MISS. 2.11
LA. 2.03
MINN. 0.36
IOWA 5.02
KANS. 2.55
OKLA. 1.72
TEXAS 2.59
N.DAK. 1.24
S.DAK. 4.13
NEBR. 3.76
COLO. 2.25
N.MEX. 2.65
MONT. 1.23
WYO. 1.09
UTAH 2.76
ARIZ. 4.24
IDAHO 2.36
NEV. 1.50
WASH. 2.51
OREG. 1.36
CAL. 1.09
ALASKA 0.84
HAWAII 1.52

* Reserves as percent of total wages.   † Highest cost rate (percent of total wages) during most recent 10-year period.   ‡ Includes advances from Federal Unem-

Actually, the states that need to rebuild their reserves can do so without requiring employers to pay heavier taxes than the tax burden in the average state. In most states, unemployment taxes are paid on only the first $3,000 of each worker's earnings. This $3,000 base represents less than 60 percent of total covered wages for the country as a whole and even less in some individual states. There is, therefore, plenty of room for securing adequate tax income by increasing tax bases. More income can also be secured by imposing higher maximum tax rates than 2.7 percent, as is being done for employers with unstable employment in an increasing number of states. Other sources of income, such as employee contributions, can be drawn upon. Alaska, which has had the highest benefit cost rate in the United States for many years, furnishes an example of what can be done to meet this problem. During the 10-year period 1955–64, Alaska's average benefit cost rate was 2.82 percent of total payrolls, as compared with an average cost of 1.27 percent for the United States. For a time, the state had used up its reserves and had to be helped with federal loans. But, by increasing its taxable wage base several times up to $7,200, imposing an employee contribution averaging 0.6 percent,[9] and by increasing the employer tax rates to an average of 2.4 percent of total wages, it collected more in taxes than it paid out in benefits in the five-year period, 1960–64. The financing of benefits is therefore within manageable bounds, even in Alaska.

UNEMPLOYMENT INSURANCE COSTS IN PERSPECTIVE

Because an amount equal to 2.7 percent of the wages taxed under the federal unemployment tax act is the maximum credit that employers can get against the federal unemployment tax, many persons think of this 2.7 percent rate as the maximum that employers can afford to pay in taxes for unemployment insurance. Applying this criterion of 2.7 percent of taxable wages to the amount of taxes needed to finance benefit expenditures in recent years, some states would appear to have excessively high benefit costs. Six of the ten highest-cost states had average cost rates above 2.7 percent of taxable wages in 1960–64, according to Table 16–2.[10]

However, when costs are stated as a percentage of *total* wages, they look less formidable. On this basis, all ten high-cost states have costs well below 2.7 percent, as will be seen from the last column of Table 16–2.

Whether costs are expressed as a percent of taxable or total wages, unemployment insurance benefit costs are relatively minor when they are put in perspective by comparing them with other costs that employers must meet.

One such comparison is between unemployment taxes and gross wages for each hour of work. For example, in 1964 average unemployment insur-

---

[9] This is the "standard" rate. Under experience rating the rate varies from 0.3 percent to 0.9 percent, varying with the employer's rate.

[10] Three of the other four states would have had rates above 2.7 percent if they had not increased their tax bases above the $3,000 federal base.

Table 16–2

Average Unemployment Insurance Benefit Cost Rates for Highest and Lowest Cost States, 1960–64 (as a percent of taxable and total wages)

	Average Cost Rate	
State	Taxable Wages	Total Wages
Ten highest-cost states:		
Alaska	2.80*	2.35
California	2.66†	1.92
Pennsylvania	3.02†	1.77
Massachusetts	2.77‡	1.75
Idaho	2.59‡	1.75
Washington	3.05	1.73
Wyoming	2.70	1.72
Vermont	2.52‡	1.68
New Jersey	3.03	1.66
New York	2.81	1.59
Ten lowest-cost states:		
South Carolina	1.22	.88
Georgia	1.30	.87
South Dakota	1.34	.86
Indiana	1.47	.84
Nebraska	1.31	.82
Florida	1.19	.78
Texas	1.16	.71
Iowa	1.10	.67
District of Columbia	1.06	.60
Virginia	.79	.52
U.S. Average	2.26	1.34

* Taxable wage base $7,200.
† Taxable wage base $3,800.
‡ Taxable wage base $3,600.
Source: U.S. Department of Labor, Bureau of Employment Security, *Unemployment Insurance Program Letter 800* (Washington, D.C.: U.S. Government Printing Office, March 5, 1965), tables 3 and 4.

ance contributions were less than $.03 for each hour worked, as compared with $2.54 average gross wages paid for each hour of work.[11] In other words, average unemployment taxes were less than $\frac{1}{80}$ of the average gross wages.

Unemployment insurance costs are also a small fraction of the total costs of "fringe benefits" now being paid by employers. In a sample survey of employers in 1963, total fringe payments were equal to 25.6 percent of payrolls.[12] Unemployment benefit costs represented 1.7 percent of payrolls

[11] Gross hourly wages from *Annual Report of the Council of Economic Advisers* (Washington, D.C.: U.S. Government Printing Office, January 21, 1965), table B–28. Unemployment insurance contribution rates supplied by Bureau of Employment Security, U.S. Department of Labor.
[12] Including private and public benefits.

in the firms surveyed, one fifteenth of the total costs for fringe benefits. The proportion of the cost of unemployment benefits to the cost of total fringe benefits was somewhat higher in manufacturing, 1.9 percent out of 24.2 percent of payrolls. It was less in nonmanufacturing, 1.4 percent out of 27.8 percent for all fringe benefits.[13]

Businessmen ordinarily look at their costs as a proportion of sales. However, we will use a more conservative comparison by looking at unemployment benefit costs in manufacturing as a proportion of the value added by manufacturing.[14] Table 16–3 shows the proportion of each dollar of value added by manufacture that unemployment insurance taxes represented in 1962, in manufacturing as a whole and in major industrial groups.

In manufacturing as a whole, wages represented only about a third of the value added by manufacture and unemployment insurance taxes less than one half a cent out of each dollar of value added. In only the lumber and wood products and the apparel and leather industries did average unemployment taxes represent one cent or more out of each dollar of value added by manufacture. In petroleum and coal products, unemployment taxes were less than a quarter of a cent out of each dollar of value added.

The costs of unemployment insurance, then, represent only a small fraction of the costs of all fringe benefits, only a few cents an hour in terms of wages, and only a fraction of a cent out of each dollar of value added by manufacture. In other than manufacturing, the costs are similarly small. Unemployment insurance costs are growing, but the amounts required for their proper financing are not large when seen in proper perspective.

Although unemployment benefit costs are relatively small as compared with other business and labor costs, millions and even hundreds of millions of dollars are involved in decisions as to the methods of financing unemployment insurance. Important issues are involved in the methods of distributing the cost among employers through experience rating. Significant effects on distribution of the cost are involved in decisions as to whether needed increases in taxes should be through higher tax rates or through an increase in the taxable wage base. Large sums of money and important political decisions are involved in determining how large a reserve a state needs and what measures are necessary to secure and preserve adequate reserves. Important questions, both of federal-state relations and of financing, are involved in any proposal to assist states that get into financial difficulty or are faced with higher-than-average benefit costs. The prob-

---

[13] Chamber of Commerce of the United States, Economic Research Department, *Fringe Benefits, 1961* (Washington, D.C., 1964), p. 9, table 4.

[14] This includes wages and salary costs, capital and management costs such as interest, taxes, insurance, advertising, and management profits. For a discussion of what costs enter into interstate competition, see Alvin H. Hansen and Merrill G. Murray, *A New Plan for Unemployment Reserves*, Employment Stabilization Research Institute, University of Minnesota (Minneapolis: University of Minnesota Press, 1933), pp. 30–33.

Table 16–3

Cost of Unemployment Insurance Taxes per Dollar of Value Added by Manufacture by Major Industry Groups, 1962

Industry Group	Average Tax Rate*	Cost of Taxes per Dollar of Volume Added by Manufacture
All manufacturing	1.41	$0.0074
Food and kindred products	1.27	0.0052
Tobacco products	1.46	0.0030
Textile mill products	1.51	0.0083
Apparel and related products	2.36	0.0137
Lumber and wood products	1.78	0.0107
Furniture and fixtures	1.60	0.0092
Paper and allied products	1.05	0.0050
Printing and publishing	1.01	0.0056
Chemical and allied products	0.91	0.0027
Petroleum and coal products	0.73	0.0023
Rubber and plastic products, n.e.c. ...	1.39	0.0073
Leather and leather products	2.13	0.0126
Stone, clay, and glass products	1.48	0.0070
Primary metal industries	1.36	0.0080
Fabricated metal products	1.44	0.0064
Machinery, excluding electrical	1.28	0.0065
Electrical machinery	1.46	0.0080
Transportation equipment	1.61	0.0087
Instruments and related products	1.33	0.0070

* As a percent of total payrolls.
Sources: United States Department of Commerce, Bureau of the Census, *Annual Survey of Manufactures, 1962, General Statistics* (Washington, D.C.: U.S. Government Printing Office), p. 30, table 1; United States Department of Labor, Bureau of Employment Security, *Unemployment Insurance Tax Rates by Industry, 1962* (Washington, D.C.: U.S. Government Printing Office, March, 1964), pp. 8–32.

lems that have developed in financing the unemployment insurance program and the arguments that have arisen over alternative solutions will be discussed in the following chapters.

SUMMARY

This review of the financial experience of the state unemployment insurance system has been given in order to provide the setting for discussion of the various problems connected with financing the program. The review has shown that, although benefit costs have been higher in recent years because of high levels of unemployment, the costs are within manageable limits. In fact, benefit costs have averaged just about half what was originally anticipated, even during recent years. The average benefit cost for the United States in the five-year period 1960–64 was only 1.28 percent of total payrolls, just about half the 2.7 percent of total payrolls provided for by the 1935 Social Security Act for state financing of benefits. Alaska is the only state that has come near the 2.7 percent figure. No other state has had average costs above 2 percent of total wages. There is, therefore, plenty of room for an adequate unemployment benefit program without placing an excessive financial burden on employers.

The financial problem of the states, then, is to provide a tax structure that will finance an adequate program of benefits. From this standpoint, the problem of experience rating is to establish schedules of tax rates that will provide the necessary income for the program. From the same standpoint, the question of the level of the taxable wage base or of tax rates is one of providing a broadly based tax structure that has the potentiality for a large increase in yield if this becomes necessary. The problem of solvency is largely a technical problem of developing actuarial techniques for estimating costs so that income and outgo will balance over a business cycle. But the maintenance of a solvent system is of vital importance in order that funds be available to pay benefits in full.

Experience rating, the tax base and tax rates, and methods of preserving the solvency of the program are thus means to a larger end—the financing of an adequate system of benefits. A number of subsidiary issues have developed around each of these aspects of financing. We hope that these issues will be considered in relationship to the main financial goal: to provide adequate funds for an adequate system of benefits.

Chapter 17

Experience Rating—
Boon or Bane?

Experience rating (that is, variation in tax rates in relation to individual employer "experience with unemployment") is provided for in every state law.[1] Its adoption was stimulated by many factors. Among these was a provision in the federal law which allowed full tax credit for reductions in the state tax rate below 2.7 percent on the basis of "experience with unemployment." Experience rating has become the most powerful force influencing the financing of unemployment insurance. To what extent, then, has it been responsible for the poor financial condition of many state unemployment insurance funds? Recent high benefit costs resulting from high levels of unemployment have contributed to the depletion of state funds. But, as we pointed out in the previous chapter, inadequate unemployment insurance taxes have been the major cause. Inadequate taxation has contributed to the depletion of reserves not only in states with high unemployment, but also in states with only moderate levels of unemployment and consequent moderate benefit costs.

It has been charged that experience rating is largely responsible for this depletion of reserves through inadequate taxation. Is experience rating responsible for the inadequate financing of many state funds? Certainly, experience rating formulas are resulting in underfinancing in some states. But is this because experience rating results in pressures for low rates that in turn result in inadequate financing? Or is it because some experience rating systems have been developed with inadequate consideration as to what tax income is needed?

If the latter is the problem, what needs to be done to improve or revise experience rating formulas so that they will result in sound financing? This chapter will explore this issue which involves such matters as minimum and maximum tax rates, "noncharging" or "ineffective" charging of benefits, and the federal standards with respect to experience rating.

[1] Except Puerto Rico.

330

Another charge laid on the doorstep of experience rating is that it helps to accentuate business cycles rather than minimize them. The increase in benefits that occurs when unemployment rises during business declines has been recognized as an important "automatic stabilizer" that lessens the business decline. On the other hand, this increase in benefits results in increases in unemployment insurance taxes under experience rating which tend to counteract the economic effect of increases in benefits. Can experience rating formulas be devised to operate countercyclically instead of cyclically? This also needs exploration.

Experience rating has other objectives than the sound financing of unemployment insurance. In fact, the sound or inadequate financing of unemployment insurance is a byproduct of the operation of experience rating. The objectives are to (1) serve as an incentive to stabilize employment, (2) result in proper allocation of the costs of unemployment benefits, and (3) encourage employer participation in the program (a) by helping "police" the system against unjustified benefit payments and (b) by influencing legislation. Although all these objectives do affect the cost and financing of the program, they also have important effects on other features of the program that cannot be ignored. Therefore, these objectives should be considered first before possible changes and improvements in experience rating are given consideration.

DEVELOPMENT OF EXPERIENCE RATING

Federal Legislation

Because President Roosevelt had insisted that the legislation proposed for unemployment insurance must promote the stabilization of employment, the Committee on Economic Security made specific recomendations for experience rating as the means of accomplishing such stabilization. Several Committee members were opposed to experience rating through individual employer accounts as provided for in the Wisconsin law. Agreement to provide for experience rating was not reached until the last meeting of the Committee, and then only after Assistant Secretary of Labor Arthur J. Altmeyer suggested that the experience rating provision include a requirement of a minimum contribution of 1 percent of wages to a state-wide pooled fund.[2]

The Committee recommended to the President in January, 1935, that lower state unemployment tax rates be permitted through allowing the employer "additional credit" against the federal unemployment tax, such additional credit to be the difference between the employer's actual contribution to the state and 90 percent of the federal tax. For example, if the employer paid his state contributions at an experience rate of 1.5 percent of payroll, he would get an "additional credit" of 1.2 percent and thus could

---

[2] Edwin E. Witte, *The Development of the Social Security Act* (Madison: University of Wisconsin Press, 1962), p. 127.

still get a total credit of 2.7 percent (that is, 90 percent) of the federal unemployment tax of 3 percent. Such additional credit could be secured for experience rating of employer contributions or taxes paid to three types of funds: a state pooled fund, an individual employer reserve account in a state fund, or a guaranteed employment account in a state fund. Additional credit would be allowed under a state pooled fund only after the state law had been in operation for five years; under an individual employer reserve account only if the reserve was equal to at least 15 percent of the employer's payroll; and under a guaranteed employment account only if it had a reserve equal to 7½ percent of the employer's payroll.

In transmitting the bill embodying the Committee's recommendations to Congress on January 17, 1935, President Roosevelt said: "An unemployment compensation system should be constructed in such a way as to afford every practicable aid and incentive toward the larger purpose of employment stabilization. . . . Moreover, in order to encourage the stabilization of private employment, Federal legislation should not foreclose the States from establishing means for inducing industries to afford an even greater stabilization of employment."

In its consideration of the original Social Security Act in 1935, the House Committee on Ways and Means deleted the additional credit provisions from the Administration bill on the ground that they were inconsistent with the basic purpose of the federal tax. In its opinion, if employer contribution rates could be varied, it would destroy the effectiveness of the federal uniform tax as a method of eliminating the interstate competition factor in the cost of unemployment insurance. Variable state tax rates would reintroduce interstate differences in tax burdens on employers. The House passed the Social Security bill in this form.

The Senate Finance Committee restored the experience rating provisions of the bill, both because Wisconsin and several other states had enacted laws with experience rating and so could not qualify for approval under the House-passed bill, and because the majority of its members were sympathetic to experience rating.

As finally enacted by Congress, the act required only three years of experience under a pooled fund plan before an employer could be given a reduced rate. For an individual employer reserve account plan, the minimum required reserve was reduced from 15 to 7½ percent of payroll, but two other conditions were added: compensation must have been payable from the account throughout the preceding year and the account must amount to not less than five times the largest amount of compensation paid out in the preceding three years. No change was made in the original size of the reserve required for a guaranteed employment plan, but a provision was added that the guaranteed work must be equal to at least 40 weeks of 30 hours each per year or the equivalent in total hours of work in a year. The requirement of a minimum contribution of 1 percent to a pooled fund was dropped.

A number of technical and clarifying amendments were made in 1939 to the experience rating provisions of the Federal Unemployment Tax Act, but none of them was particularly important. The House of Representatives passed, but the Senate rejected, amendments (1) requiring an average contribution rate of 2.7 percent of total payrolls and (2) permitting a state to reduce taxes on a uniform basis for all employers in the state.

The only other substantive change made in the federal provisions for experience rating occurred in 1954 when the required "experience with unemployment" before an experience rating could be given was reduced from three years to one. This was designed to shorten the time before a new or newly covered employee could secure experience rating and thereafter be on an equal competitive footing taxwise with older employers covered by the state law. Actually, the states have been quite uneven in the extent to which they have reduced the time before an employer can get an experience rating. As of January 1, 1966, 16 states still required at least three years of experience and only 21 had reduced the requirement to no more than one year of experience.[3]

STATE LEGISLATION

Original Provisions. All but 11 states originally provided for experience rating of some sort in their unemployment insurance legislation, despite bitter arguments over whether experience rating was desirable or not. Only seven states provided for individual employer reserves of the Wisconsin type and two of these established individual employer reserve accounts within a state pooled fund. All these were of the "reserve ratio" type under which the employer's "contribution" or tax rate was determined by the size of his reserve ratio. This ratio was set by subtracting all benefits charged to the employer's account from all contributions he had made to it and dividing the remainder by the employer's annual payroll. Of the 11 states without experience rating provisions, nine provided for a study of the subject.

The specific experience rating provisions differed greatly in detail. A number of states copied some of the provisions in the Social Security Board's draft bills, but the states departed from the draft bill provisions much more frequently with respect to experience rating than with respect to other provisions. Originally, the requirements for rate reduction were much higher than they are today. Fifteen of the pooled fund states provided that there would be no reduced rates unless the total fund's assets exceeded benefits paid out in the previous year and that no rate could be less than 1.8 percent of payroll unless the total fund's assets were twice benefits paid out. Most of the pooled fund states required minimum reserves of 7½ percent for individual employer accounts and some states

---

[3] A minor amendment in 1961 permitted successor employers to pick up the unemployment experience of their predecessors (Public Law 87–321, approved September 26, 1961).

required even higher reserves. Twenty-three of the states with pooled funds provided for higher tax rates than 2.7 percent, up to 4.0 percent in some states. Four of the employer reserve account states provided for rates higher than 2.7 percent.

No state originally had more than one schedule of rates and the maximum number of rates in any law was five. Twelve states provided for zero rates; that is, no contributions from an employer with little or no unemployment; 25 states provide for 0.9 or 1.0 percent as the minimum rate and two for 1.5 percent as the minimum. Higher rates were usually 1.8, 2.7, and 3.6 percent of payrolls. The states varied in the method of charging benefits against the employer's account, 23 charging in inverse chronological order of employment and 13 charging the most recent and the next most recent employer. Only two charged all benefits to the last employer.

Changes in Experience Rating

Over the years, the states' experience rating provisions have become more and more varied and increasingly complex. In 1966, it took 31 printed pages, including eight detailed tables, for the Bureau of Employment Security to describe the state experience rating provisions.[4] Limitations of space will permit us to describe only the major features and differences in current experience rating provisions.

All the jurisdictions (except Puerto Rico) now provide for experience rating, and all do so within state pooled funds. The states with individual employer reserve account plans, after experimenting with partial pooling of employer contributions, have all completely pooled their funds and use individual employer accounts only as bookkeeping accounts to determine experience rates. This pooling of funds brought at least two advantages. First, money is always available to pay benefits as long as any money is left in the state fund as a whole. Secondly, the very general federal requirements for pooled funds permit more flexibility in experience rating plans than the rigid and difficult-to-meet requirements for individual employer reserves plans. As for guaranteed employment plans which are permitted under federal legislation, none has ever been used in any state, so far as the authors know.

Different Types of Experience Rating

As of January 1, 1966, the formulas for experience rating under pooled fund systems fall into five types: reserve-ratio (32 states), benefit-ratio (eight states), benefit-wage-ratio (six states), payroll variations (four states), and compensable-separations (one state). A few states have combinations of these types.

Reserve-Ratio Formulas. These were the earliest and still are the most

---

[4] United States Department of Labor, Bureau of Employment Security, *Comparison of State Unemployment Insurance Laws*, BES No. U–141 (Washington, D.C.), pp. T 7–21, TT 1–16.

common formulas for experience rating. For each employer an account is set up, to which his contributions are credited and against which benefits paid to his former employees are charged. The ratio of the resulting balance to the employer's annual payroll is then determined. This is the reserve-ratio. The balance (reserve) is usually carried forward from year to year, and represents the excess or deficit of contributions over benefits since the program began. The payroll factor used to determine the reserve-ratio is the annual average of total payrolls in the last three years.

The employer's reserve must reach a specified minimum ratio to annual payroll before reduced rates are assigned. A schedule of reduced rates is then applied, with the rate lowered as the reserve ratio ascends in size. Most of these states have several rate schedules, the schedule in effect depending on the size of the entire state fund, with a higher schedule going into effect if the total fund is depleted to a specified level and vice versa.

Benefit-Ratio Formulas. Under these formulas, benefits are directly related to payrolls, without taking contributions into account. Contribution are varied according to the ratio of benefits to payrolls, the theory being that if each employer's contribution approximates his benefit ratio, benefits will be adequately financed. Rates are varied according to several schedules in most of these states, depending on the size of the state fund.

Benefit-Wage-Ratio Formulas. These formulas measure the relative experience of different employers by the number of separations of workers who draw benefits. The duration of benefits paid to these is not a factor. The number of such separations from an employer times the total wages that have been paid to the separated workers during their "base-periods" are recorded for each employer as his "benefit wages." The ratio of these "benefit wages" totaled over the last three years to his total payroll during this period is determined once a year for each employer. This is the employer's "experience factor." A "state experience factor" is then determined by calculating the ratio of total benefit payments to total benefit wages in the state in the preceding three years. Each employer's tax rate is then determined by multiplying his experience factor by the state experience factor, according to a table. The rates in this table are designed to replenish the fund annually for all the benefits paid. The length of time an individual worker draws benefits is not taken into account in determining the rate for the individual employer. Through the application of the "state experience factor," each employer shares in the cost of the average state-wide duration of benefits. The cost of each separation varies with the wages paid to the separated worker, but not with the worker's individual duration of benefits.

Compensable-Separations Formula. Connecticut uses compensable separations as a means of determining an employer's experience rate, a system somewhat like the benefit-wage ratio formula. Separated workers' weekly benefit amounts are entered on the employer's experience rating record and are aggregated for three years. The employer's aggregate payroll for three years is then divided by this aggregate benefit amount to determine his index. Employers are then arrayed in the order of these indices and tax rates are assigned in the same order, with the lowest rates going to employers with the highest indices. One of six different tax rate schedules is applied, according to the size of the fund.

Payroll Variation Plans. Finally, a few states determine tax rates on the basis of variations in payrolls, without any reference to whether benefits were paid to the employer's former workers. The theory is that payroll declines indicate an employer's "experience with unemployment," which is the measure specified in the federal act. Payroll declines are determined on a quarterly or annual basis. The quarterly basis indicates the amount of seasonal unemployment; the annual basis only general business declines. Each state uses a different method of determining rates on the basis of the amount of any decline in each employer's payroll over the specified period.[5]

Features of Experience Rating Plans

Cutting across the various experience rating formulas are various other features of the plans.

Minimum Fund and Solvency Requirements. As of January 1, 1966, 27 state laws, as compared with 15 in 1937, require some minimum fund balance before any reduced rate may be allowed. About one half of these have a "solvency" requirement in terms of a percentage of payrolls in specified past years. Ten states set the minimum in specified millions of dollars. Only three express the minimum balance required as a multiple of benefits paid, the only realistic measure.

Rate Schedules. Thirty-four states provide for two or more schedules of tax rates depending on the size of the state fund: lower schedules come into effect when the fund increases in size; higher schedules as it decreases. These multiple schedules are so varied as to defy comparison.

Maximum Tax Rates. For a time, there was a trend for states to eliminate maximum tax rates above 2.7 percent for employers with the poorest experience; in 1957, for instance, only ten states had higher rates. As state reserves have decreased, more states are again providing for higher maximum rates so that as of January 1, 1966, 35 states provided maximum rates above 2.7 percent, close to the original number. In 1963 alone, 11 states raised their maximum rates. The maximum rates vary from 2.9 percent to 7.2 percent. In some states these maximum rates come into effect only in the higher or highest schedule of rates. The maximum rate of 7.2 percent (in Texas) would come into effect only if the state fund was exhausted.

Minimum Tax Rates. On the other hand, minimum rates on the whole are now lower than at the beginning of the program. In the most favorable tax schedules, 15 states have zero rates. Thirteen states have minimum rates of 0.1 and 16 have rates from 0.2 to 0.5 percent. Only four states

---

[5] Montana has three factors: annual payroll declines, the "age" of the employer, and a ratio of benefits to contributions. Its plan is therefore also called a "benefit-contribution-ratio" formula.

have minimum rates of 0.5 percent or more. Three states have no specified minimums.

Voluntary Contributions. About half of the states now permit voluntary employer contributions so that an employer can secure the next lower rate[6] by making more than his required contribution for the year. This is designed for employers whose reserves if slightly larger would entitle them to a lower rate.

Methods of Charging Benefits. Differences have developed in the methods of charging benefits to employers' accounts for the purposes of experience rating. Twenty-six states charge benefits in proportion to the worker's previous wages earned from each employer in his base period. Twelve states charge employers in the inverse chronological order of employment. Ten states charge the most recent or principal employer.

Noncharging of Benefits. "Noncharging" of benefits to any individual employer is another development. This practice has developed in connection with benefits paid for unemployment for which employers feel that they are not directly responsible. Sometimes this has been the result of a legislative compromise in which employers first proposed that benefits be completely denied in some types of situations, such as voluntary quitting, and later agreed to withdraw their proposal if no benefits paid in voluntary quit cases were charged to their experience rating accounts.

THE OBJECTIVES OF EXPERIENCE RATING

Experience rating was originally designed to serve as an incentive for employers to stabilize their employment. Two other functions or objectives of experience rating have emerged in the years since its inception. One is to secure proper allocation of costs in the program, a function that has been given more or less emphasis from the beginning. More recently, it has been stressed that experience rating promotes the employer's active interest and participation in the program, especially in "policing" the system so as to prevent unwarranted payment of benefits.

Stabilization of Employment

The original basic purpose of experience rating was to provide an incentive for the regularization of employment. Professor John R. Commons, the originator of the idea, framed the original unemployment compensation bill introduced in the Wisconsin legislature in 1920.[7] Commons argued that,

[6] In Minnesota, an employer can voluntarily contribute enough to get the minimum rate.

[7] It is interesting that Commons at this time emphasized the overexpansion of credit as the main cause of unemployment. At the hearing on the bill in the Wisconsin Assembly Chamber in February, 1921, he said: "hard times are not brought about by financial conspiracy. This period is brought on by over-expansion two or three years ago. Banks are still inflating credit two years after the War was [sic] over. This bill, by making every employee a liability to the employer, would make banks go slower on granting credit and would prevent periods of over-expansion." (*Milwaukee Sentinel*, February 16, 1921.) Quoted by John B. Ewing, *Job Insurance* (Norman, Okla.: University of Oklahoma Press, 1933), pp. 30–31.

just as placing the cost of workmen's compensation directly on the employer had served as an incentive for employers to provide safer working conditions, ". . . the employer be made responsible for stable employment by creating against the employer the right of action on the part of the employees for compensation for a certain period of time in case he was laid off solely on account of lack of work."[8] This concept was expressed more precisely by Paul A. Raushenbush who helped to draft, and later administer, the Wisconsin Act: "Just as employers are now required by law to pay workmen's compensation for accidents, so they should in future pay limited unemployment compensation to laid off workers. Both accidents and unemployment are *industrial* hazards and genuine production costs to be prevented where possible but compensated for where unavoidable."[9]

In putting back into the Social Security Act the "additional credit" provisions for experience rating which had been deleted by the House of Representatives, the Senate Finance Committee emphasized that their purpose was the stabilization of employment. In the words of its report,

. . . we propose, as a further amendment, a provision that the Federal government shall recognize credits in the form of lower contribution rates which may be granted by the States to employers who have stabilized their employment. . . . In his message dealing with the subject of social security, the President urged that unemployment compensation should be set up under conditions which will tend toward the regularization of employment. All unemployment cannot be prevented by any employer, but many employers can do much more than they have done in the past to regularize employment.[10]

In a publication of the National Association of Manufacturers in 1952, employment stabilization was still stated as the primary purpose of experience rating: "The experience rating provisions of the Federal act were calculated to encourage employers to combat short-term unemployment through the stabilization of production and the exercise of other techniques in employment stabilization."[11]

Methods of Stabilization. No doubt there are many ways in which employers can stabilize employment; many employers have put forth considerable effort to regularize their operations. Herman Feldman and Donald M. Smith listed no less than ten methods that employers could use to stabi-

[8] Testimony by John R. Commons in *Unemployment in the United States*, Hearings before the Committee on Education and labor, United States Senate, 70th Cong., 2nd sess. pursuant to S. Res. 219 (Washington, D.C.: U.S. Government Printing Office, 1929), p. 217.

[9] Paul A. Raushenbush, "The Wisconsin Idea: Unemployment Reserves," *Annals of the American Academy of Political and Social Science*, Vol. 170 (November, 1933), p. 72.

[10] Senate Report No. 628, 74th Cong., 1st sess., p. 14.

[11] Industrial Relations Division, National Association of Manufacturers, *Unemployment Compensation in a Free Economy*, Economic Policy Divisions Series, Number 52 (July, 1952).

lize their employment.[12] Dr. Harold C. Taylor has reported that studies by Charles Gibbons and Henry Thole for the Upjohn Institute showed that good management throughout a business organization was more important and fundamental in minimizing business fluctuation than "formula-type" proposals such as listed by Feldman and Smith.[13]

Limitations on Stabilization. While stabilization is a desirable goal, it is a difficult one to achieve. Some of the difficulties have been described by Professor Harry M. Wagner:

The variables influencing whether an employer is to retain or fire an individual certainly include the value product of the individual's labor, an uncertain future demand schedule, and inventory holding costs. . . . Given the inherent nature of these factors, in all but trivial cases, working out an optimum employment schedule over future periods is a very difficult if not impossible problem . . . the very complexity of working out a theoretically optimal pattern is such as to leave one to believe that present day employers do the best they can by relying to a large part on intuition, which probably balances the costs of varying employment with alleged savings in payroll deductions and lower inventory costs.[14]

The possibilities of an employer's regularizing his employment are largely confined to smoothing out seasonal peaks and valleys and reducing other employment irregularities. Even reduction in seasonal unemployment is limited by factors outside the employer's control such as weather conditions or seasonal variation in the demand for many products that do not lend themselves to regularizing production. An employer can minimize technological unemployment to some extent by phasing the introduction of technological improvements and by reducing his work force through the attrition of resignations, retirements, etc. But some unemployment can be avoided only by holding up the introduction of technological improvements. Cyclical unemployment is almost entirely outside the control of the employer. The most he can do is to keep workers on the payroll by spreading the work, but this in actuality only means spreading unemployment or underemployment.

To what extent has experience rating actually been an incentive for employers to stabilize their employment? After a field study in Wisconsin in the late 1930's, Charles A. Meyers found that about 10 percent of the firms he interviewed had stabilized employment to an appreciable degree. The possibility of securing a lower contribution rate served as a psychological, as well as a financial, incentive to stabilize. He found, however, that stabilization through hiring fewer workers at peaks of activity, by

[12] Herman Feldman and Donald M. Smith, *The Case for Experience Rating in Unemployment Compensation, and a Proposed Method* (New York: Industrial Relations Counselors, 1939), pp. 5–6.

[13] Harold C. Taylor, *What the Individual Firm Can Do to Contribute to Business Stabilization* (Kalamazoo: W. E. Upjohn Institute for Employment Research, 1962), p. 14.

[14] Harry M. Wagner, "A Reappraisal of Experience Rating," *Southern Economic Journal*, April, 1959, pp. 459–69.

working overtime,[15] or by refusing orders had resulted in unemployment or less work for about 2 percent of the labor force that he studied.[16] Writing again in 1945, however, Meyers reported that, while the Wisconsin Act had an initial effect of stimulating employers to stabilize employment, this effect soon wore off.[17]

Meyer's investigation was made a generation ago. To our knowledge, no field investigations have been made in recent years of the effect of experience rating on employment stabilization. In his address to the Interstate Conference of Employment Security Agencies in 1964, Marion B. Folsom, Director of the Eastman Kodak Company, said: "Although it is difficult to obtain facts, the impression in industry is that employers are doing a better job in planning production, preventing seasonal layoffs and stabilizing employment, and experience rating has been an important factor in this development."[18]

For the most part, experience rating to stabilize employment has operated to give low rates not on the basis of merit or effort, but on the basis of factors beyond the employer's control. As P. L. Rainwater, who was then administrator of the Mississippi agency, put it in 1951:

The most probable result of merit rating in operation will be a rate structure which will impose low rates on all employers who participate in the production of goods for a relatively stable market, high rates on all employers who take part in the production of goods for a market subject to severe fluctuations. . . . The reward of rate reduction will go to the employers who have done nothing to earn it. The penalty of high rates will be imposed upon employers who are not so much inefficient as unlucky. Thus merit rating will bear little or no relation to merit. Their determination will depend less upon good management than upon good fortune.[19]

Undesirable Employment Practices. In order to minimize the payment of benefits to their workers, employers can engage in employment practices that have nothing to do with stabilization of employment. Clinton Spivey has listed such practices as hiring ineligible workers (students or workers with little or no prior wage credits); laying off the workers with the lowest accumulation of wage credits; and hiring or laying off workers at such times as will prevent the paying of partial benefits during a

---

[15] It would be interesting to know whether the extensive use of overtime in recent years is partly motivated by the savings in unemployment benefits that an employer can achieve by avoiding the hiring of additional workers during peak periods of activity.

[16] Charles A. Meyers, *Employment Stabilization and The Wisconsin Act,* Employment Security Memorandum No. 10 (Washington, D.C.: Social Security Board, September, 1940).

[17] Charles A. Meyers, "Experience Rating in Unemployment Compensation" *American Economic Review,* Vol. XXXV (June, 1945), pp. 337–54.

[18] Marion B. Folsom, "Where We Stand in Unemployment Insurance," *Proceedings of 28th Annual Meeting of Interstate Conference of Employment Security Agencies* (Miami, Florida, October 7, 1964), p. 62.

[19] P. L. Rainwater, "The Fallacy of Experience Rating: The Rebuttal," *Labor Law Journal,* Vol. 2 (October, 1951), p. 760.

week.[20] No one knows to what extent such practices are indulged in, perhaps not enough to make much difference in the system.

On the other hand, it is probable that undesirable practices by some employers to increase benefits for their employees would develop if experience rating did not exist to curb them. This is evidenced by some practices on the part of employers whose experience rates are at the maximum, so that the payment of additional benefits does not affect their rate. For example, cases have been cited of employers in highly seasonal industries who held out the possibility of drawing unemployment benefits at the close of the season as an inducement for workers to seek employment with them. It can well be maintained that without experience rating there would be more of such practices, perhaps even active connivance between employers and workers to maximize the benefits they can draw.

What does this all add up to in the appraisal of stabilization of employment as an objective of experience rating? Certainly, no one would question the desirability of stabilizing employment to the maximum extent possible. There is no doubt that experience rating has served as an incentive to stabilize employment, but the extent to which it has so served has fallen short of expectations and has not been sufficient to justify experience rating on that ground alone. To a large extent, employers' experience rates are determined by the inherent stability or instability of their industry.

Allocation of Costs

Another stated purpose of experience rating is that it is designed to result in a proper allocation of the costs of unemployment compensation. This argument for experience rating was advanced by Paul A. Raushenbush in 1933:

The perennial major problem of organized society is so to devise its legal and economic rules that the price system will adequately reflect social costs and conserve social standards. The social and human costs of irregular employment should properly be charged against and compensated by each employing unit. Only in this way can consumers be assured that a low price is not a misleading and parasitic price, and that the competitive (or other) system is really functioning in the public interest. The economic truth of this point is being increasingly admitted where sweatshop daily and weekly wages are involved, but has not yet been so clearly recognized where irregular employment and yearly earnings are concerned.[21]

Stated in economic rather than social terms, this argument has been succinctly set forth by another strong advocate of experience rating, Stanley Rector: "The competitive free enterprise system for its proper func-

---

[20] Clinton Spivey, *Experience Rating in Unemployment Compensation*, Bureau of Economic and Business Research, University of Illinois, Bulletin No. 84 (Champaign, 1958), p. 92.

[21] Raushenbush, *op. cit.*, pp.72–73.

tioning requires that the costs of production and distribution be rather accurately reflected in the ultimate purchase price. Consumers, with their dollars as ballots, elect the course of commitments of our capital, labor and resources. Certainly the cost of industrial unemployment is a production cost—in whatever manner it may be met."[22]

Limitations on Shifting of Tax by Employers. The allocation of costs argument is based on the assumption that the costs of unemployment compensation will be passed on to the consumer in higher prices. Richard A. Lester, however, has accumulated considerable evidence that experience rating tends to prevent or retard any shifting of the unemployment tax. To begin with, Lester points out that a firm with a given employment experience will pay different rates in each state if it operates in several states, as well as a different rate over a period of time within a state, partly because of differences in the experience rating systems in the several states and partly because of variations in costs in each state due to the differences in their benefit structures. As a result, the tax burden on competing firms varies greatly from state to state and within states.

Lester points out that the tax rate variations for competing firms within a single state are also marked. He found, for example, that of the 62 industry categories with rated accounts in Minnesota, all but two of the categories had accounts varying from the extremes of 0.1 percent to 2.7 percent. Lester also found that the year-to-year uncertainty and fluctuations in unemployment tax rates reduces the possibilities and likelihood of the tax being shifted forward in higher prices. As an example, he gives jumps in the average tax rate from 1958 to 1959 in California from 1.14 to 2.10 percent, in Delaware from 0.63 to 1.82 percent, in Virginia from 0.42 to 1.30 percent, and similar jumps in other states.

A third factor pointed out by Lester is that a number of the more stable, lower-taxed industries are among the more monopolistic ones, such as public utilities, and, on the other hand, many of the competitive industries such as contract construction and textiles are more apt to pay the higher tax rates and have a wide dispersion in rates among employers in the industry. In his words:

> . . . the industries that seem least likely to be able to shift the tax are more fully represented in the higher tax brackets. That is partly because the tax rate distribution of employers in those competitive industries appears to lack, in most cases, a clear central tendency. Absence of a central tendency makes shifting of the tax to consumers more difficult and less likely than is the case in more stable lines of business where firms tend to be bunched at the low tax rates. . . . Under the circumstances, only a fraction of the unemployment compensation tax would seem to be potentially shiftable.[23]

[22] Stanley Rector, "The Frailty of the 'Fallacy' of Experience Rating," *Labor Law Journal*, Vol. 2 (May, 1951), p. 346.

[23] Richard A. Lester, *The Economics of Unemployment Compensation* (Princeton: Industrial Relations Section, Princeton University, 1962), p. 65. For his full discussion and statistical presentation, see pp. 60–67.

Finally, Lester says that "the relatively minor size of the unemployment compensation tax among total payroll costs and of expansions in such costs reduces the possibility of shifting the tax." Lester thinks that probably "some fraction of the tax is ultimately shifted to employees in the sense that the unemployment tax may slightly enhance the difficulty for unions to negotiate a large wage increase, or as large a wage increase in a particular firm as would have been the case if the company's profits had not been curtailed by the tax."[24]

Lester does not stand alone in questioning the extent that the employer can pass on his unemployment compensation tax. For example, in contrasting the incidence of federal OASDI taxes (which are paid at a uniform rate) with unemployment insurance taxes, Dr. Eveline M. Burns writes, with respect to the latter, "Here, the probability is greater that the tax (at least the differential above the minimum payable by any employer) will fall upon profits and not be shifted."[25]

Finally, a basic inconsistency between the stabilization argument and the allocation of costs argument for experience rating has been pointed out by Clinton Spivey,

If experience rating is to allocate costs it must do so through increased prices to consumers. A perfect allocation would result in the complete unloading of the tax by employers. On the other hand, if the payroll tax serves as an incentive for stabilization then the employer is assumed to bear the tax. If the employer bears the burden he cannot shift it; if he shifts it he cannot bear it. Similarly, if the payroll tax is shifted to the workers then there is no basis for maintaining that the tax would provide an incentive to stabilize employment. The incentive for employment stabilization may be through profits rather than by way of the tax burden. Assuming the tax is shifted, those paying less than the maximum rate get larger profits.[26]

Effects on New Employers. New employers and employers newly covered under the system bear a disproportionate share of the cost of unemployment insurance under experience rating as now constituted. This is due to the required period of waiting during which they are accumulating "experience with unemployment" before they can get an experience rating. This period varies from one to three years, depending on the state. In some

---

[24] *Ibid.*, p. 66.
Without taking into account the consequences of experience rating, Hansen and his co-authors concluded that if the employer tax is passed on, it will be passed back to the employee rather than forward to the consumer. For the many complexities involved in determining the incidence of an employer tax see Alvin H. Hansen, Merrill G. Murray, Russell A. Stevenson, and Bryce M. Stewart, *A Program for Unemployment Insurance and Relief* (Minneapolis: University of Minnesota Press, 1934), pp. 46–51.

[25] Eveline M. Burns, *Social Security and Public Policy* (New York: McGraw-Hill Book Co., Inc., 1956), p. 162. See also, Carl S. Shoup, *The Prospects for a Study of the Economic Effects of Payroll Taxes* (1941); Harry A. Millis and Royal E. Montgomery, *Labor's Risks and Social Insurance* (1938), p. 162; Edwin T. Teple and Charles G. Nowacek, "Experience Rating: Its Objectives, Problems and Economic Implications," *Vanderbilt Law Review*, Vol. 8, No. 2 (February, 1955), p. 379, footnote 6.

[26] Spivey, *op. cit.*, p. 91.

states a considerable part of the total tax load has been borne by such employers, especially in states that have a large proportion of their employees at zero or very low minimum rates.[27] This fact caused Congress in 1954 to permit the states to shorten from three years to one year the period that a new employer is required to wait before getting an experience rating. While this has lessened the burden on new employers in states that took advantage of the Congressional amendment, the problem still exists in many states that did not shorten the period before new employers can get experience rates.[28]

Increasing Employer Interest and Participation

The third function that experience rating serves, and the one now urged the most, is to provide an incentive for employers to take an interest in and participate in the unemployment insurance program. Such participation takes three forms, as set forth by Emerson P. Schmidt, former Director, Economics Research Department, of the Chamber of Commerce of the United States. As he has written: "With one group in society (employees) receiving all the benefits, and another group (employers), in all but four States) paying the tax contributions, experience rating is highly essential to encourage a proper balance in establishing benefit levels and benefit formulas, to stimulate an employer interest in the administration of the program, and in general to act in a policing capacity to prevent the program from degenerating into a relief program."[29]

The National Association of Manufacturers has advised employers to do the following: (1) become informed as to the law, its administrative procedures, and the employer's obligations, rights and functions as an employer, if possible assigning these duties to one individual; (2) inform employees of their rights and assist those who have valid claims to receive their full benefits; (3) stabilize employment; (4) scrutinize all notices of claims filed by his employees to make sure they have not been filed under disqualifying circumstances; (5) protest claims that are believed to be unwarranted; (6) scrutinize claims of former employees (made possible in several states by the employer receiving a copy of every benefit check issued to a former employee and charged to his account); (7) analyze the annual statement of the employer's account in the fund to determine improper charges; and (8) participate in the appeals procedure when the employer finds legitimate grounds for protest, especially in cases that may set a precedent.

[27] See *Unemployment Insurance*, Hearings before the Committee on Ways and Means, House of Representatives, 83rd Cong., 2nd sess. (Washington, D.C.: U.S. Government Printing Office, 1954), p. 75, table 12.

[28] In states with reserve-ratio experience rating formulas, the one-year provision could have no effect because of the time needed to build up a reserve large enough to permit a reduced rate, unless the reserve required is 2.7 percent of taxable payroll.

[29] Emerson P. Schmidt, "Experience Rating and Unemployment Compensation," *Yale Law Journal*, Vol. 55, No. 1 (December, 1945), p. 242.

In its introduction to the discussion of these activities, the National Association of Manufacturers stated:

It should be noted that the suggested steps stress the direct economic effect on the employer of lower tax rates. This is an honest and forthright objective which should not be prejudiced by cries that labor standards and benefit rights are being undermined. However, there is another powerful sanction to vigorous employer interest. It rests in his responsibility to protect the system so it will function properly whenever his own employees need the protection for which he has helped pay.[30]

When carried out in the proper spirit, the suggested activities can be beneficial both to the system and to the employees of the employer who are filing legitimate claims. The administrators of unemployment insurance need the cooperation of employers in getting full information on which they can make sound judgments both in the award and denial of claims. The administrative agency must have prompt and accurate information from employers in order to award legitimate claims promptly and in the proper amount. It also needs the cooperation of the employer in uncovering falsification and malingering. Unfortunately, many employers have pursued only such activities as would prevent benefit payments and thus save them money. This has happened most frequently when an individual or even an outside agency has been hired to contest claims in which there is some prospect of denial. While it may result in some savings in taxes to the employer, overzealous activity of this nature arouses resentment among workers and fortifies their criticism of experience rating.

It is also unfortunate that this negative type of activity has come to be emphasized more than the positive goal of stabilization of employment. Such "policing" of the system by employers hardly saves enough money to the state unemployment fund to justify the huge amounts in taxes that are in a sense rebated to the employer through experience rating. It is also doubtful whether such activitiy protects the fund substantially, since the number of unjustified claims uncovered by employers would not be large enough to seriously deplete the fund even if they were paid. Unwise reductions of taxes has had far more to do in bringing about the present inadequacy of many state funds than the payment of unwarranted claims.

Criticisms of Experience Rating as a Stimulus to Employer Activity. Organized labor has been critical of experience rating on the ground that it has provided the incentive for employers to oppose increases in benefits and to seek more stringent disqualification provisions in the state laws. Employers would prefer such statements as that of the former chief economist of the Chamber of Commerce of the United States, Emerson P.

[30] National Association of Manufacturers, *Unemployment Compensation in A Free Economy*, Economic Policy Division Series No. 52 (New York, July, 1952), p. 35. See also article by E. R. Bartley, Director of the Industrial Relations Department, Illinois Manufacturers' Association, "How to Reduce Your Unemployment Compensation Costs," *Industrial Review*, Vol. 28, No. 2 (August, 1953).

Schmidt, that "experience rating is highly essential to encourage a proper balance in establishing benefit levels and benefit formulas."[31] They also would contend that such influence as experience rating has had on benefit and disqualification provisions has been all to the good; it has curbed the payment of benefits to those who should not receive them and has prevented undue liberality in benefits that would both weaken the system financially and weaken the incentive to work. The extent to which experience rating has resulted in deliberalizations in the program is difficult to document. Many instances can be cited in which employers have joined labor on agreed bills in state legislatures which provided for increased benefits. Many employers sincerely want an adequate benefit program. But too frequently bills have included a reduction in unemployment taxes that employers have secured as the price for their agreeing to an increase in benefit amounts or duration. Reductions in taxes often have not been justified, as evidenced by dangerously low reserves in a number of states.

Labor's criticism has been joined by the criticism of many students of the program. The effect of experience rating on state unemployment insurance legislation led Clinton Spivey, after making the most comprehensive study of experience rating in recent years, to conclude:

Considering the objectives of unemployment compensation it would seem those administering the program would be chiefly concerned with the payment of benefits. But benefits are not the major issue. Today, most unemployment compensation problems at both the legislative and administrative levels are directly involved with, if not subordinated to, experience rating. Proposals to extend coverage, to liberalize benefits, to make determinations of seasonal industries—these and similar measures are tested for their effect upon a possible reduction in the employer's tax rate through experience rating. In short, employers and many administrators in their preoccupation with experience rating are converting the present system into a tax program rather than one designed to pay benefits to unemployed workers.[32]

Unfortunately, there appears to be much truth in Spivey's conclusion.

Effect on Interstate Competition

Any discussion of the effects of experience rating would be incomplete without a consideration of the effect of experience rating on the position of employers in interstate competition. The initial purpose in the federal unemployment tax, as has been repeatedly emphasized, was to enable states to enact unemployment insurance laws without fear that the cost would place their employers at a disadvantage in interstate competition.

The inconsistency of including provision for experience rating in the federal unemployment tax legislation was recognized by Congressman Jere Cooper in the hearings on the bill before the House Committee on

[31] Emerson P. Schmidt, "Experience Rating and Unemployment Compensation," *Yale Law Journal*, December, 1945, p. 242.
[32] Spivey, *op. cit.*, p. 88.

Ways and Means. The colloquy between Congressman Cooper and Edwin E. Witte, who was presenting the case for the bill, is worth quoting:

MR. COOPER: Doctor, I understand the underlying principle supporting the idea of a Federal tax, it is to make it uniform throughout the entire country?
MR. WITTE: Yes, sir.
MR. COOPER: Thereby meeting a difficulty that would naturally arise on account of the element of competition.
MR. WITTE: Certainly.
MR. COOPER: That is, competition between certain business enterprises. If the system is to make allowances for certain industries to have special accounts, does not that strike at the very principle that is supposed to prevail through the whole system?[33]

Because of this inconsistency, Mr. Cooper prevailed upon the Committee on Ways and Means to strike out of the bill the "additional credit" provisions which would permit experience rating; the bill passed the House without them. (The additional credit provisions were restored in the Senate and agreed to in conference with representatives of the House Committee.)

How has this inconsistency worked out in practice? The variation in average unemployment tax rates of all industries combined between the various states has been wide, as has already been brought out in the preceding chapter. More significantly, tax rates of employers within individual industries vary widely from state to state. For example, in the textile mill products group, tax rates averaged 2.56 percent of total wages in Pennsylvania and 0.47 percent in South Carolina in 1962. These differences in tax rates have been due to differences in economic conditions and differences in the benefit provisions of the state laws, but the differences have also been due to the differences in the experience rating formulas in the various states.[34]

Unemployment insurance taxes are relatively small in comparison with other costs to the employer. These differentials in tax rates between states, therefore, should not be important to the average employer. On the other hand, experience rating makes it difficult for the employer to shift the tax by an increase in prices as is brought out earlier in this chapter. Because of this, as Dr. Lester concludes, "interstate differences in unemployment taxes can be of considerable significance to certain types of industries operating on small and fluctuating margins."[35]

Interstate differences in cost may affect an employer's decision (1) to move out of the state; (2) to expand plant within the state; or (3) to go into

---

[33] *Economic Security Act*, Hearings before the Committee on Ways and Means, House of Representatives, 74th Cong., 1st sess. on H.R. 4120, p. 145.
[34] For an estimate of the effect of the experience rating formulas on state differences in taxes paid, see Rachel S. Gallagher, "State Differences in Unemployment Compensation Employer Taxes," *Social Security Bulletin*, October, 1945, pp. 15–16.
[35] Lester, *op. cit.*, p. 95. See Lester's full discussion of interstate competition in chapter 6 of his book.

a new state. As to the extent that interstate competition does affect employer's decisions in any of these three ways, Dr. Lester found considerable difference of opinion. In perusing the hearings on unemployment insurance before the House Ways and Means Committee in 1959, he found that employer representatives who testified belittled the importance of the cost of unemployment insurance as an interstate competitive factor,[36] but, in their own states, emphasized its importance.[37] He also found that the governors of a number of states were concerned about the effect of unemployment insurance costs on attracting industry to their states.[38]

Another factor influencing an employer's decision to come into a state is the "climate for business." Differences in experience rates in different states, as well as differences in the provisions of state laws with respect to benefit amounts and duration, eligibility conditions, and disqualifications, enter into this business climate. Dr. Lester concludes that:

Perhaps as influential in a State as the calculated interstate differences in tax terms is the argument in terms of business climate. Employers associations and management spokesmen are prone to emphasize that particular provisions of the State's law show a pro-business or anti-business attitude and hence encourage or discourage business expansion and location in the State. Obviously, assessment of this intangible factor is practically impossible. Nevertheless, those with political and legislative experience in the States recognize that this contention has force.[39]

To the extent that employers strive for low benefits, and consequently low taxes, in order to provide a "good" business climate, the introduction of this consideration into the picture can have detrimental effects on unemployment compensation in a state.

POSSIBLE IMPROVEMENTS IN EXPERIENCE RATING

Whether or not one believes that experience rating has been a boon or a bane to unemployment insurance, one must recognize that experience rating is so firmly embedded in the unemployment insurance system and in the thinking of employers that it is likely to remain part of the system. How can any bad effects of experience rating be minimized and how can its contribution to sound financing of the unemployment insurance system be maximized? A discussion of this problem will include (1) examination of ways to revise experience rating provisions so as to secure countercyclical

[36] *Unemployment Compensation,* Hearings before the Committee on Ways and Means, House of Representatives, 86th Cong., 1st sess. (April 7–16, 1959), pp. 188, 776, and 719.

[37] *Ibid.,* pp. 188–89, 345.

[38] *Ibid.,* pp. 214–15, 776, 821.

[39] Lester, *op. cit.,* pp. 95–96. As an example of employer representatives using this as an argument, the *State Journal* of Frankfort, Kentucky, on April 17, 1957, contained this dispatch from Louisville, "Rayburn Watkins, managing director of the AIK (Associated Industries of Kentucky), described the law as 'liberally written,' generally administered and 'so expensive to employers' that it has created a 'bad business climate' in Kentucky." (Hearings, *op. cit.,* p. 345.)

financing; (2) consideration of what other changes in experience rating would strengthen financing of the program, such as changes in minimum and maximum rates; and finally, (3) determination as to whether the federal legislation should be changed so as to permit states more freedom of choice as to how they may vary tax rates.

Countercyclical Financing

Unemployment compensation has been increasingly recognized as being a "built-in" stabilizer of the economy, since the total amount paid out in benefits expands as workers are laid off during a business decline, a process which occurs without the necessity of legislative action. But, after pointing out the effect of unemployment compensation as an automatic stabilizer, Professor Albert G. Hart has written, ". . . grafted onto the process is a destabilizer—Merit Rating. . . . Hence, heavy unemployment, draining the reserves, leads to an increase in contribution rates—which tends to make unemployment worse. This destabilizing arrangement is not enough to cancel the stabilizing effect of the unemployment insurance system, but it does weaken it."[40]

Clinton Spivey had an empirical study of each state made for the period from 1946 to 1955 in order to study the timing of the financial load and benefit payments under experience rating. Two tests were made: (1) changes in taxable payrolls were correlated with changes in the average contribution rate in order to determine whether an increase in payrolls was accompanied by a change in tax rates; and (2) changes in benefit payments were correlated with changes in the average contribution rate to determine whether an increase in benefits paid was accompanied by a decrease in tax rates. Most of the states showed a poor correlation. Only eight states under the first test, when payrolls and average tax rates were correlated, had a coefficient high enough (0.576) to be positive; four of the 33 reserve-ratio plans; three of the five benefit-ratio plans; one of the six benefit-wage-ratio plans. Under the second test only six met the criterion of a negative coefficient of correlation (below minus 0.576) when changes in benefits were correlated with average tax rates: three reserve-ratio and three benefit-ratio plans. Spivey concluded: "This indicates that most of the financing systems under experience rating aggravate rather than mitigate the fluctuations produced by cyclical unemployment."[41]

There is usually a time lag between the onset of a recession and the annual adjustment in tax rates. This factor, no doubt, influences the results of Spivey's study. The countercyclical effect of experience rating will vary depending on the time of the year that a recession begins and also on the duration of the recession. Richard A. Lester tabulated the direction of change in the states' average tax rates from the previous year for the

---

[40] Albert G. Hart, *Money, Debt, and Economic Activity* (New York: Prentice-Hall, Inc., 1948), pp. 475–76.

[41] Spivey, *op. cit.*, p. 68.

period from 1946–60, totaling the number of states in which the average tax rates rose, fell, or remained unchanged each year. While he found that tax rates rose and fell in connection with recessions, the timing of the tax changes varied. Tax rates generally rose from 1949 to 1950 during the 1949–50 recession. The time lag in the annual adjustment of tax rates served to reduce rates generally in 1954, during the 1953–54 recession. In the 1957–58 recession the upward adjustment of rates in some states and the downward adjustments in other states balanced out.[42]

Russell A. Hibbard maintains that the reserve-ratio formulas, the most common type of experience rating, tend to work out countercyclically. According to Hibbard:

If properly worked out, this type of plan will actually raise rates in good times and lower them in bad times. . . . Under this formula, an increasing payroll lowers the reserve ratio and raises the tax rate; and a declining payroll increases the reserve ratio and lowers the tax rate. In actual practice, of course, reserve balances increase as payrolls rise. However, study of actual cases shows that payrolls tend to fluctuate farther and more rapidly than reserve balances, with the result that the net effect of the interaction of the forces is a counter-cyclical incidence of taxes. This has been proved by actual study.[43]

While recognizing this tendency, Lester points out that in practically all of the reserve-ratio states, if the state fund falls below certain levels, there may be a general rise in all employer tax rates as a higher tax schedule becomes effective.[44] He also points out another factor that weakens the countercyclical tax tendency is the limited taxable wage base, which covers only the first $3,000 of annual earnings in most states. Since total wages in covered employment averaged about $5,200 in 1963, "taxable payrolls do not vary as much cyclically as total payrolls and are a lower percentage of total payrolls in boom periods than in recessions. In recessions the tax burden is likely to rise as a percentage of the employer's total payroll, and thus would be cyclically accentuating. In prosperous times, the narrow tax base and the buildup of reserves serve to reduce the tax burden in terms of total payroll."[45]

Countercyclical Devices. Several methods of making experience rating operate countercyclically, or at least of neutralizing its cyclical effect, have been tried or suggested. In 1951, Wisconsin adopted a provision that brought a reduced schedule of tax rates into effect when total wages in covered employment declined 5 percent or more from the previous calendar year. This was revised in 1958 to provide that the reduced schedule would come into effect if benefit payments exceeded 1 percent of total

[42] Lester, *op. cit.*, pp. 68–70.
[43] Russell A. Hibbard, "Minimizing State Unemployment Compensation Taxes," *Proceedings* 9th Annual Conference, Tax Executives Institute (Bedford Springs, Pa., September 21, 1963), p. 10.
[44] Lester, *op. cit.*, p. 69.
[45] *Ibid.*, pp. 70–71.

covered payrolls plus $10 million. This occurred in 1958, and the average employer tax rate in Wisconsin declined from 1957 to 1959, at the same time that it increased in 42 states. The provision applied, however, only with respect to reductions in tax rates. No offsetting device was provided for increasing taxes when there were extraordinary increases in average payrolls. Wisconsin has since abandoned the provision.

Another device is the "tax credit" system formerly used in New York and currently used in the State of Washington. Such a tax credit plan, which would operate countercyclically, was described in detail in the 1958 report of the Benefit Financing Committee of the Interstate Conference.[46] This plan would lower the tax of the employer whose payroll was dropping and raise the tax of the employer whose payroll was increasing. Under this plan, an employer would receive a tax credit equal to the difference between his taxes that year and an amount equal to 2.7 percent of his taxable payroll. This dollar amount of credit could be applied against the contributions due the following year, based on a rate of 2.7 percent on his taxable payroll.[47] The effect will be to both reduce his taxes more during a recession than under present experience rating systems and to have no lag, such as now occurs, in the change in his tax rate. In another discussion of the tax credit device in 1961 the Benefit Financing Committee thought that over a ten-year period, the average employer's total taxes would be about the same as under present experience rating systems.[48]

Another plan, suggested by Nathan Morrison of the New York State agency, would provide for a uniform surtax, independent of experience rating, that would be triggered in or out or varied by an economic indicator. Such an indicator might be a ratio of unemployment claims to covered employment or a ratio of benefit payments to total or taxable wages. The level of the surtax would depend on benefit cost fluctuations, on the trigger or economic indicator level, and on the length of the periods of depression and periods of prosperity. The trigger levels could also be used to reduce the regular tax schedule during a recession.[49]

The only states that have as yet experimented with a countercyclical financing plan are New York, Washington, and Wisconsin, as described

---

[46] *Financing Unemployment Benefits,* Report of the 1958 Committee Benefit Financing to the Interstate Conference of Employment Security Agencies, September 30, 1958, pp. 16–17.

[47] For example, if his experience rate is 1.5 percent on $100,000 payroll, he will receive a tax credit equal to 1.2 percent or $1,200. If his payroll remains unchanged the following year, he can apply the $1,200 toward his $2,700 tax (2.7 percent of taxable payrolls) and pay $1,500 or 1.5 percent, the same amount as the previous year. If his payroll increases to $200,000 his tax will be $5,400 at the 2.7 rate. Applying the $1,200 credit, he pays $4,400 or 2.2 percent of taxable payroll. On the other hand, if his payroll is only $50,000, he pays 2.7 percent of that or $1,350 less his tax credit of $1,200 or only $150.

[48] *Minutes of Benefit Financing Committee* (Washington, D.C.: Interstate Conference of Employment Security Agencies, May 16–18, 1961), pp. 21–22.

[49] Nathan Morrison, *Proceedings of the Eleventh Annual Conference on Labor,* 1958, p. 328; and *Minutes of Benefit Financing Committee, op. cit.,* p. 20.

above. In addition to difficulties of developing an acceptable plan, Professor Lester believes that there are other obstacles to secure acceptance of a plan: "The political difficulties mainly stem from the unwillingness of State legislatures to delegate the power to make tax increases as well as decreases and from employer resistance (perhaps shortsighted for well-established firms) to tax rate increases in good times (partly for fear that large reserves will lead to higher benefit levels)."[50]

A Stable Rate Structure as an Alternative. In the meantime, Arizona has tried another approach which at least minimizes any undesirable cyclical movement of rates under experience rating. Under this plan, Arizona first projected estimates of average benefit costs over a ten-year period. It then set up a number of tax schedules that would come into play at different reserve fund levels so as to maintain reserve fund levels at or above a target level. Costs were kept under constant surveillance and changes in cost served as a basis for changes in the financial plan. Stability in tax rates was achieved by fairly accurate projections of annual costs over each planning period. The general plan was adopted by Arizona in 1953. In the eight-year period from 1954 through 1961, the average employer tax rate fluctuated between 1.26 perecent and 1.35 percent. Such a program of tax rate stability has been recommended to other states by the Bureau of Employment Security, which assisted Arizona in working out its plan.

Noncharging of Benefits and "Ineffective Charging"

Certain types of benefit payments are not charged to any employer, such as benefits paid after a worker has served a temporary disqualification period; benefits paid during an appeal period when the initial award is finally reversed; reimbursements under "wage-combining plans" for interstate claims; and payments of dependents' benefits. This "noncharging" has grown up because of the feeling of employers that they should not have to pay for benefits for which they are not *directly* responsible.

Noncharging of some types of benefits exists in practically all states except those under payroll-variation experience rating plans. The extent of noncharging, however, varies. It is most frequent in cases where benefits are paid after a temporary disqualification: for voluntary leaving (37 states as of January 1, 1966) or discharge for misconduct (35 states), or for refusing suitable work (11 states). In about two thirds of the states, if a worker has been awarded benefits and on appeal by the employer his award has finally been reversed, benefits paid in the interim are not charged to the employer. In about half the states, if a worker has filed an interstate claim under which wages earned in two or more states are combined to determine the amount of benefits payable, any part paid by the state is not charged to the employer with whom the worker earned the wages. For example, if

[50] Lester, *op. cit.*, p. 73.

a worker earned $200 of his wages with Employer A in State X and $300 of his wages with Employer B in State Y, Employer B's account would not be charged with benefits paid on the basis of the $300 in wages he paid, if his state did not charge such benefits. In seven of the 11 states paying dependent's benefits, there is no charging of the payments to the employer's account or experience rate. There are other types of noncharging scattered among the states.

The amount of noncharging varies widely from state to state. In 1962, the proportion of benefits that were not charged varied from less than 1 percent in a few states to 41.7 percent in one state.

"Ineffective Charging." When the total amount of benefits that would be "chargeable" to an employer exceeds his tax payments, which usually occurs when he is paying the maximum rate, the excess results in what the technicians call an "ineffective charge." The same term is applied when an employer's reserve account is exhausted and benefits that are charged to his account place it in the red or result in "negative charges." In all these cases, the benefits are paid from the state fund as a whole.

In most of the states no provision is made for any financing of benefits that are "noncharged" or "ineffectively charged." While they are paid out of the state fund, employers' reserve accounts are treated as if none of the taxes that they have paid has been used for noncharged or ineffectively charged benefits. As a result, in a state with a reserve-ratio system of experience rating, the sum total of the amounts credited to all employer accounts is much larger than the actual money in the state fund. These "paper reserves" have led to underfinancing of some state funds.

The volume of benefits that are "ineffectively charged" will be reduced by either a higher tax base or higher tax rate, both of which will permit more effective operation of experience rating. There will always be some "ineffectively" charged benefits because there are practical limits to how high maximum tax rates can be pushed. To this will be added any "noncharged" benefits resulting from noncharging provisions in the state law. To finance these "socialized costs" several states have a supplementary tax, a balancing tax, a contribution to a solvency account, or some similar surtax for financing ineffectively charged and noncharged benefits. West Virginia does not credit a portion of each employer's tax to his account, from 0.3 to 0.7 percent depending on the condition of the fund. Another method is to array all employers so that the rates they pay will produce adequate income to finance the "socialized costs." In the absence of any of these measures, employers at minimum rates will be financing the socialized costs. If the minimum rate is zero, the socialized costs go unfinanced and deplete the state fund as a whole. Definite provisions should therefore be made in every state law for all employers to share in "socialized costs." While we are not competent to judge what is the best method, it would seem best to integrate the financing of "socialized costs" into the experience rating system, rather than imposing a special tax to finance them.

Minimum and Maximum Tax Rates

Seventeen states provide for zero rates and 14 for minimum rates of 0.1 percent in their most favorable tax schedules as of January 1, 1965. In such states, employers at these rates are escaping or almost entirely escaping the "socialized costs" of benefits unless some sort of surtax finances such costs.

As it was introduced in 1935, the Social Security Bill provided for a minimum contribution of 1 percent, but this was dropped by Congress from the bill.

The Advisory Committee on Social Security to the Senate Committee on Finance in 1948 recommended a minimum contribution rate of 0.6 percent for both employers and employees. In its report, the Council said,

The present arrangement permits the States to compete in establishing low contribution rates from employers and therefore discourages the adoption of adequate benefit provisions, since proposals to provide more nearly adequate benefits in a given State are weighed against the effect of increased contribution rates on the competitive position of employers in that State. . . . The Council's proposed minimum contribution rate is a return to the principle of assuring relative equality among employers in the various States. It will remove an important barrier to the liberalization of benefits by requiring that all covered employers and employees throughout the Nation pay a minimum rate.[51]

A minimum contribution rate by itself, however, cannot assure an adequate program of benefits. Nor will it assure adequate financing of benefits. Adequate financing depends on an adequate tax structure, which includes a reasonably high taxable wage base, and minimum and maximum rates which permit the effective operation of experience rating.

The minimum contribution rate should be varied upward and downward along with other rates in the various tax schedules in the state law so that the most stable employers will share in any necessary general increase in taxes. The minimum should also be large enough—we would recommend 1 percent—so that employers at the minimum will bear their share of the social obligation to meet some of the benefit costs of employers who, because of the nature of their business, cannot stabilize their employment.[52] Some states accomplish this through some form of surtax applicable to all employers.

Maximum Tax Rate. Twenty-five of the 40 states with experience rating had maximum benefit rates above 2.7 percent in 1937, varying from 3.6 to 4.0 percent. This fell short of the original expectation that all states under experience rating would provide rates both above and below the "standard" rate of 2.7 percent so as to achieve an average rate of approxi-

[51] *Recommendations for Social Security Legislation,* Reports of the Advisory Council on Social Security to the Senate Committee on Finance (Washington, D.C.: 1949), p. 167.

[52] See Marion B. Folsom, "Where We Stand in Unemployment Insurance," *Proceedings of the 28th Annual Meeting of the Interstate Conference of Employment Security Agencies,* October 7, 1964, p. 62, in which he discusses a similar, but not identical proposal.

mately 2.7 percent.[53] Until recent years, there was a tendency for states to repeal rates in excess of 2.7 percent. Recently a number of states have enacted higher rates, the number totaling 31 as of January 1, 1964.

The question of having rates above 2.7 percent has become entangled with the question of increasing the taxable wage base. The relative merits of raising taxes by increases in the base or by increases in rates will be discussed in the following chapter. Whether or not the taxable wage base is increased, it is desirable to have tax rates in excess of 2.7 percent for high-cost employers. There are practical limitations, however, to the extent that employers with high rates of unemployment can absorb the full cost of the benefits paid to their laid-off employees because of the interstate competitive factor, unless there is a general increase in maximum tax rates in all states.

The trend toward higher maximum tax rates is sound and desirable within limits. If experience rating is to be practiced, it should work both ways, raising tax rates for employers with higher-than-average unemployment, as well as lowering rates for those with below-average unemployment. However, there should be limits at both ends of the scale. Employers fortunate enough to have steady employment should bear part of the cost of the program and other employers unfortunate enough to be in unstable industries should not have to bear all the costs of unemployment caused by the economy as a whole.

Federal Experience Rating Standards

If a state wishes to lower taxes because of excess reserves, it has no way to do so under the present "additional tax credit" provisions of the Federal Unemployment Tax Act, except through an experience rating system. This is because the federal provisions permit credits for reduced taxes only if such reductions are based on the *individual* employer's "experience with unemployment." Reductions cannot be made uniformly for all employers. Consequently, several states that objected to experience rating in principle had to adopt an experience rating plan after World War II in order to pare down excess reserves.

It has therefore been suggested that the present standards for experience rating in the federal act be repealed and any type of experience rating or uniform reduction in the tax rate for all employers in the state be permitted. This would be in keeping with the philosophy of the present federal legislation that states should be allowed maximum freedom for experimentation in their state laws.

Such a change would also be desirable for states that prefer to keep experience rating, but in a form not permitted by present federal standards. At present, the standards in the federal act for individual employer reserves are no longer used, since those states that started out with such systems have pooled their funds and have individual employer reserves only as

[53] Ewan Clague, "The Economics of Unemployment Compensation," *Yale Law Journal*, Vol. 55, No. 1 (December, 1945), p. 59.

bookkeeping accounts for rate making purposes. The guaranteed employment standards have never been used. As a result, only the standard for a pooled fund is used by the states. This standard is simply that the experience rate be based on the employer's "experience with respect to unemployment risk during not less than the three years[54] immediately preceding the computation date" for setting employer's rates.[55] The determination as to whether all the elaborate experience rating systems meet this seemingly simple requirement has consumed much time and effort and has resulted in many disagreements between the federal and state agencies. The disagreements often arise over some highly technical question.

The federal requirement also prevents experimentation with new methods of rate making that might be highly desirable. For example, one state was prevented from adopting a plan of tax rebates that had much merit in it.

Both federal and state personnel would heave a sight of relief if this federal requirement for reductions in rates was wiped off the statute books. However, employer representatives have opposed any attempt to remove the federal additional credit requirements. When it has been pointed out to them that they were inconsistent in supporting this standard and in opposing federal benefit standards, they have been frank to admit that, while they are being inconsistent, they wish to preserve the federal requirements as a safeguard against the abandonment of experience rating of any state. But if experience rating cannot stand on its own feet and continue to exist on its merits, states should be free to abandon it.

SUMMARY AND CONCLUSIONS

Experience rating of employer unemployment taxes as it has developed in the states, has had a major influence on their unemployment insurance programs. Paradoxically, it has had only limited influence in stimulating the stabilization of employment, the primary reason for its introduction into the program. The second objective of experience rating, the allocation of the costs of the program on the basis of the risk of unemployment, has been more nearly achieved since unstable industries have borne a greater share of the cost of benefits than stable industries. Experience rating, however, has hampered any shifting of the cost on to the consumer, a result which many originally anticipated. In addition a disproportionate share of the cost of the program has been borne by new employers who have not yet qualified for experience rating. A third objective of experience rating, employer participation in the program, has received increasing attention. This has taken both the form of "policing" the system against unwarranted payment of benefits and of employer influence on legislation. "Policing" the system has sometimes been overzealous, but no doubt has kept down abuse of the system. The savings in benefits, however, have been small compared to the large amounts in taxes that employers have saved through

[54] Except for new employers.
[55] The Administration bill (H.R. 8282) provides for repeal of this standard.

experience rating. Employer influence on legislation has been stimulated by experience rating, and has usually been in the form of opposition to liberalizations in benefits and support of restrictive disqualification provisions. At times, employers have joined with labor in proposing benefit increases. However, this has often been in return for labor's agreements to tax reductions. Pressures to keep taxes low have resulted in underfinancing in some states.

There is a wide variation in tax rates under experience rating, both between states and within the same industry in different states. This is due not only to differences in economic conditions and benefit provisions, but also to differences in experience rating formulas in the various states. The effect of this, which places employers in a state with high rates at a disadvantage in interstate competition, is debatable. When testifying before Congress, employer representatives usually minimize the effect of unemployment insurance costs on employer's decisions to move in or out of a state. In state legislatures, employer representatives often stress the bad effects on interstate competition of liberalizations in the program. The effect of the relative liberality of a state law on the "business climate" seems to be more important than the actual costs of the law.

How can experience rating provisions be improved so as to strengthen the financing of the program? Studies of whether or not experience rating has resulting in countercyclical financing are inconclusive. Several methods of countercyclical financing have been proposed, but only one method has been tried (by Wisconsin) and it has been abandoned. The most hope seems to lie in neutralizing the cyclical effect of experience rating by long-range financial planning that is designed to minimize tax fluctuations.

The "noncharging" to any employer of certain types of benefit payments, such as benefit payments after a temporary disqualification from benefits, is a financial problem in some states. Also, in some states there is under-financing of the program because of "ineffective charging" of benefits, that is, no charging of benefits to an employer's account because the benefits to his former employees exceed the taxes he has paid. The remedy for this is to charge all employers uniformly with these "socialized costs." Several methods are possible, one being to impose a uniform supplementary tax on all employers. It would be preferable to integrate such costs into experience rating.

Many states have gone too far in the reduction of rates at the minimum, some to the extent of providing for "zero rates." Preferably, minimum contribution rates should not fall below 1 percent. At least, employers at the minimum should meet their share of the social obligation to pay that part of the cost of the program that cannot or should not be charged to any employer. Also some states should provide for higher maximum rates, although this also can be carried too far.

The present experience rating standards in the federal act should be repealed so that a state can have any type of experience rating it desires, or none at all if it prefers uniform tax rates on all employers.

Chapter 18

Increase the Tax Base
or Tax Rates?

The unemployment insurance system is in serious need of strengthening its financial condition to meet benefit costs, as has already been discussed.[1] If the upward trend in administrative expenditures continues, there will also have to be an increase in either the federal tax base or tax rate to yield enough income to meet these costs.

The need for increased tax income to finance both increased benefit and administrative costs has intensified a decade-old debate as to whether tax increases should be made through an increase in the taxable wage base or increases in tax rates for employers who have not been paying as much in taxes as has been paid to their former employees in benefits.

Since 1939, the federal unemployment tax has been imposed on only the first $3,000 of each worker's annual earnings. This tax base has remained unchanged despite a fourfold increase in workers' earnings. Spokesmen for high-wage, stable employers have steadfastly opposed increases in the tax base, especially on a federal basis, contending that it would be more equitable to raise any additional revenue needed for unemployment benefits by increases in the tax rates on unstable employers who, they contend, are also low-wage employers. The $3,000 limitation on the tax base has been an issue ever since wages increased substantially after World War II, but it has become a more important issue as the need for increased tax income has grown in recent years. The opposition to an increase in the *federal* tax base has been stronger than opposition to increases in state taxable wage bases. The opponents of a federal increase argue that each state should be left free to decide whether to increase its tax base, its tax rates, or both.

Some states have already increased their taxable wage base, most of them by modest amounts. An increasing number of states are also raising their tax rates, especially for employers who have not been "paying their

[1] See Chapter 17.

way." It is obvious, however, that much more needs to be done if the states are all to get in sound financial shape. Decisions will also have to be made in the immediate future as to whether the needs for increased federal unemployment tax income will be met through an increase in the federal taxable wage base of $3,000, an increase in the federal tax rate of 3.1 percent, or both.

The spokesmen for employer groups have generally opposed an increase in the tax base and have advocated increases in tax rates, if additional income is necessary, with the claim that increased tax rates would be more equitable. The effects of a tax base increase on employers with stable or unstable employment must therefore be determined. But while these effects should receive consideration, there are other important considerations that must also be taken into account. These include: whether present benefit levels justify an increase in the tax base, whether adequate benefit financing requires a broader tax base, and whether an increase in the tax base or an increase in the tax rate would more equitably allocate needed increases in the federal unemployment tax "take." Before considering these questions, a review of the history of the taxable wage base for the federal unemployment tax will be useful.

HISTORY OF THE TAXABLE WAGE BASE

Federal Action

Total annual wages were taxed under the federal unemployment tax when it was originally enacted in 1935. No one questioned the taxation of total wages, which was in keeping with the principle of imposing a tax that would apply uniformly throughout the country so that no state would have an advantage over another. On the other hand, since only up to $3,000 in annual earnings was used to determine a worker's federal old-age insurance benefit, the federal tax on employers and workers to finance old-age benefits was imposed only on the first $3,000 of the worker's annual earnings. Thus, there was a direct relationship between the taxes paid by the employer and worker and the monthly amount paid out in old-age benefits.

In unemployment insurance, however, there has never been a *quid pro quo* between the amount of annual wages on which taxes were paid and the amount of wages used to determine benefits. In the beginning, weekly unemployment benefits were based on the worker's full-time weekly wages without any relation to annual earnings. The taxation of total wages was therefore more logical than any other base. There is no indication that even this much reasoning entered into the differentiation between the taxable wage base for old-age insurance and for unemployment insurance. Congressional committee reports merely stated these two different bases without any explanation for their difference.

In 1939, the Social Security Board recommended that federal taxes for old-age insurance and unemployment insurance be combined so that the employer would have to make only one tax return to the federal government. More specifically, it recommended: "that the Federal payroll tax in connection with unemployment compensation be limited to the first $3,000 of annual wages, if that maximum is retained in the old-age insurance tax provisions. Though the Board recognizes that such a limitation would reduce revenue somewhat, it believes that this disadvantage would be counterbalanced by the advantages to be derived from making the Federal tax provisions identical for both programs."[2]

Congress did not combine the two federal taxes, but it did limit the tax base for the federal unemployment tax to $3,000. In subsequent years, however, Congress did not keep the tax base identical for the two programs, even though this was the expectation of the Social Security Board as implied in the phrase in its recommendation "If that maximum is retained in

Table 18–1

Ratio of Taxable Wages to Total Wages under
Federal Unemployment Tax, 1938–63

Year	Ratio (in Percent) of Taxable Wages to Total Wages
1938	98.0
1939	97.7
1940	92.8
1941	91.8
1942	90.7
1943	89.3
1944	87.7
1945	87.8
1946	86.8
1947	84.3
1948	81.7
1949	81.3
1950	79.1
1951	76.0
1952	74.1
1953	71.6
1954	70.4
1955	68.3
1956	66.8
1957	65.0
1958	63.2
1959	61.7
1960	61.1
1961	60.0
1962	59.0
1963	58.1

Source: United States Department of Labor, Bureau of Employment Security.

[2] Proposed Changes in the Social Security Act, A Report of the Social Security Board to the President and to the Congress of the United States (Washington, D.C.: U.S. Government Printing Office, January, 1939), p. 18.

the old-age insurance tax provisions." Congress increased the federal tax base for the OASDI program four times, until it reached $6,600 in 1966. The increases corresponded to the maximum wages used for successive increases in benefits, and such increases were recognized as necessary to keep pace, to some extent, with rising wages.

This was not done for unemployment insurance. At the time the $3,000 limitation was placed on the taxable annual earnings of workers covered by unemployment insurance, about 98 percent of total earnings were still taxable; as wages increased, however, a smaller and smaller proportion were taxable. By the end of 1963, the proportion of total covered wages that was taxed under the $3,000 limitation had fallen to 58.1 percent of total wages (see Table 18–1). In that year, average annual earnings in covered employment were $5,308.

The increasing spread between taxable and total wages has been recognized for some years. It was called to the attention of the Federal Advisory Council on Employment Security in the early 1950's. The federal Council, however, in 1953, recommended against an increase in the taxable wage base,[3] stating that they saw no need for it. The Council reviewed the problem again in 1956, and again agreed that federal action to raise the tax base was unnecessary. The question was once more considered in 1958, this time because the federal "take" of 0.3 percent on a $3,000 wage base threatened to be inadequate to meet the administrative costs of the program. Viewing the problem solely from the standpoint of raising federal funds for administration, the majority of the Council in 1958 recommended an increase in the tax base to $3,600. The employer members of the Council, as they had done consistently, opposed any increase.[4]

In 1959 the Eisenhower Administration recommended that the taxable wage base in the Federal Unemployment Tax Act be increased to $4,200. Under Secretary of Labor James T. O'Connell testified before the House Committee on Ways and Means that this was necessary both for administrative and benefit financing.[5] Representatives of the Interstate Conference of Employment Security Agencies made a counterproposal that the federal tax *rate* be increased by 0.1 percent to raise needed federal revenue for administrative expenses and the federal loan fund. They argued that some states did not need a tax increase and those that did should be free to increase either their tax bases or tax rates.[6] Their views prevailed and Congress increased the federal tax to 3.1 percent on the first $3,000 of earnings, leaving the maximum credit an employer could receive for contributions under state laws at 2.7 percent.

[3] Report of Benefit Financing Committee to Federal Advisory Council, October 26, 1953.

[4] For the 1956 and 1958 reports, see *Unemployment Compensation,* Hearings before the Committee on Ways and Means, House of Representatives, 86th Cong., 1st sess. (Washington, D.C.: U.S. Government Printing Office, 1959), pp. 26–41.

[5] *Ibid.,* pp. 15 ff.

[6] *Ibid.,* pp. 197 ff.

Table 18–2

Unemployment Insurance Taxable Wage Base and Tax Rate Provisions under State Laws and Rates in Effect as of June 5, 1964*

State	Taxable Wage Base ($3,000 Except as Shown)	Employer Tax Rates (% of Taxable Wages) Statutory Limits Maximum	1964 Rates† Maximum
Alabama		3.6	3.6
Alaska	$7,200 (1/1/60)	4.0	4.0
Arizona	3,600 (1/1/65)	2.7	2.7
Arkansas		4.0	3.3
California	3,800 (1/1/62)	3.5	3.5
Delaware	3,600 (1/1/55)	4.5	4.0
Florida		4.5	3.5
Georgia		4.2	4.2
Hawaii	90% stat av. ann. wage (1/1/65)	3.0	3.0
Idaho		5.1	4.5
Illinois		4.0	4.0
Kentucky		4.2	4.0
Maryland		4.2	4.2
Massachusetts	$3,600 (1/1/62)	4.1	3.9
Michigan	3,600 (4/1/63)	6.6	4.6
Minnesota		3.0	3.0
Mississippi		2.7	3.2
Missouri		5.0	4.5
Nevada	3,600 (1/1/54)	2.7	2.7
New Hampshire		4.0	4.0
New Jersey		4.2	3.9
New Mexico		3.6	3.0
New York		4.2	3.8
North Carolina		3.7	3.7
North Dakota		7.0	7.0
Ohio		4.7	4.7
Oregon	3,800 (1/1/60)	2.7	2.7
Pennsylvania	3,600 (1/1/64)	4.0	4.0
Rhode Island	3,600 (1/1/56)	3.3	2.7
South Carolina		4.1	4.1
South Dakota		4.1	3.6
Tennessee	3,300 (1/1/63)	4.0	4.0
Texas		7.2	2.7
Utah	4,200 (1/1/64)	2.7	2.7
Vermont	3,600 (1/1/64)	4.5	3.5
Washington		2.7	2.7
West Virginia	3,600 (1/1/62)	2.7	2.7
Wisconsin		4.4	4.0
Wyoming		3.2	3.2

* States with tax base of $3,000 and maximum tax rate of 2.7 percent of taxable wages are not shown.

† Represents maximum rates assigned to employers during calendar year 1964. In states where tax schedule was changed during 1964 the figures shown represent the highest rates assigned under either schedule.

Source: United States Department of Labor, Bureau of Employment Security, June 8, 1964.

The Kennedy Administration made another attempt to increase the federal tax base to $ 4,800 in 1961 and to $5,200 in 1963,[7] but the bills never got to the hearing stage. President Johnson submitted a revised bill to Congress in 1965 providing for an increase in the annual earnings base to $5,600, effective in 1967, and to $6,600, effective in 1971.[8]

State Action

For a long time, the states left the taxable wage base at $3,000. In recent years, more and more states have increased their taxable wage bases. The states were slow to take such action because of the fear of handicapping their employers in interstate competition. Nevada was the first to initiate a modest increase to $3,600, effective in 1954. By 1960, California, Delaware, Oregon,[9] and Rhode Island had taken similar action. Because of its desperate financial situation and its high wage rates, Alaska increased its base first to $4,200 and then to $7,200. As states faced the need of higher revenue following the recession of 1961, taxable wage bases were increased at an accelerated rate. As of January 1, 1966, 18 states had passed legislation raising their wage bases, 11 to $3,600. Increases in most of the other states were from $3,800 to $4,800. Effective January 1, 1966, Hawaii had enacted a flexible taxable wage base equal to 90 percent of its average annual wage. In 1966, this amounted to $4,300.

At the beginning of the program 27 states enacted tax rates above the 2.7 percent of taxable wages for which a state could receive credit against the federal tax. By 1955, only ten states provided for higher schedules. After 1958, an increasing number of states have been raising their maximum rates above 2.7 percent or if they already had higher rates than 2.7 percent, they have been raising them further. As of January 1, 1966, a total of 35 states had provisions for maximum rates above 2.7 percent. Many of these increases go into effect only when the state has moved up to higher schedules because of depletion of reserves. The maximum rates range from 3.0 percent in two states to a possible maximum of 7.2 percent in another.

Fourteen states had both tax bases above $3,000 and tax rates above 2.7 percent.

EFFECTS OF A TAX BASE INCREASE ON EMPLOYER TAXES

The Equity Argument

Opposition to increasing the taxable wage base has been largely based on arguments that it would result in inequities in taxation. The typical

[7] H.R. 7640, 87th Cong., 1st sess.; H.R. 6339, 88th Cong., 1st sess.
[8] H.R. 8282, 89th Cong., 1st sess.
[9] Oregon in addition provided for a further increase to $3,800 if its reserves fell below 6 percent of taxable wages.

argument has run as follows: stable employers usually pay higher wages than unstable employers. If the taxable wage base is increased, the high-wage, stable employer would therefore have a larger tax increase than the low-wage unstable employer. This would be inequitable, since unstable employers generally do not pay enough in taxes to finance the benefits paid to their former employees. Therefore, this argument concludes, if more tax income is needed, it should be raised by increasing the unstable low-wage employers' tax rates.

An opposing point of view argues that unstable employers are not necessarily low-wage employers. The data given in Table 18–3 substantiate this. In this table, the 26 major industrial groups covered by unemployment insurance are arranged from the industry with the lowest average tax rate to the one with the highest average tax rate. The right hand column gives

Table 18–3

Average Tax Rate as Percent of Taxable Wages, and Taxable Wages as a Percent of Total Wages, by Major Industrial Groups, 1962

Industry Group	Average Tax Rate as Percent of Taxable Wages	Taxable Wages as Percent of Total Wages
All industry groups	2.36	58.5
Petroleum refining and related products	1.65	44.4
Transportation, communication, and utilities	1.92	54.1
Finance, insurance, and real estate	1.92	58.7
Printing, publishing, and allied industries	1.93	52.2
Chemicals and allied products	1.93	47.2
Paper and allied products	1.97	53.3
Mining	1.99	54.4
Textile mill products	2.03	74.4
Wholesale and retail trade	2.12	63.1
Food and kindred products	2.15	59.2
Tobacco manufactures	2.16	67.5
Service industries	2.38	66.0
Furniture and fixtures	2.38	67.1
Lumber and wood products	2.43	73.2
Rubber and miscellaneous plastic products	2.46	56.4
Machinery, except electrical	2.54	50.3
Ordnance and accessories	2.56	47.9
Stone, clay, and glass products	2.56	57.7
Professional, scientific, and controlling instruments ...	2.60	51.2
Fabricated metal products	2.68	53.8
Electrical machinery	2.69	54.0
Leather and leather products	2.81	75.8
Primary metal industries	2.85	47.6
Construction	2.93	64.9
Apparel and other finished products	3.08	76.7
Transportation equipment	3.10	51.9

Source: United States Department of Labor, Bureau of Employment Security, *Unemployment Insurance Tax Rates by Industry, 1962*, BES No. U–221 (March, 1964).

the percentages of total wages in each industry group that is taxed under unemployment insurance. The lower the percentage taxed, the higher the wages are in the industry.

Nine of the 15 industry groups whose tax rates were above average had a smaller ratio of taxable to total wages than the average for all industries, in other words, were high-wage industries.[10]

Annual earnings have risen above $3,000 among high-cost industries in individual states as well as on a national basis. For example, Richard A. Lester calculated that in the ten New Jersey industries with the highest benefit costs, average wages ranged from 21.8 to 45.0 percent above $3,000 in 1960.[11]

These statistics seem to explode the argument that high-cost industries are low-wage industries and so would not be affected by an increase in the taxable wage base. Instead, the high-cost industries would generally pay more taxes under a wage base increase. Moreover, since most of the high-cost industries also pay high annual wages, an increase in the wage base would increase the possibility of their "paying their way" in the program.

Analysis on an industry basis, however, is of limited value because there are high-cost and low-cost employers *within* industries. In fact, in most industries some employers are paying their way or more than paying their way and other employers are not. A more realistic way to analyze the effect of an increase in the taxable wage base is to analyze the impact on employers who have paid more and those who have paid less in taxes than has been paid in benefits to their employers. This can be best done in states that use the reserve-ratio method of experience rating, since their employers who have paid more in taxes than has been paid out in benefits have "positive accounts," and those who have paid less in taxes than have been paid out in benefits that are chargeable to them have "negative accounts."

New York, which uses the reserve-ratio method, made a study of a sample of employer accounts for the calendar year 1961.[12]

Based on the New York study, Table 18–4 shows the increase in basic[13] contributions for major industrial groups that would result from the initial

[10] Benefit cost rates in each industry are not available. However, average tax rates should approximate average benefit costs. Although the industries with highest costs may have tax rates somewhat lower than costs, the comparison given here is still valid in relative terms.

[11] Richard A. Lester, *The Economics of Unemployment Compensation* (Princeton: Industrial Relations Section, Princeton University, 1962), p. 80, table 13.

[12] New York State Department of Labor, Division of Employment, *A Study of the Tax Base Under the New York State Unemployment Insurance Law* (Albany, N.Y., June, 1964).

[13] New York has a "subsidiary tax," varying from 0.2 to 1.0 percent of taxable payrolls depending on the size of the state unemployment fund, which applies equally to all employers. Since most states do not have such a supplementary tax, its exclusion from the table is fortunate in that it makes the result of its study more applicable to other states with a reserve-account formula for experience rating.

Table 18–4
Increase in Basic Contributions by Industry, Initial Impact of $4,800 Tax Base, New York, 1961

Industry	Amount of Increase (in Millions)			Percent Increase		
	All Firms	Positive Accounts	Negative Accounts	All Firms	Positive Accounts	Negative Accounts
All industries $103.8		$79.1	$24.7	32.8	35.8	25.7
Manufacturing	47.4	34.8	12.6	35.8	41.2	26.2
Metals and machinery	23.6	17.3	6.3	44.4	46.3	39.8
Apparel	5.1	2.1	3.0	21.2	25.4	19.0
Other manufacturing	18.7	15.4	3.3	33.8	39.6	20.1
Nonmanufacturing	56.4	44.3	12.1	30.7	32.6	25.2
Contract construction	8.1	2.6	5.6	29.5	31.8	28.6
Transportation and public utilities	9.3	7.8	1.5	38.4	41.3	28.2
Wholesale and retail trade ..	20.2	17.6	2.6	29.5	31.1	22.2
Finance, insurance, and real estate	7.4	7.0	0.4	32.9	33.6	23.0
Services and miscellaneous	11.4	9.3	2.0	27.5	29.6	20.9

* Excludes subsidiary tax. Detail may not add to totals because of rounding.
Source: New York State Department of Labor, Division of Employment, *A Study of the Tax Base Under the New York State Unemployment Insurance Law*, June, 1964, table 14.

impact of an increase from a $3,000 to a $4,800 tax base. It shows that both the dollar and percentage increases in taxes would initially be greater for "positive accounts" than for "negative accounts."

It must be emphasized that Table 18–4 gives the *initial* impact, which is due to the increased dollars that must be credited to each employer's account for the account to reach a percentage of taxable payroll high enough to result in a lower tax rate for the employer. The New York study spells out how it will take about three years for the readjustment to reach the point where the positive account employer, if his unemployment rate has not been changed, will not be paying any more tax dollars than before. But the report is careful to state the following in its concluding paragraph:

The foregoing analysis is based on the assumption *that the tax schedule would not* be adjusted to the new tax base. This assumption would be expected to apply in a situation where the Unemployment Insurance Fund was deemed to be in immediate need of more revenue. However, if raising the tax base were achieved in a period of relatively low need for additional taxes, an appropriate tax rate conversion formula could be written into the Law. The Size-of-Fund Index determinant and employer's account percentage table could be modified to yield whatever amount of contributions was required to finance the program. If desired, the modification could be such that most categories of employers would pay the same amount in contributions on the higher tax base as at present.[14]

In his introduction to the report, Mr. Alfred L. Green, Executive Director of the New York Division of Employment, goes on to point out: "The

[14] *A Study of the Tax Base*, etc., *op. cit.*, p. 11.

rates for most positive account employers would, of course, adjust themselves to such employers' benefit cost experience, while negative account employers would contribute more in proportion to the benefits charged to their accounts, thereby lessening the need for the imposition of subsidiary contributions."

The relative effects over a 15-year period of a taxable wage base increase and a tax rate increase have been calculated by Eugene C. McKean of the W. E. Upjohn Institute.[15] Calculations were made for low-wage and high-wage "deficit" employers who were paying less in unemployment taxes than the unemployment benefits chargeable to their experience rating accounts, for "self-supporting" employers whose tax payments equaled benefit charges, and for "no-unemployment" employers who had no benefit charges. The calculations were based on a hypothetical ABC Corporation operating under the Michigan law prior to its 1963 revision. At that time, Michigan operated on a $3,000 base. The state's maximum rate schedule, in which the maximum rate was 4.0 percent and the minimum rate was 0.5 percent, was assumed to be in effect.

For a low-wage "deficit" employer, an increase in the maximum tax rate to 6.4 percent (the maximum rate provided under Michigan's 1963 amendments) on the $3,000 base would have produced more taxes than an increase in the taxable wage base to $4,800 with no change in tax rates. However, for a high-wage "deficit" employer, such an increase in the tax base or tax rate would have worked out about equally well. After the initial operative period, during which he would build up his reserves to required levels, the "self-supporting" employer, whether high-wage or low-wage, would be paying about the same amount in annual taxes under a $4,800 tax base as under a $3,000 base. Total taxes paid during the entire 15-year period would be moderately higher under the $4,800 base. In the case of the "no-unemployment" firm, both the high-wage and the low-wage employer would have paid considerably more taxes during the 15-year period on the $4,800 base than on the $3,000 base. However, additional taxes paid by the high-wage employer would have been more than double those paid by the low-wage employer. Once the no-unemployment employer was subject to the minimum tax rate, however, the tax rate would be much more important than the tax base in determining the firm's annual tax load.[16]

Actually, it is beside the point to determine the relative merits of an increase in the tax base or tax rates, on the basis of the relative increase in taxes on different types of employers. The whole argument is based on the assumption that there is some rationale for a $3,000 base. There was a rationale for moving from a tax base of total wages to $3,000 in 1939, administrative convenience with only a small loss in tax income. Such a rationale has completely disappeared now that taxable wages are less than

[15] Eugene C. McKean, *The Taxable Wage Base in Unemployment Insurance Financing* (Kalamazoo, Mich.: W. E. Upjohn Institute for Employment Research, 1965).
[16] *Ibid.*, pp. 51–53.

60 percent of total wages. An equity analysis should be based entirely on whether, *once reserve accounts or reserve requirements are adjusted to the increased wage base*, high-cost employers will be bearing a larger or smaller share of the total benefit load than before the increase took effect.

Implicit in the whole equity argument is the assumption that "equitable treatment" means apportioning benefit costs to individual employers on the basis of all the unemployment for which they are "responsible." But it has already been pointed out that the kinds of unemployment that are within the control of the individual employer, those for which he is responsible, are quite limited. Testing tax policy solely on the basis of equity, therefore, is using a shaky foundation. As Professor Lester has stated:

The equity notion of requiring employers to pay unemployment taxes according to their individual responsibility for unemployment, though it has a superficial plausibility, raises more questions than it settles. Responsibility for unemployment is a profound and involved subject. . . . Its very complexity, nevertheless, raises serious doubts concerning the possibility and practicality of enforcing tax payments according to a theory of individual responsibility. Who knows the extent to which particular unemployment is due to employer policies, to consumer buying patterns, to technological change and other innovations, to policies of employees and their unions, or to various exogenous factors, ranging from crop failures to shifts in the currents of international trade? Who is responsible for a declining industry, and over what time-span does that responsibility extend? As such questions indicate equity considerations involving un-employment are highly complicated in a private enterprise economy.[17]

The Effective Tax Rate

The true impact of the unemployment tax on an employer can be best measured in terms of his total wage bill. This effect can be seen most clearly in connection with the federal unemployment tax since it is not complicated by experience rating. The present amount that employers pay under the federal unemployment tax is equal to 0.4 percent of taxable wages. An employer who pays each of his employees $3,000 a year has an effective tax rate of 0.4 percent, since his taxable payroll equals his total payroll. But suppose an employer pays each of his employees $6,000 a year? He pays exactly the same amount to the federal government as the other employer, 0.4 percent of $3,000, for each employee. But this represents an *effective* tax rate of only 0.2 percent of total payroll. Thus, any taxable wage base that is less than total wages bears more heavily on the employer paying lower wages.

With respect to state unemployment taxes, the effective tax rate argument is particularly significant for "deficit" employers; that is, employers whose benefit charges are more than the taxes they have paid to the state fund.

A high-wage deficit employer will have a lower effective tax rate than

17 Lester, *op. cit.*, pp. 81–82.

a low-wage deficit employer. Take, for example, a state that still has a $3,000 tax base. In it, deficit Employer A employs his workers at uniform annual wages of $3,000 each, and deficit Employer B employs his workers at uniform annual wages of $6,000 each. Employer A and Employer B are both paying the state's maximum tax rate of 4.0 percent. Employer A has an effective tax rate of 4 percent, but Employer B has an effective tax rate of only 2 percent. If the tax base were raised to $4,500, Employer A would still have an effective tax rate of 4 percent, but Employer B's effective tax rate would be increased from 2 to 3 percent. Both would have the same effective tax rate only if the tax base were raised to $6,000.

This illustration is oversimplified since it does not take into account that many $6,000 employees would earn much less because of unemployment, if they were working for a "deficit" employer with a 4 percent tax rate. Also, the high-wage employer's tax rate would be lowered to the extent that he has labor turnover. To take an extreme example, if Employer B, although paying wages at an annual rate of $6,000 has two employees on every job, each for six months, he would pay $3,000 to each and have an effective tax rate of 4 percent.

Effect on New Employers

An increase in the tax base can have different effects on new and older employers. Initially, an increase in the tax base will affect new and older employers alike, but, as has been said, within a few years state experience rating schedules can be adjusted so that older employers will pay the same amount in taxes as they did before the change. But after such a readjustment, new employers must bear the full brunt of an increase in the tax base until they get an experience rating. On the other hand, if a state raises its tax rates above 2.7 percent, the increases are applied only to "older" employers with high benefit costs.[18] New employers would not be affected by such an increase at all. This should have weight in any consideration of a change in the state unemployment tax base, although it should not be the decisive factor. The higher taxes on new employers may be justified because of the high mortality of new employers during their first few years of operations and the resulting unemployment of their employees. Of course, if the new employer has stable employment and is in a state with a reserve ratio type of experience rating, the reduced tax payments that he may eventually make can offset the higher payments he made before he got an experience rating.

To the extent that new employers would be at a disadvantage, the time that they are disadvantaged could be reduced by all states experience rating new employers after a year, as is permitted under the 1954 amendments to the federal unemployment tax act.[19]

[18] Unless a general increase in all rates to levels about 2.7 perecent is necessary to finance the state's benefit program.

[19] Some states have reduced the period before new employers can get an experience rating but few states have reduced the period to the permitted minimum of one year.

The disadvantage could be removed entirely by permitting the states to retroactively "experience rate" the new employers who have had stable employment. This could be done through tax rebates or through tax credits against future taxes. A change in the federal legislation on requirements for experience rating would be necessary to enable the states to give such retroactive experience rating. (This might be a desirable amendment, whether or not there is a change in the federal tax base or rate.)

The foregoing analysis has been made with respect to the taxes that new employers pay under state laws. An increase in the federal taxable wage base would affect new and older employers equally, however, so far as the portion of the tax paid to the federal government is concerned, since the federal portion is not subject to experience rating.

Effect on Experience Rating

Advocates of an increased wage base contend that a low taxable wage base may narrow the range of rates under which experience rating can operate, thus lowering its effectiveness. The argument is that if the tax base is unrealistically low, and more revenue is needed, minimum rates must be raised when maximum rates reach a practical limit. By contrast, a broader tax base permits a wider range of rate variation between the minimum and maximum even when added yields are necessary. This can be put more concretely as follows: If a state needs more tax income and increases neither its tax base nor its minimum tax rates, it must resort to a higher tax schedule.[20] Thus a state may move from tax schedule A that varies rates from 0.1 to 2.7 percent to tax schedule B that varies rates from 0.9 to 2.7 percent, and eventually may have to move to a schedule in which there is little or no variation in rates. Even if the rate schedule is not changed, reserve requirements will force rate changes for individual employers so that the total effect is that nearly all employers will pay high rates. If, on the other hand, the taxable wage base is increased, more taxes flow into the fund under the lower tax schedules, so that it may be unnecessary to move to higher tax schedules where there is a narrower range of rates.

Alternatively, if the state increases its maximum rate above 2.7 percent, it can raise more money and, at the same time, increase the spread in experience rates. If it becomes necessary to go to a higher rate schedule, this may restore the range in rates to something like what it was originally. But there is a practical limit to how maximum rates can be pushed in an individual state. As costs go up, a state may have to go to a high enough tax schedule that the spread in rates is compressed.

Russell L. Hibbard of General Motors Corporation has maintained that

---

[20] Thirty-four states have more than one tax schedule. The schedule that is in effect any given time depends on the size of the state's reserve.

an increase in the taxable wage base would narrow rather than widen the range of experience rating:

This way of increasing fund revenue cannot restore the necessary scope of experience rating, because it tends to narrow further, rather than widen, the range between minimum and maximum tax rates. The employer whose employees receive pay for 52 weeks per year will tend to have a greater percentage increase in his taxable payroll as a result of an increase in the wage base ceiling than an employer whose employees average substantially fewer weeks per year. Consequently, increasing the tax base results in a bigger percentage increase in tax liability for stable employers paying the minimum rate than for unstable employers paying the maximum rate.[21]

Mr. Hibbard's argument applies only when a state fund is in good condition, so that a low tax schedule is in effect. It might be observed, also, that "stable employers paying the minimum rate" were subject to a tax rate of zero or 0.1 percent under the most favorable schedule in 28 states as of January 1, 1966, and the minimum rate actually in effect in April–June, 1964, was less than 0.5 percent in 21 states.[22] A substantial tax base increase at such low rates would not narrow experience rating significantly.

Even if the fund is in good condition and the rate of unemployment remains constant, there will be a steadily increasing cost related to taxable payrolls because of the continuing rise in wage levels. As a result, there will be a steadily narrowing gap between the average contribution rate and the maximum rate. Unless the maximum rate is constantly increased, the distribution of employers at the various tax rates becomes more and more constricted as a larger and larger percentage become taxable at the higher rates.

Richard A. Lester has pointed out one other effect of a limited tax base on experience rating that is not usually recognized; namely, that under a $3,000 tax base the bulk of the unemployment taxes are paid in the first two quarters of each calendar year, since large numbers of workers earn $3,000 or more during this period. As he puts it: "The theories used to justify experience rating assume that each employer's tax burden is distributed evenly productwise. Heavy concentration of the tax liability on production in the first part of each calendar year undermines the structure of theoretical support for experience rating, leaving it in a state of intellectual distress."[23]

So far, the discussion has been confined to arguments from a tax or ex-

---

[21] Russell L. Hibbard, "As Industry Sees It" *Unemployment Insurance Review* (Washington, D.C.: BES, U.S. Department of Labor, January, February, 1964), p. 6. (From an address to National Tax Association, Milwaukee, Wisconsin, November 12, 1963.)

[22] *Unemployment Advisors, Inc.*, Research and Education Bulletin No. 58, March 13, 1964, p. 3.

[23] Lester, *op. cit.*, p. 75.

perience rating standpoint. There are other considerations, however, which also need to be thrown into the balance.

RELATION TO BENEFITS

In 1939, the federal OASI tax base was increased to $3,600. The Bureau of Employment Security was interested in the increased tax base because of the implied promise in 1939 that the tax base for unemployment and old-age insurance would be kept the same. At the time, practically no increases were being made in unemployment compensation weekly amounts and it was feared that no progress could be made until the taxable wage base was also increased.

But it was difficult to demonstrate any connection between the maximum wage base and maximum benefits. In many states there was no statutory relationship between the wages that were taxed and wages used for benefits. Even in the 14 states that were using only taxable wages as a basis for determining benefits, none needed to use as much as $3,000 under its formula. Also, although some states based benefits on annual earnings, no state was using all of the $3,000 that was being taxed to determine even maximum benefits.

The relationship between taxable wages and benefits has become closer as benefits have been increased in recent years. As benefit maximums have increased, a higher and higher amount of annual earnings has been required. Thus in West Virginia, which bases the benefit amount on annual earnings, only $1,250 in annual earnings was required in 1941 to qualify for the maximum weekly benefit of $15; as of January 1, 1965, $3,650 in annual earnings was necessary to qualify for the maximum of $35 a week. By 1965, the annual earnings required to receive the maximum weekly benefit amount in the eight states with annual wage formulas ranged from $2,900 to $4,000; five of the states required more than $3,000. It would certainly be logical for the states using more than $3,000 in wages in determining benefit amounts to tax at least the maximum annual earnings used. But two of the five states requiring annual earnings of over $3,000 for maximum benefits still have annual taxable wage bases of $3,000.

In the states using high-quarter wages or average weekly wages to determine the weekly benefit amount, there is no explicit relationship between annual earnings and weekly benefits. The states with variable duration of benefits, however, limit the total benefits payable (weekly benefit amount times duration) either specifically or practically by annual earnings in the base period. For example, in 1964, Indiana paid a maximum of $36 a week for a maximum of 26 weeks or potential total benefits of $936. But it limited total benefits to one fourth of base year earnings. Therefore, a worker had to earn at least four times $936 or $3,744 during his base year to qualify for the maximum total benefits. In a similar manner, 26 states, as of January 1, 1965, required more than $3,000 a year in annual earnings for a worker to receive the maximum potential benefits. The amounts required ranged up to $4,860 in Wisconsin.[24] It is again curious that only eight of these 26 states had taxable wage bases in excess of $3,000. Apparently, these states are paying little attention to the relationship of the amount of annual wages that they tax to the annual wages that they require to receive maximum benefits. More attention to the relationship of wages used for benefits and wages that are taxed would promote sounder financing of the program.

There were still one third of the states, as of January 1, 1966, that required less than $3,000 in earnings in order for a claimant to get the maximum amount and maximum duration of benefits.[25] For these states, one other argument remains for a higher wage base because of increased benefits. This argument derives from the fact that the maximum weekly benefit in practically every state is now based on earnings which would exceed $3,000 on an annual basis. Thus, if the maximum benefit is $30 and the benefit is equal to 50 percent of wages, the maximum is based on $60; in turn, $60 a week represents an annual wage of $3,120. All but two of the states and Puerto Rico have a maximum of $30 or more, eight states as of January 1, 1965, provided for basic maximum benefits (not counting dependents' benefits) of $50 a week or more. New York, for example, has a $50 maximum weekly benefit amount. As Mr. Green put it in his introduction to the New York study of the tax base previously referred to: "with a maximum benefit rate of $50 per week, individual earnings up to the rate of $5,200 per year are involved in the process of creating potential liabilities for the payment of unemployment benefits."

Finally, a worker might actually be unable to qualify for any benefits in some states with a $3,000 base because his earnings are too high. For example, in such states if a worker earns $3,000 in each of four calendar quarters, and the state law required *taxable* earnings in two calendar quarters in order to qualify for benefits, he would be able to use only $3,000 in the first calendar quarter, since that is all that is taxable, and so could not qualify for benefits.

In summary, the arguments for increasing the wage base because of the increases in the amount of wages on which benefits are based, while not conclusive, are becoming increasingly pertinent.

EFFECTS ON BENEFIT FINANCING

When the question of an increase in the tax base was debated in the 1950's, those who opposed an increase were able to argue that an increase

---

[24] Michigan, altogether not counted among these 26 states because its maximum benefit for a single person required maximum annual earnings of only $1,134.14, required maximum annual earnings of $4,088.28 for a claimant with four dependents to receive maximum benefits.

[25] These included the eight states that provide the same maximum potential duration of benefits to all claimants and determine the benefit amount on annual or quarterly wages.

was not necessary to finance benefits, since reserves and tax rates were adequate in most states. The situation was drastically different following the 1961 recession. Reserves were low in many states. Benefits costs had increased from an average of 1.26 percent of average taxable payrolls in the period 1951–54 to an average of 2.26 percent in the five-year period 1960–64. During the latter period, 23 states had average cost rates of more than 2 percent and six states had average cost rates in excess of 2.7 percent of taxable payrolls. As a result, tax income had to be drastically increased in many states to meet current costs as well as to rebuild depleted reserves. Average tax rates had been increased in many states by 1964, with 12 states having average tax rates of 2.7 percent or more in that year. The average tax rate for the United States as a whole was 2.2 percent. Yet 17 states still paid out more in benefits than they collected in taxes in 1964. All but one had average tax rates of less than 2.7 percent.

The explanation for the failure of so many states to adequately increase their tax yield can be partly blamed on the reluctance of some states to face up to their financial problems. It is also no doubt due to a reluctance to increase either their tax base above $3,000 or to increase their maximum tax rate above 2.7 percent.

The authors are not competent to estimate how high the taxable wage base would have to be raised, at different levels of insured unemployment, in order for a state to raise adequate funds to keep in a sound financial condition. Certainly there is plenty of room between present taxable wages and total wages to secure the needed income except in a state with as extremely high unemployment as Alaska. In the other states, including those who have increased their tax bases somewhat, state taxable wages ranged from 51 percent to 74 percent of total wages in 1965.

Nor are we competent to estimate how high tax rates would have to be pushed in some states with high rates of unemployment, if sole reliance were placed on increasing tax rates. Our guess is that, in a state with an insured unemployment rate of 5 percent or more, the states would have to impose rates so high that no legislature would enact them. Norman Barcus has estimated [26] that a national insured unemployment rate of 5 percent means a cost rate to total payroll of about 1.7 percent. In 1946, this would have required an average tax rate of 1.96 percent; by 1955 of 2.5 percent. By 1959, an insured unemployment rate of 5 percent would have required an average contribution rate in excess of 2.7 percent and by 1964 of 3 percent or more. This would have been the situation despite the fact that some states have increased their tax bases somewhat during this period. If Barcus' analysis is correct, 5 percent insured unemployment would have required maximum tax rates in excess of 4.5 percent in 1963, and if the trend in wages continues and the tax base is not increased, Barcus estimates that some states will need maximum rates in excess of 7 or 8

[26] In comments to the authors on March 3, 1965.

percent in a few years to finance unemployment at the average levels of recent years.[27]

Nor would it be economically sound to enact such high rates. As Professor Lester has brought out, experience rating makes it difficult for an employer to pass on increased costs to the consumer, and industries with high costs are highly competitive industries, which makes it even more difficult for them to pass tax increases on. If priority is given to the interests of general health of the economy over attempts to finance increased benefit costs by reliance on higher tax rates in the interest of experience rating, some of the increased benefit costs must be met through increases in the taxable wage base.

We think it is an inescapable conclusion that large revenue capacity, which will be adaptable to rapid increases in tax yield, demands a broad tax base, even if a state also chooses to have high tax rates for high-cost employers. The broader tax base will apply to all employers and thereby give a broader basis for any additional revenue needed through higher tax rates on some employers.

This is one of the reasons Mr. Green of the New York agency recommended a higher tax base despite the showings of the New York study that the immediate impact would be heavier on low-cost than on high-cost employers. In Mr. Green's words: "Keeping the tax base in step with potential liabilities of the fund is less a matter of immediate solvency . . . than a matter of preservation of capacity as a safeguard against possible future uptrends in benefit outlays."[28]

THE TAXABLE WAGE BASE AND ITS EFFECT ON FEDERAL UNEMPLOYMENT TAX NEEDS

We have thus far centered our discussion of the limited taxable wage base largely on its effect on state tax income. The federal "take" from the federal unemployment tax, however, is, and will continue to be, increasingly important. First, it was necessary in 1960 to increase the federal "take" from 0.3 to 0.4 percent, or by one third, in order to provide funds to finance the increasing costs of administering the program and to rebuild the federal loan fund. The federal unemployment tax was temporarily increased by another 0.4 percent in 1962 and by 0.25 in 1963, to finance the Temporary Extended Unemployment Compensation program of 1961. It appears inevitable that there will be some permanent legislation to finance extended benefits, at least in recessions, and that this will be financed at least partially out of federal unemployment taxes. A program to assist states with high cost through reinsurance or "matching grants for excess benefit costs" such as are proposed in the 1965 Administration bill (to be discussed in the next chapter), may also be enacted and require federal financing.

---

[27] The actual rates necessary in individual states will depend upon the benefit structure in the state.

[28] A Study of the Tax Base, etc., op. cit., introduction.

When more federal funds are needed, the question of whether the taxable wage base should be widened or the tax rate should be increased assumes much more importance than when state taxes are being changed. This is because the part of the federal unemployment tax paid to the federal government is at the same rate for all employers.

Since the federal unemployment tax is a flat tax, *already* large numbers of employers with low state experience rates are paying more in taxes to the federal unemployment trust fund than they are paying to their state unemployment insurance funds.

Administrative Costs

The ever-increasing administrative costs of the employment security program makes an increase in the taxable wage base or a further increase in the federal unemployment tax rate imperative as long as the costs are financed through grants under Title III of the Social Security Act.

Administrative costs of the employment security program have been expanding more rapidly than increases in income from the federal unemployment tax under the limited tax base of $3,000 (see Table 18–5).

The appropriation requested by the President for fiscal year 1966 was $13 million more than the estimated federal unemployment tax receipts, and $39 million more than the ceiling of 95 percent of tax receipts that can be used for administration. The appropriation request asked that the $39 million excess be advanced from general Treasury funds to be repayable as Congress might provide. Congress cut the appropriation for state administrative grants to $492 million from the Unemployment Trust Fund to keep within the 95 percent ceiling and appropriated $10 million from general Treasury funds.

Table 18–4

Administrative Costs of Employment Security Program
Fiscal Year 1961–65

Fiscal Year Ending June 30	Grants to States	Federal Adm. Costs	Total Adm. Costs	Federal Tax Receipts
1961 ....$326		$13	$339	$343
1962 405		16	421	452
1963 412		18	430	471
1964 425		19	444	489
1965 455		21	476	500
1966 .... 502*		22*	524*	518†

* Appropriation.
† Estimated.

There are, of course, alternative methods of meeting the mounting administrative costs. Much of the increase has gone for expansion and improvement of the Employment Service; some of this might be financed out of general funds, as is discussed in Chapter 21. Or the financing of administrative costs might be shared by the states, as is discussed in Chapter 20.

Other Federal Costs

It appears inevitable that some program of extended unemployment benefits will be enacted that will be at least partially financed through the FUTA. Possibly some plan of reinsurance or grants to assist states with heavy benefit costs will be enacted. If such programs are enacted, and are partly or wholly financed by the federal unemployment tax, it will again become necessary for a decision to be made as to whether the financing will be through an increase in the federal tax rate or tax base.[29]

SUMMARY AND CONCLUSIONS

Unemployment taxes were originally paid on total payrolls. In 1939, the federal unemployment tax was limited to the first $3,000 of each worker's earnings to conform with the taxable wage base for the federal old-age and survivors insurance program. This $3,000 has remained the base for the federal unemployment tax for a quarter of a century, although the tax base for OASI has been increased to $4,800.

Efforts have been made to increase the wage base but with only limited success because of the argument that increases in tax rates are more equitable. Statistics show that most high-cost employers also pay high wages, and that average annual wages in most if not all industries now exceed the $3,000 base, so that a tax base increase would also yield more taxes from high-cost employers. Within industries, low-cost employers initially (until their reserves were built up) would have their tax bills increased more than high-cost employers. Unless tax rate schedules are adjusted, an increase in the taxable wage base would therefore be less equitable, at least temporarily, than an increase in tax rates on high-cost employers. The equity argument, however, is based on employer responsibility for unemployment, while in most cases, employer control over unemployment is quite limited. Also, the equity argument assumes that there is some rationale for a $3,000 base. Such rationale as originally existed for this argument has disappeared, now that taxable wages are less than 60 percent of total wages.

One consideration from an equity standpoint has more validity: that a low taxable wage base can result in a high-wage employer paying a lower *effective* tax rate (when measured against his total payroll) than a low-wage employer whose benefit cost rate is no higher.

Increases in the taxable wage base would fall more heavily on new than older employers who have lower rates through experience rating. Some

[29] These decisions will not have to be made program by program. If the tax base were increased to $5,600, as proposed in the 1965 Administration bill, a smaller increase in the tax rate would be necessary.

relief might be provided through retroactive tax credits for new employers with stable employment experience.

Those advocating a higher tax base argue that a low tax base forces states with high costs to narrow the range of their experience rates. Experience rating advocates say the solution to this is to have higher tax rates for unstable employers. There is a limit, however, to how high tax rates can be pushed, particularly for employers in highly competitive industries.

Almost one half the states now use more than $3,000 in determining maximum benefit rights, but only part of these states have increased their wage bases above $3,000. The tax base should be increased at least enough to tax all the wages used in determining benefits.

Another important consideration is that a low wage base limits the ability of states with higher benefit costs to raise enough taxes to finance benefits. Most important of all, states, whether high-cost, or not, should have a broadly based tax structure in order to quickly expand tax income if this becomes necessary.

The federal unemployment tax income also needs to be increased to meet rising administrative costs. It is also probable that a program of extended benefits will be enacted that will be at least partially financed from the federal unemployment tax. A federally financed program to assist high-cost states is also a possibility. Since the part of the federal unemployment tax that is collected by the federal government is a flat rate tax, an increase in the tax rate bears more heavily on low-wage than high-wage employers. The federal taxable wage base should therefore be increased as well as the tax rate to provide needed increases in federal unemployment tax revenues.

In short, we believe the arguments for a substantial increase in the taxable wage base for unemployment insurance outweigh the arguments for raising all additional funds needed through increased tax rates. Some increase would be desirable in state tax rates above 2.7 percent (the maximum for which an employer can get credit against the federal tax) in order that high-cost employers would pay more of their share of total costs but tax rate increases should not be pushed to unreasonable limits while the tax base remains obsolete.

Chapter 19

Maintaining the Solvency
of State Unemployment
Insurance Funds

The maintenance of a solvent unemployment insurance program was one of the major concerns in framing the original state laws. The planners of the American system, cognizant of the large debt accumulated in the 1920's by the British unemployment insurance fund, were extremely cautious as to the income-outgo relationship between contributions and benefits. In determining how much could be paid in benefits under the proposed 3 percent payroll tax, the actuaries of the Committee on Economic Security heavily loaded their cost estimates to allow for unforeseen contingencies. Unemployment was generally considered to be unpredictable, and any actuarial estimates, although based on past experience, were thought of as little more than guesses. Combined with the extremely low unemployment rates during World War II, the cautious actuarial estimates of the Committee and the very modest benefits that were accordingly recommended and enacted resulted in the system being in a very strong financial position at the end of the War.

The high reserves that the states had built up by 1945 led many of them to reduce tax rates during the prosperous years that followed. These tax reductions caused little concern until the higher levels of unemployment during and following the 1954 recession drew down the reserve of many states to levels that endangered the solvency of the programs.

As in most insurance schemes, it was expected that there would be a need to build reserves in relatively good times that would be available to the unemployment insurance program during business slumps. From the beginning of the program it was also recognized that provisions should be built into the state laws to prevent the state funds from becoming insolvent. With many state reserves at low levels, the need for adequate provisions in the state laws to protect the solvency of their funds has assumed renewed importance. It has also become important that the state

379

fund levels under which different tax schedules come into effect in states with more than one tax schedule are set high enough so that the fund will be kept in a sound condition.

For many years, the technicians have recognized the importance of making long-range economic and actuarial studies in order to assure that income and outgo from the state unemployment fund will balance over time. These studies, largely ignored by policy makers until lately, are receiving increased consideration. Nevertheless, some states whose reserves were low in such prosperous years as 1963 and 1964 were still raising less in taxes than they were paying in benefits, or were doing little to rebuild depleted reserves. Unless there is vigorous corrective action by such states, the need for federal solvency standards may become a more serious issue.

Considerations of solvency led to the recognition that, under the federal-state system of unemployment insurance, individual states in financial difficulties may need federal assistance. A federal loan fund—"the George Fund"—was therefore enacted in 1944. Although it expired from disuse in 1952, a new plan—"the Reed Fund"—was enacted in 1954. Many have long felt that such repayable loans as were provided by these two plans represent an inadequate solution to the problems of states whose reserves become depleted because of high benefit costs over an extended period of time. Accordingly, federal "reinsurance" grants were proposed in the early 1950's as an alternative to loans. A recent plan developed by the Committee on Benefit Financing of the Interstate Conference of Employment Security Agencies would provide for temporary reinsurance against sudden rises in a state's cost experience. An alternative to reinsurance, a plan of "Matching Grants for Excess Benefit Costs," was proposed by the federal Administration in 1965. This would provide federal grants to finance most of a state's benefit costs above a given level. The form in which federal financial assistance should be provided to states in financial difficulty is likely to continue to be an issue even if the 1965 Administration proposal is enacted.

STATE MEASURES TO PROTECT SOLVENCY

Minimum Reserve Requirements

Concern with solvency is not a new idea. The early concern to assure the solvency of the state unemployment insurance funds is shown by inclusion in the Social Security Board's original draft bills of provisions under which experience rating would not take effect until the state fund reached specified levels. The recommended provisions did not allow reduced tax rates unless the total assets of the fund exceeded benefit payments in the preceding year, and allowed no rate of less than 1.8 percent of payrolls unless the assets exceeded twice the preceding year's benefit payments. Twenty-seven of the original 38 states with experience rating followed the recommendation in the draft bills. Several of the remaining states had even higher reserve requirements for experience rating to be operative.

By 1951, with experience rating in operation in all states, 33 of the 51 required a minimum state fund balance before experience rating could be operative. New and less stringent tests of solvency had been developed. Only seven states had a minimum solvency measure in terms of a multiple of benefit payments, the measure originally enacted in most states. Eight states suspended experience rating or put the highest schedule of rates into effect when the reserve fell to a stated number of millions of dollars. Eleven states took this action when the reserve as a percentage of payrolls fell to a stated level. Seven had alternative tests in terms of multiples of benefits or payrolls, whichever required the higher reserve.

The variety and obvious inadequacy of some of the requirements led the Federal Advisory Council in 1952 to initiate a study by its Committee on Benefit Financing of the state provisions and sound solvency requirements. In terms of dollars, some of the reserve requirements were obsolete because of increases in payrolls; others just didn't make sense. In a report to the Council on October 26–27, 1953, the Committee on Benefit Financing agreed that the most effective solvency measure is one that evaluates the reserve as a multiple of the state's average annual benefit costs. The Council accepted the report and transmitted it to the Secretary of Labor with the request that it be distributed to the state employment security administrators for their consideration and the consideration of their state advisory councils.

The 1959 report of the Committee on Benefit Financing of the Interstate Conference concluded that the highest-cost consecutive 12-month period (rather than the average cost rate) should be used as a base, and that 1½ times the cost in such a period should be considered as a minimum adequate reserve.[1]

The recommendations of the Council and the Interstate Conference Committee had little effect. By 1966, the number of states with "solvency" requirements had been reduced to 28. The number using a multiple of benefit payments (which the Council had recommended) had fallen to three and the number using a percentage of payrolls had increased to 15. There was some improvement in the provisions. Several of the ten states using a dollar requirement had raised the amount required; for example, Georgia had increased the minimum requirement from $12.5 million to $75 million. Still, in 1962, three states paid out two or three times as much in benefits as their minimum dollar requirement. Using a percentage of past payrolls, several states had reduced their requirements.

The reduction in the number of states with a minimum solvency measure may have been due to another development, the use of "multiple" experience rating schedules. By 1966, 34 states had tax schedules that, in effect, were determined by the size of the state's reserve—the higher the

---

[1] *Report of the Committee on Benefit Financing,* Interstate Conference of Employment Security Agencies, August 11–13, 1959, p. 22. The Committee has since qualified its advocacy of this measure, saying that other factors should be considered by individual states.

reserve, the lower the tax rates and vice versa. As of January 1, 1966, 21 states still have a minimum solvency measure which requires experience rates to be suspended, but provides for multiple schedules of rates when the state reserve is above the solvency measure. Thirteen other states have multiple tax schedules, but when reserves fall below a prescribed level the highest tax schedule goes into effect. In all of these states, except Virginia, the highest tax schedule provides for rates above 2.7 percent. In some of these states, the aim is to produce an average of 2.7 percent or more through the range of rates in the highest schedule.

A sound experience rating system would require rates both above and below 2.7 percent, the maximum for which tax credits can be secured against the federal tax. This is superior to providing for suspension of rates when reserves fall to a dangerously low level. Suspension of experience rates disrupts an experience rating system, especially of the reserve-ratio type. Under a reserve-ratio system, if experience rating is suspended, stable employers will build up excessive reserve ratios and there will be a concentration of employers at the minimum tax rate when the reserve rises to where experience rating is reactivated.

Provisions for suspension of experience rating when reserves fall below a prescribed level have come into effect from time to time in a few states. Rates have been suspended in Rhode Island in every year since 1949. Rates were also suspended in West Virginia from 1960–62 and in Washington from 1959–62. Alaska first suspended experience rating in 1953, later repealed it, and then reinstituted it but with a rate schedule that produces collections averaging above 2.7 percent of a taxable wage base of $7,200. Six states had suspended experience rating in 1963,[2] and six states had higher rates schedules in effect that yielded average tax rates above 2.7 percent of taxable payrolls.

State Experience in Preserving Solvency

In many states neither the fund solvency measures nor multiple tax schedules have been sufficiently effective to prevent their reserves falling to dangerously low levels. As has been previously brought out, at the end of 1964 there were 20 states with reserves lower than 1.5 times their annual benefit costs in the highest cost per year in the preceding ten years. Of these, six states had reserves of less than 1.0 times their highest annual benefit cost. Of the 23 states with low reserves, nine still collected less taxes in 1963 than they paid out in benefits that year, and several other states had average tax rates only slightly higher than their benefit costs. This was during a prosperous year when reserves should have been substantially rebuilt. Of the eight states still running a deficit, only three passed any corrective legislation in 1963 to provide for a higher tax base or higher tax rates.

This failure of many states to improve their financial situation is not due to an unawareness of the need for action. In 1949, the Bureau of Employ-

---

[2] In addition, experiencing rating was not in effect in Puerto Rico.

ment Security began to stimulate and assist the states in making long-range actuarial and financial studies in order to forecast and take corrective action if financial trouble lay ahead. Practically every state made such a study, but for some time, only a few states took legislative action based on the recommendations in their studies. In recent years, some states, including Alaska, Oregon, Utah, and Vermont, have used their financial studies as a basis for improving the financing of their programs. Most other state studies probably have had some influence, but have not been followed by legislation to carry out their recommendations.

The actuaries of the Bureau of Employment Security and a few of the states have also done a great deal of work to improve actuarial techniques for projecting cost estimates. The BES actuaries are constantly assisting the states in actuarial studies. Training seminars have been conducted which covered techniques for cost estimation, tax schedule development, and other matters pertaining to benefit financing. Such seminars have been attended by research and administrative personnel from practically all the states. It is to be hoped that through such education and stimulation, the states that have financial problems will act to put their funds in a sound condition.

Is a Federal Solvency Standard Necessary?

If state actions to preserve solvency are inadequate, some federal compulsion may become necessary. The federal responsibility in this area was set forth by the Federal Advisory Council. Following the recession of 1958, the Council, at its October, 1959, meeting, took note of the declining reserves of some states and appointed a committee to study the matter. On the basis of the Committee's study, the Council at a meeting on March 11, 1960, passed a resolution which read in part:

The Council believes there is a Federal interest and responsibility to see that these principles (of adequate accumulation of reserve in good times to meet the financial needs of recessions) are observed in the Federal-State program.

It is the belief of the Council that each State should accumulate sufficient reserves in good times to meet at least the financial needs that experience in previous recessions indicates might be necessary to pay benefits if a recession of similar intensity recurs. . . .

The Council believes that there is a Federal interest and responsibility to see that these principles are observed in the Federal-State program. The implementation of this responsibility might possibly take the form, among others, of Federal legislation setting minimum reserve requirements to assure the solvency of State laws. . . .

Such a resolution, passed unanimously by the Council, has considerable significance. Even management representatives joined those from the ranks of labor and the public representatives in urging speedy state action and inferring that, in its absence, federal solvency standards might be necessary.

The best argument for a federal solvency standard is that the present requirements for experience rating of pooled state funds, the only requirements now used, provide only that the experience rating be related to the employer's "experience with unemployment or other factors directly related to unemployment." The federal requirements for state funds that segregated individual employer reserves in separate accounts had definite standards as to how large the employer's reserve would have to be before he could get an experience rating. But the few states that adopted such plans have abandoned them (with employer reserve accounts kept only for bookkeeping purposes). Since all the state funds are now pooled, it would be logical to have a standard as to how large the state fund should be before any experience rates can be given to employers.

The usual argument against any further federal standards is that they would be a step toward federalization. Others argue that so long as the states are responsible for financing their programs, why should the federal government worry about the status of state funds? This latter view fails to recognize, however, that in the long run the status of a state's reserves is bound to affect its attitude toward the relative adequacy of its benefit provisions. It is therefore important to have an adequate reserve in order that adequate benefits will be enacted.

No formal proposals for a federal solvency standard have been made (as of the time of writing).[3] A standard might take the following form: if a state's reserve falls below what is generally recognized as a minimum adequate reserve, it should not give credit for any state taxes (which would result in a state increasing its tax rates to the full amount that employers can receive in credit; namely, 2.7 percent of federal taxable wages). The minimum adequate reserve might be the criterion commonly used by the Bureau of Employment Security; namely, a reserve equal to 1.5 times the benefit costs in that year during the past ten years when a state's costs were highest. Such a criterion might be adjusted to take into account such factors as the maximum contribution rate, the ratio between the costs in the year in which costs were the highest to the average costs over a business cycle, the relationship of noncharged and ineffectively charged benefits to the total volume of benefits, etc. Or the measure of fund solvency might be the fund-raising capacity of the state's tax structure. The development of a specific fund solvency measure is a technical matter that could be developed when the need for a federal solvency standard became evident.

Some states have taken measures to improve their financial condition,

---

[3] In the 1939 Social Security Amendments, the House of Representatives passed the following standard which a state would have to meet before additional credit would be given under the federal unemployment tax act for a reduced state tax rate: the amount in the state fund would have to be not less than one and one-half times the highest amount paid into such fund with respect to any one of the preceding ten calendar years or one and one-half times the highest amount of compensation paid out of such fund within any one of the preceding ten calendar years, whichever is the greater.

but some of these measures have been insufficient to restore the state funds to a sound condition. Other states have taken no action and the financial condition of their funds continues to deteriorate. If a substantial number of state funds continues to be in a weak financial condition, a federal solvency standard may become necessary.

FEDERAL AID TO STATE FINANCING

There has been general recognition that federal assistance should be provided for any state unemployment insurance fund that is in danger of insolvency. There has been wide disagreement, however, as to what the nature of such assistance should be. The types of assistance advocated fall into two general groups: federal loans and federal grants. Those favoring the loan approach believe that, in the long run, each state should be financially self-sufficient, and repayable loans or "advances" should be available only for temporary emergencies. They wish to minimize federal assistance in order to avoid additional federal control. Those favoring the grants approach believe that repayable loans are of little assistance to a state that consistently experiences heavy costs, since the burden of repaying the loan will be placed on top of the state's efforts to rebuild its reserves. They are less worried about federal authority. In recent years, the advocates of federal grants fall into two subgroups. One favors catastrophic "reinsurance grants" to tide over a state that has experienced a sudden, unforeseen rise in costs until it can readjust to its new situation. The other favors matching grants to states that chronically have heavy costs because of unfavorable economic conditions. The latter believe that the costs of the states should be equalized to some extent through the federal government using national financial resources to carry some of the burden of high-cost states. We will review these approaches in detail, since disagreement still is wide on the issues involved.

The "George Loan Fund" of 1944

As World War II approached its end in 1944, there was general agreement in Congress that unemployment compensation should play a major role in providing assistance for the unemployment that was expected while the economy was being reconverted to peacetime production. No less than five Congressional committees concerned themselves with the matter. Several approaches were proposed: supplementation of state unemployment benefits out of federal funds (S. 1823); minimum federal standards designed to increase the coverage and amount and duration of benefits, with reinsurance grants to states that could not finance the increased benefits (S. 1730); and federal loans to states whose reserves became low (S. 2051). Only the latter provision was enacted into law, and came to be known as the "George Loan Fund" from the name of the sponsor of the bill, Senator Walter F. George, Chairman of the Senate Committee on Finance.

This plan provided for interest-free loans to state unemployment funds

A state could become eligible for such a loan if the balance in its unemployment fund did not exceed total contributions to the fund during the one of the two preceding calendar years in which such contributions were higher. The loan would be equal to the amount by which benefit payments in any calendar quarter exceeded 2.7 percent of taxable payrolls. A federal unemployment account was established in the Unemployment Trust Fund out of which such loans were to be made. Appropriations were authorized for this account from the excess of federal unemployment tax collections over administrative expenses of the employment security program.[4] Actually, no appropriations were ever made to the account. The provisions were allowed to expire on March 31, 1952. The recommendation of the Advisory Committee on Social Security to the Senate Committee on Finance in 1948 for a revised but essentially similar loan plan was disregarded.[5]

The George Loan Fund was allowed to lapse because no state became eligible for a loan during the time its provisions were in effect. Benefits exceeded contributions in several states during 1949, notably in Rhode Island whose benefits equaled 6.21 percent of taxable payrolls and whose reserves fell to 4.94 percent of taxable payrolls. Massachusetts' benefit costs were 3.12 percent of taxable payrolls in 1949 and its reserves fell to 3.44 percent. Rhode Island's and Massachusetts' reserves were still high enough, however, so that neither was eligible for a loan.

Proposals for Reinsurance Grants

Rhode Island's precipitate fall in reserves, however, kept the question of a federal loan fund alive. The idea of federal reinsurance grants, proposed in one 1944 bill,[6] was also revived and became a rival idea to the loan idea. The Federal Advisory Council studied the two approaches but could reach no agreement, although members agreed on a document in 1952 setting forth the relative advantages of loans and reinsurance grants. Reinsurance was usually proposed in connection with proposals for federal minimum benefit standards. If a state system could not finance the benefits required by the standards through its own income and its reserves fell, the federal government would make reinsurance grants to the state to assist it in remaining financially solvent.

Along with other proposals on unemployment insurance, a proposal for reinsurance grants was included in a special message to Congress by President Truman in April, 1950; an Administration bill (H.R. 8059) was introduced to implement the President's message. The reinsurance plan proposed in H.R. 8059 provided that a state would be eligible for a grant if its unemployment reserve at the end of any calendar quarter was less than

---

[4] A new Title XII of the Social Security Act included the loan provisions. Amendments to Title IX provided for financing of the loans.

[5] Advisory Council on Social Security, *Recommendations for Social Security Legislation*, Senate Document No. 208, 80th Cong., 2d sess. (Washington, D.C.: U.S. Government Printing Office), pp. 168–70.

[6] Plans for reinsurance were studied by the Committee on Economic Security in 1934 and were studied by the Social Security Board in the early 1940's.

benefit expenditures in the preceding six months. The grant would be equal to three fourths of benefit expenditures which were over 2 percent of taxable wages in the quarter. The bill also provided that a state would need to have a specified minimum contribution rate as a safeguard against irresponsible financing by the state.

The basic argument in favor of reinsurance grants instead of loans was that some States have higher rates of unemployment because of the nature of their economies. If high benefit costs persist and their reserves become depleted in such states, the state should be assisted in meeting such costs. If only loans are available, these must be repaid, and such repayments when combined with high contribution rates, would worsen the competitive position of employers in a state securing a loan.

Typical arguments against reinsurance grants were, first, that each state should stand on its own feet financially. If it was unwilling to raise enough taxes to finance its program, there was no reason for the federal government to permanently subsidize it out of funds that really belonged to all the states. Secondly, reinsurance grants would not prevent and probably would encourage irresponsible benefit practices. Third, the federal controls that must be written into a reinsurance plan to prevent abuse would be a first step toward federalization of the program.

Hearings on the Administration's reinsurance proposal were held by a Subcommittee on Unemployment Insurance of the Committee on Ways and Means in December, 1950, but no action was taken by the Subcommittee.

Criticisms leveled during the hearings at the reinsurance proposal in H.R. 8059 caused the Department of Labor to revise the plan so as to make it less vulnerable to charges that it would be misused. Under the revised plan, a grant would not be available unless the balance in a state's fund fell below the amount paid out in benefits in that quarter of the preceding eight in which benefit expenditures were highest. No grant could exceed such high quarter benefit expenditures. Adjustments would be made at the end of the year so that the total grants in a year could not exceed 2.7 percent of the state's annual taxable payrolls. To be eligible, the state must have suspended reduced experience rates when its fund dropped below the greater of 6 percent of taxable payrolls or three fifths of the total benefit expenditures during the preceding five years. The revised bill (H.R. 6954) was introduced by Aime J. Forand, Chairman of the Subcommittee on Unemployment Insurance. Hearings were held in 1952 on this as well as other measures, including H.R. 4133, a bill sponsored by the Interstate Conference which provided for a new federal loan fund. The changes in the reinsurance plan did not weaken the opposition to it on the basis of this hearing,[7] and no report was made by the Subcommittee.

[7] A bill (H.R. 3547) was introduced by Congressman Thaddeus M. Macrowicz in 1959 which was similar to the bill introduced in 1950 for reinsurance grants. Extensive hearings were conducted on this and other unemployment insurance bills by the Committee on Ways and Means in April, 1959, but no action was taken by the Committee.

The New "Reed" Loan Fund Plan

On April 14 and 15, 1953, the full Committee on Ways and Means held hearings on rival plans for federal loans and for reinsurance grants.[8] The arguments pressed for the loan approach were (1) that it would preserve state responsibility for financing its own program, which was consistent with the basic principles on which the federal-state program was founded; (2) the requirement for repayment would serve as an incentive to corrective financial action; (3) it could be kept free from additional and burdensome federal controls.

Although the Department of Labor supported the reinsurance proposal, the Treasury Department expressed preference for the loan approach in a letter asking for revisions in other parts of H.R. 3530–3531 which provided for "earmarking" federal unemployment tax receipts. The Committee reported out a bill which included the new federal loan plan, and this bill was approved by Congress and became law on August 5, 1954.[9]

This Act provided for a new Title XII, in place of the expired act. Under its provisions, a state became eligible for an interest-free advance[10] if its reserves at the end of a calendar quarter had fallen below the amount paid out in unemployment compensation in the four calendar quarters ending on that date. The advance could not exceed the highest amount of benefits paid out in any of such four quarters. If not repaid in the meantime, repayments would be effected through a reduction in tax credits of employers of the state equal to 5 percent of the federal tax in the fourth year following the loan, 10 percent the fifth year, and so on until the advance was repaid.

In contrast to the 1944 act, which merely authorized appropriations, this act provided for automatic financing of the federal loan fund. The federal unemployment tax income was earmarked, and any excess remaining at the end of a fiscal year over federal and state employment security administrative expenses was transferred to the federal unemployment (loan) account until that account totaled $200 million.[11]

Alaska soon qualified for a loan (1955) and for additional loans in several years thereafter until the amounts advanced to it reached a peak of

[8] The loan plan was included in bills introduced by Wilbur D. Mills (H.R. 3530) and Noah Mason (H.R. 3531). The reinsurance grant plan was embodied in a bill introduced by Congressman Forand (H.R. 2261). These bills were identical with the bills on which the Subcommittee on Unemployment Insurance had held hearings the preceding year.

[9] Employment Security Administrative Financing Act, Public Law 83–567.

[10] The term "advance" rather than "loan" was used in the Act because in the hearings questions were raised as to whether some state constitutions prohibited these states from securing a loan.

[11] Any excess taxes thereafter were distributed to the state funds on the basis of their taxable payrolls, to be used for administration or benefits.

$8,765,000. During the 1958–59 recession, Michigan secured an advance of $113 million and Pennsylvania qualified for an advance of $112 million.[12]

As it turned out, neither Michigan nor Pennsylvania needed to use the advances they received during the 1958–59 recession, although Pennsylvania used its advance for short periods in 1961 and after. There was no incentive to repay the advances because they bore no interest.

Because of this experience, the Interstate Conference of Employment Security Agencies became convinced that the requirements for a federal advance should be considerably tightened. A bill, worked out jointly with the Department of Labor and eventually enacted into law,[13] provided that a state will not become eligible for a loan until its reserve fund and its estimated tax receipts fall to such a point that, without a federal advance, it cannot meet its estimated benefit payments in the ensuing month. The advance is equal to the amount estimated to be needed to make up the deficit. Federal advances can thus be made only when a state fund actually becomes bankrupt.

These provisions are extreme and should be modified. A loan might be available, for example, when a state's reserve is below one half of the benefit expenditures in the preceding 12 months. As a minimum, the advances should be made for estimated needs of the state for the ensuing three months instead of the ensuing month.

The repayment provisions were also considerably tightened. They now provide that if the advance is not repaid by the state by the second January after it receives a loan (instead of the fourth January), the tax credits of the employers of the state will be reduced by 10 percent instead of 5 percent. For each succeeding year, the reduction will be 10 percent more (instead of 5 percent) until the loan is repaid. The amendments provide for additional reductions if the state has not increased its taxes to specified levels which were designed to "induce" a state to get its fund back on a sound financial basis. An additional reduction will be made if in either the third or fourth years after the loan is made, the state has failed to collect taxes equal to at least 2.7 percent of its employers' taxable payrolls. The reduction in tax credit (payable the following year) will be equal to the difference in the state's average tax rate and 2.7 percent. For example, if the state taxes equaled 2.3 percent of taxable payrolls, the additional reduction in tax credit would be 0.4 percent. Although the additional 0.4 percent that the state's employers would pay the federal government would be applied toward repayment of the state's loan, it was assumed that the employers would prefer to pay this additional amount to rebuild the state's fund and so would have their state law revised to increase taxes by the necessary amount.

[12] Pennsylvania initially received $96.4 million, since that amount exhausted the balance remaining in the federal unemployment account. Subsequently Pennsylvania received the rest of the $112 million as small amounts accrued in the federal unemployment account.

[13] Public Law 86–778, approved September 13, 1960.

If the loan was not repaid by the fifth year, an even stiffer provision would be applied. The state would have to collect taxes equal to its average annual benefit costs in the first five of the six preceding years. If it failed to do so, the federal tax credits of the state's employers for any year would be reduced by the difference between the state's average annual benefit costs and the average tax rate paid by employers in that year. For example, if its annual benefit costs were 3.5 percent and it collected 2.0 percent, the employers' tax credit would be reduced 1.5 percent. If the state had average costs of less than 2.7 percent, the state would still have to collect taxes equal to 2.7 percent, or its employers' federal tax credits would be reduced as in the third or fourth years. These very complicated provisions, in short, would "induce" a state needing a loan to raise unemployment taxes equal to 2.7 percent in the second and third years after securing a loan, and to raise taxes equal to the higher of its average annual benefit costs, or 2.7 percent in the fourth or succeeding years until the state's loan is repaid. The intent was to motivate the state to get its fund back into a sound condition.

The "Catastrophic" Reinsurance Proposal of the Interstate Conference

The reenactment of a federal loan plan did not permanently close off discussion of reinsurance. In its annual report in 1959 the Interstate Conference Benefit Financing Committee revived the idea in a different form. Although the Committee made no recommendations, it pointed out three weaknesses in the loan plan. First, the incidence of unemployment among the states is very uneven, striking some industries in one recession and other industries in another. This places heavy drains on certain states for which a loan gives no permanent relief. Second, federal loans might give temporary assistance, but the necessity of their repayment would only increase the tax burden of employers in states securing such loans. Third, unemployment insurance was designed primarily for noncyclical unemployment and there is a point at which a loan does not meet interstate responsibility for severe recession unemployment. So ran its argument. The Committee suggested that the Interstate Conference might well examine the principle of reinsurance and its application to the abnormal risks of recession unemployment.[14]

The 1960 Benefit Financing Committee made a detailed study, continued in 1961, of some 90 different formulas for reinsurance. The 1961 Committee emphasized that, as in other types of insurance, the reinsurance should be against catastrophic loss.[15]

[14] *Report of the Committee on Benefit Financing*, Interstate Conference of Employment Security Agencies, September, 1959, pp. 24–25.

[15] The idea of an interstate plan for reinsurance to which states would contribute was first put forward by Milton O. Loysen, then administrator of the New York agency. On March 19 and 20, 1953, Mr. Loysen invited New England and North Atlantic state administrators to a conference at West Point, New York. Mr. Loysen proposed a reinsurance plan to deal with catastrophic losses that came suddenly, such as significant shifts in government procurement, atomic attack or other developments outside a state's

This Committee selected a plan which seemed to work best on the basis of 1950–58 experience. The National Executive Committee of the Interstate Conference approved this plan at a meeting on September 28–30, 1961, and directed the Committee on Benefit Financing to develop a questionnaire for polling the states on the proposal. In the course of developing the questionnaire, the 1962 and 1963 Benefit Financing Committees revised the plan. As finally developed, the catastrophe reinsurance plan provided for a reinsurance payment to a state equal to the excess in its benefit cost above 1.6 times its average benefit cost rate. The amount of the payment would be equal to only 60 percent of benefit expenditures above this. The average costs for the five-year period, ending December 31 of the fourth year preceding the year in which the state qualifies for reinsurance, would be used for averaging the state's cost rate.

The purpose of the catastrophic reinsurance plan was to meet extraordinary or unexpected costs of the state's unemployment insurance program until it could readjust its financing if the increase in costs proved to be permanent. As one of the members of the Benefit Financing Committee, Nathan Morrison of the New York agency, pointed out, an advantage in such a plan is that a state could safely operate with a somewhat lower reserve, since a state would not need to take into account possible catastrophic contingencies in fixing the desirable size of its reserve fund.

In the course of its further consideration of plans, the Committee had concluded that only the poor risks would come into the plan if it were financed on a voluntary basis. Consequently, in the questionnaire prepared in 1963, five alternative methods of financing were presented: (1) a uniform increase in the federal unemployment tax; (2) a small uniform increase in the federal unemployment tax plus a surtax on employers in states receiving reinsurance payments if the costs of the program exceeded the proceeds of the uniform tax; (3) an employee payroll tax; (4) federal general revenue; and (5) a combination of two or more of the first four methods.[16]

The "Matching-Grants-for-Excess-Benefit-Costs" Proposal of the Administration

In 1961, the Kennedy Administration came out with a new approach to the problem of high benefit costs, namely, a plan for "equalization grants." This plan was embodied in a bill introduced in 1961, 1963, and 1965 (H.R.

---

control. It was the consensus of the conference that the technical problems involved in developing a voluntary plan should be explored by experts not subject to the pressure of employer and labor interests such as state administrators were subject to, and that some impartial foundation or university should be asked to make the study. Nothing further came of this.

[16] It was estimated that the cost of the Committee's proposal if it had been in operation in the nine years from 1954 to 1962 inclusive, would have been $1,207 million. Most of the cost of the proposal would have been concentrated in the recession years 1954, 1958, 1960, and 1961. All but five of the states would have received a reinsurance payment under the plan (all except Arkansas, New Hampshire, Rhode Island, Utah, and Washington).

8282). The aim of the "matching-grants-for-excess-benefit-costs" plan, as it was called in the 1965 bill, was to assist states in meeting high benefit costs due to differences in economic conditions, whether or not such states are in a weak financial condition. By reducing the amount of revenue a state would otherwise have to raise, the grants would put a state eligible for them in a better competitive position with states that have more favorable economic conditions.

Briefly stated, the 1965 proposal provided that if a state's costs exceeded 2 percent of total payrolls, two thirds of the excess cost would be met through a federal grant. If the benefit costs in all states (during a recession) exceeded 2 percent of total payrolls, then the grant would be based on the excess of the individual state's costs above the national average. In order to qualify for a grant, a state would have to meet the standard for weekly benefit amounts prescribed in the bill. The grants would be financed by an increase in the federal unemployment tax.

Thus, this plan had as one of its aims the encouragement of the states to provide adequate benefits by assisting them in meeting excessive costs. Its sponsors maintained that, while cost differentials between states may be partly due to differences in benefit formulas, the cost differentials are primarily due to differences in the incidence of unemployment over which there is little control. The incidence of unemployment, and therefore benefit costs, vary widely from state to state. At present, the state with higher-than-average costs can keep its costs down to some extent by providing inadequate benefits. The "grants-for-excess-costs" would encourage states with high unemployment to provide adequate benefits. Another value of the plan would be that it would lessen the competitive disadvantage that employers in high-cost states have because they are paying higher unemployment taxes than employers in lower-cost states.

Actually, the modest proposal for grants in the Administration bill would not result in much equalization in the costs of the states, although it would materially help a few states with very high costs.

The difference between the approaches of catastrophic reinsurance and grants for excess costs is as follows: the reinsurance approach would give assistance to a state to meet either a temporary unusual cost or a sudden increase in cost, but if the state permanently experienced a higher level in costs it would have to readjust its financing to the new cost level. On the other hand, the grant approach would assist a state with high costs experienced either on a temporary or long-range basis, if such costs are substantially higher than costs experienced by most states. The reinsurance approach is essentially like reinsurance for other types of insurance; namely, to meet unusual "catastrophic" costs. The "matching grant-for-excess-costs" approach is, as its name implies, the spreading of the risk of high benefit costs on a national basis.

There is, however, an important difference between the reinsurance plan considered by the Interstate Conference and usual reinsurance plans. In other types of insurance, reinsurance is designed for nonrecurring catastrophies such as a hurricane. The great bulk of reinsurance payments under the Benefit Financing Committee plan would go to pay part of the cost of recessional unemployment, which recurs periodically. It would pay practically nothing between recessions, except to the extent that a state experiences a business slump somewhat earlier or later than the country as a whole. Thus, it is essentially a plan for subsidizing states with extraordinarily high costs during recessions. Such subsidies also would be paid in states whose costs were not high, if their costs between recessions were low.

The 1963 Committee on Benefit Financing concluded that there was nothing incompatible between a reinsurance and an equalization plan, and in its questionnaire would have given the states the choice of voting for a reinsurance plan,[17] an equalization plan, or both. There would, of course, be a good deal of overlapping if both plans were enacted.

The plans pose these alternatives: should states be aided only when they have sudden rises in costs so that they will have time to readjust their financial system to increased costs, or should states that have a long-range, high-cost problem because of the nature of the economies of their states be given some federal financial assistance to lessen the competitive disadvantage with other states under which their employers operate? One's attitude toward these alternatives will determine whether he thinks the reinsurance plan or the cost equalization plan is "better." Or perhaps one may believe both reinsurance and cost equalization grants are desirable. On the other hand, if one believes that every state should be self-sufficient, one would probably say that the present federal loan provisions give enough protection.

SUMMARY AND CONCLUSIONS

The framers of the unemployment insurance program were very careful to be sure that the recommended program would be solvent. The limited benefits provided because of this cautious attitude and the very low unemployment during World War II resulted in very high reserves in most states by 1945. Many states, however, used up most of their reserves during the following years, mainly through reducing tax rates more than was justified, and also because of the increased unemployment beginning in 1954.

Although most states originally had fairly high reserve requirements below which experience rates were suspended, the requirements in many states were lowered to where they no longer protected the solvency of their funds. Most states now have multiple tax schedules, the highest schedule being a substitute for suspension of experience rating when reserves fall to a given level. If the tax schedules and the fund levels in which different schedules operate are properly framed, solvency will be protected. The

[17] The cost equalization plan presented by the Benefit Financing Committee was similar to the 1965 Administration plan.

condition of many state funds, however, indicates that their minimum reserve requirements and tax schedules need revision.

For many years, research and actuarial personnel in the federal and state agencies have recognized the need for long-range financial and actuarial studies to assure that income and outgo from the state unemployment fund would balance over the business cycle. Actuarial studies have been made in all the states, but only recently have they been taken seriously by policy makers in many states. Despite depleted reserves and the availability of detailed actuarial studies, some states have taken no action or inadequate action to regain a strong financial position.

One of the questions that may have to be faced is whether some compulsion through a federal solvency standard may be necessary for states that are not facing their financial problems. It is our belief that a federal minimum solvency requirement should be enacted if it is the only way to prevent some state funds from becoming insolvent. We would hope, however, that all the states will face the necessity of putting their financial houses in order before federal compulsion becomes necessary.

Because of the unpredictability of unemployment and the wide variations in the incidence of unemployment among the states, it was also recognized early in the program that some types of federal financial assistance should be available to states that got into financial trouble. At the end of World War II a federal loan fund was created in anticipation of heavy unemployment during the reconversion period. This was allowed to lapse because of disuse, but the idea remained alive. Federal "reinsurance grants" became a rival idea. While a new federal loan plan was enacted in 1953, there has been renewed study of the reinsurance grant approach in recent years.

Emphasis has been placed on reinsurance of extraordinary and unforeseen increases in costs in a plan developed by the Committee on Benefit Financing of the Interstate Conference. An alternative "grants-for-excess-costs" approach has been proposed by the federal Administration in recent years. This approach is for the federal government to subsidize states with very high costs through grants which would pay the major part of benefit costs above 2 percent of the state's total covered payrolls. Since the reinsurance and cost equalization approaches are aimed at different goals, the determination as to which is a better plan depends on one's attitude toward these goals. Possibly both plans are needed, as well as the present federal loan fund. The question as to what type of federal assistance should be given to high-cost states and whether it should be provided only for unexpected increases in costs or for chronically high costs is a major issue in unemployment insurance. It is our belief that the "grants-for-excess-costs" plan is the sounder approach, since it would lessen the competitive disadvantage (even though this may be exaggerated) in which employers in high-cost states are placed.

Part V

Problems
in Relationships

Chapter 20

Federal Financing
of State Administration

Title III of the Social Security Act provides that the Secretary of Labor award grants of sufficient funds to each state employment security agency to meet its needs "for proper and efficient administration." Such grants are made if the state agency meets specified requirements. This 100 percent financing of state administration by the federal government has largely accomplished its purpose of assuring adequate funds for efficient administration of the state programs. It has raised the level of state administration above what it might otherwise have been. At the same time, it has inevitably created problems in the relationships between the federal and the state agencies. The federal agency has had the responsibility of securing adequate appropriations for administration, and, also, of allocating the appropriated funds in a manner that the states consider to be equitable. In the process, the federal government has had to assure proper expenditure of funds without creating resentment on the part of the states that there is too close oversight of their operations.

The wisdom of the federal government paying 100 percent of the cost of administration has been questioned from time to time. Alternative plans have been proposed which would give the states more responsibility for financing administration. These alternatives have raised basic questions regarding how extensive a role the federal government should play in the program. From time to time questions are also raised regarding the allocation of administrative funds on the basis of each state's needs for proper and efficient administration rather than on the basis of the federal unemployment taxes paid by employers of the state.

Thus, the 100 percent financing of state administration by the federal government has both created difficult administrative problems and raised important issues as to the federal-state relationship in the employment security program. The importance of these issues in financial terms is indicated by the amounts appropriated for administration, amounting to $502 million for the fiscal year 1966.

397

In 1935, the Committee on Economic Security recommended that the Social Security Act provide for federal grants to meet the cost of administering the state unemployment insurance laws because Committee members were concerned that the state legislatures would not vote adequate funds for administration. They recognized that a great deal of the success of the unemployment insurance program would depend on good administration of the laws and that adequate funds were necessary for good administration. They thought that the 10 percent of the federal unemployment tax that would be paid to the federal government (assuming all employers got 90 percent credit against the tax for their contributions to state unemployment insurance funds) would be a convenient source of funds for federal and state administration. They also believed that the 10 percent income would be quite adequate for this purpose.

In addition to its concern that the state agencies should have adequate funds for administration, the Committee was also concerned that the states should administer their laws properly and efficiently. It was possible in the legislation to require proper standards of administration as a condition for receiving grants for administration.

The Committee also saw a third value in providing for federal financing of administration; it would permit a degree of flexibility that would not be possible if the state unemployment insurance agencies were dependent on appropriations for administration from state legislatures. Unemployment is constantly fluctuating and it is impossible to predict business slumps with any degree of accuracy, so it might well occur that a state agency would be short of administrative funds between legislative sessions because of a sudden increase in unemployment. This could happen even if the state legislature had made available what appeared to be an adequate amount at the time of the appropriation. On the other hand, since Congress meets annually, its appropriations from year to year could be adjusted to the volume of unemployment. Furthermore, if sudden increases in unemployment did occur between these annual appropriations, it would be possible to go back to Congress for supplemental or deficiency appropriations if necessary.

This plan for 100 percent grants for administration has worked reasonably well, although its operation has presented some knotty problems. The principal problem has been to develop procedures for determining how much each state should receive in administrative funds. Although the Bureau of Employment Security has developed procedures over the years that result in a high degree of objectivity and impartiality in the granting of administrative funds, these are by no means perfect. At times, the methods of distribution have resulted in rather strong federal-state disagreements. Questions are still raised as to the basis of distributing funds, and even the basic premise on which funds are distributed, what is necessary for proper and efficient administration, is sometimes questioned. Nevertheless, on the whole, the close consultation of recent years between federal and state officials has resulted in comparatively good relations in working out the allocation of administrative funds to the states.

Another constant problem has been to estimate in advance the amount that will be necessary for administration and to persuade the Budget Bureau to approve and Congress to appropriate what is estimated to be necessary. The amounts requested have frequently been reduced, often as a part of a general government drive for economy. For some years, the federal unemployment tax receipts were a part of the general funds of the federal government; in fact, it was originally thought necessary to completely divorce the grants provisions in Title III from the Unemployment Tax provisions in order to get a favorable constitutional decision from the Supreme Court. However, the Supreme Court decision on the unemployment features of the Social Security Act was so broad that it was evident that the proceeds of the federal unemployment tax could be earmarked for employment security purposes. The belief grew that if the tax proceeds were so earmarked, considerations of general government economy and budget balancing would not influence the amount appropriated for state employment security administration. Legislation was accordingly secured in 1953 which earmarked the tax. The hope that both the Budget Bureau and Congress would thereafter loosen their controls over employment security appropriations proved to be illusory. Further legislation was therefore secured in 1960 which appropriated all unemployment tax receipts directly to the Unemployment Trust Fund and provided that employment security appropriations for administration would be made from the Trust Fund. This removed both receipts and expenditures from the conventional part of the federal budget, as is the case for other trust fund operations.

Congress has continued to be concerned over the increasing costs of administration. While most of the increases have been due to rising prices and salaries, to the growth in the number of workers and employers covered by the program, and to the additional and more complex programs given the states to administer, Congress is constantly suspicious that the program could be administered more economically. One question that is latent, though not often expressed, is whether funds would be administered more economically if the federal government did not pay the entire cost of administration. Would the state employment security agencies be more circumspect in their requests for administrative funds if they had to persuade their own state legislatures to appropriate part or all of their administrative funds? Although this issue has not been specifically raised for some years, we believe it should be looked at.

In this chapter, we will first review the experience with the financing of administration of the employment security program under present legislation, and then discuss several basic issues regarding such financing. These will include such questions as (1) whether the total appropriation should be considered, as it is at present, as a national pool out of which funds are granted to the states without regard to how much has been received in taxes from each state; and (2) whether 100 percent grants for administration with no matching of state funds is sound and preferable to the customary matching of grants in other federal-state programs, or preferable to exclusive state financing. A third basic question: namely, whether the public employment service should be financed on the same basis as unemployment insurance, will be discussed in the next chapter dealing with the relationship of unemployment insurance and the public employment service.

REQUIREMENTS FOR ADMINISTRATIVE GRANTS

Title III of the Social Security Act contains certain administrative requirements that a state must meet in order to be entitled to a grant for administration. These include (1) such methods of administration (including personnel standards) as are reasonably calculated to insure full payment of unemployment compensation when due; (2) payment of unemployment compensation solely through public employment offices or such other agencies as the Secretary of Labor may approve; (3) opportunity for a fair hearing before an impartial tribunal for all individuals whose claims for benefits are denied; and (4) the making of such reports as the Secretary of Labor may require. Most of the other requirements under Title III are the same as those under the Federal Unemployment Tax Act. The Secretary can withhold grants if, after reasonable notice and opportunity for hearing, he finds that there has been (1) denial, in a substantial number of cases, of benefits to which individuals are entitled, or (2) a failure to comply substantially with any of the requirements listed above.

In the early years, the federal government had a most salutary influence in getting the states to develop personnel administration on a merit basis. While a few states had civil service systems when the Social Security Act was passed, most of them did not. The original Social Security Act gave the Social Security Board authority to require proper methods of administration. However, it exempted administrative methods "relating to selection, tenure of office, and compensation of personnel." The Social Security Board interpreted this to mean that it was prohibited from participating in the actual selection of personnel but that it could prescribe personnel standards. This was confirmed by Congress in a provision in the 1939 Social Security Amendments which gave the Board specific authority over "methods relating to the establishment and maintenance of personnel standards on a merit basis, except that the Social Security Board[1] shall exercise no authority with respect to the selection, tenure of office, and compensation of any individual employed in accordance with such methods. . . ." Under this authority, the Social Security Board required the states that did not

---

[1] Now, the Secretary of Labor, in accordance with the President's Reorganization Plan No. 2 of 1949, which transferred the Bureau of Employment Security to the United States Department of Labor.

have civil service systems to establish public boards to administer a merit system for personnel of their state employment security agencies. This was so successful that it became a model in many states for the establishment of merit systems in other state departments or the establishment of state civil service systems. This aspect of federal supervision has operated with comparatively little friction, although there have been disputes with individual states over specific cases, where the merit regulations have not been followed.[2]

The original legislation required that the state law provide for "Payment of unemployment compensation solely through public employment offices in the state or such other agencies as the Board may approve."[3] The Social Security Board made an early ruling that unemployment compensation would be paid only through public employment offices. This did not mean the benefit checks would have to be physically paid through the local employment offices, although this is done in several states. It did mean, however, that claims for benefits were to be filed in local employment offices and claimants were required to register for employment with the local employment office.

Since Title III authorized the payment of unemployment compensation through public employment offices, the Social Security Board interpreted this to mean that it was also authorized to pay the cost of administering the public employment service. Therefore, under agreement with the United States Employment Service, the Board took over a large part of the financing of the federal-state system of employment offices, although the offices continued to operate under the Wagner-Peyser Act of 1933. The requirement of paying unemployment compensation through public employment offices plus financing of the offices through Title III resulted in close integration of the two activities, usually under the same state agency. (The problems created by this integration are discussed in the next chapter.)

The provision that the state agencies must make such reports as the federal agency requires has resulted in the collection of very complete operating statistics on a comparable basis for all states, as well as the collection of much valuable labor market information. In the early years, the states leaned heavily on the Bureau of Employment Security in developing methods of administration "reasonably calculated to insure full payment of benefits when due," as required by Title III. After the states had gained sufficient experience, there was only general federal supervision over state administration. The role of the Bureau of Employment Security is largely

---

2 The state merit systems for unemployment compensation and public assistance were administered jointly, and after the transfer of the Bureau of Employment Security to the Department of Labor, the Department of Health, Education, and Welfare and the Department of Labor have continued to jointly administer the merit system under a cooperative agreement.

3 Sec. 303 (a) (2), Social Security Act, Public Law 74–271, approved August 14, 1935.

one of consultation and technical assistance. It has developed administrative standards and an elaborate manual of approved administrative practices. It also evaluates and audits administrative operations of the states and audits their operations. It develops administrative tools such as occupational tests, the Dictionary of Occupational Titles, and procedures for making "nonmonetary" determinations of unemployment insurance claims. It develops new programs and procedures for carrying them out, such as special programs for youth, older workers, and the handicapped. It advises the states on legislation, particularly as to its conformity with federal requirements. In recent years, the Bureau has probably been most effective through group conferences with state technicians on specialized problems of administration.

The problem of compliance with the requirements in Title III has arisen with considerable intensity in several states; however, these requirements, with one or two exceptions, have not been an important problem. The main problem has been the severity of the penalty in cases of noncompliance, namely, the total withdrawal of administrative grants. In view of this severe penalty, the states resent the fact that there is no further recourse, if the Secretary of Labor finds a state out of compliance with Title III requirements. The states feel that they should be able to appeal his decision to the courts. These issues will be discussed in the chapter on federal-state relations.[4]

FEDERAL DETERMINATION OF ADMINISTRATIVE GRANTS

The Secretary of Labor is directed, under Section 303 (a) of Title III of the Social Security Act, to make grants to each state with an approved unemployment insurance law in such amounts as he "determines to be necessary for the proper and efficient administration of such law." The Secretary is also directed to base the amount of the grant on "(1) the population of the State; (2) an estimate of the number of persons covered by the State law and of the cost of proper and efficient administration of such law; and (3) such other factors as the Secretary of Labor finds 'relevant.'"

Since there were no standards or guides at the beginning, the Bureau of Employment Security based the grants on "line-item" budgets submitted by the states. These budgets listed every job and every desk, chair, and typewriter that was needed. This resulted in strained relations between the Bureau and from the beginning there were endless arguments over what specific items each state needed.

After the Bureau of Employment Security had accumulated some experience, it adopted a system in 1941 of budgeting by functions. An estimate was made of the work load for each function and the cost of performing each work load unit where this was feasible. For example, the cost of processing a quarterly tax return was multiplied by the estimated

---

[4] These two problems also apply to the requirements under the Federal Unemployment Tax Act, and so can be discussed with respect to both Title III and the Federal Unemployment Tax Act at the same time.

number of employers covered by the state law. Time studies are made of routine work load items. For operations that could not be standardized, such as the examination of claims for benefits, the average time allowed was based on experience. Beginning with fiscal 1963, the "work load time factor" system was abandoned for the Employment Service. "Position allocations" to broad functional areas, to special projects, and to metropolitan office areas were substituted. The "work load time factor" basis was retained for unemployment insurance functions, but functions were grouped so as to have fewer items to budget. Overhead costs have never been standardized, although by experience, the Bureau is able to judge when they are excessive. A crucial figure, basic to the building of the budget request, is the estimated volume of insured unemployment that will occur in the year for which the appropriation request is made.

It is a long time from the beginning of the process of estimating how much will be needed in federal appropriations to the end of the fiscal year in which the appropriated funds are actually spent; this process takes about 30 months. For example, work began in December, 1963, on the appropriation for the fiscal year ending June 30, 1966. Because this lead time is so long and because conditions can change even after the appropriation is made, for some years Congress has been appropriating a contingency amount, usually about 5 percent of the total budget, for (a) changes in work loads; (b) changes in state legislation; and (c) changes in state salary rates. This makes it possible for the federal bureau to grant additional funds to individual states during the fiscal year to meet unforeseen contingencies.

In spite of more than a quarter century of experience, the determination of the amount that should be granted to each state is far from a scientific process. There has been a tendency to use an historic basis to develop the amounts for unmeasurable functions and overhead costs in each state's annual grant; that is, the state must show why it has increases over the previous year's costs. Some states claim that this has resulted in their being penalized for being efficient. If they have carried on an economical operation, it is difficult to get as much as a comparable state that has been less efficient in the past. Some states charge that a premium is placed on inefficient operations. It is difficult to substantiate or disprove such allegations. In any case, only a small proportion of the state's grant would be in areas in which the size of the grant would be affected by inefficient operations, such as in administrative overhead. The bulk of the grant is based on estimated work loads, which, of course, vary from state to state. Other differentials that affect the amount granted are also largely uncontrollable, such as differences in rental rates and state salary levels.

THE STRUGGLE FOR ADEQUATE APPROPRIATIONS FOR ADMINISTRATION

Throughout most of its history, the unemployment insurance program has been in a chronic crisis over appropriations for administration. For constitutional reasons, administrative grants under Title III of the Social Security Act originally were financed through appropriations from general federal funds. Although it was understood that the source of these funds was the federal unemployment tax, there was no legal connection between the taxation provisions and the grant provisions.

This meant that funds for administration were secured through the regular budgetary and appropriation process. The federal Bureau first received budgetary requests from the states and, on the basis of these, compiled a consolidated request for funds. Formal requests were made for funds from the Budget Bureau which, after hearings and negotiations, recommended an amount to be included in the President's budget. In the process, the amount requested was usually pared down. The request for administrative funds went to Congress as a part of the general federal budget and was subjected to hearings by the Appropriations Committees of both Houses of Congress and to floor debate. Congress also usually pared down the appropriation request received in the President's budget. The result was the appropriation of an amount considerably less than the Bureau originally requested; and much less than was originally requested by the states.

Since the appropriations for administration were part of the general federal budget, broader considerations than the needs of the employment security program entered into the amounts appropriated. Arbitrary cuts were constantly made both by the Bureau of the Budget and Congress as a part of the process of trying to balance the federal budget.

Since the work loads and therefore the expenses of administering unemployment insurance were determined by the volume of employment and unemployment and were largely beyond the control of the state agencies, any substantial cuts in appropriation requests usually meant that a deficiency or supplemental appropriation request would have to be made to Congress. In fact, several supplemental appropriation requests have had to be made during a number of years. If there were any shortages in funds, amounts for the employment service were usually cut, since the employment service could expand or contract certain of its activities such as contacting employers to solicit job openings, while unemployment insurance work loads could not be reduced.

For many years, this appropriation process resulted in less being appropriated for administration than was collected in federal unemployment taxes. As a result, it was estimated in 1952 that up to that time the excess of collections of federal unemployment taxes over appropriations for administrative expenses totaled from $570 million to $1,128 million, depending on what expenses were included.[5]

[5] F. F. Fauri, *Study of Administrative Costs of Changes in State Employment Security Laws, Fiscal Years 1948–1952*, submitted to Subcommittee of Committee on Appropriations, House of Representatives (Washington, D.C.: United States Department of Labor, Bureau of Employment Security, January 15, 1953), p. 4, table A.

Earmarking of Federal Unemployment Tax

The difficulties in securing adequate appropriations led the federal and state employment security agencies to agree that the federal unemployment tax receipts should be earmarked for the employment security program. Furthermore, it was believed that if the taxes were earmarked, the Bureau of the Budget and the Congress would be more disposed to review appropriation requests on their merits rather than to be influenced by budget balancing or general fiscal policy considerations.

Beginning in 1949, the Bureau of Employment Security and the state agencies both sponsored bills, which, although they differed in many respects, were in general agreement on the objectives of earmarking the federal taxes solely for employment security purposes.

Both bills provided that the total receipts of the federal unemployment tax would be appropriated to the federal unemployment account in the Unemployment Trust Fund and that appropriations for administration would be made out to this account. However, the law enacted in 1954 provided that federal unemployment taxes would continue to go into the general funds of the Treasury, and appropriations for administration would be paid out of general funds. At the end of such fiscal year, the excess of tax collections would be appropriated to the Federal Unemployment Trust Fund.

The Interstate Conference and Administration bills differed as to the disposition that should be made of excess tax collections. The Interstate Conference bill provided that 80 percent of the surplus would be distributed to the states in proportion to their taxable payrolls and could be used either for benefits or for administration expenditures. The other 20 percent of the surplus would be left in the federal unemployment account until a reserve of $100 million had been accumulated for federal loans to states whose benefit reserves fell below a prescribed amount.[6] The Administration bill, on the other hand, provided that all surplus tax collections be accumulated without limit in the federal unemployment account for loan purposes. The bill enacted by Congress provided that excess funds would be appropriated to the federal unemployment account until a loan fund of $200 million was built up; thereafter, any excess tax collections would be distributed to the states for benefit or administration expenditures. Such funds could be used for administration, however, only if appropriated by the state legislature for specific purposes.[7]

This new method of financing provided by the 1954 Act apparently had little influence on appropriations. Since the appropriation requests were still part of the regular federal budget, they were subjected to the

---

[6] See Chapter 19 for details on the loan provision.

[7] *Employment Security Administration Financing Act of 1954*, Public Law 83–567, approved August 5, 1954.

same scrutiny as before.[8] Accordingly, on the joint request of the federal and state administrators, Congress was asked in 1960 to take the further step of providing that the federal unemployment tax receipts would be automatically appropriated to the Federal Unemployment Trust Fund and expenditures for administration would be paid out of such funds. The proposed bill was a modification of the bills proposed by the Administration and the states in 1953. Congress this time agreed to the proposal.[9] This changed the appropriation process to a trust fund operation similar to that for federal old-age, survivors, and disability insurance. Appropriations requests are subject to the same review as before by the Bureau of the Budget and Congress, but because they do not enter into the conventional federal budget they are not subjected to budget balancing and other general fiscal policies. As a result, as will be seen in Table 20–1, the Bureau of the Budget estimate submitted to Congress has been practically the same amount as what the Bureau has requested in recent years.

Table 20–1

Grants to States for Unemployment Compensation
and Employment Service Administration

	Budget Request*	Budget Estimate†	Appropriation
1955	$299,687,000	$263,156,000	$229,500,000
1956	287,622,000	251,480,000	250,000,000
1957	270,500,000	265,000,000	250,000,000
1958	314,000,000	303,000,000	292,814,000
1959	374,970,000	349,600,000	325,600,000
1960	337,000,000	328,684,000	315,819,000
1961	436,805,000	394,919,000	378,924,000
1962	420,995,000	407,695,000	405,000,000
1963	428,500,000	424,900,000	400,000,000
1964	429,608,000	432,570,000	425,000,000
1965	459,150,000	455,076,000	455,076,000

* Amount requested by the Department of Labor that the Bureau of the Budget include in the President's budget.
† Amount in the President's budget submitted to the Congress.

[8] Actually, although the states had habitually complained about receiving inadequate appropriations, little if any use of the surplus taxes distributed to the states were used for administrative purposes, except for the construction of office buildings. In turn, the federal bureau agreed to amortize the cost of these buildings, by granting funds for what it would have cost to rent these buildings. In spite of much hue and cry, the state agencies evidently have not felt the pinch of inadequate funds sufficiently to attempt to secure supplementary state appropriations out of these excess funds.

[9] Public Law 86–778, Title V, approved September 13, 1960. The statutory arrangements are quite complex, and need not be described for our purposes, except to say that the amendments raised the amount to be built up in the loan fund to $550 million or an amount equal to 0.4 percent of the federal unemployment tax, whichever is larger, and for a $250 million administrative fund to be built up to take care of increases in administrative costs during recessions. As a result, for some years, the states have received none of the surplus federal unemployment tax collections.

The "Ceiling" on Administrative Costs

For a few years, efforts to secure adequate appropriations were complicated by a limiting factor in the 1960 amendments. In this act, Congress included a ceiling of $350 million on the amount that could be appropriated for state administrative grants because of its concern over the steadily mounting costs of administering the state employment security programs. This also stemmed from the position taken by the House Ways and Means Committee that part of the federal unemployment tax receipts should go to the federal loan fund which was exhausted at the time. The same act increased the federal unemployment tax from 3 to 3.1 percent and the Committee wanted the additional 0.1 percent to go into the loan fund. Because of the increased claims load due to the 1961 recession and the additional administrative costs of the extended benefits paid under the Temporary Unemployment Compensation Act of 1961, the following year the ceiling was temporarily increased to $385 million for fiscal year 1961 and $410 million for the fiscal year 1962. Finally, in 1963, an act was passed which provided for a ceiling on state administrative grants equal to 95 percent of estimated tax receipts instead of the $350 million ceiling set by the 1960 amendments.[10] This increased the ceiling to an estimated $475 million for fiscal 1965. For that year Congress, for the first time, appropriated the amount in the President's budget, $455,076,000 (see Table 20–1). This indicates that, once the limiting factor of the $350 million ceiling was removed, the 1960 amendments had their effect of causing Congress to appropriate what was requested.

ALTERNATIVES TO 100 PERCENT FEDERAL GRANTS

The payment of the total administrative expenses of the state employment security systems by the federal government has been challenged from time to time and alternatives which would give the states more financial responsibility have been proposed.

Proposals for States to Pay All Administrative Costs

After World War II, employer groups began to press for changing the program to provide for a 100 percent credit against the federal tax instead of the 90 percent credit allowed for taxes paid each state. It was assumed that employers would thus pay to the state the 10 percent of the tax now paid to the federal government. States would finance their own costs of administration out of the additional unemployment taxes collected from employers by the state. Title III of the Social Security Act would be repealed.

This proposal was thoroughly debated in the late 1940's in the meetings of the Interstate Conference of Employment Security Agencies. The rep-

[10] Public Law 88–31, approved May 29, 1963.

resentatives of the state agencies appeared to favor retaining 100 percent grants, but with distribution of surplus federal taxes to the states as provided in modified form in the 1954 Administrative Financing Act. The states believed that the receipt of surplus taxes would make available to them funds to supplement any federal grants that might be inadequate. Other considerations may have influenced their decision to pursue this course rather than the 100 percent offset route. As one of the best friends of the Interstate Conference wrote at the time: "I suspicioned that many (State) Administrators thought they could do a better job getting money out of Washington than they could in getting it out of their own State legislatures. Others, with a sincere regard for the welfare of State programs, thought that unsympathetic legislatures might scuttle the State laws through providing inadequate financing."[11]

The shifting of responsibility to the states of financing their administrative costs was revived in 1955 by a majority of the Study Committee on Unemployment Compensation and Employment Service of the President's Commission on Intergovernmental Relations. The Committee members recommended a 99 percent credit against the federal unemployment tax. The 1 percent of the tax that would still be collected by the federal government would finance federal administrative expenses, the federal loan fund, and any excess costs of administration in a state above 0.3 percent of its taxable payrolls.[12]

In view of the recent enactment of the 1954 Administrative Financing Act, at its 1955 annual meeting the Interstate Conference voted opposition to the Study Committee's recommendation "pending adequate operating experience. . . ."[13] After considering the Study Committee's recommendation, as well as the alternatives of complete operation by the federal government, and operation on a 50-50 matching arrangement, the Commission on Intergovernmental Relations recommended that the 90 percent credit against the federal unemployment tax and provisions for federal grants of total state administrative costs under Title III be retained. The Commission did recommend some administration changes such as the use of a state's auditing, purchasing, and other fiscal controls if the Secretary of Labor determined that they afforded adequate protection of the national interest in the proper expenditure of federal funds. The Bureau of Employment Security now approves the use of certain centralized state services such as purchasing and printing. However, the Bureau has not relinquished its fiscal controls, including the auditing of federal grants, because of the Secretary of Labor's responsibility for determining amounts necessary for proper and efficient administration.

Although the 100 percent federal grant for administration has ceased to

[11] Stanley Rector, writing in *The Advisor* (Washington, D.C.: Unemployment Benefit Advisors, May 25, 1951), '51–5, p. 5.

[12] *A Study Committee Report on Unemployment Compensation and Employment Service*, submitted to the Commission on Intergovernmental Relations, June, 1955, p. 7.

[13] Resolution adopted at the Annual Meeting of the Interstate Conference of Employment Security Agencies, October 14, 1954.

be a live issue, we believe it desirable to appraise how it has worked and to consider whether an alternative method of state administrative financing would be desirable. Apparently, the method has worked reasonably well and the federal and state agencies have worked out methods of consultation so that it is no longer a strain on federal-state relationships. The principal question is whether it has resulted in more costly administration than would have been the case if each state agency had had to secure its appropriations wholly or partly through its state legislature. Congress has been concerned with the constantly mounting costs of the state programs and in 1952 and 1958 requested formal reports from the Bureau of Employment Security to determine the reasons for the huge amounts required for administration. In both instances the Bureau has been able to show that the increases have been due to state-wide increases in state salaries, rising costs of "nonpersonal" items, and increases in the number of employers and workers covered by the program. In 1958 and thereafter, administrative costs have also been higher because of increased claims costs, and, since 1961, because of expansions in the public employment service. We are in no position to judge whether the system could have been operated at lower costs. Perhaps an inquiry by a nongovernmental research organization should be made of the growing costs of state administration.

Pros and Cons for Present System

It might be of value, however, to review the pros and cons of the present system of 100 percent grants as compared with the alternatives of the states securing all their funds for administration through appropriations from their state legislatures, or operating under a system of grants on a 50-50 matching basis.

The advantages of the present system of 100 percent financing by the federal government were stated in 1955 by Robert C. Goodwin, Administrator of the Bureau of Employment Security: (a) It assures that the national interest in a properly and efficiently administered system of unemployment insurance and a nation-wide system of public employment offices will be realized. (b) It gives the federal government means of assuring that the operations of the program meet federal requirements. (c) It provides a flexible and adjustable mechanism for appropriating and allocating administrative funds, essential in view of the unpredictability and wide fluctuation in work loads of the employment security program, and the urgent and undeferrable nature of the work load. (d) It has resulted in higher personnel and administrative standards than would otherwise have been obtained in many states. (e) It permits a pooling of administrative funds so that adequate funds can be granted to each state without regard to the amount of taxes paid in each state.[14]

The arguments against 100 percent grants were stated succinctly by the

---

[14] For Mr. Goodwin's detailed statement, see his minority views in the Report of the Study Committee of the Commission on Intergovernmental Relations, *op. cit.*, pp. 41–65.

majority of the Study Committee of the President's Commission on Intergovernmental Relations in 1955:

> The majority believes . . . that the Federal Government now has more discretionary power over the States than it needs to meet this responsibility. It believes that the Federal power to determine the amount of money to be spent for State administration of the program and to determine the amounts to be expended by the States for various parts of the program creates an unsound and undesirable situation within the States, under which neither the State legislature nor State administrator can be called to account by citizens of the State for locally objectionable policies which may be imposed on them by limitations on Federal grants for administration or by the allocation of such grants to the functions to be performed by the State agency.[15]

We might add that the scrutiny of the request of such state agency by its state budget bureau, governor, and state legislature might result in more economical administration.

The majority of the Study Committee believed that even though it granted no funds to the state, the federal government could exercise sufficient supervision and control over state administration by giving the Bureau of Employment Security the authority to submit a recommended budget to the state governor. If the state appropriation was so much lower than the recommended budget that it resulted in performance below the standards set by the Bureau of Employment Security, the inadequate appropriation could form the basis for withdrawal of federal tax credit from employers of the state. The Majority Report of the Study Committee also proposed that any pertinent existing federal standards required for grants be retained as additional requirements for federal tax credits. In his minority views, Mr. Goodwin argued that this would inject the Bureau into state affairs more than under the existing Title III provisions. He also stated that withdrawal of tax credit would be too extreme a sanction for protecting federal interest in day-to-day administration.

Matching Grants as an Alternative

In its Annual Report for 1944, the Social Security Board recommended that both unemployment insurance benefit and administrative financing be placed on a grant-in-aid basis, with the federal government paying half the cost. This recommendation was repeated in Annual Reports through 1948. With respect to administrative grants, the 1948 report said that "The Social Security Administration has been concerned with the fact that 100-percent Federal financing does not create sufficient interest in economical administration."[16] The report went on to say that the existing federal budgetary procedures required frequent deficiency appropriations, since these procedures are not flexible enough for the changing economic

---

[15] *Ibid.*, p. 18.
[16] *Annual Report of the Federal Security Agency*, Social Security Administration (Washington, D.C.: U.S. Government Printing Office, 1948), p. 154.

conditions with which unemployment insurance had to deal. Thirdly, the report said that the states felt that Congress had not appropriated sufficient funds for the program. "On the other hand, the existing provision has permitted the State systems a more adequate administration than many other purely State functions have been able to achieve."[17]

There is no doubt that if a state had to run the gamut of the state budgetary process, it would not only have a greater interest in economical administration, but would probably be forced to exercise economics beyond measures now taken under the present system. It is not clear, however, how a grant-in-aid system would result in greater flexibility in financing, since most state legislatures meet only biennially and many of them only briefly. The federal appropriation process is cumbersome, but it can move with surprising speed in emergencies and Congress in recent years has been in almost continuous session. There is also the question as to whether the state legislatures would always appropriate sufficient amounts, when added to federal grants, to enable the state employment security agencies to operate efficiently.

A federal matching grant plan would be far superior to transferring the financing entirely to the states. There are advantages in federal financial participation that are too numerous to list. Federal participation not only assists in keeping administration on an efficient level, but enables the federal bureau to initiate policies and programs to expand and improve the system. These advantages can be secured either through a matching grant plan or the present financing of the entire cost of administration by the federal government. Matching grants may be superior from a theoretical standpoint. But after 30 years of experience under the present system, there would be danger, if a matching grant plan were substituted, of losing the advantages of the present system.

DISAGREEMENTS OVER ALLOCATION OF GRANTS TO THE STATES

Periodically, complaints are made that some states get less in administrative grants than their employers pay in federal unemployment taxes, while other states get more in grants than their employers pay in taxes. For example, in 1964, during the course of hearings on the appropriation for fiscal 1965 by a subcommittee of the House Committee on Appropriations, Congressman Winfield K. Denton of Indiana said he had just received a telephone call from the Indiana Manufacturers Association complaining that the Indiana agency received back in administrative grants only 50 percent of the total amount that Indiana employers paid under the federal unemployment tax.[18] At the same hearing, the Ohio Congressional delegation submitted for the record a letter to the Secretary of Labor complaining

---

[17] *Ibid.*, p. 155.

[18] *Departments of Labor and Health, Education, and Welfare Appropriations for 1965*, Hearings before a Subcommittee of the Committee on Appropriations, House of Representatives, 88th Cong., 2d sess., p. 526.

about cuts in the budgetary allocation to Ohio. This letter stated that Ohio ranked 47th among the states in the ratio of grants for administration to federal unemployment tax collections from employers in the state.[19]

It is true that there are wide differences from state to state in the ratio of funds granted for administration in proportion to federal unemployment taxes collected. The range in 1963 was from 50 percent in Indiana to 337.6 percent in Alaska. Twenty-two states received more in grants for administration than were received in federal unemployment taxes from their states. In 1952, there were 15 states; in 1961 (a recession year) there were 33 states. With the increase in the federal collections from 0.3 to 0.4 percent of taxable payrolls beginning with fiscal 1962, the number of states getting more than 100 percent of their employers' payments of federal unemployment taxes dropped back to 21 in 1962 and 22 in 1963 (see Table 20–2).

Table 20–2

Estimated Federal Unemployment Tax Receipts and Federal Funds Allocated to States for Administration during Fiscal Year 1963

(dollar amounts in thousands)

State	Federal Unemployment Tax Collections*	Federal Funds Allocated to States (Incl. Postage)	Ratio of Funds Allocated to Tax Collections (Percent) by Fiscal Year		
			1963	1962	1961
United States	$471,395	$411,725†	87.3	89.5	108.7
Alabama	5,848	4,950	84.6	88.4	112.9
Alaska	518	1,749	337.6	343.6	374.2
Arizona	3,176	5,150	162.2	171.5	201.8
Arkansas	2,693	4,001	148.6	157.5	191.6
California	48,327	50,513	104.5	104.4	127.8
Colorado	4,428	4,153	93.8	96.4	115.1
Connecticut	8,733	6,311	72.3	77.8	92.6
Delaware	1,381	969	70.2	69.8	75.9
District of Columbia .	2,762	3,278	118.7	122.7	166.0
Florida	10,805	7,761	71.8	73.4	90.9
Georgia	8,500	5,428	63.9	67.4	83.0
Hawaii	1,588	1,697	106.9	96.2	96.6
Idaho	1,208	2,553	211.3	214.1	250.5
Illinois	32,307	19,580	60.6	61.1	67.8
Indiana	13,260	6,636	50.0	51.3	63.7
Iowa	5,076	3,627	71.5	72.4	89.9
Kansas	4,073	3,076	75.5	75.6	89.5
Kentucky	5,109	4,274	83.7	90.3	111.9
Louisiana	6,164	5,414	87.8	90.1	105.1
Maine	2,140	1,934	90.4	89.2	114.5
Maryland	7,284	6,500	89.2	91.1	116.0
Massachusetts	17,018	14,417	84.7	92.5	112.0
Michigan	21,230	17,280	81.4	86.6	111.5
Minnesota	7,422	5,413	72.9	74.4	87.8

[19] *Ibid.*, p. 547.

Table 20–2 (Continued)

State	Federal Unemployment Tax Collections*	Federal Funds Allocated to States (Incl. Postage)	Ratio of Funds Allocated to Tax Collections (Percent) by Fiscal Year 1963	1962	1961
Mississippi	2,972	3,769	126.8	138.1	185.7
Missouri	11,236	7,295	64.9	65.2	80.4
Montana	1,243	2,142	172.3	158.0	205.5
Nebraska	2,728	1,962	71.9	79.5	84.5
Nevada	1,174	1,780	151.6	159.1	205.8
New Hampshire	1,740	1,531	88.0	93.3	114.4
New Jersey	19,400	15,998	82.5	80.1	102.3
New Mexico	1,691	2,388	141.2	143.7	167.8
New York	58,030	61,626	106.2	106.2	127.0
North Carolina	10,320	7,091	68.7	73.8	91.6
North Dakota	800	1,598	199.8	209.3	228.1
Ohio	27,270	17,368	63.7	67.7	84.4
Oklahoma	4,349	5,438	125.0	127.9	171.2
Oregon	4,315	5,073	117.6	124.0	135.2
Pennsylvania	31,793	29,992	94.3	97.7	114.4
Puerto Rico‡	1,933	2,957	153.0	165.7	....
Rhode Island	2,520	3,666	145.5	155.3	183.3
South Carolina	4,892	3,833	78.4	79.6	108.7
South Dakota	967	1,199	124.0	135.8	159.0
Tennessee	7,620	4,824	63.3	67.4	87.5
Texas	20,815	16,231	78.0	79.9	95.2
Utah	2,037	3,820	187.5	193.6	221.4
Vermont	759	1,162	153.1	164.1	165.6
Virginia	8,308	4,247	51.1	53.7	68.0
Washington	7,042	7,611	108.1	115.3	135.0
West Virginia	3,659	3,122	85.3	84.5	100.9
Wisconsin	10,080	5,995	59.5	59.5	71.5
Wyoming	652	1,195	183.3	156.8	175.0

* State distribution estimated on basis of data from the 1962 ES–202 reports—*Employment, Wages, and Contributions,* the ES–202 Taxable Wage Supplement for calendar year 1962, and *Employment and Wages,* first quarter 1962.

† Includes allocations to Virgin Islands—$126,000, and Guam—$25,000.

‡ Puerto Rico became part of the federal-state unemployment insurance system beginning January, 1961.

Source: Bureau of Employment Security, U.S. Department of Labor.

In response to questions raised in the 1964 hearings on fiscal 1965 appropriations, the Bureau explained that the differences in the proportionate amount of grants in the various states were due to many factors, including:

1. More sparsely settled states have higher costs because of the higher overhead of small, widely scattered local offices. (Of the 19 states receiving 100 percent or more in grants in each of the six years ending in 1963, all but California and New York were rural or relatively sparsely settled states.)
2. Variations in work load, mainly due to variations in the rate of unemployment.
3. Differences in salary rates. (Annual salaries averaged $6,178 in California and $5,605 in New York as compared with $4,553 in Indiana and $4,678

in Ohio, the latter two states being the ones that raised complaints at the hearing.)

4. Differences in nonpersonal costs, especially rents.

5. The relative complexity of the state law, particularly with respect to experience rating and the method of determining eligibility for benefits. States covering more employers than are covered by the federal tax also have higher administrative costs.

6. More intensive programs of the employment service for youth, veterans, minority groups, and older workers.[20]

The above will indicate the complexity of the factors that enter into the determination of the amounts granted. Since the whole basis for the operation of Title III is challenged by such criticisms as those raised by Indiana and Ohio in 1964, it is appropriate to examine the principles involved and the soundness or unsoundness of the provisions of Title III as to how grants shall be determined.

Such complaints as that of Indiana, of course, are based on a misunderstanding of, or disagreement with, the basic purpose of Title III, which is to create a national pooled fund out of which each state is granted what is needed for proper and efficient administration. The position of such states as Indiana is that administrative grants should, in effect, be rebates of the amount of federal unemployment taxes their employers pay. Their position is understandable in view of the fact that *in effect* 2.7 percent of the 3.1 percent federal unemployment tax[21] is "rebated" for benefit purposes. Since employers get credit equal to 2.7 percent against the 3.1 percent federal tax if they are covered by an approved state law, they ask why their state cannot get the remaining 0.4 percent they pay to the federal government, which largely goes for administrative expenses.[22]

States taking this attitude feel that all the unemployment taxes are state money.[23] It must be stated unequivocally that the 0.4 percent of the federal unemployment tax that is paid to the federal government by employers is federal money to which the states have neither a legal nor moral claim. It must be emphasized that there is actually a 3.1 percent federal excise tax on the first $3,000 of each employee's annual wages, and credit for an amount equal to 2.7 percent of this is allowed an employer if he is covered by a state unemployment insurance law that meets federal requirements. If the state does not meet these requirements, the law provides that the

---

[20] *Ibid.*, pp. 527–33.

[21] Since the 1960 amendments, the 90 percent credit applies to only 3.0 percent of the 3.1 percent federal tax, and so still equals 2.7 percent of taxable wages.

[22] In fact, the provision for distribution of excess federal unemployment tax collections to the states on the basis of their taxable payrolls, as provided in the "Reed Act" of 1954, is a concession to this point of view.

[23] This was a major issue in the Senate debate on the 1961 Temporary Extended Unemployment Compensation Act, in which an amendment by Senator Byrd proposing that any surplus remaining of the temporary increase in the federal unemployment tax to finance the TEUC program be rebated to the states in proportion to their taxable payrolls was defeated by a narrow margin.

employer will pay the entire 3.1 percent to the federal government. Furthermore, from the beginning the law has provided that the granting of funds to the state shall be based on the amount it needs for administration on the basis of several factors, *none of which has ever been the amount of taxes paid by the state's covered employers to the federal government.*

Given the program of 100 percent grants, the allocation of costs on the basis of what is necessary for proper and efficient administration is the only method that makes sense. It is natural that there will be differences in state costs in a national economy. With the great variation in the demographic characteristics of the states, the wide differences in work loads because of differences in the rate of unemployment, the different salary scales, the great differences in the state laws, and all the other factors that are taken into consideration in determining how much shall be allocated, the administrative grants cannot coincide with the tax receipts from a state. With the pooling of the federal unemployment tax receipts, the grant can be tailored to the needs of each state.

It is probable that most of the "gripes" regarding inadequate allocation of grants to individual states arise from the fact that Congress has frequently appropriated an inadequate over-all amount, rather than from any inequitable or improper allocation of funds by the Department of Labor.

Nevertheless, it must be recognized that after a quarter of a century of trial and error, the methods for allocating funds to the states for administration are still unavoidably imperfect. As Dr. Eveline M. Burns has written:

The disadvantages of a system of 100 percent grants have long been evident in the unemployment insurance program, where the Federal government pays all of the cost of administration of programs over whose nature and content it has little or no control. Here differences of opinion between the two levels of government have inevitably prevailed as to the sums needed for "proper and efficient administration," and the States have no financial incentive to moderate their requests or to give appropriate weight to the administrative costs of various proposed changes in the law, because these costs are met by the Federal government.[24]

SUMMARY AND CONCLUSIONS

The Social Security Act provided federal grants to meet the entire cost of state administration because of the fear that the state legislatures would not provide sufficient funds. Providing grants for administration also made it possible for the federal government to impose requirements designed to secure good and proper administration.

These requirements have resulted in relatively efficient administration, a personnel merit system in all states, coordination with the public employment service, and highly valuable national statistics on operations and

[24] Eveline M. Burns, *Social Security and Public Policy* (New York: McGraw-Hill Book Co., Inc., 1956), pp. 240–41.

labor market information. The Federal Bureau interprets federal objectives, develops and recommends procedures and systems, provides technical assistance in the installation of its recommended procedures, conducts training on programs and procedures, evaluates operations, allocates funds, and issues policies, principles, and standards. Acceptance of the federal leadership in these activities is obtained more through consultation than through coercion.

Over the years efforts have been made to achieve an equitable basis for granting administrative funds to states. For a number of years, grants were determined largely on the basis of work loads and time allowances for accomplishing the projected work load, with other objective factors being considered. More recently, the work load and time-factor system has been replaced by other objective considerations, but the methods for determining grants are still far from scientific.

There has been a continuous struggle to get adequate federal appropriations. At first, appropriations were paid out of general federal funds. Changes in the law in 1954 to earmark federal unemployment tax collections for employment security purposes apparently had little tangible effect in securing more adequate appropriations. Further legislation to treat unemployment taxes as a trust fund freed them from federal budgetary limitations. However, only after Title III was amended in 1963 to change the authorization from a fixed ceiling on appropriations of $350 million to a ceiling equal to 95 percent of federal unemployment tax collections was the ceiling raised to a level above the appropriation requested for administration. The total amount in the President's budget was appropriated for 1965.

The soundness of the 100 percent federal grant for administration has been questioned from time to time. Proposals have been made for a 100 percent credit against the federal tax, or a 99 percent credit, with the states then being responsible for meeting their own administrative expenses. The state administrators have not favored such a change, and as an alternative, have secured federal legislation providing that excess federal unemployment taxes be distributed to the states for either benefit or administrative use. The excess funds distributed to them, however, have not been used to supplement federal grants. Instead, they have been used almost exclusively to build employment security office buildings which are amortized out of federal grants.

The system has been criticized as providing no incentive for the state agencies to economize. As an alternative, federal matching grants have been proposed. Theoretically, federal-state sharing of costs would have the advantage over the present total financing by the federal government. Grants would assure continuing federal supervision but would require state administrators to justify their costs to their own state legislatures, which should result in more economic administration. Practically, however, it would be wiser to preserve the present system with all its disadvantages, rather than to risk a shift to an untried system of financing.

The present system of administrative grants has apparently worked fairly well. Although Congress has been concerned about rising costs of the program, the Bureau has been able to justify these increases, which are largely due to growth in the program and to salary and price increases.

There are periodic complaints that in the allocation of administrative funds, the states do not get back what their employers contributed in taxes. Funds are allocated on the basis of many factors, including the density of population and industrialization of the state. Other factors are differences in unemployment rates and salary scales. Complaints that grants to a state should be equal to tax collections from that state have no legal or moral basis. We are not impressed with the argument that federal unemployment tax collections are state money that should be returned to the state. The federal unemployment tax, like all federal taxes, is a national tax, to be used for national purposes. It is natural that, within a national economy, there will be differences in state costs. The pooling of the tax on a national basis and allocation of funds on the basis of needs for proper and efficient administration meets the states' needs better than if each state were given what their employers contributed. Actually, most complaints as to allocation of state grants are due to inadequacy in the total federal appropriations. Nevertheless, the allocation of grants is unavoidably imperfect. The task, then, is to secure better Congressional understanding of the program's needs and to strive for improvement in the process of allocating funds to the states so that they can properly and efficiently administer their programs.

Chapter 21

The Relationship
of the Employment Service
and Unemployment Insurance

The goal of the employment service as conceived now is the development on a local, state, and national basis of a manpower utilization program. In addition to registration of applicants and their referral to jobs, this involves a comprehensive knowledge of manpower requirements and manpower supply, selection and referral of workers to training programs, facilities for research and analysis, testing and counseling, and a host of similar techniques essential to a community manpower program.

It is clear that the development of a comprehensive manpower program is the present objective of the USES and state employment services. It is equally clear that this is an ideal or goal unfortunately quite far from reality in many states.

Our concern in this chapter is to trace the relationship of the employment service to unemployment insurance. Increasingly the registration of applicants for unemployment insurance benefits, the determination of eligibility, the application of the "work test," and other devices to administer the unemployment compensation program represent only a facet, although an important one, of the employment service responsibility. This facet has been criticized for absorbing too much time and energy and personnel to the detriment of the essential manpower functions of the employment service. Some persons in the United States, as well as in the United Kingdom, have therefore suggested that the administration of unemployment insurance payments should be separate from the employment service. However, the proposal for complete separation has not been practical. The problem, therefore, is the protection of the basic goals of the employment service while it simultaneously participates in the administration of the unemployment insurance program.

When the Social Security Act was passed in 1935, the desirability of coordination of unemployment insurance and the public employment service was taken for granted and was made a condition for the states receiving Title III grants. Such coordination had been standard practice in countries with compulsory unemployment insurance systems such as the United Kingdom and Germany.

Unemployment insurance claimants are required by legislation to file claims for benefits and register for work at the local public employment offices. This requirement attempted to facilitate getting claimants back to work as soon as possible, and to test the availability for work of unemployment insurance claimants by their referral to suitable jobs. Claimants who refused offers of suitable work without good cause could be denied benefits, and in this way, it was assumed that the public employment service could apply a "work test" to unemployment insurance claimants.

It was recognized that the required registration of unemployment insurance claimants with the public employment offices would bring large numbers of qualified workers to the offices. It was also expected that employers covered by unemployment insurance would hire workers through the employment service in order to get claimants off the unemployment insurance rolls. This expectation has been only partially fulfilled. Not all employers use the employment service regularly; some use it only as a last resort if they cannot find workers elsewhere.

It was also believed that a desirable flexibility in the use of staff in the local employment offices would result from the coordination of unemployment insurance and the employment service. In periods of high unemployment when job openings were scarce, employment service personnel could be shifted to assist in taking claims. This did occur, but too frequently the processing of unemployment insurance claims so overwhelmed local employment service staffs that activities related to the employment placement function almost reached a standstill. Employment service officials increasingly argued that employment service staff should be left free of unemployment insurance duties so that they could "develop" job openings and give adequate attention to filling job orders. They also contended that the preponderance of unemployment insurance claimants in public employment offices had given them the reputation as "*un*employment offices" and had degraded the public image of the employment service. Despite arrangements for the hiring of temporary personnel for peak periods for "claims taking," there has continued to be a feeling that the employment service is handicapped in its operations by the presence of unemployment insurance activities in many local offices. This became a problem especially in large metropolitan areas which contain 50 or 60 percent of wage and salary employment in the nation and where the claims loads are greatest.

Beginning in 1962, the Bureau of Employment Security secured appropriations for improvement and expansion of employment service operations. This included the physical separation of local employment office functions from unemployment insurance, at least in the larger cities. Is this a sound move and, if so, how far should it be carried? Should there eventually be a separation of the public employment service and unemployment insurance at all local levels, as well as at the state and federal levels? Or is there some middle course? This chapter will be concerned largely with these questions.

DEVELOPMENT OF THE PUBLIC EMPLOYMENT SERVICE

The history of the United States Employment Service and its affiliated offices need only be summarized here since it has been detailed elsewhere.[1] Some local and state employment services were established in the late nineteenth and early twentieth centuries and several moves were made toward establishing a national system during and following World War I.

Beginning in 1907, the Bureau of Immigration and Naturalization began to distribute labor market information to immigrants through a Division of Information, but made few actual placements. In 1913, the Immigration Service was transferred to the newly created Department of Labor. The necessities of directing workers into war industries and agriculture during World War I resulted in the expansion of the Division of Information into the United States Employment Service and its establishment as a separate bureau in the Department of Labor. Provision of federal funds enabled expansion of the Employment Service to 773 offices in 605 cities. In fiscal 1918–19, the United States Employment Service registered six million workers, received notice of ten million job openings, and made about five million placements.

Historians of that period recognized that the public employment offices made valuable contributions in meeting the nation's manpower requirements.[2] With the end of the war, and the return to "normalcy," appropriations were stopped and an overwhelming number of offices were closed overnight. The few remaining public offices were in cities that had prewar experience with good local offices: Rochester, Cincinnati, Milwaukee.

During the period from 1919 to 1932 attempts were made to secure legislation for a nation-wide employment service, but without success. Finally, in 1931, New York's Senator Robert F. Wagner introduced a bill for a federal-state system of public employment offices. The bill was passed by Congress but was vetoed by President Hoover, who favored a national system of employment offices. A few weeks later, the Secretary of Labor reorganized what remained of a federal employment service, setting up federal offices without regard to the existing state and local employment

---

[1] See William Haber and Daniel H. Kruger, *The Role of the United States Employment Service in a Changing Economy* (Kalamazoo: W. E. Upjohn Institute for Employment Research, February, 1964), chap. iii; "The Public Employment Service System, 1933–1953," *Employment Security Review*, Vol. XX, No. 6 (June, 1953) entire issue; and "Public Employment Service in the Nation's Job Market, 1933–1963," *Employment Security Review*, Vol. XXX, No. 6 (June, 1963), entire issue.

[2] D. H. Smith, *The United States Employment Service*, Institute for Government Research Monographers of United States Government, No. 28 (Baltimore: Johns Hopkins Press, 1923), pp. 13–28. Harrison and Associates, *Public Employment Offices* (New York: Russell Sage Foundation, 1924), p. 624.

offices. As a result, 53 of the 96 federal offices were located in cities where state or local offices were already in existence.[3] The available funds were spread so thin that inadequately staffed and poorly housed offices resulted. The personnel was also inferior, since many were appointed for political reasons rather than for their ability to perform a placement function.

The Wagner-Peyser Act of 1933

The inefficiency and limited coverage of federal offices, the wastefulness of their duplication with state and locally financed employment services, and the stimulus of the need for finding jobs for the unemployed during the depression led to the enactment in 1933 of a revised employment service bill. The Wagner-Peyser Act of June 6, 1933,[4] provided for a jointly financed federal-state system of public employment offices. At the time it was passed, there were only 192 public employment offices in 120 cities affiliated with 23 state systems. These 23 state employment services almost immediately affiliated with the United States Employment Service under the Wagner-Peyser Act, and by the end of 1935, the number of state organizations had increased to 36, with 232 local or district offices. However, the state and local employment offices existing in 1933 were inadequate to meet the immediate pressing problems of placing workers on federal public work and work relief programs. Consequently, a few months after the passage of the Wagner-Peyser Act, a federally financed National Re-employment Service was established to fill the gap. In almost all states with public employment offices, the director of the State Employment Service served also as the state director for the National Re-employment Service. In states without a public employment service, the National Re-employment Service was organized to deal with this problem. Thus a nation-wide public employment service was in existence when the Social Security Act was passed in 1935.

Unemployment Insurance Causes Employment Service Expansion

In order to receive a grant of administrative funds for unemployment insurance, Title III of the Social Security Act provided that the state would have to pay unemployment benefits solely through the public employment offices in the state.[5] The Social Security Board interpreted this requirement as authorizing the financing of local employment offices through Title III grants. All states expanded their offices, largely by taking over National Re-employment Service offices. By July, 1939, all the states had affiliated with the United States Employment Service and were paying unemploy-

---

[3] Ruth Kellogg, *The United States Employment Service* (Chicago: University of Chicago Press, 1933), p. 83.

[4] 48 Stat. 113.

[5] The provision also contained the phrase "or such other agencies as the (Social Security) Board may approve." The Board decided to approve only public employment offices.

ment benefits through local employment offices. As a result, the National Re-employment Service was liquidated. It was also not long before Title III funds were paying for the entire operation of the state employment services and the provisions for matching federal funds with state funds in the Wagner-Peyser Act were repealed.[6]

In all the states, unemployment insurance and the State Employment Service were placed in the same administrative agency. In 14 states this is an independent commission or board; in 18 states, an independent department; in 20 states, a division of the Department of Labor or workmen's compensation agency.[7]

Frequent Shifting of United States Employment Service

For some years, the federal part of the public employment service lived a wandering career. The Wagner-Peyser Act had placed the United States Employment Service in the Department of Labor and the Social Security Act had made the Social Security Board (which was responsible for unemployment insurance) an independent agency. A cooperative agreement was reached, however, between the Secretary of Labor and the Social Security Board on March 30, 1937. This provided for integrated operation of the United States Employment Service and Unemployment Insurance as a single agency. Then, on July 1, 1939, in accordance with the President's Reorganization Plan No. 1, the United States Employment Service was transferred to the Federal Security Agency (established by this Reorganization Plan) and made a part of a new Bureau of Employment Security encompassing both the Employment Service and Unemployment Insurance. The anticipated manpower problems created by the country's participation in World War II led to the "nationalization" of the 48 state employment services by Presidential Order on December 19, 1941. These were "borrowed" for the duration of the War and managed by the United States Employment Service as the operating arm of the War Manpower Commission. At the close of the War, after the dissolution of the War Manpower Commission in 1945, the United States Employment Service was again returned to the Department of Labor and the states resumed the administration of the state public employment service systems in 1946. On July 1, 1948, the United States Employment Service was again transferred to the Federal Security Agency and again became a part of the Bureau of Employment Security. In 1949, the President's Reorganization Plan No. 2 transferred the entire Bureau of Employment Security, includ-

---

[6] Public Law 81–775.

[7] Arizona and Wisconsin were exceptions. In Arizona, which has an Employment Security Commission, the Directors of the Unemployment Insurance Division and the Employment Service Division are top executive officers, answering directly to the Commission. In Wisconsin, both unemployment compensation and the employment service are under the Wisconsin Industrial Commission but are separate divisions largely autonomous in operation.

ing the Employment Service and Unemployment Insurance, back to the Department of Labor, where they have remained ever since.

This frequent shifting of the United States Employment Service was not without its effect on its personnel. Certainly at the national level, Employment Service personnel paid little attention to unemployment insurance. Even after they were placed in the same Bureau, the two groups never worked as a completely unified team. For some years, the Employment Service staff was divided into three units in the Bureau of Employment Security; the Farm Placement Service and Veterans Employment Service operated as separate units. The legislative complexities and pressing problems of unemployment insurance received the major administrative attention in the Bureau.

Reorganization of Bureau of Employment Security

In February, 1962, the Bureau of Employment Security was reorganized in order to give both the Employment Service and Unemployment Insurance Service much more authority and independence. The head of the Employment Service was again given the title of Director of the United States Employment Service. Emphasis in the reorganization focused on separating the two services as much as possible, although they continued to be in one Bureau and under the same over-all administrator.[8]

Concurrent with this reorganization, the Bureau launched a campaign to improve employment security operations in 55 metropolitan areas. This included the establishment of a proper office structure, internal office organization, and a better management system designed to better serve the employment needs of the area. The new office structure provided for a separation of unemployment insurance claims and Employment Service operations. The intent was to introduce similar reorganizations in smaller cities wherever feasible and desirable. Specialized employment offices were established on an industrial-occupational basis, usually with separate offices for professional and commercial workers, industrial workers, service workers, and unskilled labor. These offices were located where these types of employment were concentrated; for example, professional and commercial offices were located in the center of the city. This was a move which represented a significant change in operating policy regarding the relationship of Unemployment Insurance and the Employment Service.

SHOULD EMPLOYMENT SERVICE AND UNEMPLOYMENT INSURANCE FUNCTIONS BE SEPARATED?

The arguments for and against separation of the Employment Service from Unemployment Insurance administration have usually been discussed from the standpoint of the advantages to the Employment Service.[9]

---

[8] In a further reorganization in December, 1962, the Farm Labor Service was organized as a separate unit in the Bureau.

[9] See Haber and Kruger, *op. cit.*, pp. 71–73.

Application of the Work Test

The purpose of coordinated unemployment insurance and employment service operations has been to assure the maximum exposure of claimants to jobs, and through this, a concrete test of the claimants' availability for work.[10] The most objective test of availability is whether the claimant accepts the offer of a suitable job. If the employment office offers a claimant a suitable job and he turns it down or fails to apply for it, there is objective evidence as to whether or not he is available for work. The Employment Service is the only public agency through which such a test can be applied. If the job offer is refused, the Employment Service can find out the reasons for the refusal and notify the unemployment insurance personnel so that it can determine whether a disqualification should be imposed.

How well has this worked out in practice? Few statistics are available on the number of jobs offered to unemployment insurance claimants since it is the established policy of the Employment Service to refer registrants to jobs in terms of their qualifications without reference to whether or not they are unemployment insurance claimants. An indication of the extent to which the Employment Service participates in job recruiting is given by the placement "penetration rate," the number of nonagricultural placements per 100 workers in nonagricultural employment. In 1960, the national placement rate was 12.0 percent. The rate varied from 5.1 percent in Delaware to 34.9 percent in Nevada.[11] However, about one third of nonagricultural placements are temporary—2 million out of 6.3 million placements in 1964.

In turn, placement of unemployment insurance claimants represents only a fraction of total nonagricultural placements. In Ohio, for example, in January–June, 1964, placement of claimants totaled 10,126 or 17.4 percent of the total of 58,184 nonagricultural placements exclusive of placements of casual labor and household workers.[12]

These figures were given in a letter dated August 31, 1964, from Robert C. Goodwin to Congressman Elmer J. Holland, Chairman of the Select Subcommittee on Labor. Data were also given showing that in May, 1964, only 56,400 or 41.9 percent of the estimated total of 134,900 unemployed in Ohio were drawing unemployment compensation; an estimated 37,700 or 27.9 percent were covered by unemployment compensation but had exhausted benefits, had been disqualified, or had delayed filing for benefits. The balance, an estimated 40,800 or 30.2 percent, had worked in non-

[10] For a discussion of the requirement that unemployment insurance claimants be available for work, see Chapter 14.
[11] Haber and Kruger, *op. cit.*, pp. 82–83. The authors warn that this is only a rough measure of penetration, as there are significant variations in turnover and types of placements made in the states.
[12] *Public Employment Service*, Hearings of Select Subcommittee on Labor, Committee on Education, House of Representatives, U.S. Congress, 1964, p. 182.

covered employment. While these statistics are not comparable with the placement figures, it does indicate one reason why so small a proportion of the placements were of claimants; about 60 percent of the registrants for jobs were not drawing unemployment compensation at the time. Mr. Goodwin pointed out a number of other factors that influenced the small proportion of claimants to the total placed. For example, the average Ohio claimant was unemployed only 6½ weeks and a significant number were unemployed for even a shorter period. As has been pointed out elswhere, many of these are on short-term layoff with a promise of a call back to work and therefore other employers were not willing to hire them. In fact, when the claimant knew that he was on a short-term layoff, he was usually unwilling to accept a job on which he could stay only a week or two.

Based on the modest record of the employment service in applying the "work test," no one could contend that registration of unemployment insurance claimants with the Employment Service should be abandoned. The real question is whether the Employment Service's record of placing claimants would be poorer or better if the local employment office were separated from the local unemployment insurance operation. Application of the "work test" requires close collaboration and communication between Unemployment Insurance and Employment Service staff. After steps to separate the functions commenced in 1962, federal unemployment insurance officials expressed the belief that where Employment Service and Unemployment Insurance operations have been physically separated, there has been an improvement in collaboration and communication. When the two staffs were located together, there was often an assumption that collaboration was going on, although in fact it was practically nonexistent. When the two functions are physically separated, it is necessary to set up definite procedures for clearance of information and coordination, and it is easier for supervisors to check on whether such procedures are being carried out.

Provision of a "One-Stop" Service

An argument advanced for housing the unemployment insurance and employment service functions together has been that the worker can file a claim for benefits and register for work at a saving of both time and travel expense. Over the years, the tendency has been to locate metropolitan branch offices closer to claimants' homes in order to distribute the claims load evenly. However, since many claimants do not live near where they work, branch offices were located to a large degree in areas other than where jobs were available, usually in the central section of the city. One method that has been attempted to expose workers to jobs outside their neighborhoods has been to clear job orders with other branch offices if the order-receiving office cannot fill the job from its own registrant file. This was attempted on an elaborate scale in Chicago, but the results were not satisfactory. There was a tendency for the job-receiving office to hold the order for several days until the possibilities of filling it were exhausted. It was then circulated to other branch offices. By the time the other branch offices received the job order, a week might have elapsed. In the meantime, in a large number of cases, the employer had filled the order by other means.

The general pattern that is being encouraged by USES in metropolitan areas is to set up branch unemployment insurance offices in areas convenient to the claimants' homes, and to establish specialized employment offices for different occupational or industrial groups in the area where most of the job openings will occur. This means that, in most instances, the claimant will have to file for benefits and register for work in different areas. It has been argued that this will involve considerable transportation expense, particularly for claimants living in the suburbs who will have to go into the center of the city to register for work. However, it is necessary to register for work only once, unless the nature of the work, such as stevedoring, requires frequent contact with the employment office. Since some states permit mass *pro forma* registration in temporary layoffs such as for model changes in automobile production, separation of the insurance and employment offices results in no inconvenience to the claimants in these cases. On the other hand, unemployment insurance offices can be located near the worker's home to minimize his transportation expense in filing weekly benefits claims. This system has been used in New York City for many years with marked success. Liaison officers are placed in both the neighborhood unemployment insurance offices and the specialized and centralized employment offices to assure that proper coordination between unemployment insurance and employment service operations is maintained. Claims offices are also located in the same buildings as the employment offices so that workers whose residence and occupational branch of the employment service are in the same area have a "one-stop" service.

The early results of the reorganization of metropolitan offices were quite promising. Nonfarm placements rose 22 percent in the 55 largest metropolitan areas in 42 reorganized areas, but they rose only 14 percent in the 13 areas that had not been reorganized.[13]

It may be questioned whether this greater increase in placements was due solely to reorganization. Increased appropriations made possible a large increase in employment service staff in these offices. Between 1961 and 1963, staff was increased by 35.2 percent in the local offices of the 55 metropolitan areas. The following increases and decreases took place in these local employment office activities for September–November, 1963, as compared with January–March, 1961:[14]

[13] Haber and Kruger, *op. cit.*, p. 109.
[14] *Report of First Meeting*, Committee on Employment Service Programs and Operations, Interstate Conference of Employment Security Agencies (Washington, D.C.: March 31, April 1, 2, 1964), pp. 39–40.

Activities in Metropolitan Employment Offices

Activity	January–March, 1961	September–November, 1963	Percentage Change
New applications for work	1,489,936	1,331,040	−10.7
Counseling interviews	234,568	245,036	4.5
Employer visits	138,166	193,196	39.8
Openings received	719,645	976,871	35.7
Total placements made	609,075	843,504	38.5
Professional placements	29,186	46,358	58.8

These are noncomparable periods, both on the basis of seasonal and cyclical factors. September–November is normally an expansionary season, while January–March is normally characterized by contraction. Also, January–March, 1961, was the trough of the business cycle, while September–November, 1963, occurred during the recovery phase of the business cycle. Nevertheless, from this data it can be inferred that the increases in placements were largely due to the increases in employer visiting and more thorough placement activity made possible by the increased personnel, rather than to separation of employment service and unemployment insurance functions. Employment service officials, however, assert that the reorganization of the offices was also an important factor.

The "Image" of the Employment Service

It is said that unemployment insurance operations in local offices have hurt the "image" of the Employment Service negatively. No doubt the presence of large numbers of unemployment insurance claimants in the local employment offices, especially during recessions, has created the impression that the offices are principally concerned with taking claims and not with seeking employment opportunities for those who need them. Among workers, as well as employers, the public employment offices are often referred to as "unemployment offices." This may be partly due to the fact that only a small portion of the claimants get job offers through the local employment office, so for them it *is* an "unemployment office," a place to file unemployment insurance.

Employment offices have greatly improved over the past ten years. The funds made available under Title III, and particularly the increases since 1961, have made it possible to expand and improve the services provided. The requirement in Title III of merit selection of personnel has greatly improved the quality of its employees. During the last decade, the states have also made extensive use of the surplus federal unemployment tax funds distributed to them under the "Reed Act" of 1954 to obtain many attractive and well-located local employment offices. The national leadership provided under the Wagner-Peyser Act has also contributed to the improvement of the public employment service.

There is another reason, however, for the poor image of the Employment Service. During the depth of the depression of the 1930's, the Employment Service had no alternative but to give most of its energies to the job needs of relief recipients, and to assign them to publicly sponsored jobs under the many alphabetical programs which prevailed, such as the PWA, CWA, WPA, NYA. After World War II, the Employment Service, either through legislation or public pressures, was concerned with special programs for handicapped workers, older workers, inexperienced youth, migratory labor, minority groups—in short, programs for those who had difficulty in finding jobs. This emphasis on disadvantaged groups, when added to the traditional preponderance of unskilled and casual workers among those placed by the Employment Service, created an image that would attract neither skilled job-seekers, especially professional, semi-professional, and while-collar workers, nor employees who needed such talent.

Since 1950, the Employment Service has been steadily increasing the number of placements of white-collar workers. Placements of professional and managerial personnel have increased from 87,500 in fiscal 1951 to 249,100 in fiscal 1964. Clerical and sales placements increased from 755,000 to 995,000 in the same period. The proportion of all white-collar placements to total nonagricultural placements increased from 13 to almost 20 percent during this period.

The proportion of casual and domestic workers placed to total workers placed has gradually declined, although in fiscal 1964 casual workers placed were still 393,000 or 6 percent and day workers in domestic service were still 619,000 or over 9 percent of total placements. Placements of unskilled workers have also declined, but total 1,924,000 or almost 30 percent of total placements. The Employment Service evidently is still looked on by many as a source of supply for only such workers.

The "image" of the Employment Service that we have been discussing is largely an employer image. Although some white-collar workers may also hold this poor image, surveys of worker attitudes do not indicate that the claims-taking function of the Employment Service influences their use of it. A 1962 survey of attitudes toward the public employment service in Ohio revealed that when workers were actually searching for jobs, the state employment service ranked second among the preferred methods of looking for a job. Only direct application to the employer ranked higher. Twenty percent of those who responded to the question as to their first preference gave the state employment service, compared to about 25 percent who listed direct application to employers.[15]

A 1964 study conducted in Erie, Pennsylvania showed essentially the same results. When the blue-collar workers surveyed were asked to select

[15] Research Foundation, The Ohio State University, Use of and Attitude toward the Ohio Bureau of Unemployment Compensation: A Research Report, Project 1472 (Columbus, 1963), p. 16.

from a list of ways to get a job which way they thought was best, 33 per-cent indicated direct application to the employer compared to 31 percent who selected the state employment service.[16]

It was concluded in the Ohio study that the reason more workers did not use the Ohio State Employment Service was simply that it was not the customary way of finding a job.

It was found in the Ohio study, however, that many employers did not use the Employment Service because of the image they held of it. The close integration of the Employment Service with unemployment compen-sation contributed to this image in two ways. Many employers believed that some workers were drawing unemployment compensation who did not need it. (The report said that "shockingly large numbers of employers were found to be either uninformed or misinformed about the system.") Secondly, many employers assumed that most job applications referred to them by the Employment Service are frequent claimants for unemployment com-pensation.[17] Here again, although the employers were misinformed, the Employment Service image was hurt nevertheless.

Evidently, then, the separation of the Employment Service from the unemployment insurance program have more influence on employers than on workers. It should remove any adverse attitudes that employers carry over from unemployment insurance to the Employment Service. Separation still would not remove the prevalent conception of the Employment Service as a source for supply mainly for casual, unskilled, and household workers. Freed of any handicap that employment insurance may give it, the Em-ployment Service will still have to prove its worth as a placement agency[18] especially to employers.

Diversion of Employment Service Personnel to Taking Unemployment Insurance Claims

Unemployment insurance and employment office operations were orig-inally unified at the local office level to give some flexibility in the utiliza-tion of personnel. If there was a sudden influx of unemployment insurance claims because of an increase in unemployment, it was assumed that job openings would decline and Employment Service personnel could be shifted to help take claims for benefits. Experience has proved, however, that too much shifting has occurred, to the detriment of the Employment Service.

[16] The authors were given this data from a study shortly to be published which was conducted by the W. E. Upjohn Institute for Employment Research.

[17] Research Foundation, The Ohio State University, *op. cit.*, pp. 158–59.

[18] For further discussion of the separation of local employment service and unem-ployment insurance functions, see Haber and Kruger, *op. cit.*, pp. 70–74. Also, see *The Role and Mission of the Federal-State Employment Service in the American Economy*, report prepared by the subcommittee staff of the Select Subcommittee on Labor, Com-mittee on Education and Labor, House of Representatives, 88th Cong., 2d sess. (Decem-ber, 1964), pp. 37–39 (Washington, D.C.: U.S. Government Printing Office, 1964).

Employment Service officials maintain that placement personnel should be kept on their regular work assignments in order to place the maximum number of claimants possible. They argue that during periods of heavy unemployment, it is all the more important that Employment Service personnel be left free from claims taking so that they can more intensively develop job orders and refer registrants to them.

Because of complaints about the diversion of Employment Service personnel during the 1950's, the Bureau of Employment Security obtained contingency appropriations for temporary personnel to meet peak claims loads. The Bureau also urged the states, under their civil service rules, to adopt procedures for maintaining and using rosters of personnel to secure temporary claims takers. By the end of fiscal 1957, most of the states had done so. An important source of such temporary personnel has been former female claims takers who have married. This source of emergency workers reduced the amount of training that was necessary for such temporary personnel and alleviated the need for transfer of employment service personnel from their regular duties.

Specialization of Personnel

Another reason why diversion of employment service personnel to unemployment insurance operations is undesirable is that both unemployment insurance and employment service functions have become highly specialized operations. The unemployment insurance laws and regulations have become so detailed and complex that it takes a great deal of training and much practice for unemployment insurance claims takers to properly apply the unemployment insurance laws and rules to individual cases. On the Employment Service side, the program has also become complex and highly specialized. There are many specialists in the local employment offices, including counselors, labor market analysts, employer relations specialists, and so on. Even if transfer of personnel to claims taking is confined to placement personnel, these usually have specialized knowledge in a limited industrial or occupational field and have established working relationships with employers in their specialized area. Even temporary transfer to claims taking disrupts the day-to-day communication with employer "accounts" that is necessary if the Employment Service is to render prompt and efficient services to such employers. If Employment Service personnel are also to perform unemployment insurance functions, they must be trained in two quite different fields. From an unemployment insurance standpoint, the shifting of Employment Service personnel may also be undesirable and inefficient. Employment Service personnel probably will take little interest in their unemployment insurance claims taking if they know that there are employer orders for workers lying on their desks. And they probably will take less interest in learning the technicalities of unemployment insurance than personnel who are specially hired for unemployment insurance purposes, even if hired on a temporary basis. It is therefore inefficient to shift personnel from one operation to the other, except in emergency situations.

Expansion of Employment Service into a Manpower Agency

The responsibilities of the public employment service have been expanded, especially in recent years, to where it has become a manpower agency with basic and far-reaching responsibilities for implementing the manpower programs and policies of the government. As for the local employment office, Secretary of Labor Willard Wirtz wrote in 1963, "For the Employment Service, the basic challenge ahead is one of becoming, in a true sense, the 'Community Manpower Service Center' in every labor market area which USES serves."[19] At the time that it was originally decided in the 1930's that there should be integration of unemployment insurance and the Employment Service functions, the Employment Service was largely a labor exchange. Farsighted persons saw the need for widening Employment Service functions to testing and counseling, and to the development of labor market information, but no one foresaw the many uses these functions would serve, or all of the manpower services that are now expected of the Employment Service. Testing and counseling has not only greatly increased the service that the Employment Service can give to such groups as veterans, the handicapped, older workers, and youth in helping them find work; it has also enabled the Employment Service to provide services not directly related to placement. For example, a large proportion of high school students not planning to go on to college are given occupational tests and are counseled as to available jobs that will use their special talents.

The collection of labor market information by the Employment Service has been greatly expanded over the years and is used in many ways not originally foreseen. Its monthly classification of the extent of unemployment in labor areas has become one of the most important economic indicators. The classification of jobs in the Dictionary of Occupational Titles, originally developed as a guide to placement workers in understanding the requirements of specialized jobs for which they receive orders, has come to be used for many purposes by a variety of public and private users.

In recent years, the Employment Service has conducted a large number of area skill surveys which not only provide information on the skills being used in the community, but also provide projections of the skills that will be needed in the future. Short-range projections of local manpower needs for the next two to four months are also secured monthly by the local employment office. This has also made it possible for the community to plan its vocational education programs to meet the needs of its industries.

The labor market information developed by the Employment Service has enabled local offices to participate in community development plan-

[19] *Employment Security Review*, Vol. XXX, No. 6 (June, 1963), p. 1.

ning. Information as to skills available in the community has helped community development organizations to attract industries, especially important to areas in need of redevelopment. The Employment Service has also been able to provide individual employers with local labor market information that will aid them in the location of plants.

Another manpower activity of the Employment Service has been advance planning for mobilization in case of threats to the national security or actual attack. This planning has also enabled local offices to quickly marshall the forces of the community in peacetime disasters such as floods.

In the last few years, the Employment Service has been given large additional responsibilities. It has a major role in the training and retraining programs developed under the Manpower Development and Training Act. Because of the information it has collected on local skill and occupational needs, it helps decide the type of training projects that will be initiated. Because of its testing and counseling techniques and skills, it has been given the responsibility of selecting the trainees. The Employment Service also plays a major role in the youth programs provided under the "poverty program." In this program, the Employment Service selects youth for the Job Corps, for Neighborhood Youth Corps, and for work-training programs for part-time work in state or local government departments and nonprofit establishments. It has also been made responsible for seeking out disadvantaged youth for counseling and motivation to get additional schooling or training and for assistance in finding work. In order to provide a well-rounded program of employment services for youth, it is experimenting with "Youth Opportunity Centers" in major areas. These additional responsibilities have heavily taxed the resources of the Employment Service.

In short, both nationally and locally, the Employment Service has developed from a labor exchange to a manpower agency that assists in meeting the manpower needs of modern industry in a rapidly changing technology and economy.[20]

Employment Service activities are now so wide that integration of the Employment Service with unemployment insurance in order to apply the "work test" is placing two highly differentiated services together because of only one servicing function of the Employment Service. Nevertheless, since placement of workers on jobs continues to be the main function of the Employment Service, application of the work test of unemployment insurance claimants should still be its special responsibility. There should, therefore, continue to be coordination between the two services. Fortunately, the physical separation of local offices has improved coordination to some extent and does not imply elimination of the work test by the Employment Service.

[20] For a full discussion of the Employment Service as the key agency in a manpower program, see E. Wright Barke, *A Positive Labor Market Policy* (Columbus, Ohio: Charles E. Merrill Books, Inc., 1963).

FINANCING THE EMPLOYMENT SERVICE FROM THE UNEMPLOYMENT TAX

The greatly expanded activities of the Employment Service, in addition to moves toward the separation of the Employment Service from unemployment insurance, have raised questions as to the extent that the Employment Service should be financed out of the federal unemployment tax funds. It is true that it has been given additional monies from general appropriations for its new manpower services under the MDTA and poverty programs, but the bulk of its funds are provided from Title III grants. As its general manpower activities expand, the Employment Service may have to seek a greater part of its appropriations out of general funds. Although this would be primarily a problem for the Employment Service, the unemployment insurance program also has a vital concern in the adequate financing of the Employment Service. If unemployment insurance is to get real service in the application of the "work test," there must be an efficient public employment service. The possibility of inadequate appropriations for the placement side of the employment security equation must therefore be avoided.

The financing of the Employment Service is already under discussion because of its increasing manpower functions that have no direct relationship to unemployment insurance. While some of these functions, such as participation in retraining programs, are partially if not wholly reimbursed by the agencies administering these programs, an increasing portion of Title III grants to the Employment Service are utilized for services that only remotely contribute to the re-employment of workers covered by unemployment insurance. For example, in the staff report of the House Select Subcommittee of Labor prepared after the Subcommittee's 1964 hearings, the question was raised as to whether the costly and time-consuming special services for "disadvantaged" workers, such as the physically handicapped, older workers, youths entering the labor market, and nonwhite workers should not be financed out of general revenues. This report stated: "Consideration should also be given to financing other employment service activities, which are not immediately related to the placement of unemployment insurance recipients, at least partially out of general revenues."[21] A strong case could be made for financing of many such functions wholly or at least partially out of general tax funds. It also might be a healthy thing for the Employment Service to justify more of its services to the general community by having to secure appropriations from general funds. This would put the Employment Service more on its mettle to demonstrate that

[21] *The Role and Mission of the Federal-State Employment Service in the American Economy, op. cit.,* p. 70. This report was transmitted by the Chairman of the Subcommittee, Congressman Elmer J. Holland, to the Chairman of the Committee on Education and Labor, Congressman Adam C. Powell, for the consideration of the entire Committee, but without recommendation.

it is doing an effective job. It would also emphasize that the Employment Service is more than an "*un*employment office."

How Can the Employment Service Be More Useful to Unemployment Insurance?

So far we have been considering the relationship of the Employment Service to unemployment insurance from the standpoint of whether physical separation of the two programs will hurt unemployment insurance. The relationship of the two programs should also be looked at to explore ways in which the Employment Service can be of greater service to unemployment insurance.

First and foremost is the need to secure greater utilization of the Employment Service by employers covered by unemployment insurance in their recruitment of workers. With the emphasis on minimizing benefit payments in order to save taxes, one would think that covered employers would go first to the Employment Service with their job openings so that claimants of unemployment compensation would be re-employed as quickly as possible. Perhaps many employers fail to do so because they are interested primarily in the claimants whose benefits are being charged to their accounts, who can be called back to work directly. But with the large proportion of the cost of unemployment compensation that is "pooled" in the sense of being a common charge on the state unemployment fund, savings through more rapid employment of *any* claimant will eventually be reflected in savings to individual employers contributing to the state fund. All covered employers, therefore, have a financial stake in utilization of the Employment Service.

One possible way of getting greater employer utilization of the Employment Service would be to amend the Wagner-Peyser Act to require all employers to register all openings with the public employment offices. This is done in other countries. But such compulsion is not in the American tradition. Nor would Congress countenance such a proposal. A more practical approach was the initiation in 1964 of a job vacancy collection program by the Employment Service on an experimental basis in a selected number of metropolitan areas. Periodically, employers in these areas will be asked to provide the number of job openings by occupation. If this experiment is successful and expanded nation-wide, the Employment Service will have an opportunity to volunteer information on the availability of qualified applicants registered with the Service, and permit a broader application of the "work test" for unemployment insurance claimants. The Subcommittee on Employment and Manpower of the Senate Committee on Labor and Public Welfare has made another proposal, namely, to require employers engaged on government contracts to list all job vacancies with the Employment Service. Although such listing would be mandatory, the employer would not be required to place job orders with or accept referrals from the Service. The Subcommittee thought that "The complete listing would allow more intelligent occupational decisions and job search and furnish important labor market information not now available."[22]

Two minority members of the Subcommittee, as well as the minority members of the Joint Economic Committee, made a somewhat different, but more comprehensive recommendation, for the establishment of a national clearing house on emerging skill requirements, existing skill needs, and obsolescent skills. The minority members, Senators Winston L. Prouty and Len B. Jordan, recommended that "The clearinghouse should also keep an up-to-date list of job vacancies for the use of the U.S. Employment Service, employers, private employment services and others so that jobs and men can be brought together."[23] As recommended by the majority of the Subcommittee, the listing of job vacancies by defense contractors could be enforced by making such listing a part of the contract. It is not clear how the minority recommendation could be enforced.

Midway between compulsory and voluntary listing of job openings would be the provision of incentives for employers to list their jobs with the Employment Service. One alternative, aimed at the employers covered by unemployment insurance, has been suggested by Dr. Sar A. Levitan, who proposed that "Voluntary registration of vacancies might be encouraged by offering employers inducements through adjustment of their unemployment insurance rates. Such incentives would have to be applied carefully in order to avoid serious reductions in unemployment insurance taxes."[24] This proposal ties in with the argument above that covered employers should hire through the Employment Service in order to reduce payments of unemployment compensation from the state unemployment fund. If such benefit savings were passed on more directly to employers in the way of tax savings, there would be more of an incentive for them to use the Employment Service. The proposal was included in the recommendations of the Senate Subcommittee on Employment and Manpower.[25] It would probably be very difficult, however, to devise a practicable plan for implementing this idea. One of the principal problems would be defining what constitutes a vacancy. There would also be the administrative difficulty of checking whether an employer listed *all* his vacancies. Despite these and other problems, the idea should be fully explored.

The Employment Service could perform other valuable services to un-

---

[22] *Toward Full Employment: Proposals for a Comprehensive Employment and Manpower Policy in the United States,* A Report Prepared by the Subcommittee on Employment and Manpower Together with Minority and Individual Views of the Committee on Labor and Public Welfare, United States Senate, Committee Print (Washington, D.C.: U.S. Government Printing Office, 1964), p. 97.

[23] *Ibid.,* p. 107.

[24] Sar A. Levitan, *Federal Manpower Policies and Programs to Combat Unemployment* (Kalamazoo: W. E. Upjohn Institute for Employment Research, February, 1964), pp. 10–11.

[25] *Toward Full Employment, op. cit.,* p. 97. This was also endorsed by Senator Jacob J. Javits in his individual views included in the report (p. 147).

employment insurance such as giving attention to identifying, counseling, and referring for training or retraining those claimants who have no prospect of returning to their former occupations. If the Employment Service is in close touch with claimants from the beginning, much could be saved in benefits through early identification of those who need counseling or training. This is important because of the number of workers being displaced through automation and other technological changes.

SUMMARY AND CONCLUSIONS

Unemployment insurance and the public employment service have been operated on an integrated basis in order to maximize exposure of unemployment insurance claimants to jobs and, thereby, to offer suitable work as a test of claimants' availability for work. From the beginning the Social Security Board granted funds to the states to enable them to expand their employment services so that their local offices could both take unemployment insurance claims and apply the "work test" to claimants.

In practically all the states, unemployment insurance and the Employment Service are administered by one agency. In 1949, after a number of moves, the United States Employment Service became a part of the Bureau of Employment Security of the United States Department of Labor. In 1962, the Bureau was reorganized in order to give greater autonomy to both the United States Employment Service and the Unemployment Insurance Service. At the same time, a drive was started to get the states to reorganize their offices in metropolitan areas, with separation of unemployment insurance and employment service the major goal.

At the time of writing, it is too early to know how far the process of separation of unemployment insurance and employment service will or should go. From the standpoint of the Employment Service there are strong arguments for separation. From the standpoint of unemployment insurance, the considerations favoring separation are not as clear-cut although, on balance, some separation seems desirable. The Employment Service is needed for application of the "work test" to claimants, but with proper coordination this can be accomplished as effectively, or even more effectively, in separate offices. Actually, separation of some offices has forced coordination where it did not exist when the offices were integrated. The provision of a "one-stop" service for the unemployed in securing unemployment compensation and registering for work has not worked well in large cities; the combined task did not produce either good applications for employment or good claims for benefits.

It is argued that the Employment Service should operate separately because its association with unemployment insurance hurts its public image. Surveys indicate, however, that the image held by employers, rather than by workers is adversely affected, although this is based on misconceptions. Some employers feel that unemployment insurance is paid to many workers who do not need it (both irrelevant and a misconception of the purpose of the system) and that claimants of poor quality are referred to jobs.

Another reason given for separating the services, the practice of assigning Employment Service personnel to claims taking during rush periods, has largely been taken care of through the use of contingency appropriations to hire temporary personnel to take claims. An important reason for keeping Employment Service and Unemployment Insurance personnel confined to their own duties is the increasing complexity and techincal character of both Unemployment Insurance and Employment Service operations. The conversion of the Employment Service from a labor exchange to a manpower agency has made cooperation with unemployment insurance through application of the "work test" a minor phase of its operations. There is danger that the placement of claimants may not receive adequate attention because of the preoccupation of the Employment Service with the additional manpower functions recently assigned to it.

It is possible that if separation goes far enough, this development, combined with the increase in manpower activities unrelated to unemployment insurance, may raise questions as to whether some of these unrelated activities should not be financed out of general revenues, rather than by the Federal Unemployment Tax.

Whether or not the Employment Service and unemployment insurance are separated administratively, the Employment Service could be of greater usefulness in exposing claimants to jobs. Its usefulness could be improved if employers covered by unemployment insurance utilized the Employment Service to a greater extent. Compulsory listing of job openings with the Employment Service has been suggested, at least for defense contractors. The Employment Service has a pilot project to secure listings on a voluntary basis in major cities. Some direct tax incentives for covered employers to hire claimants (in addition to their former employees) has also been recommended.

The Employment Service could also be more useful to unemployment insurance if it gave particular attention to claimants who have no prospect of return to their former occupations, by counseling and referring them to retraining if necessary.

Chapter 22

Issues in
Federal-State Relationships

The creation of the vast federal-state program of unemployment insurance has inevitably resulted in problems in federal-state relationships. Over-all issues in federal-state relationships are principally concerned with three types of questions. The first has to do with the proposals designed to convert the unemployment insurance system into a national or exclusively federal plan. The second is concerned with less ambitious proposals designed to expand the rather nominal present requirements which state legislatures must meet, including federal standards on benefit amounts and duration, disqualifications, and other substantive standards. The third question is concerned with so-called "conformity issues" which grow out of changes in state legislation, the effect of which raises questions as to whether the state law is out of conformity with the federal requirements. Closely allied are questions of "compliance" with federal requirements in the interpretation or administration of state laws.

It is clear that any one of these three categories of questions could introduce strained relations between the federal and state agencies concerned. The first one, namely, any proposal for outright federalization, would of course pose a clear threat to the existence of the state plans. It would be and has been most vigorously resisted by the state administrators. The second one, namely, federal benefit standards, while not representing an outright assault on the sovereignty of the state plans, does, nevertheless, increase the anxiety of the state administrators, since such proposals are interpreted as an entering wedge to federalization of the program. The third category deals with *ad hoc* problems that arise as a result of amendments to the state legislation or of administrative actions by the state agency which may require a review (and possibly a hearing) by the Secretary of Labor as to conformity or compliance with federal requirements. This third category has been a substantial source of difficulty and irritation and has often led to strained relations.

PROPOSALS FOR A FEDERAL SYSTEM

Chapter 6 has described the disagreements in the Committee on Economic Security as to whether a federal system of unemployment insurance should be proposed. Even though they lost the battle, many of the advocates of a federal system continued to argue for it.[1]

Federalization of the unemployment insurance program was proposed as a part of a unified and enlarged social security program in the report of the National Resources Planning Board on *Security, Work, and Relief Policies*, published in March, 1943.[2]

The Social Security Board came out officially in favor of a federal system in 1942 and again in its 1943 and 1944 Annual Reports.[3] In arguing for a national system, the Social Security Board stated that the crux of the problem was to pool the reserves of the states so as to assure that the system could finance the anticipated increase in unemployment benefits in the postwar readjustment period. The Board also emphasized that the employment service, which had been temporarily nationalized during the war, would need to operate on a national basis following the war to relocate demobilized soldiers in civilian jobs and demobilized workers in war industries. It stated: "The Social Security Board is convinced that nothing less than a nationally uniformly operated employment service, sustained by an adequate and soundly financed federal unemployment insurance system, will meet the needs of the period immediately following the war and the longer-range objectives of social security."[4] In its 1944 *Annual Report*, the Social Security Board emphasized the desirability of a national system of unemployment insurance as a part of a comprehensive system of social insurance.

The Congress of Industrial Organizations (CIO) also took up the cudgels for federalization of unemployment insurance. It supported the Wagner-Murray-Dingell bill, introduced in 1943, for a comprehensive system of social insurance, including a national health program and a national unemployment insurance system. This system would have provided all-inclusive coverage of all employees, uniform and increased benefits throughout the country, and a uniform maximum duration of 26 weeks.[5]

[1] See for example Bryce M. Stewart, "Federal and State Unemployment Insurance," *Proceedings of the Academy of Political Science*, June, 1935, pp. 74–92. William Haber and J. J. Joseph, "Unemployment Compensation," *Annals of the American Academy of Political Social Sciences*, Vol. CCII (March, 1939), p. 33.

[2] Dr. Eveline M. Burns was the principal author and William Haber was chairman of the Committee. This report was made by the Committee on Long Range Work and Relief Policies of the National Resources Planning Board. A summary of the report, which President Franklin D. Roosevelt transmitted to Congress on March 10, 1943, bore the title *Post-War Planning*.

[3] *7th Annual Report*, Social Security Board (Washington, D.C.: U.S. Government Printing Office, 1942), pp. 15–17; *8th Annual Report* (1943), p.p. 34–38; and *9th Annual Report* (1944), pp. 15–16.

[4] *7th Annual Report, op. cit.*, p. 17.

[5] S. 1161, 78th Cong., 1st sess. (1943).

The Wagner-Murray-Dingell bill was reintroduced with few changes in 1945. It was actively supported by the Social Security Board as well as the CIO, but opposed by the Interstate Conference of Employment Security Agencies and the Council of State Governments. The bill never came to a hearing, and the Social Security Board shifted its support in 1945 to a system of federal grants-in-aid. Organized labor, however, continued to be in favor of a national system,[6] although it has given active support to federal minimum standards for benefits as an alternative.

Advantages of Federalization

The advantages and disadvantages of a federal system over the present federal-state system have been set forth many times.[7]

The arguments for federalization are:

a) Unemployment is a national problem and no respector of state lines. Its causes are national and international. The degree of unemployment varies widely from state to state, thus placing an unequal financial burden on different states.

b) A federal system would permit uniformity of coverage of workers in all states and uniformity of benefit protection. The great diversity in state provisions has little relation to the differences in the state economies.

c) Under experience rating, an employer in one state with identical experience with an employer in another state will have a different tax rate. This is due either to differences in benefit provisions or differences in the rate of unemployment or both. Improvements in state benefits are hampered because of arguments that the increased costs will handicap the state's employers in interstate competition.

d) The nation-wide pooling of funds under a federal system would give greater assurance of solvency. Under the present system, individual state funds could become insolvent while billions of dollars are still in the Unemployment Trust Fund, credited to the accounts of other states.

e) A federal system would permit economies in the collection of contributions and in record keeping. Tax collection and record keeping could be unified for unemployment insurance and the federal OASDI program.

f) Further economies would be achieved through the reduction in administrative overhead costs which are inevitably higher under 52 separate organizations.

g) Difficulties and conflicts in administration that arise from the division

---

[6] See, for example, Resolution No. 17, "Unemployment Insurance and the Public Employment Service," Eleventh Constitutional Convention of the Congress of Industrial Organizations, Cleveland, Ohio, October, 1949.

[7] For a statement of both advantages and disadvantages, see *Issues in Social Security*, Report to the Committee on Ways and Means, House of Representatives, U.S. Congress by the Committee's Social Security Technical Staff (Washington, D.C.: U.S. Government Printing Office, 1946), pp. 454–55. For a statement of the advantages see also *Annual Report* of the Social Security Board, 1943, pp. 34–38.

of responsibilities between the federal and state governments would be eliminated.

Advantages of the Present System over a Federal System

The arguments for the present system are:

a) The present system gives greater opportunity for experimentation. The entire unemployment insurance system would not be damaged if ideas which are tried out in individual states do not work.

b) The state programs can be adapted to local conditions. This particularly applies to different wage levels and living costs.

c) The state systems result in decentralized administration which can be more responsive to local conditions and thinking. It also permits quicker settlement of questions than would be possible if all the decisions had to be made in Washington.

d) Federalization would bring centralized control and would further the present undesirable trend toward centralization of government.

e) The states all have a large enough number of covered workers to satisfy the general insurance law of large numbers in spreading the risk; with proper financial policies all states can remain solvent.

f) The present billions of dollars in the Unemployment Trust Fund are state money in individual state accounts. It would be unfair to states which have been prudent in their financing and have relatively large reserves to have their reserves pooled with the relatively small reserves of other states, some of which have been improvident. It would also be confiscatory and unconstitutional. This argument is probably the most realistic argument of all.

g) Any fundamental change in a system that has been in operation for almost a third of a century should come only in the event of the financial collapse of the present system or some other extreme emergency. As the Staff Report of the Committee on Ways and Means stated in 1946: "the question at issue is whether conditions of such compelling importance exist as to require that a 'going' system be wiped out and another system substituted for it."[8] No such compelling conditions have as yet appeared. Although the authors believe a federal system would have been better, we recognize that unless there were a breakdown in the present system, to propose a federal system now would be unrealistic.

FEDERAL MINIMUM BENEFIT STANDARDS

Proposals for federal minimum benefit standards can be ranked next to federalization of the program as the most controversial area of federal legislation because they would enlarge federal authority and pose a threat to state prerogatives to determine the basic provisions of their programs. In its 1945 and 1946 *Annual Reports* the Social Security Board recom-

[8] *Issues in Social Security, op. cit.*, p. 455.

mended minimum benefit standards either as a part of a grants-in-aid program, or if that were not enacted, under the present federal-state system. By 1948, the *Annual Report* of the Social Security Administration put the emphasis on minimum benefit standards, barely mentioning a grants-in-aid plan.

Federal minimum benefit standards were included in several bills during the late 1940's, but did not become official Administration policy until President Harry S. Truman in April, 1950, sent a special message to Congress proposing federal minimum standards for benefit amount and duration and maximum qualifying requirements and disqualification provisions, along with a number of other proposals such as extension of coverage and reinsurance.[9] The standards proposed by President Truman were incorporated in a bill introduced by Congressman McCormack of Massachusetts (H.R. 8059). Hearings were held on this bill by a subcommittee of the House Ways and Means Committee, but there was such strong opposition to it that the subcommittee did not even write a report.

Minimum benefit standards remained a major legislative issue until President Eisenhower took office. During his two terms of office, Administration support of federal legislation providing federal standards was withdrawn. Nevertheless, federal interest in adequate state benefits continued. In his Economic Report for 1954 and subsequent years, President Eisenhower recommended that the states meet goals with respect to benefit amount and duration, similar to those formerly proposed as federal standards.[10]

The Commission on Intergovernmental Relations appointed by President Eisenhower also stated that "the National Government has a proper and important interest in State standards of unemployment benefits" and recommended that ". . . the President and the Secretary of Labor, from time to time as deemed appropriate, recommend to the States minimum standards for inclusion in State laws. These recommendations should cover the amount and duration of benefits and eligibility and disqualification provisions."[11]

Bills providing for federal standards continued to be introduced by Democratic Congressmen during the Eisenhower Administration. There was no serious consideration of them, however, until 1959 when the Committee on Ways and Means[12] held general hearings on unemployment

[9] House of Representatives, Document No. 547, 81st Cong., 2d sess., April 6, 1950.

[10] See Chapter 11 for a detailed discussion of his recommendation on the benefit amount.

[11] Commission on Intergovernment Relations, *Report to the President* (Washington, D.C.: U.S. Government Printing Office, 1955), pp. 206–7. Senators Hubert Humphrey and Wayne Morse and Dr. William Anderson of the University of Minnesota expressed a preference for uniform nation-wide benefit standards, saying "The Commission's recommendation in this area merely supports the existing practice, with its demonstrated inadequacies, that have been in operation for a number of years."

[12] *Unemployment Compensation*, Hearings before the Committee on Ways and Means, House of Representatives, 86th Cong., 1st sess. (April 7–15, 1959), 1167 pp.

insurance. During these hearings, organized labor and others strongly supported a bill providing for minimum benefit standards introduced by Congressman Frank M. Karsten of Missouri (H.R. 3547).[13] Those on the Committee supporting federal standards failed by only one vote to secure approval of the Karsten bill.

The Democratic Administrations under Presidents Kennedy and Johnson again included benefit standards in their bills. The 1965 bill (S. 1991 and H.R. 8282, 89th Cong.) included the following standards that a state would have to meet in its law as a condition for its employers to receive full federal tax credit:

a) A weekly benefit amount equal to at least 50 percent of average weekly earnings, exclusive of dependents' benefits;

b) A maximum weekly benefit equal to at least 50 percent of the state-wide average wage by July 1, 1967, 60 percent by July 1, 1969, and 66⅔ percent by July 1, 1971;

c) A qualifying requirement of not more than 20 weeks of employment or its equivalent;

d) Twenty-six weeks of benefits for claimants meeting such a qualifying requirement; and

e) A maximum of six weeks of disqualification, except for fraud, labor disputes, or conviction of a crime arising in connection with the claimant's work; prohibition of the reduction or cancellation of benefit rights in connection with disqualification.

Organized labor and many economists who are students of the program have supported federal benefit standards, but with only a few notable exceptions, employers have strongly opposed them. Federal Administration officials have favored standards, but the great majority of state employment security administrators have been against them.[14]

Arguments for and against Standards

The principal argument given for federal benefit standards is that many of the states have failed to provide adequate protection and always will in the absence of federal standards. Supporters of benefit standards also argue that standards would not change the character of the system, since they would merely be additions to the standards or requirements already in the federal unemployment tax act. A third argument is that federal standards would bring up to a level of minimum benefit protection those states that hesitate to increase benefits because the cost may place their employers in an unfavorable competitive position.

[13] The bill provided for maximum weekly benefits of at least two thirds of state-wide average covered wages, duration of at least 39 weeks, qualifying requirements of not more than 20 weeks, and prohibition against reduction or cancellation of benefit rights in connection with disqualifications.

[14] In a special meeting on January 25–26, 1966, in Phoenix, Arizona, the Interstate Conference of Employment Security Agencies endorsed recommendations (*a*) and (*b*) above, except that the approval of the maximum benefit standard was limited to a maximum of 50 percent of the state-wide average weekly wage.

The principal argument in opposition to federal benefit standards is that it would extend federal control over the system. Some go further and argue that federal standards would be an entering wedge toward federalization, or would even amount to *de facto* federalization of the program. The following quotation gives an indication of feelings expressed on this point:

Federal controls are not desirable: Federal standards mean Federal controls. The imposition of Federal minimum standards is a long step toward nationalization of the unemployment insurance system. Once the principle of Federal standards is accepted, additional requirements might be anticipated in the future which may remove from the State any real discretion in this area. Federally imposed benefit standards cannot adequately take into consideration the real differences among the States in general economic conditions and in wage structures. The determination of benefit formulas should be left to the States whose legislators are familiar with their local economies and wage structures and can best determine benefit adequacy. Federal control of benefit formulas is not desirable because it would impair or destroy State initiative.[15]

Less semantically charged arguments against federal standards are that the states can be depended on to provide adequate protection, and that standards would reduce state benefits to a common level and tend to keep benefits at lower levels for some states that would otherwise provide more adequate benefits than the federal standards require.

Professor Frank T. DeVyver of Duke University summarized the two points of view as follows:

An examination of Congressional hearings indicates that the advocates of stronger Federal standards have generally stressed what may be called the social aspects of unemployment insurance. . . . Those who would retain only the most mild Federal controls are generally advocates of what may be called the business aspects of unemployment compensation. Here is the fundamental difference of opinion. Since the Federal administrators of unemployment compensation have consistently shown that they are believers in the social aspect of insurance, those who advocate the business concept have fought against any increase in Federal control. Actually, unemployment compensation, like other types of social insurance, is bound to be part social and part business rather than being clearly one or the other.[16]

The severity of the federal penalties if a state does not meet federal standards has led the Department of Labor to search for means of securing the objectives of federal standards by less drastic means. Thus, in the Administration bills of 1961, 1963, and 1965, the standards for benefit amount and duration carried a sanction of reduced tax credits if the standards were

---

[15] Statement of E. Russell Bartley, Director of Industrial Relations, Illinois Manufacturer's Association, *Unemployment Compensation*, Hearings before the Committee on Ways and Means, House of Representatives, 86th Cong., 1st sess. (April 7, 1959), p. 134.

[16] Frank T. DeVyver, "Federal Standards in Unemployment Insurance," *Vanderbilt Law Review*, Vol. VIII, No. 2 (February, 1955), p. 435.

not met. The reduced tax credit would be equal to the state's average cost rate over the preceding four years, or 2.7 percent, whichever is lower. For example, if a state did not meet this standard and its average costs were 1.6 percent of taxable payrolls, the state's employers could get a tax credit of only 1.6 percent instead of 2.7 percent.

Years of discussion of standards has led the Department of Labor to propose that a state be allowed to phase its increases in benefits over several years. Also, its latest proposal recommended that the maximum benefit amount be attained as a percentage of average wages, instead of a stated dollar amount. This would recognize differences in wage levels in different states and permit all the states, as more and more states are doing, to enact a "flexible" maximum which would automatically increase the dollar maximum as general increases in wages occur. These latest proposals are less severe in their sanctions and more flexible in their application to individual states.

In our view, benefit standards are justified, at least as to the amount of benefits that a state shall provide, because of the inadequate maximum benefits discussed in Chapter 11. In addition, we believe benefit standards are justified in principle as a condition for giving employers credits against the federal unemployment tax. All the federal-state programs have minimum federal standards in order to get the benefits of the federal legislation. But with the exception of the so-called "labor standard," which prohibits denial of benefits under certain conditions, the federal government prescribes no substantive standards as to the unemployment benefits paid under the state program. A state can pay any amount, for any duration, and under any conditions it pleases. And since employers, under experience rating, can save taxes if they hold down benefits, it is surprising—almost incredible—that the states have provided as adequate benefits as they have, under such loose arrangements.

There may have been some excuse for the few standards in the original Social Security Act. There was a grave question as to whether *any* federal unemployment insurance legislation would be upheld by the Supreme Court, and it was thought each added requirement would further endanger its constitutionality. However, the Supreme Court decision was so favorable that there is little question but that benefit standards would have been upheld.

In the beginning there were good grounds for permitting the states to experiment since so little was known about unemployment insurance, and especially about how much protection could be provided under the system of tax credits. Enough experience has long since been accumulated so that there is an adequate basis for the federal government prescribing the minimum amount of protection the states should provide.

Minimum benefit standards could still leave the states a great deal of discretion. States could provide more liberal benefits. Standards have been proposed only for the most critical provisions, especially those relating to amount and duration of benefits, and they have been *minimum standards.*[17]

An active consideration of benefit standards would strain federal-state relations because of the opposition of most State administrators to such proposals. But if enacted, the administration of benefit standards need not put a strain on federal-state relations. The amount of strain would depend on the character of the standards. If the standards are specific and conformity with them can be easily verified, no difficulties in federal-state relations should arise. If the standards are subject to different interpretations or compliance with them is difficult to verify, strained relations could result.

PROBLEMS IN CONFORMITY ISSUES

The severity of the penalty involved is the principal problem when a question arises as to conformity or compliance by a state with federal requirements. If a state's unemployment insurance law does not conform to the federal requirements listed in Title III of the Social Security Act, or if the state does not substantially comply with these requirements, the penalty is withdrawal of federal administrative grants. If a state's law is out of conformity with the requirements of the federal unemployment tax act, the penalty is both withdrawal of administrative grants and denial to the state's employers of credit against the federal unemployment tax. If its experience rating system is out of conformity, employers in the state can get credit only for actual taxes paid the state. A violation of Title III requirements may therefore involve millions of dollars in administrative funds, and a violation of federal unemployment tax requirements may involve tens or hundreds of millions of dollars in taxes.

The severity of these sanctions for nonconformity or noncompliance has made federal officials very reluctant to apply them, and state officials very wary of doing anything that will result in their application. It has also put a strain on federal-state relations when a conformity or compliance issue arises. State officials may feel that the question raised is too trivial in the light of the severity of the penalty. On the other hand, federal officials may be resentful if they are criticized for raising such questions when they are only doing their duty. They are especially resentful when they give a warning to the state and the state persists in its noncompliance, knowing that the federal government will hesitate to come to a showdown on the question. For example, despite technical defects in their experience rating provisions which states fail to correct, the Bureau of Employment Security has continued to recommend that the Secretary of Labor certify such states for administrative grants and tax credit. Or the question may be procedural. Picked at random, the following is illustrative: in 1963, an issue was raised with a state as to whether it was complying with the fair hearing require-

---

[17] As to the *need* for standards, the reader is referred back to Chapter 11 and 12, in which the inadequacy in many states and great unevenness in benefit protection in many states is discussed in detail.

ment because of certain rules and practices of its Review Board (a separate organization from the agency), such as how long before a hearing a party could request a subpoena.

If state and federal officials are unable to resolve an important conformity or compliance question, the Secretary of Labor gives the state agency a formal notice and holds a hearing on the issue. In practically all compliance cases, the issue is settled through discussions between federal and state officials. In the case of proposed legislation, if they learn in time of a bill that may raise a conformity question, federal Bureau officials warn the state officials of this question. Frequently, the proposal is modified in order to remove the conformity question, or a proviso may be added to the proposed legislation that it will only take effect if approved by the Secretary of Labor as meeting federal requirements.

A limited number of conformity or compliance questions have been raised during the history of the program and only a few have come to a formal hearing stage. In 1964, the Legislative Committee of the Interstate Conference wrote all state agencies (except Puerto Rico) asking them to send information on the conformity and compliance questions that had been raised in their states. Twenty-six of the 51 states replied, nine saying that no issue had been raised in the state. It can be presumed that a substantial number of states that did not reply had no issues raised with them. Twenty-six specific conformity or compliance questions were described in the replies of the 17 states which reported that one or more issues had been raised. Three reported that issues had been raised which had been resolved, but did not give the number of issues.[18]

As to formal application of federal sanctions, in only two cases have Title III administrative grants been withheld. In 1939, administrative grants were withheld from South Dakota when it proposed to pay unemployment compensation through the state public welfare offices instead of through public employment offices as required by federal standards under Section 303 (a) (2) of the Social Security Act. In 1941, administrative grants to Arizona were denied because it did not have an Employment Service Director devoting his full time to these duties. During the time required for Arizona to hold merit examinations for and appoint a new Employment Service Director, the United States Employment Service operated the offices.[19]

---

[18] *Minutes of the National Executive Committee* (Interstate Conference of Employment Security Agencies, March 17–18, 1964), appendix c. For additional cases, see DeVyver, *op. cit.*, pp. 417–24.

[19] In a third case in Kentucky, a conformity issue was not involved, but rather difficulties under Kentucky's constitution in connection with transfer to the Railroad Retirement Board under the Railroad Unemployment Insurance Law of railroad employee contributions prior to July 1, 1939. Kentucky thought these contributions should not be transferred because worker contributions were not required in other states. Until this problem was worked out, federal administrative grants were withheld and Kentucky's administrative contributions were paid out of employer contributions diverted to Kentucky's administrative fund. (See DeVyver, *op. cit.*, p. 422.)

Conformity Cases

As to conformity issues under the requirements of the Federal Unemployment Tax Act, one of the few cases that has resulted in a formal decision by the Secretary of Labor (as of time of writing) was a case in California involving the interpretation of "new work" under the so-called labor standards requirement in Section 3304 (a) (5) of the Federal Unemployment compensation to maritime workers who had been laid off prior to a strike of West Coast maritime unions in 1948. Some of the workers were actually drawing benefits when the strike began. The California agency ruled that an offer of employment on the struck work was an offer of "new work" to such unemployed workers.[20] The Secretary of Labor called a formal hearing on the issue in December, 1949, but stopped the hearing when California offered to reconsider its position.

The California agency subsequently revived its interpretation of "new work" and was upheld by the Supreme Court of California in 1955. The Secretary of Labor again formally raised a conformity question on the basis that the state interpretation did not conform with the Department of Labor's interpretation. After a formal hearing by a hearing officer delegated by the Secretary of Labor, the Secretary asked an informal panel of high legal authorities to review the findings of the hearing officer and advise him on the ruling he should make. On their advice, the Secretary of Labor ruled that the state had not violated the federal standard.

An earlier case reaching the hearing stage involved experience rating. This was a 1947 amendment to the Minnesota law permitting employers to make voluntary contributions so as to increase their reserve accounts enough to get a lower experience rating. After a hearing, this amendment was found to be out of conformity with the experience rating requirements of the federal act. Minnesota's way out was to secure an amendment to the Federal Unemployment Tax Act[21] making such a practice permissible.

The Secretary of Labor held two hearings in 1964, one on a substantive issue and the other on a procedural matter. The substantive issue involved an amendment to the South Dakota law which would have increased the waiting period for benefits to seven weeks for a worker with base period earnings of from $6,000 to $6,999. The amendment provided for an additional waiting period of two weeks for each additional $1,000 earned up to a waiting period of 13 weeks for workers with earnings of $9,000 or more. The amendment was reputedly designed to cut down benefits to construction workers during the winter season. The Bureau of Employment Security raised a conformity question on the basis that this introduced a

---

[20] A conformity question was raised on a similar issue in Washington involving a carpenters' union but Washington changed its ruling to conform to the federal interpretation of "new work."

[21] Section 3303 (d). 61 Stat. 416 (Act of July 24, 1947).

needs test into the law so that it would no longer be a genuine unemployment compensation law. The bill containing the amendment included a provision that if the Secretary of Labor did not notify the Governor of South Dakota by January 8, 1964, that the amendment made the law out of conformity, it would take effect on January 15, 1964. The Secretary so notified the Governor on January 7. Then South Dakota passed another measure declaring that the legislature did not consider the Secretary's communication to the Governor as a finding, as required by the federal act, and also declaring the amendment in question to be in effect as of January 15. However, the amendment was made inoperative until July 1 in order to give the Secretary of Labor time to hold a hearing on it. A Hearing Examiner of the Secretary of Labor held a hearing on the amendment on July 7, 1964, and recommended that the amendment be found out of conformity. The ground for such a finding was that the South Dakota law no longer contained the provisions specified in Section 303 (a) (5) of the Social Security Act and Section 3304 (c) (4) of the Internal Revenue Code that money withdrawn from the Unemployment Trust Fund shall be used solely in the payment of unemployment compensation. It was based on the argument that the waiting period amendment introduced an income test into the South Dakota law so that it no longer was a genuine unemployment compensation law. The Secretary of Labor on September 25, 1964, adopted the Hearing Examiner's recommendation as his decision.[22]

The other case arising in 1964 involved a New Hampshire practice in appealed cases in which the claimant was awarded benefits, of mailing his checks to him at his attorney's address if the claimant so requested. Evidently in such cases, the attorney representing the claimant had reached an agreement with the claimant that this would be done so that the attorney had greater assurance of collecting his fee. The questions raised were whether this violated the federal requirement that money withdrawn from the Trust Fund shall be used solely for the payment of unemployment compensation, and also whether it was an infringement of the federal requirement that the state have "such methods of administration as are found by the Secretary of Labor to be reasonably calculated to insure full payment of unemployment compensation when due" (Section 303 (a) (1) of the Social Security Act). A hearing was held on May 12–13, 1964, at which representatives of six other states appeared or submitted briefs. These representatives revealed that other states were following New Hampshire's practice or were mailing checks to other than the beneficiary, in one state to the public assistance agency if the claimant was on relief. Instead of issuing a finding on the basis of the hearing, the Secretary dismissed the case and directed the Bureau to investigate the various practices followed by the states in payments delivered to persons other than claimants, including their attorneys, and to prepare for his consideration a standard which

[22] 29 Federal Register 7621.

would be applicable to all states. Before issuing the standard, the Secretary said that he would submit the proposed standard to the states for their comments.[23]

The "Knowland" Amendment

The initial hearing in California in 1949 involved the question as to whether the Secretary of Labor could raise a conformity question if a state "changed" its law by interpretation or could only raise a question if a state changed its law by legislative amendment. California also raised a question as to whether the Secretary could intervene until the state's interpretation of its law had been passed on by its highest court.

To resolve these questions, Senator William Knowland of California introduced an amendment as a rider to the 1950 Social Security bill, during the Senate floor debate on that bill, which was passed after very brief debate. The amendment prevented the Secretary of Labor from raising a compliance issue until the highest court in the state to which an appeal was taken had ruled on a state agency's interpretation of its law. The amendment also prevented the Secretary of Labor from calling a conformity issue on changes in *interpretations* of a state law, confining him to raising a question only on *amendments* to the state law. The amendment further provided that, in case of an adverse finding by the Secretary, a state will have 90 days in which to amend its law to comply substantially with the Secretary's interpretation of the federal requirements. Although the conference committee recognized that the amendment was ambiguous, it was agreed to on the understanding that it would be reviewed at the next session of Congress. Negotiations broke down between representatives of Department of Labor and Interstate Conference officials over a revision of the amendment and no further action has ever been taken on the amendment.

The Knowland amendment undoubtedly has hampered and delayed the Secretary of Labor in raising conformity and compliance questions. A case in point is that of California. After the passage of the Knowland amendment, the Secretary was unable to reopen the issue of the state agency's interpretation of "new work" until the Supreme Court of California had upheld the interpretation five years later, in 1955.

While the Knowland amendment is seldom mentioned today, the Department of Labor would probably ask for its revision if there were active consideration by Congress of judicial review—an issue to be discussed later in this chapter.

Lesser Sanctions

Because of the severity of the consequences of a ruling of noncompliance or nonconformity with federal requirements, during the 1950's the Secretary of Labor asked the Bureau of Employment Security to study the possi-

[23] Federal Register Document 64–7807, filed August 3, 1964.

bility of providing for sanctions short of stopping administrative grants or withholding the certification of the state law for tax credit purposes. The Bureau was unable to suggest any lesser measure that the Secretary felt would be effective.

One device the Bureau uses with respect to improper use of funds for administration is to take audit exceptions to improper expenditures and require their restoration, as provided under Section 303 (b) (9) of the Social Security Act.[24] Such restoration of funds is usually made only after long negotiations which sometimes absorb more expenditure of time and money by federal and state officials than the expenditures in question. The practice, however, probably results in the state agencies exercising more care than they otherwise would in the use of granted funds only for employment security purposes and under the rules and policies of the federal bureau.

Because of the lack of lesser sanctions (other than the restoration of funds mentioned above), most issues are resolved through negotiations between federal and state officials. On the federal side, there has been a reluctance to carry questions to a formal hearing unless an important issue is involved and it is clear that the issue cannot be resolved by negotiation. On the other hand, state officials complain that they often give in and agree to the federal position rather than risk being called out of compliance or conformity. If satisfactory lesser sanctions could be devised, it no doubt would improve federal-state relations.

Although the problem of requiring conformity to or compliance with federal requirements has been a source of bad federal-state relations, no satisfactory alternative for the present legislation seems forthcoming. In its report in 1955, the President's Commission on Intergovernmental Relations recommended that ". . . administrative action be taken to provide that the Secretary of Labor consult the states before adopting rules, regulations, and standards materially affecting the program of the states. Consultation should include discussions with governors and other appropriate state officials as well as with directors of state employment security agencies."[25] This recommendation has not been followed. It probably would not help the situation, since unfortunately most disagreements arise over questions that have not been foreseen in such standards as the Secretary of Labor has issued.[26]

The other recommendation of the Commission was that "Administrative provision should be made for a hearing board to advise the Secretary of

[24] States usually restore such monies from their interest and penalty funds, which do not have to be deposited in the Unemployment Trust Fund.

[25] *Report to the President, op. cit.*, p. 205.

[26] Neither the Social Security Board nor the Secretary of Labor has issued rules and regulations with respect to unemployment insurance, although they have with respect to the employment service. "Standards" issued by the Secretary cover such areas as the frequency of tax collections and benefit payments, registration of claimants with the employment service and retroactive filing of partial unemployment claims. Detailed fiscal management standards have also been issued.

Labor on conformity and compliance cases before he renders a decision."[27]

As related above, the Secretary of Labor did just this in the California case. Because of the infrequency of formal hearings, it would be impracticable to appoint regular hearing boards: *ad hoc* advisory boards would be more advisable.

This raises another issue; namely, whether the decisions of the Secretary of Labor in conformity and compliance cases should be subject to federal court review.

SHOULD THERE BE FEDERAL COURT REVIEW OF SECRETARY'S FINDINGS?

The consequence of an adverse finding by the Secretary, possibly involving millions of dollars in administrative grants or employers' unemployment taxes, has raised the question as to whether the Secretary of Labor's finding of nonconformity or noncompliance with federal requirements should be subject to federal court review. Expressing themselves through the Interstate Conference, state administrators have increasingly contended that, in view of the powers given the Secretary, a state should be able to appeal his findings to a federal court. While it can be argued that the Secretary's findings are subject to the provisions for court review in the Federal Administrative Procedures Act, there has been no official determination on this.[28]

In a speech at the annual meeting of the Interstate Conference in 1955 in St. Louis, Missouri,[29] Secretary James P. Mitchell stated that he favored judicial review of the Secretary of Labor's decisions. Department of Labor officials followed up Secretary Mitchell's speech by attempting to work out a mutually satisfactory judicial review bill with representatives of the Interstate Conference, but negotiations have always broken down. The differences have revolved around three questions on which neither side has been willing to give in to the other.[30] The Interstate Conference secured the introduction of its draft of the bill in Congress and has had it introduced in each succeeding Congress.[31] While it would be beyond the province of this book to go into all the technical differences and issues on which this bill differs from the views of the Department of Labor lawyers, we

---

[27] *Report to the President, op. cit.,* p. 205.

[28] Professor Reginald Parker of Willamette College has expressed the opinion that the Secretary's finding is not subject to the procedure of the Administrative Procedures Act because the Social Security Act does not require that the Secretary's decision be made upon the record of the hearing, as required by the Administrative Procedures Act. See his article, "Administrative Law Problems in the Unemployment Insurance Program," *Vanderbilt Law Review,* Vol. VIII, No. 2 (February, 1955), p. 440.

[29] *Proceedings* of the 19th Annual Meeting of the Interstate Conference of Employment Security Agencies, St. Louis, Missouri, September 22–25, 1955, p. 4.

[30] These involve what federal court should have jurisdiction, whether court review should be confined to the record, and whether stay of the Secretary's ruling should be mandatory or discretionary with the court.

[31] See H.R. 4947, 88th Cong.

should discuss one because it involves a broad policy issue. If a finding of the Secretary is appealed to judicial review, should there be a "stay" of the Secretary's finding until the court has ruled on the case? The nub of the problem involved in a "stay" grows out of the delays that would necessarily result from a court review of the Secretary's findings. (It should be borne in mind that probably several years would elapse before the issue would go through the state's administrative and court reviews.)

To see what this would mean let us examine a case involving withholding of administrative grants. Should grants be withheld pending the court's decision? If so, the state, if it is going to continue to operate its employment security program, would have to get special appropriations from its state legislature, with the accompanying difficulties and delays this would entail. On the other hand, if grants are continued, but the court upheld the Secretary's finding of noncompliance, how could the grants made in the meantime be recovered? Certainly, there is no way that the federal government could force repayment. Probably the only practical course would be to provide that the Secretary continue to certify grants during court review, but if this were done it would virtually assure that a state would appeal any adverse finding, since it would have nothing to lose by doing so.

Even more difficult problems would be created by conformity issues under the Federal Unemployment Tax Act. If the Secretary finds a state out of conformity and it does not amend its law to bring it in line with federal requirements by the end of the calendar year (or within 90 days if the finding is near the end of the year) employers covered by the state law cannot receive tax credit for that year. If court review of the Secretary's findings were available, the question would arise whether or not employers should continue to receive tax credit pending the court's decision. If employers were given tax credit and the court decision upheld the Secretary's finding, taxes for which credit was given would have to be collected retroactively. In the meantime, many employers would have gone out of business. On the other hand, if no tax credit was given until the court rendered its decision, the employers of the state would have to pay the full federal tax as well as their unemployment taxes to the state. This would be a hardship for many employers operating on a narrow margin, even if the court reversed the Secretary's finding and tax refunds were made.

If a conformity issue involves beneficiaries, as in the California case, under the "labor standards provision" (Section 3304 (a) (5) of the Federal Unemployment Tax Act), the problem of delay resulting from court review would also be serious. If workers to whom benefits have been denied under the state law would be entitled to receive benefits under the Secretary's ruling, further delay in the payment of benefits would be a hardship. A few more months (or years) delay would not have made much difference in the case of the workers who raised the issue of denial of benefits since they probably had already waited several years and managed to "get along." But what about new cases arising while the issue is pending in the court?

These would be cases of workers currently unemployed for whom retroactive payments would be due if the Secretary's ruling were upheld, but who would have to find some other means of surviving without unemployment benefits in the meantime. In short, life does not stand still under the unemployment compensation program and court review would make it more difficult than at present to unscramble cases where a state has been denying benefits under a state provision that was not in conformity with federal requirements.

Some kind of provision for a stay of the Secretary's finding would probably have to be included in a judicial review bill, but it was the view of the Department of Labor lawyers that this should be discretionary with the court. This would enable the court to fit the "stay" to the circumstances of the case. For example, if denial of benefits were involved, it could specify that the state hold all rulings on claims involving the question at issue in abeyance pending the decision of the court.

Aside from specific questions, there is much to be said for the principle of judicial review. An increasing number of laws involving federal grants to states include provision for judicial review, in case the federal agency withholds grants because it finds the state is not complying with federal requirements.

Undoubtedly, it would improve federal-state relations if court review of the Secretary's decision were available. Under the present situation, state agencies frequently give in on a conformity issue because they assume that if it is important enough, the issue has already been discussed with the Secretary and a hearing would probably make little difference in his final decision. But if the issue were important, and especially if it involved large amounts of money in benefits, the state, represented by its agency, might be more inclined to insist on its side of the case if it knew that court review of the Secretary's decision was eventually available. This raises the question of whether there would be many more compliance and conformity issues brought to the hearing stage. It is our opinion that there would not be many. The long-established practice of discussion and negotiation over a compliance or conformity issue, which in almost every case has resolved issues, would go on. But the availability of court review would remove the feelings of resentment and frustration that no doubt often accompany a state agency's arguments with the federal "people" over a compliance or conformity issue.

SUMMARY AND CONCLUSIONS

Relationships between the Federal Bureau of Employment Security and the state employment security agencies have never been completely harmonious and frequently have been quite strained. In recent years, relationships have improved but conflict is always latent. This arises partly from the natural tendency for the federal bureau to look at problems from a national standpoint in contrast to the state agencies which view problems from a local perspective. It is also due to the human tendency to oppose any threat to one's prerogatives. Also, basic economic interests are often at issue. Federal proposals for improvements in the program and many conformity issues involve higher or lower benefit costs. For this reason, employers are often aligned with state officials and labor with the federal bureau on the issues involved.

The issues on which there have been the greatest strains on federal-state relationships have been those that would lead to federalization of the program and abolish the state systems. Proposals for federalization of the system made by the Social Security Board in the early 1940's created a lasting suspicion on the part of state administrators that any proposal by the federal government that would enlarge federal authority or jurisdiction is a move toward federalization of the system. Proposals for federal minimum benefit standards have fared no better. Rather than being considered on their merits, they have been opposed by most states as an intrusion on state prerogatives to determine their own benefit standards and as a move toward federalization of the program. The federal proposals have usually been supported by organized labor, and employer organizations have backed state opposition.

While there are strong arguments for federalization of the program, it is our conclusion that nothing short of bankruptcy of the present system or a national catastrophe would or probably should open the way to serious consideration of so drastic a change. On the other hand, federal minimum benefit standards appear to be necessary if the program is ever going to adequately meet the needs of the unemployed. The federal government can appropriately require that a state meet adequate standards as a condition for receiving the billions in federal tax credits to employers covered by state unemployment insurance laws. As embodied in the Administration bill of 1965, the most recent federal proposals for minimum benefit goals have not been tested in the legislative arena at the time of writing. If past experience is any indication, the proposals will be as strongly opposed as have stronger federal benefit standard proposals in past years.

Federal-state relationships are constantly being strained by questions raised by the federal bureau as to conformity or compliance with federal requirements, even though federal officials are only carrying out their duty. Almost all of these are settled through negotiation, but this is often because of the severity of federal sanctions—loss of administrative grants or credits against the federal unemployment tax. In some cases, the state agencies give in because of these sanctions; in other cases, the federal agency hesitates to "crack down" because the issue is not important enough to apply the federal sanctions. Only a few cases have gone as far as the stage of a formal hearing by the federal authority, and in only two cases have federal grants been temporarily withdrawn until the state "got in line" again.

Because of the severity of federal sanctions, a search has been made for "lesser sanctions" but with scanty results. The state administrators have felt that there should be federal judicial review of the Secretary of Labor's decisions, because of the great powers given him through the federal sanctions for nonconformity or noncompliance with federal requirements. Negotiations between federal and state officials to reach agreement on a court review bill have always broken down. After the last failure, the states secured the introduction in Congress of their own bill. While there is considerable justification for judicial review of the Secretary's conformity or compliance decisions, it could create serious problems. Employers would be hurt if there was not a stay of the Secretary's decision pending court review; beneficiaries could be hurt if there was a stay. Judicial review would appear to be undesirable unless some satisfactory solution to these problems is worked out.

APPENDIX

The Interstate Conference of Employment Security Agencies

Any discussion of federal-state relations under the unemployment insurance program would be incomplete without a discussion of the activities of the Interstate Conference on Employment Security Agencies and its relationship to the Bureau of Employment Security and the federal-state program in general.

The principal medium for collective communication between the Bureau of Employment Security and the state administrators is the Interstate Conference of Employment Security Agencies. This organization is perhaps unique among interstate organizations in federal-state programs in the power and influence it has had. It also has been a target for criticism by organized labor both because of its activity on federal legislation and because of the "hold" it allegedly has, in labor's opinion, on the Bureau of Employment Security's administration of its responsibilities.

After several informal meetings of the representatives of state organizations in 1936 and 1937, the Interstate Conference was formally organized and adopted a constitution at a national meeting in Washington on October 20, 1937. The stated objectives of the Conference are (1) to improve the effectiveness of the employment security program; (2) "to foster a closer professional relationship and the exchange of ideas among the Administrators"; (3) to promote proper and efficient administration; (4) to encourage cooperative research among the state agencies; and (5) to develop and propose federal and state legislation in the field of employment security.[32]

The Conference operates through an annual meeting, a President who is elected annually, a National Executive Committee composed of 13 regional vice-presidents, and various committees appointed by the Executive Committee. It has a full-time Executive Secretary, whose salary and office expenses are financed by the Bureau of Employment Security, and who is a Special Assistant on Federal-State Relations to the Administrator of the Bureau. The policies developed and promoted by the Conference are either adopted through resolutions at its annual meetings or by interim polls of the states between annual meetings.

Between its annual meetings the Interstate Conference works through meet-

[32] *Constitution,* Interstate Conference of Employment Security Agencies, Article II.

ings of its National Executive Committee and a number of committees to deal with various aspects of the employment security program. Most of these committees have operated for many years, but other committees are appointed from time to time to work on functions of special interest. In addition to the National Executive Committee, the Committee on Interstate Benefit Payments is the only permanent committee provided for in the Constitution of the Conference. Working under the instructions of the National Executive Committee, the activities of the Legislative Committee have been the principal source of any strained relations between the Interstate Conference and the Bureau of Employment Security.

Activities of the Interstate Conference. On the positive side, the Interstate Conference has provided an organized forum for the exchange of ideas among the state agencies, and between the states and the Bureau of Employment Security. Most of its committees have been technical working committees which discuss current issues and problems. For example, the Administrative Grants Committee works closely with the Bureau's officials on detailed policies governing the annual grants for administration.

Other committees of the Conference have done constructive work. These include the Employment Service Program and Operations Committee, the Benefit Financing Committee, and the Fraud Prevention and Detection Committee.[33]

In most instances, there is a close working relationship between the committees of the Conference and the technical staff of the Bureau. The Bureau is represented by its technical and regional staff on the committees of the Conference. Because it is usually working to oppose legislation proposed by the Bureau or on proposals to which the Bureau is opposed, the Legislative Committee does not cooperate as much as other committees. This committee calls in a Bureau representative only on technical questions but excludes him from discussions of policy issues.

The Committee on Interstate Benefit Payments has been an operating committee which has worked out interstate agreements providing for uniform treatment of claims and for uniform coverage arrangements that have prevented overlapping of coverage of workers operating across state lines. Altogether, eight interstate agreements have been worked out by the Committee and practically all of the states have adopted most of them.

Federal legislation is an activity of the Interstate Conference in which it has often worked independently of or at odds with the federal bureau. At times, the Interstate Conference has drafted and promoted its own bills. At other times, it has opposed proposals of the Bureau, particularly when these would enlarge or strengthen federal authority. Its officials have not only appeared at Congressional hearings, but have arranged conferences with Congressional Committee chairmen to oppose federal proposals for legislation or to promote their own legislative proposals. Individual state administrators have also communicated their views to their own Congressional delegations. Through such activity, the Conference has had a significant influence on federal legislation in the field of employment security. In the area of appropriation legislation the Conference has

---

[33] In 1965, there were 13 committees, which, in addition to those named above, included committees on farm placement, interstate benefit payments, legal affairs, legislation, manpower training, personnel management, and research and statistics. There is also a program committee to plan the next annual meeting of the Conference.

more frequently worked cooperatively with the Bureau, since usually the federal and state agencies have a mutual interest in securing their appropriation request.

Issues Regarding the Interstate Conference

Legislative Activity. The most controversial activity of the Interstate Conference has been in this field of legislation.[34] According to one's viewpoint, the Conference, through its opposition to many federal legislative proposals, has been the most obstructive influence against changes in the program, or has been the greatest protector of the states' rights. The Interstate Conference has taken upon itself the role of a collective spokesman for the states on federal employment security legislation and is so regarded by Congress. This has drawn the fire of organized labor and liberal Congressmen who have questioned whether the State administrators, speaking as representatives of the Interstate Conference, are stating their personal views or the official position of the state government.[35] Organized labor has also accused the Interstate Conference of always taking the employers' point of view.[36]

In 1954, labor members of the Federal Advisory Council on Employment Security charged the Interstate Conference officials with using federal grants to finance trips to Washington to lobby against federal legislation proposed by the Bureau. After long study, the Advisory Council adopted a report in which detailed recommendations were made for Bureau policy governing federal legislative activity by State Employment Security administrators. The policy recommended that the expenditure of granted federal funds be permitted (1) to present the views of the state to the state's Congressional representatives on the request of such representatives; (2) to present the views of the state to any other member of Congress on the member's request; (3) to present the views of the state at a public hearing of a committee of Congress; or (4) to arrange for the introduction of legislation agreed to by the Conference, acting as a representative of the Interstate Conference. It recommended that the use of granted funds be denied if the legislative activity was not in accordance with these guides or was used to prompt other state agencies or others to influence Congressmen regarding legislation. The Bureau of Employment Security adopted the recommendations of the Advisory Council with some changes.[37] This policy, however, has not re-

[34] While one of its stated objectives is to improve state legislation, the Conference has largely confined its legislative activity to federal legislation.

[35] During the 1959 hearings of the Committee on Ways and Means, the President of the Interstate Conference, the late John Morrison of Kansas, testified that the majority of the state agencies, by a poll of the Conference, were opposed to federal benefit standards. When questioned by Congressmen Thaddeus M. Machrowicz as to whether opposition to standards represented the views of Mr. Morrison's agency or the views of the governor of the state, Mr. Morrison confessed that he had not discussed them with the governor. Thereupon Mr. Machrowicz, to Mr. Morrison's embarrassment, read into the record a telegram from George Docking, Governor of Kansas, urging the enactment of federal legislation for minimum benefit standards. *Unemployment Compensation*, Hearings, *op. cit.*, p. 212.

[36] State Employment Security Officials, Resolution No. 36, *Proceedings*, Seventy-Second Annual Convention of the American Foundation of Labor (St. Louis, Missouri, 1953), p. 405.

[37] The Bureau of Employment Security's latest revision of its statement of policy was issued in 1962.

strained Congressional activities of the Interstate Conference to any noticeable degree.

Financing of Conference Activities. The travel and other expenses of state personnel attending meetings of the Interstate Conference and its committees are paid out of federally granted funds under Title III. This includes the expenses of the host state in connection with annual meetings of the Conference and the printing of its proceedings. The Secretariat of the Conference is on the payroll of the Bureau of Employment Security. It is rather paradoxical that the Interstate Conference, representing the legislative and political interests of the states, is financed by a Bureau of a federal department with whose legislative objectives it is frequently in conflict.

The financing of the Secretariat of the Interstate Conference out of Bureau funds also seems paradoxical, because of the legislative activity of the Conference in opposition to Bureau proposals. On the other hand, there are distinct advantages in having the Secretary of the Conference on the Bureau staff. Not only is the great bulk of the committee work of the Conference of a cooperative nature between the Bureau and the states, but the Executive Secretary of the Conference serves as a liaison between the Conference and the Bureau. Closely associated with state administrators, he is also able to interpret state thinking on problems to the Bureau as well as to interpret Bureau thinking to the officials of the Conference.[38] Because of this function, the Secretary also serves as Special Assistant for Federal-State Relations to the Administrator of the Bureau.

The Bureau is often put on the defensive at meetings of the National Executive Committee when some new or controversial matter is under discussion. Individual state administrators sometimes act as self-appointed inquisitors. On the other hand, the meetings of the Interstate Conference and its committees serve as a medium through which the Bureau can interpret its policies and actions to the states. The committees also serve as a medium for discussion of current problems. Therefore, their financing through federally granted funds has considerable justification. The financing of legislative activity with federal funds is the most questionable practice.

Does the Conference Pre-empt Bureau Functions? The Bureau has several other media by which it communicates directly with the states. There are, of course, a great number of individual contacts between national staff of the federal bureau and state staff. There is a close and continuing relationship between the regional offices of the Bureau and the state agencies. The most commonly used medium for communication with the states by the federal Bureau consists of identical letters sent to the states by the administrator of the Bureau or its major units. The Bureau calls regional or national meetings of specialists for consultation and training in new programs in various aspects of the employment security program. When a new national program is introduced, the Bureau usually calls a national meeting of all state administrators to explain and discuss the problems involved in it.

The Bureau constantly faces the question, however, as to whether it should take the initiative in calling conferences with the states, rely on liaison with the

[38] While regional administrators of the Bureau have a closer day-to-day relationship with the state administrators in their regions, a composite view of nation-wide opinion of state administrators cannot be secured from them except at periodic conferences of the regional administrators.

states by the regional offices, or use the Interstate Conference and its committees as a means of conferring with the states. Because of the activities of the Interstate Conference, the Bureau is often put on the defensive concerning its position of national leadership. Some state officials who resist such leadership, look on the Conference as a means of counterbalancing federal influence. The Interstate Conference has also been criticized by organized labor for acting as a collective body for the states in bringing pressures on the Bureau of Employment Security and the Secretary of Labor when its leaders disagree with policies or even with the internal organization of the Bureau of Department of Labor. The problem is to keep the activities of the Conference within proper limits so that it plays a constructive role in being a medium of consultation between the states and between the states and the Bureau.

The Interstate Conference has undoubtedly exerted a powerful influence on the unemployment insurance program. As the collective voice for the state administrators, its views have great weight with Congress. Since its leadership has usually been conservative, it has often successfully opposed Administration proposals for liberalization of the program. It has also frequently served as a collective bargaining agency for the state agencies when issues have arisen between the Bureau of Employment Security and the state agencies.

Chapter 23

Coordination
with Other Programs

While the Social Security Act of 1935 contained a variety of programs, it fell short of providing for a comprehensive system of social insurance. It provided for only two social insurance programs: for unemployment and old age. The Committee on Economic Security report discussed all the hazards for which social insurance is provided in most industrialized countries, but only proposed such programs as appeared to be attainable at that time in the United States.

Since 1935, there has been a considerable expansion of social insurance. Protection has been added to the federal old-age insurance program for survivors in the case of death of the wage earner and for permanent and total disabilities suffered by workers. A few states have provided temporary cash benefits for non-work-connected disabilities. Workmen's compensation for work-connected disabilities has been expanded in coverage and scope. Social insurance in the United States, nevertheless, is incomplete in the risks it protects. The most serious gaps have been in the protection against sickness and disability. Unlike other modern industrial societies, our society provides no social insurance for medical care and hospitalization of employed workers suffering from nonindustrial illness or injury.[1] Because of the gaps in social insurance protection, pressures have been put on the unemployment insurance system to partially fill some of these gaps. For example, continuing benefits to unemployed workers when they become ill is practiced in some states.

Such social insurance programs as exist are largely uncoordinated, or coordinated on a piecemeal basis. This is generally true of the coordination of unemployment insurance with other programs.

States have followed no consistent policy with respect to the relationship

---

[1] The hospitalization insurance for retired persons, and government subsidized voluntary insurance for medical care for such persons, added to the OASDI program by the 1965 Social Security Amendments (Public Law 89–97, approved July 30, 1965) still leaves employed workers unprotected.

of unemployment compensation to any other social insurance program. If a worker is receiving workmen's compensation, for example, some states deny unemployment compensation, others reduce the amount of unemployment compensation by the amount of workmen's compensation, and still others have no statutory provision.

In addition, an individual state may vary in its policies regarding the relationship of unemployment compensation to different social insurance programs. For example, some states deny or reduce unemployment compensation if a worker is receiving workmen's compensation, but pay unemployment compensation in full if a worker is receiving a federal old-age insurance benefit. The policies governing the relationship of unemployment compensation need to be examined program by program.

The start of several new federal programs closely allied to unemployment compensation necessitates additional coordination. These include the program for training allowances provided under the 1962 Manpower Development and Training Act and the readjustment benefits provided to workers displaced through trade policy under the 1962 Trade Expansion Act. The problem is not only whether duplication of benefits should be prevented, but whether or not training or readjustment allowances should have priority over unemployment insurance if a worker is eligible for both. There is also the question as to whether an unemployment insurance claimant should be denied benefits if he refuses an offer of suitable training.

There is the question of the relationship of unemployment insurance to public assistance. In this area, the problem of coordination is minor because relatively few able-bodied unemployed are eligible for public assistance in most states. The major problem is to secure nation-wide provision of public assistance for the needy unemployed who have exhausted their unemployment compensation or are not covered by unemployment insurance.

Unemployment compensation is provided through separate programs for each of the 50 states, the District of Columbia, Puerto Rico, and federal programs for federal civilian workers, ex-servicemen, and railroad workers. These programs need coordination to prevent overlapping or gaps in coverage and benefits. Although this has been largely attempted through uniform definitions in the laws or by interstate agreements, nevertheless, the coordination is incomplete and needs review.

Finally, supplementary unemployment benefits (SUB) are payable to several million workers under collective bargaining agreements. While these are private programs, they involve questions of coordination with unemployment insurance. Such SUB programs therefore will be discussed in this chapter.

COORDINATION OF UNEMPLOYMENT INSURANCE LAWS

So far as unemployment compensation is concerned, the first and primary need has been for coordination between the unemployment compensation laws. Problems of coordination have largely arisen because great numbers of workers move across state lines while working or after they become unemployed.

Coordination of Coverage

Interstate coverage problems were among the first issues that faced the states. The most obvious problem was to prevent a worker, such as a traveling salesman who works in more than one state on the same job, from being covered by two or more state laws. The solution was to have all his wages credited to one state and his employer pay contributions with respect to his earnings in that state. This has been accomplished through the adoption by all the states of a uniform definition of "localization" of work. If a worker's services cannot be localized in any one state, his entire services can still be covered in one state, namely, the state from which he is directed if he does some work there.

Most states have also adopted legislation which enables them to enter into reciprocal arrangements with other states so that an employee who works successively in two or more states can have continuity of coverage. The reciprocal arrangements worked out among 47 of the states permit an employer to cover all the services of such a worker in any state in which any part of his service is performed, in which he resides, or in which his employer maintains a place of business. These reciprocal arrangements normally cover services performed by individuals who contract by the job and whose various jobs are in different states. The coverage of interstate workers, therefore, presents no current issues.

Another coverage problem arises when an employer does not have enough localized employees in one or more states for them to be covered because of size of firm exclusions. Thus, he may have one employee in New Hampshire, which covers only employers with four or more workers, but he has enough workers in Maine to be covered by the Maine law. Thirty-six of the states permit the employer to elect the coverage of such an employee under the state law which covers the employer. However, all but eight require that the employee reside in the state of election. This limits the election almost entirely to employees working in states adjacent to the state covering the employer. For many years there has been no change in the number of states with these election provisions. Evidently, there are not enough workers involved who are still not covered to call attention to this problem.

Coordination of Benefits

The first problem in the area of benefits for interstate workers was to prevent duplication of benefits. Practically all state unemployment compensation laws provide that their own benefits will not be paid in any week in which a worker is receiving or seeking benefits under any other state or federal unemployment compensation law. If it is finally determined that the worker is not eligible for any week under the other law, under most of these provisions the disqualification does not apply. The uncontroversial aim of such provisions was to avoid duplication of unemployment compensation payments.

Looking at the other side of the picture, the states have gone a long way toward assuring that an unemployed worker will not suffer from having been covered successively by two or more unemployment compensation programs instead of just one. The first step was to develop an interstate plan under which each state would act as the agent for other states in taking the claims of unemployed workers who had moved to the agent state and had had enough employment in another state to qualify for benefits. All states participate in a uniform interstate benefit payment plan.

The next step was to enable a worker to combine his wage credits earned in two or more states, if he had not worked long enough to qualify for benefits in any single state. All but three states have agreed to a plan to permit such combination of credits, termed "Basic Arrangements for Combining Wages."

A plan was then developed which combined the wages earned in all states of an interstate worker who qualified for benefits in one state if this would produce a larger benefit. The states were slower to join this "Extended Arrangement for Combining Wages" but as of December 1, 1965, all but seven states had subscribed to this plan.

If all states agreed to these wage-combining plans, one of the major disadvantages of a system of separate state unemployment insurance systems will have been overcome.[2]

Reduction of Benefits to Interstate Claimants

Three states discriminate against their claimants if they file in another state. Alaska limits benefits to a maximum of $25 and pays no dependents' benefits. Ohio pays claimants who have gone to another state either the benefit they would have received if they had remained in Ohio or the average benefits being paid in the state in which they file a claim, whichever is lower. Wyoming pays either 75 percent of the benefit payable in the state or the maximum in the state where the claim is filed, wherever is lower. The Administration bill of 1965 would prohibit such reductions, under penalty of loss of FUTA tax credit.

COORDINATION WITH SUPPLEMENTARY UNEMPLOYMENT BENEFITS

Supplementary unemployment benefit plans were first negotiated by the United Automobile Workers with the automobile companies in 1955. The following year, the United Steel Workers negotiated a similar but more liberal plan with the steel and car companies. In 1962, over 2.5 million workers were covered by SUB plans. Besides auto and steel, the largest

[2] Other plans have been developed: for cooperation with Canada in taking claims, and for interstate reciprocal arrangements for maritime workers and for Great Lakes seamen.

groups with SUB plans include workers in rubber and plastics, women's and children's garments, and the General Electric and Westinghouse Electric Companies.[3]

Although these plans vary in their provisions, the original automobile and steel plans set the general pattern.[4] The 1955 Ford and UAW plan provided for supplementation of state unemployment compensation up to 65 percent of take-home pay, or $25, whichever was the lesser, for 26 weeks. The steel companies–USW plan provided the same amounts for 52 weeks. The automobile–UAW plan as amended in 1961, provides benefits up to 62 percent of gross pay plus $1.50 per dependent up to four, with an overall maximum of $40 a week for 52 weeks. The electric companies-IBEW plans supplement duration only.[5]

In order to draw supplementary unemployment benefits, the worker must be eligible for state unemployment compensation. The plans provide for subtraction of the amount of state unemployment compensation from the gross supplementary benefit amount. If the worker exhausts his public benefits, the SUB is payable in full. With some exceptions, the disqualifications are stricter than in some state unemployment insurance programs. For example, all voluntary quits, regardless of cause, are disqualifying for the duration of unemployment. In some plans, disqualification in connection with a strike is broader than in state unemployment insurance laws. On the other hand, SUB is more liberal in that it may be payable even if the worker has earned more in a week than the amount allowable under the state program.[6]

When supplementary unemployment benefits were first agreed upon in 1955 and 1956, a major battle threatened as to whether or not unemployment compensation would be denied or reduced by the amount of SUB received.[7] Since supplementary unemployment benefits were designed to augment and not substitute for unemployment compensation, all but six states have taken action to permit supplementation without its affecting unemployment compensation. Five states have taken no formal action,[8] and Virginia by statute does not permit receipt of unemployment compen-

[3] Joseph M. Becker and Virginia Kyner Boman, "Suppmentary Unemployment Benefits" in Joseph M. Becker (ed.) In Aid of the Unemployed (Baltimore: Johns Hopkins Press, 1965), chap. 6, pp. 115–16, table 6–2. This chapter gives a full description of the history, provisions, and experience of SUB plans, as well as an appraisal of their success and significance for unemployment insurance.

[4] For a description of the original plans, see: United States Department of Labor, Bureau of Employment Security, Supplementary Unemployment Benefit Plans and Unemployment Insurance, BES No. U–172 (1957).

[5] For detailed descriptions, see United States Department of Labor, Bureau of Labor Statistics, Digest of Nine Supplemental Unemployment Benefit Plans, Early 1963 (Washington, D.C.: U.S. Government Printing Office, May, 1963).

[6] Becker and Boman, op. cit., pp. 115–18 and table 6–3.

[7] For a discussion of the issues involved, see John G. Turnbull, C. Arthur Williams, Jr., and Earl F. Cheit, Economic and Social Security (2nd ed.; New York: Ronald Press Co., 1962), pp. 214–15.

[8] New Hampshire, New Mexico, Puerto Rico, South Carolina, and North Dakota.

sation in a week in which supplementary unemployment benefits are received.

Since SUB has been accepted by almost all the states, no particular problem of coordination exists. Supplementary unemployment benefits have served a useful purpose in providing more security to the covered workers, particularly in those states where unemployment insurance benefits are low. As in the case of private pensions, SUB can provide another layer of protection even in states with "adequate" benefits, since unemployment insurance is designed to provide for only the minimum essentials of living.[9]

The state agencies have no administrative problem of coordination with SUB, since the companies paying SUB adjust such payments to what is received in unemployment compensation.

COORDINATION WITH TEMPORARY DISABILITY INSURANCE

Since unemployment insurance is payable only to able-bodied workers who are involuntarily unemployed, sickness, that is, inability to work, is a standard disqualification from benefits for covered workers. Four states have social insurance programs providing for temporary disability benefits for workers suffering nonoccupational illness or disability.

Cash benefits during absence from work due to temporary disability are more closely related to unemployment compensation than to any other social insurance benefits. This is reflected in three of the four state laws that provide for temporary disability benefits which were initially financed in whole or in part by the transfer of employee contributions from their unemployment insurance plans. In 1942, Rhode Island provided that its employee contributions for unemployment insurance should be used to finance the payment of cash temporary disability benefits. California followed suit in 1946, except that it also stipulated that part of the cost of temporary disability benefits be paid through an employer contribution. Shortly thereafter, in 1948, New Jersey took similar action to that of California, except that a small part of the employee contribution continued to be used for unemployment insurance. In 1949, New York, which had no employee contribution for unemployment insurance, enacted a temporary disability insurance law which differed substantially from unemployment insurance and was separately administered.[10] In the late 1940's, several other states considered TDI legislation, but took no action.[11]

The four state temporary disability laws are of three types. Rhode

[9] See Becker and Boman, op. cit., pp. 132–36.
[10] There is also a federal temporary disability law for railroad workers which is coordinated with their unemployment insurance law.
[11] In the states that had diverted employee contributions to temporary disability insurance, the question arose as to contributions made by employees prior to the enactment of these laws. In 1946, Congress amended the Federal Unemployment Tax Act so as to make it possible for employee contributions previously made for unemployment insurance to be used for temporary disability insurance (60 Stat. 978 [1946]).

Island has an exclusive state fund. California and New Jersey have state funds, but permit the contracting out of private plans that provide at least as much protection. New York permits insuring of employed workers by private insurers, by a competitive state fund, or through self-insurance by the employer. New York insures unemployed workers through a state fund to which all employers must contribute. This contribution also is used to defray state administrative expenses.

These different types of plans require different kinds of coordination with unemployment insurance. There is complete coordination in Rhode Island, with the same coverage and benefit formula for the two programs and administration by the same agency. In New Jersey, the coverage is the same. Disabled unemployed workers and unemployment insurance claimants are paid under the same benefit formula, with a somewhat different formula for disabled employed workers. The combined duration of benefits for a worker drawing both unemployment compensation and temporary disability benefits is limited to 150 percent of the duration for either program separately. In California, the coverage is the same for both programs, but benefits are higher for temporary disability. In both California and New Jersey, the state employment security agency administers the programs, which prevents duplication of benefits to claimants paid from state funds. The employer who has contracted out should be able to prevent duplication of benefits to his employees, since he will be notified regularly by the state agency of unemployment compensation payments and will be notified of temporary disability claims by his insurance company.

New York presents an entirely different situation. Not only do coverage and benefit provisions differ, but the temporary disability program is administered by a different agency, the state workmen's compensation division. There has been little coordination with the unemployment insurance program, except to check whether unemployed TDI claimants are simultaneously filing claims for unemployment insurance.

Benefits during Maternity

Temporary disability insurance laws differ in the extent to which they provide benefits during pregnancy or in the weeks following childbirth. Only Rhode Island and New Jersey pay benefits before and after childbirth. California pays benefits only for disability occurring 29 days or more after termination of pregnancy. New York pays no benefits for maternity and requalifies a woman for temporary disability benefits for other causes only after she has returned to covered employment for at least two consecutive weeks following termination of pregnancy.[12] Because of these limitations on benefits during and after pregnancy, California and New York have no particular problem of overlapping of temporary disability and unemployment benefits during and after pregnancy. New Jersey pre-

---

[12] The railroad social insurance system provides specifically for maternity benefits for 115 days beginning 57 days before childbirth.

vents overlapping by specifically disqualifying a woman for unemployment compensation four weeks before and four weeks after childbirth. State unemployment compensation laws differ widely in their treatment of pregnant women.[13] This is an area that badly needs greater uniformity of treatment.

Payment of Unemployment Compensation during Illness

When no insurance is provided for a specific risk, there is a general tendency for some other type of insurance to move in to fill the gap. In some states, if a worker becomes ill while drawing unemployment compensation, he is allowed to continue to draw it unless he has an offer of a suitable job. At a meeting on December 13–14, 1964, the Federal Advisory Council discussed this tendency and debated whether to recommend it as a policy for all states without temporary disability programs. Instead, it reached the following conclusion: "Without, at this time, taking a position for or against temporary disability insurance, it is our belief that the approaches to the problem of unemployed claimants who become disabled can be more appropriately taken into account in any consideration of temporary disability insurance rather than in connection with unemployment insurance." While TDI is the ideal method of protecting unemployed workers when they are ill, realism would seem to dictate that unemployment insurance be continued in states that do not provide TDI protection.

Should Temporary Disability Insurance Be Coordinated with Unemployment Insurance or Federal OASDI?

No state has enacted legislation for temporary disability insurance since 1949. This may be due to the growth of such insurance in private industry as a part of "fringe benefit" programs often associated with collective bargaining. Protection under voluntary plans has slowed down in recent years, however, and in 1960, it was estimated that 22.8 million out of 53.9 million wage and salary workers were neither under voluntary nor compulsory plans. Consideration has therefore been given within the federal government to proposing a federal program that would stimulate coverage of all workers under some type of temporary disability insurance. The question has arisen in these discussions as to whether such proposed legislation should provide for coordination with unemployment insurance or with federal old-age, survivors, and disability insurance. The principal argument for coordination with unemployment insurance focuses on programs for temporary risks, in which prompt and weekly payments of benefits are essential to make the programs effective. Since temporary disability or illness can occur during unemployment, it is also easier to coordinate the administration of the two programs. The arguments for coordination of temporary and permanent disability programs are also strong. A worker who is permanently disabled must first draw benefits under a temporary

[13] See Chapter 14.

disability program if it is available and then shift after the sixth month to the permanent disability program which has different qualifying conditions and different rates of benefits. From an administrative standpoint, it is desirable that the administrative agency for permanent disability insurance be able to observe the disability from its inception, rather than to have to rely on affidavits from doctors six months later when the worker files for permanent disability insurance. In many cases, prognostication of permanent disability might be made months earlier if the same agency administered both temporary and permanent disability insurance. Furthermore, a program of rehabilitation and retraining of cases susceptible to such treatment could be started much earlier if the same agency administered both temporary and permanent disability insurance. Federal functions in the unemployment insurance program and the OASDI program are in separate departments of the federal government, and as yet no agreement has been reached on this issue between the two departments. It is our opinion that temporary disability insurance is more closely related to unemployment insurance than to permanent disability insurance.[14]

COORDINATION WITH WORKMEN'S COMPENSATION

Presumably, an unemployed worker who is drawing workmen's compensation for temporary total disability is unable to work and will be disqualified from unemployment compensation in all states. Yet six states reduce the unemployment compensation payment and eight deny it if a worker is receiving workmen's compensation for total temporary disability. The states differ in their treatment of partial disability (temporary or permanent) and of permanent total disability cases. Twenty-four state unemployment compensation laws have specific provisions with respect to workmen's compensation payments, as of January 1, 1966. Nineteen of these states deny or reduce the unemployment compensation payment by the amount of any workmen's compensation payment for temporary partial disability, since these are the cases in which the unemployed worker is most likely to be able to prove that he is able to work. Sixteen states deny or reduce unemployment compensation in cases of temporary total disability. Two states deny and two states reduce the benefits of a worker receiving workmen's compensation for permanent partial disability; and four states reduce and three states deny benefits if a worker is receiving workmen's compensation for permanent total disability (see Table 23–1).

It is the authors' view that there is no justification for reducing or denying unemployment compensation if a worker is drawing either partial or total permanent disability benefits. If a worker is able to secure employment and qualify for unemployment compensation despite an injury for

---

[14] In the railroad system, in which all types of insurance programs are administered by the Railroad Retirement Board, unemployment and temprorary sickness benefits are paid out of one fund and have the same qualifying requirements and benefit provisions, while permanent disability annuities are paid out of the retirement fund.

Table 23–1

Effect on Unemployment Compensation of Receipt of Different Types of Workmen's Compensation, as of January 1, 1966

State	Type of Workmen's Compensation			
	Temporary Partial	Temporary Total	Permanent Partial	Permanent Total
Alabama	R	R		
Colorado	R	R		
Connecticut	D	D		
Florida	R	R		R
Georgia	D	D		
Illinois	R	R		
Iowa	R	R		
Kansas		D		D
Louisiana	R	R		R
Massachusetts*	D	D	D	D
Michigan	R	R	R	R
Minnesota	R	R	R	R
Missouri	R			
Montana	D	D	D	D
Nebraska	R			
New Hampshire	R			
Ohio	R			
Rhode Island	R			
South Dakota	R			
Tennessee	D			
Texas	D	D		
Vermont	R			
West Virginia		D		
Wisconsin		D		

"R" means weekly unemployment compensation benefit is reduced by weekly prorated amount of the payment.
"D" means no benefit is paid for the week of receipt.
* Except weekly payments for dismemberment.
Source: United States Department of Labor, Bureau of Employment Security, *Comparison of State Unemployment Insurance Laws* (Washington, D.C.: U.S. Government Printing Office).

which he is still drawing workmen's compensation, he should be eligible for unemployment compensation if he suffers wage loss due to unemployment. For example, a man may be blinded in an explosion, but may be rehabilitated so that he is able to engage in gainful employment, although at perhaps somewhat less income. To deny such a worker unemployment compensation if he loses his job would be inconsistent with the emphasis in public policy on rehabilitation and employment of the handicapped. If the worker drawing permanent disability payments is unable to work, he should, of course, be disqualified under the "able to work" provisions in unemployment insurance laws. Specific disqualifications because of temporary *total* disability payments under workmen's compensation also seem unnecessary, since workers receiving such payments presumably are unable to work and so can also be disqualified under the "able to work" requirements of unemployment insurance laws. On the other hand, such specific disqualifications do no harm. Workers drawing temporary *partial* disability benefits under workmen's compensation present a different problem. Presumably, the worker's capacity to work is reduced while he is eligible to draw such benefits. He may, however, be unable to find any kind of work while partially disabled. If he is qualified for unemployment compensation, supplementation of his partial workmen's compensation payment with unemployment compensation will relieve hardship and would seem to be socially justified. Provisions for reduction or denial of unemployment compensation exist because the total cost of unemployment insurance is assessed against the employer. At the most, the unemployment compensation should be reduced by the amount of the workmen's compensation payment and not be denied entirely if the claimant is available for work, except in the case of temporary total disability. In short, none of the provisions in unemployment insurance laws reducing or denying unemployment compensation because of the receipt of workmen's compensation seems necessary or justified, except possibly a reduction in unemployment compensation in the case of partial temporary disability benefits.

COORDINATION WITH FEDERAL OLD-AGE INSURANCE BENEFITS

When the two programs began, it was expected that there would be much more coordination of unemployment insurance and federal old-age insurance than has occurred. Coverage was almost identical, except that old-age insurance covered employers of one or more, while the federal unemployment tax covered employers of eight or more. In 1939, the taxable wage base for unemployment insurance was made the same as for old-age insurance ($3,000), in order to simplify tax payments under the two programs.[15] For a time, most employers were able to file identical tax returns to the federal and state governments for the two programs. As the programs matured, however, they diverged more and more both in coverage and in their taxable wage bases. Federal OASDI now covers practically everyone who works, except federal government employees who are covered by the civil service retirement plan, and many state and local government employees. Unemployment insurance, on the other hand, covers only about three fourths of all employees. The wage base for OASDI was increased to $6,600 in 1966, as compared with the federal unemployment tax base of $3,000. Collaboration between the two programs is limited to the use of federal OASDI wage records by some states as a means of checking claimants who have had earnings while drawing unemployment compensation, and in the use of OASDI statistics for research purposes.

Originally, the general policy was to deny unemployment compensation to anyone drawing federal old-age insurance benefits. Following recommendations in the Social Security Board draft bills, 44 states enacted provisions denying unemployment compensation to anyone currently receiv-

15 See Chapter 18.

ing federal old-age benefits. Over the years, there has been a change in public attitude toward this, however. As of January 1, 1966, only 19 states took account of the receipt of federal old-age benefits and all but one provided for *reduction* of the weekly unemployment benefit by the amount received in old-age benefits, rather than outright denial. The question as to whether duplication of federal old-age insurance benefits and unemployment compensation should be permitted was put squarely up to Congress in connection with the pension amendment to the Temporary Extended Unemployment Compensation Act of 1961 (see Chapter 13). This amendment reduced extended unemployment compensation by the amount of any public or private pension to which a "base period" employer had contributed. Federal old-age insurance benefits were specifically exempted from the provision. This established a precedent in federal policy that unemployment compensation should not be denied to persons drawing federal old-age insurance benefits.

The TEUC amendment reflected the general long-prevailing attitude of Congress that federal old-age beneficiaries should be leniently treated with respect to other income because of the low level of old-age benefits. In December, 1964, the average old-age benefit was only $77.57 a month and the average benefit for a wife was $40.23. It is true that a maximum of $187.50 a month for husband and wife was payable at that time, but even those drawing the maximum were well below the $3,000 a year used by the Johnson Administration as the "poverty level."

Congress has therefore allowed beneficiaries to earn more and more without a reduction in old-age benefits. Under the 1965 amendments, an old-age beneficiary can earn $1,500 a year without any reduction in his old-age benefit, and then have a reduction of only $1 for each $2 of earnings up to $2,700 a year. Furthermore, he still will have no reduction in benefits for any month in which he has no earnings, no matter how much he earned in other months. After attaining age 72, there is no reduction in benefits, no matter how much he earns.

This Congressional attitude that a federal old-age beneficiary should be able to supplement his benefits to a certain extent with current earnings is reflected in the repeal of the provisions in most of the state laws which denied or reduced unemployment compensation without respect to workers drawing federal old-age benefits.[16]

To what extent do federal old-age insurance beneficiaries work and earn money? In 1962, a comprehensive study was made of the work experience and earnings of old-age beneficiaries.[17] Some work experience in 1962 was reported by 39.7 percent, or about 2,080,000, of male beneficiaries and 19.0

---

[16] The tide has turned, however. The number of states reducing or denying unemployment benefits grew from 10 to 18 in the three years 1963–65.

[17] Erdman Palmore, "Work Experience and Earnings of the Aged in 1962: Findings of the 1963 Survey of the Aged," *Social Security Bulletin*, Vol. XXVII, No. 6 (June, 1964), pp. 3–14.

percent, or about 1,250,000, of female beneficiaries. Most of them reported working at full-time jobs, but only 7.3 percent of the men and 2.6 percent of the women were on a full-time year-round basis. The mean average earnings of all male workers were $1,352 and of full-time male workers were $1,871. Women had lower earnings: a mean of $1,015 for all female workers and $1,513 for full-time workers. Of course, large numbers earned less than the average amount, but it would appear that most old-age beneficiaries who worked earned enough to qualify for unemployment compensation.

To what extent do federal old-age insurance beneficiaries file for unemployment compensation? A sample study of pensioners among claimants for regular unemployment benefits was made in 13 states in May and September, 1961, and January, 1962. Eight percent of the claimants were receiving some kind of pension and 7 percent were receiving federal old-age insurance (popularly called "social security") benefits, as will be seen from Table 23–2. A slightly higher proportion of male claimants was receiving a "social security pension." The proportions varied widely in the 13 states, ranging from 2 to 11 percent of all claimants. In two states, 12 percent of the male claimants were "social security" beneficiaries.

Almost twice as many claimants for extended benefits under the TEUC program of 1961 were receiving federal old-age benefits. Twelve percent were receiving "social security" benefits, of which 5 percent were also receiving another pension. The percentages in individual states ranged from 1 to 26 percent.[18]

The proportions of claimants drawing federal old-age benefits were high enough in most of the states to raise the question as to how many of these drew unemployment compensation immediately after retirement. A New York agency study of retirees drawing unemployment benefits showed that about 40 percent had qualified for benefits on the basis of wages earned after retirement.[19] Also, how many were seriously looking for work? The age handicap of the retirees certainly makes it difficult for them to find re-employment. One question is whether their combined income from federal old-age insurance and unemployment compensation was high enough in many cases to lower their incentive to actually seek other employment. This question becomes particularly important for those who were also receiving a private pension from their former employers. It can be presumed that most of the 3 percent shown in Table 23–2 who were receiving a non-social security pension were also receiving a "social security pension."

These are casual observations and a much more intensive study of claim-

[18] United States Department of Labor, Bureau of Employment Security, *Family Characteristics of the Long-Term Unemployed*, BES No. U–207–4, p. 119, table 16a.
[19] New York Department of Labor, Division of Employment, *Pensioners and Unemployment Insurance*, February, 1960.

Table 23–2

Pensions among Unemployment Insurance
Claimants, 13 States, 1961–62*

	Percent of Claimants Receiving		
State	Any Pension	Social Security Pension	Non-Social Security Pension
All Claimants:			
Arizona 4	2	1
California 7	5	3
Georgia 4	3	1
Illinois 8	7	3
Indiana 7	7	5
Louisiana 3	2	2
Maryland 9	8	4
Michigan 6	5	3
New York 12	11	5
Ohio 6	4	2
Oregon 7	6	2
Pennsylvania 9	8	5
Vermont 13	10	4
13-state total .. 8	7	3
Male Claimants:			
Arizona 5	3	3
California 8	6	4
Georgia 4	4	1
Illinois 9	7	4
Indiana 7	6	5
Louisiana 1	1	2
Maryland 9	7	5
Michigan 6	5	3
New York 14	12	6
Ohio 6	4	3
Oregon 8	7	3
Pennsylvania 11	10	8
Vermont 16	12	6
13-state total 9	7	5

* May and September, 1961, and January, 1962.
Source: United States Department of Labor, Bureau of Employment Security.

ants drawing social security benefits seems indicated. Although we with-hold judgment pending further study, we believe there is a serious question as to whether unemployment compensation and federal old-age benefits should be paid simultaneously. If unemployment compensation and old-age insurance benefits are both inadequate so that an unemployed worker needs both, then the basic remedy is liberalization of old-age benefits rather than a liberal policy toward the simultaneous receipt of both bene-fits. On the other hand, realism as to the possibility of either program pro-viding adequate benefits perhaps justifies a liberal policy toward duplica-tion of benefits.

COORDINATION WITH PUBLIC RETIREMENT SYSTEMS

Coordination of unemployment compensation with pensions received under public retirement systems should be reviewed, even though government retirement pensions are not strictly social insurance. Federal civil service annuities are principally involved, since only a small proportion of state and local government employees are covered by unemployment insurance.[20]

In 1960, the U.S. Comptroller General recommended that former federal civilian employees drawing benefits under Title XV of the Social Security Act be disqualified if they have voluntarily retired and are drawing a Civil Service annuity.[21] His recommendations were based on a survey made by his office in the District of Columbia during the week ending February 7, 1959, in which it was found that 36 percent of 1,610 former federal employees drawing unemployment compensation were Civil Service retirees and 298 or 18.5 percent had retired voluntarily. The Comptroller General was particularly concerned about this since Title XV unemployment compensation as well as more than half of the cost of Civil Service annuities is entirely financed by the federal government.

In a reply to the Comptroller General dated August 9, 1960, Secretary of Labor James P. Mitchell said that a survey covering the entire year of 1958 had established that 23.8 percent of the claimants in the District of Columbia were retirees, but that only 7.4 percent of federal claimants in the country as a whole were retirees and only 3.4 percent were voluntary retirees. He pointed out that all states have disqualifications in varying degree for voluntary quits and that claimants are required to be available for work. He maintained that many who voluntarily retire quite the government for several reasons: to take another job because of the need to do less strenuous or less hazardous work, because the agency moves to another city, or for reasons other than retirement. The Secretary of Labor accordingly opposed the amendment.

In 1962, Congress amended the District of Columbia law to prohibit the payment of unemployment compensation to former federal civilian employees who had *voluntarily* retired.[22] The restriction of the amendment to those who had voluntarily retired was based on the presumption that such retirees (who would be eligible for unemployment compensation in the District of Columbia from five to ten weeks after a voluntary quit without good cause) were not genuinely seeking work. This left those who were

[20] Many state and local government employees are covered by federal OASDI and to the extent they draw unemployment benefits, they would fall under the preceding section.

[21] For statements of the Comptroller General and the Secretary of Labor referred to in what follows, see *Unemployment Compensation*, Hearings before the Committee on Finance, United States Senate, 87th Cong., 1st sess. on H.R. 4806 (Washington, D.C.: U.S. Government Printing Office, 1962), pp. 160–69.

[22] Public Law 87–424, approved March 30, 1962.

compulsorily retired (which is at age 70 under the federal Civil Service retirement system) free to file for unemployment compensation immediately after retirement if they can establish that they are able to work and available for work.

Is it sound to distinguish between those who have voluntarily retired and those who are compulsorily retired? It is true that there is a greater presumption that one who has waited for compulsory retirement cannot live on his retirement annuity and so may have to seek work after retirement. But many who retire voluntarily have good reason to do so and still need supplemental income. It would have been sounder, in our opinion, to have followed the principle established in the TEUC amendment; namely, that the unemployment compensation would be reduced by the amount of the pension unless the work on the basis of which the worker qualified for employment was other than government employment on which the pension was based.[23]

COORDINATION OF UNEMPLOYMENT COMPENSATION AND RETRAINING ALLOWANCES

The need for retraining of large numbers of the unemployed displaced by technological changes has become increasingly evident in recent years. This need was first publicly recognized by the inclusion of provisions for retraining of the unemployed in depressed areas in the Area Redevelopment Act of 1961.[24] The need for retraining on a much wider scale throughout the country was recognized by the passage of the 1962 Manpower Development and Training Act.[25] Until these acts were passed, unemployed workers who undertook vocational training or retraining were almost universally denied unemployment compensation on the theory that they were not available for work while taking training. Three states were exceptions: Michigan and Massachusetts provided unemployment compensation during training, with Massachusetts providing for the payment of 16 additional weeks of benefits if this was necessary for the worker to complete his training. The District of Columbia went further and provided that a worker would be denied benefits if he refused training recommended by the Unemployment Compensation Board. Several other states by regulation permitted a claimant to take training, provided that he stopped his course if necessary in order to take a job. These provisions and interpretations, however, were seldom, if ever, used.

Because of these restrictions on the receipt of unemployment compensation during training, Senator Paul Douglas secured inclusion of a provision in the Area Redevelopment Act that a worker receiving training under the Act could receive "retraining subsistence payments" if he was

---

[23] For a discussion of coordination with private pensions, see Chapter 15.
[24] Public Law 87–27, approved May 1, 1961.
[25] Public Law 87–415, approved March 15, 1962.

not seeking or receiving unemployment compensation under a federal or state act. The amount of the payment was equal to the average weekly unemployment compensation payment in the state in which the worker was receiving training. Such payments were available for a maximum of 16 weeks.

The ARA provisions for retraining payments set a precedent for the enactment of similar provisions in the 1962 Manpower Development and Training Act. One of the criticisms of the ARA provisions was the limitation on the duration of the training allowances to a maximum of only 16 weeks, since many types of training that were anticipated under the Manpower Development and Training Act would take up to a year or more. Under the 1962 Act, the MDTA accordingly provided for the payment of training allowances up to a maximum of 52 weeks.[26]

The provisions for coordination with unemployment compensation in the Manpower Development and Training Bill followed the wording of the Area Redevelopment Act that training allowances will not be payable if the trainee was *seeking* or *receiving* unemployment compensation. In addition, the MDTA provides for reimbursement of a state if it paid unemployment compensation to a worker while he was undergoing training. Provision for such reimbursement was designed to avoid penalizing those states that permitted training while drawing unemployment compensation. These two provisions for coordination with unemployment compensation set contradictory policies. The reimbursement provision set a policy that training allowances should be paid from public funds rather than from the unemployment insurance funds that were financed by employers. The other provision for denying a training allowance if a trainee was seeking or receiving unemployment compensation set a policy of giving primary responsibility to unemployment insurance to pay benefits while an insured worker was taking training. However, under the latter provision, the insured worker can draw training allowances by simply not filing a claim for unemployment compensation.

In actuality, the great majority of insured workers have drawn training allowances. Prior to the 1963 and 1965 amendments to MDTA, the exceptions were mainly those whose unemployment insurance payments were higher than the MDTA allowance which was equal to the average unemployment insurance allowance in the state, or those who were not heads of households and so were ineligible for an MDTA allowance. Under the 1963 amendments,[27] a worker receives an MDTA allowance equal to the weekly amount he is entitled to receive as unemployment compensation if that is larger than the regular MDTA allowance. With this change, prac-

---

[26] The training provisions of the ARA are repealed as of June 30, 1965, by the 1965 amendments to MDTA, which authorized training and training allowances in redevelopment areas under the MDTA.

[27] Public Law 88–241.

tically all the trainees choose to receive the MDTA allowance, if eligible for it.[28] In addition, under the 1965 amendments, the training allowances may be increased up to $5 a week for each dependent over two up to a maximum of six dependents, or $20 a week. The 1965 amendments to MDTA also increased the maximum duration of allowances to 104 weeks.[29]

Under the Area Redevelopment Act and under the original Manpower Development and Training Act, many trainees who were entitled to unemployment compensation would get less than the training allowance provided or would exhaust their rights to training allowances before completing their training. As of January 1, 1965, 23 states have amended their laws to provide that a claimant will not be denied unemployment compensation because he is undergoing training or retraining approved by the employment security agency. The 1963 and 1965 MDTA amendments made these state provisions less necessary, since they provided that a trainee can get a training allowance equal to the unemployment compensation to which he is entitled or even more. Also, the possibility of exhausting MDTA training allowances and still being eligible for regular unemployment compensation is almost nil. There are some circumstances, however, in which a worker taking training is not entitled to an MDTA allowance. An example is a secondary worker in a household, the head of which is employed, unless it is determined that such payments are necessary for the individual to undertake or continue in training.

Refusal of Training

Should an unemployment insurance claimant be denied benefits if he refuses to take an appropriate training course as provided in the District of Columbia law? This was included in the 1965 Administration bill as a provision in its plan for *extended* benefits. There is a good case for such a provision when a worker is drawing extended benefits since he has been unemployed long enough to indicate he may need to change his occupation. It is questionable, however, whether a claimant should be *required* to take training while drawing regular benefits. The need to take retraining may be clear in some cases from the beginning of a worker's unemployment, and in such cases he should be given the *opportunity* to take training. But he should not be immediately required to, if he has not yet become convinced that his old job is obsolete.

TRADE READJUSTMENT ALLOWANCES

On October 11, 1962, a program was enacted for the payment of special unemployment allowances to workers who became unemployed as a result of an increase in imported products due to a trade concession. This program was included in the Trade Expansion Act of 1962. It had been advo-

[28] To prevent hardship, any trainee may have his allowance increased up to $10, taking into account any increase by reason of eligibility to a higher unemployment compensation payment.

[29] Public Law 89–15, approved April 26, 1965.

cated by organized labor as a counterpart to the provisions in the Act for assistance to companies adversely affected by trade concessions under the Act.

Description of Trade Readjustment Allowances

Trade readjustment allowances would be equal to 65 percent of the average weekly wages of eligible workers up to a maximum of 65 percent of the average weekly wage in all manufacturing. They are also payable for partial unemployment when earnings are reduced more than 25 percent so as to bring the combined income from wages, readjustment allowances, and any unemployment compensation received up to a total of 75 percent of wages. The allowances are payable for a maximum of 52 weeks whether or not a worker is undergoing training. An additional duration of 13 weeks is possible for workers 60 years of age or older, and an additional duration of 26 weeks is payable to a worker of any age who is undergoing training if the additional weeks are needed to complete his training course. No allowances will be payable if the worker refuses to undertake training unless he changes his mind and agrees to take training.

In order to be eligible for the trade readjustment allowances, a displaced worker must have been employed at some work for 18 months out of the three years preceding his unemployment, and for six months in the last year in work for an employer adversely affected by imports. He can draw allowances only within the two years following his last import-affected layoff, or within three years if he receives an additional allowance because of age or attendance at a training course.

The provisions regarding the relationship to unemployment compensation are the same as those in the Manpower Development and Training Act; that is, if the worker is seeking or receiving unemployment compensation, the amount of unemployment compensation is deducted from the trade readjustment allowance.[30] If a worker eligible for trade readjustment allowances does draw unemployment compensation, the state will be reimbursed for such payments. Thus, the unemployment resulting from a trade concession is recognized as a national government obligation.

Before an unemployed worker becomes eligible for trade readjustment allowances, there must be an official finding that his unemployment is due to increased imports resulting from a trade concession. Up to the time of writing, no finding of adverse effect of any industry had been found by the Trade Commission, although many applications for a finding have been made. As a result, no trade readjustment allowances had become payable.

Implications for Unemployment Compensation

The provisions for coordination of trade readjustment allowances and unemployment insurance are similar to those of training allowances, which

---

[30] If the application for unemployment compensation is finally denied, the worker is paid the full readjustment allowance retroactively.

have already been discussed. For example, unemployment compensation benefits seem to have priority, but in practicality, a worker can become eligible for TRA simply by not filing for unemployment compensation. Moreover, because the trade readjustment allowance would usually be larger in amount, they usually would be drawn in preference to unemployment compensation. Trade readjustment allowances also establish a new principle; namely, that there is a government responsibility for relieving the unemployment that results from its policies.[31] As pointed out by the opponents of the program, the same policy could logically be applied to the relief of unemployment growing out of the cancellation of government contracts. If this were done, it would have much larger implications for unemployment insurance than the trade readjustment allowance program.

Despite these implications for unemployment insurance, the Trade Readjustment Allowance program has as yet had no noticeable effect on the older program. Perhaps this is because TRA has been nothing more than a paper program thus far. If significant amounts of trade readjustment allowances should become payable, the story may be different.

POVERTY PROGRAM

There is no direct relationship between the unemployment insurance program and the Economic Opportunity Act of 1964,[32] although both programs are aimed at the prevention of poverty. The poverty program is principally designed to assist disadvantaged persons, particularly youth, to secure education, training, or other assistance that will fit them for gainful employment and enable them to rise above the poverty level. Unemployment insurance, however, is designed for those who have been in gainful employment. It is no doubt true that many unemployed workers who qualify for unemployment insurance have had such poorly paid work that they are at the poverty level. Extension of coverage of unemployment insurance to agricultural and household workers would help such workers to avoid extreme poverty when they are unemployed. Unemployment compensation enables others to avoid sinking to the poverty level when they become unemployed and in a broad sense can be considered to be one of the programs that assists in the "war against poverty." There are, however, no problems of duplication or coordination between unemployment insurance and the programs provided by the Economic Opportunity Act.

PUBLIC ASSISTANCE FOR THE UNEMPLOYED

In many places public aid is sadly deficient or nonexistent for the unemployed who exhaust benefits, who are not covered by unemployment insurance, or whose unemployment compensation is inadequate. Several federal grant-in-aid programs act as a floor of protection for those who fall

---

[31] If state unemployment benefits are paid to a worker eligible for trade readjustment allowances, the state is reimbursed for such payments.
[32] Public Law 88–452, approved August 20, 1964.

through any of the several nets of federal social insurance for old-age, survivors, or permanent and total disability. To help such persons are the programs of old-age assistance, aid to needy families with children, and aid to the permanently and totally disabled. There is no corresponding program of federal grants for aid to the needy unemployed (except for an unemployed parent under the program of aid to needy families with children).

In the absence of the stimulation of a federal grants-in-aid program, many states and communities made little or no provision for the needy unemployed. As of January, 1959, only 26 states had state-wide programs of general assistance available to unemployed persons or the families of such persons. Of these 26 states, 11 limited their protection in one way or another, such as to emergency situations only or to a temporary period. Another 11 states provided that general assistance might be given to unemployed persons or their families, but the extent to which this was done varied among the local jurisdictions of the state and was affected by the availability of local funds and local economic conditions. In Maryland, for example, some counties do not participate at all. In 16 other states, general assistance was not available to any unemployed persons or their families.[33] General assistance, where it is payable to the unemployed, averages only about half of the amounts paid under old-age assistance and other public assistance programs. In November, 1960, the average amount of general assistance was $69.88 a month *per family*, while the average for old-age assistance was $68.82 *per individual*.

Aid to Needy Families with Children and Unemployed Parent

Until 1961, no federal grants were made for aid to needy families with children under Title IV of the Social Security Act if both parents were residing with the family. The original intent was to assist needy children when the breadwinner had died or had deserted the home. If a father was unable to support his family, his only recourse in order for the family to qualify for aid to dependent children, was for him to leave the home. During periods of unemployment, large numbers of fathers are reported to have left home so that their families could get some relief under the program. This problem became so acute that during the recession of 1961, Title IV of the Social Security Act was temporarily amended to provide that families with unemployed breadwinners could become eligible for assistance provided the unemployed parent is not receiving unemployment compensation, registers for work at a public employment office, and does not refuse employment in which he is able to engage if it is offered to him by the public employment office or an employer.[34] These provisions were

---

[33] *Characteristics of General Assistance in the United States* (Washington, D.C.: Department of Health, Education, and Welfare, Social Security Administration, Bureau of Public Assistance, 1959), Public Assistance Report No. 39.

[34] Public Law 87–31, approved May 8, 1961.

extended to June 30, 1967, by the 1962 Public Welfare Amendments.[35]

Limited at least in part by the temporary character of the extension, only some of the states have participated in this extension of the program. In January, 1965, only 18 states were providing aid to families with an unemployed parent. Only 77,000 families with a total of 442,000 recipients, including 296,000 children, were being assisted. If all states had been participating, the number of recipients would have been twice this number.

What Proportion of Unemployment Insurance Beneficiaries Need Assistance?

It is not known what proportion of unemployed workers who exhaust unemployment benefits would secure public assistance payments if they were universally available to unemployed employable persons. This would depend to a considerable extent on the liberality of the eligibility rules. With the prevailing practice of requiring relatives to provide support if possible, the proportion would probably be small. Scattered surveys indicate that the proportion of exhaustees of unemployment compensation who would be eligible for public assistance would range from about 6 to 10 percent. Universal provision of public assistance for the needy unemployed, especially of those who had been eligible for unemployment insurance, certainly would not be prohibitive in cost.

Absence of public assistance for the unemployed in many states and localities brings pressure on the unemployment insurance program to provide for longer and longer duration of benefits and lower eligibility requirements because the unemployed have no other place to turn for income maintenance. Therefore, the integrity of unemployment insurance requires a complementary program of unemployment assistance. This problem becomes particularly acute in times of recession when unemployment becomes prolonged for large numbers of workers.

The temporary extended unemployment compensation programs of 1958 and 1961 did much to alleviate the problem of long-term unemployment of unemployment insurance beneficiaries. Under both programs, however, the extended benefits still did not meet the entire problem, as indicated by the fact that over 60 percent exhausted their extended benefits. The provision of extended benefits for any worker who has qualified for *any* unemployment compensation drew the criticism that many received extended benefits who did not need them. The proposal in the 1965 Administration bill for Federal Unemployment Adjustment Benefits, payable only to those with a record of considerable employment during the past three years, would largely eliminate those with marginal attachment to the labor market. The extension of duration to 52 weeks would also greatly reduce the number who would exhaust their benefits before they were re-employed. Nevertheless, even if their program is enacted, large numbers of unemployed workers would still exhaust their benefits or not

[35] Public Law 87–543, approved July 25, 1962.

be covered by unemployment insurance. Of these, many would be in need of some type of public aid, especially during recessions. Also, even more who did not meet the qualifying requirements for extended benefits would need public assistance.

How Should Public Assistance Be Provided for the Unemployed?

There are several ways in which public assistance could be made universally available to the needy unemployed. One approach would be to add a new category of public assistance for the needy unemployed, similar to other categories of public assistance for which federal grants are made. While in line with other special public assistance programs, this is probably the most unrealistic alternative because of the spotty acceptance of public responsibility for the needy unemployed and the widespread attitude during periods of prosperity that the needy unemployed are shiftless. A separate program would also be handicapped by a case load which fluctuated both seasonally and cyclically much more than other public assistance programs.

Many public assistance specialists would prefer the alternative of a single federal grant-in-aid program of public assistance for all needy persons, including the unemployed, in place of the present special public assistance programs for the aged, the blind, and other categories. While this would be the ideal approach, and was the one eventually adopted by the United Kingdom, its acceptance is doubtful in this country at this time.

Authorized by the Social Security Amendments of 1958 the Advisory Council on Public Assistance recommended that the states be given "freedom of choice as to whether public assistance should be administered as a single program, or as separate categorical programs."[36] This would open the way for acceptance of the idea of a single public assistance program on a state-by-state basis.

Federal grants for a residual program of general assistance for those not assisted through the specific public assistance programs, including the unemployed, would seem to be the most feasible alternative and most needed. Such a program was also recommended by the Advisory Council on Public Assistance: "The Social Security Act should be amended to add a new provision for Federal grants-in-aid to States for the purpose of encouraging each State to furnish financial assistance and other services to financially needy persons regardless of the cause of need (including, for example, the unemployed, the underemployed, and the less seriously disabled)."[37]

Since there is already partial inclusion of the needy unemployed under general assistance programs, it should be feasible to require as one condition of federal grants-in-aid to states that the employable unemployed who

[36] *Report of the Advisory Council on Public Assistance*, Senate Document No. 93, 86th Cong., 2d sess. (January, 1960), p. 3.
[37] *Ibid.*, p. 3.

need financial aid be eligible for general assistance. Because of the greater public acceptance of the program it would also be desirable to continue to include unemployed heads of families in the Aid to Needy Families with Children Program as well.[38]

SUMMARY AND CONCLUSIONS

The social insurance programs with which unemployment insurance should be coordinated are federal, federal-state, and state programs, which currently have only limited interrelationships. Each of these social insurance programs presents different problems of coordination.

At the beginning of the program, the state unemployment insurance programs themselves needed cooperative agreements so as to meet the coverage and benefit problems presented by interstate workers. In only a few areas is coordination still incomplete.

The supplementary unemployment benefit (SUB) plans, negotiated by unions with their companies in a limited number of industries, present no problem of coordination with unemployment insurance, except in one state that does not permit payment of SUB without denying unemployment compensation. Since the companies involved adjust the SUB payments to what is paid in unemployment compensation, no administrative problem for the states is involved.

Three of the four state temporary disability insurance programs are administered by the state employment security agencies so that the benefits are closely coordinated with unemployment compensation. Under the railroad system, unemployment and temporary disability insurance are financed out of the same fund. In New York, temporary disability insurance is administered by the workmen's compensation agency and there is little coordination. There is no consistency among the state temporary disability insurance laws or unemployment insurance laws in the treatment of pregnancy and maternity cases. In some states that do not have TDI laws, unemployment compensation is continued if the unemployed worker becomes ill, which illustrates the tendency for one social insurance program to fill a gap left by the absence of another program. If any national program of TDI is proposed, there are strong arguments for coordination of temporary disability insurance with unemployment insurance; there are also strong arguments for placing TDI and permanent disability insurance together. On balance, we believe the case is stronger for coordination of temporary disability insurance with unemployment insurance, particularly since there are already several states with temporary disability insurance laws. A case could even be made for paying unemployment compensation if a worker is drawing temporary partial workmen's compensation if the worker can demonstrate ability to work.

[38] These conclusions may be placing political expediency above what is theoretically best, but the authors believe that what can receive the greatest public acceptance is the most desirable program in a democracy.

Many states deny or reduce unemployment compensation by the amount received in workmen's compensation. The most common provision is to reduce unemployment compensation if a worker is drawing workmen's compensation for temporary total or partial disability. A few states disqualify a worker who is receiving permanent disability benefits under workmen's compensation. If such a worker is rehabilitated and is able to secure employment and earn enough to qualify for unemployment compensation, he should be able to draw unemployment compensation.

On the recommendation of the Social Security Board at the beginning of the social security program, most states denied unemployment compensation to anyone drawing old-age benefits. Only 19 states now have such provisions, and all but one merely reduce the unemployment benefit by the amount of old-age benefits received. Congress exempted old-age insurance beneficiaries from an amendment to the 1961 TEUC Act, which denied extended unemployment compensation to pensioners. Studies indicate that there should be some tightening up on the present tendency to pay both benefits. An intensive study of this question would be desirable in view of the increasing number of federal old-age insurance beneficiaries.

Coordination of unemployment compensation and public service retirement annuities is largely a problem of the duplication of unemployment compensation for federal workers under Title XV of the Social Security Act and federal civil service retirement annuities. In 1962, Congress amended the District of Columbia Unemployment Insurance Act to disqualify *voluntary* retirees from unemployment compensation. It would have been sounder to treat voluntarily and compulsorily retired workers alike and to reduce the unemployment compensation by the amount of the annuity received, unless the worker qualified for unemployment compensation on the basis of other than federal employment.

The training allowances provided under the Area Redevelopment Act and the Manpower Development and Training Act raised a new problem of coordination for unemployment insurance. Both acts provided that if a worker is seeking or receiving unemployment compensation, he will be denied a training allowance. The MDTA also has a somewhat contradictory provision providing for reimbursement of states which pay unemployment compensation during training. In actuality, practically all trainees qualify for training allowances merely by not filing a claim for unemployment compensation. Nevertheless, 22 states have amended their laws to permit the payment of unemployment compensation during training, since there are cases in which a worker who is qualified for unemployment compensation cannot qualify for training allowances.

The higher benefit amounts and longer duration provided for the trade readjustment allowances payable under the 1962 Trade Expansion Act created a new type of problem of coordination with unemployment compensation. So far there has been no noticeable effect on the unemployment insurance program, probably because no allowances have yet been certified.

There are no interrelationships between the poverty program under the Economic Opportunity Act and the unemployment insurance program. While the two programs have the common aim of preventing poverty, unemployment compensation assists unemployed workers from sinking into poverty, while the Economic Opportunity Act assists people to rise out of deprivation.

At present there is only a limited problem of coordination of unemployment compensation with public assistance because so few who are drawing or have exhausted unemployment compensation either need or are able to qualify for public assistance. About half the states and large numbers of communities deny general assistance to any employable unemployed person or his family. A partial filling of this gap was accomplished by the 1961 amendment to the Needy Families with Children program which provided for federal grants-in-aid to families in which one of the parents was unemployed. However, only part of the states have taken advantage of this amendment. A federal grant-in-aid program for all the needy unemployed should be provided. This could take several forms: (a) a special program of public assistance program for the unemployed; (b) a single comprehensive public assistance program which includes provision for the unemployed; or (c) a federal-state program of general assistance with a requirement that employable unemployed persons and their families be eligible for assistance if in need. The latter seems the most feasible and practicable program.

Chapter 24

The Summing Up: Progress, Problems, Recommendations

Unemployment insurance has become an accepted part of the American scene. Strongly opposed by many before its enactment, hardly anyone now suggests its repeal. Yet, although it helps millions of workers every year, hardly anyone is content with it. Organized labor is critical of its inadequacies in coverage and benefits. Labor blames the program's shortcomings largely on experience rating, which often gives the employers a direct interest in holding down benefit payments. While most labor representatives would prefer a federal system, they urge that there should be at least minimum federal standards to assure an adequate program in every state. Most management representatives are also critical of the program, maintaining that it is not sufficiently "tight" in its eligibility and disqualification provisions. In management's opinion, too many are being paid benefits for unemployment for which the employer is not responsible. There is a general public impression that the program is surrounded with a great deal of abuse. This is often based on isolated cases or on the reading of a critical newspaper or magazine article. But on the whole, in spite of the serious qualms held by many, unemployment insurance is widely accepted and taken for granted.

Public interest in the program fluctuates. It is rather lethargic under normal conditions of employment; it increases rapidly during a recession when the volume of unemployment rises. At such times, unemployment insurance is expected to automatically provide a ready, available means of meeting the needs of the unemployed. Congress, which during "good times" usually ignores appeals for improvement in the program, suddenly turns to it and, as it did in 1958 and 1961, hastily enacts a temporary program for the extension of benefits during the recession. More fundamental reforms are postponed. Further study is suggested. But once unemployment recedes, it is difficult either for organized labor or even for a friendly President or Secretary of Labor to stir up interest in permanent improvements. Meanwhile, the state legislatures are continuously amending their legislation. The changes, however, represent compromises with respect to benefits and other substantive features to meet labor's demands, or to provide tax concessions and stricter disqualifications to appease employers.

Our review has shown that the program falls considerably short of the needs of the unemployed and is imperfect in other ways. There is a lack of general agreement concerning almost every feature, and the issues that have arisen are not easy to resolve.

In addition to the shortcomings that have existed since the program began, substantial adjustments in important features are required if recognition is to be given to the vast changes that have occurred in the labor force, in employment, and in the character of unemployment since World War II. The outstanding facts of this period as they impinge on unemployment insurance are the continuing high levels of employment, the persistence of a substantial degree of unemployment, the large number experiencing a relatively long duration of joblessness, the increased proportion of the labor force composed of women workers, and the increased volume of part-time work.

The increased benefit costs that have accompanied these developments call for considerable improvement in the methods of financing the program. The large numbers who experience relatively longer spells of unemployment, either because of recessions and technological change or inadequate growth of the economy, have led many to ask whether this program, originally designed to provide for short-term layoffs, should not be extended to also include longer-term joblessness, and what form such extension should take.

In seeking to revise the program in ways that meet the needs of the unemployed and are fair to the views of management and labor organizations, the experts and legislative policy makers have been handicapped. One reason for this is the absence of sufficient information on which solid judgments can be based. There are, of course, masses of statistics. Most of the data, however, are too general in nature to be of much use in specific policy decisions. Relatively few studies "in depth" have been made. In addition, the mere presence of more statistics would be of limited value. The questions which face us involve basic attitudes rather than more facts. Certainly, the matter of what is an "adequate" benefit is much more than a statistical question. These problems have been spelled out in detail in the preceding chapters.

We have attempted to present the historical developments and the facts to guide the reader to form his own judgments. We have also, where possible, indicated the pros and cons of alternative approaches and outlined the direction in which these analyses have led us. Our conclusions assume that the basic features of the unemployment insurance system in this country are likely to remain. While our economy is increasingly assuming a national character so that a national rather than a federal-state system of unemployment insurance could well be defended, nevertheless, we recognize that the broad outlines of the present federal-state system will probably not be seriously revised, except perhaps for the adoption of additional federal standards particularly concerned with weekly benefit amounts, duration, and similar provisions. We also recognize that use of experience rating in assessing employer contributions, while one of the more controversial features of the system, is so widely accepted by management and so firmly embedded that little purpose would be served by debating whether our unemployment insurance system would be better or worse if experience rating were not to remain a basic feature of the plan.

In the pages that follow the recommendations for improvement of the unemployment insurance program are therefore proposed within the established framework of the system.

EXTENSION OF THE COVERAGE OF UNEMPLOYMENT INSURANCE

The most obvious improvement needed in the unemployment insurance program is to provide for universal coverage. Only about three fourths of those who work for others are protected by unemployment insurance; those not now included could be provided such protection without much difficulty.

Coverage of Small Firms

The least defensible gap in coverage is the exclusion by the federal unemployment tax law of employees of firms with less than four employees. Twenty states have demonstrated that coverage of employers of one or more workers is administratively feasible. Since the remaining states show little inclination to extend coverage to small firms, federal coverage seems to be necessary. If federal coverage were extended, state coverage would automatically follow.

Employees of Nonprofit Organizations

Employees of nonprofit organizations are another large and growing group for which coverage would be administratively simple. While the risk of unemployment is smaller in most of these organizations, it is not absent. In fact, the small incidence of unemployment among nonprofit organizations makes their coverage all the more feasible, since such action would impose no substantial cost on these organizations. Their coverage on a reimbursable basis, that is, the payment only for the actual cost of benefits to their employees without any advance contributions, would remove the need for building unnecessary reserves. Obviously, some exemptions from coverage would have to be made; these would include members of the clergy and of religious orders and part-time employment of a minor character. Federal initiative in the coverage of employees of nonprofit organizations appears to be essential, including an amendment to permit the states to cover them on a reimbursable basis.

Employees of State and Local Governments

The largest and easiest group to bring under employment insurance are employees of state and local governments. Coverage of federal employees has demonstrated that there is a small but real problem of unemployment among government workers. Few states cover their employees on a compulsory basis. While an increasing number of states provide for optional coverage of both state and local governments, few governmental units have actually elected coverage. Since financing could be through reimbursement of the unemployment fund of the actual cost of benefits, coverage would create only a minor financial problem. While compulsory coverage of state and local government workers through federal action would be desirable, constitutional obstacles prevent such action.

Agricultural Employment

The coverage of agricultural workers is a more complex and difficult problem. The large amount of seasonal employment, most of which is performed by local women and students during vacations or by migrants who move from state to state, imposes special problems for the average farmer or agricultural employer. However, the increasing concentration of farming in larger units may make the coverage of agricultural workers for such units somewhat more feasible. A beginning in coverage could therefore be made by starting with large employers of agricultural labor. This should also include the coverage of processing workers, hundreds of thousands of whom are defined as agricultural workers, and are thus exempted although they are really working in agricultural "factories."

Domestic Service

The coverage of household workers also presents some special problems. A good deal of the employment is casual. The increasing employment of workers for one or two days a week by individual households would complicate the collection of contributions for such workers since large numbers of female workers in domestic service piece out full employment through working for several households. New York and Hawaii have nevertheless found coverage feasible; in both states for employers of one or more and a minimum quarterly payroll. This is a nelgected problem partly because of the lack of unionization or reform groups interested in improving the working conditions of such workers.

Borderline Employees

Finally, there are several hundred thousand workers in the grey area between self-employment and job holding for whom there is no consistent policy of coverage throughout the country. These include commission salesmen, agent drivers of milk, bread, and other household supplies, and similar workers—not employees under the common law but employees in economic reality. While most of the states cover these workers to a greater or lesser degree, it would be desirable to amend the federal act so that such workers are covered throughout the country.

THE WEEKLY BENEFIT AMOUNT

The adequacy of the weekly benefit amount has been one of the principal bones of contention in the unemployment insurance program. This is natural, since the amount and duration of benefits are the most important provisions in the program. It has also been difficult to find a consensus on the weekly benefit amount because the concept of "adequacy" of benefits is elastic; it is related to one's views about incentives to work and hold a job; and it is a critical item in the cost of unemployment insurance. The matter of "adequate" benefits is largely influenced by individual judgment and social philosophy.

Fifty percent of weekly wages has been the generally accepted norm for the weekly benefit amount. Such research as has been done, a few sample studies some years ago, appear to indicate that 50 percent of the average weekly wage is frequently not enough even for single persons, and is clearly inadequate for heads of households with dependents.

Dependents' Benefits

A few states have solved this problem by providing for dependents' benefits. There is some objection to this concept, since in the minds of some persons it introduces a "needs test" into the program—a program which is designed to relate benefits only to employment and wages and which provides benefits as a matter of right. On the other hand, much of social insurance is based on presumptive need. Another advantage of dependents' benefits is that they can be provided for workers with families without raising the level of benefits for secondary or single workers to such a level as might adversely influence work incentives.

Maximum Benefits

Limitations on the maximum weekly benefit amount provided under the state laws has been the most serious check on weekly benefits. Wages rose rapidly after World War II. On the other hand, the maximum weekly benefit amount changed rather slowly. As a result, so large a portion of beneficiaries were receiving the maximum benefit amount in some states that the program was in danger of becoming a flat benefit system. In recent years, the maximums have been repeatedly increased in many states. In most states, however, these increases have barely kept pace with continuing increases in wages. In order to avoid the need for continued review of this controversial topic by the legislatures, a good number of states have provided for an automatic annual adjustment of the weekly benefit maximum to a prescribed percentage of average weekly covered wages in the state, usually 50 percent. We believe that this method should be adopted in all states.

We believe also that a maximum equal to 50 percent of state average wages is too low. Unless the maximum is set at two thirds of the average weekly wages of all covered workers in a state, or at least 60 percent, too large a proportion will have their benefits cut off by the maximum. These goals should be sought.

DURATION OF BENEFITS

With the greatly increased number of wage earners who experience a relatively long duration of unemployment especially during recessions, two programs of unemployment benefits rather than one appear to be necessary. As originally contemplated, the first is for short-term unemployment. Our present federal-state program was designed for that purpose. A second program, with which this country has had some experience during the 1958 and 1961 recessions, is designed to provide extended benefits for those with longer-term unemployment. Practically all the states now provide a maximum duration of at least 26 weeks for short-term, that is, "normal" unemployment. A few states provide longer benefits on a variable basis under their regular programs and some states pay extended benefits when the percentage of unemployment reaches certain levels. Our analysis suggests the desirability of a uniform maximum duration for the regular program of 26 weeks of benefits in any 12-month period. An extended benefit program would be superimposed on that.

Uniform versus Variable Duration

With respect to regular benefits, the important issue is whether all claimants who quality for any benefits should be eligible for the maximum duration, or whether the duration of benefits should be proportioned to the amount of previous employment or wages, that is, should be variable. We believe that all claimants should be uniformly eligible for the maximum duration of benefits. We recognize that workers with casual attachment to the labor force should be excluded altogether. Regularly attached workers, however, who have been unable to secure regular employment need benefits just as long, or perhaps longer, than workers who have had full employment before losing their jobs. Also, the variable duration formulas result in too high a proportion of claimants exhausting their benefits before finding employment.

Extended Duration

The type of program that should be provided for the long-term unemployed has been vigorously debated since the Temporary Extended Unemployment Compensation program of 1961. There appears to be a consensus for a permanent program of extended benefits. There is disagreement, however, on several issues regarding such a program. One of these is whether extended benefits should be available only during recessions or for eligible workers at all times. We believe it would be sounder to provide extended benefits at all times. The reasons for long-duration unemployment are complex and diverse; they are not solely related to economic recessions. Industrial mergers, technical changes including automation, migration of industries, obsolescence of products and materials, and similar types of economic change occur all the time. Workers affected by these developments, particularly if they are over 45 years of age, are likely to be jobless, even in an active labor market, for more time than the "normal" period for which unemployment benefits are available. The claimant should be required to have had a record of long and substantial qualifying employment over a period of several years. Such a requirement would eliminate many whose attachment to the labor force has not had sufficient continuity.

There is also some difference of opinion as to whether extended benefits beyond the "normal" period should be for 13 additional weeks or longer. The 1961 legislation provided for extended benefits for a maximum of only 13 weeks. The experience under this program indicates that benefits were for too short a period for too many unemployed. It has been observed that those who have been attached to an occupation which may have become obsolete often need a long period of readjustment if they are to change to another type of work. Many need retraining. Extended benefits should be paid if retraining is not available or impractical. We therefore recommend a maximum duration of extended benefits of 26 weeks.

Another issue is whether extended benefits should be exclusively a federal program or a federal-state program. A program of extended benefits that is in effect at all times would not be advisable on a state basis. The cost would fall too unevenly on different states due to state variations in the levels of unemployment. On balance, the issue as to whether the program should be exclusively federal or whether it should be a federal-state sharing of the cost, in our judgment, is not crucial. However, we believe that it would be more desirable to rely on federal financing of the program. If the program is partially financed by the states, it would inevitably have to be optional. States participation would therefore not be assured. Federal financing also creates the opportunity for changing the method of meeting the costs of the program. Employers should not be expected to finance such benefits in full, nor would it be desirable. Much long-duration unemployment is due to general economic causes. Government participation in meeting its costs is justified.

ELIGIBILITY FOR BENEFITS

With reference to the short-term program, available data and experience suggest that about 20 weeks of employment or its equivalent in wages as a qualifying requirement is the maximum that can realistically be required. Less than that period will qualify too many who should not be entitled to a long period of benefits because of their inadequate attachment to the labor force. It is clear that many states need to tighten their qualifying requirements.

As to requirements for continuing eligibility for benefits, experience has shown that mere registration at the local public employment office is not enough; the worker needs to look for work on his own, as well. However, formal requirements which insist that an unemployed worker must present evidence of a prescribed number of applications for work each week are, in our judgment, neither equitable nor desirable. The concept that the applicant must "actively seek work" is sound; the manner in which it is applied, however, needs to be fitted to the individual worker and the conditions of the labor market. For example, it does not make sense to require that an employee laid off for three or four weeks because of a "model changeover" or for a similar purpose should be required to visit a half dozen establishments and seek alternative employment as a condition for receiving benefits.

DISQUALIFICATIONS

Some of the disqualifications from benefits need to be appraised in the light of changes in the labor market. The liberal view has always been that the three major types of disqualification—refusal of suitable work, discharge for misconduct, and voluntary quitting without good cause—should be temporary in nature. A short disqualification period is based on the theory that after a few weeks, continued unemployment of the worker is not due to the reason for which he was disqualified. There are many reasons that a worker may refuse a job; and whether the worker did not have good cause to refuse the work is often debatable. Consequently, in our view, permanent disqualification during the entire period of unemployment appears to be an unreasonable penalty for refusal of suitable work. We favor a temporary period of six or eight weeks, after which the worker again becomes eligible for benefits.

With regard to disqualifications for voluntary quitting without good cause and for discharge for misconduct, we believe that, while harsh, disqualifying the individual involved for the duration of his unemployment is not unjustified. Such unemployment resulted from the employee's own actions. Readmitting a person to benefits after a short period when the unemployment was due to a voluntary action without good cause or discharge for misconduct can lead to considerable abuse. We recognize that the increased number of women in the labor force creates opportunities for those who have no serious intention of returning to work to register for work, file a claim, and draw benefits after a short period of disqualification, while avoiding opportunities to work. This, in our view, is not the purpose of unemployment insurance. Public confidence in the program would be increased if this frequent and potential source of abuse were removed.

At the same time, in the case of voluntary quits without good cause we recommend disqualification for the duration of unemployment with some hesitation because of the very narrow interpretation of "good cause" applied by some states. We believe that the language in some state statutes which limits "good cause" to causes attributable to the employer or connected with the work are too restrictive. There are many cases in which compelling personal reasons for quitting justify the payment of benefits. In the same vein, the many arbitrary statutory disqualifications for specified periods before and after childbirth or for temporarily quitting to fulfill marital obligations can result in serious inequities.

No Cancellation of Benefit Rights

We also believe that provisions that reduce or cancel benefit rights when a person is disqualified from benefits are unjustified. We strongly recommend that the benefit rights of the disqualified individual be preserved so that when he gets another job and is then laid off for lack of work, his eligibility for benefits can be restored. There is no justification for the reduction or cancellation of benefit rights in connection with any disqualification except as a penalty for fraudulent misrepresentation in order to obtain benefits. In the case of an employee who has been discharged for cause or who has quit without good cause and later becomes eligible for benefits as a result of unemployment due to a new job, there is a question whether the cost of such benefits should be charged to the former employer. There is much merit to the employer's view that his account should not be charged with such benefits. Many states have existing arrangements for such costs to be charged to the fund as a whole rather than to the individual employer.

Labor Disputes

As a general rule, employees involved in a strike should be disqualified from benefits. Unemployment insurance funds should not be used to finance labor disputes. A case can be made for the payment of benefits in connection with plant shutdowns resulting from lockouts. It can also be argued that benefits should be paid to employees on strike when the strike resulted from the fact that the employer was violating the law or breaking a collective bargaining agreement. In our view, it would be wise to follow the policy of not providing unemployment benefits to those directly involved in a strike, whatever the cause. We do not, however, believe that this should be extended to plants where layoffs are necessary because of a strike in supplier plants.

FINANCING UNEMPLOYMENT INSURANCE

For many years, the financing of unemployment insurance was not a serious problem. With the very low rate of unemployment during World War II, state unemployment reserve funds were built to high levels. For a dozen years after the War it was possible for many states to finance benefits with very low contribution rates. From 1958 on, however, the high rates of unemployment have required considerable increases in employer contribution rates in most states. Even in the states with the highest benefit outlays, however, unemployment insurance costs have remained a relatively small proportion of total payrolls. Benefits can be increased to adequate levels without unduly burdensome tax contributions to finance them.

The unemployment insurance program has been almost wholly financed by employers. While some states had employee contributions in the early years, only three states now have such contributions and they are at low rates. In theory, it would be desirable to have employee contributions, but as long as employer contributions are related to experience rating, the case for employee contributions is more difficult to defend.

Experience Rating

The most important influence on the financing of unemployment insurance has been the experience rating of employer contributions. While it is difficult to find concrete evidence that experience rating has had any permanent effect in stimulating employers to stabilize their employment, it has served to allocate the costs of unemployment insurance among industries according to their risk of unemployment. Such allocation of costs has not been rigid. Many states have recognized the social insurance character of the program and have required all employers to pay some part of the cost even if their employment has been quite stable. A third purpose of experience rating, to give employers a direct interest in helping to police the system against unjustified claims and fraud, has received the most attention from employers. This has been helpful to the program when it has not been carried to such extremes as contesting practically every claim. There is considerable basis for organized labor's belief that experience rating has also given employers an incentive to oppose liberalizations in benefits and especially to secure the enactment of unduly restrictive and severe disqualification provisions.

Whether or not one is critical of experience rating, one must recognize that it is an established part of unemployment insurance. Therefore, our position is that any reforms in experience rating should be in the direction of maximizing its contribution to sound financing, or, at least, of minimizing any harmful effects it may have on financing.

It would be desirable to structure experience rating in such a way that contribution rates would fall during recessions and rise during prosperous times. There is some evidence that the most common type of experience rating, the so-called "reserve ratio" plans, operates in a countercyclical manner to a limited extent. No specific device has been thought of that would effectively result in countercyclical financing. Perhaps the most that can be done is to minimize fluctuations in tax rates so that they do not rise much during business recessions or fall during periods of prosperity.

We believe that some states have gone too far by providing minimum tax rates of zero or 0.1 percent of taxable payroll. Employers who qualify for such rates should at least pay their share of the "socialized costs," that is, the cost of benefits that have not been charged to any employer's experience account. Part of these uncharged costs are due to limitations on maximum tax rates. There are practical limits, however, as to how high maximum rates can be set, especially under state systems that cover employers in interstate competition. Other uncharged costs include benefits paid after temporary disqualifications and dependents' benefits. We believe that a minimum contribution rate of 1 percent, as proposed by the Committee on Economic Security in 1935, would be desirable to finance uncharged costs and to strengthen the financing of the system.

While we do not advocate the abolition of experience rating, the present federal provisions that govern experience rating should be amended so that a state is able to lower rates equally for all employers if it prefers. In addition, it would be desirable to abolish the very general, but circumscribing, standards for experience rating that exist in the federal act so that the states are free to experiment with types of experience rating now prohibited, such as a system of rebating of taxes.

Taxable Wage Base

The limitation of the taxable wage base to the first $3,000 of each worker's annual earnings, effective for the federal unemployment tax and most states' unemployment taxes, is increasingly limiting the tax-raising capacity of the states to finance unemployment insurance benefits. In the last few years, the taxable wage base of $3,000 has covered less than 60 percent of total payrolls, and the base is constantly narrowing in relation to payrolls as wages increase. Some of the states have recognized the need to increase the base, but most have hesitated to increase it to more than $3,600, although a much higher base is justified. A return to the taxation of total payrolls, as was done at the beginning of the program, would be ideal. This is not likely to take place, however. A wage base approximating weekly earnings on an annual basis would be more realistic. If this were adopted, the base would be at least $5,200. Failure to increase the base will require some states to impose high tax rates. While some states should increase their maximum tax rates, a higher base will permit more modest maximum rates.

Federal Assistance to Financing

Interest in the solvency of the unemployment insurance system has been strong from the beginning. Aware of the heavy debt that the British system had accumulated in the 1920's, the framers of the original legislation were perhaps oversolicitous about solvency. Proposals for some type of federal assistance to state financing were considered from the beginning. Strong opposition developed, however, to any system of federal reinsurance because of the fear that it would lead to federal control. The alternative concept of federal loans prevailed, and a federal loan fund was finally enacted in 1944 and again in 1954. The 1954 plan was, perhaps, too lenient in its requirements and the pendulum swung to a rather stringent plan in 1960. Under the present act, a state fund must be practically insolvent before it can secure a loan, and loans would be "doled out" on a month-by-month basis. It would be desirable if somewhat less stringent provisions were enacted.

A federal loan, however, gives only temporary help. Interest continues in the provision of some type of federal financial assistance to states that experience unusually high costs. "Reinsurance" plans are strongly resisted and are viewed as a threat of federalization. We recommend the enactment of grants to states with unusually high costs.

Federal assistance to states having financial difficulties cannot take the place of sound and adequate financing by the states to the extent of their ability. In recent years, a number of states have allowed their reserves to fall to dangerously low levels, either through inadequate tax bases and schedules, through increased costs, or through both causes. As this is written, some states have taken steps to improve their financial position, but others have not.

Basic to sound financing of unemployment insurance are long-range economic, financial, and actuarial studies, and use of them by the policy makers in the states.

FINANCING OF ADMINISTRATION

The financing of total administrative costs of the state unemployment insurance systems through federal grants was designed to assure proper and efficient administration. This was quite a different method of securing state cooperative action than the tax-credit method of securing legislative action to establish unemployment insurance laws. The grants for administration were to be financed out of the 0.3 percent portion of the federal unemployment tax that was paid to the federal government, 0.4 percent since 1960.

From the beginning of the program, there has constantly been a problem of securing adequate appropriations for administrative grants. In 1963, the ceiling on administrative grants was raised by Congress to 95 percent of federal unemployment tax receipts. As this book is written, that ceiling already appears to be inadequate to meet growing administrative costs unless federal unemployment taxes are increased. If the tax base were increased as we recommend, it would solve this problem. It may also become necessary, if not desirable, to provide for financing out of general government funds of some of the new and expanded manpower functions of the public employment services that are not related to servicing unemployment compensation claimants.

Another problem with which the Bureau of Employment Security has struggled from the beginning has been to devise methods by which each state's needs for administrative grants can be objectively and scientifically determined. Objective standards have been worked out in consultation with the state agencies, but are still far from perfect. One principle that has been consistently adhered to is to make the grants in accordance with the volume of administrative work rather than with reference to the amount of federal unemployment taxes collected from each state. Occasionally, some state that is receiving in administrative grants less than is collected from employers in the state under the federal tax complains about the discrepancy. The Bureau of Employment Security follows the policy that grants to the states should be related to the volume of work of each state agency and not to the amount of taxes collected from employers of a particular state. We believe the Bureau's policy in this respect is sound.

Alternative Methods of Financing Administration

For a time efforts were made to secure a change in the method of administrative financing. After World War II, proposals were made to transfer to the states the full responsibility for financing their administrative costs. These efforts, however, have been abandoned. It has also been proposed—at one time by the Social Security Board—that administrative financing be changed to a system of grants-in-aid by the federal government, with the states paying one half or some such fraction of their administrative grants. It was thought that such a plan, which would require the states to appropriate part of their administrative costs, would increase their incentive to seek economies in administration. While this approach would be logical, there is an overriding national interest in the proper administration of the program. Most state legislatures meet only biennially; Congressional review of appropriation requests takes place every year. We believe the present system has worked fairly well and has provided the flexibility needed in a program as sensitive to economic changes as unemployment insurance is.

RELATIONSHIP TO THE PUBLIC EMPLOYMENT SERVICE

Since the time that unemployment insurance operations were coordinated with employment service operations, the functions of the employment service have been greatly expanded. It is increasingly becoming a manpower agency rather than a labor exchange. The function for which the two programs were coordinated, the exposure of unemployment insurance claimants to jobs and the application of the "work test" through the referral by the employment service to job openings, has become a relatively minor function in total employment service operations. The extent to which the employment service has been able to apply the "work test" has been disappointing; a small percentage of claimants are actually placed on a job. At the same time, payment of unemployment insurance claimants through local employment offices has hurt the image of the Employment Service, especially as viewed by employers. It has also resulted in the diversion of employment service personnel to help out in rush periods when claimants have crowded the local offices. Although the states have been encouraged to build up registers of temporary personnel to be hired during periods of heavier claim loads, this has not entirely solved the problem. Accordingly, beginning in 1962, the United States Employment Service encouraged the states to reorganize their metropolitan offices so that employment service operations were separated from unemployment insurance operations as much as possible. While this has not resulted in as much of an increase in job placements as had been hoped for, it has resulted in better operations and, surprisingly enough, better coordination between unemployment insurance and employment service functions.

We believe that this move toward physical separation of unemployment insurance and employment service operations was needed and should be carried as far as possible. In small offices, however, it would be expensive and inefficient. Where administration is physically separated, the two programs should continue to be closely related, so that maximum exposure to jobs is continued. It will also be desirable to maintain a close relationship in order to facilitate counseling of those claimants who have difficulty finding jobs, a function that would especially important if a program of extended benefits is provided for the unemployed.

FEDERAL-STATE RELATIONSHIPS

Although the relationships between the Bureau of Employment Security and the State Employment Security Agencies have been strained at times, particularly in the early years, on the whole their working relationships have been remarkably good in recent years. Most of the tension and differences in viewpoints has been aroused by proposals for federal legislation. This has been true particularly when the federal Administration has proposed legislation that would impose any restrictions on the freedom of the states to legislate as they see fit.

Federal Benefit Standards

More specifically, there has been strong disagreement over proposals for federal legislation requiring minimum benefit standards. The resistance of state officials has been reinforced by employer opposition. We believe that such opposition is not justified when the states fail to provide adequate benefit programs. The use of the sanction of tax credit to assure that the states are meeting minimum standards of benefit adequacy, we believe, would be consistent with the original objectives of the tax-credit device; namely to remove the fear on the part of a state that if it provides adequate benefits the cost of such benefits will place its employers at a disadvantage in interstate competition.

Conformity Questions

Another occasional source of friction between the federal and state agencies has been over questions of conformity with federal requirements. Most differences are negotiated, and few have come to a point where a formal hearing by the Secretary of Labor is necessary. This is partly due to the "life or death" character of the federal sanctions if a state does not meet federal requirements, withdrawal of tax credit for state employer taxes or withdrawal of grants for administration. Because of this, the state agencies have often "given in" although they did not agree with the interpretation of the federal requirements by the Department of Labor. On the other hand, the Department of Labor has been reluctant to apply the federal sanctions because of their sweeping character and, at times, has shown great patience in waiting for a state to bring itself into conformity with federal requirements.

Judicial Review

For some years, the state agencies have sought to secure legislation that would provide for federal judicial review of findings by the Secretary of Labor, if the Secretary finds a state out of conformity or compliance with federal requirements. Although there have been extended negotiations between federal and state officials, they have not been able to agree on the form of such judicial review. One of the problems is that, if the issue involves the benefit rights of workers, many workers may lose benefits during the inevitable delay before a federal court can review the Secretary of Labor's finding. Unless this problem is solved, we believe federal judicial review would be undesirable. On the other hand, if a satisfactory plan of judicial review of the Secretary's findings in conformity and compliance cases can be found, it would be desirable to have such review in the interests of improved federal-state relations.

COORDINATION WITH OTHER PROGRAMS

There remains the problem of coordination of unemployment compensation with other forms of social insurance. Such coordination as exists has been on a piecemeal basis and varies from state to state. The possibility of overlapping and duplication of benefits exists between unemployment insurance and the federal old-age insurance program, federal and state retirement systems, private pensions, workmen's compensation, temporary disability insurance, and supplementary unemployment benefits.

The problem is that a claimant may be receiving any one of these benefits and file a claim for unemployment insurance on the basis that he has met the qualifying requirements and is able to work and available for work.

Temporary Disability Insurance

The simplest problem has been the coordination of unemployment insurance and temporary disability insurance. In three of the four state programs of temporary disability insurance, the same agency administers unemployment insurance and the programs are closely coordinated to prevent overlapping in benefits. The same is true of the Railroad unemployment insurance and temporary disability insurance programs.

In states that do not have temporary disability insurance, the problem arises as to what policy should be followed if a worker becomes disabled while drawing unemployment compensation. A few states continue benefits if no suitable work is available. We would say that if no temporary disability program exists in a state, this is the only humane and realistic policy to follow.

Should temporary disability insurance programs be coordinated with unemployment insurance or with the federal disability insurance program? Since the latter is geared to monthly payments for long-range risks, we believe it is more realistic for temporary disability insurance to be coordinated with unemployment insurance.

Workmen's Compensation

Workmen's compensation presents many problems of coordination because of the different types of payments a worker may be receiving. There are temporary total and temporary partial benefits; there are permanent total and permanent partial benefits. Clearly, there should be no duplication between temporary total workmen's compensation and unemployment compensation; the latter should be denied. Unemployment compensation should be reduced by the amount a worker is drawing in temporary partial workmen's compensation, but the reduced amount should be paid if the worker is able to demonstrate ability to work. As for workmen's compensation for permanent disabilities, we believe that a worker should be eligible for unemployment compensation if he has been able to find employment and qualify for unemployment compensation subsequent to his injury.

Pensions

In the case of retired workers who are drawing federal old-age insurance, public retirement annuities, or private pensions, we believe that a common policy should prevail. If a worker is drawing a pension contributed to by the employer with whom he has worked and from whom he has secured wage credits for unemployment insurance, his unemployment compensation should be reduced by the amount of that pension. On the other hand, if the worker has retired, and especially if he has been compulsorily retired, and finds a new job, he should be eligible for unemployment compensation if he works long enough on the new job to qualify for it and demonstrates that he is able to work and is available for work.

RETRAINING ALLOWANCES

The development of training and retraining programs for the unemployed which pay allowances during training, especially under the Manpower Development and Training Act, required coordination with unemployment insurance. We believe that it is desirable that the training programs should be primarily responsible for such allowances. If an unemployed worker takes a type of training which does not carry an allowance with it, the state should award unemployment compensation and waive the requirement that he be available for work until he can complete training, if such training has been previously approved by the unemployment insurance agency.

SUPPLEMENTARY UNEMPLOYMENT BENEFITS

Almost all of the states pay full unemployment compensation when supplementary unemployment benefits are payable. To do otherwise is a denial of the very purpose of SUB payments. The one state that still denies benefits by the amount of supplementary unemployment benefits for which a worker is eligible should change its policy to conform with other states.

PUBLIC ASSISTANCE

There is no problem of overlapping of unemployment insurance and public assistance payments. The problem is that a number of states and a larger number of local government units deny public assistance to unemployed but employable workers. Some states provide assistance under the special provisions in the federal-state program of aid to needy families with children, if one of the parents is unemployed. But even if all states have taken advantage of these federal provisions it would meet only part of the problem. There are many unemployed who do not have children and who are in need.

Since unemployment compensation is limited in both amount and duration, we believe that public assistance should be available to every unemployment insurance beneficiary if unemployment compensation does not meet his needs. Public assistance should also be available to the needy unemployed if they do not qualify for or are not covered by unemployment insurance.

Proposals for Unemployment Assistance

Some believe that it would be desirable to have a special program of unemployment assistance, perhaps with a limited means or income test, for those who exhaust regular unemployment insurance benefits. They advocate such a program as an alternative to extended unemployment compensation. We believe, however, that such a proposal is unrealistic. When large parts of the country do not even provide general public assistance to the needy unemployed, it would be impossible to marshall public support for a special program for the needy unemployed to be paid out of public funds, especially if only a limited needs test were proposed. The attitude that "anyone can find work if he wants to" is still too prevalent.

Federal-State General Assistance

We would therefore recommend that efforts be concentrated on securing legislation to make public assistance available throughout the country to any unemployed person who is in need. In order to encourage those states that still deny public assistance to employables, we would recommend that a federal grant-in-aid program be provided for general public assistance for those who are not covered by the special federal-state programs of public assistance, and that one requirement for a federal grant be that employables be eligible for assistance. A program of federal-state general assistance is necessary anyway, either to cover all categories of the needy or as a "catch-all" for those not covered by special programs. And the needy unemployed should be covered by such a program.

NEED FOR HIGH LEVEL REVIEW

As this book is written, unemployment is still one of the important problems facing the country. While the unemployment situation has been improving and we hope will continue to improve, some unemployment will always exist and unemployment insurance will continue to be one of our important public programs. But in spite of the need for improvement of the program to more effectively meet the need of the unemployed, the program merits an objective review at the highest level. There is statutory provision for a Federal Advisory Council on Employment Security reporting to the Secretary of Labor, but it has been difficult to secure enough persons of sufficient standing on this Council so that its recommendations, when able to agree on recommendations, would receive attention at the highest policy-making levels in the federal Administration, in Congress, and in the states. A high-level commission should be periodically appointed by the President, possibly in cooperation with Congressional leaders, of persons of the highest standing in the ranks of management, labor, and the general public, to give a comprehensive view of the major policy issues regarding unemployment insurance. Progress can be made with respect to many of the issues discussed in this book without such high-level consideration. But at least those issues that require national action should receive such a review.

SOME CONCLUDING OBSERVATIONS

Observing the development of unemployment insurance for more than thirty years, one is impressed with its dynamic character. It deals with one of the most significant and pervasive forms of instability in our economy. This is a job economy. The overwhelming proportion of workers are dependent upon the contractual relationship to the job giver, the employer. The vicissitudes of economic life increase the hazard faced by the job holders. With all of its faults, unemployment insurance provides the best method we have so far developed for providing some underpinning in the form of income security when the job ceases to exist. The critics may like to dwell on the weaknesses of the system, its limitations, and even its abuses. However, it should never be forgotten that, these criticisms to the contrary, millions of wage earners are dependent upon it and sustained by its benefits at one time or another. Our task, therefore, is to subject the unemployment insurance program to continuous analysis so as to improve its benefits, to finance it more soundly, and to relate it to the economic and income changes that are continually taking place in the American economy.

Appendixes

Appendix A

Significant Benefit Provisions
of State Unemployment Insurance Laws,
January 1, 1966

The almost unlimited variations in the state unemployment insurance laws present a confusing array of features which often cloud, rather than light up, the scene. The data below are therefore limited to the amount and duration of benefits. Even so, the table indicates the great variety of detail and the difficulty of describing the unemployment insurance program in the 50 states, the District of Columbia, and the Commonwealth of Puerto Rico. For tables on all the provisions in the state laws, see the latest issue of the *Comparison of State Unemployment Insurance Laws*, BES No. U–141, issued by the Bureau of Employment Security, United States Department of Labor.

State	Weekly Benefit Amount for Total Unemployment		Weeks of Benefits in 52-Week Period for Total Unemployment	
	Minimum	Maximum	Minimum‡	Maximum
Alabama	$ 12	$ 38	13	26
Alaska	10–15*	45–70*§	15	26
Arizona	10	43	10	26
Arkansas	15	38	10	26
California	25	65	12–14++†	26†
Colorado	14	51	10	26
Connecticut	10–15*	50–75*	8+–26†‡	26†
Delaware	7	50	11+	26
District of Columbia	8–9*	55	17+	34
Florida	10	33	10	26
Georgia	8	35	9	26
Hawaii	5	62	26†	26†
Idaho	17	48	10†	26†
Illinois	10	42–70*	10–26†‡	26†
Indiana	10	40–43*	12+	26
Iowa	9	49	11	26
Kansas	10	49	10	26
Kentucky	12	40	15	26
Louisiana	10	40	12	28
Maine	9	34	26	26

State	Weekly Benefit Amount for Total Unemployment		Weeks of Benefits in 52-Week Period for Total Unemployment	
	Minimum	Maximum	Minimum‡	Maximum
Maryland	10–12*	48	26	26
Massachusetts	10–16*	50–*	8+–25+‡	30
Michigan	10–12*	43–72*	10+	26
Minnesota	12	38	18	26
Mississippi	8	30	12	26
Missouri	3	45	10+–26+‡	26
Montana	15	34	13	26
Nebraska	12	40	11	26
Nevada	16–24*	41–61*	10	26
New Hampshire	13	49	26	26
New Jersey	10	50	12+	26
New Mexico	10	36	18	30
New York	10	55	26	26
North Carolina	12	42	26†	26†
North Dakota	15	46	18	26
Ohio	10–13*	42–53§	20	26
Oklahoma	10	32	10	39
Oregon	20	44	11+	26
Pennsylvania	10	45	18†	30†
Puerto Rico	7	20	12†	12†
Rhode Island	12–15*	47–59*	12	26
South Carolina	10	40	10	22
South Dakota	12	36	16	24
Tennessee	12	38	12	26
Texas	10	37	10+	26
Utah	10	48	10–22‡	36
Vermont	10	45	26†	26†
Virginia	15	36	12	26
Washington	17	42	15+	30
West Virginia	12	35	26	26
Wisconsin	11	57	14+	34
Wyoming	10	47§	11–15‡	26

* When two amounts are given, higher includes dependents' allowances. Higher for minimum WBA includes maximum allowance for one dependent; Michigan—for one dependent child or two dependents other than a child; Ohio—for a dependent spouse or a dependent child if there is no spouse. In the District of Columbia and Maryland, same maximum with or without dependents. In Massachusetts maximum augmented payment not shown since such augmentation is limited only by the claimant's weekly wage. In Alaska no dependents' allowances are paid to interstate claimants.

† Benefits are extended when unemployment in state reaches specified levels: California, Connecticut, Hawaii, Idaho, Illinois, Pennsylvania, and Vermont, by 50% and in North Carolina, by eight weeks. In Puerto Rico, benefits are extended by 40 weeks in certain industries, occupations, or establishments when a special unemployment situation exists.

‡ For claimants with minimum qualifying wages and minimum WBA. In states noted, range of duration applies to claimants with minimum qualifying wages in base period: longer duration applies with the minimum WBA; the shorter duration applies with maximum possible concentration of wages in the high quarter, and therefore the highest WBA possible for such base-period earnings.

§ In Alaska, maximum for interstate claimants is $20; in Ohio and Wyoming, maximum amount for interstate claimants may be less than that shown.

Source: United States Department of Labor, Bureau of Employment Security, *Significant Provisions of State Unemployment Insurance Laws, January 1, 1966.*

Appendix B

Selected Unemployment Insurance Financial Data, Calendar Year 1964

The table below is designed to give a picture of state unemployment insurance transactions in one year. The last year available is 1964. The table shows the total amount collected in contributions, the amount distributed in benefits, the reserves at the end of 1964, and the percentages which each of these represents of the total covered payrolls in the state.

State	Contributions Collected* Amount (in Thousands of Dollars)	Estimated Average Employer Tax Rate† (Percent of Total Wages)	Benefits Paid Amount (in Thousands of Dollars)	Benefits Paid Percent of Total Wages	Reserves December 31, 1964‡ Amount (in Thousands of Dollars)	Reserves December 31, 1964‡ Percent
United States ..	$3,047,560	1.3	$2,522,089	1.10	$7,296,315	3.17
Alabama	33,498	1.1	18,744	.74	78,858	3.13
Alaska	8,704	2.4	5,486	1.94	11,267	3.98
Arizona	12,829	.9	14,238	.98	66,486	4.58
Arkansas	13,076	1.1	13,127	1.09	28,862	2.39
California	504,271	1.9	511,037	1.93	656,011	2.47
Colorado	18,478	.9	12,410	.61	57,436	2.84
Connecticut	51,457	1.1	47,451	1.05	180,068	4.00
Delaware	10,037	1.2	7,336	.93	19,558	2.47
Dist. of Columbia	7,478	.6	10,066	.68	63,525	4.32
Florida	41,236	.8	24,326	.51	157,086	3.30
Georgia	31,823	.9	19,622	.54	173,934	4.76
Hawaii	10,973	1.6	7,691	1.12	19,282	2.81
Idaho	8,520	1.5	8,068	1.50	28,411	5.28
Illinois	164,826	1.0	115,128	.72	489,900	3.06
Indiana	44,498	.6	34,463	.53	164,887	2.55
Iowa	10,702	.5	10,258	.45	112,049	4.87
Kansas	14,987	.8	16,182	.91	62,149	3.49
Kentucky	27,001	1.1	25,609	1.12	111,814	4.90
Louisiana	32,715	1.1	25,430	.89	113,598	3.96
Maine	11,591	1.5	9,133	1.08	30,160	3.57
Maryland	64,123	1.8	35,024	.95	148,658	4.02
Massachusetts .	133,524	1.8	132,460	1.70	197,936	2.54
Michigan	187,232	1.5	78,513	.66	414,401	3.49
Minnesota	28,612	.8	36,296	.96	23,031	.61
Mississippi	19,121	1.6	11,309	.98	49,597	4.30

State	Contributions Collected* Amount (in Thousands of Dollars)	Estimated Average Employer Tax Rate† (Percent of Total Wages)	Benefits Paid 'Amount (in Thousands of Dollars)	Benefits Paid Percent of Total Wages	Reserves December 31, 1964‡ Amount (in Thousands of Dollars)	Reserves December 31, 1964‡ Percent
Missouri	43,063	.8	37,321	.70	220,055	4.12
Montana	5,196	.9	7,267	1.35	20,034	3.73
Nebraska	9,224	.8	8,979	.78	42,119	3.68
Nevada	12,644	1.8	9,978	1.40	29,407	4.12
New Hampshire	7,416	1.1	6,744	.99	25,968	3.80
New Jersey	132,777	1.3	150,926	1.58	292,330	3.06
New Mexico	6,597	.9	8,171	1.01	35,109	4.35
New York	428,187	1.4	406,287	1.37	1,172,276	3.96
North Carolina ..	43,869	1.0	34,864	.86	217,091	5.36
North Dakota ...	5,335	1.6	5,605	1.70	7,608	2.30
Ohio	208,989	1.4	108,300	.76	232,727	1.63
Oklahoma	18,048	.9	15,413	.80	44,270	2.30
Oregon	36,271	1.6	25,193	1.14	85,861	3.89
Pennsylvania ...	293,073	2.0	175,664	1.15	238,641	1.56
Puerto Rico	18,280	2.3	15,722	2.18	50,708	7.04
Rhode Island ...	20,492	1.9	14,881	1.37	46,246	4.26
South Carolina .	18,491	.9	14,905	.80	86,855	4.67
South Dakota ...	2,334	.6	3,331	.95	15,132	4.30
Tennessee	39,378	1.2	28,856	.89	87,062	2.70
Texas	54,695	.5	56,343	.60	237,923	2.54
Utah	9,662	1.0	12,594	1.25	38,274	3.81
Vermont	4,572	1.4	5,977	1.72	6,793	1.96
Virginia	22,224	.5	13,208	.37	136,919	3.84
Washington	52,976	1.5	62,167	1.72	199,861	5.53
West Virginia ..	14,327	.8	14,705	.86	59,713	3.50
Wisconsin	41,943	.9	46,368	.95	199,935	4.09
Wyoming	6,185	1.9	2,909	.92	8,436	2.65

* Contributions collected include contributions and penalties from employers, and employee contributions in states which tax workers (Alabama, Alaska, and New Jersey).

† Estimated by Bureau of Employment Security.

‡ Reserves include advances from Federal Unemployment Account to Alaska, Michigan, and Pennsylvania.

Source: United States Department of Labor, Bureau of Employment Security.

Bibliography

Selected Bibliographical Notes

The following bibliographical notes are designed to provide a guide for the reader to sources for further reading or reference. Additional references on special aspects of the unemployment insurance program will be found in footnotes to the chapters on specialized subjects.

("USDL" denotes United States Department of Labor; "BES" denotes Bureau of Employment Security; "GPO" denotes U.S. Government Printing Office; and "UI" denotes unemployment insurance.)

A. BOOKS

1. Social Security in General

While the primary purpose of the biblographical references cited below is to call attention to significant writings dealing with unemployment insurance, it is relevant to call attention to some books which deal with the over-all subject of social security and particularly with its historical development. Among these, the following are especially significant:

ARMSTRONG, BARBARA N. *Insuring the Essentials: Minimum Wage, Plus Social Insurance–A Living Program.* New York: Macmillan Co., 1932.

A critical review of the evolution of social insurance in different parts of the world, together with an analysis of their trends and probable future.

BURNS, EVELINE M. *The American Social Security System.* Boston: Houghton, Mifflin, Co., 1949.

Includes general discussion of need for, principles, and issues regarding social insurance and public assistance in the United States; chapters 6 and 7 on unemployment insurance.

DOUGLAS, PAUL H. *Social Security in the United States: An Analysis and Appraisal of the Federal Social Security Act.* 2d ed. New York: McGraw-Hill Book Co., Inc., 1939.

Explains the Social Security Act of 1935 and records accomplishments through 1938.

EPSTEIN, ABRAHAM. *Insecurity: A Challenge to America. A Study of Social Insurance in the United States and Abroad.* 2d rev. ed. New York: Random House, 1938.

Discusses the risks social insurance is designed to meet and action taken in

511

the United States and other countries. Includes information on developments in this country to July, 1938.

HARRIS, SEYMOUR EDWIN. *Economics of Social Security.* New York: McGraw-Hill Book Co., Inc., 1941.

Effects of American social security program on savings, investment, monetary conditions, and economic fluctuations; methods of financing the program; incidence of payroll taxes.

MERIAM, LEWIS. *Relief and Social Security.* Washington, D.C.: Brookings Institution, 1946.

Critical study of American relief and social security programs. Describes British efforts for universal coverage, comprehensiveness, and coordination, and considers the major issues in social security.

PRESIDENT'S COMMITTEE ON ECONOMIC SECURITY. *Social Security in America. The Factual Background of the Social Security Act as Summarized from Staff Reports to the Committee on Economic Security,* Social Security Board Publication No. 20. Washington, D.C.: Social Security Board, 1937.

Section on UI includes foreign experience, actuarial basis, role of federal government, standards for provisions.

RUBINOW, I. M. *The Quest for Security.* New York: Henry Holt &. Co., 1934.

Presents the need of society for protection from financial losses incidental to accidents, illness, old age, and unemployment; and philosophy of government action through social insurance.

SOCIAL SECURITY TECHNICAL STAFF. *Issues in Social Security: A Report to the Committee on Ways and Means of the House of Representatives.* 79th Cong., 1st sess. Washington, D.C.: U.S. Government Printing Office, 1946.

Describes the social insurance and public assistance programs and evaluates the purpose, effect, and cost of proposed changes. Issues still current in UI discussed.

WITTE, EDWIN E. *The Development of the Social Security Act.* Madison: University of Wisconsin Press, 1962.

Detailed history of work of President's Committee on Economic Security in developing recommendations for Social Security Act.

———— *Social Security Perspectives* (ed. Robert J. Lampman). Madison: University of Wisconsin Press, 1962.

Selection of his writings on social security. Part I on general considerations of Social Security; Part IV on unemployment insurance.

Among more recent treatises on social security are:

BURNS, EVELINE M. *Social Security and Public Policy.* New York: McGraw-Hill Book Co., Inc., 1956.

An analysis of the factors influencing policy decisions in the field of social security. Considers four major groups of issues—types of payment and amount and eligibility conditions, risks covered, financing, and administration.

CARLSON, VALDEMAR. *Economic Security in the United States.* New York: McGraw-Hill Book Co., Inc., 1962.

Evolution of social insurance as an imperative in American market-oriented economy. Cost and impact of the system on the economy.

GAGLIARDO, DOMENICO.   *American Social Insurance*. 2d ed. New York: Harper & Bros., 1955.
Textbook treatise on principles, provisions, and experience of social insurance programs in the United States.

GORDON, MARGARET S.   *The Economics of Welfare Policies*. New York: Columbia University Press, 1963.
Flow of public funds to welfare programs, and income distribution through such programs. Chapter 5 on unemployment compensation.

MEYERS, ROBERT J.   *Social Insurance and Allied Government Programs,* chap. 12. Homewood, Ill.: Richard D. Irwin, Inc., 1965.
Factual description of principles and features of American social insurance and public assistance programs. Emphasizes financial aspects.

SCHOTTLAND, CHARLES I.   *The Social Security Program in the United States.* New York: Appleton-Century-Crofts, 1963.
Description of American social insurance and public assistance programs by former Commissioner of Social Security.

TURNBULL, JOHN G., WILLIAMS, C. ARTHUR, JR., and CHEIT, EARL F.   *Economic and Social Security, Public and Private Measures against Economic Insecurity.* New York: Ronald Press Co., 1957.
Considers each of the major problems of economic insecurity—death, old age, unemployment, disability, substandard conditions—and the public and private methods of combating these problems.

2. Unemployment Insurances

ALTMAN, RALPH.   *Availability for Work: A Study in Unemployment Compensation.* Cambridge: Harvard University Press, 1950.
Comprehensive analysis of statutory provisions and principles regarding availability for work and related eligibility requirements.

ATKISON, RAYMOND C.   *The Federal Role in Unemployment Compensation Administration.* Washington, D.C.: Social Science Research Council, 1941.
Study of federal administrative experience in early years of program and recommendations for improvement. Relative advantages of federal or federal-state system.

BECKER, JOSEPH M.   *The Problem of Abuse in Unemployment Benefits: A Study of Limits.* New York: Columbia University Press, 1953.
Study of experience following World War II under unemployment compensation and servicemen's Readjustment Allowances.

———   *Shared Government in Employment Security: A New Study of Advisory Councils.* New York: Columbia University Press, 1959.
The theory of advisory councils, experience under State employment security programs, and anaysis of their effectiveness.

DOUGLAS, PAUL H.   *Standards of Unemployment Insurance.* Chicago: University of Chicago Press, 1933.
Analysis of controversial issues still applicable.

EWING, JOHN B.   *Job Insurance.* Norman: University of Oklahoma Press, 1933.
History of early voluntary efforts and attempts at legislation. Detailed history of passage of Wisconsin Act.

HANSEN, ALVIN H., MURRAY, MERRILL G., STEVENSON, RUSSELL A., and STEWART, BRYCE M.   *A Program for Unemployment Insurance and Relief in the United States.* Employment Stabilization Research Institute, University of Minnesota. Minneapolis: University of Minnesota Press, 1934.

Discussion of fundamental issues in development of a UI program and outline of a plan for emergency benefits. Problem of investment of reserves.

INDUSTRIAL RELATIONS COUNSELORS, INC. *An Historical Basis for Unemployment Insurance.* Minneapolis University of Minnesota Press, 1934.

History of British, German, Swiss, Belgian systems and early American voluntary plans.

INTERNATIONAL LABOUR OFFICE. *Unemployment Insurance Schemes.* Studies and Reports, New Series No. 42. Geneva, Switzerland: 1955.

Description of development of national programs, and discussion of principles and experience of different countries with coverage, benefits, eligibility, etc.

LESTER, RICHARD A. *The Economics of Unemployment Compensation.* Princeton, N.J.: Princeton University, Industrial Relations Section, 1962.

Economic significance of benefits, implications of labor force changes, impact of unemployment taxes, proposals for improvement of program.

WOYTINSKY, W. S. *Principles of Cost Estimates in Unemployment Insurance.* Social Security Administration, Bureau of Employment Security. Washington, D.C.: GPO, 1948.

Analyses effect of labor market, statutory, and administrative factors on operation of UI and presents methodology to measure costs of program over a hypothetical business cycle.

B. ARTICLES, PAPERS, AND PAMPHLETS

AMERICAN ENTERPRISE INSTITUTE FOR PUBLIC RESEARCH. *Legislative Analysis: Proposed Federal Unemployment Compensation Legislation,* Analysis No. 14. Washington, D.C.: August 17, 1965.

Explanation of major proposals in Administration bill of 1965 and Recession Unemployment Compensation bill (H.R. 7476, H.R. 7477), and discusses issues.

BECKER, JOSEPH M. "The Adequacy of Benefits in Unemployment Insurance," *In Aid of the Unemployed,* chap. 4. Baltimore: Johns Hopkins Press, 1965.

———— and BOWMAN, VIRGINIA KYNER. "Supplementary Unemployment Benefits," *In Aid of the Unemployed,* chap. 6. Baltimore: Johns Hopkins Press, 1965.

Description of SUB plans and discussion of experience under them.

———— "Twenty-five Years of Unemployment Insurance, An Experiment in Competitive Collectivism," *Political Science Quarterly,* Vol. LXXV, No. 1 (December, 1960), pp. 481–99.

BLOOM, MARVIN K. *Measuring the Effect of Unemployment Benefits on the Economy.* Publication No. 102. Chicago: Research Council for Economic Security, 1954.

Estimates of replacement by UI of income loss due to unemployment.

BRANDEIS, ELIZABETH. "The Federal Threat to State Progress in Unemployment Compensation." *American Labor Legislation Review,* Vol. XXX (December, 1940), pp. 151–58.

BROCKWAY, RICHARD C. "Federal Policies on Unemployment Insurance—What Are They and What Should They Be?" *Proceedings of the Eleventh Annual Conference on Labor.* New York University, 1958, p. 308.

COHEN, WILBUR D. "Some Major Policy Issues in Unemployment Insurance and General Assistance" in *Studies in Unemployment*, prepared for the Special Committee on Unemployment Problems, United States Senate, pursuant to S. Res. 196, 86th Cong. Washington, D.C.: GPO, 1960.
   Examines deficiencies in UI program and proposals for overcoming them.

FELDMAN, HERMAN, and SMITH, DONALD M. *The Case for Experience Rating in Unemployment Compensation, and a Proposed Method.* New York: Industrial Relations Counselors, 1939.
   Arguments in favor of experience rating.

GORDON, MARGARET S., and AMERSON, RALPH W. *Unemployment Insurance.* Berkeley: University of California, Institute of Industrial Relations, 1957.
   Brief treatment "to provide the reader with an understanding of the main features of the existing program and of major issues."

GRAY, HERMAN. *Should Unemployment Insurance Be Federalized?* New York: American Enterprise Association, 1946.
   Arguments for federalization of system.

HABER, WILLIAM, and JOSEPH, J. J. "Unemployment Compensation," *Annals of the American Academy of Political and Social Science*, Vol. 202 (March, 1939), pp. 22–35.
   Critical evaluation of early experience of UI program.

———— and KRUGER, DANIEL H. *The Role of the United States Employment Service in a Changing Economy*, pp. 70–75. Kalamazoo: W. E. Upjohn Institute for Employment Research, 1964.
   Discusses question of separation of the Employment Service and unemployment compensation.

HALSEY, OLGA S. "British Experience in Supplementing Duration of Unemployment Benefits," *Monthly Labor Review*, Vol. 83, No. 3 (March, 1960), pp. 249–56.
   Review of British experience, 1918–57.

LESTER, RICHARD A. "Issues in Unemployment Insurance," *Proceedings of the Social Security Conference*, pp. 19–27. East Lansing: Labor and Industrial Relations Center, Michigan State University, 1958.
   Discusses eligibility requirements, benefit levels, structural defects in UI and their remedies.

———— and KIDD, CHARLES V. *The Case against Experience Rating in Unemployment Compensation.* New York: Industrial Relations Counselors, Inc., 1939.
   Arguments against experience rating.

LEWIS, WILLARD A. *Unemployment Compensation Law in Labor Disputes.* Michigan Compared with Seven Selected States, 1936–64. Kalamazoo: W. E. Upjohn Institute for Employment Research, 1964.
   Examines judicial interpretation of Michigan's UI labor disputes provisions and compares with interpretation in other states.

MACKIN, PAUL J. *Extended Unemployment Benefits.* Kalamazoo: W. E. Upjohn Institute for Employment Research, 1965.

Discussion of issues in extended UI, with special reference to implications of family characteristics of claimants under TEUC program of 1961.

MALISOFF, HARRY. "The Emergence of Unemployment Compensation," *Political Science Quarterly*, Vol. LIV (September and December, 1939), pp. 237–88, 391–420, 577–99.

Historical account of early federal and state UI legislation.

———— *Cost Estimation Methods in Unemployment Insurance, 1909–1927.* New York: New York Department of Labor, Division of Employment, June, 1958.

Review of development of actuarial methodology for unemployment insurance.

———— *The Financing of Extended Unemployment Insurance Benefits in the United States.* Kalamazoo: W. E. Upjohn Institute for Employment Research, April, 1963.

Discusses alternatives of employer, employee, and government contributions.

———— *The Insurance Character of Unemployment Insurance,* Unemployment Insurance Monographs. Kalamazoo: W. E. Upjohn Institute for Employment Research, December, 1961.

Discusses principles of unemployment insurance with special emphasis on insurance characteristics.

MORRISON, NATHAN. "Financing Unemployment Compensation," *Proceedings of the Eleventh Annual Conference on Labor.* New York University, 1958, pp. 319–28.

Discusses issues in financing.

MUNTS, RAYMOND. "A New Role for Unemployment Insurance," *AFL-CIO American Federationist,* June, 1965.

Discusses Administration bill of 1965 in the light of shortcomings of present unemployment insurance system.

MURRAY, MERRILL G. "Unemployment Insurance: Risks Covered and Their Financing," *In Aid of the Unemployed,* chap. 4. Baltimore: Johns Hopkins Press, 1965.

Description of coverage, eligibility, disqualification, and financial provisions of state UI systems.

———— *Proposed Federal Unemployment Insurance Amendments,* Public Policy Information Bulletin. Kalamazoo: W. E. Upjohn Institute for Employment Research, February, 1966.

Discusses pros and cons of issues raised by amendments proposed in Administration bill of 1965.

NATIONAL ASSOCIATION OF MANUFACTURERS, INDUSTRIAL RELATIONS DIVISION. *Unemployment Compensation in a Free Economy.* Economic Policy Division Series, No. 52. New York: July, 1952.

Statement of employer policies regarding UI.

PAPIER, WILLIAM. "The Role of Unemployment Compensation," *Proceedings of the Second Annual Conference on Social Security,* pp. 51–65. Ann Arbor: University of Michigan, 1959.

Discusses need for broad scale review of state and federal UI statutes. Questions federal role.

RECTOR, STANLEY. *The Advisor*. Washington, D.C. Unemployment Benefit Advisors, Inc.

Occasional letters to subscribers on UI legislation and issues.

ROHRLICH, GEORGE F. "Public Policy Implications of Unemployment Insurance Financing," *Proceedings of the Eleventh Annual Meeting of the Industrial Relations Research Association*, 1958.

Questions inflationary influence of UI, advocates re-evaluation of rate-making, tax, and reserve policies.

SMIGEL, E. O. "Public Attitudes toward Chiseling with Reference to Unemployment Compensation," *American Sociology Review*, Vol. XVIII (February, 1953), pp. 59–67.

Report on results of a sample survey.

SPIVEY, CLINTON. *Experience Rating in Unemployment Compensation*. Bulletin 84 of the Bureau of Economic and Business Research, University of Illinois, Urbana: 1958.

Critical study and evaluation of experience rating.

WAGENET, R. GORDON. "Twenty-five Years of Unemployment Insurance," *Social Security Bulletin*, Vol. XXIII, No. 8 (August, 1960).

Discusses general character, changing role, program developments, and issues.

C. SYMPOSIA, READINGS, PROCEEDINGS

AMERICAN ASSEMBLY, THE. *Economic Security for Americans; An Appraisal of the Progress During the Last 50 Years*. New York: Graduate School of Business, Columbia University, 1954.

Background papers by experts and findings of group convened in Third American Assembly. Excellent papers on UI.

HABER, WILLIAM, and COHEN, WILBUR J. *Readings in Social Security*, readings 17–28. New York: Prentice-Hall, Inc., 1948.

Reprints or excerpts from significant publications on unemployment insurance. Introductory readings on problems of insecurity, theory, and development of social security.

——— *Social Security; Programs, Problems and Policies* (Selected Readings), readings 20–34. Homewood, Ill.: Richard D. Irwin, Inc., 1958.

More recent reprints or excerpts from significant publications on UI. Introductory readings on persistent issues, historical developments, and emerging concepts in social security.

INTERSTATE CONFERENCE OF EMPLOYMENT SECURITY AGENCIES. *Annual Proceedings*.

Includes speeches by experts and representatives of management and labor, panel discussions, and resolutions.

SPECIAL COMMITTEE ON UNEMPLOYMENT PROBLEMS, U. S. SENATE. *Readings in Unemployment*, pp. 1301–482. 88th Cong., 1st sess. Washington, D.C.: GPO.

Selected papers on UI; also papers on all aspects of unemployment.

U. S. DEPARTMENT OF LABOR, BUREAU OF EMPLOYMENT SECURITY. "Helping the Long-Term Unemployed," *Employment Security Review*, Vol. XXIX, No. 12 (December, 1962), entire issue.

Articles on problems in providing extended duration of unemployment benefits.

———— "The Role of Unemployment Insurance Today and Tomorrow," *Employment Security Review*, Vol. XXIX, No. 8 (August, 1962), entire issue. Articles by outside experts and staff of BES.

———— "Twenty Years of Unemployment Insurance in the U.S.A., 1935–1955," *Employment Security Review*, Vol. XXII, entire issue. Includes articles on history of coverage, benefit financing, benefits, disqualifications, administration, the changing role of unemployment insurance, and issues for tomorrow.

———— "Unemployment Insurance in the U.S.A., 1956–60," *Employment Security Review*, Vol. XXVII, No. 8 (August, 1960). Articles on history of coverage, etc. for five years following issue on "Twenty Years of Unemployment Insurance."

———— "Unemployment Insurance—A New Look," *Employment Security Review*, Vol. XXI, No. 8 (August, 1954), entire issue. Articles on current issues in unemployment insurance.

VARIOUS AUTHORS. "A Symposium on Unemployment Insurance," *Vanderbilt Law Review*, Vol. VIII, No. 2 (February, 1955). Articles on development of UI, coverage, eligibility, disqualifications, labor disputes, experience rating, federal standards, administrative law, guaranteed annual wage, interstate aspects of UI.

———— "Unemployment Insurance," *Yale Law Review*, Vol. XV, No. 1 (December, 1945), entire issue. Articles on development, socio-economic objectives, and economics of UI, able and available for work, eligibility, disqualifications, refusal of suitable work, employment relation, employer fault, experience rating, labor's views.

———— "Unemployment Compensation," *Law and Contemporary Problems*, entire issue. Articles on coverage, benefits, actuarial problems, worker contributions, employer reserves, pooled funds, guaranteed employment plans, administration, employment service, federal-state system, constitutionality, relief, history of UI in Social Security Act.

D. GOVERNMENT PUBLICATIONS

1. Advisory Reports

ADVISORY COUNCIL ON SOCIAL SECURITY. *Final Report . . . December 10, 1938.* Sen. Doc. 4, 76th Cong., 1st sess. Washington, D.C.: GPO, 1939. Recommendations became basis for far-reaching amendments of 1939 to Social Security Act.

ADVISORY COUNCIL ON SOCIAL SECURITY TO SENATE COMMITTEE ON FINANCE. *Recommendations for Social Security Legislation.* Sen. Doc. 208, 80th Cong., 2d sess., pp. 137–80. Washington, D.C.: GPO, 1949. Part IV, recommendations on UI on coverage, financing, disqualifications, etc.

COMMISSION ON INTERGOVERNMENTAL RELATIONS. *Report to the President.* Washington, D.C.: GPO, 1955. Recommendations on UI recommended more discretion to states in administrative financing, stronger federal leadership on program aspects.

———— STUDY COMMITTEE ON UNEMPLOYMENT COMPENSATION AND EMPLOY-
MENT SERVICE. *Report submitted to the Commission on Intergovernmental
Relations.* Washington, D.C.: GPO, June, 1955.
    Majority and minority views on federal and state roles in UI.
COMMITTEE ON ECONOMIC SECURITY. *Report to the President.* Washington,
D.C.: GPO, 1935.
    Recommendations of Cabinet Committee which became the basis of the
    Social Security Act of 1935.
COMMITTEE OF INQUIRY INTO THE UNEMPLOYMENT INSURANCE ACT. *Report.*
Ottawa, Canada: Queen's Printer, November, 1962.
    History and analysis of financial operation of Canadian UI Act, conclusions
    and recommendations.
NATIONAL RESOURCES PLANNING BOARD. *Security, Work, and Relief Policies.*
Washington, D.C.: GPO, 1943.
    Comprehensive study of need for social insurance, public works, and wel-
    fare programs for U.S.

2. Annual Reports

Manpower Report of the President and *A Report on Manpower Requirements,
Resources, Utilization, and Training* of the U.S. Department of Labor, 1963,
1964, 1965. Washington, D.C.: GPO, 1963, 1964, 1965.
    Summary report of developments and recommendations of the President.
    Detailed factual presentation of manpower developments by the U.S.
    Department of Labor.
RAILROAD RETIREMENT BOARD. *Annual Reports.* Washington, D.C.: GPO.
    Include review of operations and recommendations for improvement of
    railroad unemployment insurance.
SECRETARY OF LABOR. *Annual Reports.* Washington, D.C.: GPO.
    Include annual report of Bureau of Employment Security containing review
    of operations and recommendations for improvement.
U.S. DEPARTMENT OF HEALTH, EDUCATION, AND WELFARE, SOCIAL SECURITY
ADMINISTRATION. *Annual Report of the Social Security Administration,* re-
ports for fiscal years 1936–40, issued as Annual Report of the Social Security
Board. Washington, D.C.: GPO.

3. Reference Documents

*Compilation of the Social Security Laws, Including the Social Security Act, as
Amended, and Related Enactments through December 1, 1962.* House of
Representatives Document No. 616, 87th Cong., 2d sess. Washington, D.C.:
GPO, 1963.
    Text of federal social security and related legislation.
SOCIAL SECURITY BOARD. *Draft Bills for State Unemployment Compensation
of Pooled Fund and Employer Reserve Account Types.* Washington, D.C.:
GPO, January, 1936.
    Alternative draft bills that served as basis for original state UI laws in
    many states.
U.S. DEPARTMENT OF HEALTH, EDUCATION, AND WELFARE, SOCIAL SECURITY
ADMINISTRATION. *Social Security Programs throughout the World.* Wash-
ington, D.C.: GPO, 1964.
    Tabular presentation of principal provisions in social insurance laws of all
    countries. Revised periodically.

U.S. DEPARTMENT OF LABOR, BUREAU OF EMPLOYMENT SECURITY. *Comparison of State Unemployment Insurance Laws*, BES No. U–141, Washington, D.C.

Detailed tables and description of provisions of state UI laws. Revised semiannually in odd-numbered years and annually in even-numbered years.

———— *Unemployment Insurance Legislative Policy. Recommendations for State Legislation, 1962*. BES No. U–212. Washington, D.C.: USDL–BES, 1962.

Detailed discussion of alternative substantive provisions for UI State legislation.

———— *Unemployment Insurance: State Laws and Experience*. Bes. No. U–198R (rev. February, 1965). Washington, D.C.: USDL–BES, 1965.

Graphic presentation of state UI laws and pertinent experience. Revised periodically.

———— *Handbook of Unemployment Insurance Financial Data, 1946–1963*. BES No. U–73 (rev. May, 1964). Washington: USDL–BES, 1964.

Principal financial data for U.S. and by states, by years. Annual supplements.

———— *Manual of State Employmnet Security Legislation* (rev. September, 1950). Washington, D.C.: USDL–BES, 1950.

Alternative draft legislative provisions for state UI legislation, together with commentary.

U.S. RAILROAD RETIREMENT BOARD. *The Railroad Retirement and Unemployment Insurance Systems*. Chicago: 1959.

Includes description of Railroad Unemployment Insurance program.

4. Bureau of Employment Security Reports

U.S. DEPARTMENT OF LABOR, BUREAU OF EMPLOYMENT SECURITY. *Adequacy of Benefits under Unemployment Insurance*. BES No. U–70 (R). Washington, D.C.: USDL–BES, October, 1958.

A Staff Report prepared for the Steering Committee of the Federal Advisory Council.

———— *Experience of Claimants Exhausting Benefit Rights under Unemployment Insurance, 17 Selected States*. BES No. U–178. Washington, D.C.: USDL–BES, 1958.

Summarization of 17 state postexhaustion studies.

———— *Family Characteristics of the Long-Term Unemployed*, TEUC Report Series Nos. 1–7. BES No. U–207–1 to 7. Washington, D.C.: USDL–BES, January, 1962–December, 1963.

Summary discussion and U.S. totals and detailed state tables on characteristics of samples of TEUC claimants. Reports for samples taken in May and September, 1961, and January and April, 1962.

———— *Issues Reflected in Appeals Decisions on Unemployment Benefits*. First Series, BES No. U–180, 1959; Second Series, BES No. U–201, 1961; Third Series, BES No. U–213, 1963; Fourth Series, BES No. U–236, 1965. Washington, D.C.: USDL–BES, 1959, 1961, 1963, 1965.

Reprints of articles on various issues arising out of disqualifications from benefits. Current articles in *Unemployment Insurance Review*.

———— *The Long-Term Unemployed, Educational Attainment*, Special

TEUC Report No. 1. BES No. U–225–1. Washington, D.C.: USDL–BES, 1964.

A national study of educational characteristics of claimants under the TEUC Program, 1961–62.

———— *Labor Force Status after Exhaustion of Benefits*, Special TEUC Report No. 2. BES No. U–225–2. Washington, D.C.: USDL–BES, 1965.

A 13-state study of claimants who exhausted benefits under the TEUC program, 1961–62.

———— *The Long-Term Unemployed, Comparison with Regular Unemployment Insurance Claimants*, Special TEUC Report No. 3. BES No. U–225–3. Washington, D.C.: USDL-BES, 1965.

———— *Major Findings of 16 State Studies of Claimants Exhausting Unemployment Benefit Rights, 1956–1959*. Washington, D.C.: USDL–BES, April, 1961 (Mimeo).

Summary of state postexhaustion studies.

———— *Supplemental Unemployment Benefit Plans and Unemployment Insurance*. BES No. U–172. Washington, D.C.: USDL–BES, 1957.

———— *Unemployment Insurance and the Family Finances of the Unemployed*, An Analysis of Six Benefit Adequacy Studies, 1954–58, BES No. U–203, Washington, D.C.: USDL–BES, 1961.

Summary of six state studies of benefit adequacy.

———— *Unemployment Insurance: Purposes and Principles*. Washington, D.C.: USDL–BES, 1950.

A guide for evaluating the main principles of unemployment insurance laws.

———— *Unemployment Insurance Tax Rates by Industry, 1962*. BES. No. U–221. Washington, D.C.: USDL–BES, 1964.

Detailed tables by industry groups and states of covered employment, total wages, taxable wages, and tax rates, under UI.

E. CONGRESSIONAL HEARINGS

U.S. CONGRESS. SENATE. COMMITTEE ON EDUCATION AND LABOR. *Unemployment in the United States*. Hearings pursuant to S. Res. 219, 70th Cong., 2d sess. Washington, D.C.: GPO, 1929.

Investigation of unemployment situation, and of systems for prevention and relief thereof.

———— SENATE. SELECT COMMITTEE ON UNEMPLOYMENT INSURANCE. *Unemployment Insurance*. Hearing pursuant to S. Res. 482 (71st Cong.), 72d Cong., 1st sess. Washington, D.C.: GPO, 1931.

Investigation of foreign unemployment insurance systems and union and company plans in the United States.

———— SUBCOMMITTEE OF THE HOUSE. COMMITTEE ON WAYS AND MEANS. *Unemployment Insurance*. Hearings on H.R. 7659, 73d Cong., 2d sess. Washington, D.C.: GPO, 1934.

Hearings on the "Wagner-Lewis Bill."

———— HOUSE. COMMITTEE ON WAYS AND MEANS. *Economic Security Act*. Hearings on H.R. 4120, 74th Cong., 1st sess. Washington, D.C.: 1935.

Hearings on bill resulting in Social Security Act.

———— Senate. Committee on Finance. *Economic Security Act.* Hearings on S. 1130, 74th Cong., 1st sess. Washington, D.C.: GPO, 1935.

Hearings on bill resulting in Social Security Act.

———— House. Committee on Labor. *Unemployment, Old Age, and Social Insurance.* Hearings on H.R. 2827, 2859, 185, and 10, 74th Cong., 1st sess. Washington, D.C.: GPO, 1935.

Hearings on "Lundeen Bill," a rival to social security bill.

———— House. Committee on Ways and Means. *Social Security,* 3 vols. Hearings relative to the Social Security Act Amendments of 1939, 76th Cong., 1st sess. Washington, D.C.: 1939.

Hearings resulting in Amendments of 1939.

———— Senate. Committee on Finance. *Social Security Act Amendments.* Hearings on H.R. 6635, 76th Cong., 1st sess. Washington, D.C.: 1939.

Basic material on the social security program and discussion of the 1939 amendments.

———— Senate. Committee on Finance. *Emergency Unemployment Compensation.* Hearings on S. 1274, 79th Cong., 1st sess. Washington, D.C.: GPO, 1945.

"Bill to amend War Mobilization and Reconversion Act of 1944 to provide for an orderly transition from a war to a peacetime economy through supplementation of unemployment compensation."

———— House. Committee on Ways and Means. *Amendments to Social Security Act,* 3 vols. Hearings on Social Security Legislation, 79th Cong., 2d sess. Washington, D.C.: GPO, 1946.

Volume 3 deals with unemployment insurance.

———— House. Committee on Expenditures in the Executive Departments. *Reorganization Plan No. 2 of 1949.* Hearings on H.R. 301, 81st Cong., 1st sess. Washington, D.C.: GPO, 1949.

Hearings on President's Reorganization Plan No. 2 to transfer BES from Federal Security Agency to U.S. Department of Labor.

———— Senate. Committee on Expenditures in the Executive Departments. *Reorganization Plans No. 1 and No. 2 of 1949.* Hearings, 81st Cong., 1st sess. Washington, D.C.: GPO, 1949.

Hearings on plan to transfer BES from Federal Security Agency to U.S. Department of Labor.

———— House. Subcommittee on Unemployment Insurance of Committee on Ways and Means. *Unemployment Insurance.* Hearings, 81st Cong., 2d sess. Washington, D.C.: GPO, 1950.

Hearings on President's message and bill for amending federal unemployment insurance legislation.

———— House. Subcommittee of the Committee on Ways and Means. *Unemployment Insurance.* Hearings on H.R. 3391, etc., 82d Cong., 2d sess. Washington, D.C.: GPO, 1952.

Hearings on bills to cover employers of one or more, earmark federal unemployment taxes, cover ex-servicemen, provide for reinsurance grants to states.

————House. Committee on Ways and Means. *Unemployment Insurance.* Hearings on H.R. 3531, H.R. 3530, and H.R. 2261, 83d Cong., 1st sess. Washington, D.C.: GPO, 1953.

Bills to earmark federal unemployment taxes and provide reinsurance grants to states.

————— HOUSE. COMMITTEE ON WAYS AND MEANS. *Unemployment Insurance.* Hearings on H.R. 6537, etc., 83d Cong., 2d. sess. Washington, D.C.: GPO, 1954.

Hearings resulting in unemployment compensation for federal civilian employees.

————— HOUSE. COMMITTEE ON WAYS AND MEANS. *Emergency Extension of Federal Unemployment Compensation Benefits.* Hearings on H.R. 11326, etc. 85th Cong., 2d sess. Washington, D.C.: GPO, 1958.

Hearings resulting in Temporary Unemployment Compensation Act of 1958.

————— SENATE. COMMITTEE ON FINANCE. *Unemployment Compensation.* Hearings on H.R. 12065, 85th Cong., 2d sess. Washington, D.C.: GPO, 1958.

Hearings on bill resulting in Temporary Unemployment Compensation Act of 1958.

————— HOUSE. COMMITTEE ON WAYS AND MEANS. *Unemployment Compensation.* Hearings on proposed amendments to federal laws on unemployment compensation, 86th Cong., 1st sess. Washington, D.C.: GPO, 1959.

Comprehensive hearings on Administration Bill, H.R. 3547. No action by Committee.

————— HOUSE. COMMITTEE ON WAYS AND MEANS. *Temporary Unemployment Compensation and Aid to Dependent Children of Unemployed Parents.* Hearings on H.R. 3864 and H.R. 3865, 87th Cong., 1st sess. Washington, D.C.: GPO, 1961.

Hearings resulting in passage of Temporary Extended Unemployment Compensation Act of 1961.

————— SENATE. COMMITTEE ON FINANCE. *Unemployment Compensation.* Hearings on H.R. 4806, 87th Cong., 1st sess. Washington, D.C.: GPO, 1961.

Hearings resulting in passage of TEUC Act of 1961.

————— HOUSE. COMMITTEE ON WAYS AND MEANS. *Unemployment Compensation,* 5 Parts. Hearings on H.R. 8282, 89th Cong., 1st sess. Washington, D.C.: GPO, 1965.

Hearings on the Administration bill on Federal unemployment insurance amendments.

F. PERIODICALS

RAILROAD RETIREMENT BOARD. *The Monthly Review.* Chicago.

Monthly operating statistics and special analyses.

U.S. DEPARTMENT OF HEALTH, EDUCATION, AND WELFARE, SOCIAL SECURITY ADMINISTRATION. *Social Security Bulletin.* Washington, D.C.: GPO.

Monthly operating statistics and occasional articles on unemployment insurance.

U.S. DEPARTMENT OF LABOR. *Monthly Report on the Labor Force.* Washington, D.C.: GPO.

Monthly statistics on employment and unemployment based on household data from the Census sample survey of households, sample survey of employers, and administrative statistics on unemployment insurance.

U.S. DEPARTMENT OF LABOR, BUREAU OF EMPLOYMENT SECURITY. *Employ-*

ment Security Review, Vols. I–XXX. Last issue November-December, 1963.

———— *The Labor Market and Employment Security.* Last issue October, 1963.

Operating statistics on the employment security program and articles on labor market, employment service, and unemployment insurance.

———— *Employment Service Review.* Washington, D.C.: GPO. January, 1964 ————.

———— *Unemployment Insurance Review.* Washington, D.C.: GPO. January, 1964 ————.

———— *Unemployment Insurance Statistics.* Washington, D.C.: USDL–BES. January, 1964 ————.

U.S. DEPARTMENT OF LABOR, BUREAU OF LABOR STATISTICS. *Monthly Labor Review.* Washington, D.C.: GPO.

Special labor force reports. Occasional articles on UI.

G. BIBLIOGRAPHIES

U.S. DEPARTMENT OF HEALTH, EDUCATION, AND WELFARE, SOCIAL SECURITY ADMINISTRATION. *Basic Readings in Social Security.* Publication No. 28, Washington, D.C.: GPO, 1960.

Annotated bibliography, including general section on social security and section on unemployment insurance.

U.S. DEPARTMENT OF LABOR, BUREAU OF EMPLOYMENT SECURITY. *A Selected Annotated Bibliography on Unemployment Insurance Financing.* BES No. U–216. Washington, D.C.: USDL–BES, 1963.

An extensive list of writings on all aspects of unemployment insurance financing.

H. STATE STUDIES

A large number of studies have been made for or by the state employment security agencies. These include long-range economic and financial studies, often done for the agency by university economists. They also include an increasing number of analytical studies, including studies of claimants after they have exhausted their benefits, studies of the family and other characteristics of claimants who received benefits under the Temporary Unemployment Compensation Act of 1961, and studies of coverage of excluded groups, of eligibility requirements, and of other substantive problems. The Bureau of Employment Security of the U.S. Department of Labor in cooperation with the State Employment Security Agencies periodically issues an *Employment Security Research Exchange,* which lists recently completed research projects and projects planned or in progress. The reader can receive issues of this *Exchange* by writing the Office of the Secretary, U.S. Department of Labor, Washington, D.C. 20210, and asking to be placed on mailing list No. 3046. Copies of current and past reports can be secured by writing directly to the state employment security agencies, or their reports and analysis chiefs, who are listed in the *Employment Security Research Exchange.*

Index

Index

(UI denotes unemployment insurance; OASDI denotes Old-Age, Survivors, and Disability Insurance under the Social Security Act.)

This book has been set in 10 and 9 point Caledonia, leaded 2 points. Part and chapter numbers are in 18 point (small) Univers Light #45. Part and chapter titles are in 18 point (small) Univers Bold Extended #63. The size of the type page is 27 by 46 picas 3 points.

TEXAS A&M UNIVERSITY-TEXARKANA